I0763109

Ethel Carrick

Acknowledgement of Country
The National Gallery of Australia respectfully acknowledges that we are on the Country of the Ngunnawal and Ngambri peoples of the Kamberri/Canberra region. We recognise their continuing connections to Country and culture, and we pay our respects to their Elders, past and present.

We respectfully acknowledge all Traditional Custodians throughout Australia whose art we care for and to whose lands National Gallery exhibitions and staff travel.

Warning
Aboriginal and Torres Strait Islander people are respectfully advised that this publication may contain images and words of, and references to, people who have passed away.

Aboriginal and Torres Strait Islander placenames
The National Gallery of Australia recognises Aboriginal and Torres Strait Islander cultural heritage by including First Nations placenames in the publication. The placenames are current at the time of print but may change over time.

Ethel Carrick

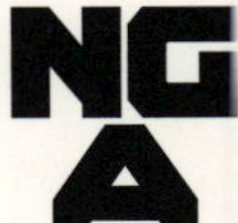

Lenders

This publication and associated exhibition have been made possible with the generous support of the following institutions and private lenders:

Institutions

Art Gallery of Ballarat, Wadawurrung/Ballarat; Art Gallery of New South Wales, Gadigal Nura/Sydney; Art Gallery of South Australia, Tarntanya/Adelaide; Art Gallery of Western Australia, Boorloo/Perth; Australian National University, University House Collection, Kamberri/Canberra; Benalla Art Gallery, Yorta Yorta Country/Benalla; Bendigo Art Gallery, Dja Dja Wurrung Country/Bendigo; Canberra Museum & Gallery, Kamberri/Canberra; Castlemaine Art Museum, Dja Dja Wurrung Country/Castlemaine; Home of the Arts, Gold Coast, Kombumerri Country/Surfers Paradise; Lawrence Wilson Art Gallery, The University of Western Australia Art Collection, Boorloo/Perth; Manly Art Gallery & Museum Collection, Cameragal Country/Manly; McClelland, Bunurong Country/Langwarrin; Mosman Art Gallery, Borogegal Country/Sydney; National Gallery of Victoria, Naarm/Narrm/Melbourne; National Library of Australia, Kamberri/Canberra; Newcastle Art Gallery, Awabakal and Worimi Country/Newcastle; Queen Victoria Museum & Art Gallery, Launceston; Queensland Art Gallery | Gallery of Modern Art, Meeanjin/Brisbane; Shepparton Art Museum, Yorta Yorta Country/Shepparton; Tasmanian Museum and Art Gallery, nipaluna/Hobart; The University of Sydney, Chau Chak Wing Museum, Gadigal Nura/Sydney; The Wesfarmers Collection of Australian Art, Boorloo/Perth

Private lenders

The Bastiaan Collection; Philip Bacon AO; Rob and Jenny Ferguson; Jim Haynes OAM and Robyn McMillan; Dr Garry Helprin; Moran Family collection; Kerry Stokes Collection, Boorloo/Perth; Collection of GR Teague; and those lenders who wish to remain anonymous and their representatives

Patrons

Major Patron
Lansdowne Foundation

Exhibition Patron
Roslyn Packer AC

Publication Partner
Gordon Darling Foundation

Supporting Patrons
Fiona Martin-Weber and Tom Hayward

Contents

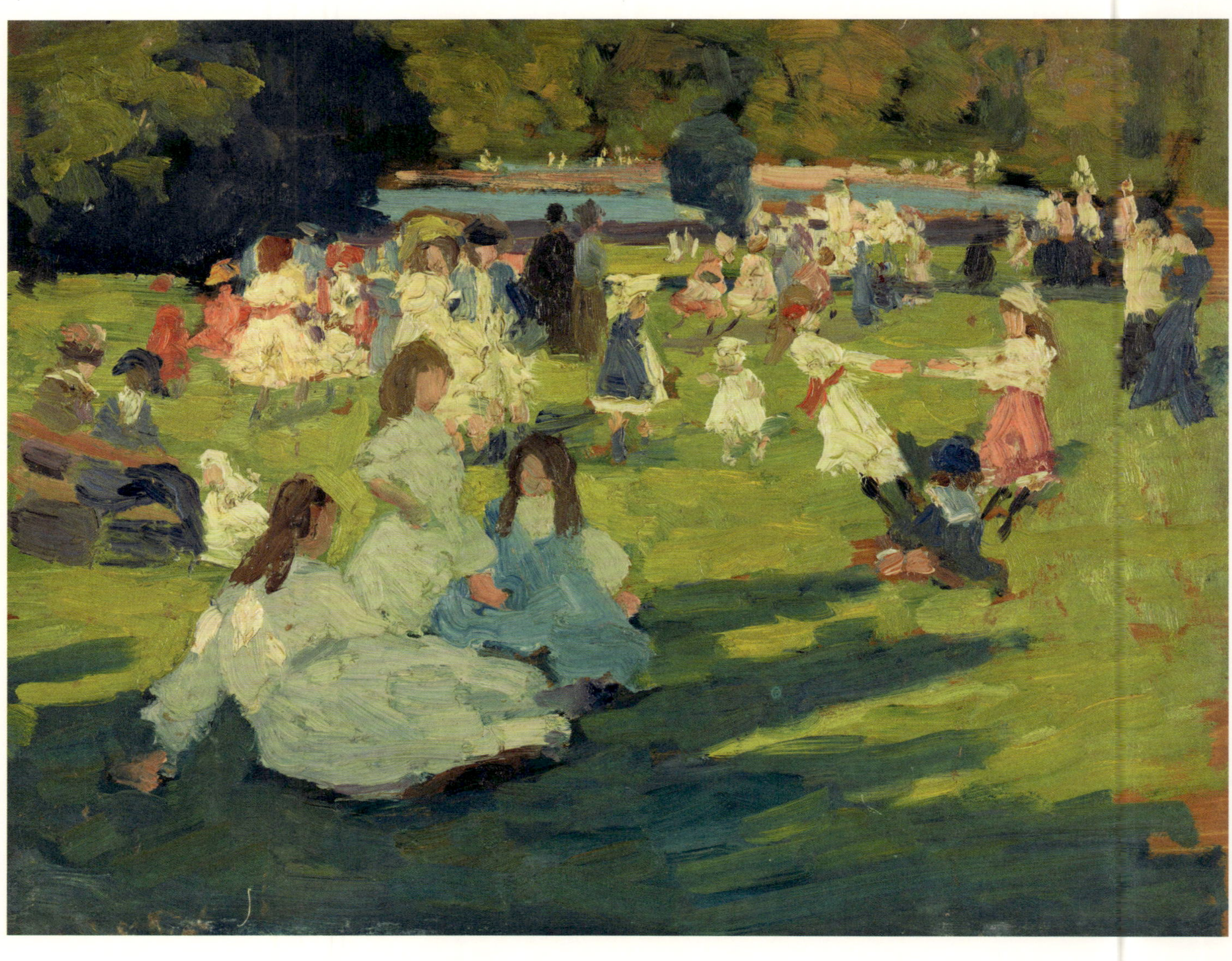

cat 1 *Esquisse en Australie* (Sketch in Australia) 1908, oil on wood, National Gallery of Australia

Foreword

The National Gallery of Australia's major retrospective exhibition of Ethel Carrick (1872–1952), together with this thorough and richly illustrated publication, brings to life Carrick's significant artistic contribution nationally and internationally over some five decades.

Born in the United Kingdom in 1872, Carrick spent most of her adult life living between France and Australia. The majority of her solo exhibitions in her lifetime were held in Australia and as a consequence she has long been considered an Australian artist. However, her impact on this country—as an artist, as well as a mentor, advocate and inspiration for others—deserves to be more widely recognised. For instance, she was among the very first artists to introduce Australia to a post-impressionist approach when she exhibited in Naarm/Narrm/Melbourne in 1908. The works exhibited included *Esquisse en Australie* (Sketch in Australia) 1908 (cat 1), of Sydney's Royal Botanic Garden, which Carrick took back to Paris and was shown in the Salon d'Automne in 1908 along with three other paintings. In 2023 the National Gallery acquired this vibrant, painterly work for the collection and all four works shown in the Salon are reunited in this retrospective for the first time in over 100 years.

This is one way among many that this project sheds light on the depth and breadth of Carrick's wide-ranging artistic contribution, transcending 'isms' and covering diverse subject matter and stylistic approaches. While her art has often been closely associated with that of her husband, Emanuel Phillips Fox, their marriage lasted only 10 years due to his untimely death in 1915, after which she continued to create her art for almost four decades until her passing in 1952 at eighty years of age. Although there have been impressive exhibitions showing their work together, this retrospective allows a clear view of her artistic oeuvre in its own right—from the earlier radical paintings that formed her reputation through to her later, great paintings of Nice, as well as the more discursive, diaristic works created during her journeys to different parts of the globe. During the years following Fox's death, her great courage and independent spirit was demonstrated in her continuing passion for travel, her endlessly enquiring mind, her desire to continually nurture friendships, and her zest for art and life.

The idea of retelling the stories of Australian art is central to the National Gallery's Know My Name initiative, which celebrates the lives and artistic achievements of women artists, in this country and internationally. We are profoundly grateful to our supporting partners for their most generous commitment to the Ethel Carrick retrospective and publication. In particular, we would like to thank our Major Patron Prue MacLeod through the Lansdowne Foundation; our Exhibition Patron Roslyn Packer AC; our Publication Partner the Gordon Darling Foundation; and our Supporting Patrons Fiona Martin-Weber and Tom Hayward. The curator of this retrospective, Deborah Hart, was a recipient of the Darling Travel Grant (International), which allowed her to travel to England and France to undertake important research and uncover new scholarship that has directly informed this project. Hart's dedicated work on the exhibition and publication has been pivotal to honouring and bringing a deeper understanding of Carrick's artistic achievements to a broad audience.

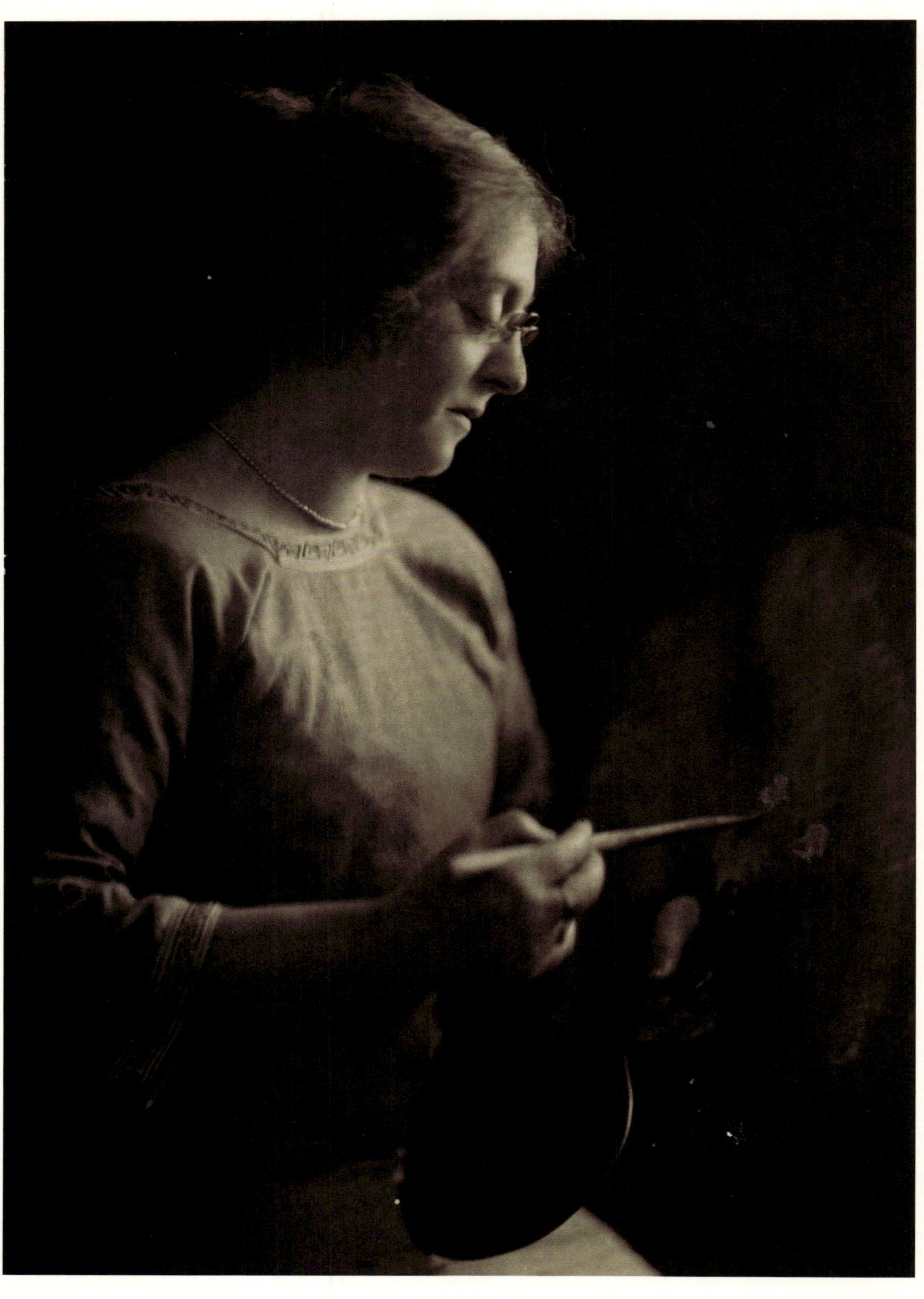

cat 2 May and Mina Moore Studios, *Portrait of Ethel Carrick*, c 1913–16, toned gelatin silver photograph, Art Gallery of South Australia

This publication provides a lasting record of the *Ethel Carrick* retrospective, as well as an in-depth exploration of her oeuvre and connections with other artists across place and time. Accompanying a major essay by Deborah Hart are engaging and informative essays by Rebecca Blake, Angela Goddard, Emma Kindred, Jenny McFarlane, Denise Mimmocchi, Juliette Peers and Catherine Speck. We are most grateful to them all for their contributions.

A retrospective on the work of Ethel Carrick is important. It is the first major showing of her work since 1979 and the most comprehensive to date, incorporating over 135 works from public and private collections. We are most appreciative of the generosity of all the lenders for their great support, which has been crucial to the success of the exhibition and the publication. Carrick's art has long enjoyed the commitment of private collectors and we recognise their kindness in parting with treasured works for the retrospective. In related ways, our colleagues in galleries around the country, as well as in auction houses, have played a crucial role in helping the National Gallery to honour Carrick's artistic legacy.

It is our hope that those familiar with Ethel Carrick's art, as well as those discovering it for the first time, will find much inspiration in engaging with the expanse of her achievements, in Australia and internationally.

Ryan Stokes AO
— Council Chair, National Gallery of Australia

Dr Nick Mitzevich
— Director, National Gallery of Australia

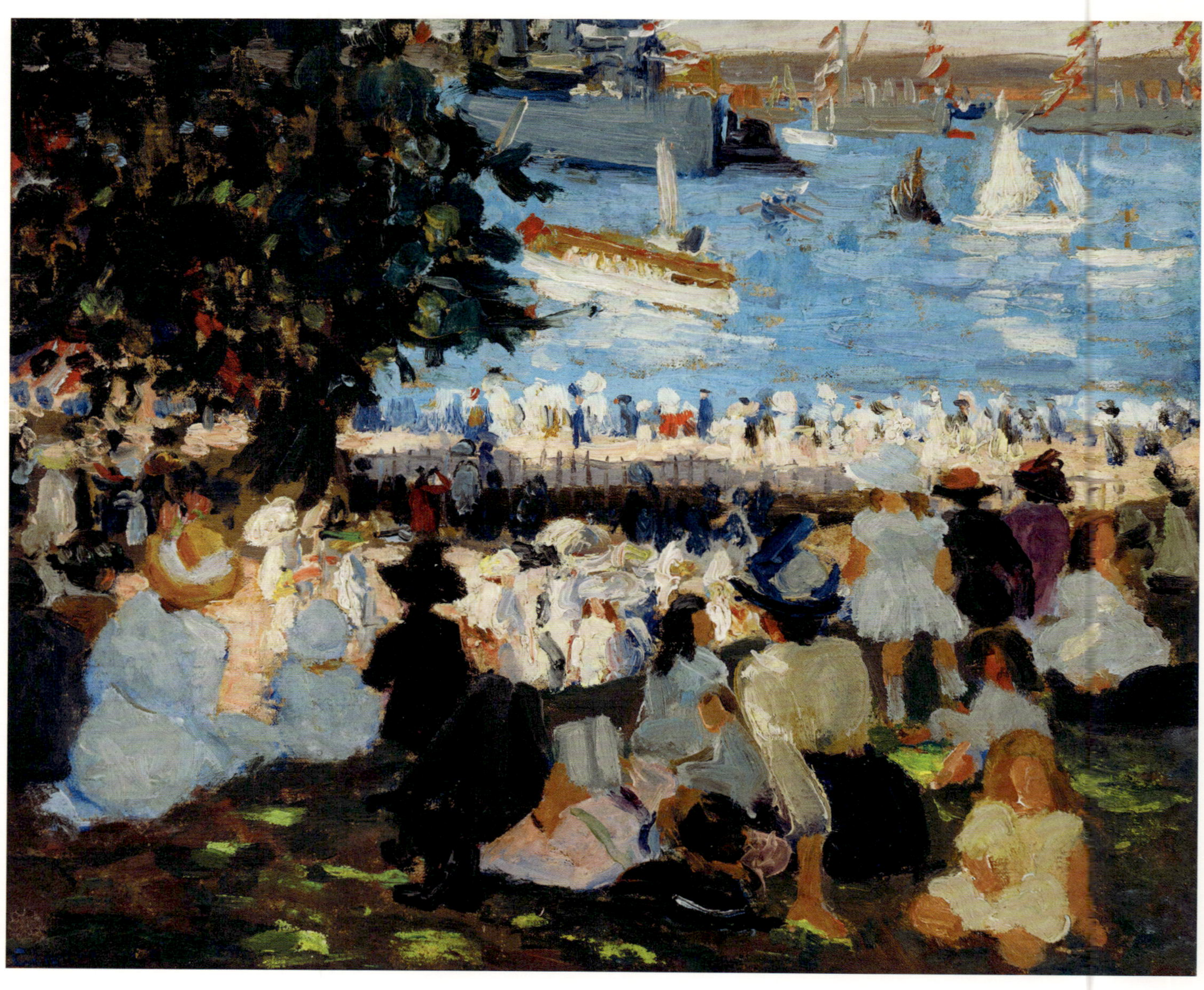

cat 3 *Watching the fleet from the Domain* 1913, oil on canvas, private collection

Introduction

I will wait until my celebrated husband's exhibition is over. Then you will see me ... for my work is me ... I think it is more me than me.[1]

— Ethel Carrick, 1913

Ethel Carrick (1872–1952) was a truly transnational artist. Born, raised and educated in Britain, she became an avid Francophile as an adult, keeping a home base in Paris for most of her life. She also spent extended periods in Australia, taking out dual citizenship in 1949.[2] She exhibited her art in all three countries over the years, with most of her solo exhibitions taking place in Australia, where she developed a solid collector base. Up until her final years, Carrick travelled widely through Europe as well as to North Africa and India—all important sites for her art. Dedication to her practice, travelling and engaging with her circles of friends, along with her philosophical and theosophical inclinations, became the mainstays of her life.

Though Carrick married late by the standards of the day, at the age of thirty-three, her artistic legacy has at times been overshadowed by the achievements of her husband, Australian painter Emanuel Phillips Fox. While his works were informed by a more academic approach to Impressionism than hers, and tended to be larger in scale, Carrick's paintings—particularly during their time together—were more adventurous and more modern. Occasionally during their travels together, his work appears directly inspired by her post-impressionist approach. By most accounts the couple had a fruitful relationship enlivened by differing viewpoints, cut short when Fox died suddenly from cancer after only 10 years of marriage. The shock of his passing and her admiration for his art meant that Carrick spent the rest of her life promoting his legacy, often putting her own work second.

This publication centres Carrick's work in the context of its times and on its own terms, shedding light on her great artistic legacy nationally and internationally.

The major essay of this book firmly positions Carrick as an artist in her own right, including her personal choices to exhibit with a diverse array of artistic groups. The challenges of documenting her development are exacerbated by her own recording practices: she does not appear to have kept diaries, and she often titled her works similarly, rarely dating them. As a result, her life and work are notoriously difficult to trace. This publication brings new scholarship to Carrick's story, drawing upon a range of primary research including letters, family accounts, archives (including those pertaining to women artists), newspapers and immigration records.[3] The narrative unfolds with an account of her familial background in Uxbridge, her early training, her meeting with Fox in St Ives and their expanding circle of British and Australian friends. Newly discovered research has also uncovered that Carrick's interest in Australia began through her brother Howard, who visited Australia before she met Fox.

Following Carrick's arrival in Paris in 1905, where she lived with Fox in an apartment in Montparnasse, she metaphorically threw open the shutters and welcomed in a new world of artistic experience. Trained at the Slade School of Fine Art in London, she now found herself in an environment conducive to evolving her distinctly modern outlook. It was the Belle Époque and artists from around the world had come to Paris, drawn by the increasing democratisation of possibilities for foreign artists offered by the Third Republic in France. This also applied to women artists, and Carrick was able to enjoy French culture and participate in an international milieu of artists.

Carrick's entry into the artworld in the late nineteenth and early twentieth centuries coincided with a loosening of the strictures of the past. In London and Paris, established rules barring the entry of women into art schools, like the Royal Academy of Arts and École des Beaux-Arts, were being overturned through the ardent efforts of those advocating for a level playing field. While it was still predominantly men who thrived in conservative establishments, Carrick found ways of showing her art in an array of venues, including the Royal Institute of Oil Painters in London and the Salon des Beaux-Arts in Paris, as well as the more contemporary Salon d'Automne, where she became a full member and the first British woman to be selected onto the jury. She also engaged with networks of female artists, such as Les Quelques and the International Art Union.

In the late nineteenth century it was considered radical for women artists to work independently outdoors, focusing not on portraits or landscapes but on the public arena. Carrick was inexorably drawn to throngs of people, to the flux of everyday experience. As a counterpoint, she found balance in her close observations of the world. When she first showed *The market, Caudebec* c 1902 (cat 4, p 16), it was noted that this 'busy scene, with stall keepers and market folk, is rendered more effective by the play of sunlight in the centre of the design. The figures in the various groups are well studied, the background architecturally excellent, and the animation in the figures arouses interest'.[4] These early impressions set the scene for what was to follow.

In Paris, the tonal variations of Carrick's prior work most often transformed into a world of colour, revealing her great abilities as a colourist and her aptitude for capturing the essence of a scene with an expressive painterly touch and a bold feeling for composition. While in overview her art defies neat categorisation, she was inspired by Impressionism and Post-Impressionism, showing with artists such as Henri Matisse, André Derain, Pierre Bonnard and Édouard Vuillard. She also exhibited with a coterie of women, including Swiss-born Martha Stettler and Latvian-born Alice Dannenberg, both of whom were founding members and directors of the Académie de la Grande Chaumière, the famous Parisian art school that endures to this day. These women artists, like Carrick, deserve wider recognition.

During Carrick's first visits to Australia (in 1908 and from 1913 to 1916), her solo shows included some of the earliest post-impressionist works to be seen and painted in the country. A pattern emerged of Carrick bringing works that had been shown in Europe to Australia with her on the ship and taking some of those created in Australia back for exhibition in France, Britain and, on occasion, Belgium. During World War I, she proactively supported the war effort as well as the plight of refugees. Her subsequent re-engagement with market scenes, including those inspired by the renowned flower markets in Nice, represent a resurgence of her strength as a painter. Likewise, her still life paintings that incorporated blooms from her much-loved garden brought the pulse of life from outdoors into her home, as sources of meditation on nature.

One of the revelations of Carrick's artistic development over time is the way that she would focus on a particular theme or subject, sometimes from different points of view and at other times from the same viewpoint, and subtly alter colour, tone and intensity of luminosity.

It was as though having grasped the essence of a scene, she sought to emphasise pictorial, abstract qualities in the making of her art to bring the poetry of the world to the fore. This corresponds with her lifelong love of music, with its myriad tonal variations to shift the mood or feeling of a composition, that was so evident in the creative output of composers she admired, like Claude Debussy and Pablo Casals.

Carrick's passion for travel in later life included visits to India (1935–37 and 1939) where she went to the theosophical headquarters in Adyar, lived on a houseboat in Srinagar, trekked into the Himalayas and exhibited with the Punjab Literary League in Lahore. At the outbreak of World War II she came to Australia, remaining until 1950. During this period, she spent some time living at The Manor (the theosophical establishment in Sydney), and in Melbourne. She also travelled to Queensland and the Australian Capital Territory, among other places, painting local landscapes as well as the Canberra Services Club (which formed part of a group of works relating to women and the war effort). Despite bouts of ill health, in her late seventies she went back to France via North Africa and visited Italy before returning to Australia near the end of her life, where she hoped to reconnect with friends and family and exhibit her art.

Such was her tenacity.

In addition to the broad overview of Carrick's oeuvre, this publication includes focused essays on key aspects of her life and work. Angela Goddard brings her in-depth knowledge of Carrick's relationship with Fox to a nuanced interpretation of their time together. Denise Mimmocchi takes us into the realm of French beach resorts, shedding light on some of the most important works of Carrick's artistic career. Emma Kindred brings original insights into Carrick's North African paintings, including stylistic shifts from one visit to the next as well as identifying precise locations where works were undertaken. Rebecca Blake examines the painting *Christmas Day on Manly Beach* 1913, reflecting upon Carrick's notion of the liberated woman and revealing new information on her friendship with artist Thea Proctor. Catherine Speck brings her scholarship to the work that Carrick undertook across both World War I and World War II, and her commitment to peace. Jenny McFarlane explores Carrick's keen interest in theosophy, drawing on extensive research and documentation. Finally, Juliette Peers brings her deep knowledge of the role of women's groups in the artworld into the broad realm of Carrick's friendships and exchanges with artists across time and place.

Contrary to several previous accounts, in her later years Carrick was not a lonely widow with a difficult temperament—rather she was vitally engaged with her varied circles of friends. As a woman artist who struggled financially later in life, she needed to be ambitious and to speak her mind. She was also keenly interested in the work of her peers and encouraged young students. Not long before she died, she wrote to her sister-in-law Irene Fox (who she called Renée) about her desire to see a substantial, well-illustrated book on Emanuel Phillips Fox's art. At the time, the possibility of seeking such recognition for her own art did not enter the picture.

This book and the accompanying retrospective (the first since 1979) are part of the Know My Name initiative to retell the stories of women artists and Australian art history. While Carrick's art is known to an extent within the artworld, she is far from being a household name in Australia, and her work is little known beyond our shores. It is our hope that Ethel Carrick's considerable artistic contribution and remarkable life, so international in its scope, becomes increasingly widely recognised.

Deborah Hart

— Head Curator, Australian Art, National Gallery of Australia

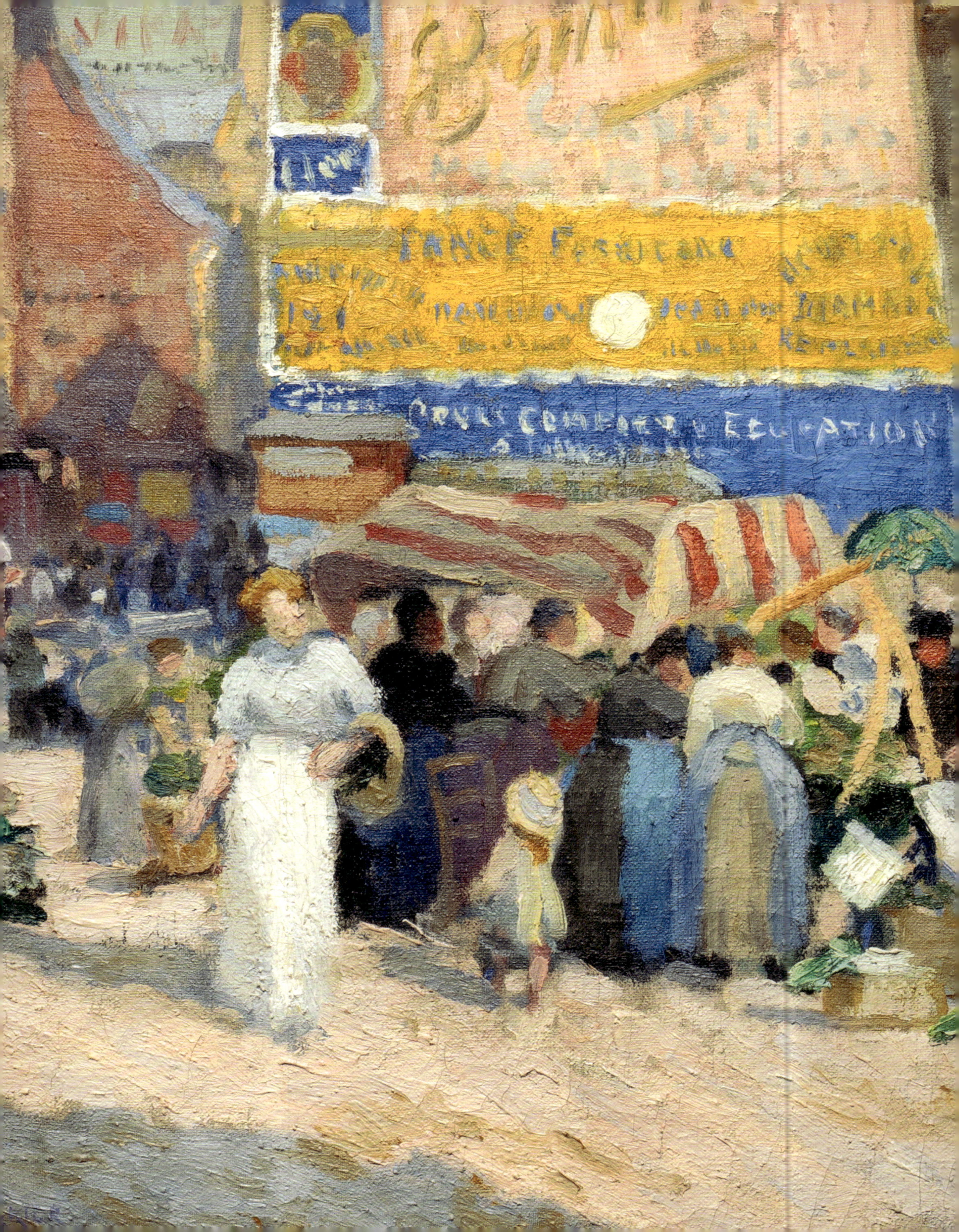

Ethel Carrick's life and art

Deborah Hart

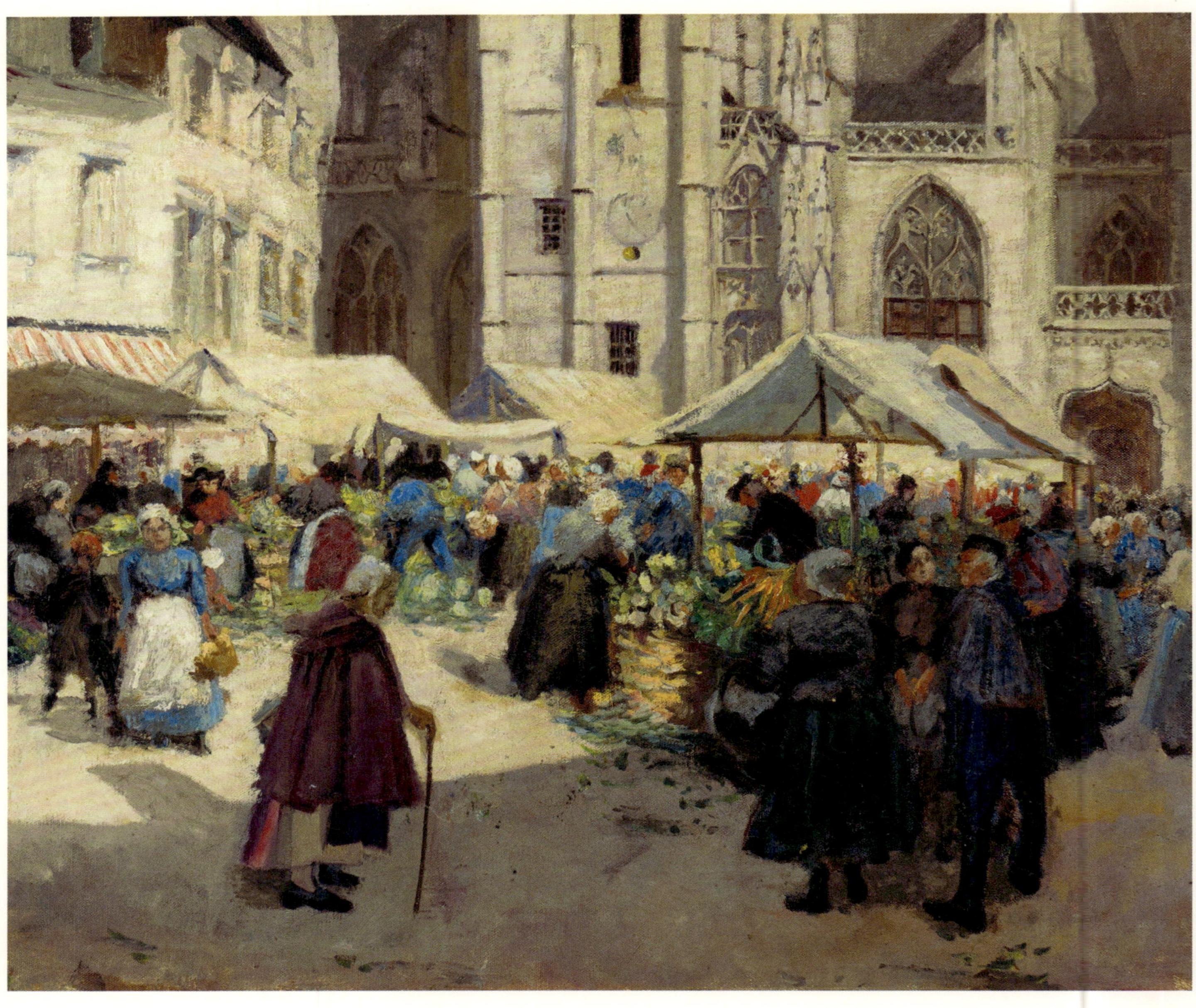

Becoming an artist: 1872–1905

I was standing shyly by the Venus de Milo, sketchbook in hand, when a very tall man [Henry Tonks] came up to me. He asked for my book, glanced through it, and remarked: 'So you are going to be a second Burne Jones?'

'No,' I replied promptly, 'a first Edna Waugh.'[1]

— Edna Clarke Hall (née Waugh)

Ethel Carrick's birth in 1872 in Uxbridge, Middlesex, which is on the outskirts of London, coincided with a time of considerable change. Just over a decade before Carrick's birth, artist Laura Herford was the first woman to become a student at the Royal Academy of Arts by submitting drawings for entry in 1860 under the name 'L Herford', thereby disguising her gender and challenging the status quo. Accepting her into the school on merit, the unknowing judges who supplied the good news to 'L Herford Esq' were caught out. With this act, the hypocrisy about women not being good enough to be in the pantheon was unmasked. Petitions for women to study at the Royal Academy had been submitted to the House of Commons since the 1840s, however resistance to change prevailed. Even in the early 1900s, many within the male bastion still regarded women as intruders.

By comparison, the Slade School of Fine Art was like a breath of fresh air for aspiring women artists in the late nineteenth century. The Slade was founded in 1871 as the result of a bequest from Felix Slade, who insisted that women students be admitted to the school on equal terms with men.[2] His progressive approach led to an influx of women, and they would soon outnumber the male students at the Slade—a situation that prevailed until World War II. This was not to say that prejudicial attitudes to women weren't present, but rather that the framework underpinning the organisation set standards in gender equity for others to follow. It was to Slade that Carrick would head as a young woman in her twenties, keen to establish a sound foundation for her artistic career.

Born on 7 February 1872, Carrick was the second daughter of nine children (one of whom died at the age of five).[3] She grew up in Uxbridge, where her father, Albert William Carrick (1841–1899), and mother,

Previous
Rue Mouffetard, Paris 1910
(detail cat 32, pp 62–63), oil on canvas,
Kerry Stokes collection

Opposite
cat 4 *The market, Caudebec* c 1902,
oil on canvas, private collection

Emma Carrick, née Filmer (1845–1938), raised their growing family across different houses, including Brookfield House, which later became a small private hotel.

The family fortunes were shaped by the astute business acumen of Albert Carrick, who progressed rapidly in his career from apprentice draper to co-manager of several stores, eventually becoming a director of Carrick and Coles with Joseph Coles. Images from the time reveal the names of the two directors emblazoned on the shopfront, signalling its importance as the largest shop in town (fig 1 and fig 57, p 241). An engraving of Carrick and Coles in the Uxbridge Directory describes the business as selling boots, hats, caps, gloves, silks, shawls, dresses, furs, carpets, linens, hosiery and lace. It also depicts the store's showrooms, a tailoring department, millenary, dressmaking rooms and mantle rooms.[4] Growing up seeing the latest arrivals in the store and being surrounded by sensuous draperies and other apparel would have an impact on Carrick, whose paintings in the years to come reveal her keen engagement with the differing fashions and dress codes of the day. As Marcel Proust wrote, 'Fashions, being themselves begotten of the desire for change, are quick to change also.'[5]

Two distinguishing characteristics of the Carrick household were the propensity to be practical and to speak one's mind—traits passed down by Albert Carrick. Although Carrick's sister Hilda claimed that Ethel had a forceful personality 'unlike anyone else in the family', others in the family were, from numerous accounts, often outspoken and 'renowned for their quarrels with one another'.[6] Carrick, like her sister Morna, showed an early talent for art, music and performance, while her brother Hartley, who trained as a barrister, ended up writing lyrics for musicals—a number of which were performed on the London stage.[7]

Carrick's youngest brother, Howard Filmer Carrick, struggled to find his way. After making it clear that he didn't want a part in his father's business, he was sent to Australia in September 1891, where he spent two years working on properties. A relative noted that Howard's love of cricket would have equipped him well for this endeavour, and his letters home would no doubt have inspired family interest in the Antipodes—including in Carrick, who at this point could not have dreamed of the deep connection this country would later hold for her.[8]

It was not the expectation at the end of the nineteenth century that middle-class women should have careers; rather, they were meant to attend to home duties. Carrick, however, was determined to continue her studies into adulthood. After being educated at home, she joined the Guildhall School of Music and Drama for lessons in singing and pianoforte.[9] Although she eventually opted for a career in art, music remained important to her. Around 1895 she began attending art classes with Francis Bate at his Applegarth Studio in Brook Green. Bate's classes included drawing from the 'antique', anatomy, life drawing (for figure and costume), still life and landscape painting. In 1887 Bate wrote *The naturalistic school of painting*, and in 1889 he exhibited with the London impressionists. His paintings reveal a conservative form of Impressionism, with figures in gardens subsumed in nature and light.[10] One of his students was Roger Fry, who coined the term 'Post-Impressionism' in 1906, applying it again in 1910 to the exhibition *Manet and the post-impressionists*.

Taking classes with Bate provided a basis for Carrick's more in-depth tuition at the Slade School of Fine Art. The signing-in books at the Slade reveal the pattern of Carrick's attendance from 1898 through

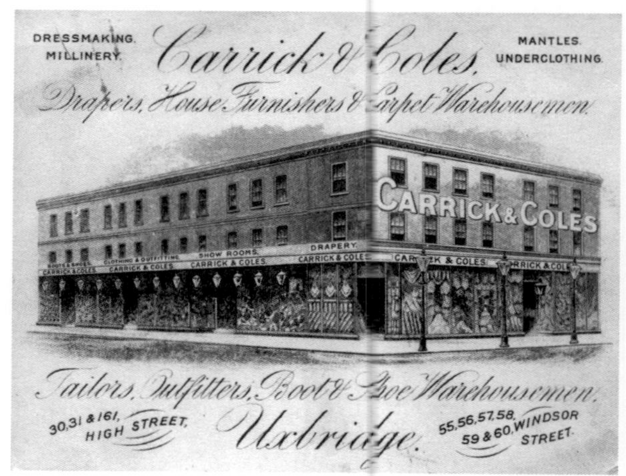

fig 1 *Carrick and Coles* c 1870, engraving

Opposite
fig 2 Robert Faulkner & Co, *Some of the students of the Slade School of Art, University College, London, taken after a strawberry tea on 23 June 1905*, photo, Slade School Archive, University College London

DEBORAH HART

to early 1904. Her first recorded address is Brookfield House in Uxbridge. After her father died in 1899, she is listed at Blakesley Avenue in Ealing, where her mother relocated. Still living at home at the age of twenty-six, Carrick was an eager student. The attendance records, divided into female and male students on opposite sides of the ledger, reveal that she was often among the first to sign in, at times attending classes on Saturdays when the numbers were down.[11] Over time, her peers included Edna Clarke Hall, Anna Airy, Muriel Coldwell, Harold Gilman and Spencer Gore.[12]

The Slade during Carrick's time under Professor Frederick Brown and the other masters, including Henry Tonks, was described as follows:

> **Every student, on entering the School, is placed in the Antique class, which they quit by completion for the Life Class. Students of both sexes are admitted, the male and female students working together in the Antique classes only. The studios are open from 9.30am till 5pm, except on Saturdays, when they close at 3pm; and in the Life School two models pose every day from 10am till 5pm for three days a week the figure or head poses for the Modelling Class.**
>
> **During every term lectures are given on Anatomy.[13]**

The annual Slade prizes, offering money or books, as well as certificates, were a source of real encouragement for the students. Carrick was awarded Third Prize in Figure Composition (1899–1900) and won the Melville Nettleship Prize for Figure Composition (1903–04).[14] Certificates bestowed to her across various disciplines over her years at the school include Antique Drawing, Head Painting, Fine Art Anatomy and Painting from Life.[15]

While there are few extant works from this period by Carrick, examples of drawings by others, including Tonks himself, convey a feeling for the teaching at the time—anatomical studies and portraits after Michelangelo Buonarroti in pencil, red chalk and ink; also drawings of draperies and apparel, including details of shoes and trousers.[16] Widely regarded at the Slade as ferocious yet influential, Tonks had been a surgeon prior to becoming an artist and teacher.[17] A man of contradictory impulses, he admired classical drawing as well as the avant-garde work of French artist Edgar Degas, who was something of a talisman for him in his approach to the subjects of daily life, and who in turn would become very important to Carrick as well.

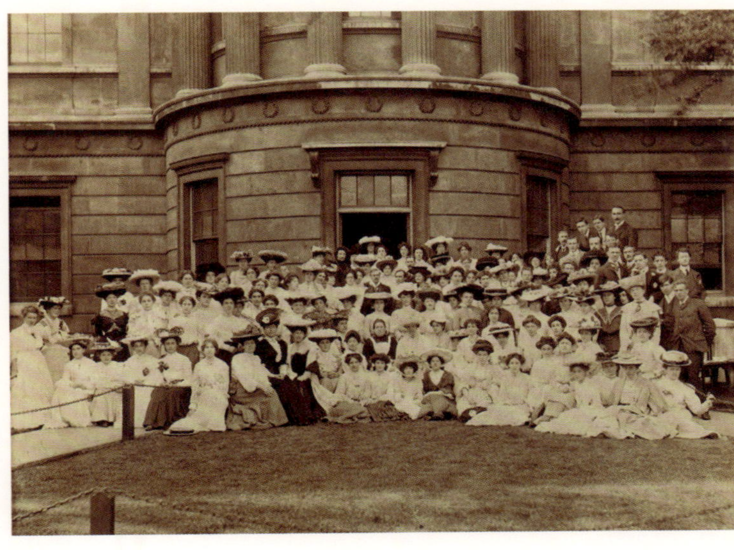

Tonks' diverse interests included fashion and etiquette, as revealed in works like *The hat shop* 1892 (fig 3). There are parallels between this painting and Carrick's *The breakfast table* 1907 (cat 91, p 140), revealing aspects of her Slade training in its luminosity, tonalities and painterly qualities. In particular, there is a striking similarity between the women in white dresses set against sunlit windows, showing white in various subtle gradations. This suggests their shared interest in James McNeill Whistler and John Singer Sargent, both American-born artists who had been exhibiting at the Royal Academy and the Paris Salons.[18] Among works of great interest was Whistler's ravishing yet controversial *Symphony in white, no. 1: the white girl* 1861–62 (National Gallery of Art, Washington DC). In Carrick's painting, the woman drawing back a delicate curtain to look outdoors stands to the side of a table that consumes the composition, becoming a stage for an array of objects: cups and saucers, a teapot on a tray, a slice of toast in a silver rack and a vase of flowers. A related painting, *The table vase* c 1907 (cat 5) depicts another contemplative woman, and is also a study of white on white and delicate tonal variations. The attention given to each object in these works conveys Carrick's interest in still life, which would emerge as a focus for her years later.

Another significant teacher at the Slade was Philip Wilson Steer, who was appointed Professor of Painting in 1893. Having been rejected by the Royal Academy as a student, Steer travelled to Paris and studied at the Académie Julian and the École des Beaux-Arts. Influenced by the impressionists in Paris, Steer's work *Boulogne sands* 1888–91 (fig 16, p 64)—depicting women and children on a beach with striped red and white beach tents in the background—is echoed in Carrick's later beach scenes. It is unclear whether she would have seen this painting when it was exhibited at the New English Art Club in 1892, but Steer's approach to the impressionist genre would no doubt have impacted her own. Steer's depictions of Richmond Castle in Yorkshire may also have been an impetus for Carrick's bold, blocky, light-filled painting of the same castle, seen from the river (cat 6, pp 22–23).

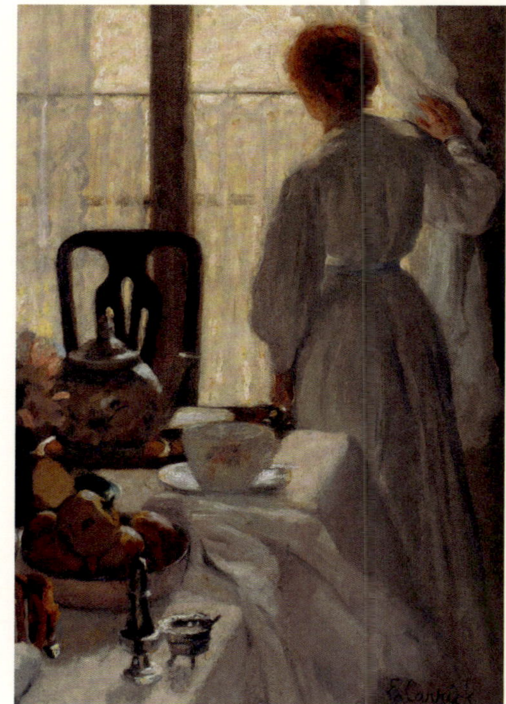

The breakfast table 1907 (detail cat 91, p 140), oil on canvas on board, private collection

Below
fig 3 Henry Tonks, *The hat shop* 1892, oil on canvas, Birmingham Museums Trust

Opposite
cat 5 *The table vase* c 1907, oil on canvas on composition board, private collection

Following
cat 6 *Richmond, Yorkshire* c 1903, oil on canvas, Art Gallery of Western Australia

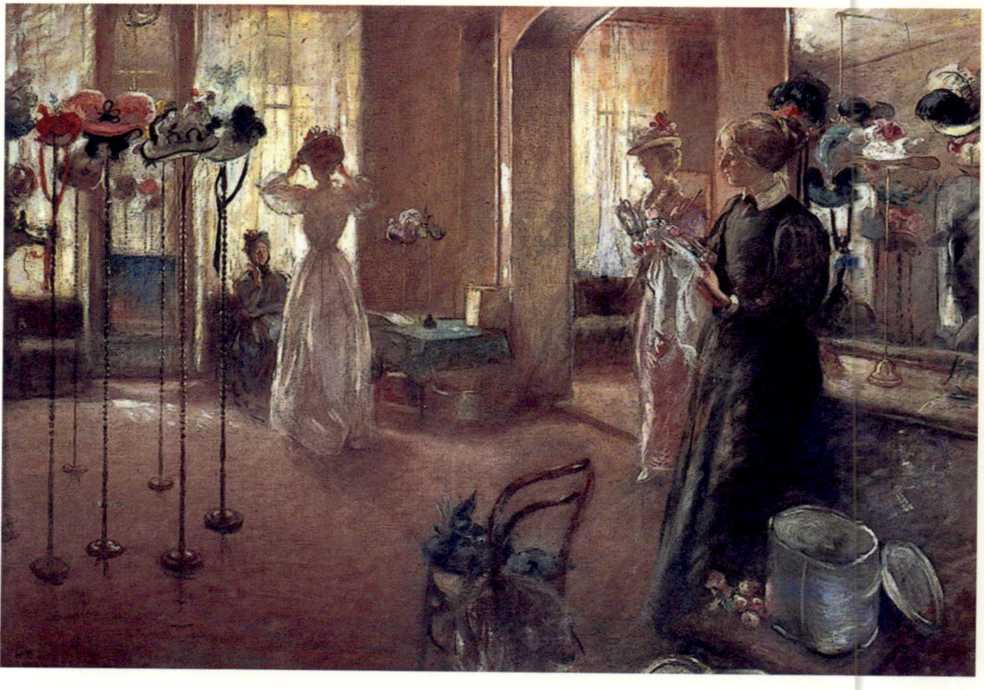

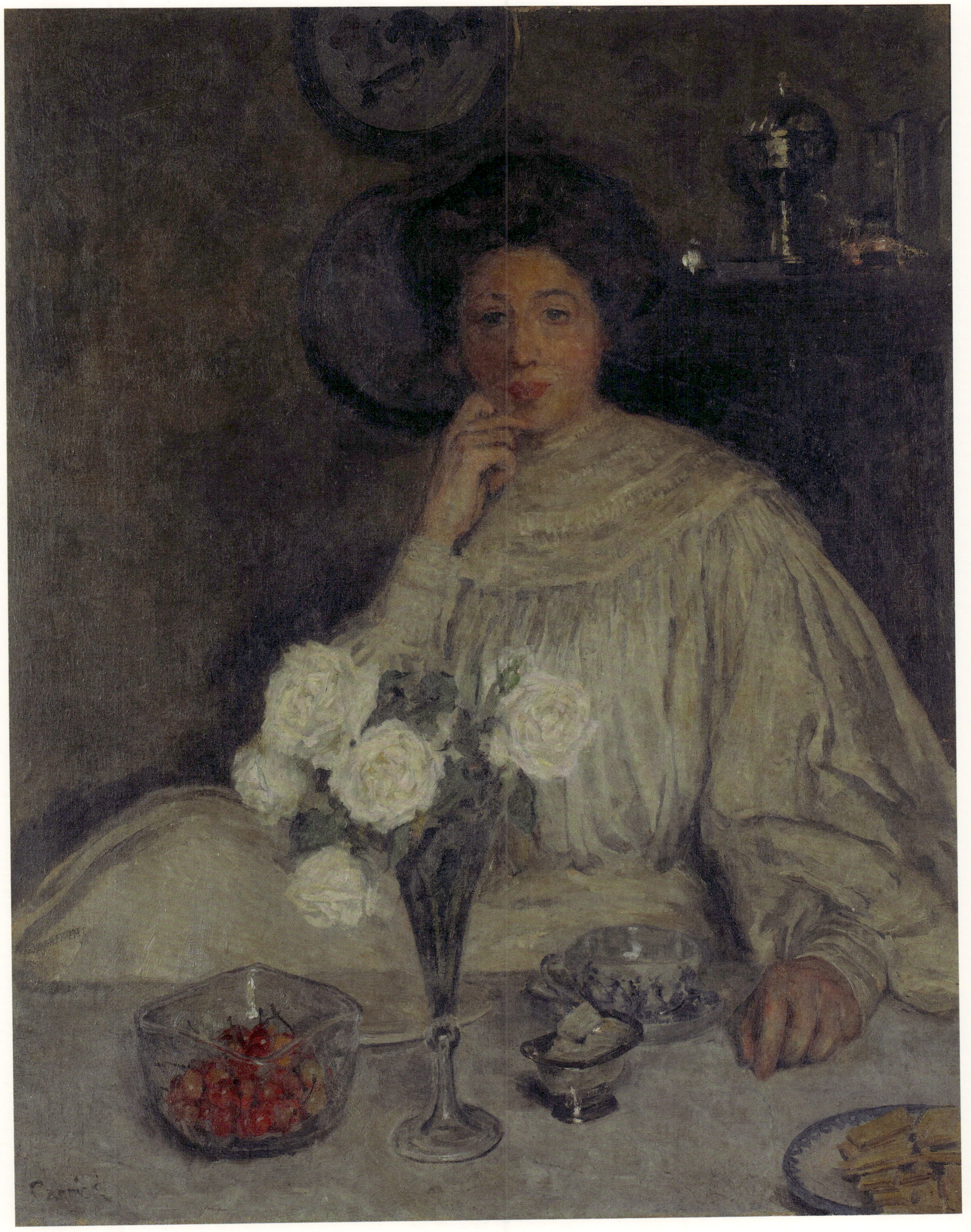

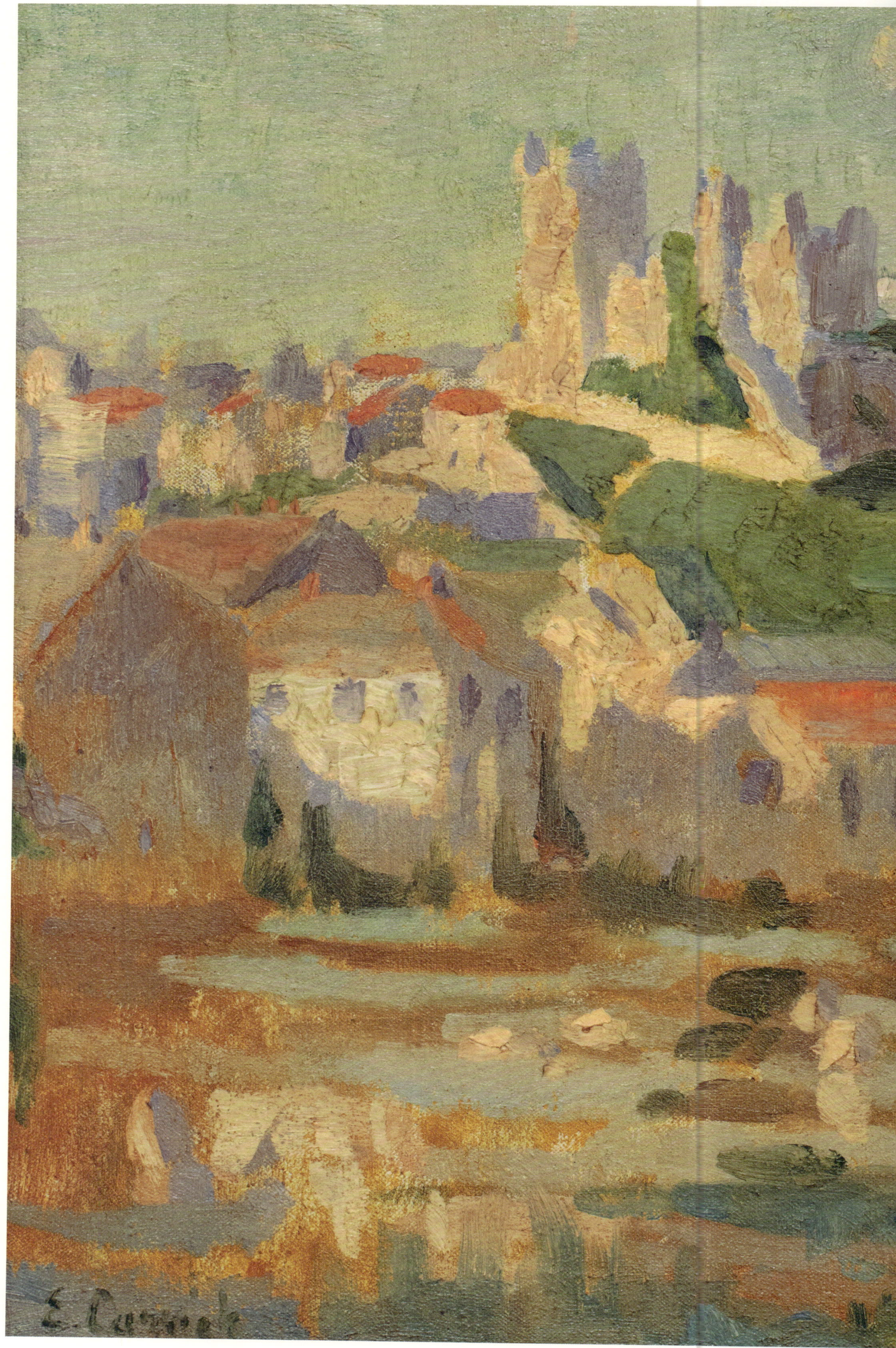

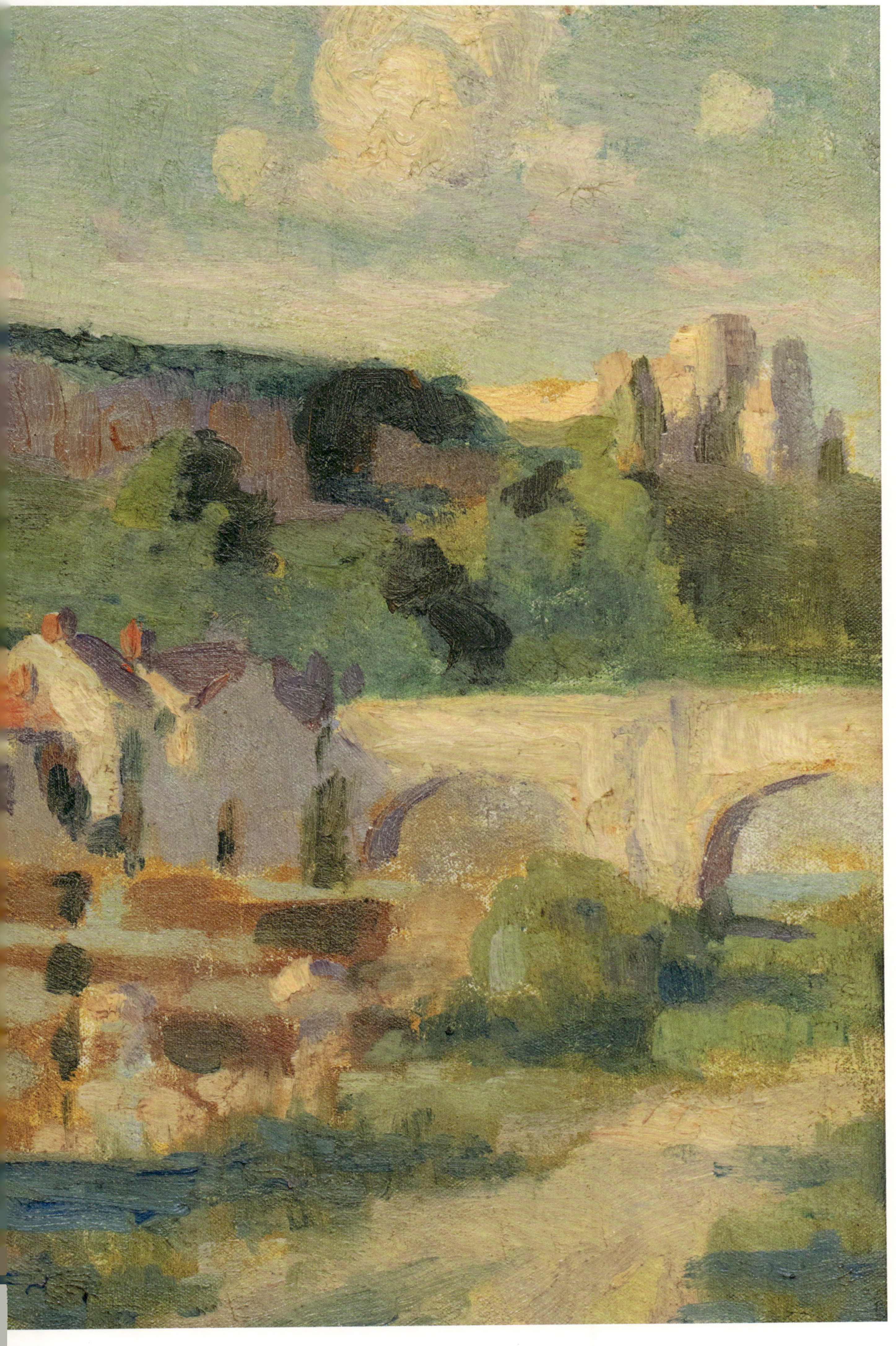

Other major inspirations for Carrick at this time were the thriving artist colonies of Newlyn and St Ives in West Cornwall, where she spent time during the summers while she was at the Slade. The colonies were known for the congenial atmosphere among artists eager to develop their skills, with many social events and much camaraderie shaping their daily lives. While the works Carrick created there have disappeared into collections over time, and there are scant details of her periods in Newlyn, the experience in Cornwall deeply influenced her life and work.

Carrick was one of 'the Slade girls' at St Ives—a group of women who mostly resided in The Cabin Studio (also known as The Cabin) in Westcotts Quay.[19] She visited the St Ives Art Club with Hilda Fearon and other Slade peers in 1899 and local papers *St Ives Weekly* and *Western Echo* reveal that Carrick stayed in St Ives from July to October in 1900, and again during the summer months in 1901.[20] Among the other artists who stayed in The Cabin were Muriel Coldwell, Agnes Vyse and Irma Richter. Conditions were basic, but the picturesque environment of St Ives, set around steep, winding streets, with its array of studios facing the sea, made it a haven for artists from all over the world. One of them, Emily Carr, a Canadian artist who spent considerable time in St Ives, noted the different customs when her landlords were surprised that she needed hot water to bathe daily rather than bathing as they did, once a week in the sea.[21] Among the Australians in Cornwall were Richard Hayley Lever, and Will Ashton who became a lifelong friend of Carrick's.

Ethel's teachers at St Ives included Julius Olsson, Louis Grier and Algernon Talmage. The mantra that many took away from their learnings was 'values', which meant an emphasis on tonal variation—very subtle shifts from dark to light, and soft, silvery greys transitioning to creamy and brighter whites. Some of these ideas had been fostered by Whistler, who spent time in Cornwall painting small poetic images abstracted from the environment. However, the teaching in St Ives tended to be more traditional and naturalistic.[22]

Insights into the teaching at this time were given by Emily Carr, who recalled that students met at the Harbour Studio first thing in the morning 'to receive "crits" on the work done the afternoon before. Both Olsson and Talmage gave the students "crits" three days a week'.[23] She found these teachers, however, to have contradictory approaches. Olsson was a tough taskmaster. Carr, who was outspoken and didn't conform to the idea of women as demure or 'decorative', remembered his disparaging remarks about a work she was proud of, calling it 'maudlin rubbish': 'Go out there ... out to bright sunlight—PAINT.'[24] Talmage's approach was, in her view, more constructive. One of his instructions, relating to her use of dark colour, was to remember that 'there is sunshine too in the shadows'.[25] This kind of idea would become very pertinent to Carrick years later.

Another influential practice—and a principal drawcard of classes in St Ives—was the opportunity to work out of doors, with the sea as a key subject. Painting out in the open with others passing by would become essential to Carrick's artistic approach and visual language. In these still formative years of her career, she evidently benefitted from setting up her easel in the landscape and painting for hours on end to capture the scenery, as well as the movement of sea and light through the day and across diverse weather conditions. Moonlight was also a favourite subject for many, including Olsson, Australian artist David Davies—who had been at St Ives earlier,[26] and Hilda Fearon who, along with her cousin,

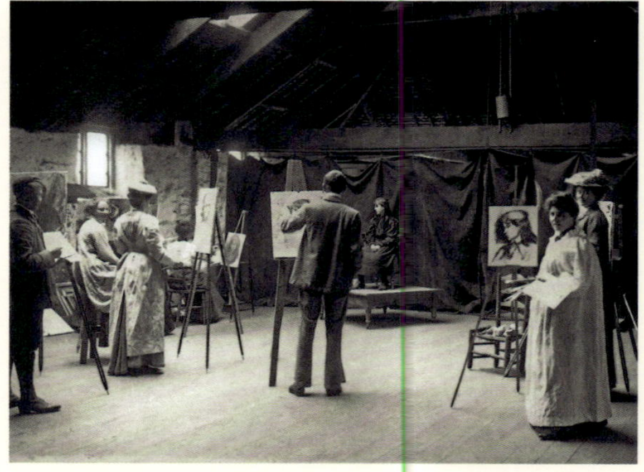

fig 4 William Herbert Lanyon, *Students at the Cornish School of Landscape and Sea Painting at work in the Harbour Studio*, c 1901, photograph, (the first three on the left, left to right) Will Ashton, Hilda Fearon and Emily Carr

Below
fig 5 Emily Carr, *And where is she at midnight* [?] *Why standing on the quay. Watching the boats with nut brown sails tossing on the sea* 1901–02, graphite drawing on paper, Royal BC Museum

Opposite
fig 6 Camille Pissarro, *Rue de l'Épicerie, Rouen* (*Effect of sunlight*) 1898, oil on canvas, The Metropolitan Museum of Art

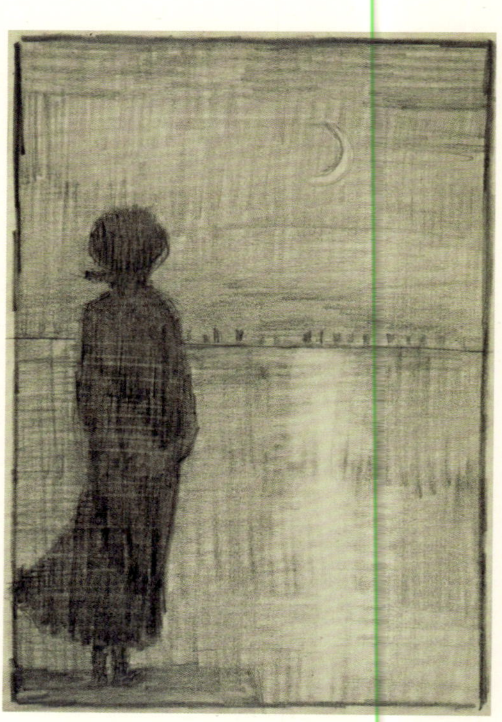

was discovered just outside The Cabin one night with her paintbox and a candle in a cigar box: 'They had been out looking for the Moon.'[27] In addition to painting outdoors, Carrick and her fellow students worked indoors at the Harbour Studio, especially on inclement days. There was a real sense of community, with the St Ives Art Club a hub of artistic and social activity.

The most important turning point in Carrick's personal life came during her time at St Ives when she met her future husband, Emanuel Phillips Fox, on one of the sketching trips into the landscape in 1901.[28]

At the time, Fox was renting the magnificent Porthmeor Studio formerly occupied by Olsson, with its expansive vista of the ocean. An Australian artist, Fox had returned to St Ives for a most unusual reason: as part of the stipulations of a commission received in his home city of Melbourne to paint Captain Cook landing on Australian shores, he had to undertake the work on British soil.[29] It says a lot about the times, with Britain still considered by many Australians as 'home'—although the idea of staging this event on the shores of St Ives is bizarre, to say the least. Fox undertook research for the painting in Australia and called upon Will Ashton to pose as one of the figures in this historical painting, which is now in the collection of the National Gallery of Victoria.[30]

It was some time before the relationship between Carrick and Fox was announced. It is possible that they were together in France with other artists in 1902 and 1903—Fox was familiar with the north-west coast of Normandy and Brittany, and both would have been aware of the classes that Norman Garstin, an artist and teacher in Newlyn, had taken to France, including to Caudebec-en-Caux.[31] It was there that Carrick painted one of her most significant early works, *The market, Caudebec* c 1902 (cat 4, p 16), a forerunner to a subject that in part defines her artistic practice: the hustle and bustle of marketplaces. In it we can already glean Carrick's delight in people gathering to purchase and sell produce under covered canopies, with a number clad in traditional local dress. The work conveys the early influence of impressionist painter Camille Pissarro, including his *Rue de l'Épicerie, Rouen* (Effect of sunlight) 1898 (fig 6).[32] In Carrick's painting, the figures appear as in a snapshot, casually going about their business—a compositional feature that would become characteristic of her approach.

Equally important was her appreciation of the architecture of Caudebec-en-Caux's famous Gothic cathedral. The detail in her depiction of the buildings conveys precise observation and drawing, which is also evident in prints undertaken in England and later in France, such as *The High Street, Oxford* (cat 7, p 26)[33] and *Houses* 1906 (cat 8, p 27). The more fluidly painted foreground cast in shadow opens onto the middle ground and a church bathed in luminosity. The figures on the far right also suggest the beginnings of Carrick's experimentation with black, which may have been inspired by Édouard Manet. This painting was shown by The Royal Institute of Oil Painters in London in 1903—her first known exhibited painting—and reproduced in the women's publication *The Queen: The Ladies' Newspaper and Court Chronicle*.

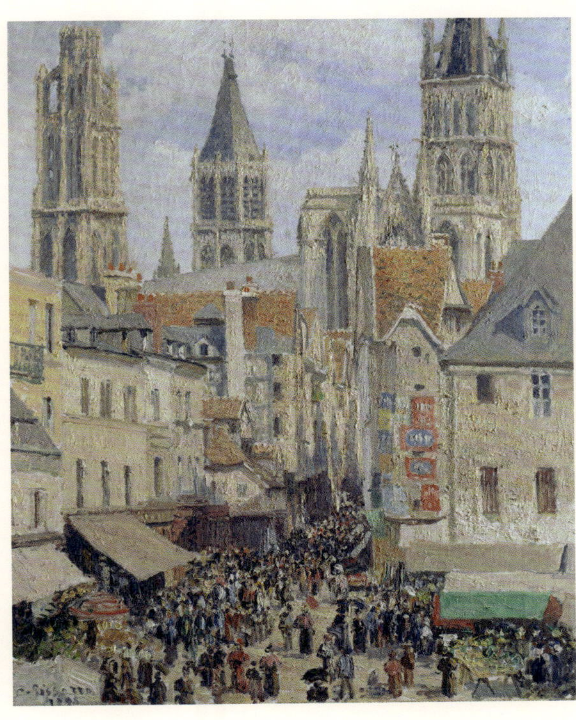

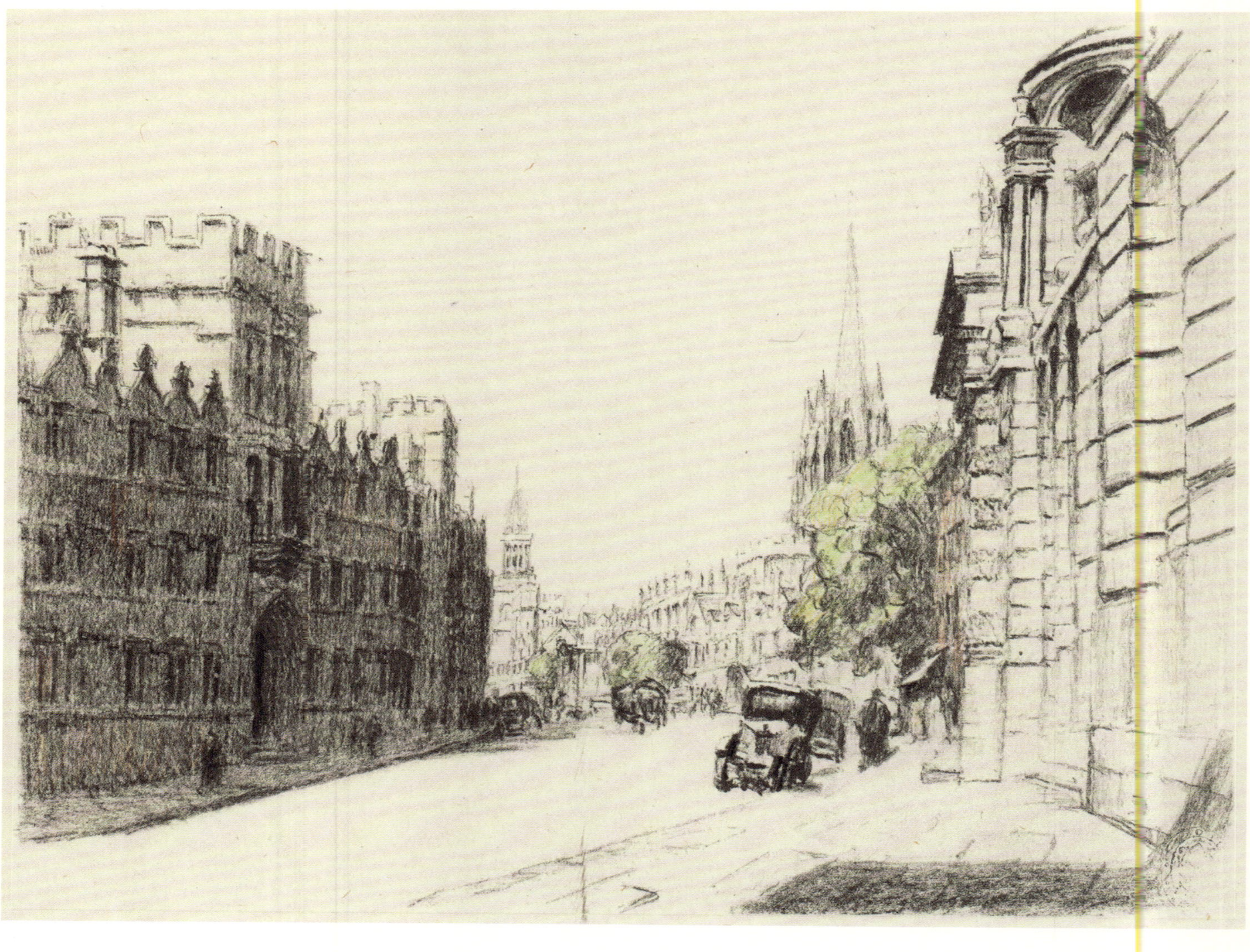

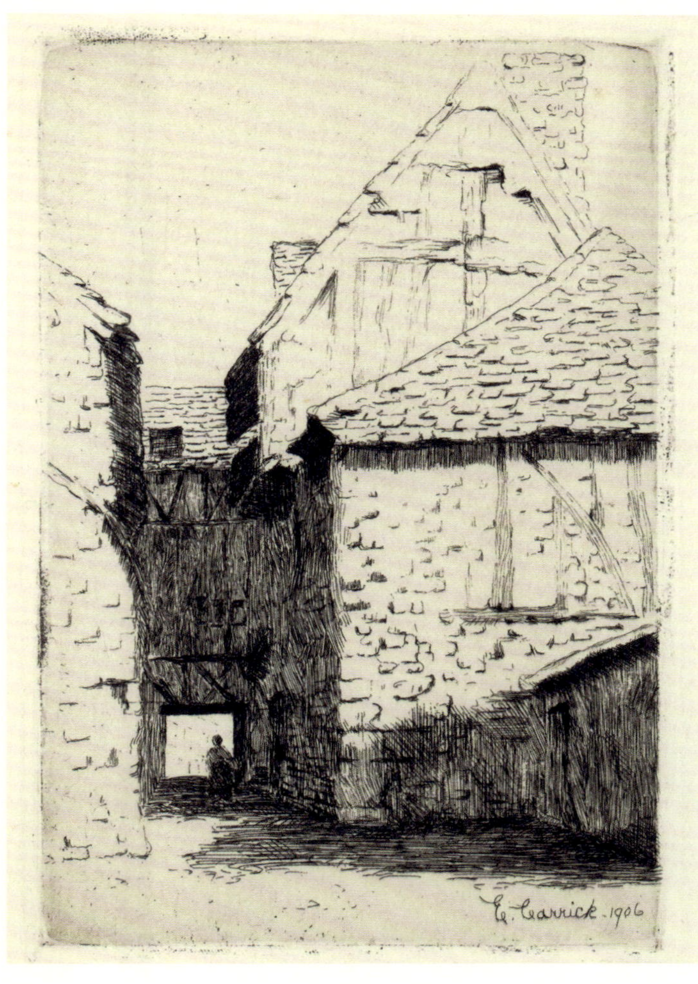

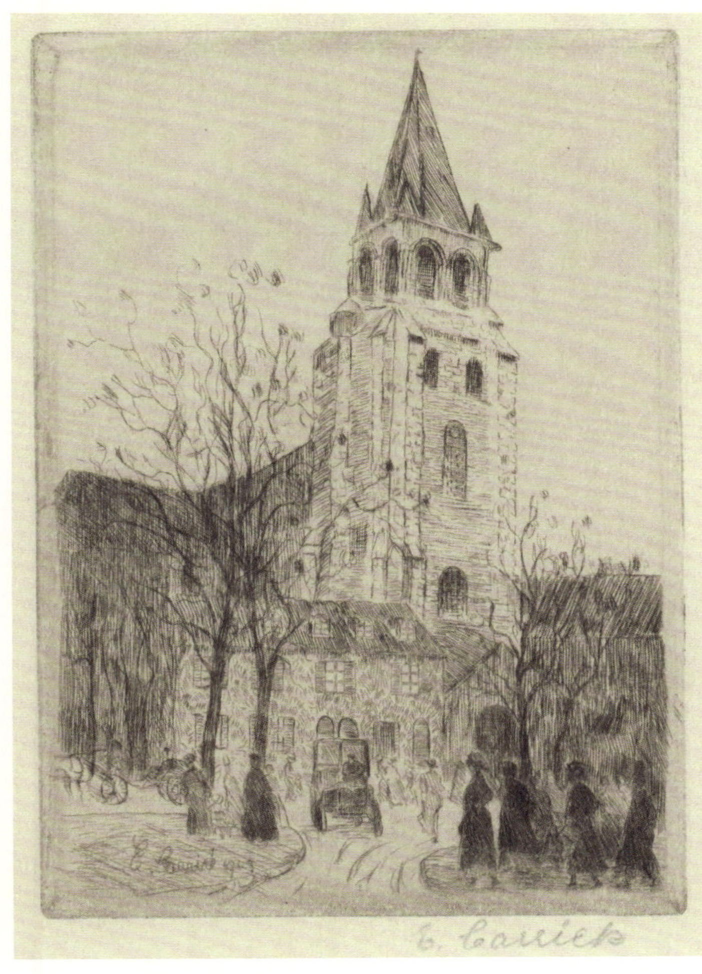

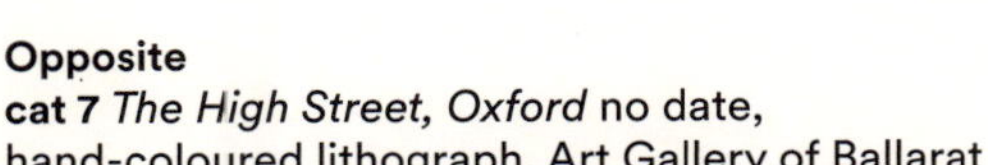

Opposite
cat 7 *The High Street, Oxford* no date, hand-coloured lithograph, Art Gallery of Ballarat

Top to bottom
cat 8 *Houses* 1906, etching in black ink on paper, Art Gallery of Ballarat

cat 9 *Saint-Germain-des-Prés, Paris* 1907, etching printed in black ink from one copper plate, National Gallery of Australia

Carrick's burgeoning fascination with marketplaces is revealed in other scenes painted in these early years, including *Pumpkin sellers* c 1903–04 (cat 11) and *Vegetable market* c 1904 (cat 12, p 30). While these works still convey the influence of her Slade teachers, the expressive, broad brushstrokes suggest Carrick's growing interest in contemporary French painting, presaging her post-impressionist works to follow. *Pumpkin sellers* also reveals her broadening interest in womanhood—in this case, women who were less privileged than herself, trying to find a way to earn a living through the abundance of nature.[34]

By 1904, Fox and Carrick's relationship had deepened and a letter from Fox to his sister-in-law Laura, dated 29 December, suggests that they were likely engaged:

> I spoke of the portrait I was painting of Ethel, whom I suppose you have discussed around the family board long ere this reaches you …
>
> I spent a very pleasant Christmas at Ealing, at the house of Mrs Carrick—They were very nice and hospitable and allowed one to amuse themselves according to their own wishes, which just suited me as I was completely fagged over the portrait—We were a party of nine, and with music, a few recitations, games of cards & billiards, we amused ourselves exceedingly well. Two of the boys were at home one from Cambridge University … The other who is younger is gaining training on a large farm …
>
> I have also spent some pleasant evenings at relations of Ethel's and we both dined with Lottie [Fox's cousin] at their pretty house, where first impressions seemed mutually favourable …
>
> Affectionately yours
>
> Mannie[35]

Below
cat 10 Emanuel Phillips Fox, *Portrait of Ethel Carrick Fox* 1907, oil on canvas on board, Art Gallery of Western Australia

Opposite
cat 11 *Pumpkin sellers* c 1903–04, oil on wood panel, private collection

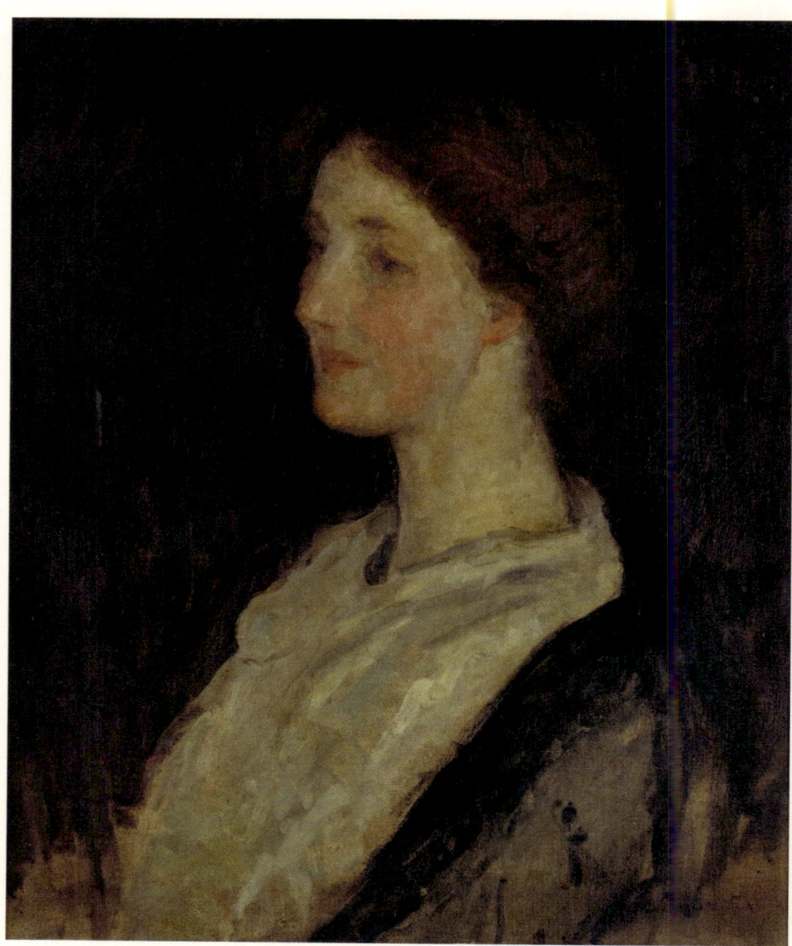

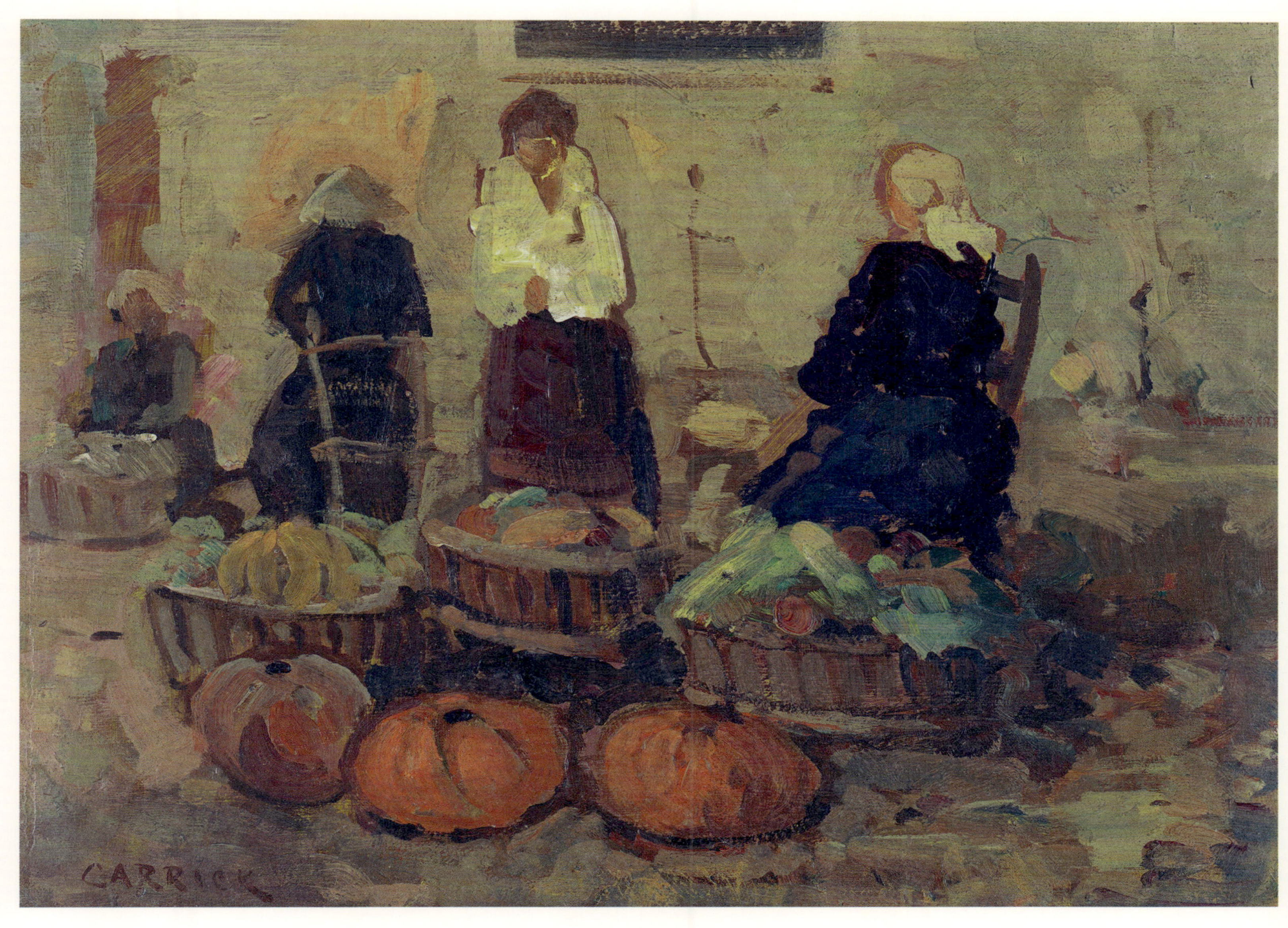
CARRICK

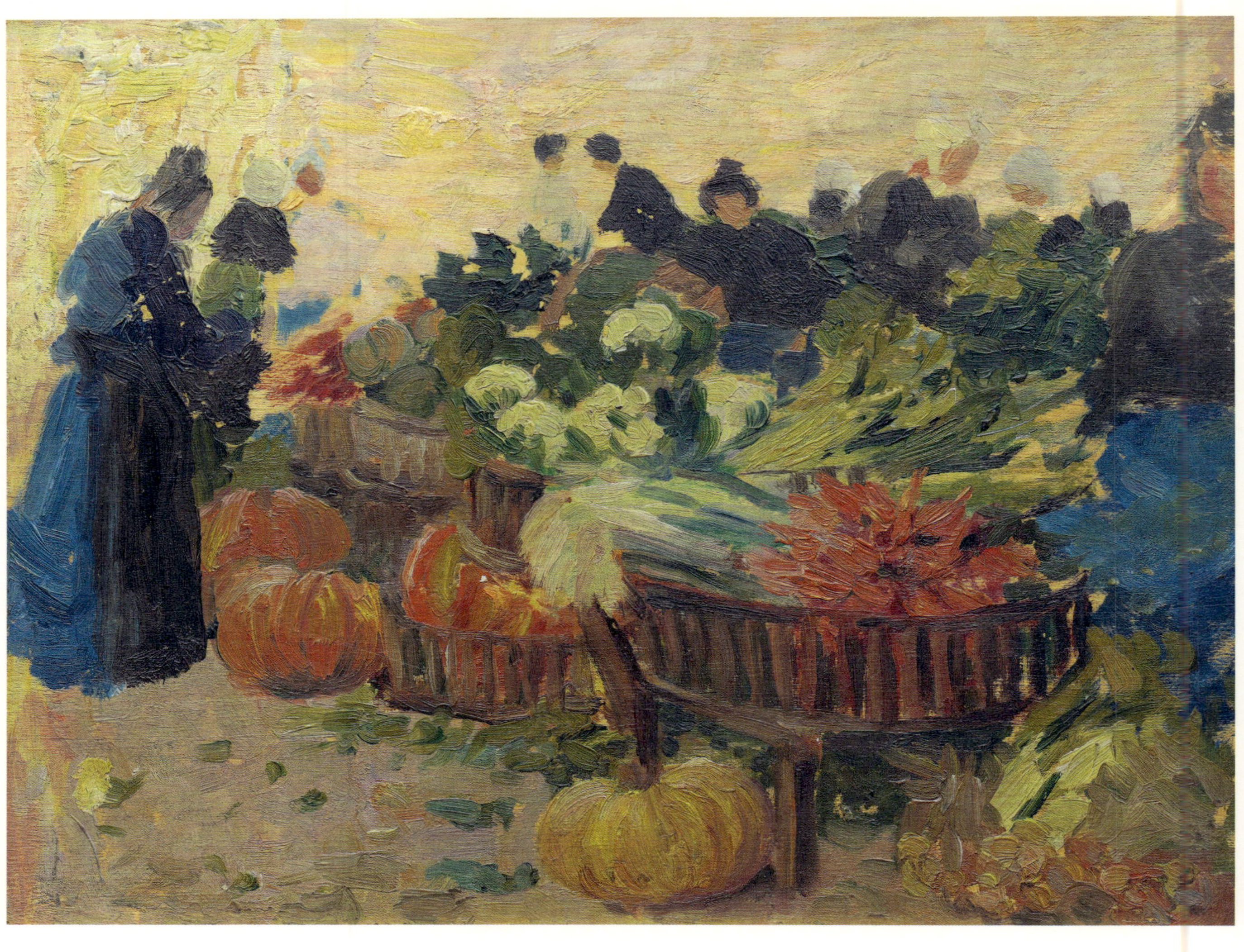

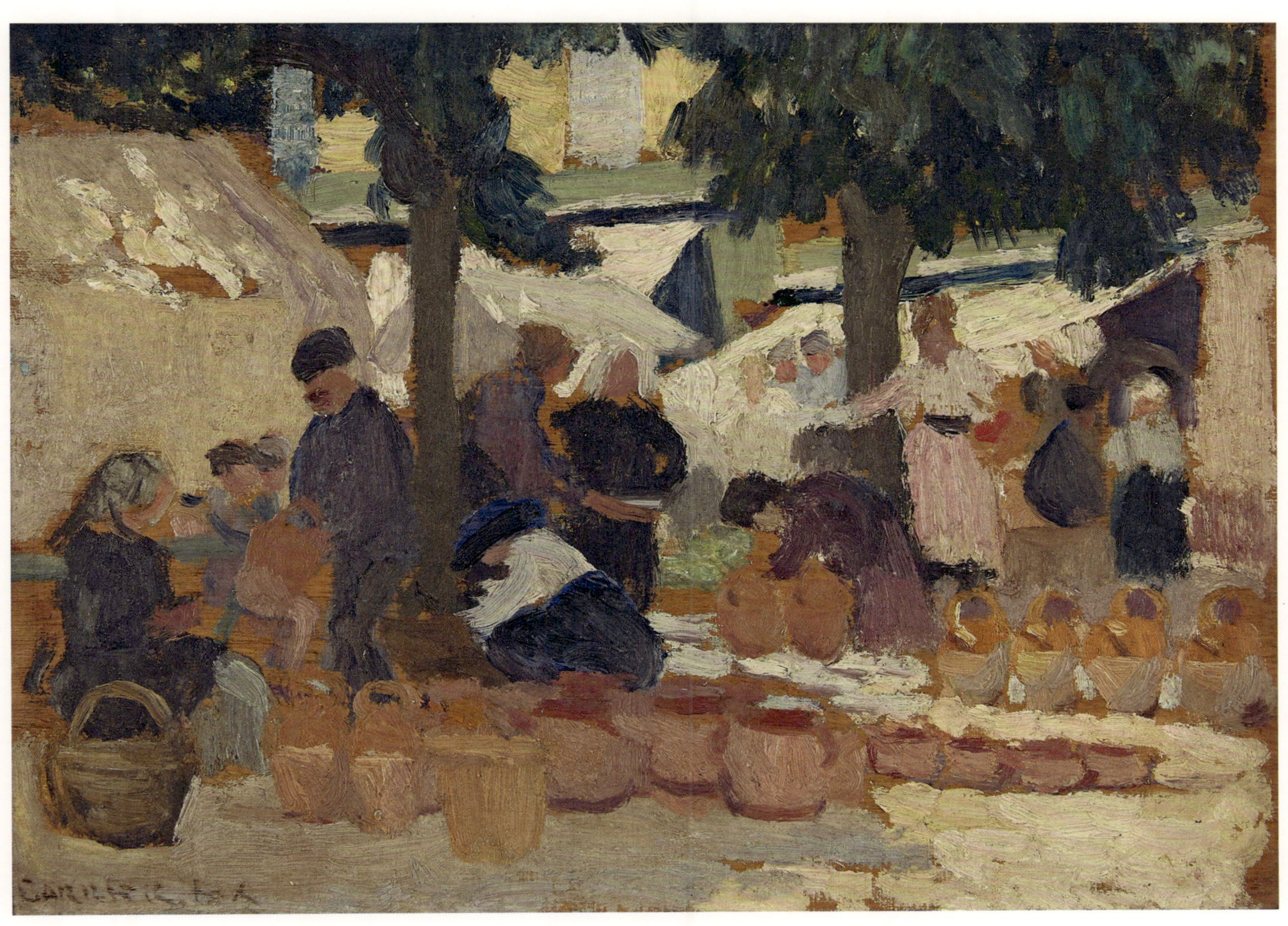

Opposite
cat 12 *Vegetable market* c 1904, oil on panel, private collection

Above
cat 13 *Market scene* c 1910, oil on board, Shepparton Art Museum

On 7 January 1905, artist Tom Roberts wrote in a letter that Fox and his fiancée, Ethel Carrick, had visited him at 39A Harrington Road, South Kensington.[36] Roberts had also made a name for himself in Australia in the latter part of the nineteenth century, and had been one of the instigators of, and exhibitors in, the *9 by 5 impression exhibition* at the Buxton Rooms in Melbourne. The show included small works painted on wooden cigar-box lids that were inspired by Whistler's innovative, non-literal approach—at times adopting the abstract language of music and envisioning works as tonal harmonies.

In January to February 1905, Carrick exhibited her painting *Harmony in grey* c 1904 at the fifth exhibition of the International Society of Sculptors, Painters and Gravers held at the New Gallery, London. Both Carrick and Fox would have been familiar with Whistler's work, especially following his death in 1903 when there were many exhibitions celebrating his achievements. It is likely that the experimental aspects of Whistler's approach were of interest to Carrick. In 1878, Whistler had won a libel suit against John Ruskin, due to the latter's disparaging comments about the artist's almost abstract *Nocturne in black and gold—the falling rocket* c 1875 (Detroit Institute of Arts Museum), shown at Grosvenor Gallery in 1877. Whistler's proclamations in his 'Ten o'clock' lecture would also have rung true to Carrick's interest in art and music, and her more modern approach to come:

> Nature contains the elements, in colour and form, of all pictures, as the keyboard contains the notes of all music.
>
> But the artist is born to pick and choose, and group with science, these elements, that the result may be beautiful—as the musician gathers his notes, and forms his chords, until he brings forth from chaos glorious harmony.[37]

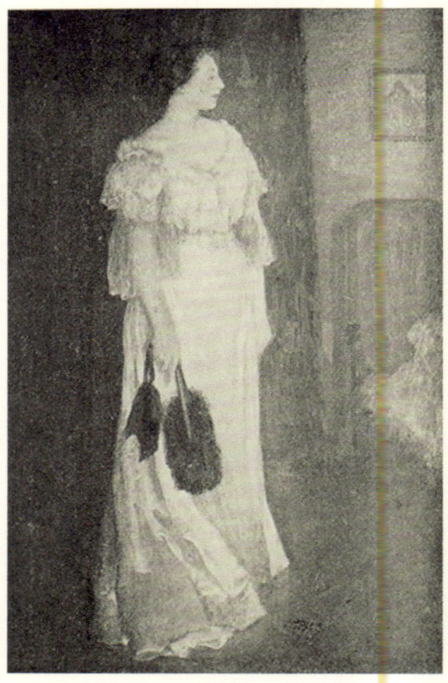

fig 7 Emanuel Phillips Fox, *Ethel, daughter of the late AW Carrick, Esq* c 1904, oil on canvas

While Carrick was open to experimentation, Fox tended towards safer aspects of Whistler's approach, such as harmonious placements of form and colour, including in portraits such as *Ethel, daughter of the late AW Carrick, Esq* c 1904 (fig 7). Known only from a reproduction in black and white and reports of the day, the painting's title indicates Fox's desire to show his wife-to-be as a dignified woman of good standing.[38] Shown at the Royal Academy in May 1905, the same month the couple married, the portrait of Carrick wearing a white silk evening dress and holding a black fan was described as a 'symphony in pearly greys and black against a deep red curtain'.[39] It is a tender tribute to a woman Fox clearly admired as being her own person.

Ethel Carrick and Emanuel Phillips Fox were married at St Peter's Church in Ealing on 9 May 1905. When the wedding bells rang out on that spring day, there was a large crowd of local, regional and cross-continental well-wishers present. Australians at the wedding included longstanding friends of Fox residing across the United Kingdom and in Paris at the time. George and Amy Lambert were there, with George as Fox's best man and witness, along with two of Carrick's siblings, Hartley and Constance Carrick. Ethel Carrick was given away by her mother and wore a 'dress of white satin ... and full court train of satin, with a wreath of orange blossom and a Brussels lace veil. She wore a handsome amethyst necklace, and carried a handsome bouquet of white roses, the gift of the bridegroom'.[40] As well as members of the Carrick family, a large contingent of the Fox family attended, including Fox's brother and sister-in-law, David and Irene Fox, along with other siblings and relatives.

After the ceremony, Carrick's mother held a reception at the family home 'Tren Crom' on Blakesley Avenue, Ealing. There was a large group in attendance. Tudor St George Tucker, with whom Fox had formed an influential art school in Melbourne, was present, along with one of their students from that time who would later become a close friend of Carrick's, Violet Teague. Other Australians listed in the *British Australasian* as being part of the occasion include 'Mr and Mrs McCubbin, Mr and Mrs Mather, Mr Bernard Hall, Mr [Arthur] Streeton, Mr and Mrs Mackennal, Mr and Mrs Geo. Coates [George Coates and Dora Meeson], Mr and Mrs Longstaff, Mr and Mrs Tom Roberts, Mr and Mrs Rupert Bunny.'[41] Also enjoying the festivities were three teachers from St Ives: Julius Olsson, Algernon Talmage with his wife (the artist Gertrude Rowe) and Louis Grier. Friends from the Slade and St Ives included Hilda Fearon, Irma Richter, Arthur Burgess and Muriel Coldwell.

Carrick and Fox spent their honeymoon in Cornwall before leaving for Paris, a move that had been planned for some time. It would open up a whole new chapter of their lives in a city where art and life enmeshed and where the couple could flourish in ways that gave them freedom to achieve their artistic ambitions, together and independently.[42]

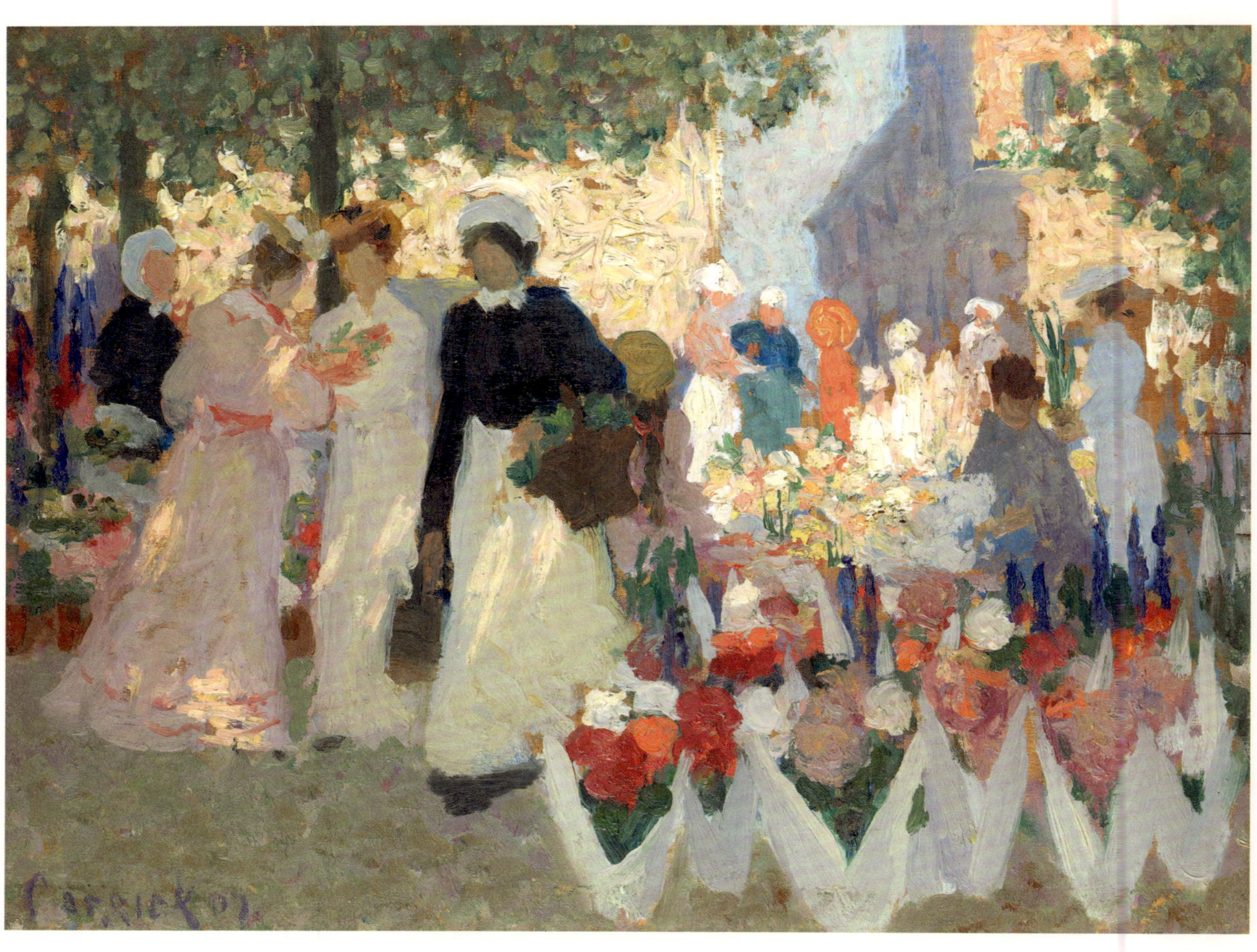
Carrick 07

Discovering her vision: 1905–1915

It's people who attract me. Crowds are to me what a magnet is to a needle. I love the color, life, movement, and individuality of a crowd ... To me it has the attraction a fine orchestra has to a musician, and often when I've been painting some of the groups ... I have felt them as musical chords.[43]

— Ethel Carrick

Opposite
cat 14 *Flower market* 1907, oil on wood panel, National Gallery of Victoria

In 1905, Ethel Carrick and Emanuel Phillips Fox moved to 65 Boulevard Arago in Montparnasse, near the Luxembourg Gardens. This would remain Carrick's abode in Paris on and off for most of her life. Situated off a wide boulevard, the complex in the artists' compound of La Cité Fleurie was entered through the main archway, where one would find 'a surprise of quaint courtyards and creepers, twisting cobble paths, wicker gates and the loveliest little gardens onto which open doors and windows of studios and flats'.[44] Comprising around 30 apartments constructed with materials from the Exposition Universelle of 1878,[45] the compound comprised two rows of adjoining half-timbered, double-storey apartments with studios.[46]

Living in Paris, Carrick and Fox enjoyed socialising and hosted many 'at home' gatherings with local artists and musicians, as well as visitors from Australia and England. Facing the courtyard, the apartments were light-filled, with windows and doors opening onto the garden. This was a source of much inspiration for Carrick and Fox in their art and daily lives. Carrick later described the feeling of a vibrant community: 'We are quite a cosmopolitan little colony of hard-working artists who have apartments in the same building, thirty different nationalities being represented.'[47] As a British-born woman residing in France married to an artist from Australia—which would later become another home—Carrick was truly a part of this international milieu.

This was the time of the Belle Époque and Paris was brimming with opportunities for culturally diverse artists, writers, musicians and intellectuals to become enmeshed in the vibrant atmosphere of the place. It was possible to visit significant collections of historical works of art alongside works of the late nineteenth century by artists such as Manet

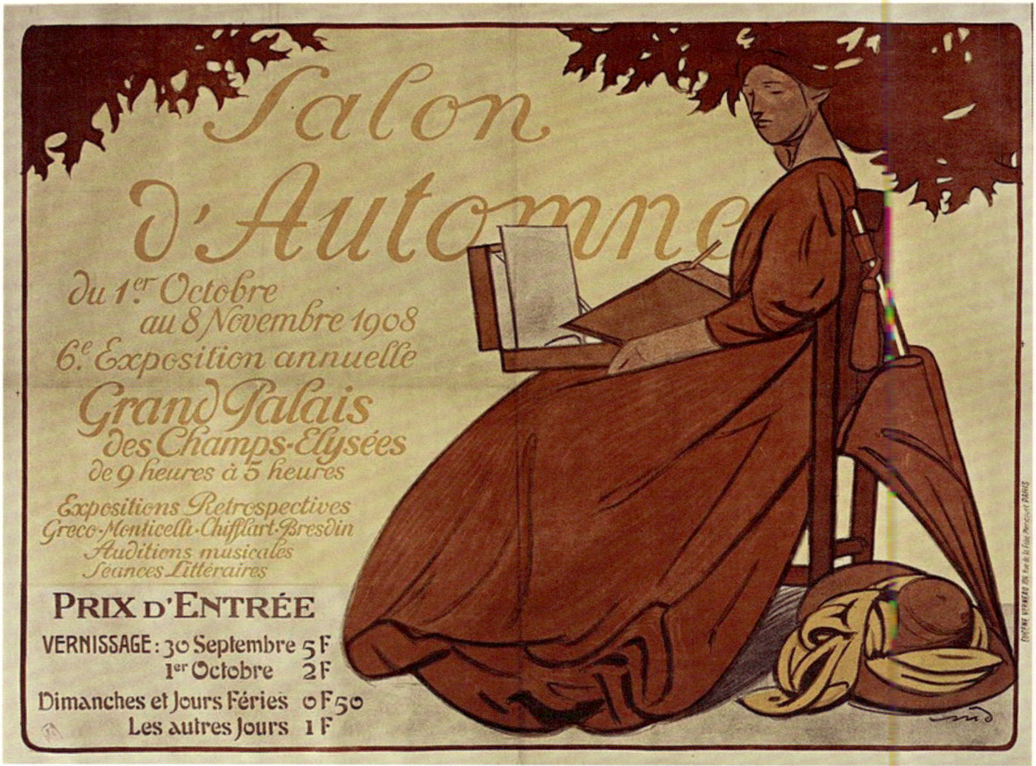

fig 8 Maxime Dethomas, *Salon d'Automne poster* 1908

and Degas, which had begun to enter museum collections. There were also many opportunities for contemporary artists to exhibit. As Carrick reflected in 'Studio Life in Paris' in 1908:

> Paris is undoubtedly the home of the art-student, the well-loved home. One is surrounded by the atmosphere of Art; there seems nothing else to live for. All one's friends are sympathetic and interested, the City and surroundings are lovely, the Louvre is a constant joy, and the Luxembourg, Salons, and various other Exhibitions, continually stimulate one's energies and interests.[48]

Studio space was an important starting point. During their first year in Boulevard Arago, Carrick and Fox shared the apartment studio space, as they did on and off for many years, although in 1906 Fox rented a separate studio nearby.[49] The couple often gave previews of their works to friends, and a report in *The Queen* on 9 March 1907 noted: 'Previous to sending their recently accomplished pictures to the Salon and Royal Academy Mr and Mrs Phillips-Fox showed them to some of their friends at their studio ... Among those who called during the afternoon were Rupert Bunny and Edith Anderson, and American artists Frederick Frieseke and Gustav Goetsch.'[50]

There were several ateliers near to La Cité Fleurie where artists could work. While Carrick doesn't appear to have attended one particular school, she remarked that there were many local studios visited by well-known professors: 'Most of them are in or near the Latin quarter ... Thus one has an opportunity of seeing work done under varied influences, and one may elect to work in that studio visited by the painter whose teaching is in sympathy with one's own outlook on things.'[51] This was true to Carrick's own desire to find those things that resonated with her as she continued to establish her own artistic sense of direction.

Carrick and Fox worked hard and were ambitious for their art, exhibiting in a range of venues in Paris, London and Australia. Among

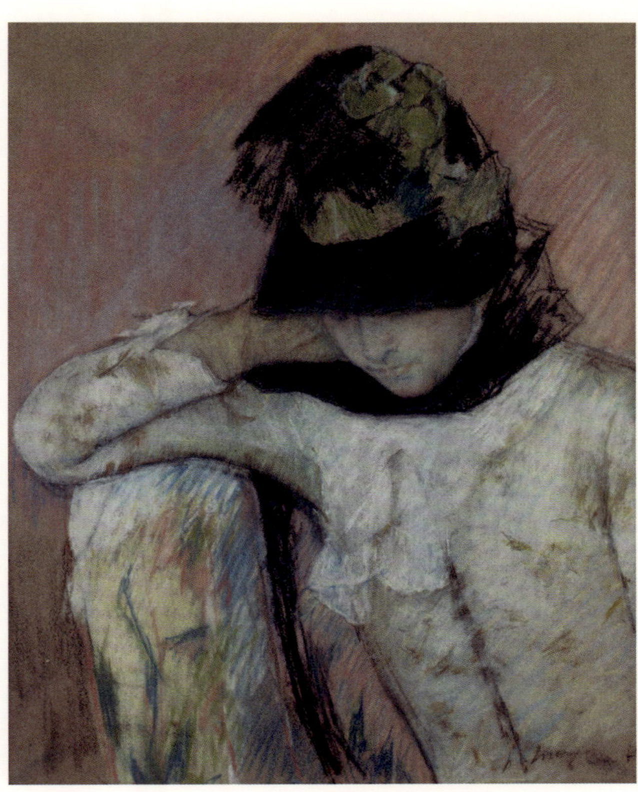

fig 9 Mary Cassatt, *Young woman in a black and green bonnet* c 1890, pastel, Princeton University Art Museum

the various Parisian Salons, the Old Salon was the most traditional; the New Salon was a more integrated affair of new and old; and the Salon d'Automne was the most radical of the three, where Carrick often exhibited. Fox, who was on the traditional end of the impressionist spectrum, considered much of the new work he saw there an affront; he was not a fan of most Post-Impressionism or Neo-Impressionism, let alone the Fauves like Henri Matisse and Maurice Denis. While the Salon d'Automne was often disparaged at the time, art history was being made there. Along with the group shows, retrospectives were held of Édouard Manet in 1905, Gustave Courbet and Paul Gauguin in 1906, and Berthe Morisot and Paul Cézanne in 1907. It was no small thing that Carrick was made a full member, a *sociétaire*, of the Salon d'Automne in 1911, as well as the first English woman to be appointed to the jury in 1912 (she was one of eight women compared to forty men).

Paris, as Carrick soon discovered, was a ferment of artistic activity—and the exhibiting options were not confined to the Salons. Women had been unable to enter the École des Beaux-Arts until 1897 and in response, late nineteenth-century Paris saw the city's first all-women art exhibitions and the establishment of the Union des Femmes Peintres et Sculpteurs (Union of Women Painters and Sculptors).[52] Founded by Hélène Bertaux in May 1881, they held annual exhibitions and fought to have women on the Salon juries.[53]

It was against this background that Carrick became closely associated with groups of women artists, including the International Art Union. Founded and supported by American philanthropist Grace Whitney-Hoff, it aimed to provide ways for American and English women artists to meet and share ideas and exhibitions, 'not as some closed circle' but together with their French peers and other nationalities.[54] The president of their first exhibition was the American-born Mary Cassatt, who had shown with the impressionists since 1877 (fig 9).[55] In 1913, Carrick told *The Herald* that she was vice-president of the women's

International Art Union.[56] She also exhibited with a group of women artists known as Les Quelques, which she described as 'a Paris club, consisting of the most prominent women painters in that city, of which Madame Cazin ... is honorary president'.[57] The work shown in forums such as Les Quelques' exhibitions was often a mix of the traditional and contemporary. Noteworthy artists included Franco-Belgian sculptor Yvonne Serruys, French painter Marie Duhem, British artist Beatrice Howe, and American artists Florence Esté and Eleanor Norcross. Norcross was the first American to have a solo exhibition at the Salon d'Automne, and also had a memorial retrospective at the Louvre in 1924.[58] Some artists like Martha Stettler and Alice Dannenberg (fig 10), made works that were very close in feeling to Carrick's distinctively modern paintings of the Luxembourg Gardens, which was a short walk from her home on Boulevard Arago.

It was to these historic gardens that Carrick often went to paint, initially with Fox. It was still relatively uncommon for women to set up outside and paint independently, and the fact that they worked together would have made it easier for Carrick. Stettler and Dannenberg, who lived together as a couple, were trailblazing directors of the Académie de la Grande Chaumière and, like Carrick, not prepared to remain shackled to traditionally female subjects or views.[59] Art historian Griselda Pollock has noted the influence of social conditioning on subject matter—even Berthe Morisot, perhaps the best-known woman impressionist to paint outdoors, mostly framed her subjects intimately and personally rather than taking in the broader public domain.[60] By contrast Carrick, like Stettler and Dannenberg, often took on a wider scope of daily experience—intimate in scale and keenly felt but often about something bigger than themselves. In their works, landscape architecture provides a stage for people, together and alone, and the spatial dimensions and luminous colour are conveyed in bold, innovative ways.

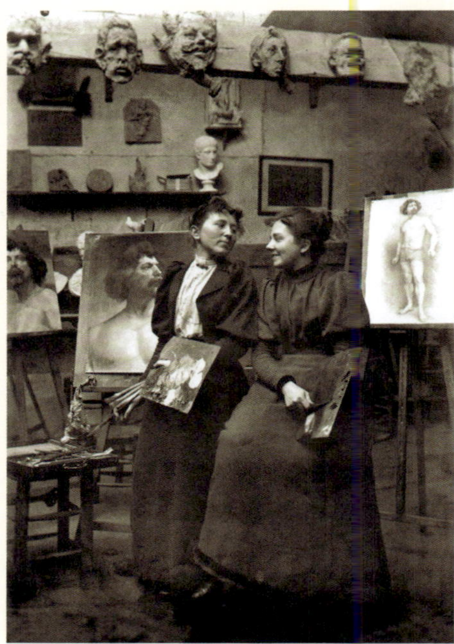

fig 10 Unknown photographer, *Alice Dannenberg* (left) *and Martha Stettler at the Académie Julian, Paris*, 1894, photograph, Kunstmuseum Bern

Below
fig 11 Martha Stettler, *Luxembourg-Park in Paris* no date, oil on canvas, Kunstmuseum Bern

Opposite
cat 15 *Sunday in the gardens* 1907, oil on canvas, Queen Victoria Museum & Art Gallery

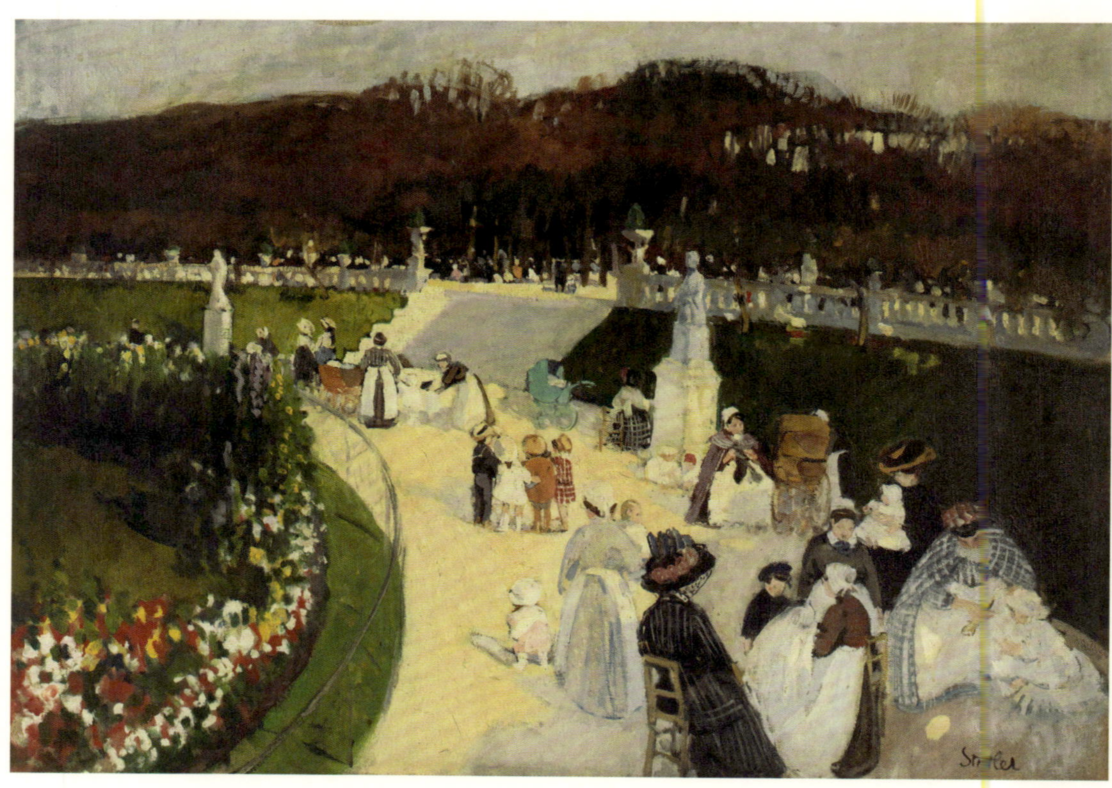

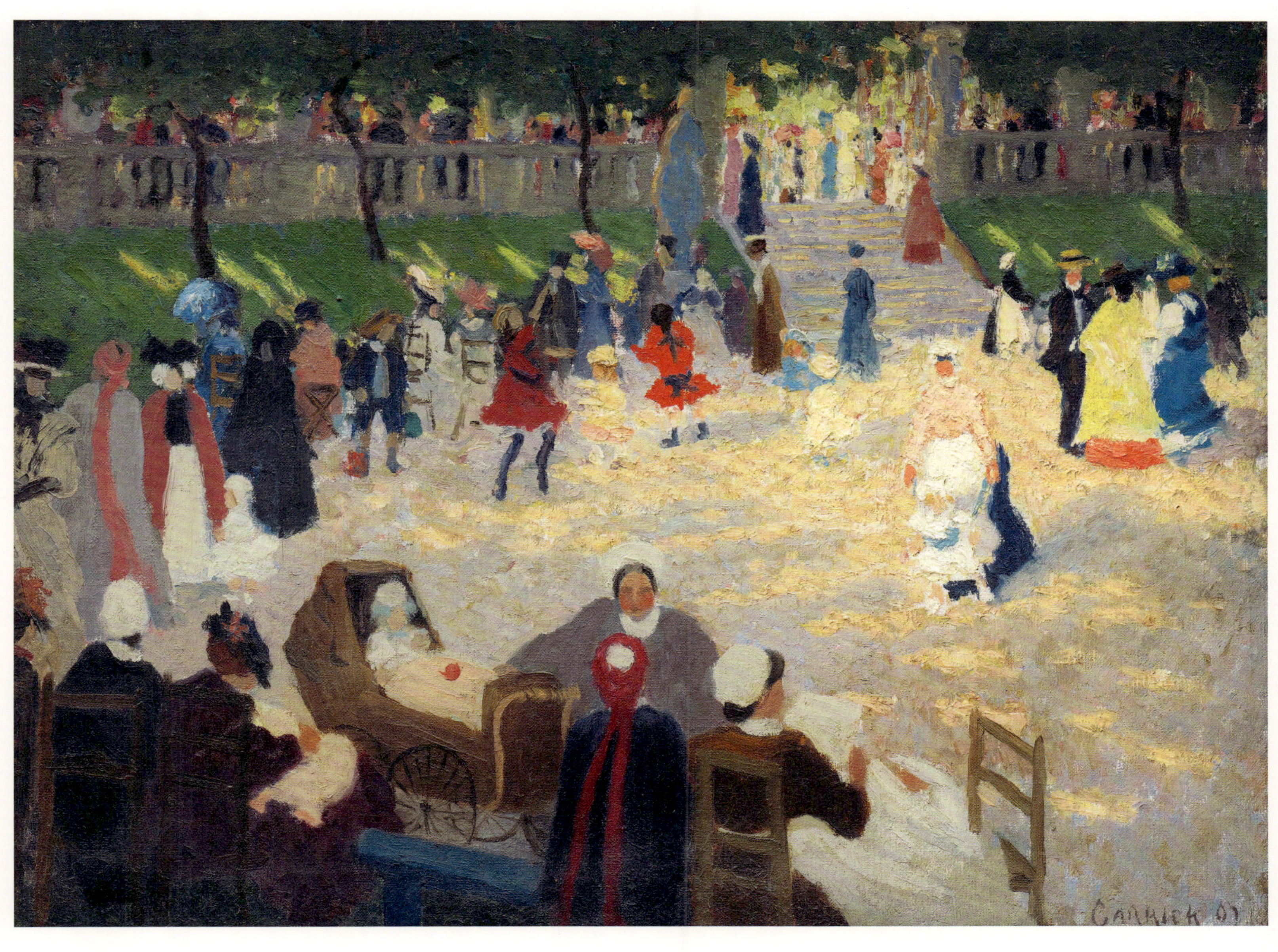

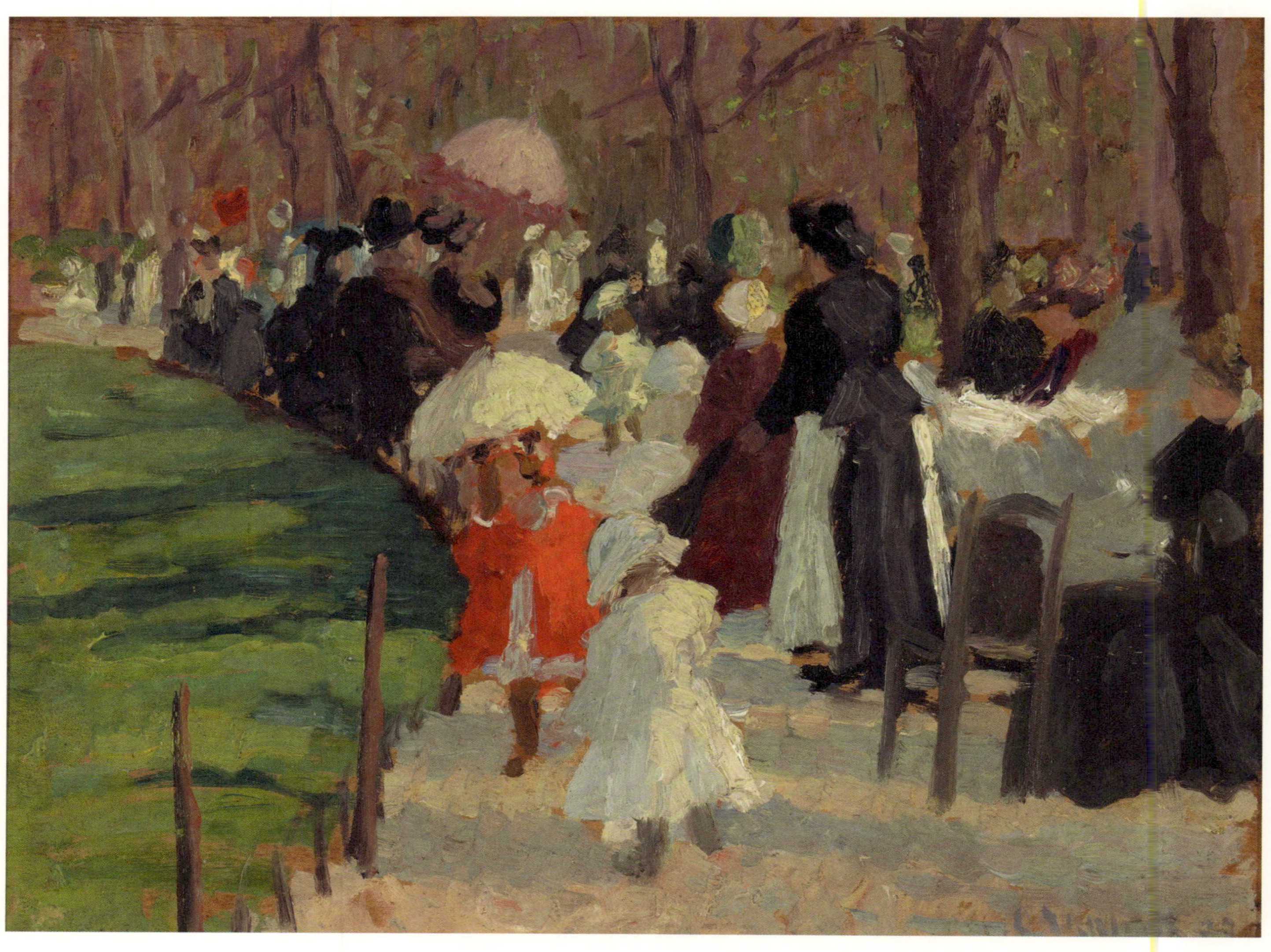

cat 16 *In springtime, Luxembourg Gardens* 1907, oil on wood panel, University Art Collection, Chau Chak Wing Museum, The University of Sydney

Opposite, top to bottom
cat 17 *Luxembourg Gardens, Paris* c 1906, oil on wood panel, National Gallery of Australia

cat 18 *Luxembourg Gardens* c 1908, oil on wood panel, private collection

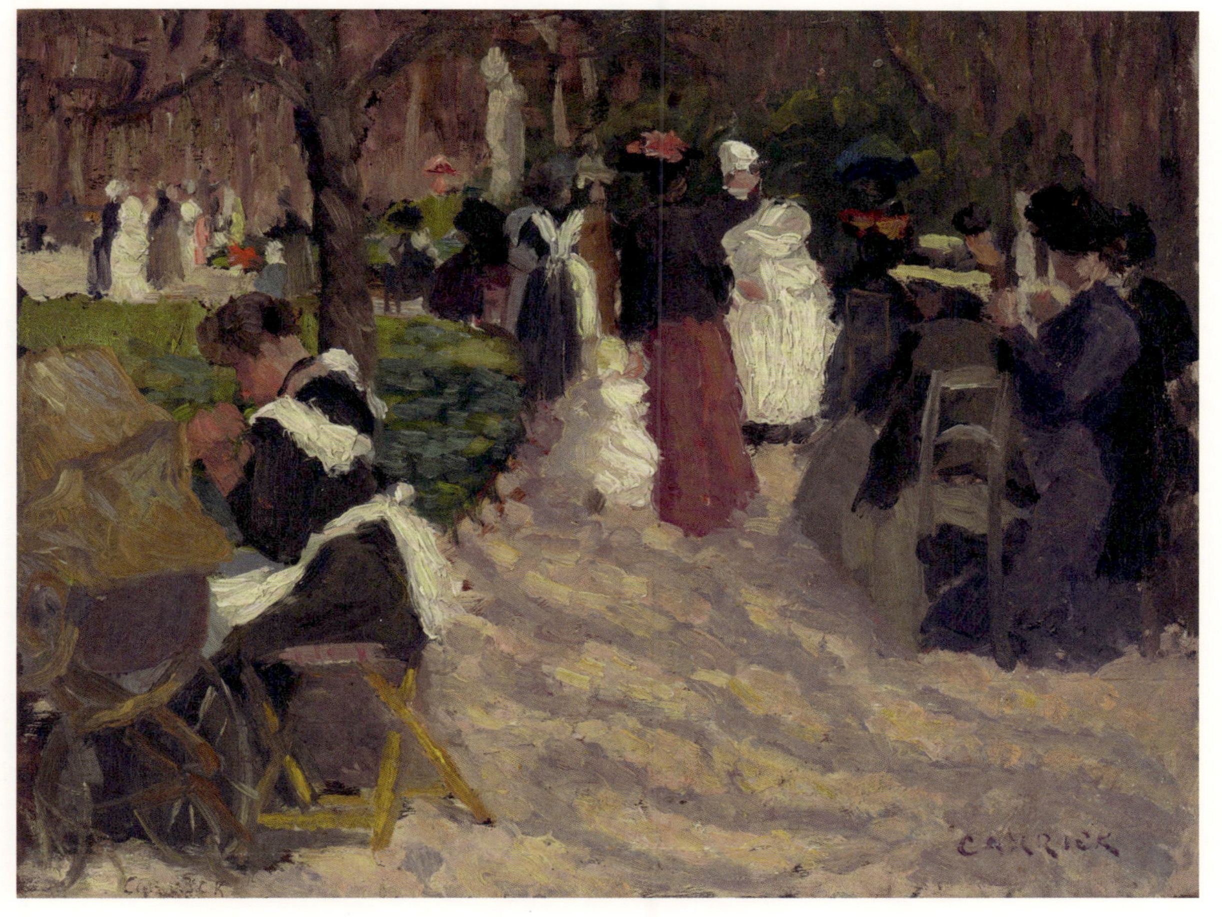
CARRICK

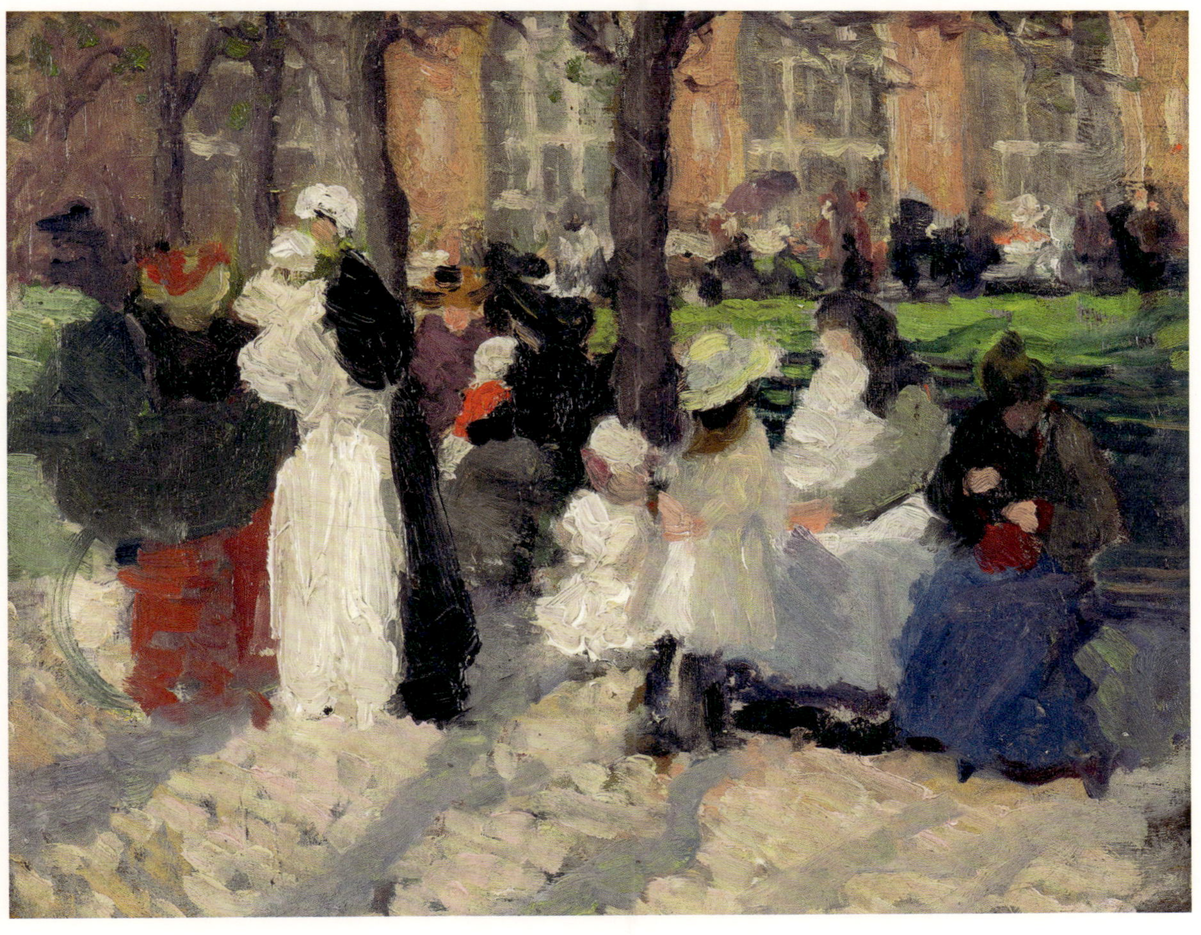

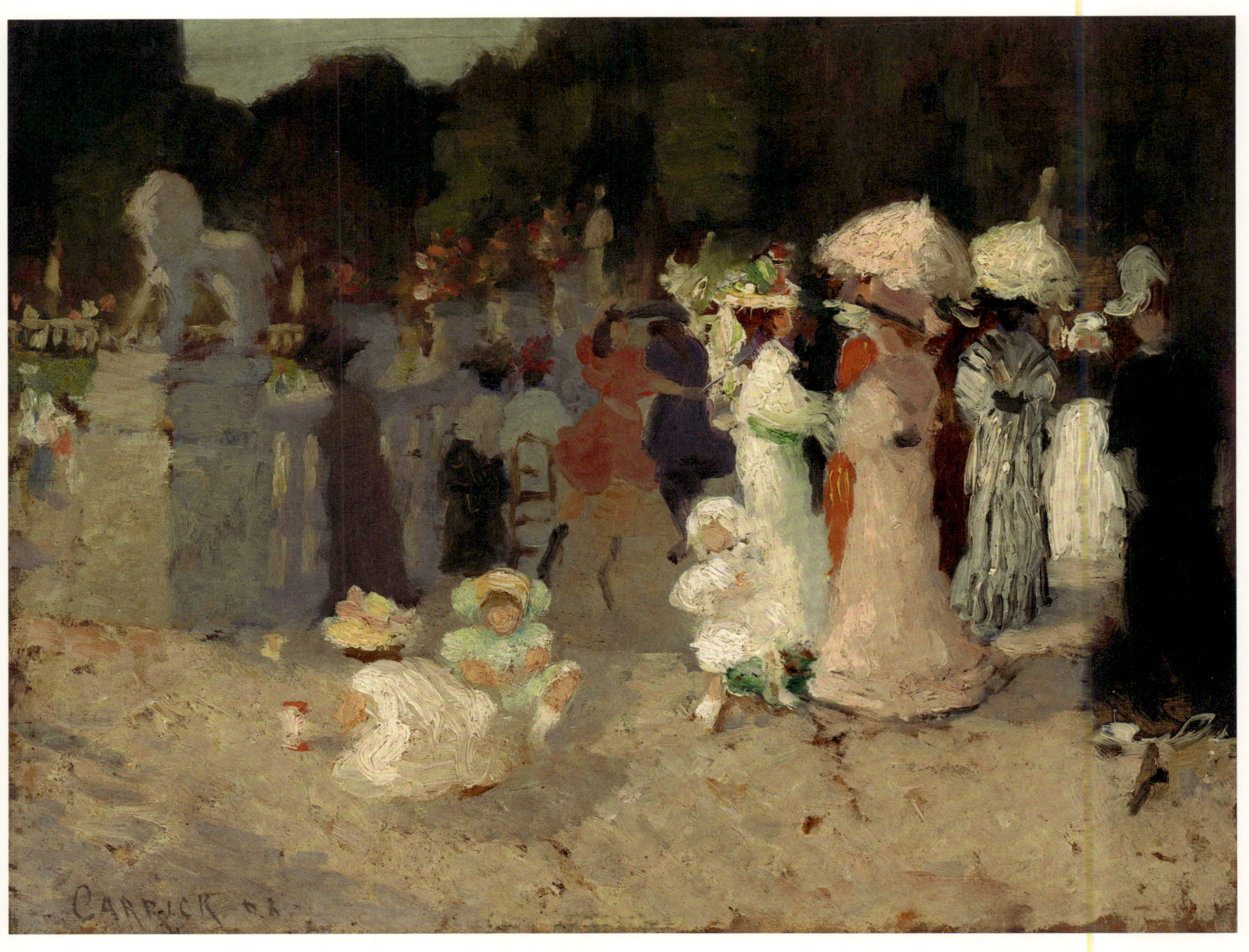
CARRICK

In 1906 and 1907, in work after work, the defining aspects of Carrick's art emerged as she painted in the Luxembourg Gardens. Her many viewpoints of the gardens offered lively, fresh impressions of women and children; people at leisure dressed in the fashions of the day against a backdrop of trees and statues, the spill of light and shadow worked as unifying factors. Her approach combined close observation with deft brushwork. She rarely did drawings and her rapidly painted sketches and finished paintings were often similar. Carrick's early, small painting *Paris park scene* 1906 (cat 19), shown in the Salon d'Automne, reveals an interplay between figuration and abstraction. The luminous, painterly foreground, which allows patches of the board to show through, is deliberately non-literal and appears to be floating. The balustrade and pillar topped with a grey leonine sculpture are set behind children playing in the sunshine. Carrick was also a keen observer of fashion, which she delicately expressed. The women in their elegant dresses on the right, some wearing hats and others holding parasols, convey the glamour of middle-class women at the time. She was also drawn to the striking black and white outfits of the nursemaids of the children in the park, who take pride of place as the protagonists in several paintings.

In childhood, Carrick had been surrounded by fashion and fabrics in her father's Uxbridge emporium, Carrick and Coles. Later, she would also have been aware of Anna Todd, her enterprising sister-in-law (for a time) who bravely set out against the odds to establish her own fashion business, Anna Goodrick Ltd, in Birmingham, keeping a watchful eye on French catalogues of the day.[61] Marcel Proust, an author who perhaps best epitomised fin de siècle fashion in his writing, reflected that he grew up with the idea that 'conservative society was fashionable, and no republicans were welcome in the smarter salons'—but the times were changing:

> People living in such a milieu could imagine that the impossibility of ever inviting an 'opportunist', much less a 'radical', was a thing that would last forever, like gas lamps and horse-drawn omnibuses. But like kaleidoscopes turning from time to time, society successively places in various ways elements which were thought to be immutable and creates a new composition.[62]

What was modern about Carrick's art was not only her interest in the changing patterns of daily life moving towards a new era, but also the ways in which she encompassed a high degree of painterly freedom. This was apparent in her unconventional compositions, often with spacious foregrounds or middle-grounds, and clusters of people moving around the edges or diagonally in space. Incidental aspects of experience and the cut-off nature of the scenes that appear to extend the action beyond the frame, as in photography, revealed her ongoing interest in Edgar Degas. Along with Carrick's realism in close observation, her broadly applied passages of colour convey the abstract construction of her compositions, reminding us of the dictum of Maurice Denis, a founder of the Salon d'Automne: 'Remember that a painting—before it is a battle horse, a nude model, or some anecdote—is essentially a flat surface covered with colour, assembled in a certain order.'[63]

Opposite
cat 19 *Paris park scene* 1906, oil on board, National Gallery of Australia

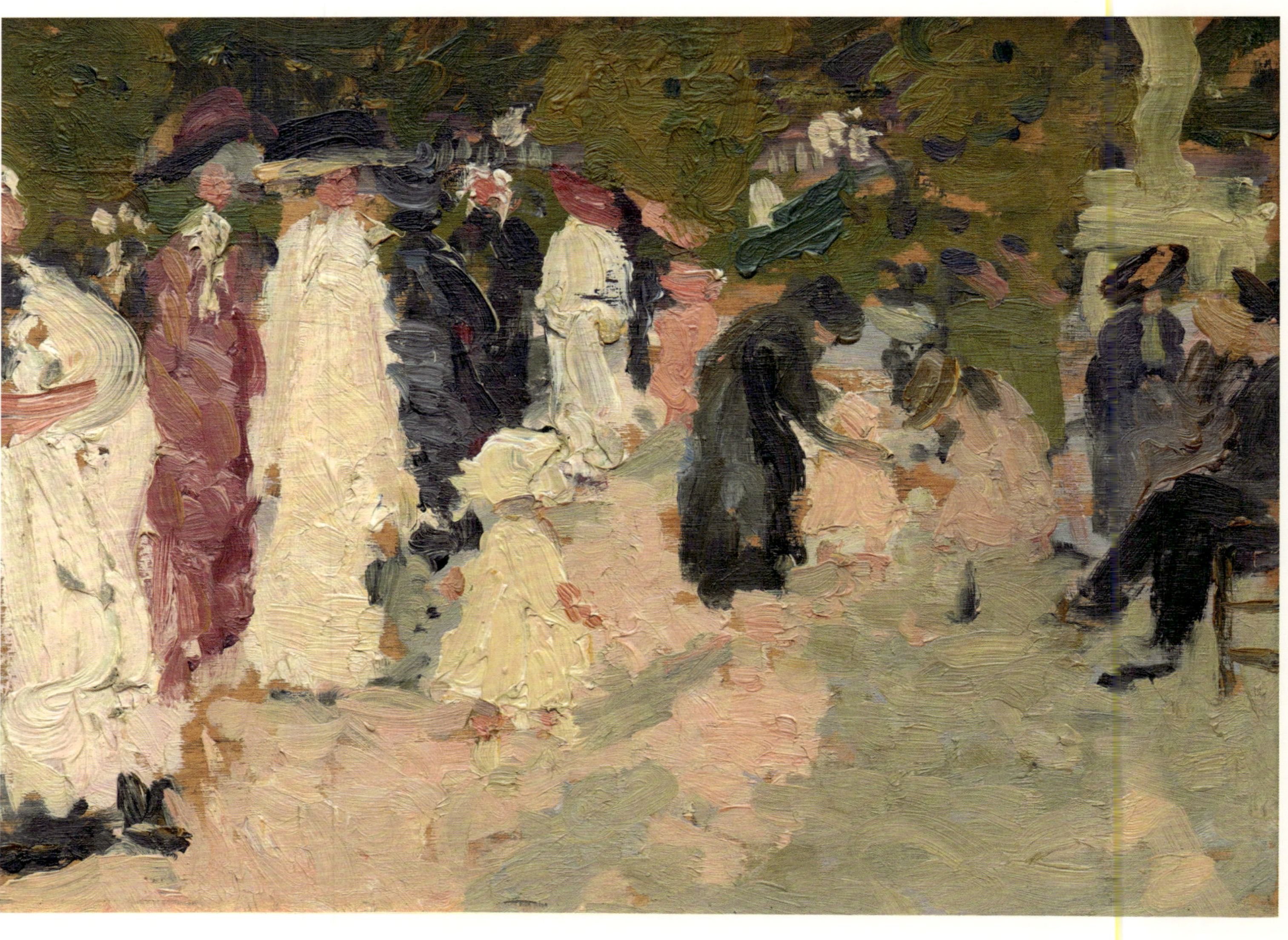

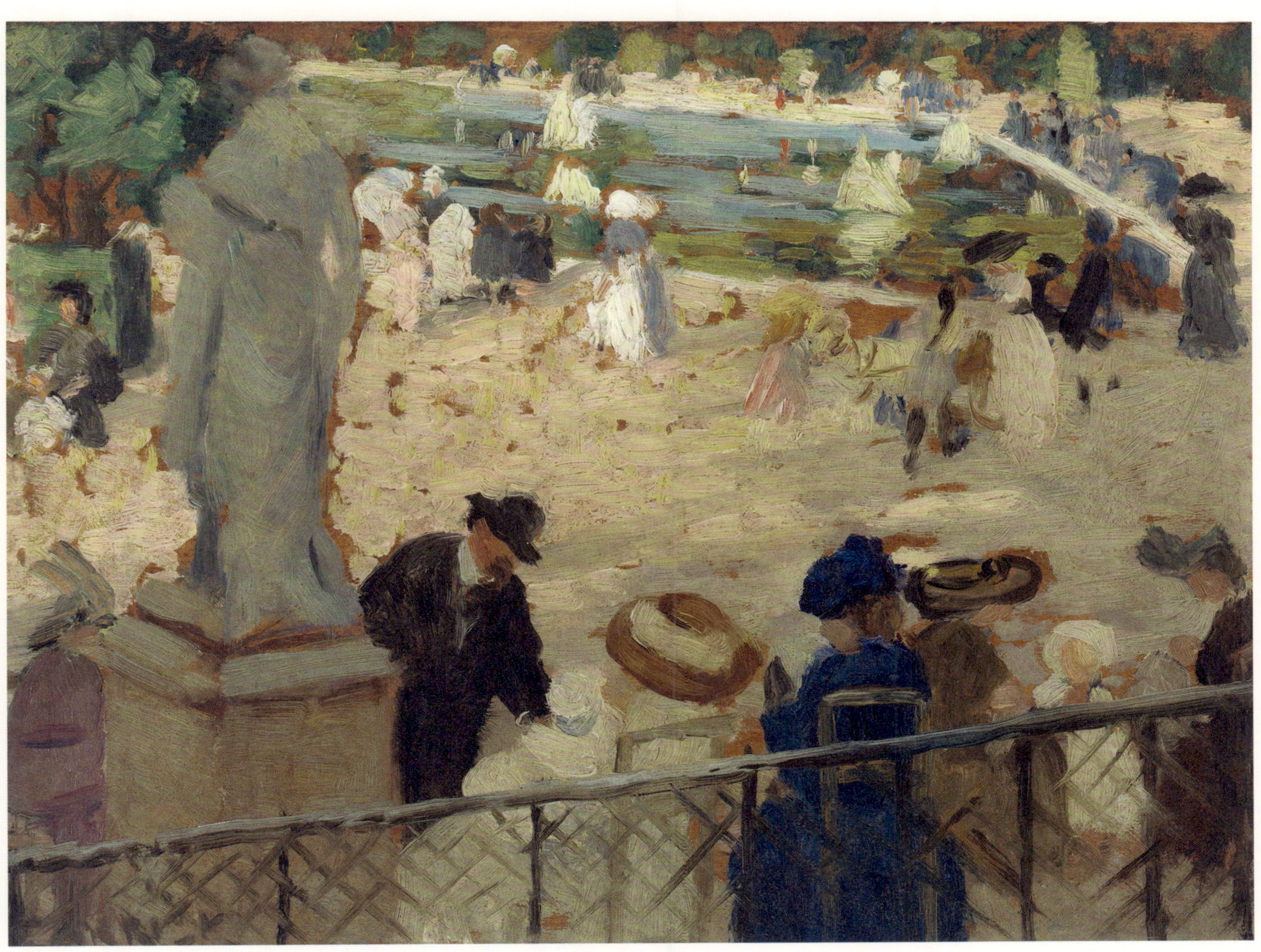

Opposite
cat 20 *Luxembourg Gardens, Paris* c 1909, oil on wood panel, private collection

Above
cat 21 *Luxembourg Gardens, Paris* c 1908, oil on board, collection of GR Teague

At times, it was as though Carrick was pushing the boundaries between abstraction and representation so far that figures appear to be on the edge of disappearing into the painterliness of their execution. However, she never wanted to lose the subject matter entirely. An influential touchstone in this dynamic interplay was Édouard Vuillard, another founder of the Salon d'Automne and member of the group known as the Nabis. Vuillard's paintings on small boards, often cigar-box lids, demonstrated that everyday subjects could convey the spirit of modernity as well as the spirit within.

In addition to small works, Carrick is likely to have seen Vuillard's great nine-panel commission, *Public gardens* 1894, when it was exhibited at the Bernheim-Jeune gallery in 1906,[64] depicting children and their caretakers in public gardens (fig 12). Across the panels, Vuillard abstracts from nature, emphasising the flow of shadows in extended patterns, with the flattened space and radical cropping likely informed by the Japanese art that was such an inspiration to French artists in the late nineteenth century. Vuillard's panel *Under the trees* 1894 (fig 18, p 73) provides parallels with Carrick's paintings, highlighting spatial interactions of figures within repeated rhythms of trees.[65]

Another parallel is the spill of light and shadow creating patterns across the ground. There are also similarities to some of Pierre Bonnard's works in other Carrick paintings, such as the casual cut-off viewpoints and everyday scenarios of the enchanting *In the Luxembourg Gardens, Paris* c 1908 (cat 22)—in this instance, a boy with a hoop playing near a girl in a check dress.

Carrick's enjoyment of velvety black, an anathema for many impressionists, reveals her interest in Manet. In October 1906, she exhibited a painting called *Le marché* (The market) at The Royal Institute of Oil Painters in London. It was noted in the *Westminster Gazette* that her painting was not hung on the line (at eye level) but was 'skied' on account of it being too much like Manet, 'but one can just see how good it is, and how captivating the little lady is'.[66] Despite the patronising tone of many reviewers, the merit in Carrick's work was seen and acknowledged. In 1907 at the Royal Academy of Arts, she exhibited a portrait of Amy Marks, who had attended Carrick and Fox's wedding.

Although portraiture would remain important to her, Carrick's predominant passion, alongside people in parks and gardens, was her developing interest in marketplaces, which moved from quite tonal works to ones brimming with colour and life with an increasingly painterly quality. In *The market* 1908 (cat 23, p 48) dappled light and shadow and the rhythm of the trees are offset by exquisite, vibrant hues, while in other examples, such as *Flower market* c 1910–12 (cat 24, p 48), the flower wrappings become prominently abstract geometric patterns.

French flower market 1909 (cat 25, p 49) is a revelatory work in its synthesis of these aspects, foreshadowing Carrick's later paintings of Nice flower markets. In this painting, the artist leads the viewer down a path, flowers bunched on either side, towards a woman in a long dress with a parasol who is screened by a row of trees in the background. Light and colour dazzle, setting a scene in which people of diverse occupations mingle.

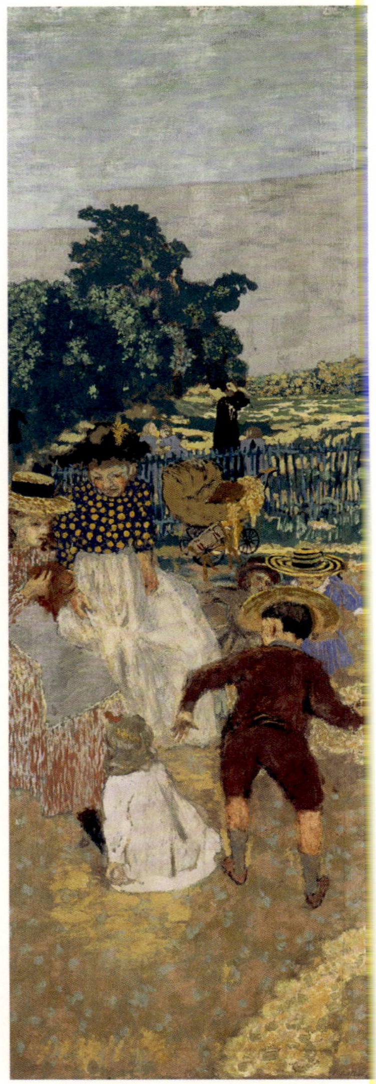

fig 12 Édouard Vuillard, *Jardins publics: la conversation, les nourrices, l'ombrelle rouge* (Public gardens: the conversation, the nurses, the red umbrella) 1894 (detail), tempera on canvas, Musée d'Orsay

Opposite
cat 22 *In the Luxembourg Gardens, Paris* c 1908, oil on canvas, National Gallery of Victoria

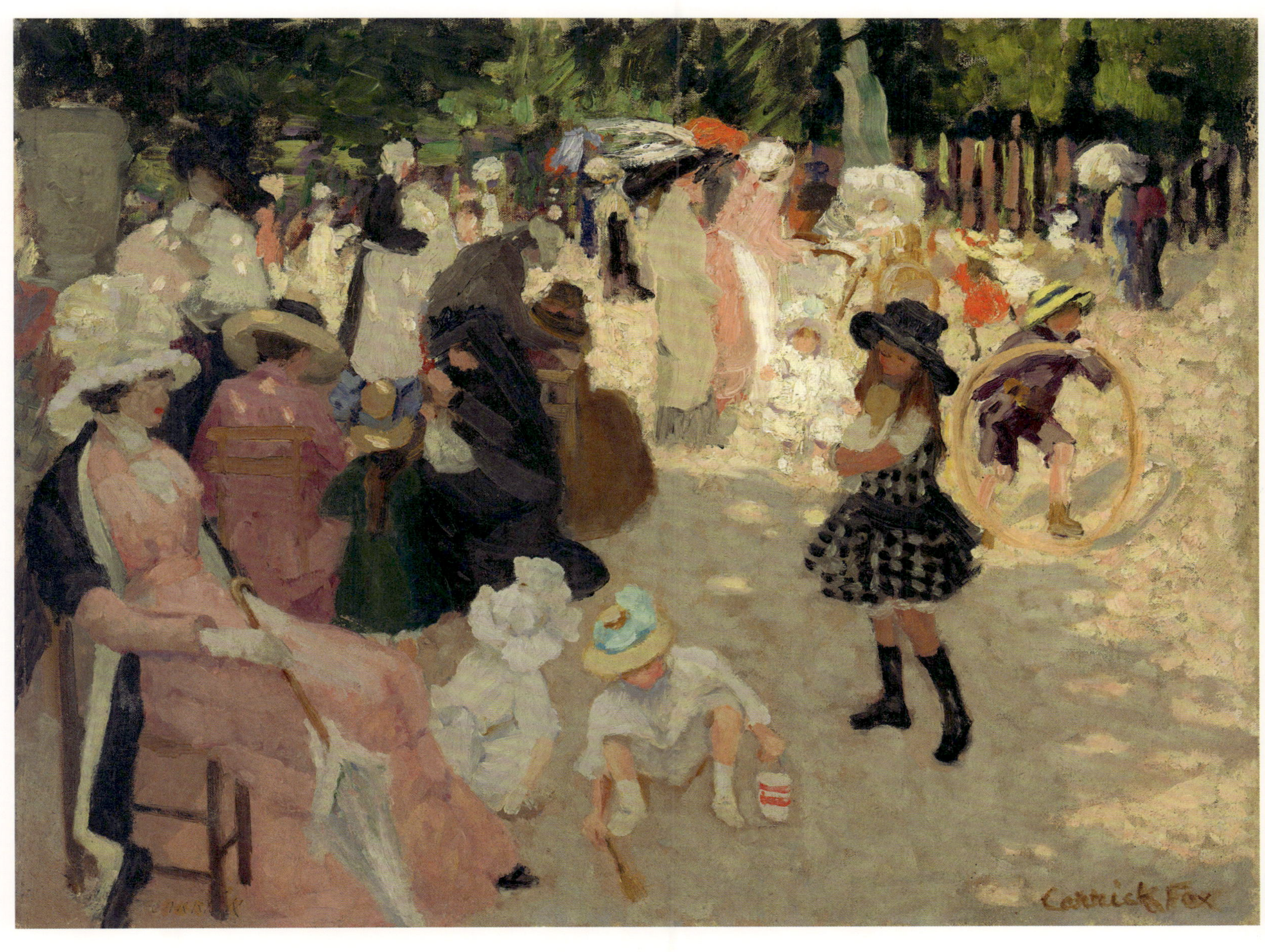
Carrick Fox

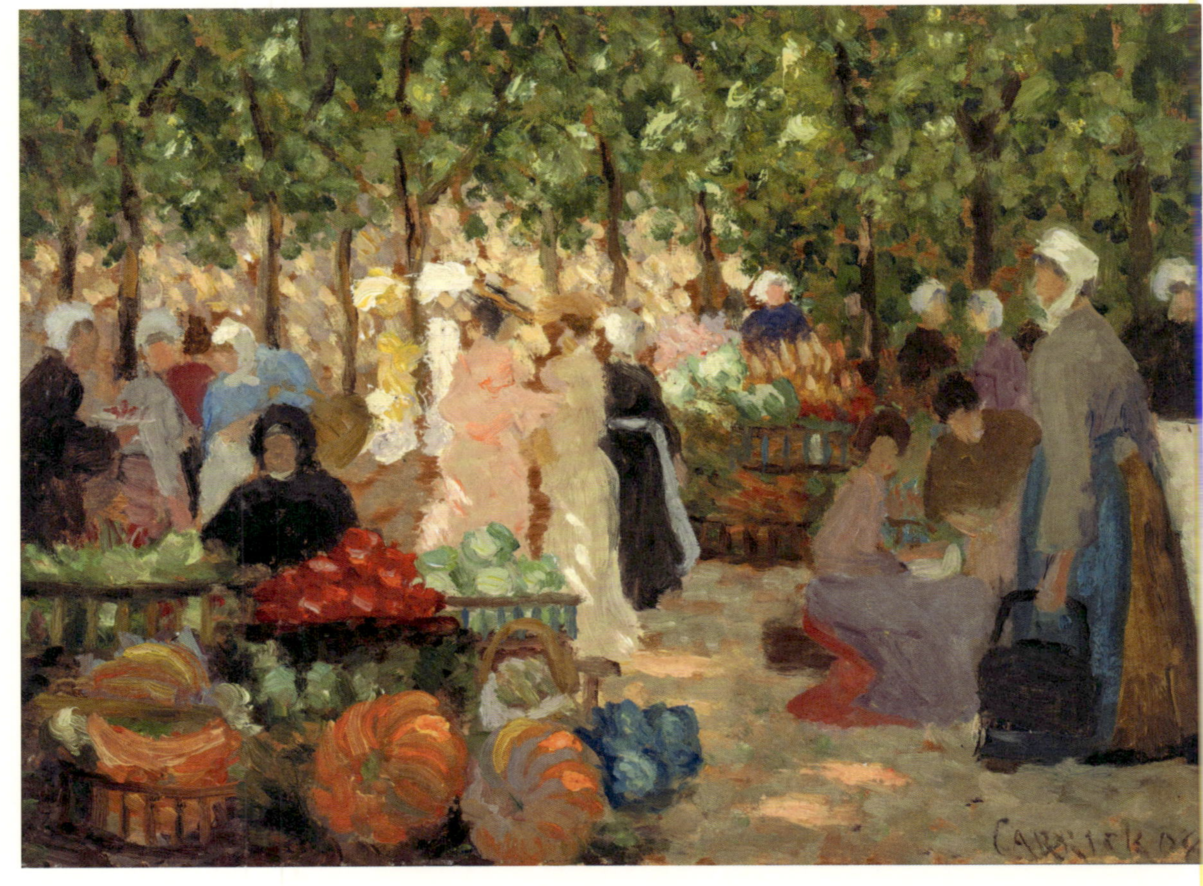

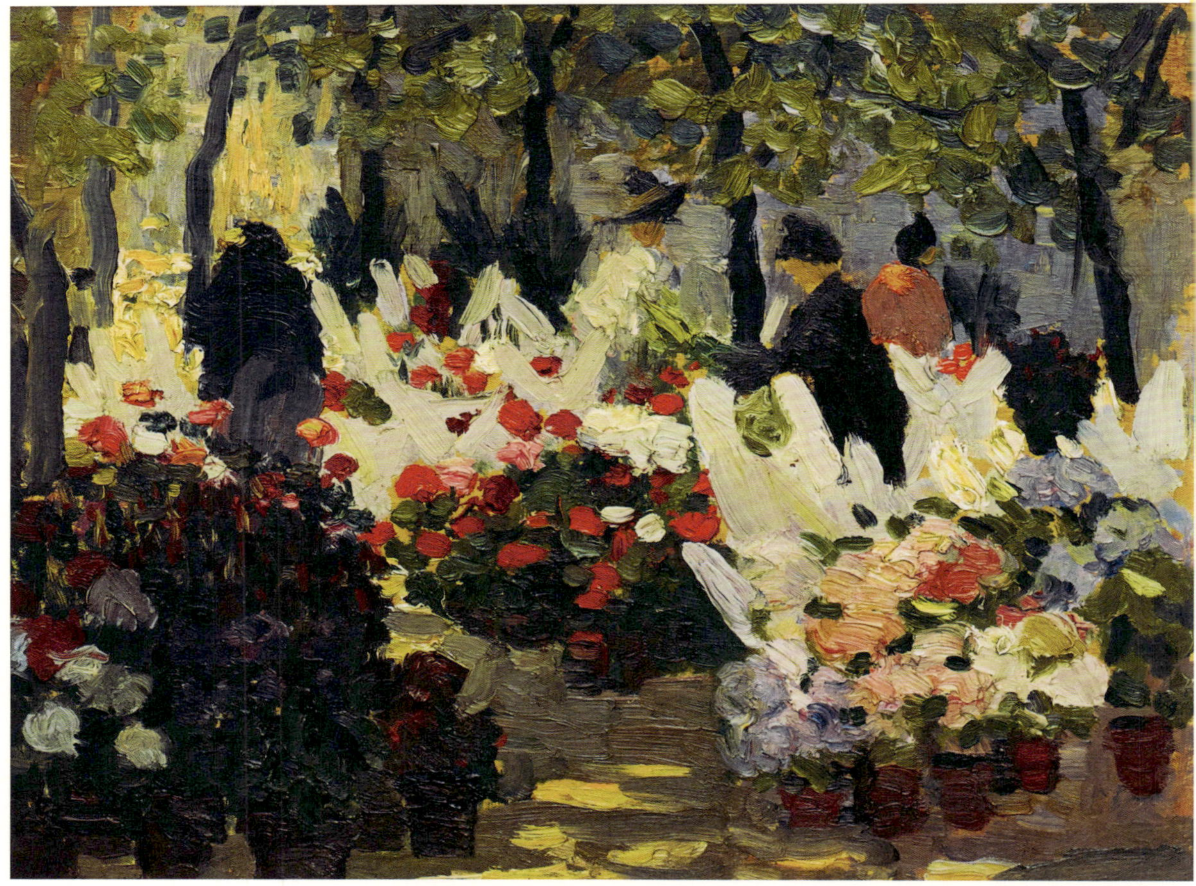

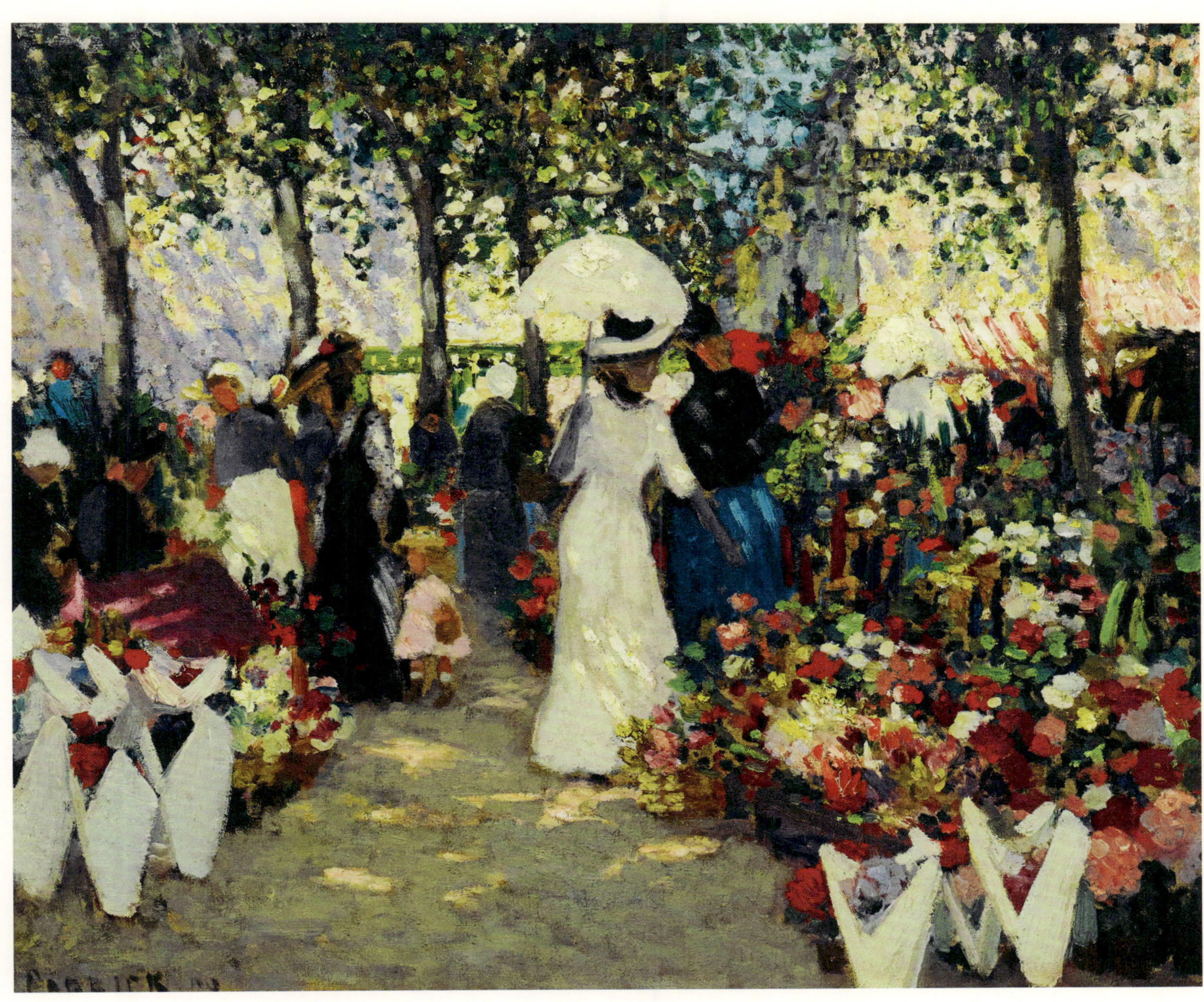

Opposite, top to bottom
cat 23 *The market* 1908, oil on wood panel, private collection

cat 24 *Flower market* c 1910–12, oil on board, private collection

Above
cat 25 *French flower market* 1909, oil on canvas, private collection

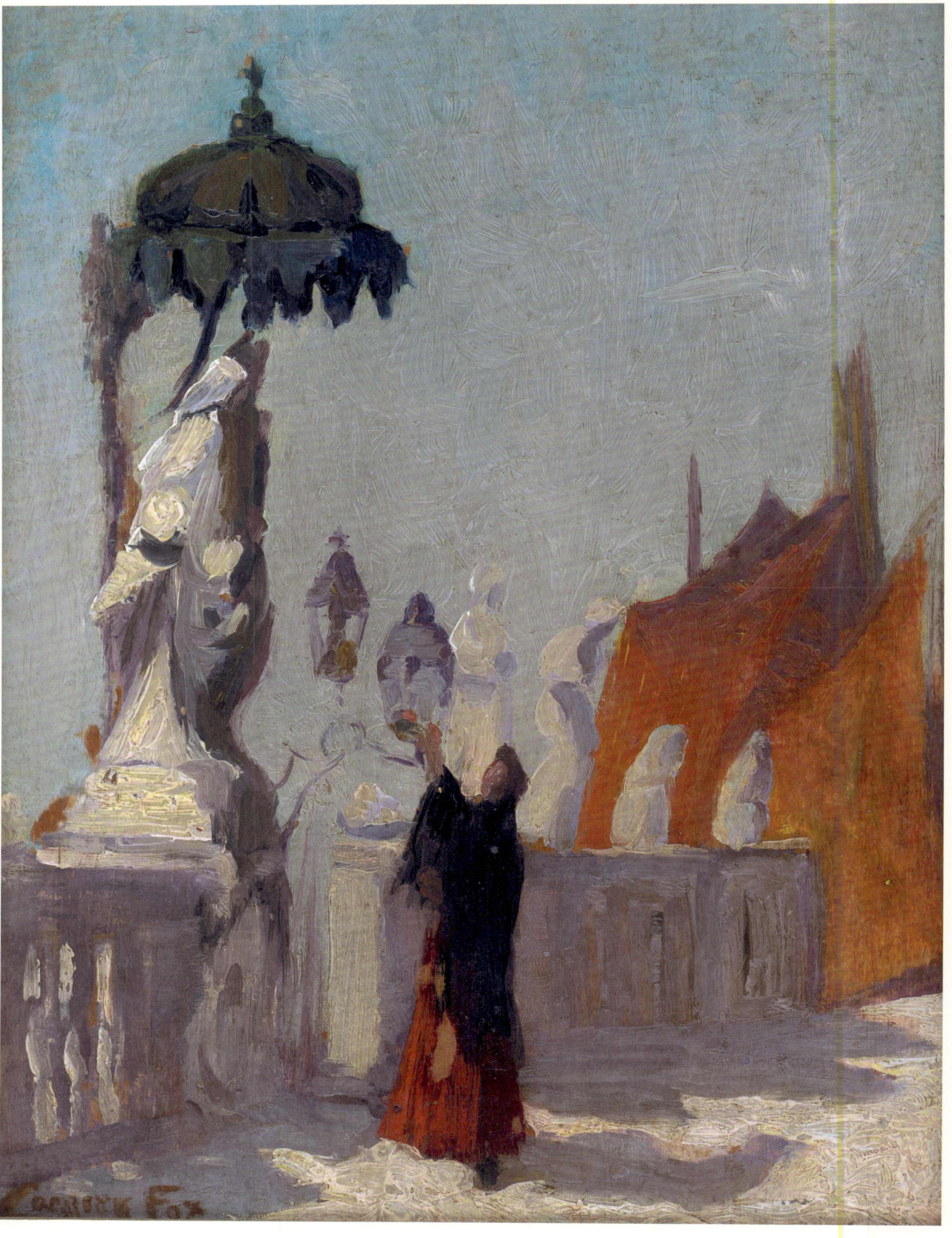

In the European spring of 1907, Carrick and Fox travelled to Venice, staying until early summer.[67] Australian artists, including Arthur Streeton, Hans Heysen and Bessie Davidson, were also enamoured by the art, architecture and natural environment of the city. On his first visit in 1902, Heysen wrote: 'Venice is a dream. It is too beautiful—all and more than I ever imagined. A photograph gives little idea of how lovely it really is ... Sometimes it looks as if the whole city hovers between water and air.[68]

While in Venice, Carrick and Fox often painted the same subject side by side. In some instances, such as in Fox's *Venice afterglow* c 1907 (cat 92, p 144) and Carrick's *St Mark's Venice* 1907 (cat 93, p 145), the results were very similar. Carrick's work reveals her ongoing passion for architecture and the movement of people bathed in light and shadow. Given the small scale and relatively loose brushwork of the painting, it is remarkable that she managed to suggest so much detail in the multi-domed basilica, down to a sense of the glowing mosaics in the alcoves of the façade and the fashions of the people in the square.

Structures anchor us, remaining like leitmotifs across time, while fashions take us back to a particular period. Light and shadow on land and water speak of transience. Carrick's numerous small-scale works of Venice capture these layers in essential aspects of place: water taking in reflections laps at the edges of paths, foliage from trees spills over walls, and pathways connect at sharp angles to reveal unexpected surprises. The small wooden panels were like a travel diary and Carrick would often paint on both sides. A poignant impression is *Chioggia, statue of the Madonna, Venice* 1907 (cat 26), which depicts a woman clad in a black headscarf and red skirt beseeching the Madonna and holding a funerary urn, while in the background red boat sails billow. Situated in the busy fishing port of Chioggia, on the end of the Venetian lagoon, the protective canopy over the figure adds to the drama of this small, poetic work. Indeed, Carrick painted a range of scenes around Chioggia, but working outdoors was not always plain sailing, as she recalled with self-deprecating humour:

> **I enjoyed being in Venice tremendously. While staying at Chioggia, which is wonderfully paintable, but woefully smelly, I had what might have been a very unpleasant experience. I was painting with my back to one of the canals, near the edge, when suddenly my camp-stool collapsed, and I was just going over the side when I was grabbed by two passers-by. I didn't feel frightened at going over; my mind was full of the awful fact that I was wearing grey stockings and black boots. I still shudder when I think of it.**[69]

In October 1907, Carrick showed paintings of Venice in the Salon d'Automne, before exhibiting them in Australia the following year. Frederick McCubbin, who stayed with Fox and Carrick in their Paris apartment, was impressed by their Venice works, acquiring two in advance for Melbourne art patrons.[70] In August, the Foxes took McCubbin to Versailles, Fontainebleau and the Sorbonne. McCubbin found Versailles a 'tremendous Palace, all marble and gold and miles of pictures, and out in the hot sun where the fountains play—a fairyland of water'.[71] He wrote in a letter to his wife, Annie, of 'a quiet stroll in the evening ... The next morning, a few pictures in the Luxembourg—the impressionists ... Manet and Monet [and] Sisley—very fine. Mrs Fox is very charming and so kind. They will be coming out to Australia for a trip—about April next.'[72]

Opposite
cat 26 ***Chioggia, statue of the Madonna, Venice*** **1907, oil on wood panel, private collection**

Following
cat 27 ***Royal Avenue, Versailles*** **c 1907, oil on wood panel, Castlemaine Art Museum**

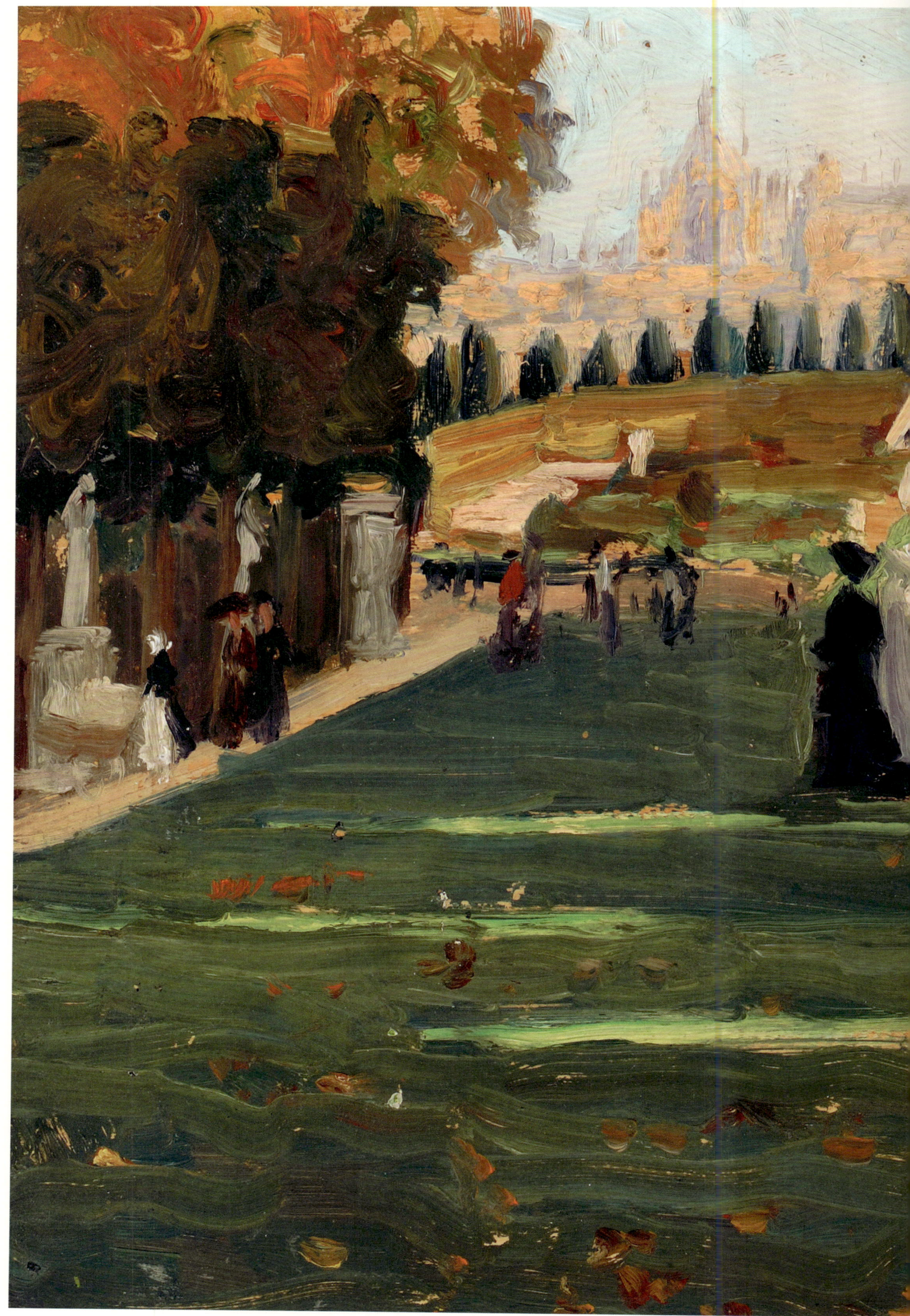

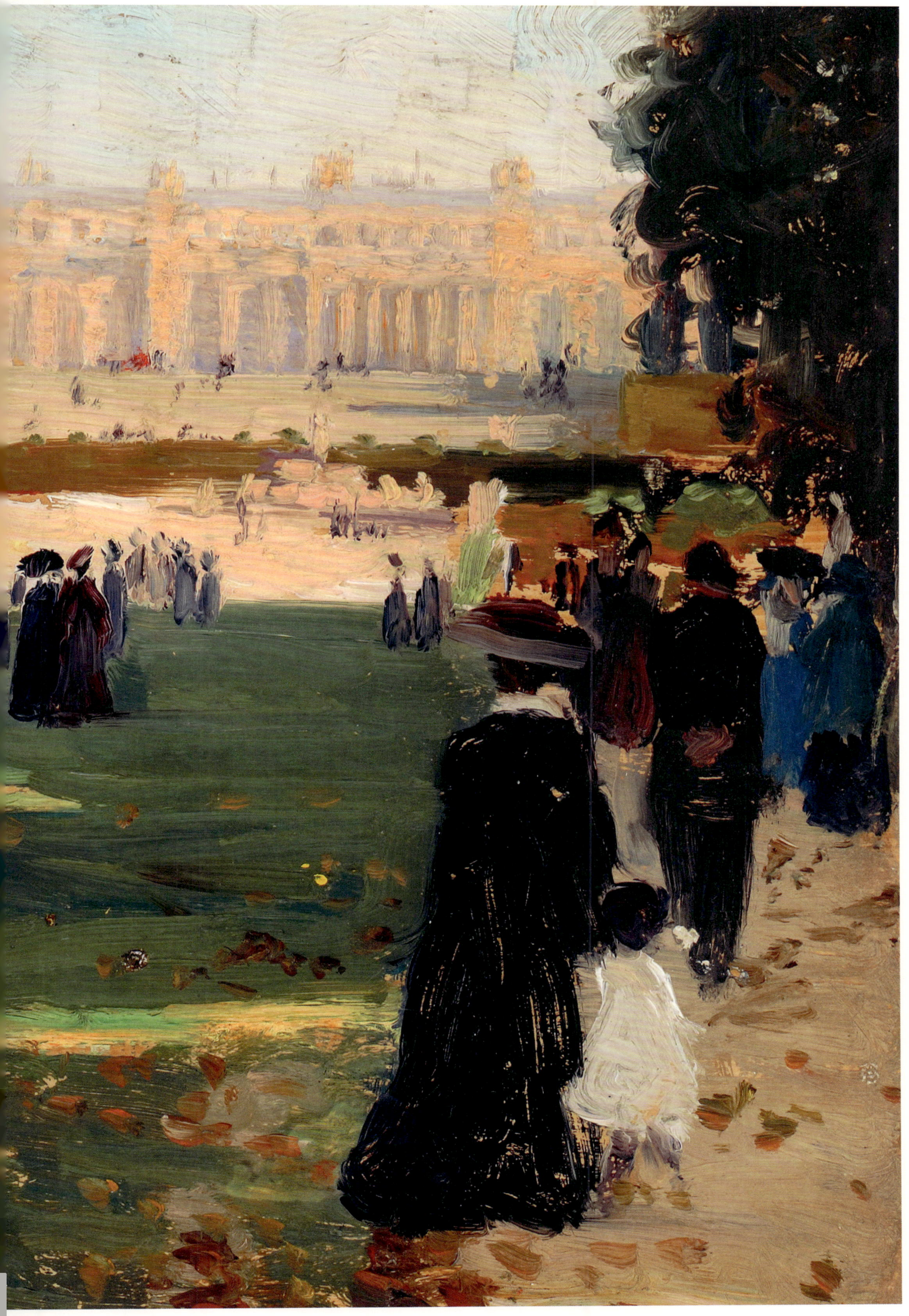

Carrick and Fox travelled to Australia in early 1908 aboard the RMS *Mooltan*.[73] For Fox, this was the first chance to introduce Carrick to his country of birth—a place she had heard much about since her brother Howard had visited, as well as from their Australian friends in London, St Ives and Paris. As an artist already well-established in Australia, Fox was keen to sustain his reputation and show work that had been exhibited at the Royal Academy and the Paris Salons. Within days of their arrival in Melbourne, he announced his availability to paint portrait commissions. While Fox exhibited at the start of their visit, Carrick held her solo show in August 1908, not long before their return to Paris.

Initially, the couple stayed with Fox's mother, Rosetta Phillips, and spent much of their time painting in the home and garden of his brother David and sister-in-law Irene Fox—'Aylmer', in East Malvern. Years later, Fox's niece, Louise Porker, who was around seven years old at the time, recalled, 'They had a beautiful partnership. Whenever Manny [Emanuel] was painting at our place, Ethel was there too. They discussed their pictures they were painting, they discussed colours, asked for one another's advice, I never heard any friction at all on that visit.'[74] Letters convey that Carrick may have painted 'directly from Fox's palette' and that some in his family did not think highly of her avant-garde work, believing there was a one-way influence from him to her.[75] Others, like Constance Ellis and Rosetta (Etta) Phillips, felt differently and gave her encouragement. Irrespective of the Fox family's feelings about her work, Carrick remained in contact with them throughout her life.[76]

Emanuel Phillips Fox was a generous-spirited, much-loved figure in his family, and he often painted close relatives, including young Louise and her three-year-old brother Len. His affection for children and interest in the subject of motherhood informed numerous, significant paintings, such as *Bathing hour (L'heure du bain)* c 1909 (fig 37, p 148). There has been much conjecture about the fact that Carrick and Fox did not have children and whether this was by choice or because they weren't able to do so. Carrick experienced repeated periods of ill health throughout her life, including ongoing rheumatoid arthritis, which may have impacted her ability to have children. Either way, as a woman who married in her thirties, she was steadfast in her commitment to her art, noting it as one of the keys to their happy marriage: 'I think one reason why we work so well together is that we always put our art before everything else. That comes first, anything else, after.'[77]

From the start, Fox and Carrick were given a warm welcome by the artistic community in Melbourne, including the Victorian Artists Society (VAS). Carrick was soon also interacting with women artists in the Melbourne Society of Women Painters and Sculptors (MSWPS).[78] Fox's reputation preceded him in Australia, while Carrick was about to become an artist to be reckoned with.

Her vibrant, mostly small paintings, many of which she brought with her from Paris, revealed a diverse, modern approach, the likes of which had not been seen before in the country. Her 1908 exhibition at Bernard's Gallery in Collins Street included some 40 paintings as well as etchings undertaken in Normandy. The range of subjects is reflected in the titles of her works: *Luxembourg Gardens*, *Washing-place at Chartres*, *Notre Dame*, *Apple blossom*, *Harmony in grey* and *French flower market*. Coverage in the press was extensive and favourable.

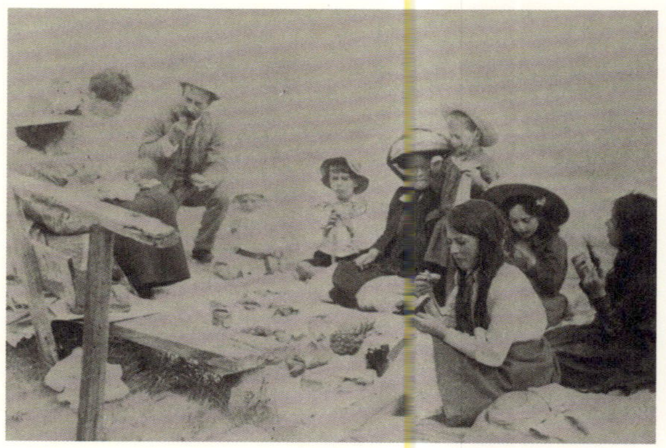

fig 13 David Fox, *Picnic, Chelsea Beach, Victoria*, 1908, photograph, (from left) Ethel Carrick, Irene (wife of David Fox) with baby Bonnie, E Phillips Fox, Len Fox, Lionel Fox, Fox's sister Carrie, Victor Fox, Louise Fox, Dorothy Fox, Rosie Fox (in front), Len Fox Papers, State Library of New South Wales

While Fox's paintings shown earlier in the year included works like *A love story* 1903 (Art Gallery of Ballarat), which revealed his feeling for 'femininity', Carrick's work surprised at least one critic for its distinctive vigour and 'masculinity'.[79] Although intimate in scale, her paintings conveyed bold impressions, dramatic compositions and a feeling for everyday life. They conveyed her awareness of recent developments in the artworld and her talent as a colourist, able to handle vibrant oranges or purples, as well as subtleties of tone. Most successful were the outdoor subjects, with groups of people giving an atmosphere and energy to the whole, including the market scenes—touchstones for Carrick's ongoing passion for this subject. On the day of the exhibition preview, a report appeared in *The Herald*:

> 'All the world loves a lover,' and it may be said with equal truth that all art lovers love a colourist. The canvases ... seem to palpitate with bright colour-schemes, but the supreme skill of the artist is found in her subtle handling of out-door groups of people in frequented parts of a populous city. A fine example is the large canvas labelled 'Le Marché,' one of a series of market scenes which form a distinct feature of the collection. There is nothing studied in the grouping of the crowd of figures which appear in the scene, and life and movement are splendidly suggested ...
>
> [In] the market pictures one may note the delicate colour of the women's dresses in 'A French Flower Market', the strong oranges and reds of a market scene in Chioggia, and the clever colour scheme of white which distinguishes the impression called 'A China Market.'[80]

A reviewer in *The Age* noted that 'Mrs Fox exhibits under the name of Miss Ethel Carrick (membre de l'Union Internationale des Beaux-Arts et des Lettres), and includes in this exhibition works which have been shown lately at the Royal Academy, Salon and other European exhibitions'. She was noted as 'an artist of the plein air school, whose methods are adapted to the interpretation of sunshine and delicate atmospheric effects':

> In *A Venetian flower market* spreading canopies shade the vendors and their wares from a blazing sun and supply rich warm tones in themselves. One of the daintiest pieces of colour is *Apple blossom* ... *Le marché* is the largest and one of the most sustained and spirited efforts: a moving, picturesque crowd at the fair, old women with white caps, nurses and children, beneath the trees' shade.[81]

In 1908, Carrick and Fox spent time in Sydney. They were keen to paint Sydney Harbour, inspired in part by Arthur Streeton, although Carrick's painterly approach was at times closer to that of Charles Conder. *The quay, Milsons Point* 1908 (cat 29, p 57) provides striking parallels with her Luxembourg Gardens paintings in the interplay between soft pastel colours and black. The composition is divided into three parts: a dusky city skyline, a blue harbour with multiple boats in view, and a small crowd of women and children in the foreground. In a related work, *Figures on a jetty* c 1908 (cat 28, p 56), a group appears mesmerised by the alluring ocean.

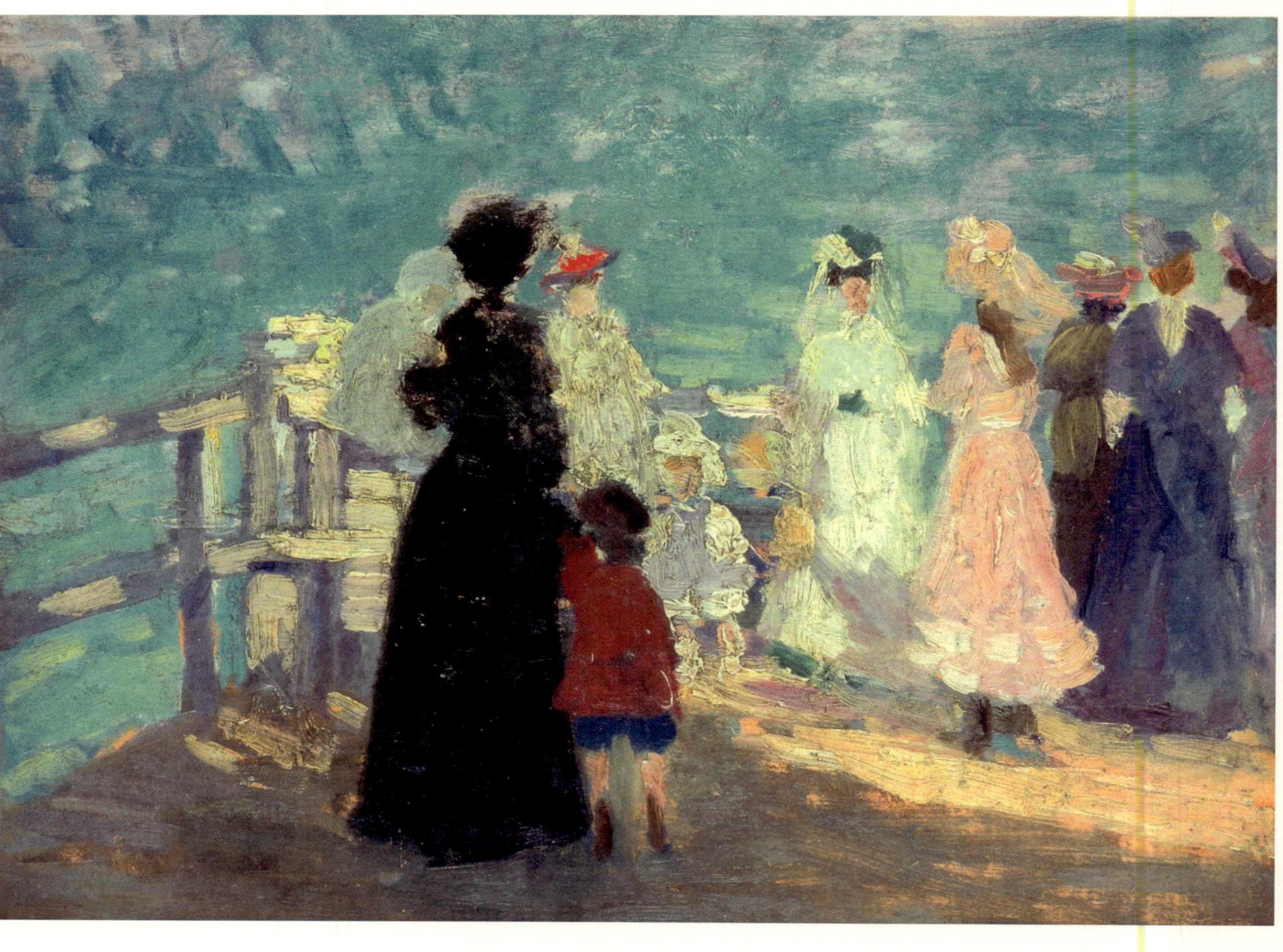

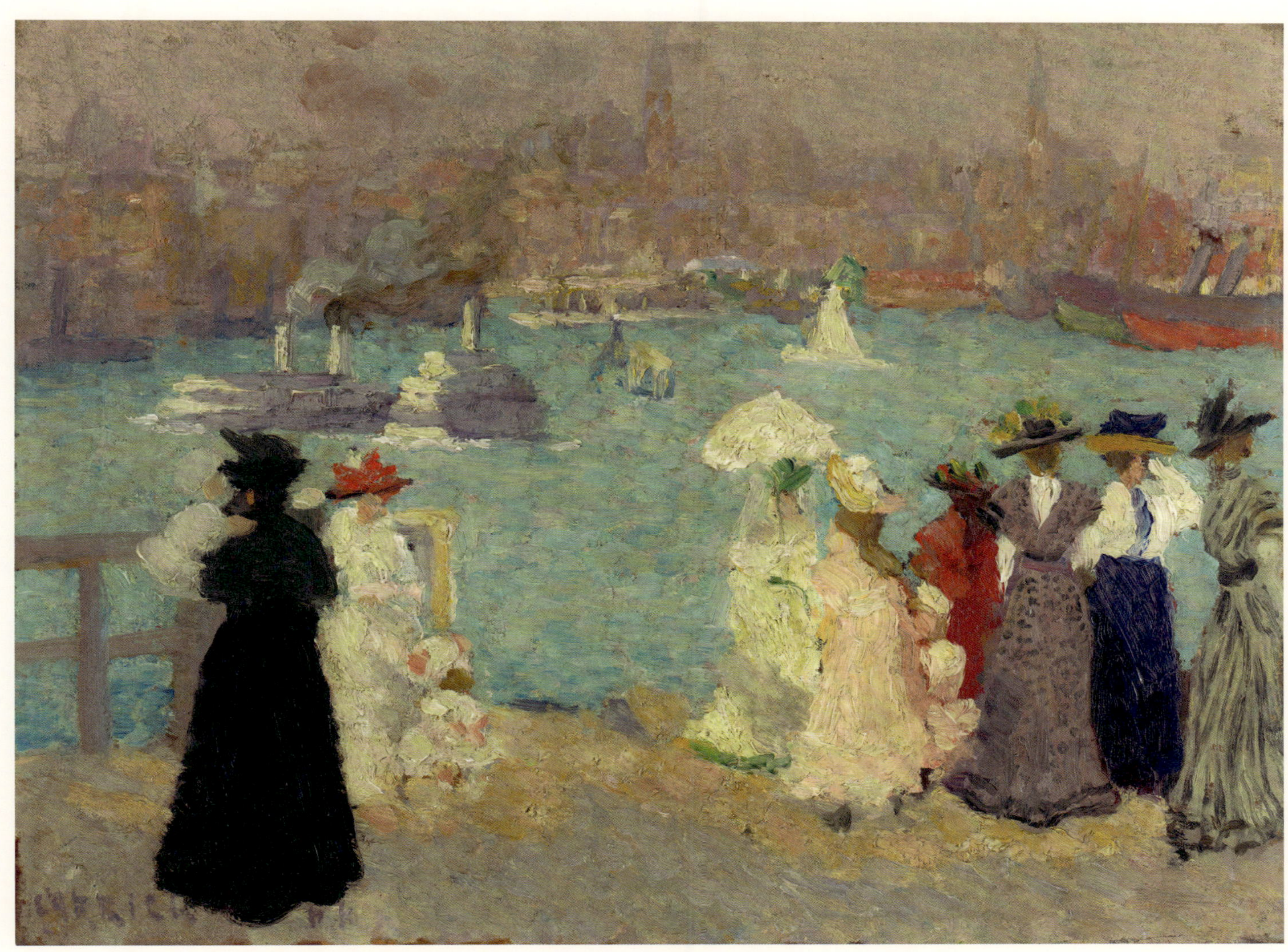

Opposite
cat 28 *Figures on a jetty* c 1908, oil on board, private collection

Above
cat 29 *The quay, Milsons Point* 1908, oil on artist board, National Gallery of Australia

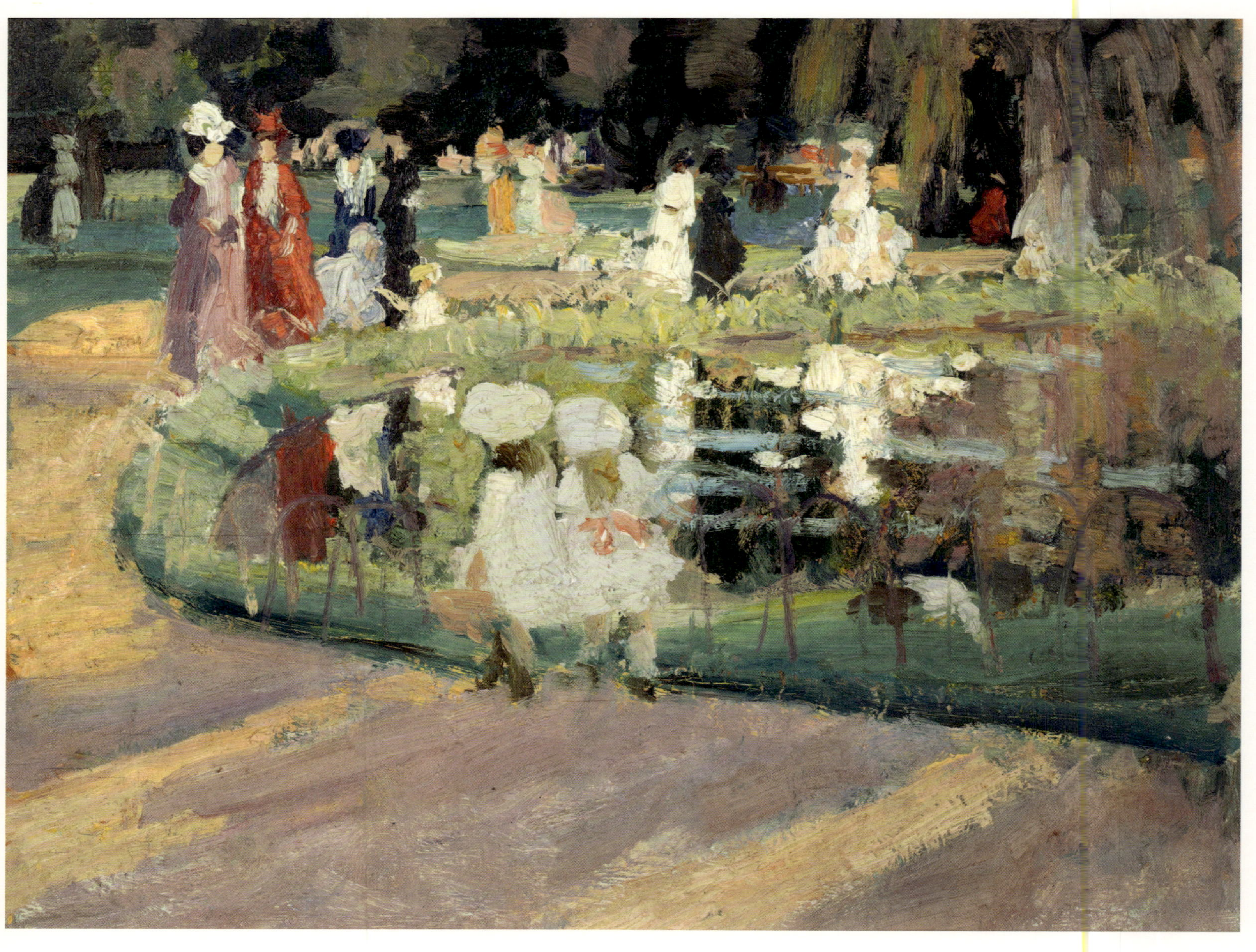

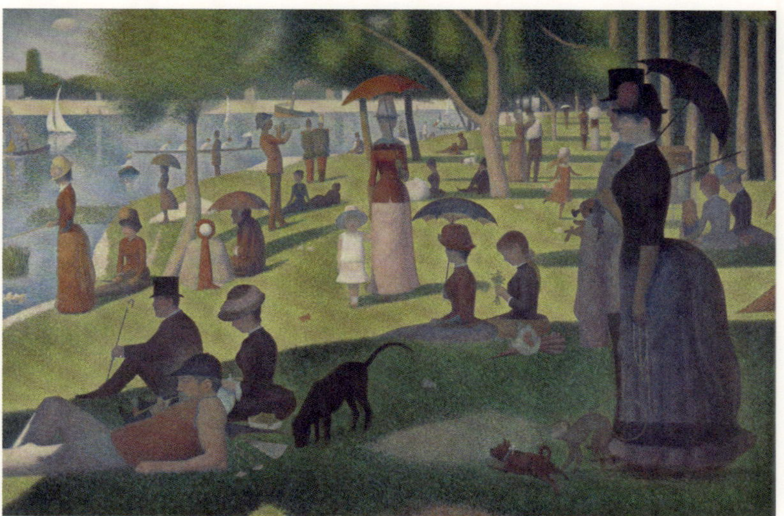

Opposite
cat 30 *Esquisse en Australie* (Sketch in Australia) c 1908, oil on board, private collection

Above
fig 14 Georges Seurat, *A Sunday on La Grande Jatte* 1884, oil on canvas, Art Institute of Chicago

Carrick's continuing interest in painting parks and gardens is evident in *Esquisse en Australie* (Sketch in Australia) 1908 (cat 1, p 6), undertaken in Sydney's Royal Botanic Garden. As one of the first truly post-impressionist works to have been created and exhibited in Australia, it is painted with such verve and such a bold palette that it would have appeared distinctly modern to local audiences. The apple-green, sunlit grass set against deep blue shadows is reminiscent of Georges Seurat's famous *A Sunday on La Grande Jatte* 1884 (fig 14), depicting people relaxing in a park just south of Paris. It is likely Carrick would have seen this painting in Seurat's retrospective at the Societé des Artistes Indépendants in Paris in 1905, and possibly even in the home of French artist Lucie Cousturier, who owned the painting for a time and with whom Carrick would later exhibit in Brussels.[82] Of course, the vigour of Carrick's paint handling is quite contrary to the precise, painterly notations of Seurat, but the subject matter and high-key palette are in harmony. Carrick took two paintings entitled *Esquisse en Australie* painted in 1908 (cats 1, p 6 and cat 30) and another striking work, *La promenade* (The promenade) 1908 (cat 120, p 200), back to Paris with her. They were exhibited at the Salon d'Automne at the start of November 1908, demonstrating the travel not only of people but also of works of art across continents.

Alongside their artistic pursuits, Carrick and Fox enjoyed the company of friends during their time in Australia, hosting several parties including one for Melbourne artists Violet Teague, Fred McCubbin, Walter Withers and art historian William Moore. Also present was Alexander Colquhoun who, like his wife Beatrix (née Hoile), was a theosophist and moved into the Theosophical Besant Lodge in Collins Street when it was formed in 1908. It was during this year that Annie Besant, then president of the Theosophical Society in Britain and a charismatic leader, gave a lecture tour in Australia. Carrick had developed an interest in theosophy in Paris and would likely have read the coverage and heard Besant talk. Prime Minister of Australia, Alfred Deakin, also attended Besant's public talk in Melbourne. His daughter Ivy Brookes and her husband Herbert were friends and supporters of Fox and Carrick, and conversations around things theosophical would have been in the air, setting the scene for what would become a keen, ongoing interest of Carrick's.

Back in Paris, Carrick was included in an exhibition of Les Quelques, which opened at the Galerie des Artistes Modernes in January 1909, a show of 'leading women artists in Paris, in which to be asked to

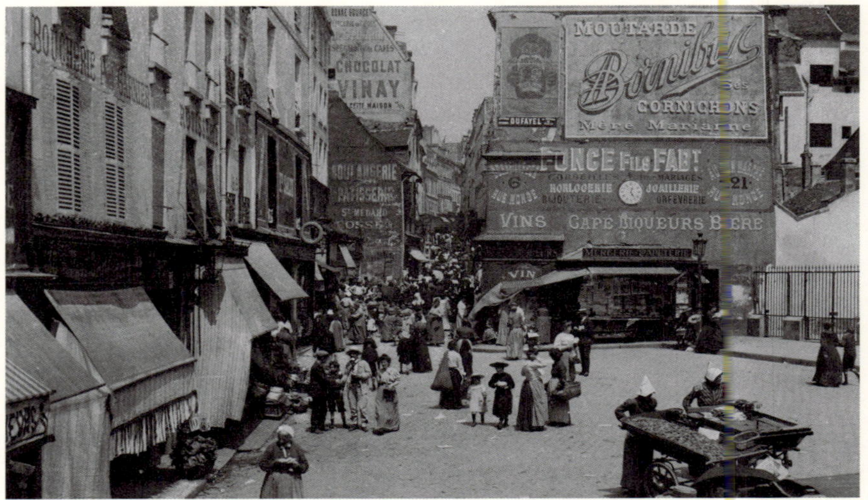

fig 15 Léon & Lévy, *La rue Mouffetard*, c 1900, photograph

Opposite
cat 31 *French village scene with figures* c 1910, oil on panel, Art Gallery of Western Australia

join was itself a distinction'.[83] Also included were French artist Lisbeth Delvolvé-Carrière, British artist Beatrice Howe, American artist Géraldine Reed Millet and Swiss-born artist Martha Stettler. Carrick's ability to convey luminosity through fragmented colour was compared with Stettler's '*delicieux tons blanches*' (delicious white tones).[84]

A number of Carrick's works from that exhibition were sent to La Libre Esthétique in Brussels in March 1909 for one of a regular number of shows instigated by director and art critic Octave Maus. In the year that Carrick exhibited, the selection of artists included Pierre Bonnard, Édouard Vuillard, Paul Signac, Odilon Redon and Maurice Denis. Fifty-one men were featured and seven women: Carrick, Anna Boch, Bessie Potter, Jane Poupelet, Mme France Raphaël, Yvonne Serruys and Lucie Cousturier, who studied under Paul Signac and wrote a monograph on Georges Seurat. In the catalogue, Maus called out public and critical hostility to neo-impressionist divisionism—and to Seurat's *A Sunday on La Grande Jatte* in particular. In something of a manifesto, he noted his aim to showcase the work of diverse contemporary artists without conforming to establishment guidelines or restricting subject matter or style:

> **What does it matter, anyway, if a painting is beautiful, whether it represents a cabbage, the St-Lazare station or the German emperor? Didn't Rembrandt make a masterpiece out of a flayed ox? And Cézanne from a basket of apples?**[85]

The 1909 catalogue listing included eight works by 'Mlle Carrick', two portraits and *Nourrices et bébés*, *Un marché aux fleurs à Venise*, *Un marché*, *Le diabolo*, *La petite rose* and *La promenade*.[86]

Soon after, Carrick painted one of her most accomplished modern works, *Rue Mouffetard, Paris* 1910 (cat 32, pp 62–63). Having escaped the massive reconstruction of Paris under Baron von Haussman in the nineteenth century, the architecture of Rue Mouffetard dates back to Roman times and provided inspiration to many authors including Victor Hugo and Ernest Hemingway. In her painting, Carrick retains the atmosphere of the old street while providing a sense of modernity by abstracting from the real, riffing off the typography on the facing wall and revealing her considerable abilities as a luminous colourist. A key focus is the woman wearing a long, white apron over her blue dress with her shopping basket slung over her arm. She appears as a vital presence walking towards the viewer, confidently inhabiting her surroundings.

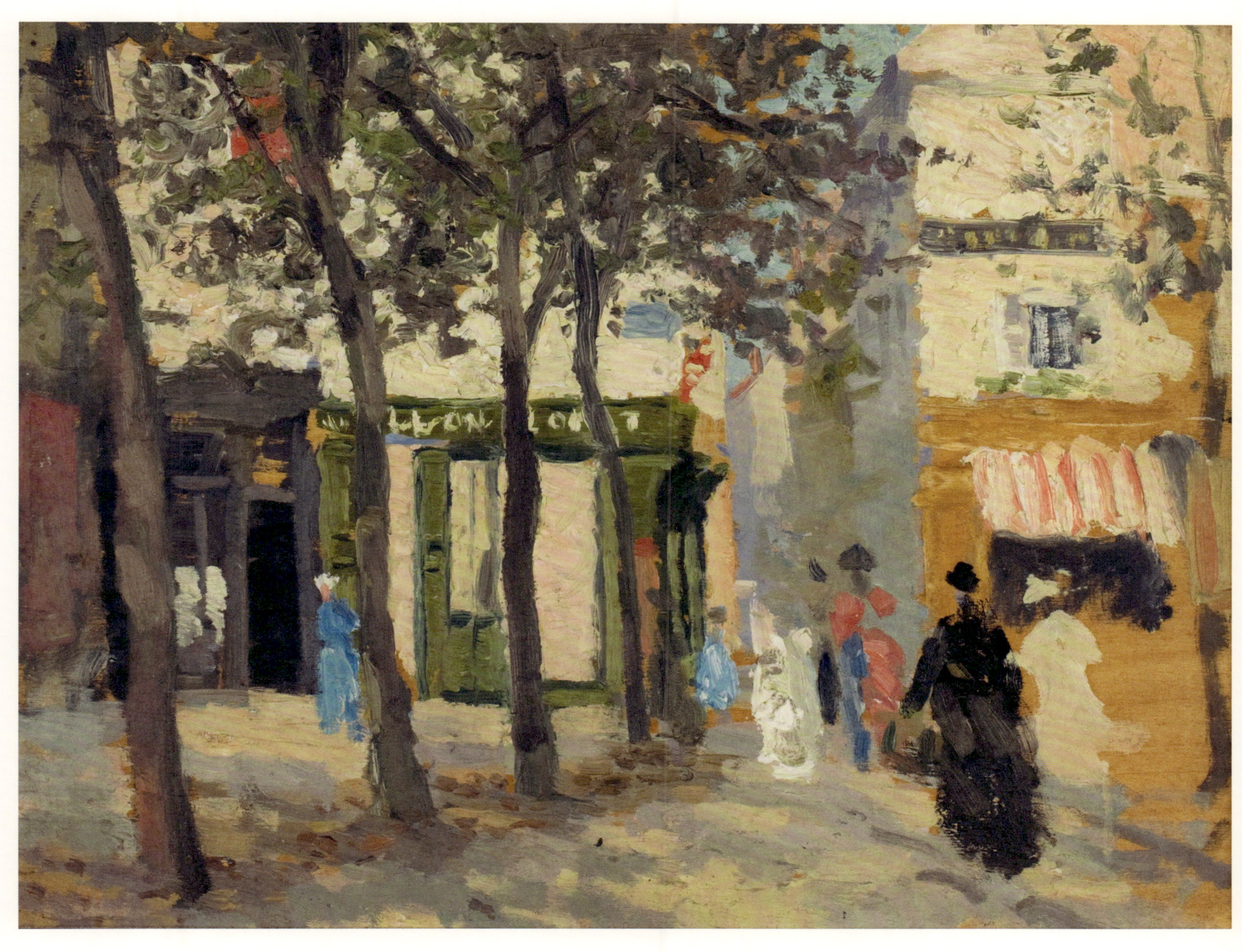

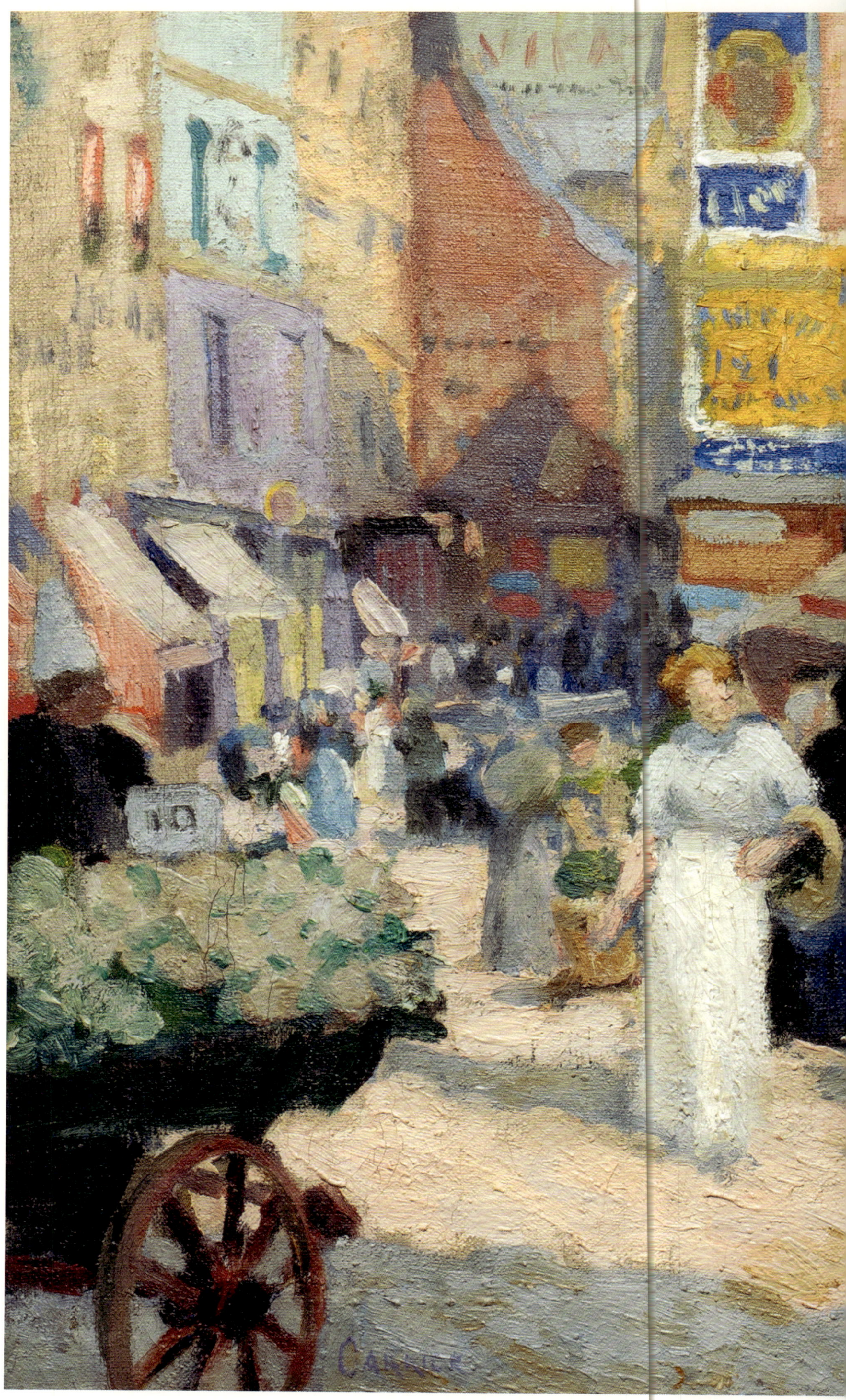

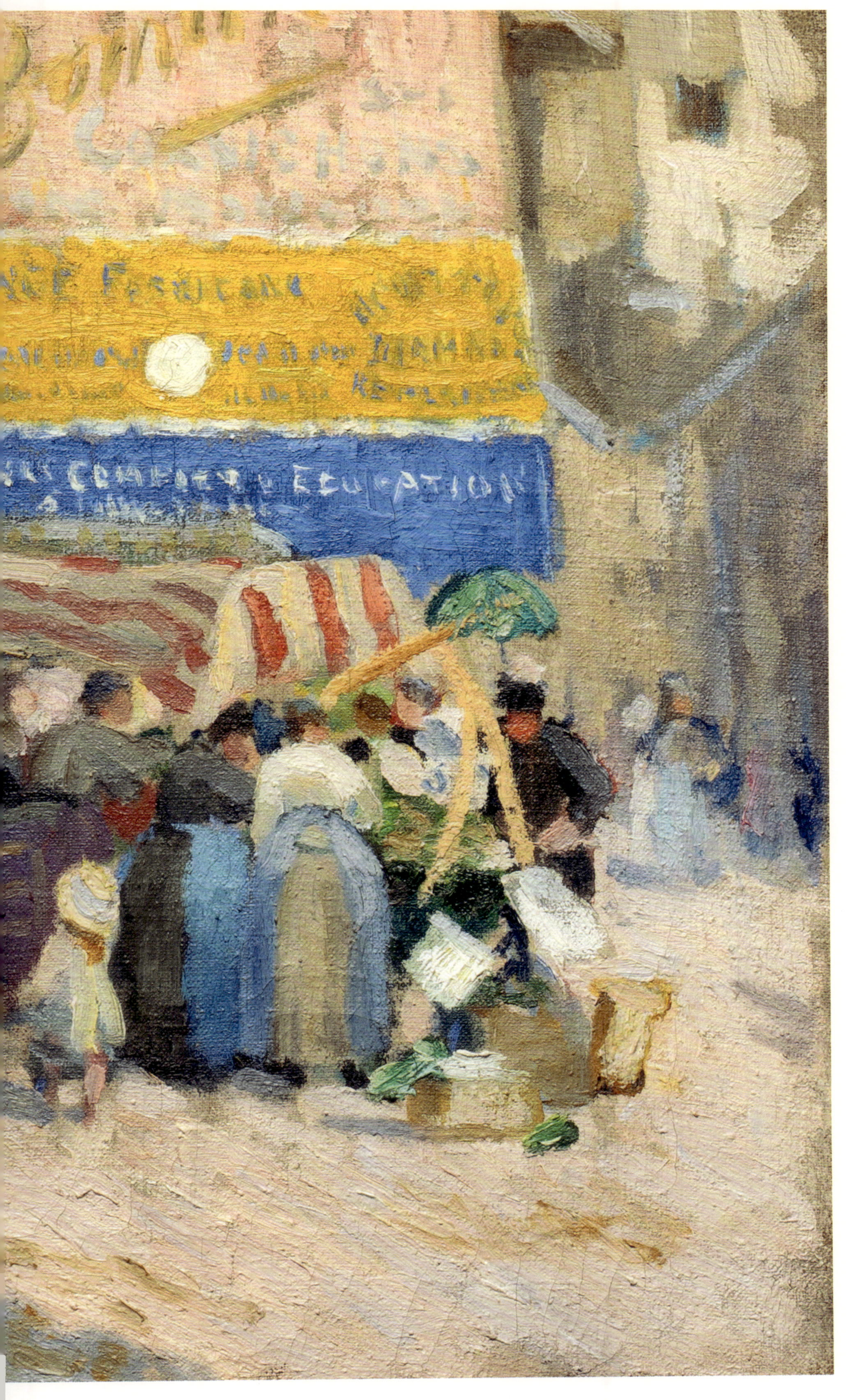

Between 1909 and 1912, Carrick and Fox embarked on a period of extensive travel in search of fresh inspiration. They visited the French beaches in Brittany and Normandy as well as a range of locations in North Africa. Carrick's work grew considerably in strength during this time, with paintings such as *Sur la plage (On the sands), Dinard* 1911 [87] (cat 97, p 149), *La marée haute à Saint-Malo (High tide at St Malo)* c 1911–12 (cat 101, p 157) and *The quay at Dinard* c 1911–12 (cat 102, p 159), as well as *Arabs bargaining* c 1911 (cat 108, p 170) and *Laveuses algériennes (Algerian women washing clothes in a stream)* c 1911 (cat 111, pp 176–77), confirming her reputation in France in group shows and in a major 1913 solo exhibition in Australia.

While Carrick and Fox enjoyed one another's company, they would likely have had lively conversations about their contradictory views. Fox's opposition to the Salon d'Automne, where Carrick showed regularly, was a case in point. As Fox wrote to Hans Heysen on 13 September 1911:

> There is a lot of talk here about the post impressionists—I am sure you would not like them, nor could you feel any interest in the Autumn Salon, which claims to be the coming art—God help it, if it turns out to be so. Strangely enough I am regarded here as quite academic, rather old hat, but at the [Royal] Academy, I am looked upon as one of the most daring revolutionists.[88]

Fox added a more conciliatory note at the end: 'My wife works away and is doing some very interesting & personal stuff—She is *societaire* of [the] Autumn Salon & is very keen on the modern outlook.'

Despite their obvious differences, they learned from one another—Carrick from his interior scenes and portraiture and Fox from Carrick's bold, innovative outdoor works. There is a real sense of delight in Carrick's painting *Sur la plage* (On the beach) 1910 (cat 99, p 154), which shows a young boy digging in the sand alongside another in a matching outfit and an array of figures doing their own thing around a striped beach tent. A distinction from Fox's very similar painting of the same title, in what feels like a game of 'spot the difference', is that Carrick's work is less sketch-like and more finished. Both artists include black as a point of definition from the light surrounds, but in Carrick's work its application is more purposeful, Fox being more interested in broad effects of light.[89]

The ubiquitous French red-and-white striped beach tents became a leitmotif for Carrick, setting up alternating tempos within individual paintings and from one work to the next. Singular tents and multiples become like the notes on a keyboard. In *Sur la plage* (On the beach) c 1910 (cat 105, p 163), the focus is placed on one tent, showing a nursemaid sheltering from the sun watching well-dressed children at play. The small, temporary shelters recall the umbrella canopies in Carrick's market scenes, and the stripe was also a recurring element across subject matter—from dress fabrics to tents—setting up dynamic linear rhythms. As Michel Pastoureau in his book on the history of the stripe writes,

> On the eve of World War I, there is no longer a beach in temperate Europe that hasn't become the veritable theatre for stripes.[90]

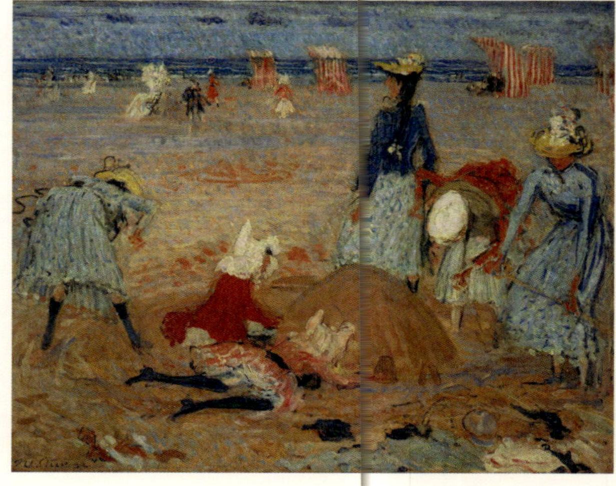

Previous
cat 32 *Rue Mouffetard, Paris* 1910, oil on canvas, Kerry Stokes Collection

Above
fig 16 Philip Wilson Steer, *Boulogne sands* 1888–91, oil paint on canvas, Tate

Opposite
cat 33 *Beach scene* c 1909, oil on canvas on cardboard, National Gallery of Australia

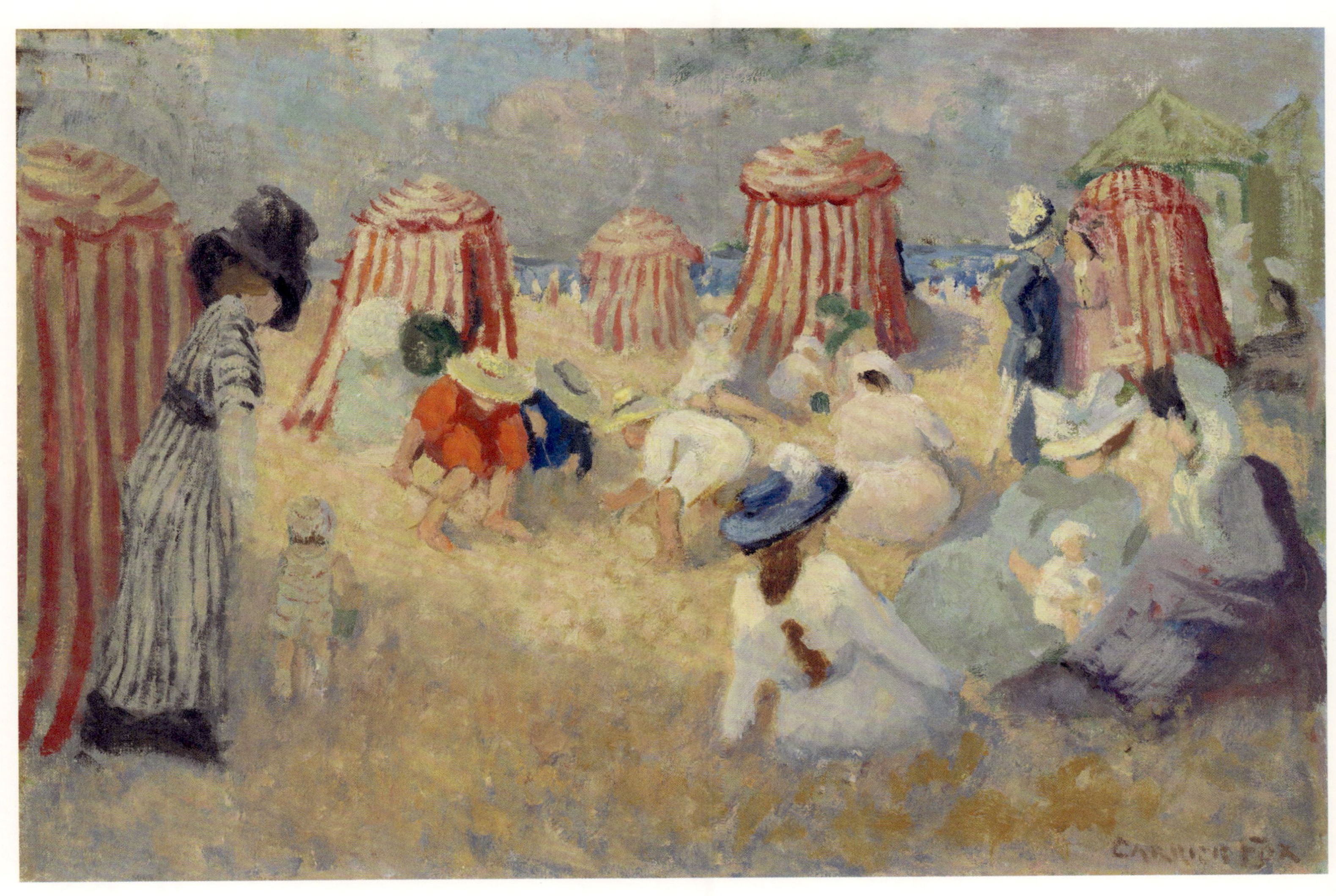

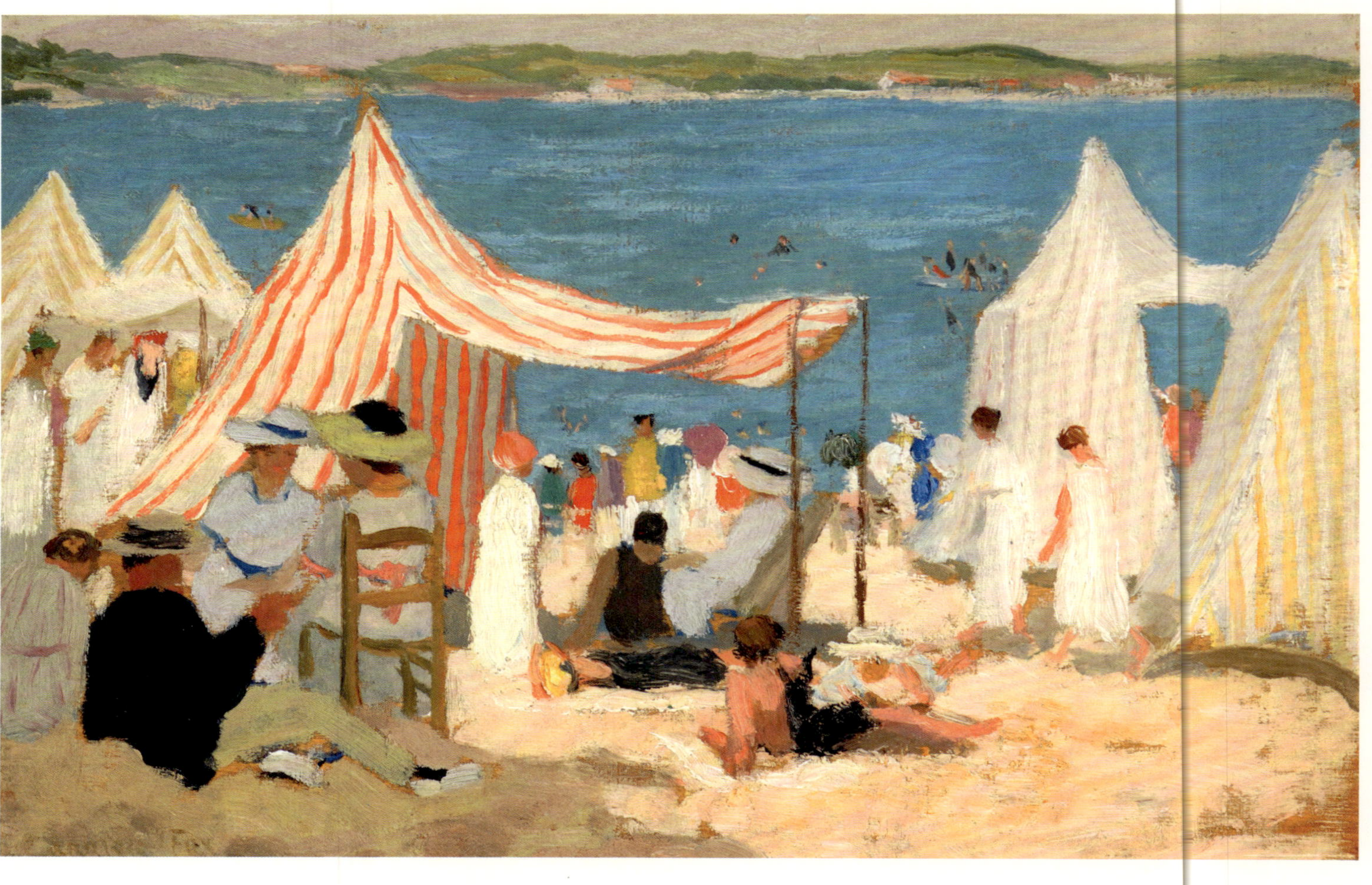

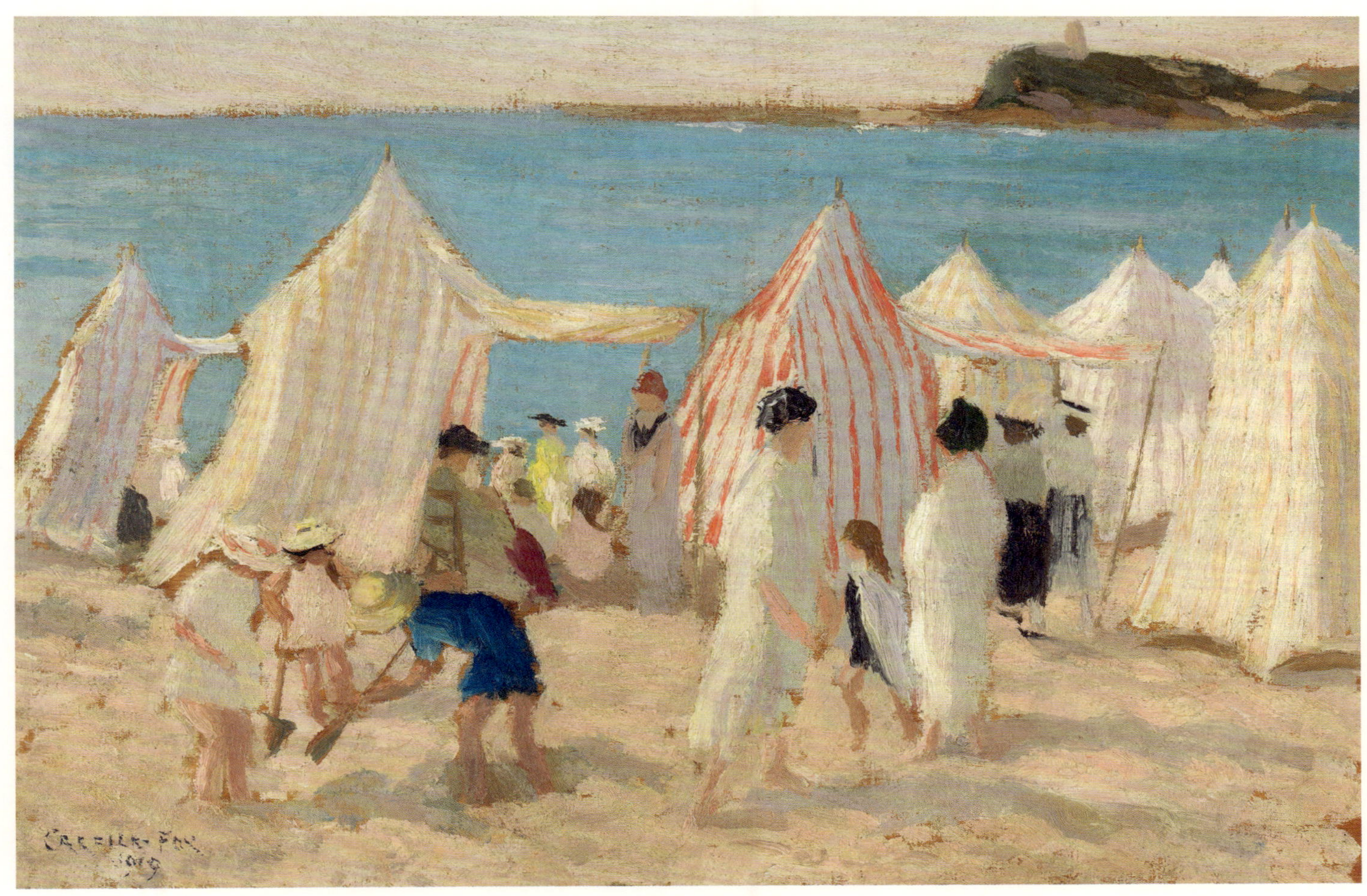

Opposite
cat 34 *French beach scene* c 1919, oil on wood panel, Castlemaine Art Museum

Above
cat 35 *La plage française* (The French beach) 1919, oil on board, University Art Collection, Chau Chak Wing Museum, The University of Sydney

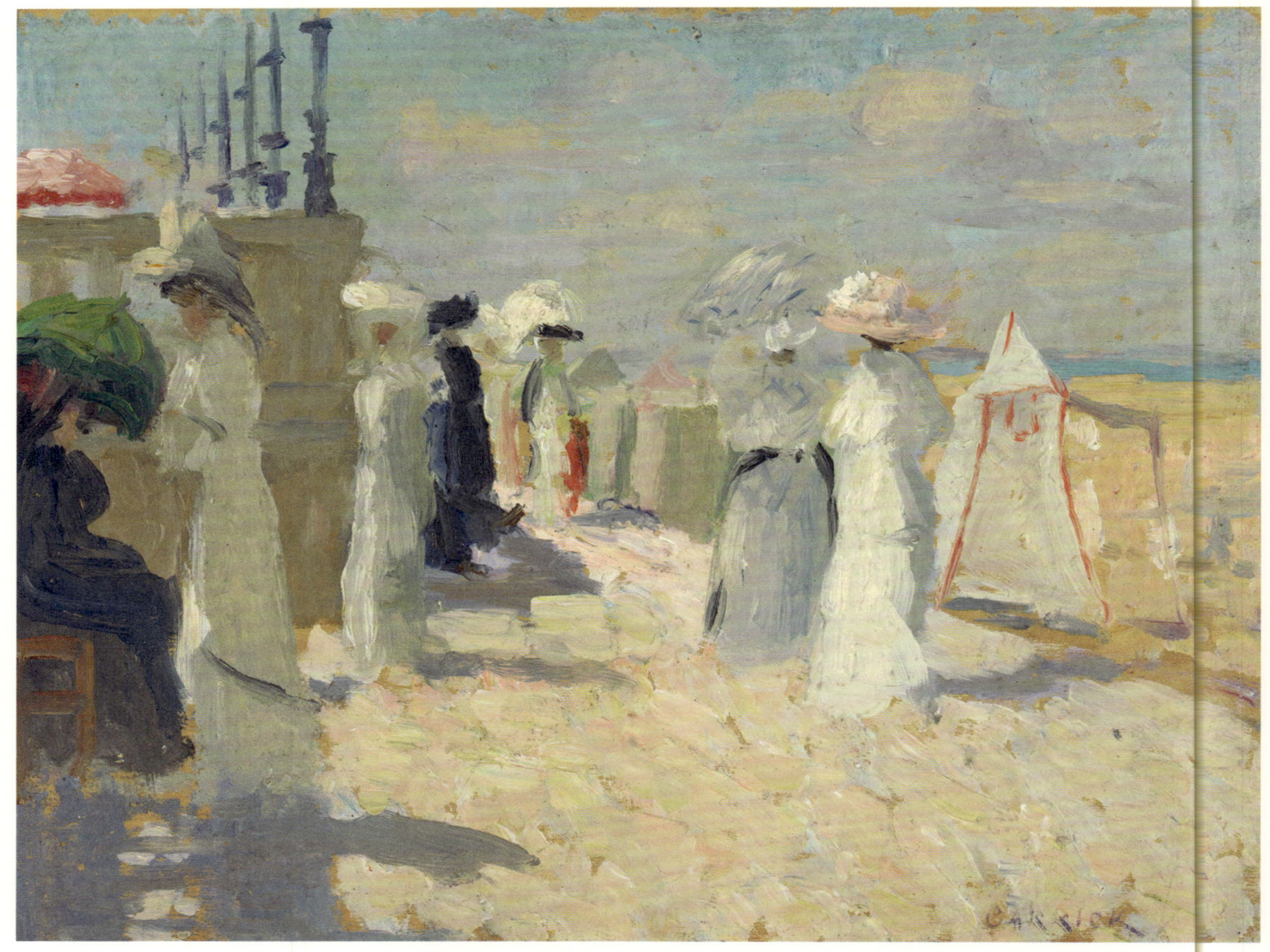

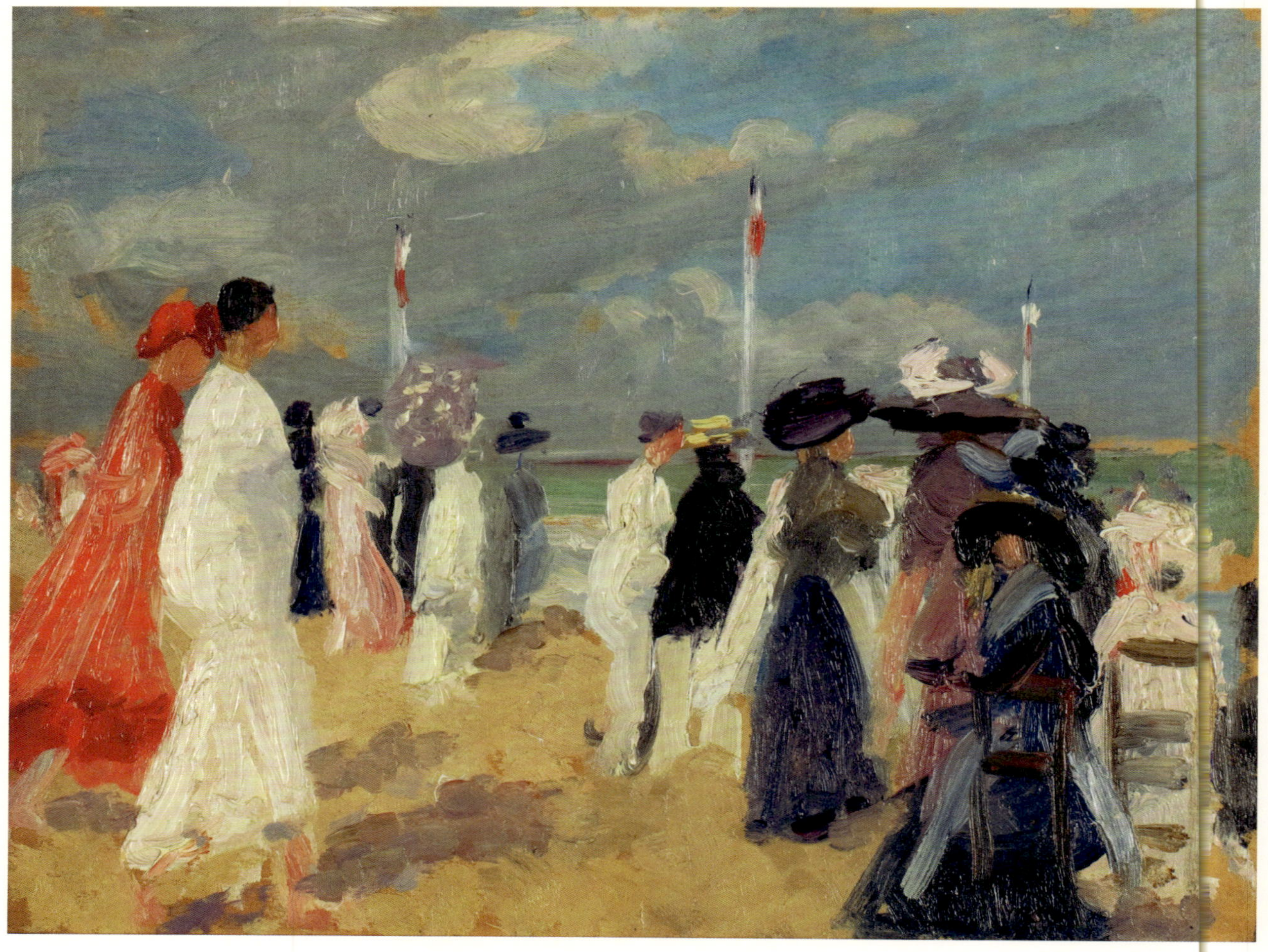

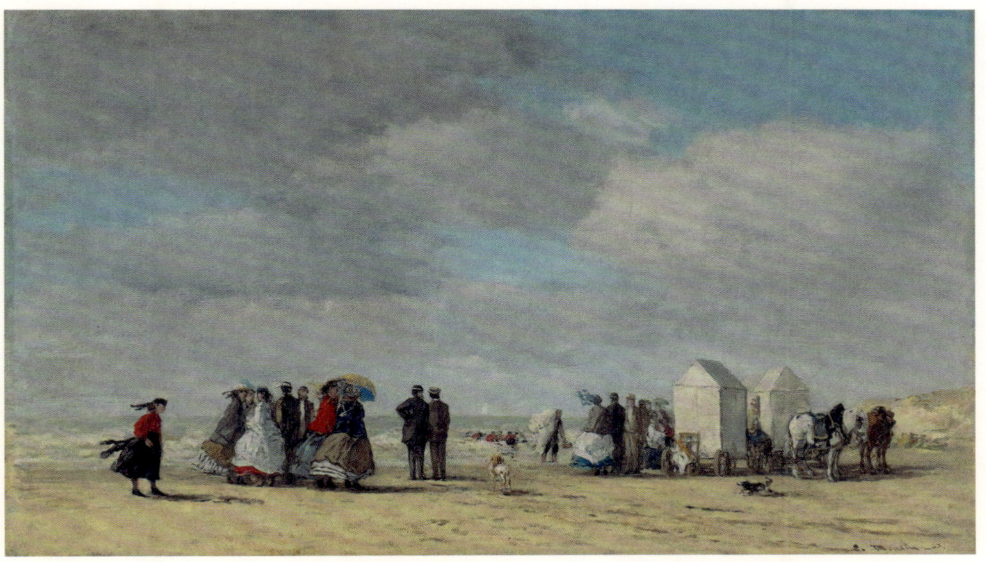

Opposite, top to bottom
cat 36 *The promenade* c 1910, oil on board, private collection

cat 37 *Seaside promenade, south of France* c 1910, oil on panel, Art Gallery of Western Australia

Above
fig 17 Eugène Boudin, *The beach at Trouville* 1865, oil on canvas, Princeton University Art Museum

While Carrick's works are about the movement and vitality of crowds, in paintings such as *On the sands* 1910 (cat 104, p 162) and *Sur la plage* c 1910 (cat 103, p 162) there is a meditative dimension, heightened by the floating luminous grounds. *Beach scene* c 1909 (cat 33, p 65), like *Sur la plage, Dinard* 1911 (cat 97, p 149), epitomises people at beach resorts—namely mothers and children accompanied by nannies or nurses. Musical analogies recur in the way that Carrick would take an identical composition and riff on it, playing with scale and subtly altering the mood by softening or deepening colour and adding or subtracting structures, like an orchestral interplay of sounds. Some of Carrick's beach paintings recall *The beach at Trouville* 1865 by Eugène Boudin (fig 17), who inspired Claude Monet's interest in the transient effects of light and weather.

Carrick's *Seaside promenade, south of France* c 1910 (cat 37) belongs to a small group of freely abstracted depictions of fashionable women, in this instance promenading in flowing long dresses—some wearing hats, a few seated—on a breezy day with clouds scudding above. A related work *The Promenade* c 1910 (cat 36) is immensely delicate, evoking a dreamlike appearance through a predominantly light-white palette brightened with touches of red, blue and black.

A defining feature of Carrick's beach paintings is the way she abstracts from the real. This is eloquently expressed in her later painting *La plage Française* (The French beach) 1919 (cat 35, p 67). In this poetic work the palette of white and palest pinks comes to the fore in the tents, with their delicately drawn stripes, along with the robed women who appear of this world and yet also ethereal. Behind them, the pale sea adds to the languid mood. In the spirit of variations on a theme, in *French beach scene* c 1919 (cat 34, p 66) the sea is a brighter, more strident blue, the stripes on the tents are stronger in warm red-white contrast, all set in the midday light of a hot summer day. These works are among the most modern of Carrick's career, demonstrating her enjoyment of the varied possibilities of modernity and an increasing confidence in her distinctive ways of working.

In *Quay at St Malo* 1911 (cat 100, p 156) and *La marée haute à Saint-Malo* (cat 101, p 157), Carrick takes an adventurous viewpoint from above, focusing on the compressed space between the high stone rampart and the small beach. Crowds of people are shown through staccato-like touches, giving an impression of the scene. It was common for Carrick to do a smaller and larger version of the same scene, capturing the essence of the subject in a fresh way prior to the more finished studio painting, in which she amplified, clarified, improvised and incorporated fine details. *La marée haute à Saint-Malo* and *The quay at Dinard* (cat 102, p 159) are large paintings for Carrick, both divided into three main compositional areas with an almost identical palette. Even details such as the black sash on the white dress of the woman on the right appears in both works. All the same, the Dinard painting is a real fashion statement, while the St Malo work, which Carrick valued highly, was more about her love of crowds in flux.

The year 1911 was a key moment in Carrick's career, involving travel to North Africa and Spain. On 13 September of that year, Fox wrote to Hans Heysen:

> **Early this year middle of Feb—having finished my work we set off for a round trip determined to get some settled sunlight ... We went first to Marseilles then across to Algiers from there South to an interior place called Bou Saada where we stayed six weeks—then back to Algiers—then to Tangiers [Tangier] & on to Cadiz—and returning home through Seville Cordova Granada Toledo Madrid. We had an enjoyable trip staying 3 or 4 days in each place following Bou Saada and working everywhere ... We both did a lot of work & I think I got some good ones ... painted at one go.[91]**

Carrick's experience in North Africa added to the lexicon of market subjects she had painted in France, Italy and Australia. Since the late nineteenth century, North Africa had become part of the colonial enterprise in which Carrick and Fox, along with many other artists, were enmeshed.[92] Another woman artist, Australian Hilda Rix Nicholas, also visited Morocco, with the American painter Henry Ossawa Tanner, a year after Carrick and Fox.[93] Like Nicholas, and in contrast to some of the male artists who painted Orientalist views, Carrick tended not to exoticise her subject matter but rather painted what she observed in front of her. Characteristically, she was interested in local attire, in this context the *thobes* (long robes) and headdresses worn by the men. In one of her most significant paintings, *Arabs bargaining* c 1911 (cat 108, p 170), buyers and sellers are shown negotiating, concentrating on their wares, against a background of milling people. Here, Carrick is intent on the formal aspects of painting. As Elena Taylor perceptively writes, 'In *Arabs bargaining*, Carrick's interest is as much in describing this commonplace market scene as in constructing a painting of abstract elements and high-keyed and vibrant colours.'[94]

Local architectural landmarks were also key reference points for Carrick's paintings. Works such as *The mosque at Tangier* c 1911 (cat 112, p 179) reveal her capacities as a most subtle colourist, the delicate hues bringing atmosphere to the old town bathed in light, shimmering with a spiritual presence. What Carrick brought most of all to her North African paintings was a search for the essence of things. She distilled her close observations of people and places, imbuing them with feeling and the constant flow of life.

A work by Carrick that extended the boundaries of perception beyond anything she had previously realised was *Laveuses algériennes (Algerian women washing clothes in a stream)* c 1911 (cat 111, pp 176–77). It is one of the most luminous abstracted paintings of her career, made more remarkable in light of the still-emerging field of abstraction. Here, Carrick brings to the fore the feeling of being immersed in the pattern of experience that is at once human, material and natural. The painting appears to palpitate with life: figures and coloured fabrics, the warm hues of rocks against flowing water, all come together through the painterliness of the artist's brush. It is the artist as medium and represents a freedom that can only come with experience, true to her inner spirit.

Carrick's interest in spiritual ideas, including theosophy, was informed by diverse sources. Since 1908 she had been a member of the Union Internationale des Beaux-Arts et des Lettres, headed by Auguste Rodin and Vincent d'Indy, whose utopian aspirations were expressed in *Les Tendances Nouvelles*, a periodical started in 1904. As art historian Jonathan Fineberg has written, this group (often referred to by the catchy name of their periodical) put into practice many characteristic ideas of Symbolism, which still held sway in the Parisian artworld during the first decade of the twentieth century:

> **Despite the broad variety of individual viewpoints published by the [*Tendances Nouvelles*] magazine the symbolist profile remained clear—in its social aspirations for art, its co-operative nature, its belief in the metaphysical unity of the various arts ... and its not infrequent forays into the mystic.**
>
> **Beyond its usefulness as an example and as a lexicon (of sorts) for lesser-known artists of the period, *Les Tendances Nouvelles* also made significant contributions to the evolution of early modern art.[95]**

Among its key philosophical concerns was the relationship between painting and music, a subject of great interest to Carrick since her studies at the Guildhall School of Music and Drama in London. Wassily Kandinsky was a regular contributor to *Les Tendances Nouvelles*, proposing that colour could exercise a direct influence on the inner life—on the soul:

> **Colour is the keyboard. The eye becomes the hammer, while the soul is a piano of many strings. The artist is the hand through which the medium of different keys causes the human soul to vibrate.[96]**

Carrick received several mentions in essays in *Les Tendances Nouvelles*, not only for her more overtly modern work, but also for her delicate flower subjects, 'her modesty of artistic approach concealing a true science of how to see, how to express with the brush and how to understand'.[97] The idea of colour vibrations eliciting psychological and spiritual resonances was associated with Carrick's feeling for the vibrancy of a crowd: 'To me it has the attraction a fine orchestra has to a musician and often when I've been painting some of the groups ... I have felt them as musical chords.'[98]

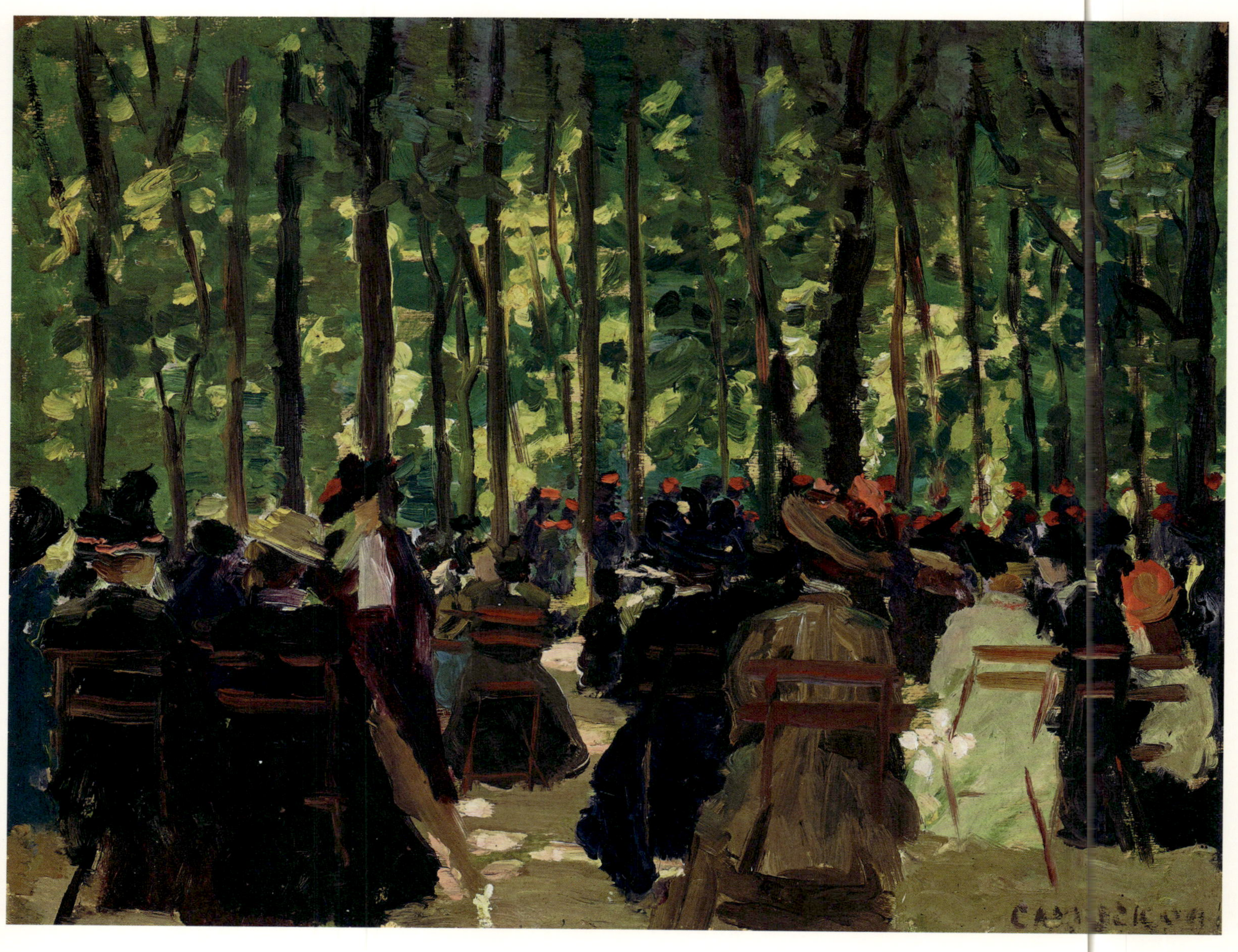

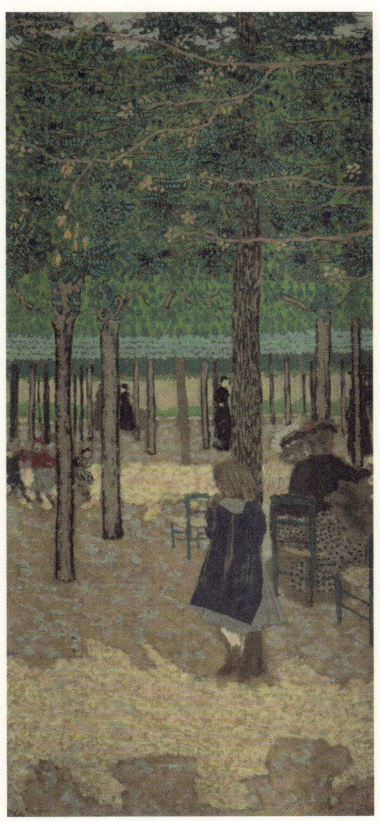

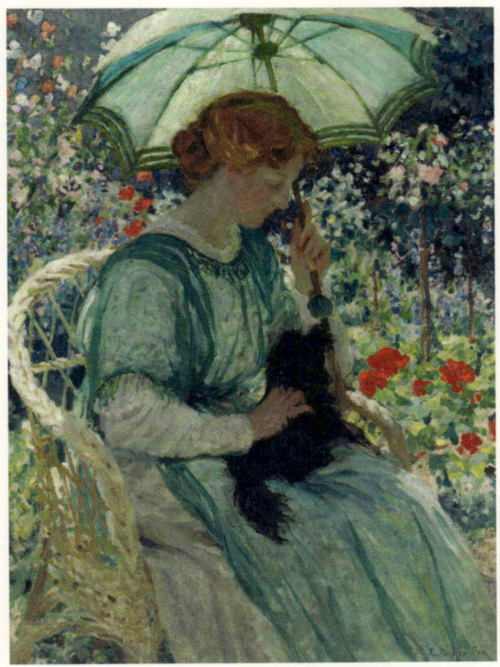

Opposite
cat 38 *Concert in the Luxembourg Gardens* 1909, also known as *Open-air concert*, oil on panel, private collection

Top to bottom
fig 18 Édouard Vuillard, *Under the trees* from *Jardins publics* (Public gardens) 1894, distemper on fabric, The Cleveland Museum of Art

fig 19 Emanuel Phillips Fox, *The green parasol* c 1912, oil on canvas, National Gallery of Australia

Over the years Carrick's interest in art and music included the act of listening. In *Concert in the Luxembourg Gardens* 1909 (cat 38) an audience on chairs is immersed in the music, the vertical tree trunks in the background setting up their own rhythm. Indeed, Carrick identified as a listener, and attended concerts in the Luxembourg Gardens, on the beach in France and in Sydney's Royal Botanic Garden. Music was also a feature of the 'at home' gatherings in her Paris apartment, and she formed close friendships with musicians such as the pianist Jean Batalla, whose portrait she painted. In the 1920s she was also interested in the colour-music theories of Roy de Maistre, coinciding with her growing interest in theosophy.[99]

On Christmas Eve 1911, Carrick and Fox held a party at 65 Boulevard Arago. The guests included New Zealand painters Frances Hodgkins, Mrs Hickman Molesworth and Owen Merton. Hodgkins recounted the festivities to her mother Rachel Hodgkins in a letter: 'I finished work at 4.30 on Xmas eve. At 9 o'clock I went off to a party at the Phillips Foxes with Mrs Molesworth, Miss Henderson & Owen Merton in a taxi—& made merry till I couldn't lift an eyelid ... Owen M played an accompaniment which marked him as a musician.'[100] It was noted that Carrick's 'delightful sketches' could be viewed on the walls.

Among Carrick and Fox's closest friends in Paris were Rupert Bunny and his wife Jeanne Morel, who lived nearby in Montparnasse. Fox and Bunny had much in common in their depictions of a feminine ideal, as seen in paintings shown at the Salons and the Royal Academy, albeit with distinctive styles. Fox's favourite model was Edith Anderson, who posed for him over a protracted period in 1912 in Carrick and Fox's Boulevard Arago home. Anderson, who was born in Brisbane and was an artist in her own right, had a special bond of friendship with Fox. While he often took selective features from different models to attain the ideal woman he was searching for in his art, Anderson had it all. She modelled in the Foxes' garden for exquisite, luminous paintings like *The green parasol* c 1912 (fig 19), and for nudes inside. It must have been something of a challenge for Carrick and it is perhaps not surprising that her portrait of Anderson, a genuinely beautiful woman, was not so flattering. A few years earlier she had exhibited a painting *Une maladie imaginaire* c 1907, referring to a metaphorical malady of the heart, and it would in all likelihood have been a relief when Fox introduced Anderson to her husband-to-be, Penleigh Boyd. Indeed, Fox and Carrick held a party in honour of their marriage and Fox gave Anderson away. Carrick also painted a portrait of Penleigh Boyd, shown in the Salon d'Automne in 1912, and they all remained friends.

While Fox would undoubtedly have learned from Carrick's innovative, small-scale, outdoor paintings (her forte), she would have learned from his portraiture and larger figure painting (his forte). In a work like Carrick's *Jeune homme contre une fenêtre* (Young man in front of a window) c 1912 (cat 40, p 75) there are clear similarities with Fox's approach. Here, the man smoking a pipe relaxes indoors on a sunny day with a view of Carrick's beloved flowering garden at Boulevard Arago behind him. When this painting was exhibited in Australia in 1913, still life elements came in for special mention: 'the syphon, lemon, and drinking requisites ... are calculated to make the beholder feel thirsty.'[101]

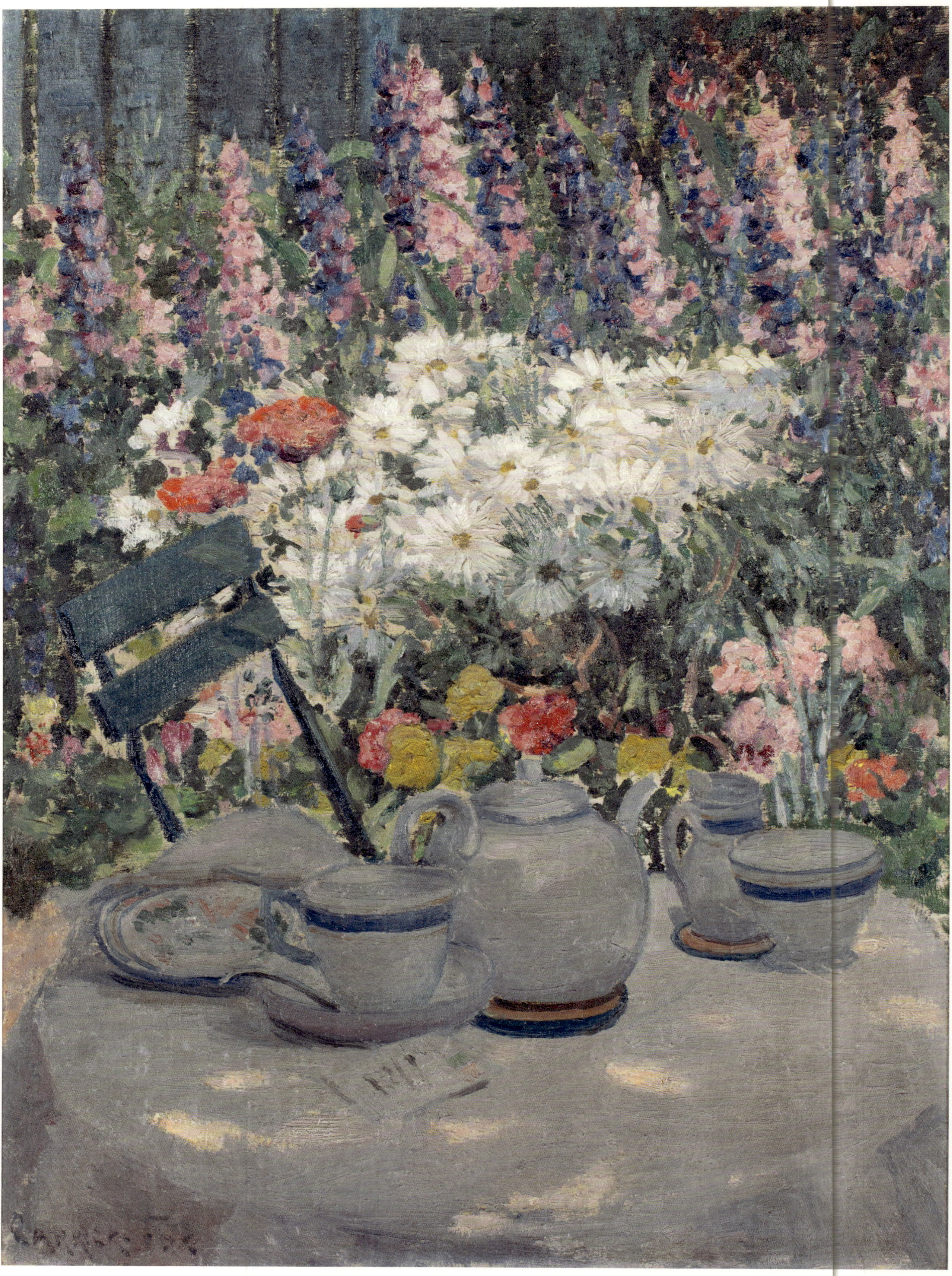

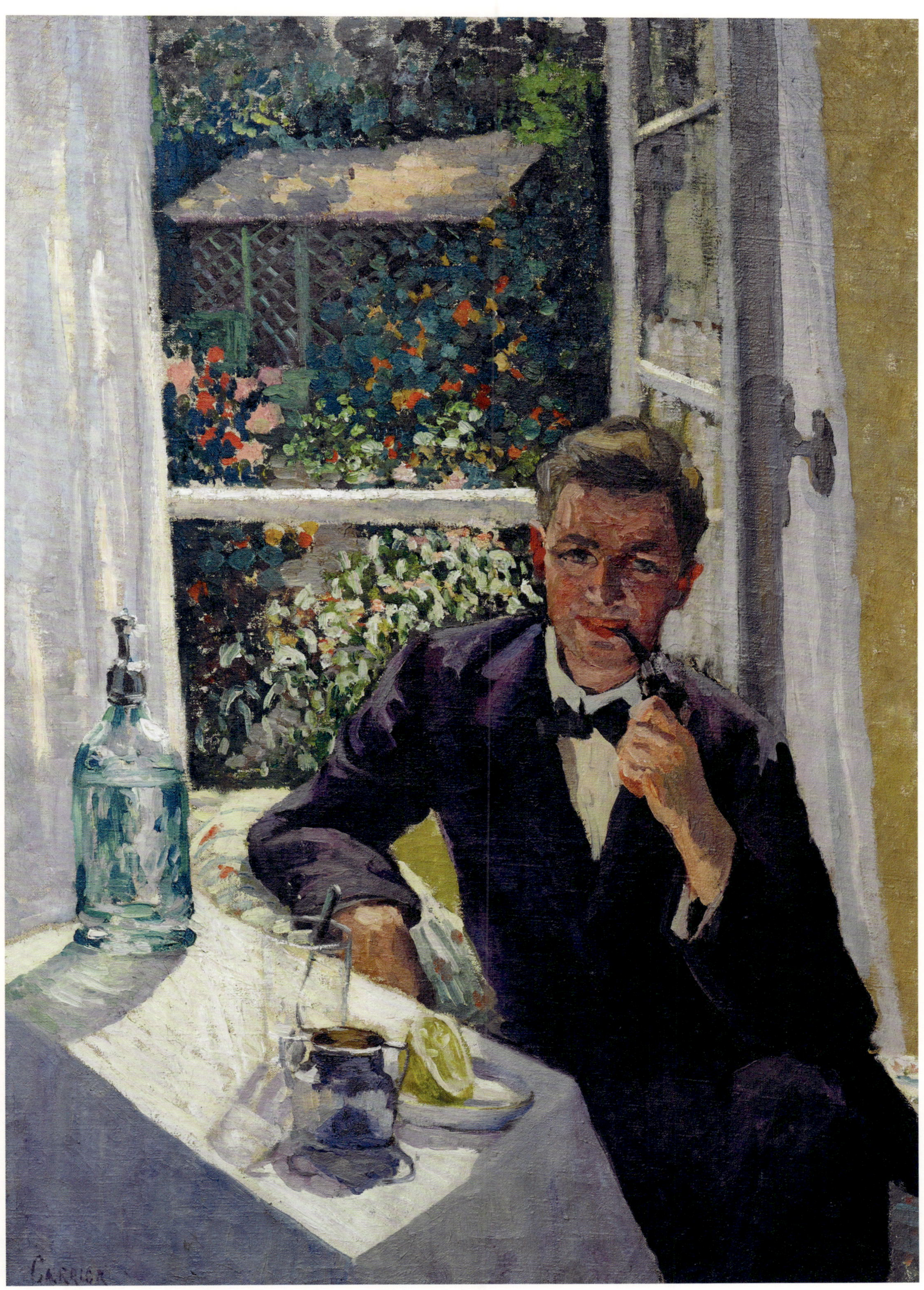
CARRICK

Over the course of 1911 and 1912, Carrick exhibited widely. In a review of an exhibition of Les Quelques in January 1912, which included work by Stettler and Dannenberg, it was noted that Carrick was showing paintings relating to life in North Africa. She also did so at the Salon d'Automne in 1911 to 1912, where again, mention was made of Algerian subjects, with one commentator writing passionately, 'I was stopped in my tracks, under something quite small ... but perfect. Signed by Mme Ethel Carrick: *Arab woman*. It is painted with breadth, verve, and extraordinary certainty; the air circulates widely ... and the colour is extremely seductive.'[102] In February 1913, Carrick showed a wide range of subjects from her time in North Africa in 1911 at the twenty-first exhibition of the Société des Peintres Orientalistes Français, at the Grand Palais, Paris including *La mosque de Tanger* (The mosque at Tangier) c 1911, and the undated works *Le Port d'Alger* (The port of Algiers), *Une rue à Tanger* (A street in Tangier), *Le marché de Bou Saada* (The market at Bou Saada) and *Le marché aux chameaux* (The camel market).

Painting in the public domain, as Carrick did—'using it effectively as her studio and principal subject matter for her art'—was still quite radical in the early twentieth century.[103] The increase in women's activism for suffrage, democratic rights and better opportunities opened up new spaces in which to experience the world. Carrick's daring painting *Bull fight at Biarritz* c 1908 (also known as *Impression of a bull fight,* cat 41) was a case in point.[104] As art historian Stephen Rainbird notes: 'For Francisco de Goya and Édouard Manet, bullfighting scenes were a conventional theme ... but for women the subject had remained off limits.'[105] While Manet's paintings of bullfight scenes were often constructed from ground level, foregrounding the matador, the embodiment of control and domination, a quite different sensibility emerges in Carrick's impression:

> Carrick has peopled the surrounding stands with spectators of both genders, but in the foreground she has prominently positioned a number of neatly hatted (probably Parisian) women. Their gaze is directed away from the artist and thus the viewer, towards the bullfight. They are engrossed in a strongly masculine spectacle that is at once relatively new and challenging, and perhaps even shocking. In presenting these women as the focus of the painting ... Carrick secured *corrida* (bullfighting) for women in the public sphere.[106]

Public spectacle was one thing, but painting on European streets and in cafes was another. Carrick spoke of the difficulty working as a woman in public places during her travels: 'Once in Cadiz I was very anxious to paint a market scene. I had no sooner settled myself to work than I was surrounded by crowds of smiling people, not in the least rude, but so interested in me that they stood right in front and I could see nothing.' After attempts to find a solution she noted: 'My husband left to sketch elsewhere. I sat down at a cafe with my back to the wall. The crowd soon gathered round again.'[107] It is most likely that Carrick found it easier to work in the midst of women in enclosed spaces. In *Women in a courtyard* c 1911–12, (cat 43, p 79), for instance, a group of women is suffused in a warm-pink glow, the atmosphere relaxed and conversational, an empty chair perhaps a gesture towards the visiting artist. In another courtyard scene featuring the characteristic whitewashed façades of the dwellings in Cádiz (cat 42, p 78), women doing the laundry go about their daily lives, unperturbed by the artist quietly engaging with the moment.

Previous left
cat 39 *Dans mon jardin (In my garden)* c 1920, also known as *A corner of my garden*, oil on canvas, University Art Collection, Chau Chak Wing Museum, The University of Sydney

Previous right
cat 40 *Jeune homme contre une fenêtre* (Young man in front of a window) c 1912, also known as *Afternoon in the studio*, oil on canvas, private collection

Opposite
cat 41 *Bull fight at Biarritz* c 1908, also known as *Impression of a bull fight*, oil on canvas, National Gallery of Australia

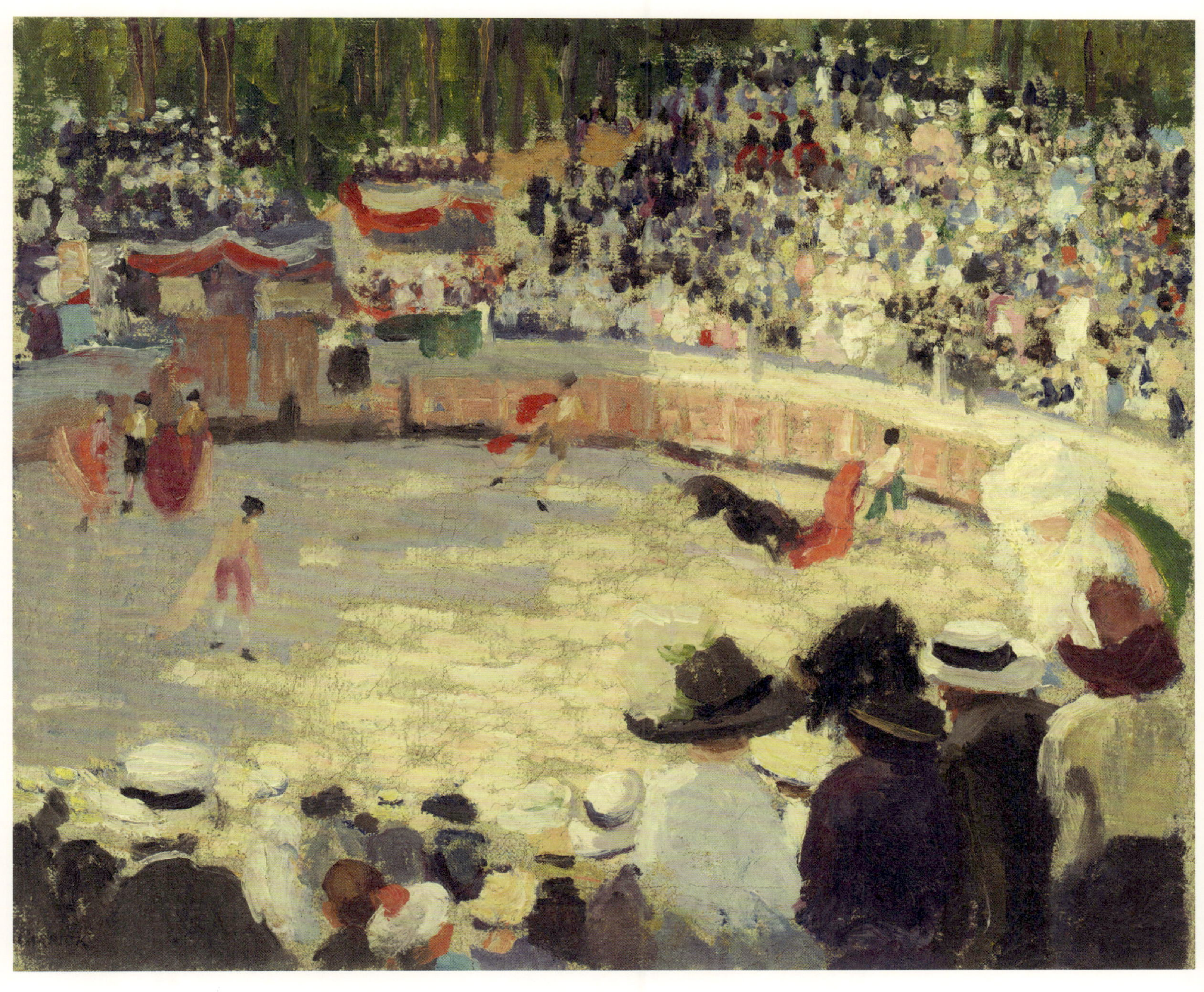

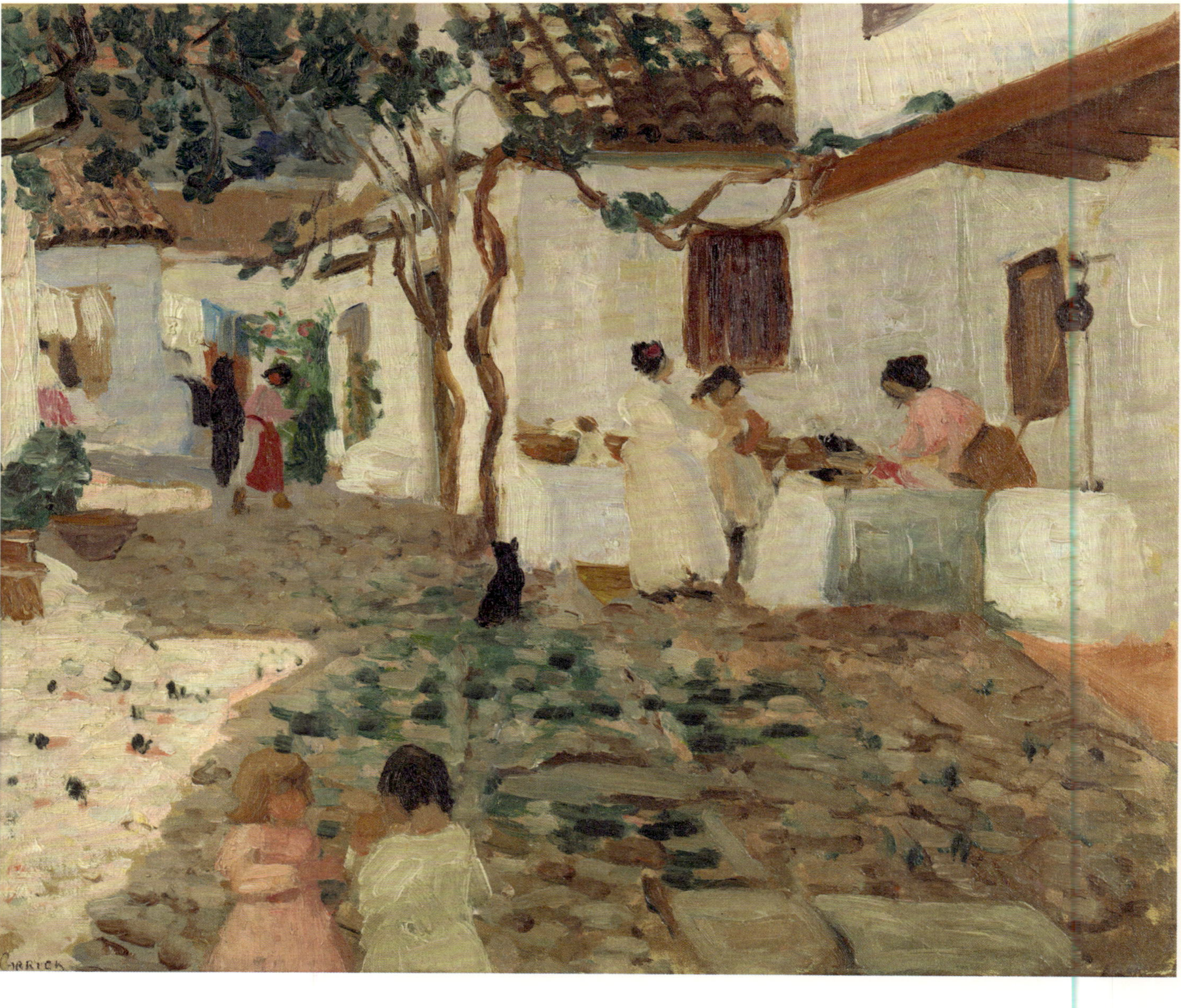

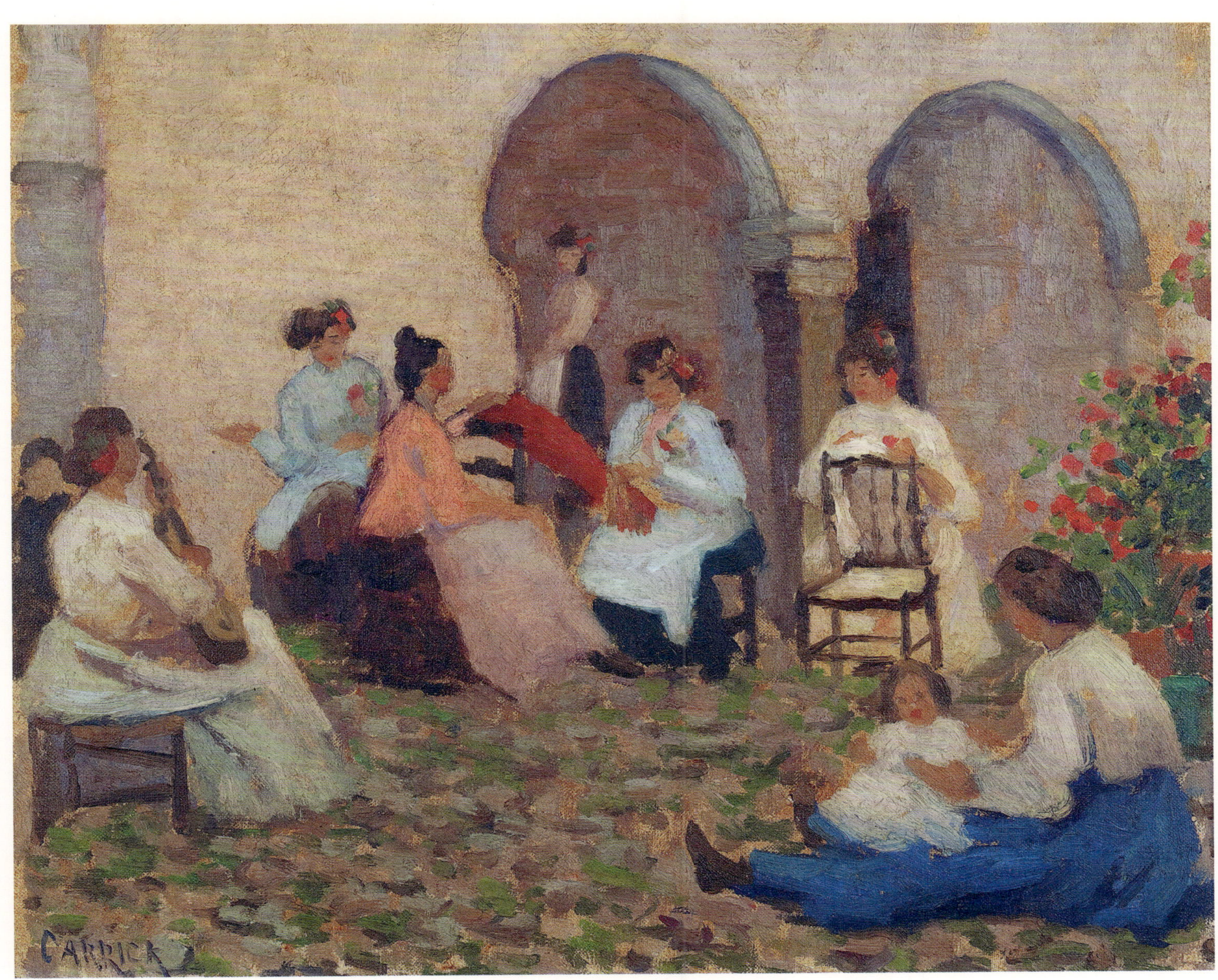

Opposite
cat 42 *The Spanish courtyard* c 1907/1911, oil on canvas, private collection

Above
cat 43 *Women in a courtyard* c 1911–12, oil on canvas, private collection

Carrick's artistic pursuits and accolades opened up possibilities for women in the public arena in art and life. In a letter to Hans Heysen in September 1912 Fox wrote, 'My wife has much improved in her work and is now a *sociétaire* of the Autumn Salon—She is serving on the jury this year—so naturally feels very important.'[108] Fox exhibited for the first and only time in the Salon d'Automne in 1912. Given that he spoke against much of the post-impressionist work he saw there, this may have been occasioned by lively debates within the Carrick–Fox household. Perhaps as a challenge, he entered conservative nudes. In the end, they made it through. As Carrick recalled in an interview in 1913:

> Years ago I was elected *sociétaire* of the Autumn Salon, where last year I had the honor of serving upon the jury in the Grand Palais, where I was called upon to judge my husband's work.
>
> 'And did you prove a severe critic?'
>
> No I was very kind to him; but the situation was amusing. I was one of eight women upon the jury, besides forty men, and I was the only Englishwoman so honoured.[109]

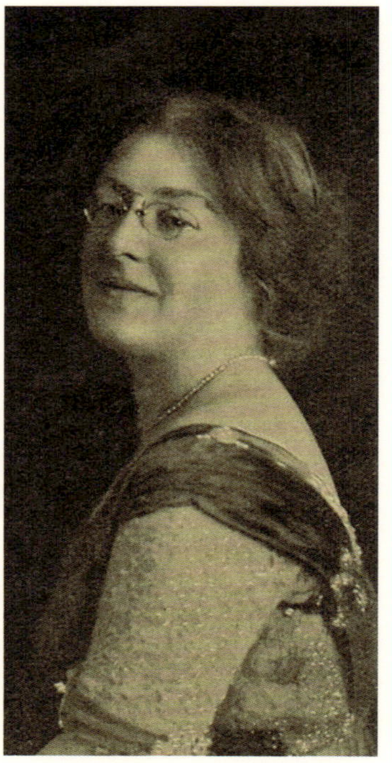

fig 20 May and Mina Moore Studios, *Portrait of Ethel Carrick* c 1913, photograph in *The Lone Hand*, 1 November 1913

While Fox was certainly not as interested in modern art as Carrick, he was mindful of the cause of women, painting a portrait referencing the subject of the suffragettes (fig 36, p 143). In addition, his beautifully realised painting championing women artists, *Art students* 1895 (fig 35, p 143), was 'one of the successes of the Salon' and among those described as shining 'in comparison with the works that surround them'.[110]

By the time Carrick and Fox departed once again for Australia, in 1913, they were at a strong point in their respective artistic careers. Their standing had grown since arriving in Paris in 1905 and they had connections in high places. On 4 July 1912, the *British Australasian* announced: 'Mr and Mrs E Phillips Fox were present on Thursday last at the reception given by the President of the French Republic and Madame Fallières, at the Élysée in Paris.'[111] By April 1913 they had gathered together key works shown over previous years, taking them on board the SS *Orvieto* bound for Fremantle and then Melbourne. Although they both had participated in an astonishing range of group shows, the chance to have large solo exhibitions seemed only possible for them back in Australia.

In 1913, Carrick and Fox rented out their Boulevard Arago apartment—initially for around eighteen months. Carrick had been unwell for a time and they delayed their departure until she was fit to travel. They arrived in Melbourne mid-May, staying initially at St Ives boarding house in Domain Road, South Yarra. They had been planning their stay for some time. While great strides had been made with their work, funds were problematic and Fox had been in communications about taking on a major commission—a portrait of Andrew Fisher, the Prime Minister of Australia, no less![112] Soon after their arrival in Australia, Fox was hard at work, and the commission would keep him preoccupied over the ensuing months. During this time, Carrick engaged with family and friends, including members of the Melbourne Society of Women Painters and Sculptors (MSWPS).

In July 1913, Carrick held her solo exhibition at the Guild Hall gallery in Swanston Street, Melbourne. This major show including works undertaken in Paris, Venice, French beachside resorts, North Africa and Spain took the artworld by storm. This show and the one that followed in Sydney were the most important of Carrick's career, establishing her artistic reputation. Public interest and extensive coverage in the press were such that the Melbourne exhibition was extended for an extra week. If her first show in Australia in 1908 had set a cat among the pigeons, introducing both her impressionist and post-impressionist works to the local scene, now she demonstrated an array of stylistic approaches. A review in *The Leader* noted that 'in her aims and methods Mrs Fox, who exhibits under her maiden name of Miss Ethel Carrick, is distinctly of the advanced school of Impressionism'.

> **Her work is a reflection of the perpetual restlessness of living things ... She notes down at high-speed ... the changeful human kaleidoscope that pass before her ... To be appreciated her work must be viewed from a distance ... so as to produce results of naturalness and beauty.[113]**

The reviewer took the position that the portraits—such as one of a man with his back to an open French window, 'which discloses a summer garden beyond'—best served 'to show the artist's manner in sustaining a theme'.

Yet it was her outdoor scenes and travel paintings that made the greatest impact. A review in *The Argus* noted Carrick's unconventional views, 'swept by an unfaltering brush': 'A group on one frame by themselves completely illustrates the artist's range of methods in dealing with outdoor effects, and the study of them will show what can be accomplished by genuinely sympathetic feeling and complete accord with the soul of things seen.'[114] Special mention was made of *La marée haute à Saint-Malo* (cat 101, p 157) and works painted in the Luxembourg Gardens: 'Altogether 87 works have been hung, and there is hardly one that is not interesting for those who will use their eyes.'[115] A commentator in *The Bulletin* wasn't quite so complimentary, writing patronisingly, 'The impressionistic little artist is especially fond of Tangier, which seems to have been designed in a hurricane and built in a fury ... Also, she has held her nose through old Cadiz, and taken her campstool and sandwiches into the leafy resorts of Paris.'[116] This perhaps wouldn't have been overly distressing to Carrick, given the comments in *The Daily Telegraph* noting the great success of the show in Melbourne:

> **She has quite eclipsed the record of any previous woman exhibitor and has out-distanced most of the men in regard to sales. There is no question of the quality of her work, and since her talent has been exercised in countries teeming with illustrable matter, the results have been a joy to the picture-seeker ... She is a very rapid worker, and her Sydney exhibition will contain, among many other things, the result of a month of hard work in and about the city.'[117]**

By mid-August 1913, Carrick had made her way to Sydney, while Fox continued to work on his portrait of the Prime Minister in Melbourne. Soon after her arrival, she was invited to a gathering of the Society of Women Painters. Excited to be in Sydney, she noted that she was preparing for plein-air trips 'to paint and paint all the beautiful things you have'.[118]

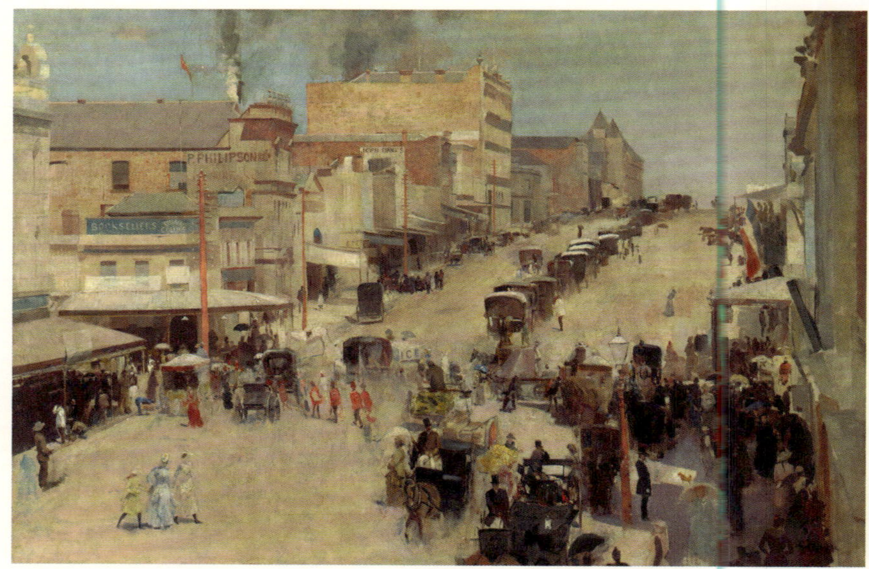

fig 21 Tom Roberts, *Allegro con brio, Bourke Street west* c 1885–86, reworked 1890, oil on canvas, National Gallery of Australia and National Library of Australia

Opposite
cat 44 *On Circular Quay* c 1913, oil on canvas on Masonite board, Art Gallery of New South Wales

Just over a month after her arrival, Fox joined her. The couple lived together in Cremorne Point on the Lower North Shore at Redcourt boarding house, with expansive views of the harbour. Around this time, Carrick was made an honorary member of the Women's Patriotic Club, which became a place for her and Fox to entertain.

Things patriotic were in the air and on the water at this time, as the Royal Australian Navy entered Sydney Harbour to show off their new fleet. In Carrick's *Watching the Australian fleet coming through Sydney Heads* 1913 (cat 45, p 84), attention is on the expectant crowd watching the vessels in the distance. A cluster of figures gathered below wave the naval flags. On the edge of the cliff, a small group makes the viewer feel included in the action, looking across with a clear-eyed view of the bright blue harbour. In another version of this event, the spectacle of waterfront activity is closer, and the large grey navy vessel is in proximity to other boats sailing over the shimmering water.

Both Carrick and Fox painted many different views of the coastal inlets around the harbour—from Balmoral, Cremorne, Rose Bay, Dawes Point, Garden Island and Manly. *On Balmoral Beach, Sydney* 1913 (cat 117, p 188) feels rather modern in the paring away of inessentials to focus on the large tree on the right with its shadow patterning the ground, set against the bright beach sand and the deepest blue ocean. By comparison, *Rose Bay, Sydney Harbour* c 1915 (cat 46, p 86) is a lyrical and delicate expression of gentle luminosity. Both Carrick and Fox exhibited views of Sydney Harbour in their 1913 solo shows in October and November respectively.[119]

A very significant painting in Carrick's exhibition was *On Circular Quay* c 1913 (cat 44). Here, the city appears in the process of modernisation, with horse-drawn carts set against electrically powered trams. At the time, Sydney's tram networks were the second largest in the world, after London. Seen from above, city-goers suggest the constant flux of life. Tall power poles lead our vision up, while trams take us back into the space of densely packed buildings beyond. The ground shimmers with hot white light while the figures are animated by brisk touches of pink, yellow, red and black. Although one commentator felt this scene to be more like Paris, parallels could be found with Tom Roberts' inner-Melbourne street scene *Allegro con brio, Bourke Street west* c 1885–86 (fig 21); Carrick echoes the mood of Roberts' musical title 'fast tempo with spirit.'

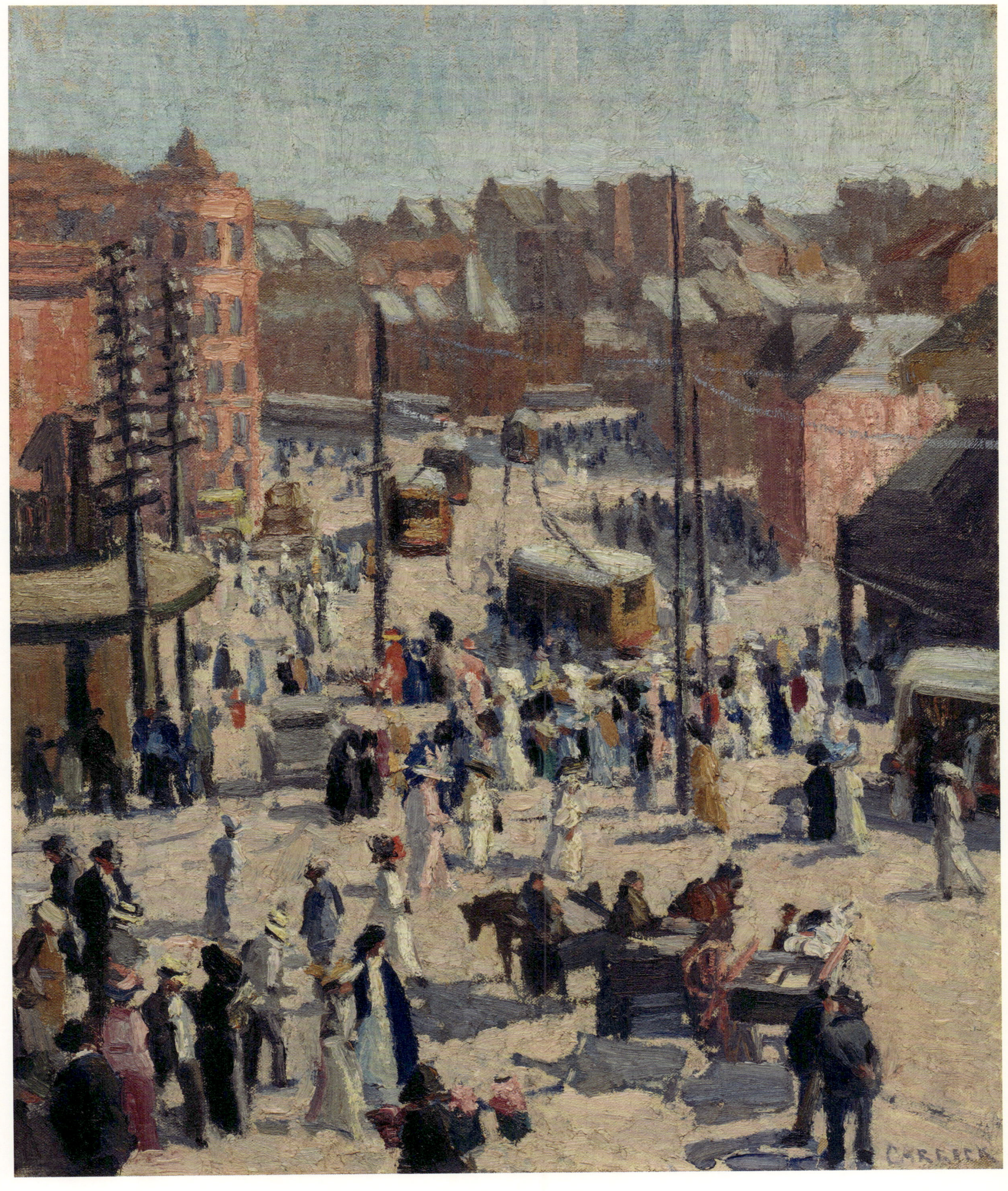

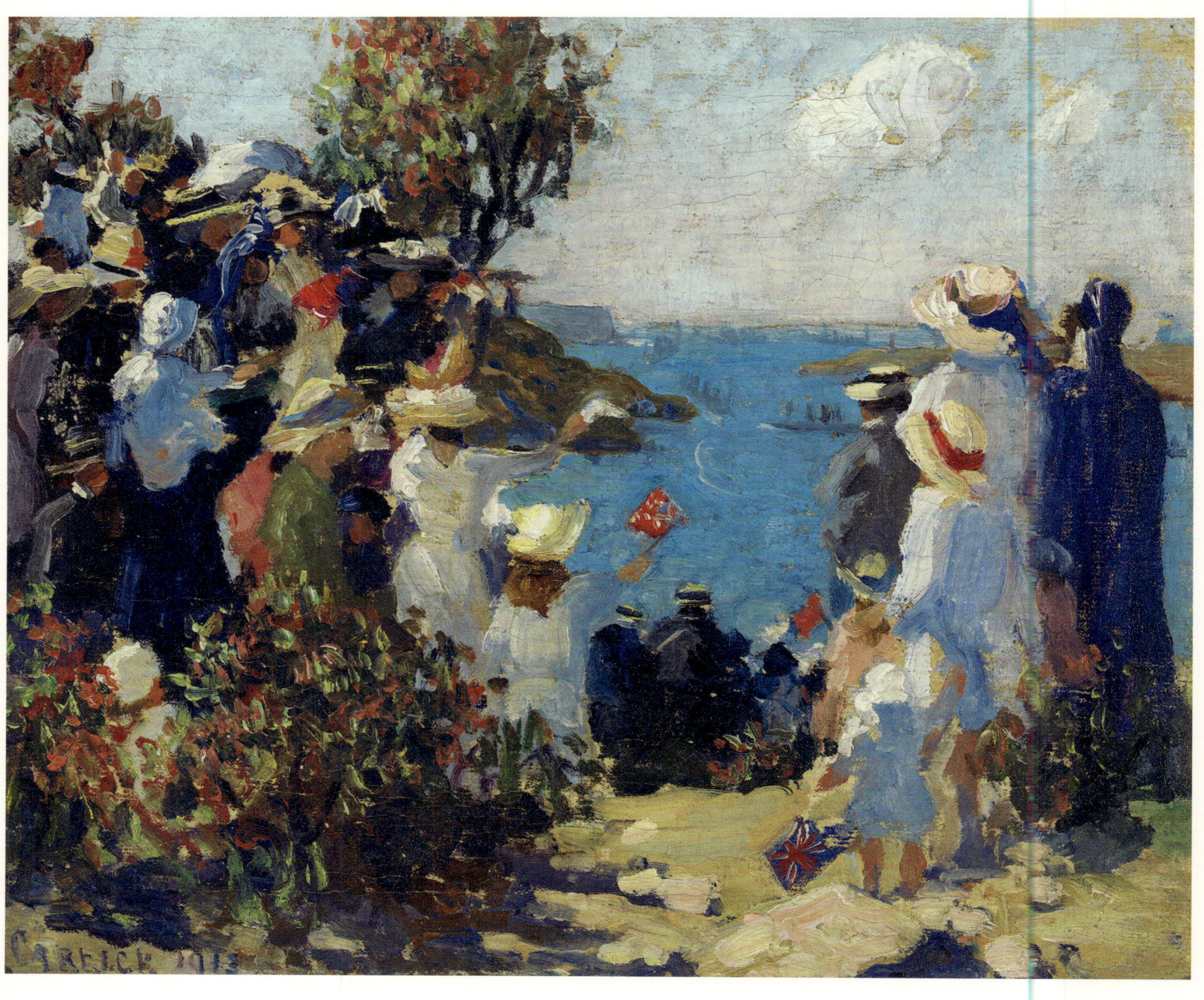

Carrick's exhibition at Anthony Hordern & Sons gallery was opened by Sir James Fairfax and included 71 works. Across a wide range of subjects, her diverse technical abilities were shown to great effect. Numerous reviews mentioned her as the wife of her very clever husband, although by this time she had the confidence to air her own views:

> **When I married my husband I had a tremendously high opinion of his work, and accepted his views without question. Now, although I still hold the same high appreciation of his artistic powers, I think for myself as well, and hear other people's views on a subject before I decide.[120]**

The reviews in Sydney were generally positive. The atmospheric effects and suggestive movement in Carrick's paintings were considered to go beyond literal depiction to convey something more evocative: 'They are as the pictures the eye sees at times in the embers of the fire; the more one looks at them the more one sees the depth of soul in the person who dared to put them from a mere dream, on to cold canvas.'[121]

As in her Melbourne show, special mention was made of *La marée haute à Saint-Malo* (cat 101, p 157): 'one almost imagines that the folks on the golden strand are actually moving about. The arrangement of the scene, too, is admirable, and the coloring exquisite.'[122] By now, some commentators in the press had become more supportive of a modern outlook, with a write-up in *The Bulletin* on 13 November stating:

> **Artist Ethel Fox dashes on her pigments with a superb contempt for lady-like or drawing-room art which must take away the breath of the veteran [conservative trustee of the Art Gallery of New South Wales, then known as the National Gallery] Du Faur. That formidable breakwind between modern art and our National Gallery is suspected of being more in touch with the early Victorian 'sampler' period when every detail was painfully attended to by the painter. Anyhow, he looked a sorrowful old gentleman as he made his exit from one of the finest one-artist shows this town has seen for a long time.[123]**

Among the many friendships that Carrick was developing around this time, one of the most influential was with Ethel Stephens, an artist intent on progressing the cause of visibility for a wide range of women artists. Stephens, like Thea Proctor, visited the solo exhibitions of Fox and Carrick. Proctor's friendship with Carrick took off in December 1913, when Fox returned to Melbourne for a few weeks and the two women went to live in 'Queensland House' in Bower Street, Manly.[124] Carrick and Proctor worked with great energy around the shores of Manly on painterly sketches from different viewpoints. Carrick's joy in the crowds interacting with each other on the beach and swimming in the ocean found its fullest expression in one of her most important works, *Christmas Day on Manly Beach* 1913 (cat 118, pp 194–95).

Alternatively titled *Manly Beach—summer is here*, how utterly different the scene would have seemed to Carrick, who had spent most of her Christmases since childhood in England (and later in France) gathered around the fire during the winter chill. In stark contrast to this 'traditional' family Christmas, the painting depicts a communal celebration in nature under the summer sun. The painting was shown in a joint exhibition with Fox at the Athenaeum Gallery, Melbourne, in May 1914, where it was widely considered her best work in the show.[125]

Opposite
cat 45 ***Watching the Australian fleet coming through Sydney Heads*** **1913, oil on canvas, collection of Rob and Jenny Ferguson**

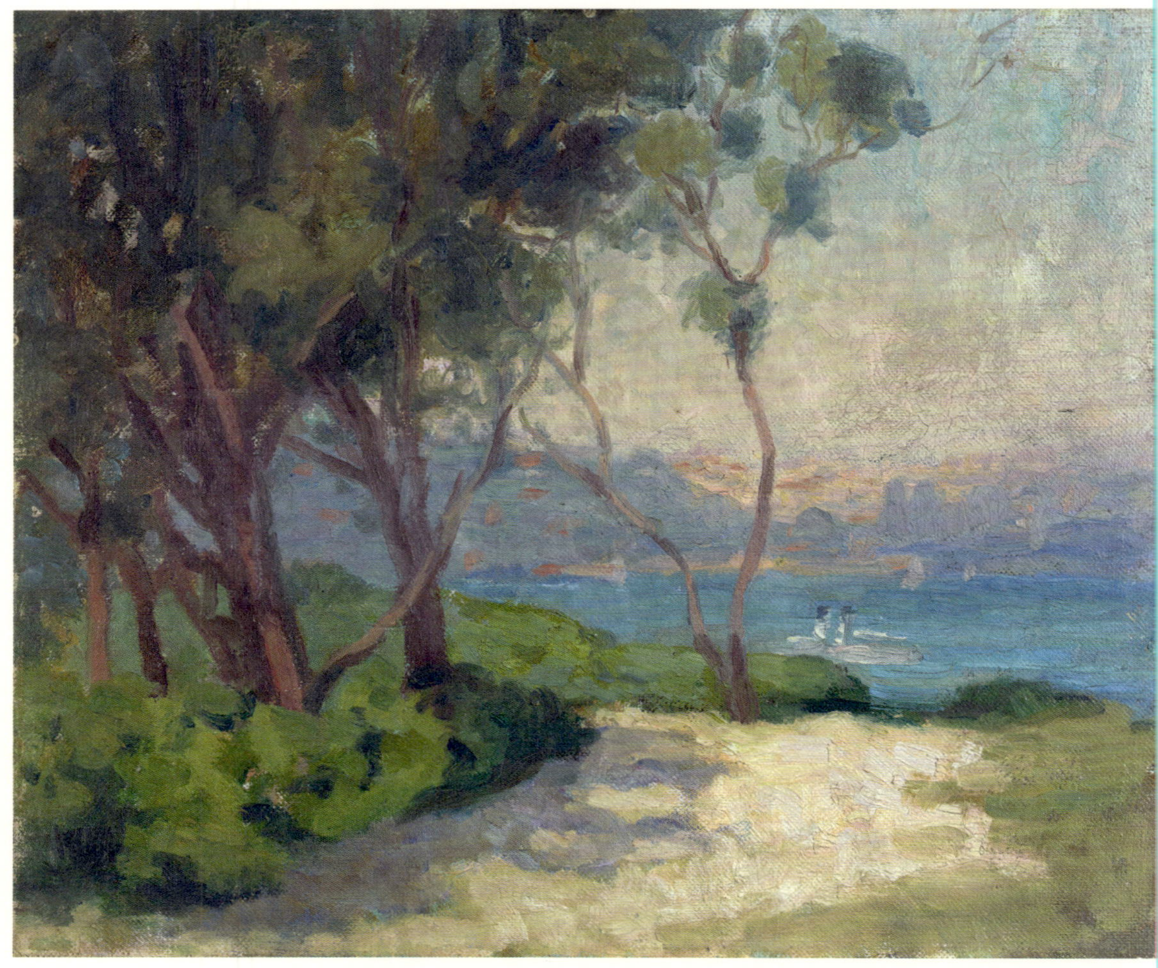

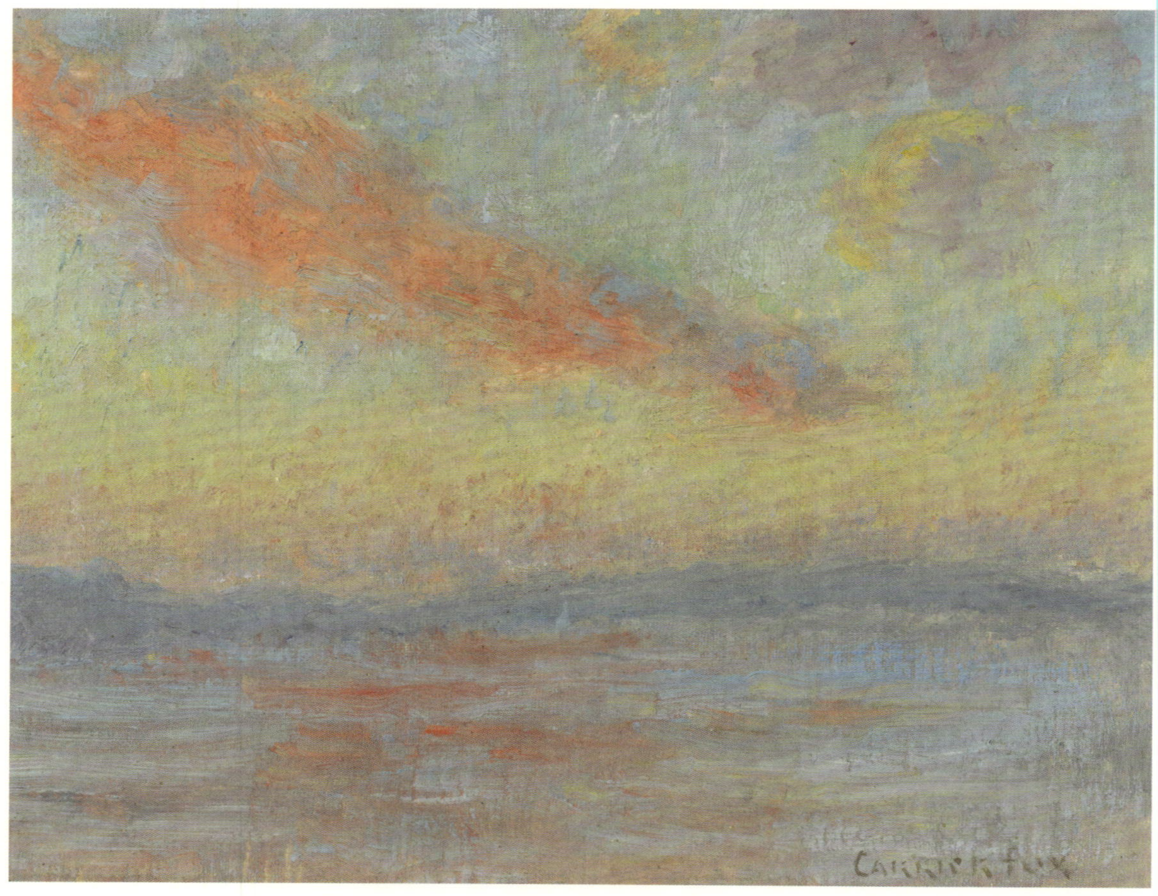
Carrick Fox

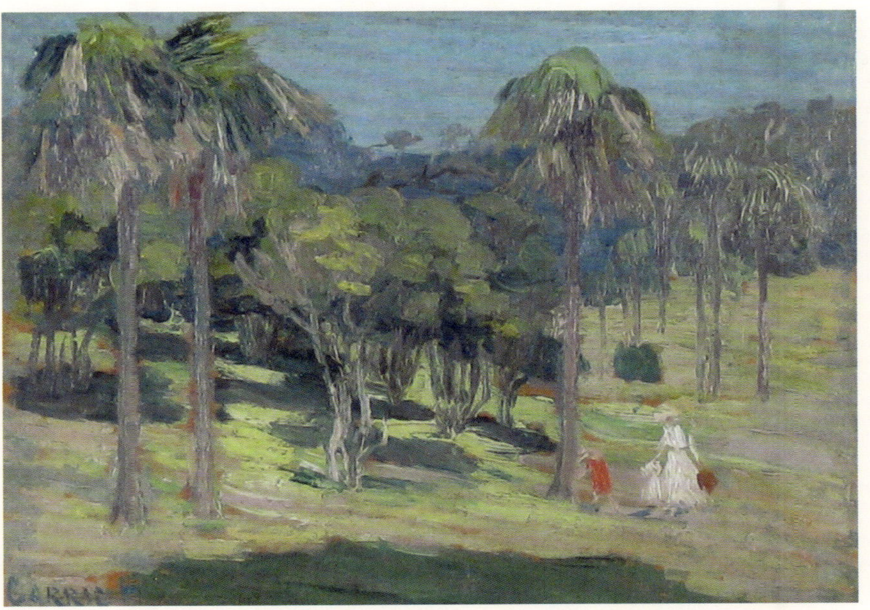

Opposite, top to bottom
cat 46 *Rose Bay, Sydney Harbour* c 1915, oil on canvas, collection of Jim Haynes OAM and Robyn McMillan

cat 47 *At sunset* 1914, oil on canvas on cardboard, National Gallery of Australia

Above
fig 22 *Stanwell Park* 1914, oil on wood, SH Ervin Gallery

The exhibition also included many of Fox's finest works: *The ferry* c 1910–11 (fig 40, p 161), *A suffragette* 1911 (fig 36, p 143), *The green parasol* c 1912 (fig 19, p 73) and *The arbour* 1910.[126] With this exhibition, it was finally becoming understood that Fox and Carrick had complementary strengths as artists. Their combined efforts were a hit. 'No two artists have struck such a high point of excellence in any show of this description, and critics are hard put to know whose work they prefer, though both artists differ widely in their treatment of subject.'[127]

In Melbourne, Carrick and Fox stayed at the Federal Hotel, close to Fox's Collins Street studio. Early in 1914, prior to their arrival, they had travelled to beautiful locations around New South Wales, including Stanwell Park, where they may have gone to the renowned thermal pool in the hope that it would help Carrick's rheumatoid arthritis. Her paintings from that trip include views of the landscape close-up and over the Illawarra escarpment. They also visited Hobart, painting local landmarks during their travels. Soon after their exhibition in Melbourne, it was noted that 'Mr and Mrs Fox are going to Tahiti, where they are likely to spend a very delightful winter. Tahiti is an artist's paradise, and the result of this particular visit will be looked for eagerly by critics on both sides of the globe'.[128] Their interest in Tahiti was most likely inspired by Paul Gauguin's work, which they had encountered in Paris.[129]

Departing on 11 July 1914, they had hoped to paint the local environment across the island, however their visit was cut short by the announcement of World War I. On 28 July 1914, a month after the assassination of Archduke Franz Ferdinand of Austria and his wife Sophie, the Austro-Hungarian government declared war on Serbia. When Germany invaded Belgium, Britain declared war on the German Empire. Instead of returning to Paris as they had planned, Carrick and Fox went back to the safer shores of Australia. In one of the few paintings from her visit to Tahiti—*At sunset* 1914 (cat 47)—Carrick painted a radiant sky and seascape, pink-lit clouds, tinged by yellow and mauve, reflected onto the waves below—almost abstract yet holding to the ephemeral beauty of nature. In retrospect, it reads as a last-ditch hope that the world could remain alive with possibilities for Carrick and Fox. Sadly, the tide was about to turn, personally and collectively, forever.

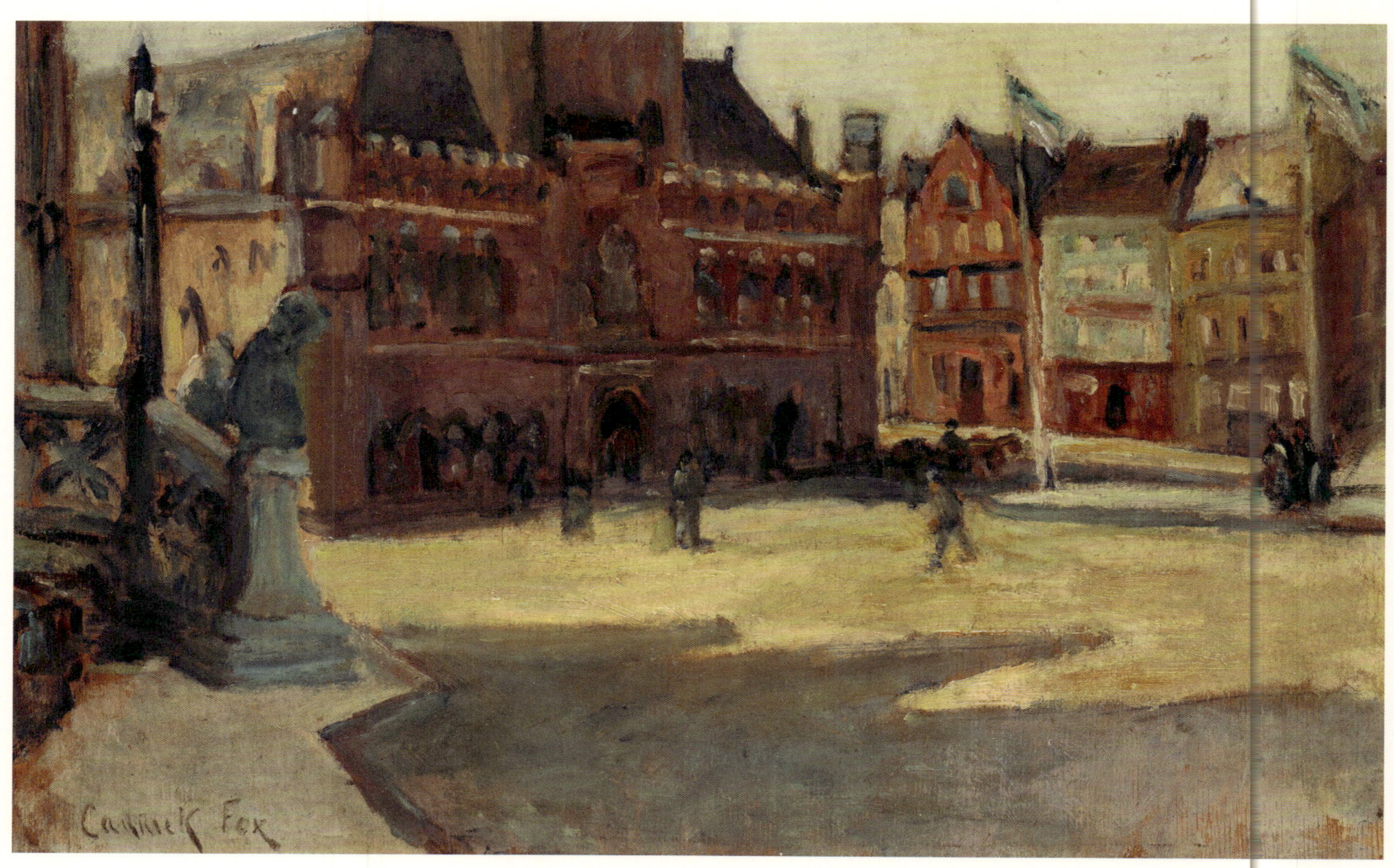

Fallow to flowering: 1915–1939

It was the age of wisdom, it was the age of foolishness,
it was the epoch of belief, it was the epoch of incredulity,
it was the season of Light, it was the season of Darkness,
it was the spring of hope, it was the winter of despair.[130]

— Charles Dickens, *A Tale of Two Cities*, 1859

When Carrick and Fox returned to Melbourne from Tahiti, they became keenly involved in the war effort. Both felt considerable anxiety about the consequences of the war for friends and family in Europe, including Carrick's relatives in England. Their shared love of France spurred them on in the ensuing year to work on fundraising projects. Fox was also working hard on portrait commissions, some large and painstaking, of people in high places—accomplished and traditional work. Carrick stood her ground in relation to modern art:

> I emphatically protest against the ... denunciation by Judge Backhouse at the annual meeting of the Repertory Theatre, when he said in speaking of the 'discovery of the cubist, the post-impressionist, and the futurist, that as a result we have the hideous and repulsive'.
>
> ... It would be better ... if those who publicly express their opinions on the subject ... would try and grasp some of the big fundamental truths that the leaders of modern art magnificently express.[131]

While Fox focused on his portraits, Carrick spent some time in Sydney working with Ethel Stephens as joint honorary secretary of the Australian Artist Workers' War Fund.[132] Carrick's commitment to the cause was such that she worked herself to a point of exhaustion. In May, it was reported that due to a sudden illness she was hospitalised at Charlemont Private Hospital in Darlinghurst, delaying her return to Melbourne. By July 1915, Carrick and Fox were working side by side on patriotic activities, such as decorating gum leaves to raise funds.[133] This enterprise, initiated by Carrick in Sydney, took off again in Melbourne where it was noted

Opposite
cat 48 *Town square* c 1919, oil on board, private collection

that '100 000 [leaves] are being treated by a band of workers, under the direction of Mr and Mrs Phillips Fox. Each leaf will bear an Australian design, or else such names as Dardanelles, Samoa, or Gabe Tepe'.[134]

By the end of September 1915, Fox was feeling unwell and it became clear that he needed an operation. Keen to finish his portrait of Sir John Forrest, he delayed the procedure. His friend Alexander Colquhoun remembered meeting him on a sunny day in Collins Street: 'In reply to the usual felicities he told me that he was suffering from an internal pain and was going to a private hospital the following day ... I wished him luck, and then, with a smile and not the personality with which I had been for so many years pleasantly familiar, he passed out of my mortal consciousness.'[135] In early October, Fox underwent an operation at Mount St Evin's Hospital, Eastern Hill, Melbourne, in the course of which bowel cancer was found. He died in hospital on 8 October 1915. The wreaths on his coffin were colourful rather than the customary white, befitting his and Carrick's shared love of colour.[136]

After Fox's sudden death in 1915, Carrick was consumed by grief. It was a shock to her system that would shift with time but never leave her. Despite a few challenges, theirs had been a close, creative, loving relationship cut short too soon.[137] Carrick stayed in Melbourne for a time with Ivy and Herbert Brookes, writing to them later: 'I would like to tell you both once more, how much I appreciate and value your kindness, you have no idea what it meant to me to be taken in.'[138] A circle of friends was there for her in Sydney too, including the painter and muralist Bertha Merfield who wrote to Brookes early in January 1916 to let her know that Carrick was improving and that Mademoiselle Augustine Soubeiran, with whom she had also stayed, managed to avert her lapses into wanting to 'pass over' with 'helpful strong talk'.[139] Carrick gained a sense of purpose in helping to organise the memorial exhibition *Pictures by the late E Phillips Fox* at the Athenaeum Gallery in Melbourne, launched on 26 February 1916. She encouraged as many of Fox's students as possible to attend.[140] Violet Teague, a former student and their close friend, wrote an obituary for *The Argus*.[141] Carrick's commitment to Fox's artistic legacy became a consuming passion, lasting until her own death in 1952.[142]

A few months after the memorial she sailed for England, visiting her mother in Ealing and spending time with immediate family. This was an important reconnection, especially with her sister Jessie Platts' two sons, who were soon after sent off to war. The younger, Edgar Lovell Filmer Platts, died at only seventeen years of age, and the older son, John Carrick Platts, passed away at twenty-two years old in a battle following the war in 1920.[143] Jessie's book *The Witness* was a 'transcription' of communications from Edgar—referred to as 'Tiny': 'These messages ... were recorded by me in 1918, my boy "Tiny," who had fallen in action on April 28th, 1917, controlling my hand. My elder son [later] ... joined him.'[144] Jessie was a spiritualist, believing in afterlives and the spirit world. 'No one gives up his earthly life for nothing; we only change from one state of existence to another, and we are all going on with our evolution in the spirit world.'[145]

In January 1917, Carrick wrote to her friend Ethel Stephens, letting her know that war shrines were being erected in London to commemorate the dead, and that she was organising one for her late husband.[146] Remembrance and reconnection were common threads; the rising interest in the spirit world after the great loss of life in World War I chimed with Carrick's personal loss and commitment to the Theosophical Society, which she joined in 1916.[147] Returning to their apartment in Paris without Fox must have been difficult for Carrick, the presence of him still there in his paintings and everyday belongings. Following his death, she almost constantly signed her works Carrick Fox, wanting her name and his to be indelibly linked.[148]

A sense of Carrick's theosophical beliefs can be found in a condolence letter dated 7 October 1919, addressed to Ivy Brookes whose father, Alfred Deakin (a theosophist), had just died: 'It is a great comfort to feel assured that the spirits of the great open-minded, are allowed to work on, to help to alter existing evil of which the world is so full.'[149] For Carrick, the idea of working for the betterment of humanity was key. During the war she felt unable to make much art, working instead with friends such as Mlle Soubeiran at the Salpêtrière University Hospital, regularly visiting consumptive patients and helping refugees from Serbia, Russia and Belgium, including many children.[150] At the end of the war, such work was recognised in the press, as relayed by Carrick:

> **What the women (and particularly the women of the invaded districts) of France have had to face during this war, and the spirit in which they have made their sacrifices, places them forever among the ranks of heroines, and it is these women with their children and parents, that the French–Australian League is helping in such a splendid way.[151]**

The winter of 1917 was bitterly cold, with coal rations and food restrictions. Carrick's little garden was a godsend, and she set about planting and harvesting her own vegetables for sustenance. In the spring of 1918, she told *The Argus* that one day, while she was in her studio, a bomb fell onto a maternity hospital close by, killing 27 patients.[152] Years later she described this terrible time:

> **When we first heard the bombs fall, we thought it was all over ... we went to the cellars and waited for an hour or so, and then, as nothing happened, we came out and went about our ordinary ways again. After that the bombs fell all day at 15-minute intervals, and one just dashed out between them to do anything one wanted to do. The armoured cars, rushing through the streets at all hours, sounded exactly as if houses were falling all about us.[153]**

Carrick's key work from this period, *Place de la Concorde* c 1918–19 (cat 49, p 92), was painted around the time of the Armistice, after a ceasefire had been agreed upon. In the wake of war, gone are the vibrant colours of the Belle Époque. Now this historic square, viewed from above, is painted in dark tonalities suffused with eerie light, the atmosphere poignantly evoking the shadowy aura of lost souls. In a small oil on panel titled *Champs-Élysées* c 1918 (cat 50, p 93), sweeping movement conveys a sense of appearance and disappearance, as the small figures seem swept inexorably on through time and space. The end of the war meant respite and remembering the fallen. A memorial in the Place de la Concorde depicted by Carrick in *Armistice Day* 1918 (cat 51, p 93), is an allegory of the city of Strasbourg, bedecked in tricolour French flags during the Armistice celebrations of 1918.

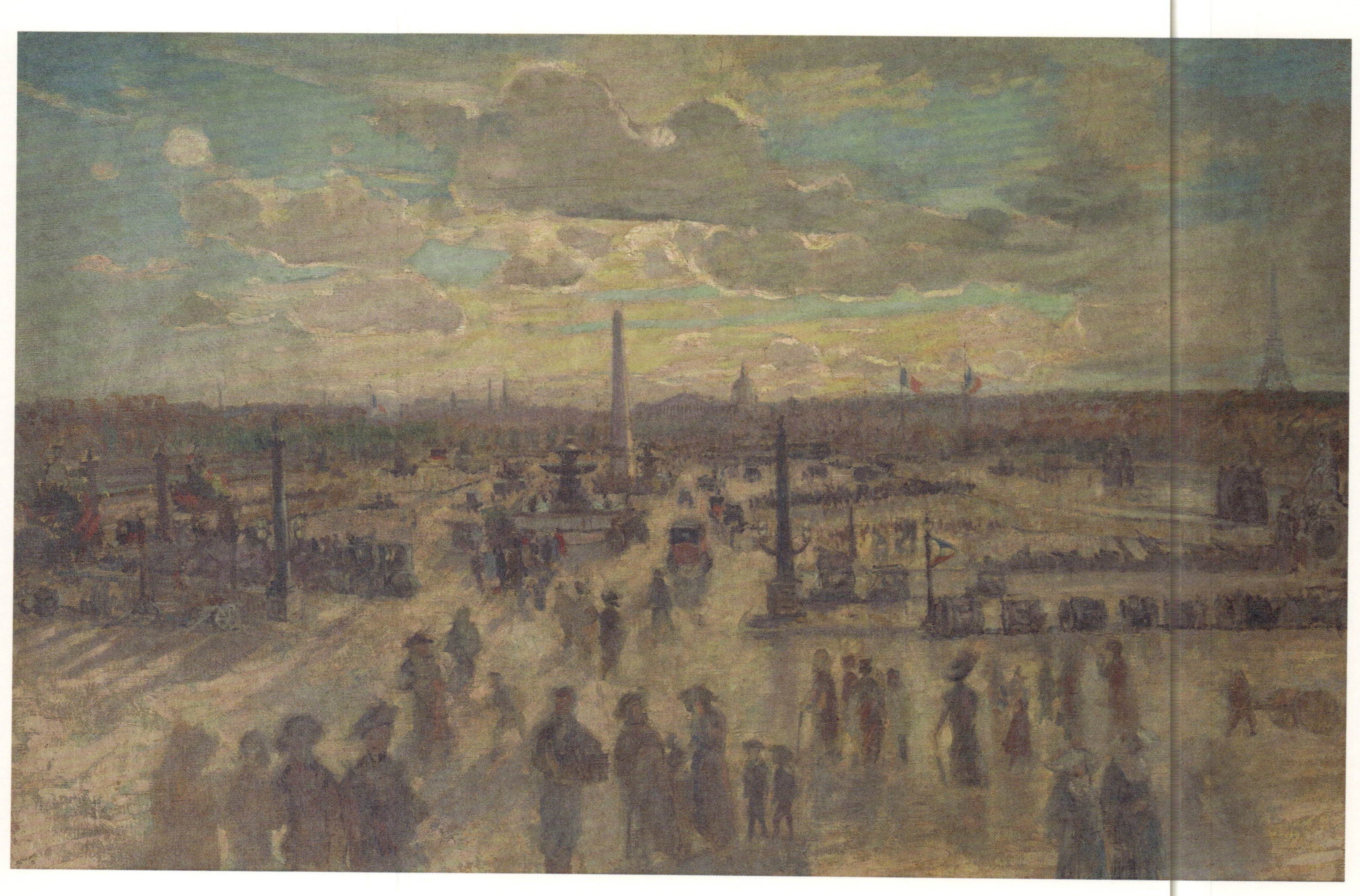

cat 49 *Place de la Concorde* c 1918–19, oil on canvas on Masonite, private collection

Opposite, top to bottom
cat 50 *Champs-Élysées* c 1918, oil on panel, private collection

cat 51 *Armistice Day* 1918, oil on wood panel, private collection

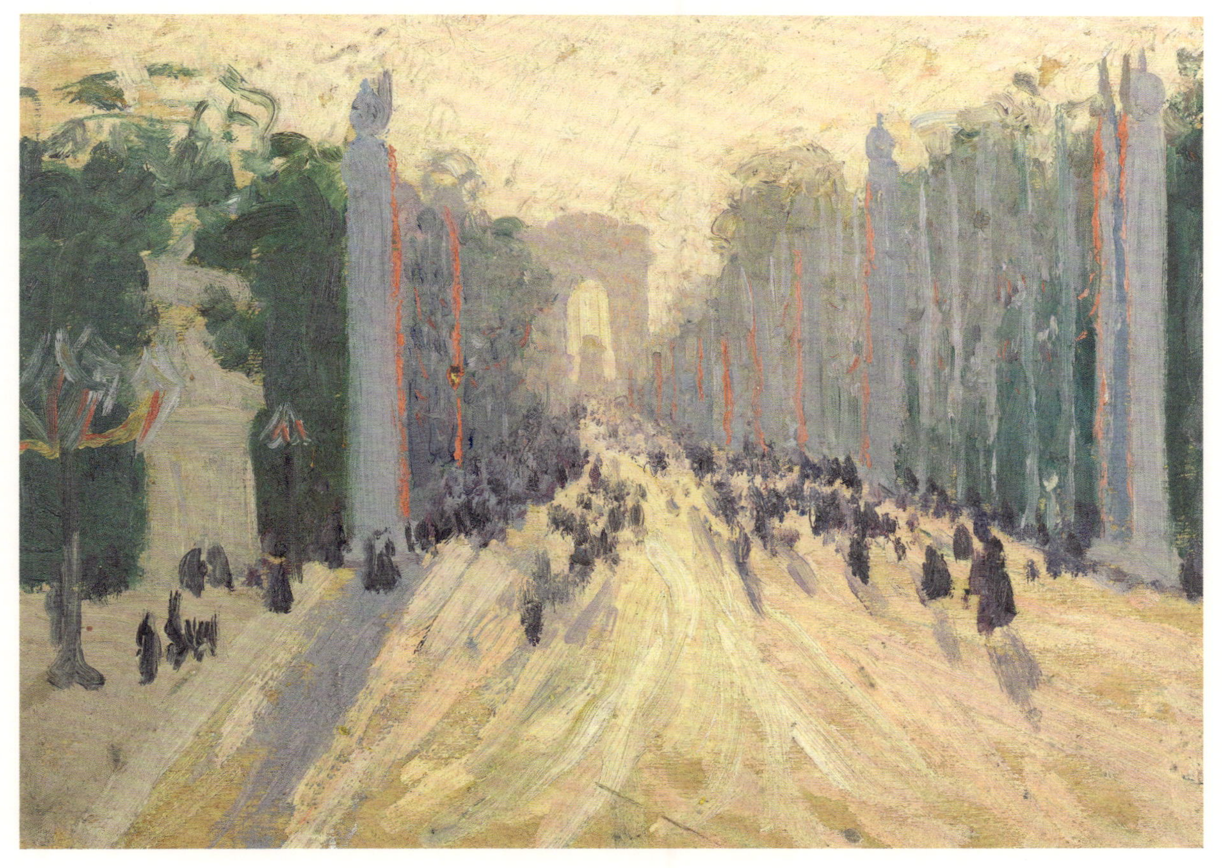

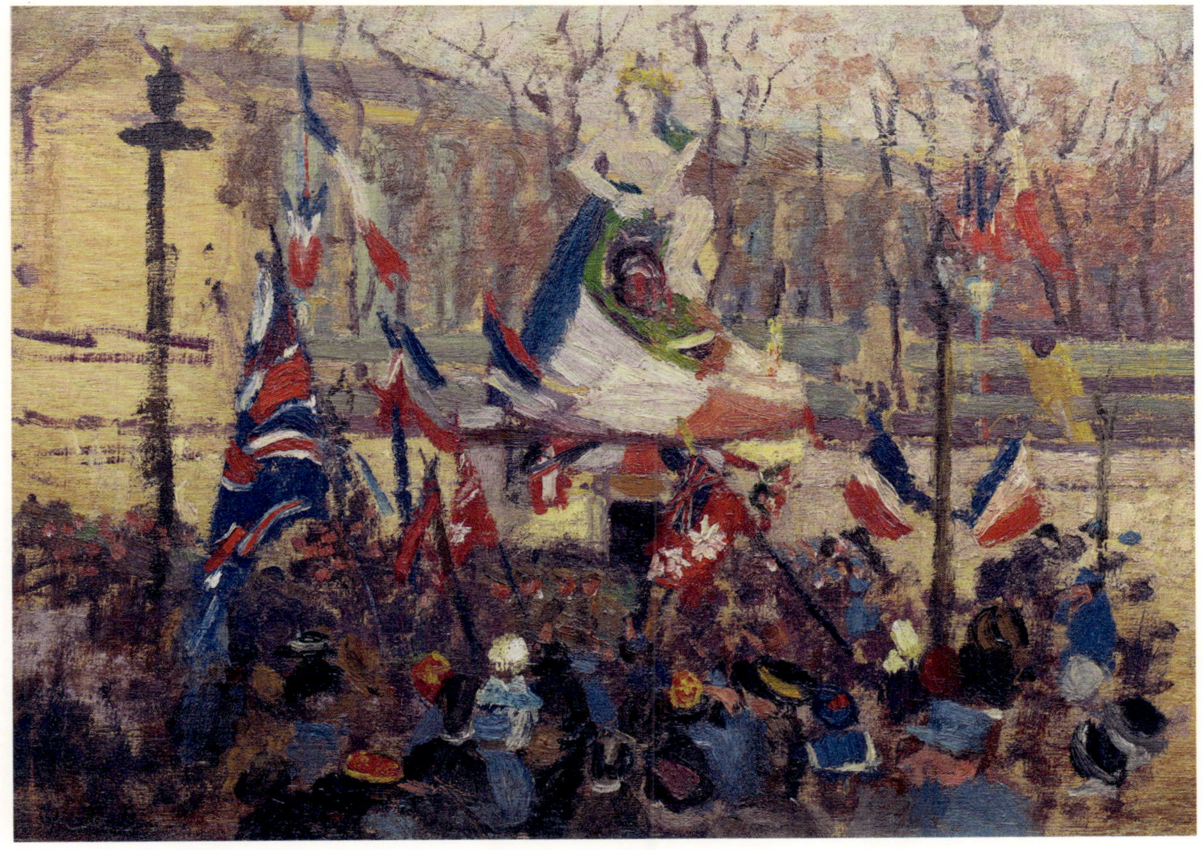

Along with Mme de Marquette, a fellow theosophist, Carrick founded the Overseas French Homes League in the autumn of 1918, with Ethel's relative Etta Phillips joining them.[154] The purpose of the League was to bring overseas service personnel into contact with the 'literary, artistic, and industrial' elements of Paris, and to give them a welcome in 'real French homes'.[155] A reception was held to support the cause, with the guest of honour being Mme Poincaré, wife of the French president and the League's Présidente d'Honneur.[156] To encourage better understanding of French culture, Carrick took groups to the studio of sculptor Antoine Bourdelle and the home of artist Lucien Simon (both of whom taught at the Académie de la Grande Chaumière). Carrick noted that Simon, 'the great painter', took them around his studio and house, which appeared in itself 'like the perfect museum'.[157]

Carrick found the cost of living high and, from 1919, worked as a private teacher, taking on a number of students including Ethel Stephens, Alfreda Marcovitch (née Goninan) and Vida Lahey (born in Brisbane).[158] Marcovitch recalled: 'Vida Lahey decided that she'd like to go too with Ethel Carrick Fox, so we used to tootle up there together ... for a couple of afternoons a week.'[159] She also remembered going on studio visits, which were 'rather lovely because Ethel took us all—her little class—two or three times for afternoon tea at [Rupert] Bunny's studio and Bunny at the time was painting his Greek sort of period. The Greek myths with lovely ladies in draperies and so forth. And we enjoyed that very much.'[160]

After the fallow period of the war came regeneration, and Carrick began painting outdoors again, returning to her favourite subjects of gardens and markets. By the time she painted *The market* 1919 (cat 53, pp 96–97), the Paris markets were back in full swing, with fruit and flower vendors selling their produce while throngs of people gathered in the gardens to enjoy the fresh air. It was a rejuvenation for Carrick, and emblematic of the times:

> Dated 1919, [this] work may actually have been conceived as a celebration of peace, almost as an allegory. A theosophist and something of a feminist, Carrick was possessed of a strong social conscience. She had worked tirelessly ... both during and after the conflict. She was very well aware of the suffering of war's victims ... In contrast to ... her bleakly autumnal armistice sketch *Luxembourg Gardens* 1918, the present work is a sunny image of natural bounty—from floral hats to giant pumpkins, and of social harmony—between bourgeoisie, domestics, peasants and nuns.[161]

The market was based both on what Carrick saw and on her reimagined realisation of the poetry of the world in peacetime.[162] Painted in the studio, it was the culmination of several studies and one of the most significant works of her career. The promise of her earlier French market scenes was fulfilled in this remarkable painting, with its mastery of dappled light, dress details, and depth and richness of colour conveying an overall sense of the joy of being alive. It was also a forerunner of things to come in her paintings of Nice flower markets.

Opposite
cat 52 *French interior with young woman* c 1919, oil on canvas, collection of Rob and Jenny Ferguson

Following
cat 53 *The market* 1919, oil on canvas, Moran Family Collection

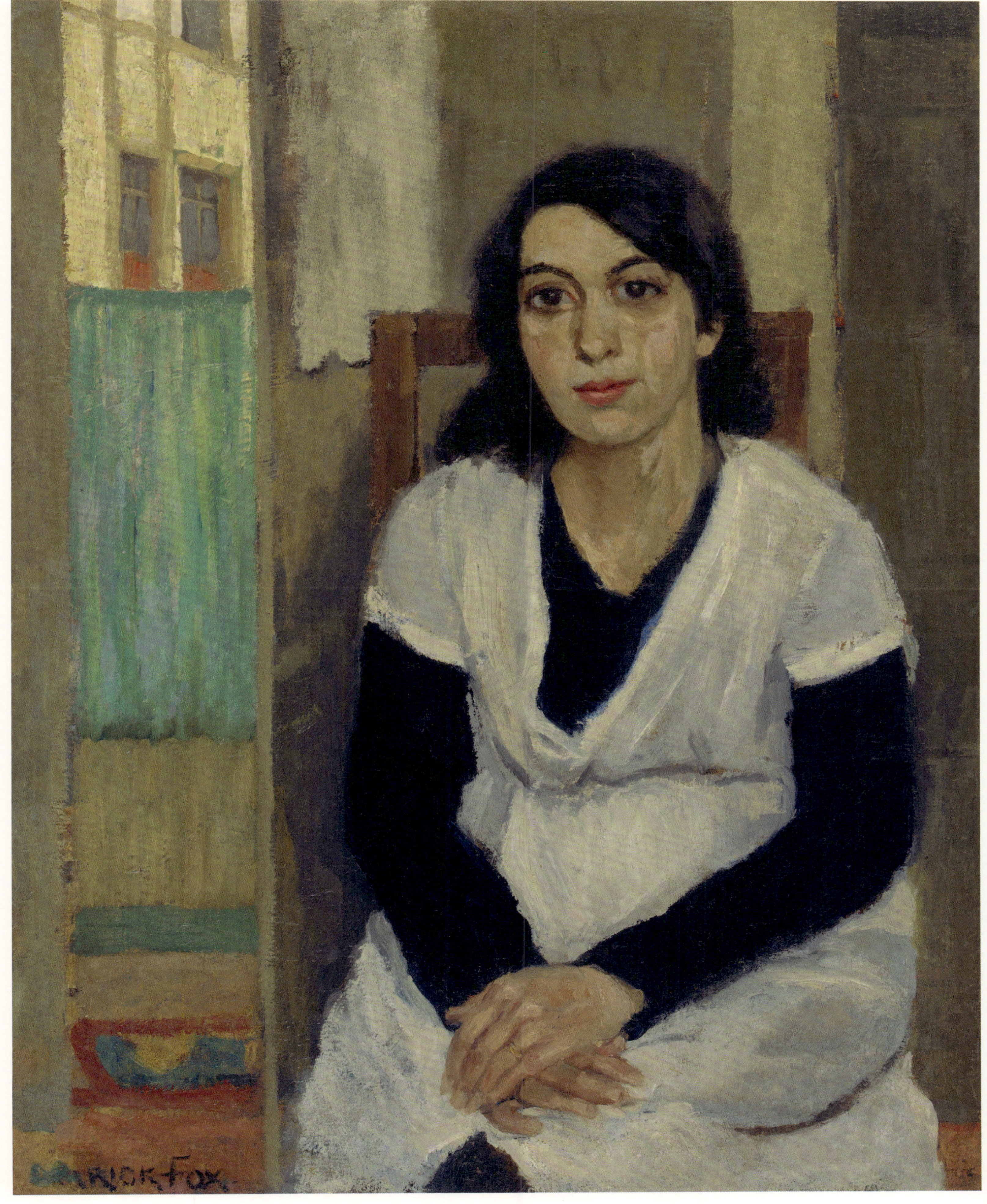

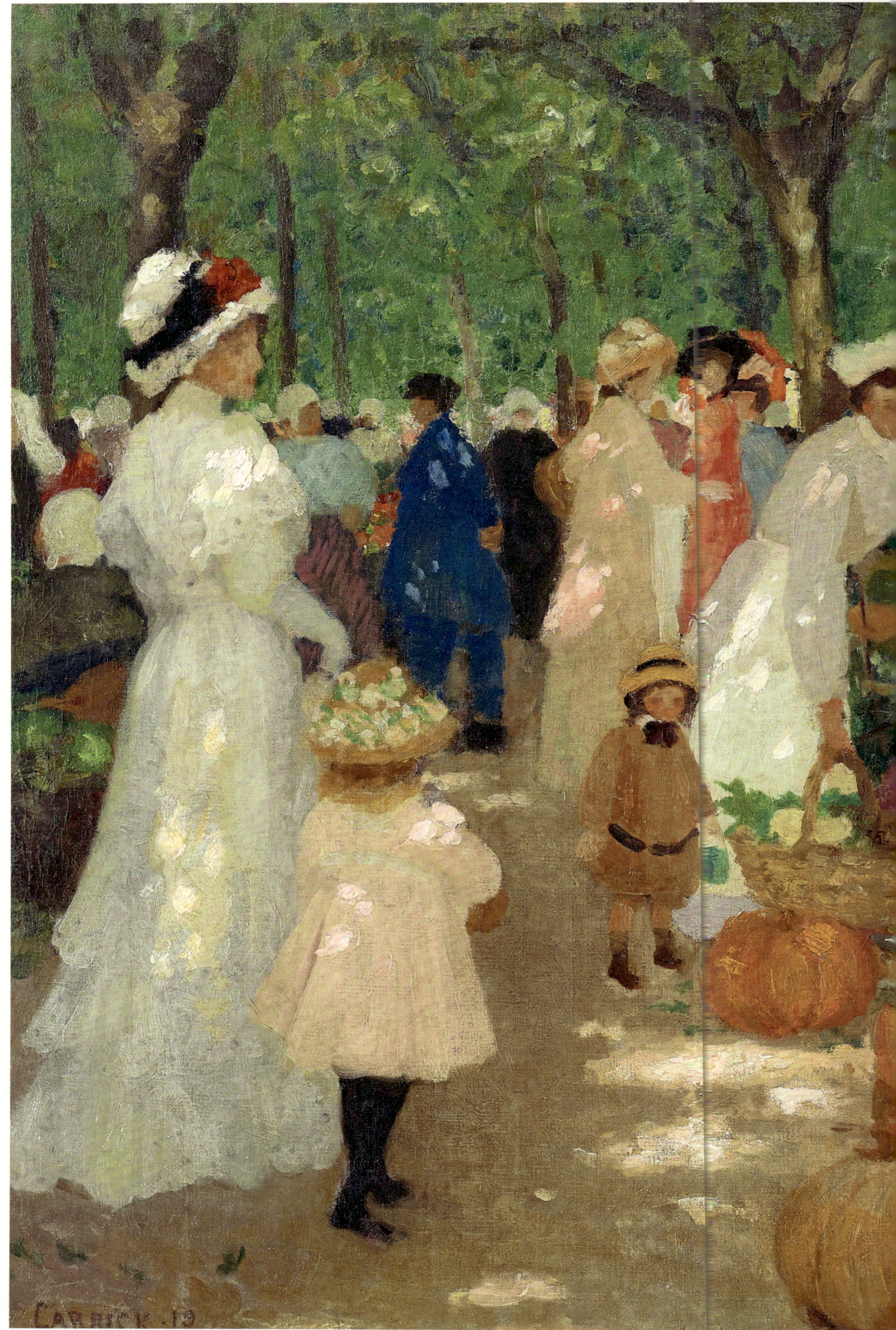

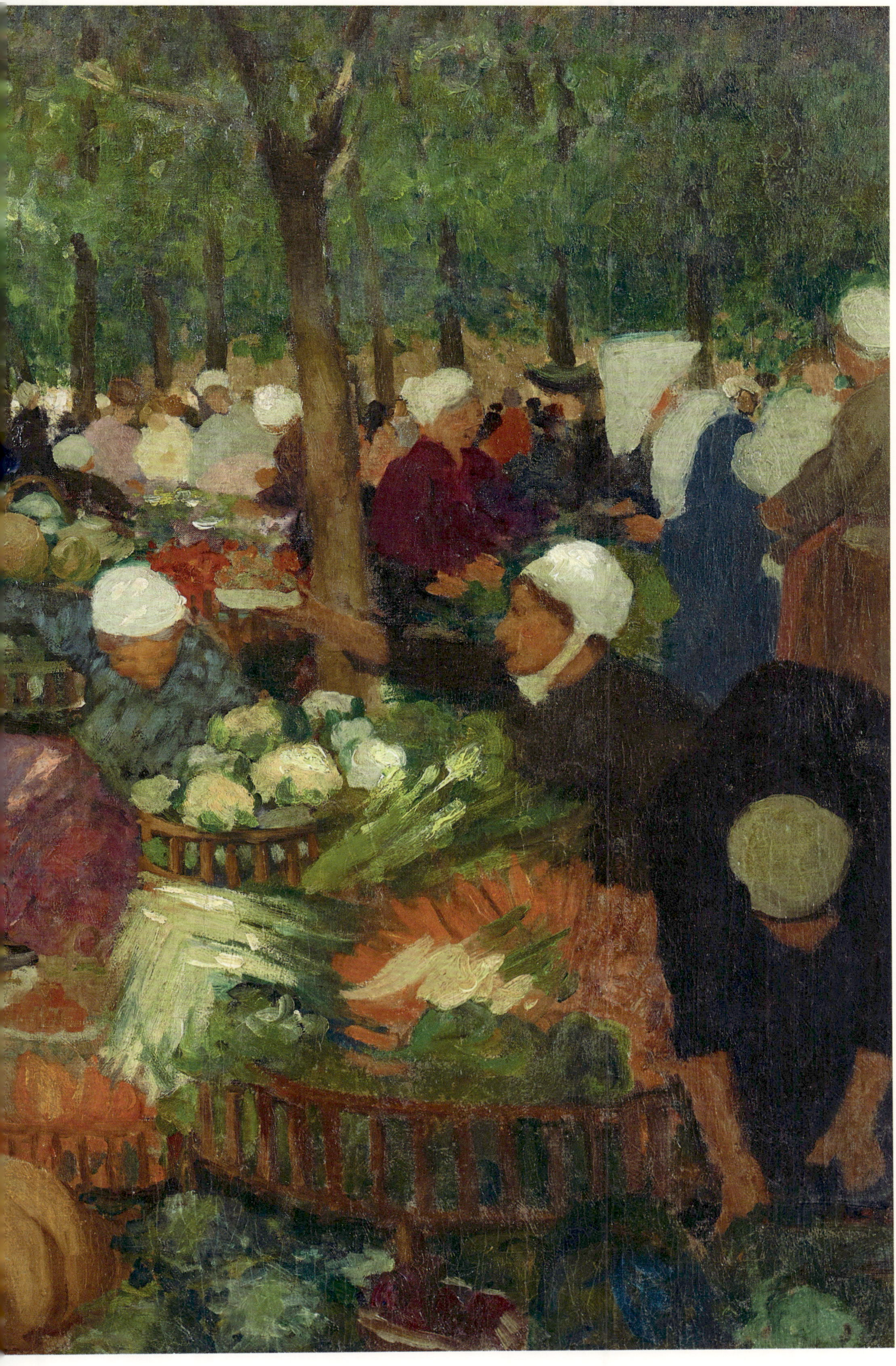

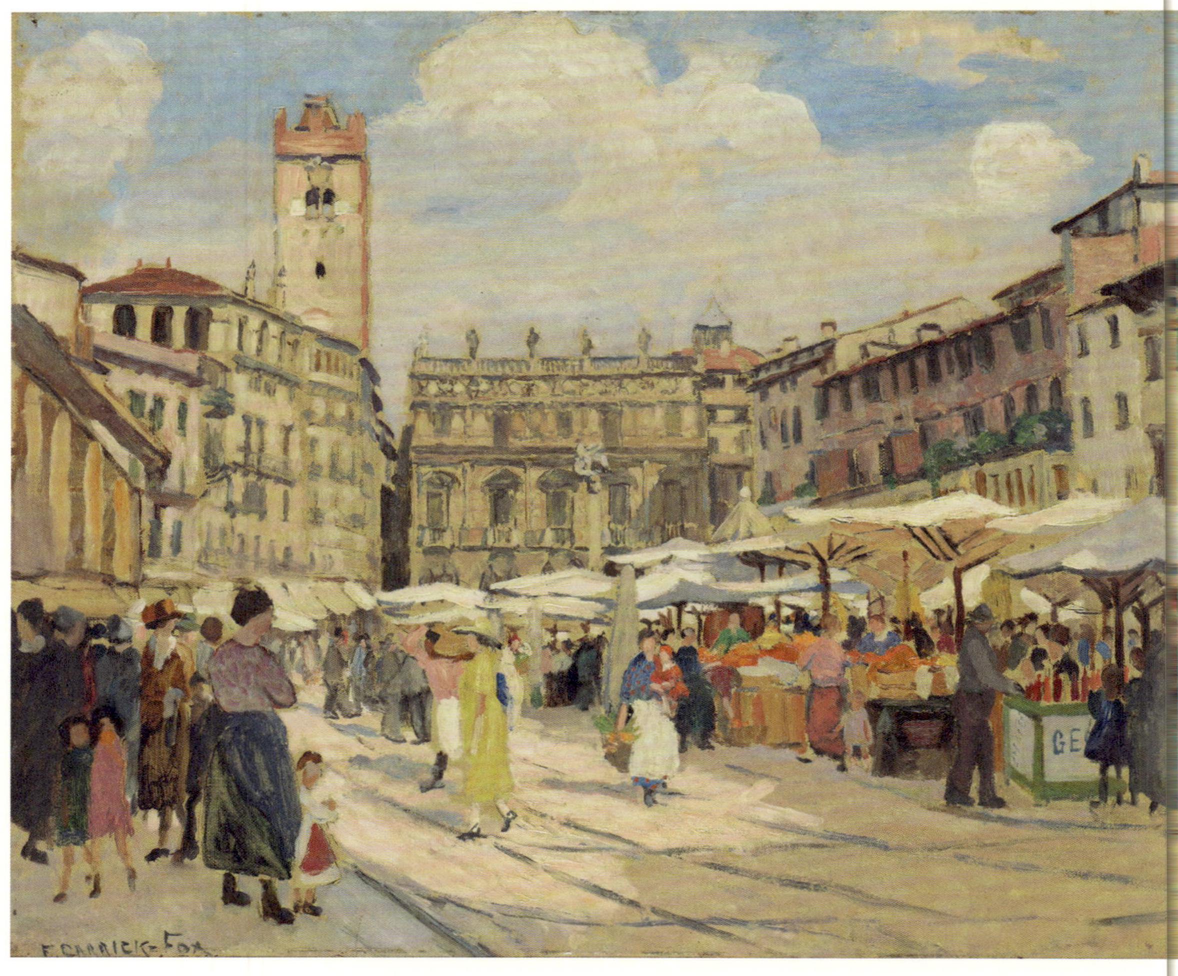

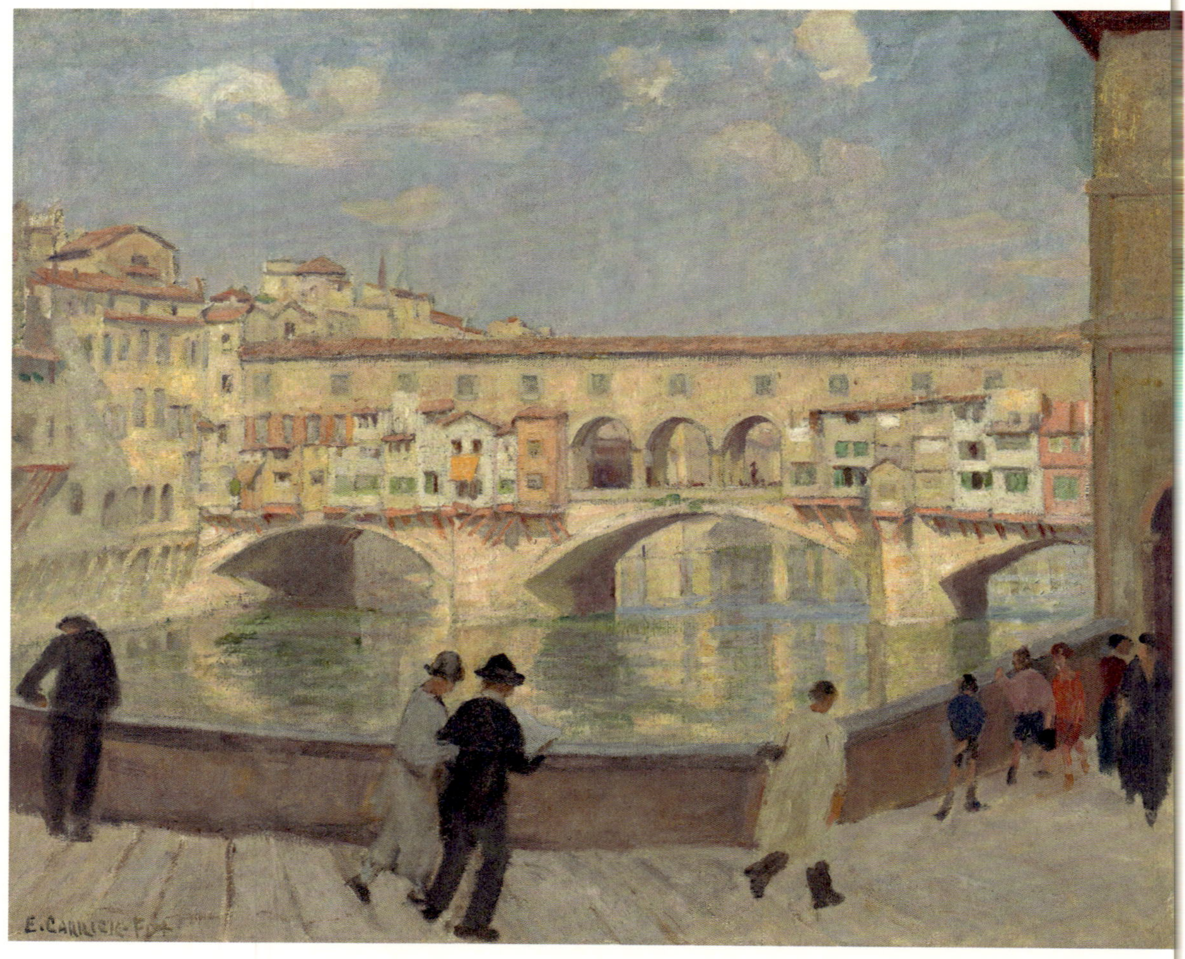

By the end of the war, Carrick was most keen to exhibit again, showing initially in March 1918 as part of the poetically named exhibition *L'arc-en-ciel* (The rainbow), the idea of spectral rainbow light suggesting transformation after despair.[163] In November 1919 Carrick exhibited four paintings at the Salon d'Automne, including a portrait of her joint Honorary Secretary in the Overseas French Homes League, Mme de Marquette. By the following year, all the Salons had re-opened, and she showed at the Salon des Indépendents, Salon d'Automne and Société Nationale des Beaux-Arts.

Over the winter of 1919 to 1920, Carrick travelled to Tunisia. It was an immensely productive visit revealing the continuing inspiration of North African subject matter, with a number of works shown in Paris the following year.[164] These paintings reveal stylistic shifts, embodying a distinctive feeling of breadth and flow, the brilliance of the sun often complemented by large leafy trees. In 1921 her portrait *Une Bretonne* (A Breton woman) was singled out for special mention, 'painted in the most truthful and best-felt way'.[165] The subject of the painting had been like a mother to hundreds of children during the war, and Carrick would have undertaken the painting with admiration for her subject.[166]

Female friendships remained a mainstay of Carrick's life. For a time in 1922, Ethel Stephens shared Carrick's studio at 65 Boulevard Arago.[167] Carrick and Stephens had both been delighted when Violet Teague was awarded a silver medal for *The boy with the palette* 1911 (fig 53, p 230) at the Salon des Artistes Français and, in her absence, Carrick collected the award on her behalf. On 28 July 1920 she wrote to Teague: 'I went to the Grand Palais to get your medal and certificate, a most solemn occasion ... As they put Monsieur Violet Teague on your certificate I asked them for a new one ... The portrait looks very well indeed.'[168] Around this period Carrick was struggling with her health and underwent treatment for rheumatism at Dax, a place famous since Roman times for its natural hot mud baths.[169]

Carrick painted two gouaches at Dax (cat 56, p 100 and cat 59, p 101), continuing in the mode of her travel works by capturing the light, colour and architecture of place from different vantage points. In 1924, she spent time painting in Tyrol and around Merano (cats 57 and 58), enamoured by the blossom trees against snow-capped mountains: 'Blossom time in the Tyrol is exquisite. I have never seen anything more beautiful than the acres of fruit trees in full bloom against a background of snow-capped mountains.'[170] By May 1924 she was travelling again, this time to Italy where she painted *Ponte Vecchio, Florence* c 1924 (cat 55), featuring the only bridge in Florence to escape bombing during the war. Showcasing an increasing interest in bridges, she depicted the closed-spandrel, segmented bridge spanning the River Arno with its glistening reflections.[171]

In 1925 Carrick travelled to Australia for the first time since Fox's death, to promote his art and show a joint exhibition of their work in Sydney and Adelaide, as well as hold a solo exhibition at the New Gallery in Melbourne. While in Melbourne she stayed with a Fox family relative, Dr Constance Ellis (the first woman to graduate as a Doctor of Medicine from the University of Melbourne, in 1903), and renewed connections with circles of friends. Not long after Carrick's arrival in Australia, she travelled to Sydney for the Theosophical Society Convention, held over Easter.

Opposite, top to bottom
cat 54 *The market place, Verona* c 1924, oil on cardboard, Tasmanian Museum and Art Gallery

cat 55 *Ponte Vecchio, Florence* c 1924, oil on canvas, National Gallery of Victoria

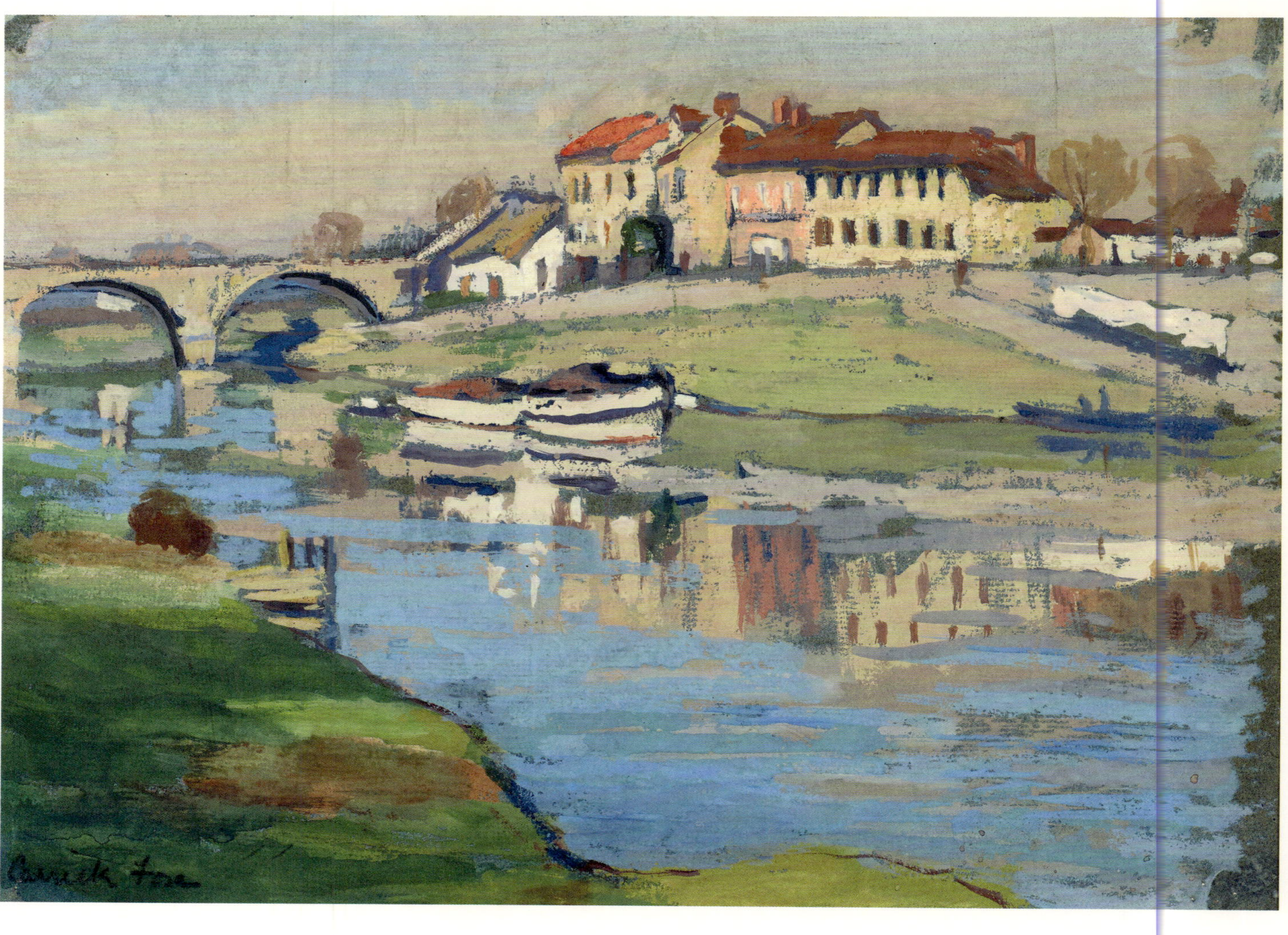

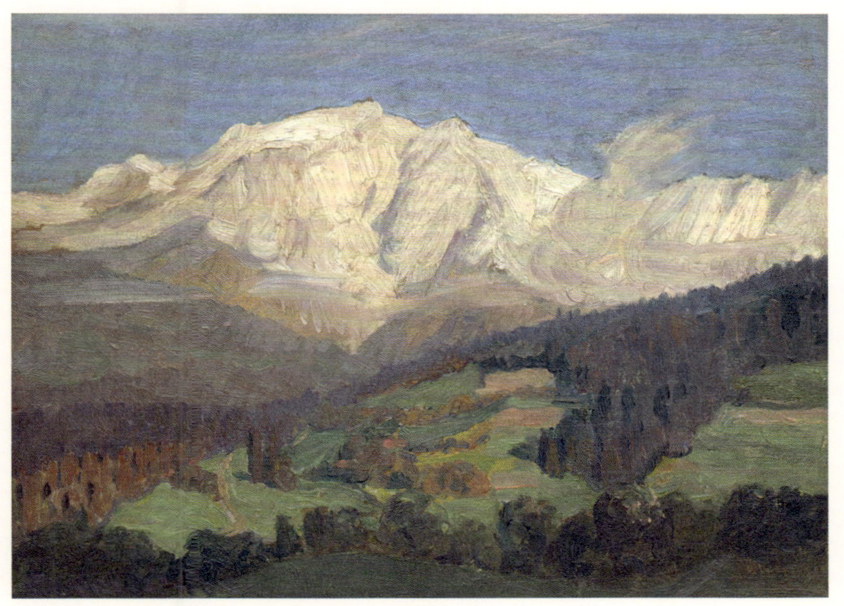

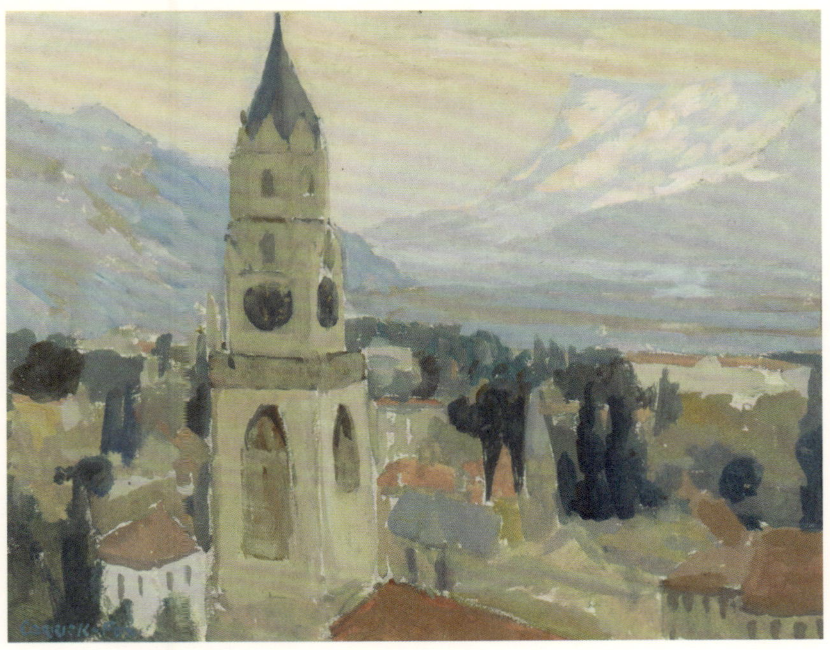

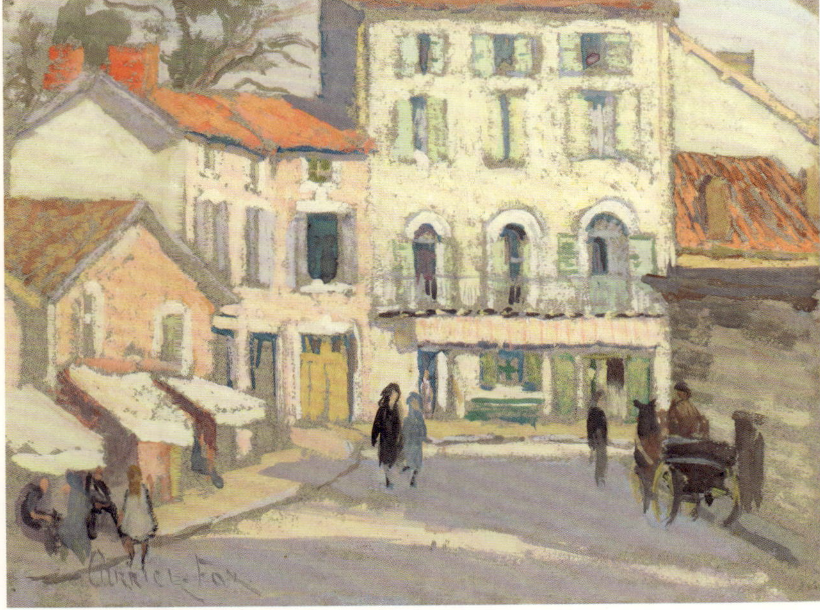

Opposite
cat 56 *Cottages at Dax* 1922, gouache on paper, private collection

Top to bottom
cat 57 *Mont Blanc* c 1924, oil on wood, collection of McClelland

cat 58 *The Church Tower, Merano* c 1924, gouache on paper, collection of McClelland

cat 59 *A street in Dax, France* 1922, gouache on paper, private collection

Lady Emily Lutyens, a close friend of Carrick's sister Jessie Platts, arrived with an Indian delegation including Jiddu Krishnamurti, who was acclaimed as the World Teacher of the Theosophical Society, and C Jinarajadasa, vice president of the Society.

Krishnamurti presented a lecture to a large crowd at the Star Amphitheatre in Balmoral, a Grecian style structure built by the Order of the Star in the East, which Carrick painted in October 1925 (fig 59, p 245).[172] Her interest in Krishnamurti's teachings on living together in harmony, beyond national boundaries, was reinforced in 1927 and 1929, when she travelled to hear him at Star Camp, Castle Eerde in Ommen, Holland, painting the castle during her first visit (fig 44, p 202).[173]

Carrick travelled to Adelaide at the beginning of July 1925 to prepare for the exhibition *Pictures by the Late E Phillips Fox and Ethel Carrick (Mrs E Phillips Fox)* at the South Australian Society of Arts gallery in Adelaide. Staying at the Queen Adelaide Club, she put her entrepreneurial skills into action. One reporter who visited noted that Carrick was 'her own manager and hanging committee', hard at work:

> It was a typically feminine touch which she was applying with a paint brush when I arrived. 'These white labels are horridly out of the picture,' she complained. So she was painstakingly going over them all with a touch of gold paint to soften the glare. Pictures of Paris, Algiers, Tunis, and forgotten corners of Morocco were on the walls, and about them all she had something personal to relate.[174]

The Verlaine Memorial, Paris c 1925 (cat 60), which had previously been displayed in the Salon d'Automne, was considered 'remarkable for breadth of treatment ... standing out against a huge tree covered with pink blossoms and the light and shade under the trees and on the paths is cleverly suggested'.[175] The sculpture in the painting—located in the Luxembourg Gardens—is a memorial to Paul Verlaine, whose poetry inspired composers like Claude Debussy, linking art, poetry and music.

Despite positive comments in the press, the exhibition didn't sell well. None of Fox's paintings were acquired by the Art Gallery of South Australia. Carrick wrote in distress to Ivy Brookes:

> I haven't written sooner because there hasn't been anything interesting to tell you about the exhibition which has not been at all successful from a financial point of view—though well-attended—there seems to be a general opinion of disgust at the gallery not purchasing (or making any offer).[176]

Soon after, Carrick wrote to Gother Mann, then-director of the Art Gallery of New South Wales, asking him to consider purchasing Fox's *Art students* 1895 for 250 guineas, noting that she was 'making arrangements to take the collection to America, as these pictures are the only fortune my husband could leave me (excepting a little money which is all gone) & I must sell them—I have Australia as the first choice, as he would have wanted—but if she doesn't want them, they must go elsewhere'.[177] In Sydney, the exhibition of Carrick and Fox's works at Anthony Hordern & Sons included 50 of her paintings undertaken in different countries. It was more successful than Adelaide, as 'several pictures were sold on the first day', including some by Fox.[178]

Opposite
cat 60 ***The Verlaine Memorial, Paris*** **c 1925, oil on canvas, private collection**

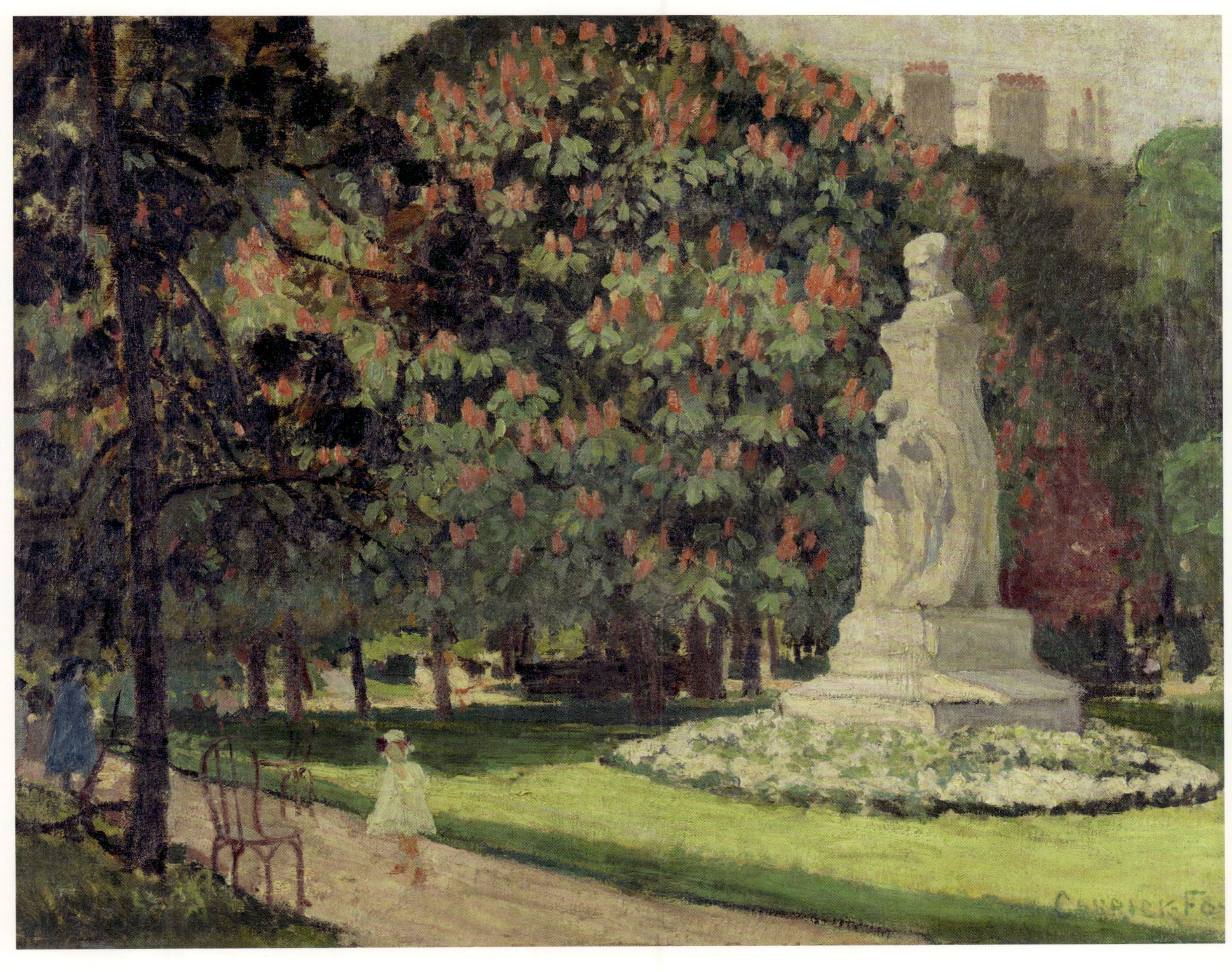

In October 1925 a reporter noted that Carrick's 'eyrie is on the heights beyond Mosman—painting the views round the harbour and its bays which charm artists from all parts of the world'.[179] While in Sydney she stayed in both Balmoral and Mosman, near the theosophical residence The Manor, where she visited friends such as Jane Price.[180] In October she wrote to Ivy Brookes:

> **It is a tiny panel of red gum flowers—painted by Jane Price, (your mother has one of hers) who was looked upon as one of the best Australian painters. She is desperately poor now. I bought a little picture of hers & Grace Officer gave her a commission. The little picture in mention is £ 5.5. anyway, I'd like you to see it.[181]**

Early in 1926, Carrick took on pupils at her studio in Bligh Street, near Circular Quay. A reporter noted: 'I found the interesting owner, conducting an art class, surrounded by dozens of her late husband's pictures, and more of her own, and putting the finishing touches to a delightful sketch of the Head, as seen from Balmoral where, for the time being, she lives'.[182] Her peripatetic life continued and on 21 April 1926, Carrick left for Paris.

Back in France, Carrick's paintings showed a renewed strength of purpose. She travelled to Nice in the south of France and was there around 1926 and 1927. On 16 April 1927 mention was made in an article that 'Mrs Phillips Fox, is staying in Nice and frequently seen working in the Old Town. Three of her paintings depicting the life of the Niçois are to be exhibited at the Spring Salon'.[183] Her delight in the local flower markets resulted in paintings that echo the boldness of her works prior to World War I, reaffirming her talent for painting outdoor subjects and her status as a wonderful colourist. In Paris in 1907 Carrick painted *Flower market* (cat 14, p 34), in which women of different social backgrounds are seen shopping for flowers; the bunches crisply wrapped in white paper form striking abstract shapes, some brushed with great verve, like musical notes. Another distinctive early post-impressionist example and a forerunner of her later Nice paintings is *Flower market (France)* c 1910 (cat 124, p 212), shows a well-dressed couple rejoicing at the sight of a vibrant mass of flowers, boldly dabbed in touches of red, pink and white to dramatic effect.

It was in Nice, at the Cours Saleya, that Carrick came upon one of the great markets of the world. The Marché aux Fleurs, established in 1897, was one of the first wholesale cut-flower markets in Europe, where local peasants and farmers brought their blooms to market in the early morning for sellers. The old quarter with its nineteenth-century buildings, one of which included Matisse's Nice apartment, ignited Carrick's imagination. In her painting *In the Nice flower market* c 1926 (cat 123, pp 210–11), bright bunches of flowers are shown on tables and amassed in baskets under stylish umbrellas, characteristic of the region. In the foreground, a seller dressed in black engages with a woman about a prospective purchase, while our vision is directed back into the space beyond where differently attired figures, including a couple of nuns, cluster against the illuminated buildings in the far distance. A colonnade of arches on the right helps to locate the scene while also providing gently curving counterparts to the angularity of the rhythmic tilting umbrellas, which animate the scene under the canopy of leafy trees.

Opposite
cat 61 ***Flower market, Nice*** **c 1926,**
oil on canvas, Art Gallery of New South Wales

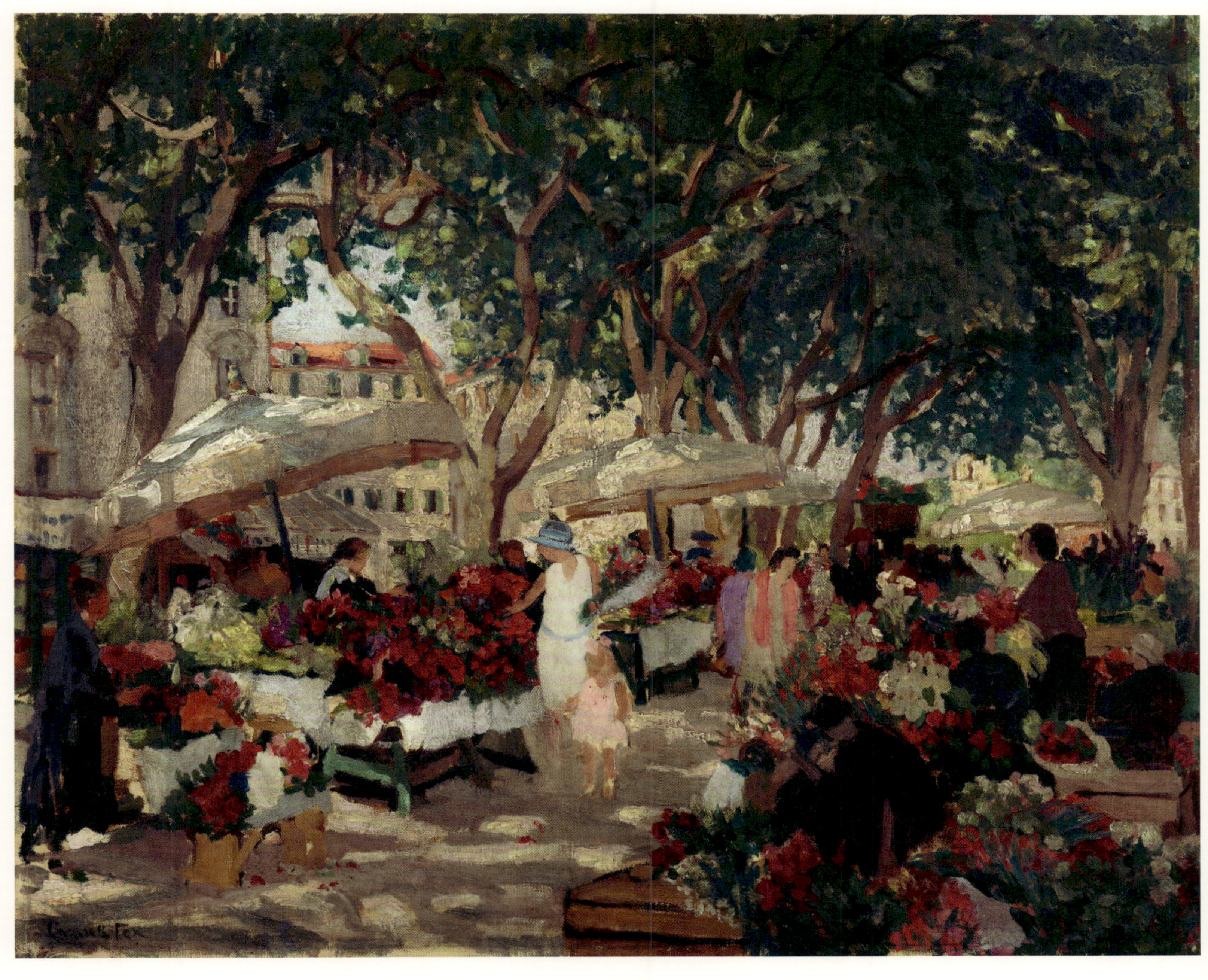

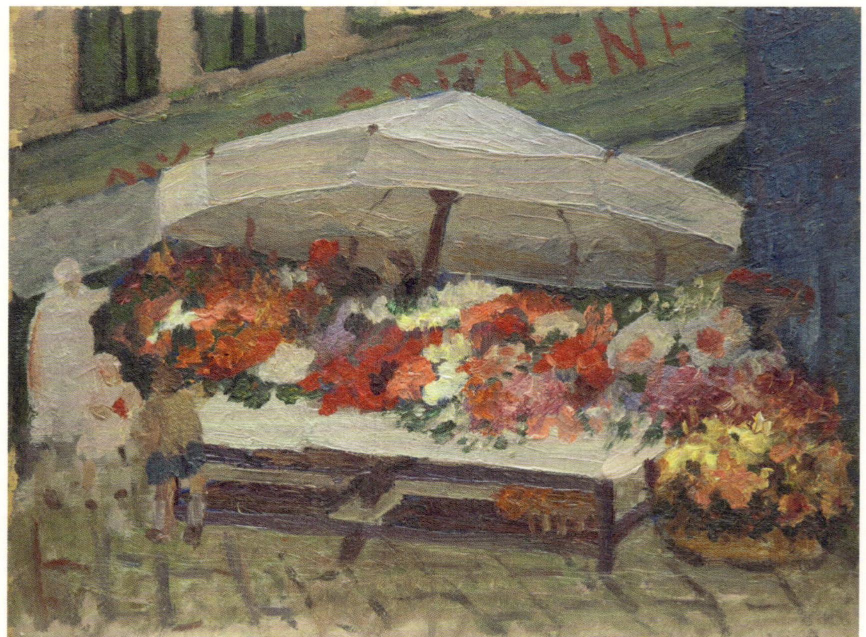

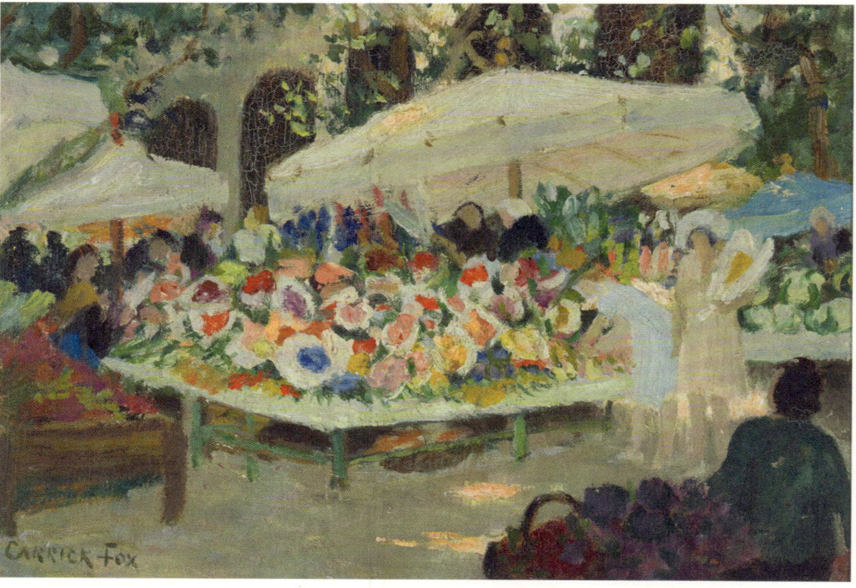

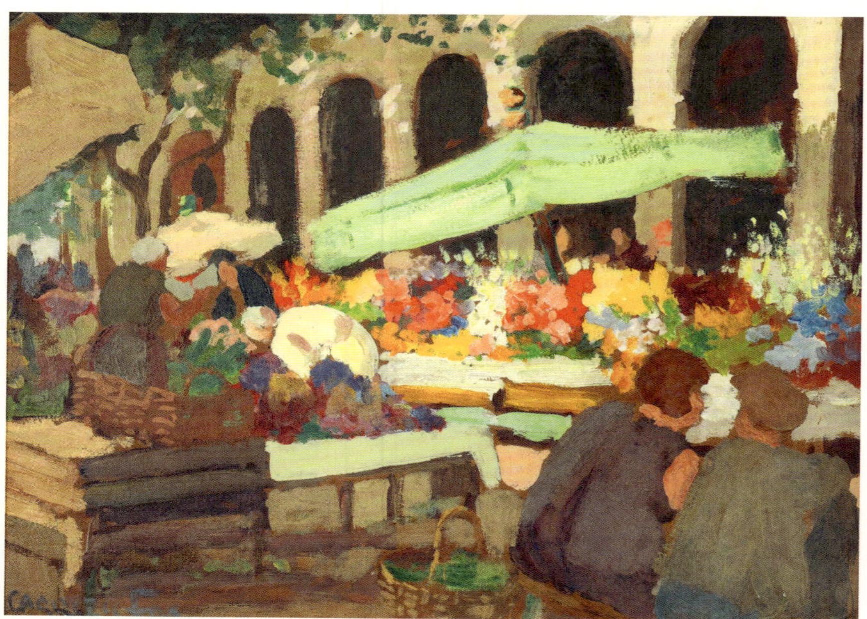

Top to bottom
cat 62 *Flower stall* c 1926, oil on wood, Bendigo Art Gallery

cat 63 *Flower market southern France* c 1935, oil on board, University Art Collection, Chau Chak Wing Museum, The University of Sydney

cat 64 *Flower vendors, Nice* c 1930, oil on cardboard, Kerry Stokes Collection

Opposite
cat 65 *Flower market southern France* c 1926, oil on board, University Art Collection, Chau Chak Wing Museum, The University of Sydney

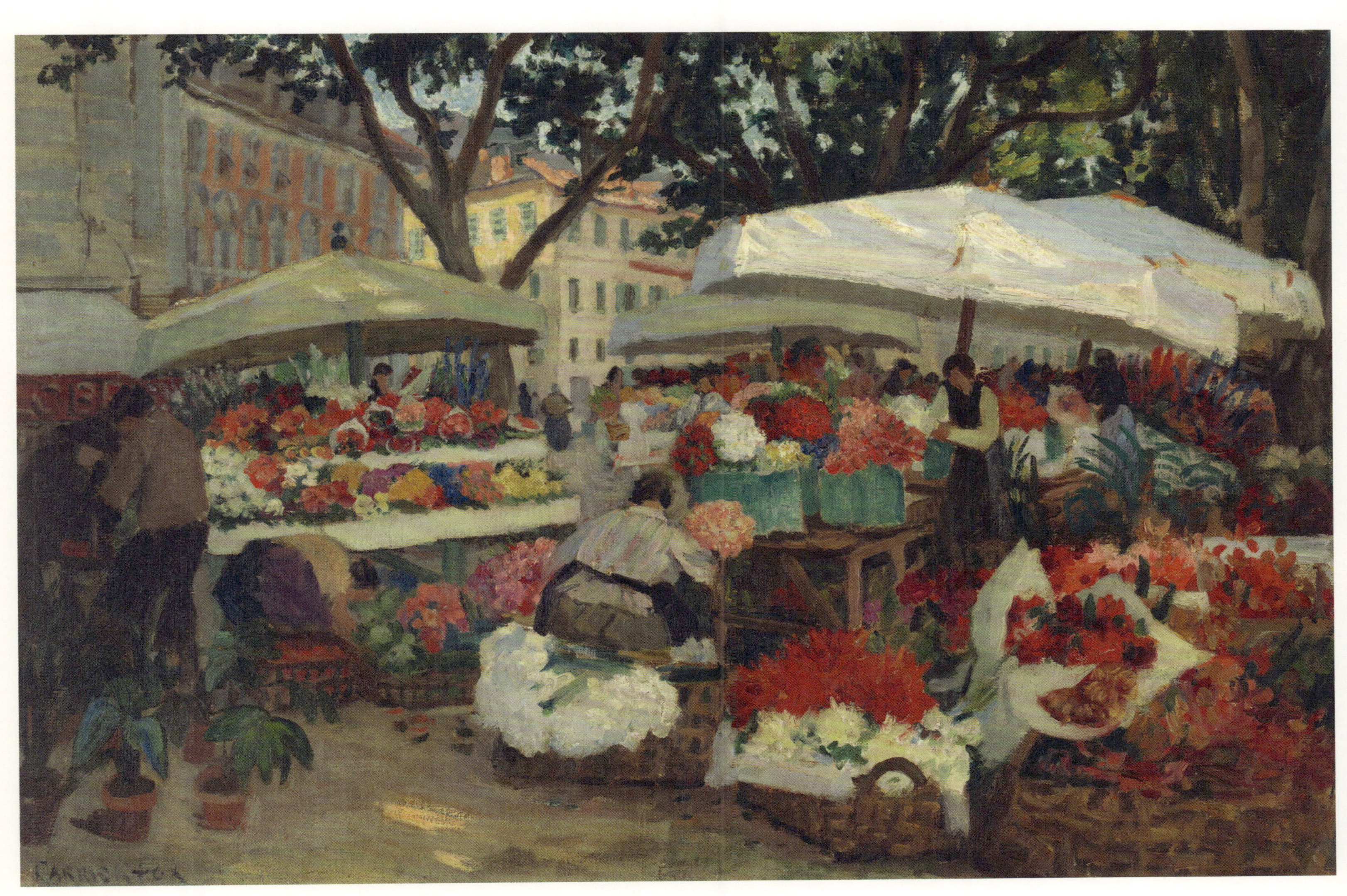

In her Nice paintings, Carrick brought great amplitude to form and space. Looked at collectively, in work after work vibrant colour and dappled light ripple across complex compositions. From one to another, it is as though she is rotating in space, enlivened by each particular viewpoint. *Flower market southern France* c 1926 (cat 65, p 107), suggests the beginning of a day, as sellers stack their produce on stands and tables and in baskets on the ground. In *Flower market, Nice* c 1926 (cat 61, p 105), the diagonals of the umbrellas add real dynamism. Here, a woman carrying a bunch of flowers and perusing a stall with a small child moves towards the viewer through dappled light, her summery white dress and bright blue hat conveying the season. Past and present, luminosity and structure, interweave. As David Thomas notes,

> **Carrick used the arcaded grandeur of the Nice market to introduce an important element of pictorial stability, a solid backdrop to the theatre of life at play. Sunlight is also at play to focus attention on bursts of colour, contrasted with the shade of tree and umbrella to shelter the shopper ... while umbrellas remain unchanged, fashion, in the length of the ladies' dresses, suggests a date in the twenties. Colour harmonies of reds and mauves are subtle, highlighted against the pale cream of the fine, arched background.[184]**

In 1927, Carrick was awarded a diplôme d'honneur for *Christmas Day on Manly Beach* 1913 (cat 118, pp 194–95) at the Exposition Internationale des Beaux-Arts de la Ville de Bordeaux.[185] In 1928, her work was included with that of Rupert Bunny and Hilda Rix Nicholas in a display of 'foreign' art at the Musée du Luxembourg. In the same year, she held a solo exhibition at the Galerie de la Palette Française, on Boulevard Haussmann in Paris, featuring 22 recent works, including those of the open-air Nice markets. The fruits of her labours were recognised not only in positive reviews but also in the announcement that her painting originally known as *Coin d'une rue, Nice* (Corner of a street, Nice) c 1928 (fig 24) would be acquired for the country by Paul Léon, Director General of Fine Arts. After years of dedicated work in France, Carrick felt her moment had arrived. An article in *The Brisbane Courier* (perhaps by her friend Frankie Payne) noted, 'The State bought one of the most attractive of Miss Carrick's works "Corner of a Street, Nice." [fig 24] And as the State is rather chary of buying foreigners' work, this was quite an honour.'[186]

Compared with her other market scenes, *Corner of a street, Nice* is more compressed, situated between two rows of buildings and framed at the back by others. The predominance of white tones reminiscent of Carrick's early works are now infused with soft greys, mauves and yellows in a delicate interplay of shadow and luminosity. These are enlivened by deep pinks, oranges and purples cleverly deployed between white umbrellas and tablecloths. Above the umbrellas, buildings of warm hue rise against the bright blue sky of the Côte d'Azur, while to the side of the composition two seated figures in shadow join the viewer in appreciating the scene.

On 9 June 1928, Georges Bal, writing for *The New York Herald*, mistook Carrick for an American (perhaps because of all the international shows she had been in), remarking that her solo show had been a great success, 'the views of the streets and markets of Nice being particularly successful, having afforded the artist an opportunity to show the wealth of her palette in very beautiful light effects'. He also noted that as

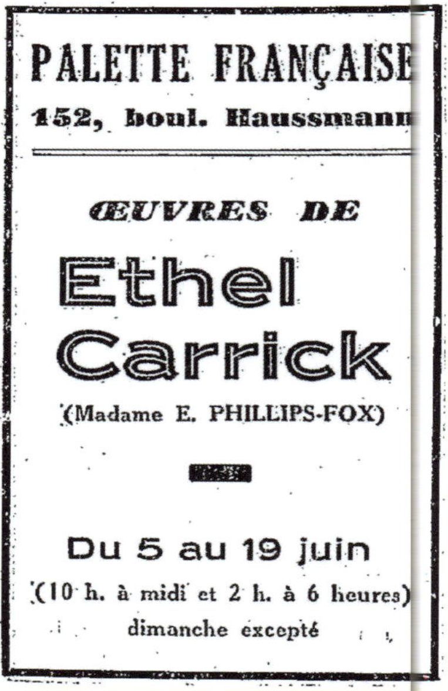

fig 23 Advertisement for Ethel Carrick's solo exhibition at Palette Française 5–19 June 1928, *La Semaine à Paris*, 1928

DEBORAH HART

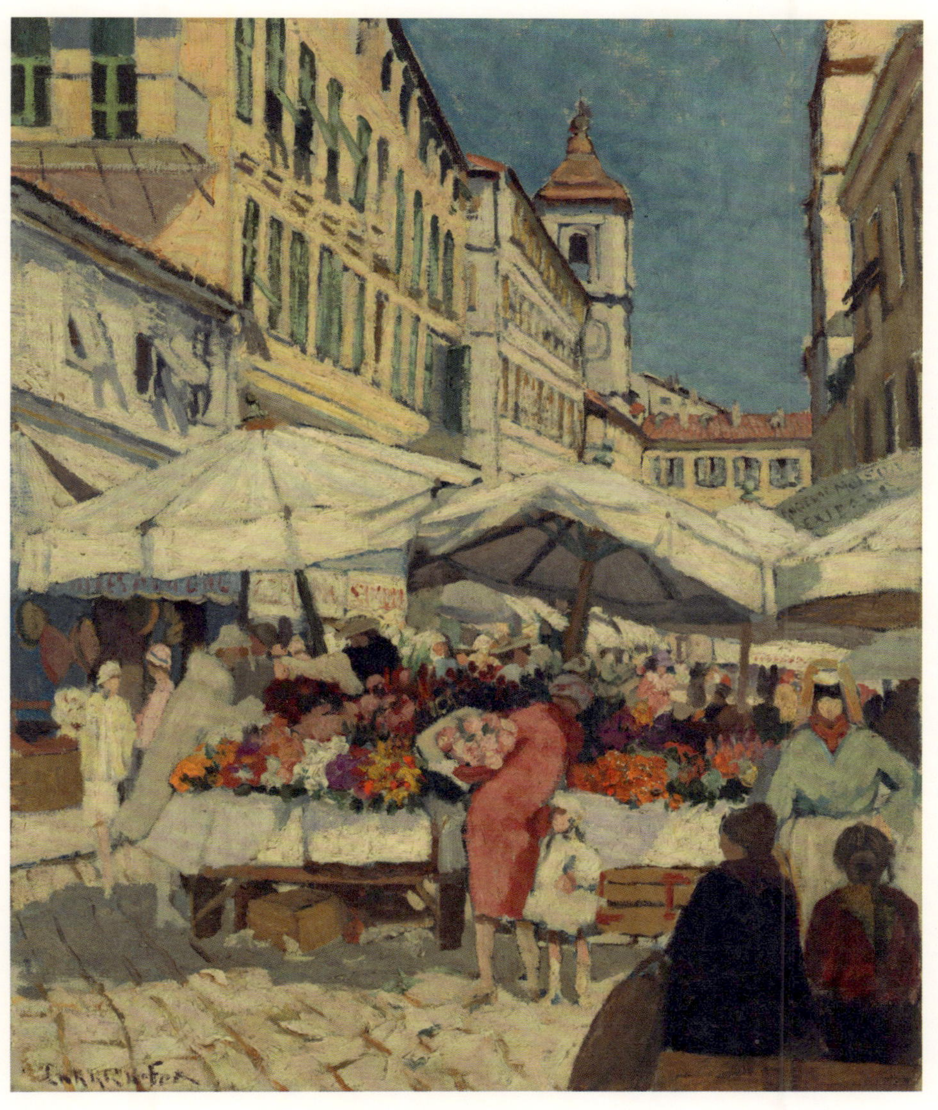

fig 24 *Le marché aux fleurs à Nice* (The Nice flower market) c 1928, originally known as *Coin d'une rue, Nice* (Corner of a street, Nice), oil on canvas, Musée des Beaux-Arts, Rouen

'a painter of flowers she succeeds with the most delicate fresh tones in rendering the many tints of anemones, tulips and other blossoms. Ethel Carrick's painting is powerful and free from any feminine finicality'.[187] While intended as a compliment, Carrick's embrace of still life as a key subject, which would continue in the ensuing years, was very much in tune with what was considered women's work and that was often downplayed as not serious enough. The title of her work *Les femmes, l'amour et les fleurs* (Women, love and flowers) suggests Carrick's embrace of the feminine in its strength, fecundity and beauty. This ode to women and flowers was shown at the Salon des Beaux-Arts in 1931.

Many of Carrick's best still life paintings were bold in conception and in harmony with the flowers themselves: she captured the ethereal delicacy of poppies (fig 25, p 111), the bowed, weighty heads of tulips creating a pattern of arabesque stems (cat 68, p 110) and the fulsome blooms of peonies (cat 71, p 111). Flowers from the marketplace or her garden—an ongoing joy since her early days with Fox—allowed for dynamic displays in vases indoors, as well as outdoors, at Boulevard Arago. It is fascinating to contemplate the ways in which the distinctive colours and shapes of a wide variety of blooms influenced the arrangements of her compositions, enlivened by varied objects of daily life and imbued with memory. A sense of time passing is evoked in her works by fallen petals, or by a set table awaiting conviviality.

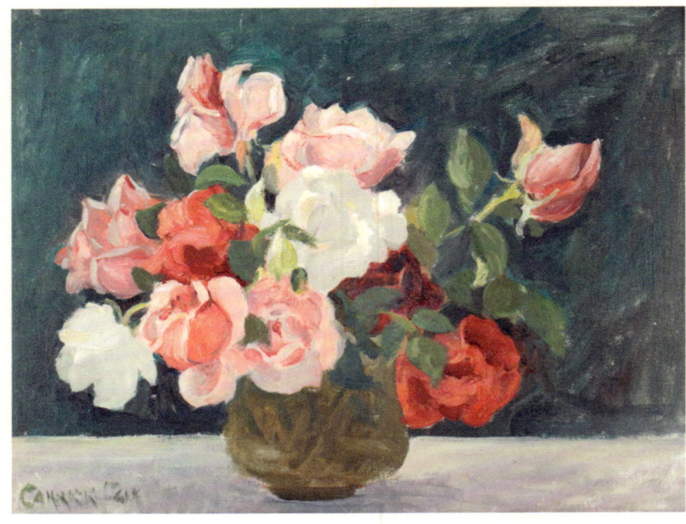

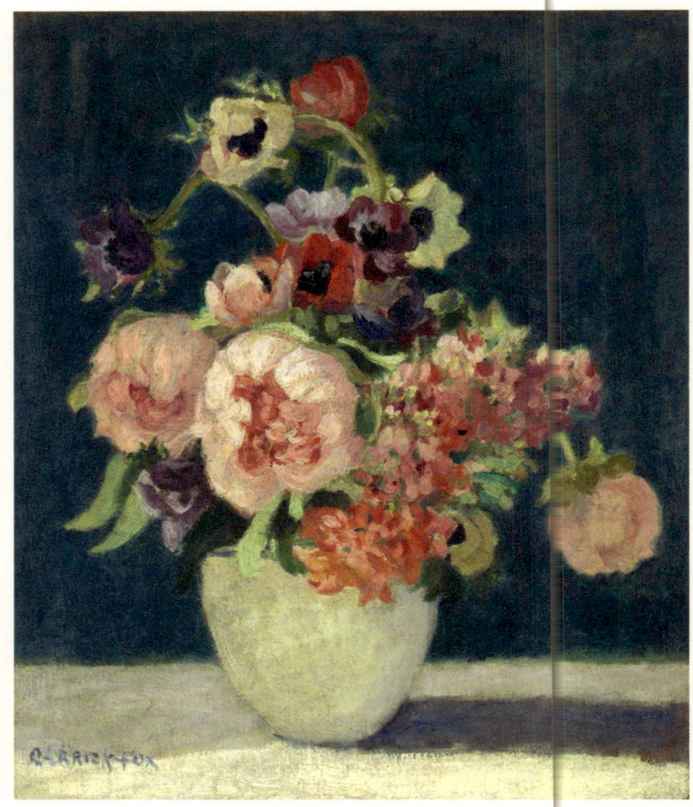

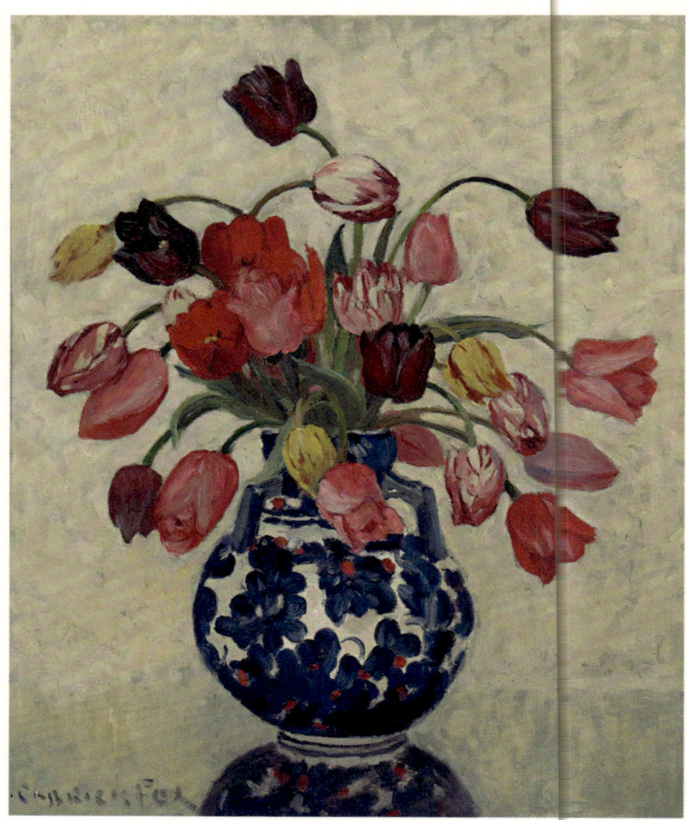

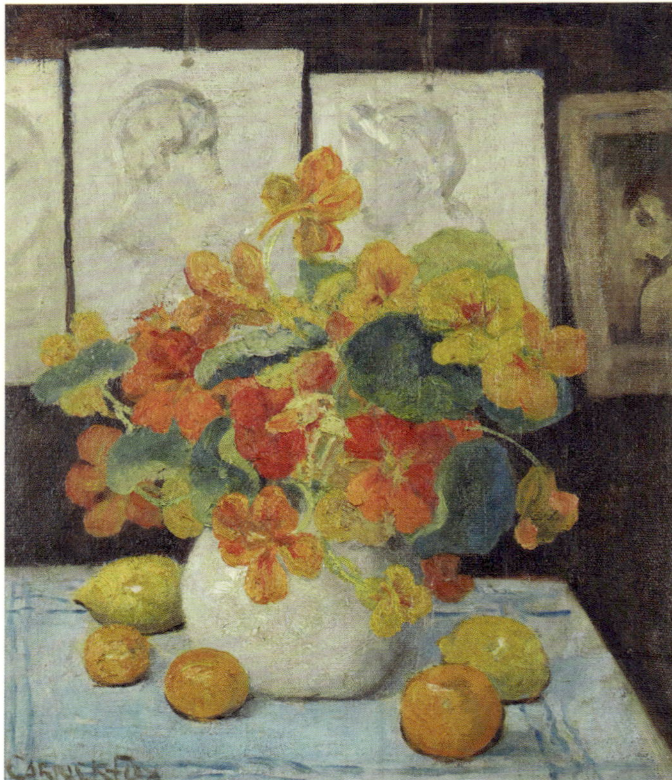

Clockwise, from top left
cat 66 *Roses* c 1938, oil on board, University Art Collection, Chau Chak Wing Museum, The University of Sydney

cat 67 *Flower piece* c 1930, oil on canvas, National Gallery of Australia

cat 68 *Tulips* c 1930, oil on canvas, private collection

cat 69 *Nasturtiums* c 1933, oil on canvas, The University of Western Australia Art Collection

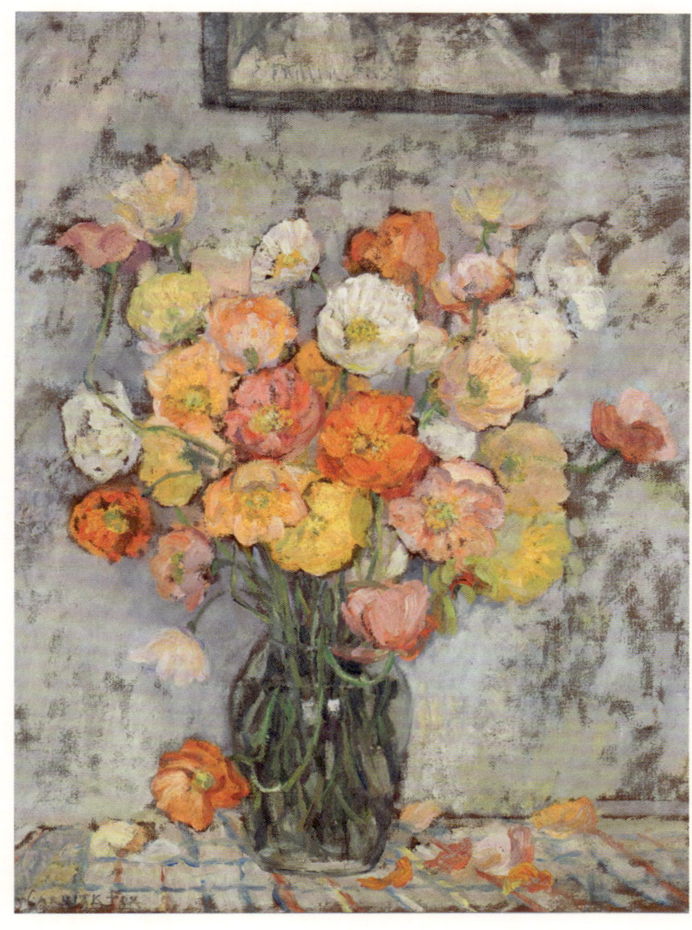

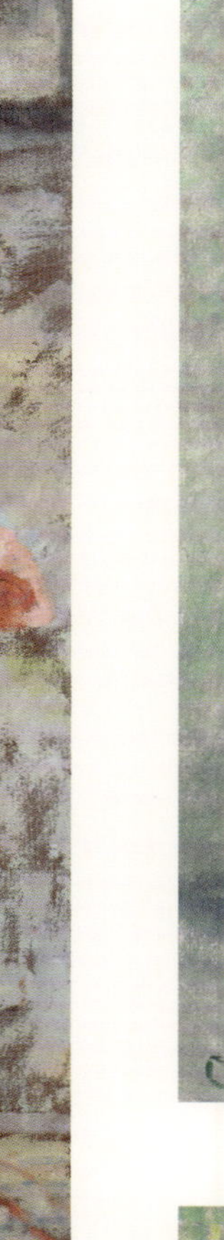

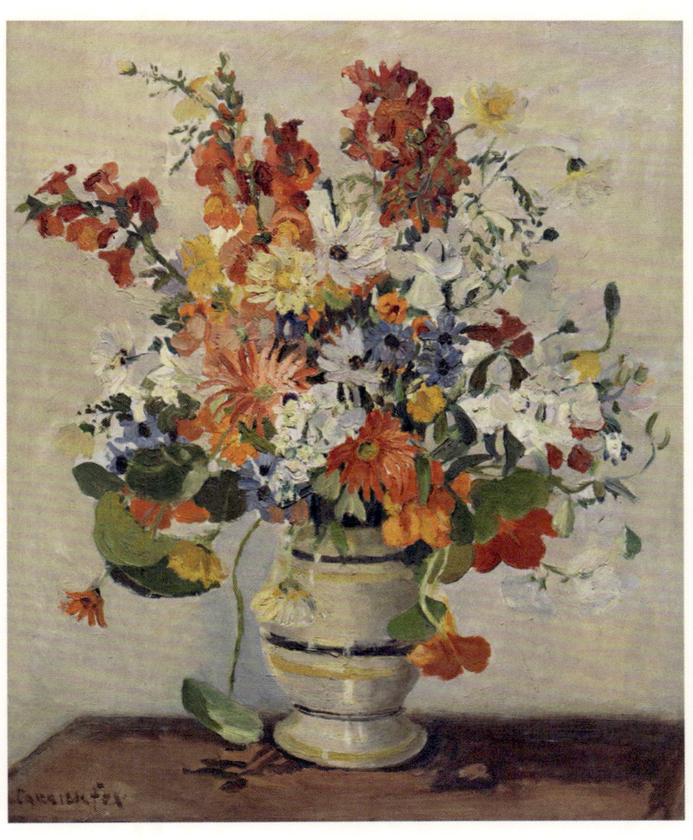

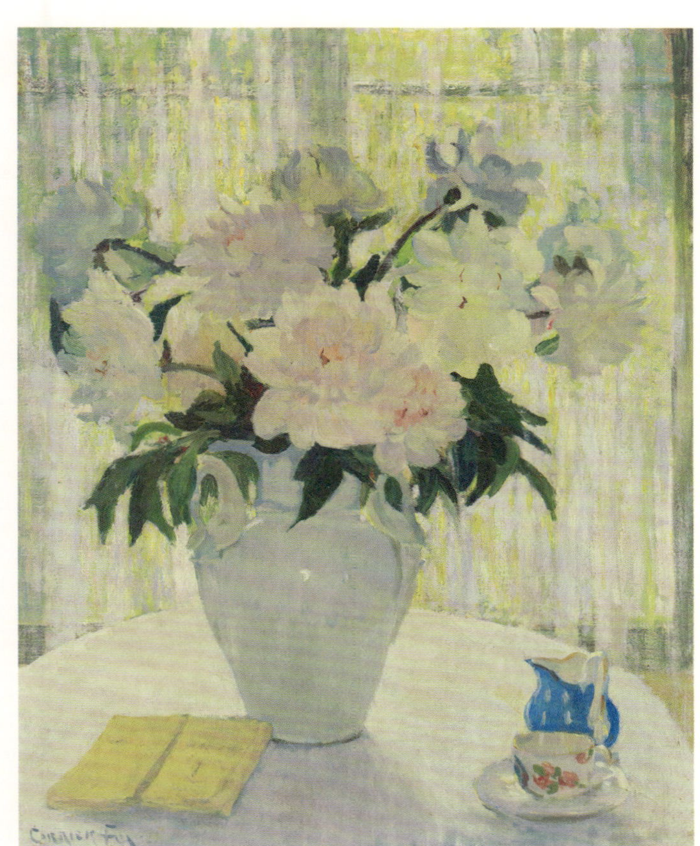

Clockwise, from top left
fig 25 *Poppies* c 1949, oil on canvas, private collection

cat 70 *Mixed flowers* c 1933, oil on canvas on board, Collection of Dr Garry Helprin

cat 71 *Peonies* c 1930, oil on canvas, private collection

cat 72 *A bunch of flowers* c 1935, oil on canvas on plywood, Queensland Art Gallery | Gallery of Modern Art

In *Nasturtiums* c 1933 (cat 69, p 110) we are reminded of the artist at work, with unfinished drawings behind the vital orange and yellow plants and fruit. Carrick's great love of flowers was expressed in an article that overflowed with specific descriptions of her garden:

> At this moment bloom pansies, mignonette, geraniums, columbines, anemones, nasturtiums, cornflowers, and roses, while the sweet peas and poppies in bud for only a few days warm sunshine to pattern the existing, green patches with embroideries of exquisite form and delicate colour ... Lovingly the plants are tended in this garden of sweet memories and loyally they respond ... Goodwill, common sense, and the best of seeds aid Nature to continue to act her eternal miracles.[188]

In an interview in Australia, where Carrick returned for a visit in 1933, she noted that she was opposed to the 'ultra-modern'. She was not against Cubism or Futurism (even if they were not for her), but she was not keen on other recent developments. Carrick wanted to distinguish 'ultra-modern' from 'modern art'. She was outspoken when asked about the National Gallery of Victoria's collection, taking issue with acquisitions of second-rate old masters for vast sums instead of acquiring great examples of modern art. She felt that it was 'a crime not to have a Degas', and advocated for an effort to be made to find works by Cézanne, Gauguin, Van Gogh and Vuillard, among others.[189] Beyond the gallery walls, she imagined 'an international League of Beauty': 'If I had my way,' Carrick said, 'I would travel all over Australia, sowing flower seeds and planting trees.'[190]

Pre-empting her visit to Australia and building interest in her art, *The Argus* noted that her pictures of fruit and flower markets 'are gorgeous in colour, yet harmonious in the whole'.[191] *The fruit market, Nice* c 1927 (cat 73) is one of Carrick's most ambitious examples of a marketplace. Depicting the bustling market outside Le Palais Préfectoral de Nice, the round shapes of many white umbrellas cascade into the background, while in the foreground people are buying and selling fruits and vegetables. By pulling back and taking an aerial view, the work emphasises the architectural stage, the action filling every inch of the composition. The animation also comes from the linear patterns formed by denuded trees against the blue sky on a sunny winter day.

In Melbourne in 1933, Carrick exhibited a range of works at Everyman's Lending Library, including some in tempera that were variously praised and criticised—as in *The Bulletin*, where the reviewer took a swipe by describing them as part of a 'Back-to-the-horse Movement'.[192] Her show was opened by Ivy Brookes, who hosted an event in Carrick's honour. During her visit, Carrick stayed at the Lyceum Club, reconnecting with family and friends. Among them were Violet Teague and Jessie Traill who, with Una Teague, had been instrumental in organising a pipeline to take water to the Aboriginal communities of Hermannsburg in the Northern Territory—an endeavour supported by Carrick, who included one of her flower market paintings in a group fundraising exhibition.[193]

Carrick and Fox's exhibition at the Athenaeum Gallery in 1934 was an extensive offering of more than 150 works—probably rather too many for the space. Overall, it was her flower studies that received special mention: 'She is seen at her best in some of her flower-pieces, "White Peonies" (49) being carried through with surprising verve.'[194]

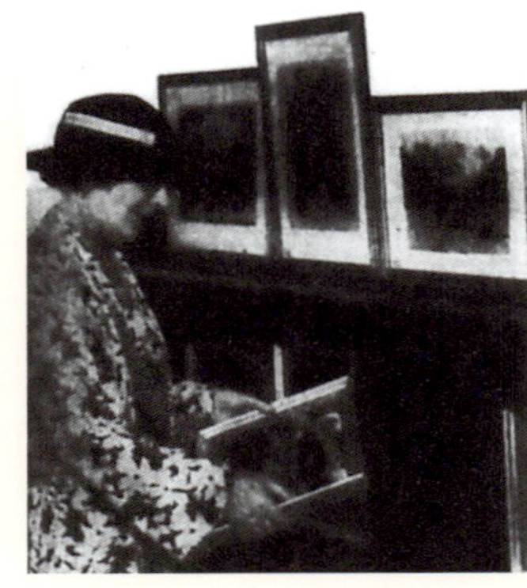

fig 26 *Ethel Carrick arranging some of her paintings for an exhibition of her work and that of the late E Phillips Fox at the Athenaeum Gallery, Melbourne*, photograph in *The Herald*, 27 February 1934

Opposite
cat 73 *The fruit market, Nice* c 1927
oil on canvas, Kerry Stokes Collection

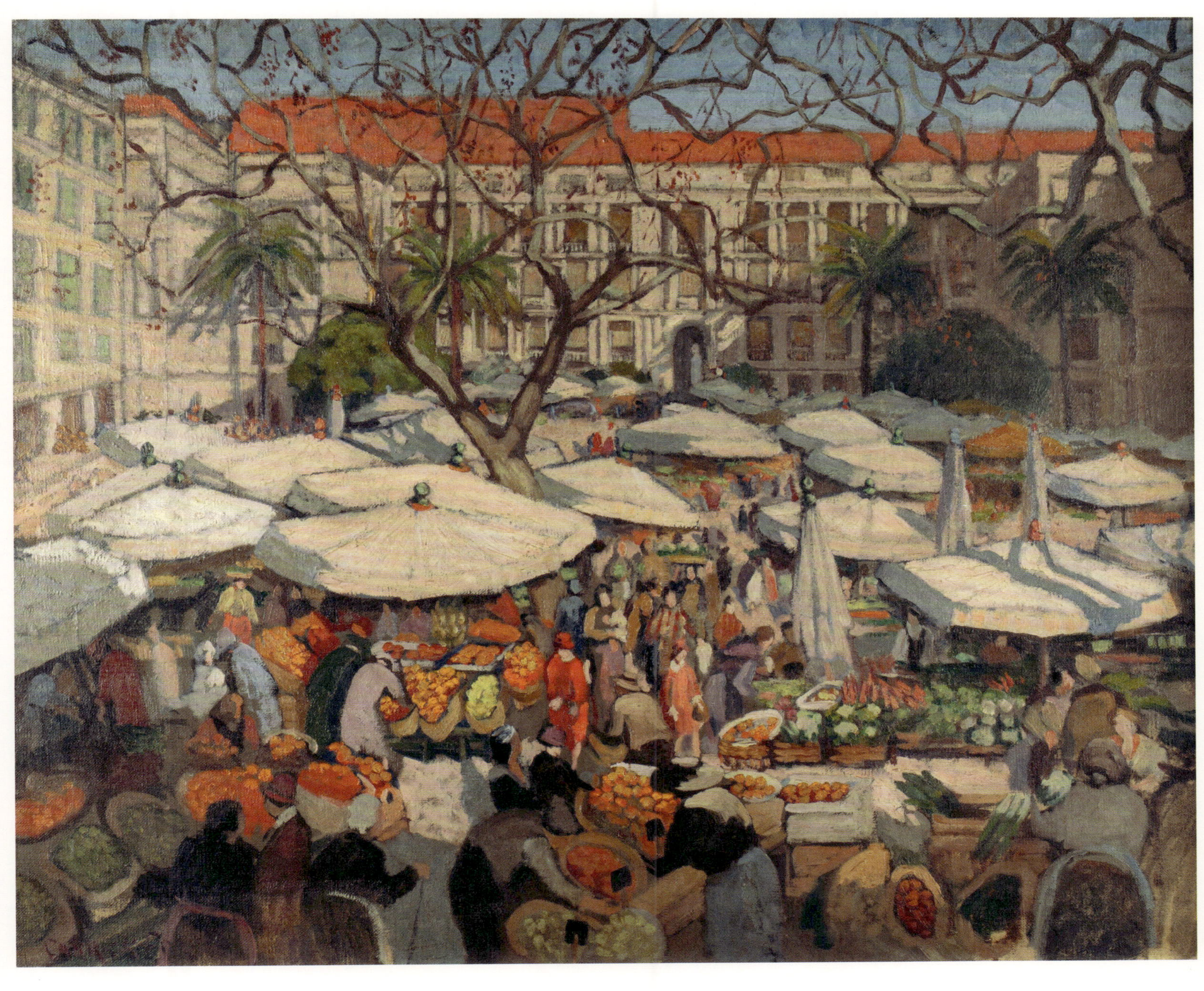

A number of these works, painted in Paris, had already been shown at the Salon d'Automne, the Salon des Beaux-Arts and even in the Paris horticultural exhibition.

Late in 1935, Carrick travelled to India, going to Adyar for the Diamond Jubilee Convention of the Theosophical Society in late December.[195] Records note that around 2000 people attended from around the world. Annie Besant, a champion of Indian self-rule and president of the Society until 1933 (the year she died) was called upon in spirit for her blessing.

Through 1936, Carrick exhibited in various venues across India, including at the Srinagar Club in Kashmir, Nedou's Hotel in Gulmarg and with the Punjab Literary League in Lahore, where her works were shown alongside those by Mr and Mrs Roop Krishna and Mr Chughtai in a 'fine arts display'.[196] Around Christmas Day in 1936, Carrick's solo exhibition launched at the club house of the Punjab Literary League, organised by the Art Circle of the League.[197] The show was opened by Lady Boyd and Mr Roop Krishna, a Punjabi artist,[198] who remarked that Carrick was a 'very famous artist' whose paintings had been exhibited in various venues in London and Paris. From a review of the exhibition, we can attain a sense of the works shown, many of which were undertaken during her visit to India:

> **The work of Mrs Phillips Fox is distinguished for its life, light, colour and character. It is a practical record of her impressions of Kashmir. One noticed [the] unfaltering decision of touch with which 'Morning on the River Jhelum' had been painted. The same combination is seen in the treatment of 'A Lilac Festival' and 'The Grass cutters'—a rhythmic composition of figures in movement and repose, rich in colour and tone. A directness of vision and insight into character that lies behind the actual mask is remarkably shown in the portrait work of this artist. 'Mahatma' and 'A Sikh Youth' may be mentioned as two examples.[199]**

During her visit, Carrick travelled through Kashmir, depicting the landscape in delicate, luminous gouaches painted at different times of day, from early morning to evening (cats 74 and 75). She conveyed the richly verdant terrain at Ganderbal in the mountains, with the wooden huts of the Gujjar people in a number of small travel paintings that would be shown alongside others from different locations in her exhibition at Cooling Galleries, London, in June 1938. This included *Kashmir, India* c 1939 (fig 28). Carrick also made lithographs depicting the great sights of India, including the historic Taj Mahal, the mausoleum on the river Yamuna in Agra and the Ganges. *Pilgrims bathing at Benares* c 1937 (cat 78, p 120) showcases her dexterity in capturing the atmosphere of place. Benares, also known as Varanasi, is a pilgrimage site located on the river Ganges where devotees come to bathe in the waters at least once in their lives. Viewed from the water, Carrick paid close attention to the temples on the banks, layered high above and leading down the *ghat* (stairway) to the Ganges. For all her attention to detail, Carrick drew with fluency, capturing a sense of the mystical in the throngs of people seen from a distance moving towards the river of salvation.[200]

Carrick's travels in India from 1935 through to 1937, and again in 1939, included time spent with family and friends. On one occasion she spent a few days with her niece, Maureen Tweedy, daughter of her brother Howard Filmer Carrick and the enterprising Anna Todd, who had started her own fashion business.

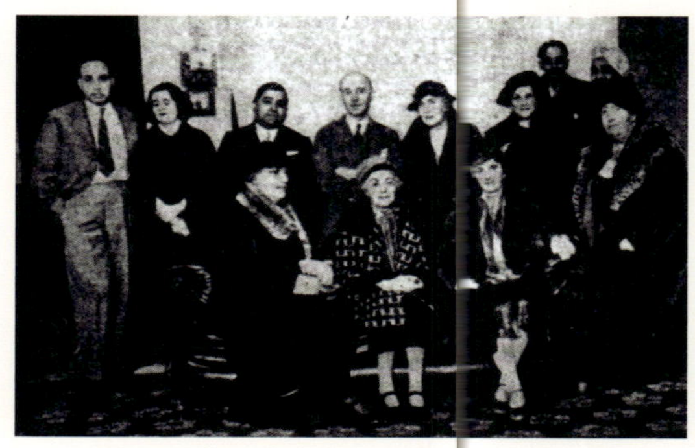

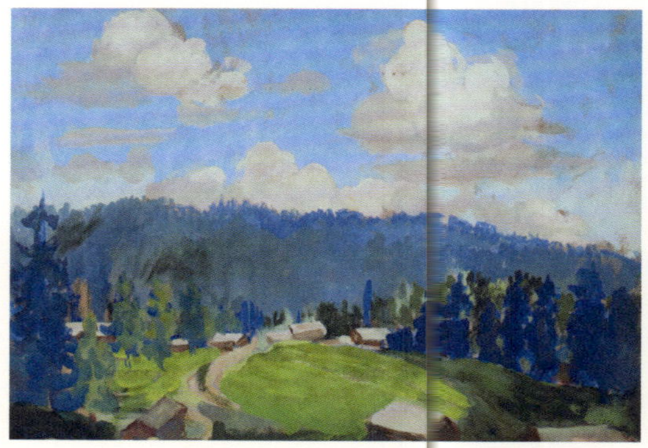

Top to bottom
fig 27 Unknown photographer, *The opening of Ethel Carrick's solo exhibition at the Punjab Literary League, Lahore*, 23 December 1936 (front row, seated, left to right) unknown woman, Mrs Phillips Fox (Ethel Carrick), Lady Boyd and Helen Mary Boulnois, *Civil & Military Gazette*, 25 December 1936

fig 28 *Kashmir, India* c 1939, gouache, private collection

Opposite, top to bottom
cat 74 *Early morning in Kashmir* 1935, gouache on paper, Newcastle Art Gallery

cat 75 *The wooden bridge* 1935, gouache on paper, Newcastle Art Gallery

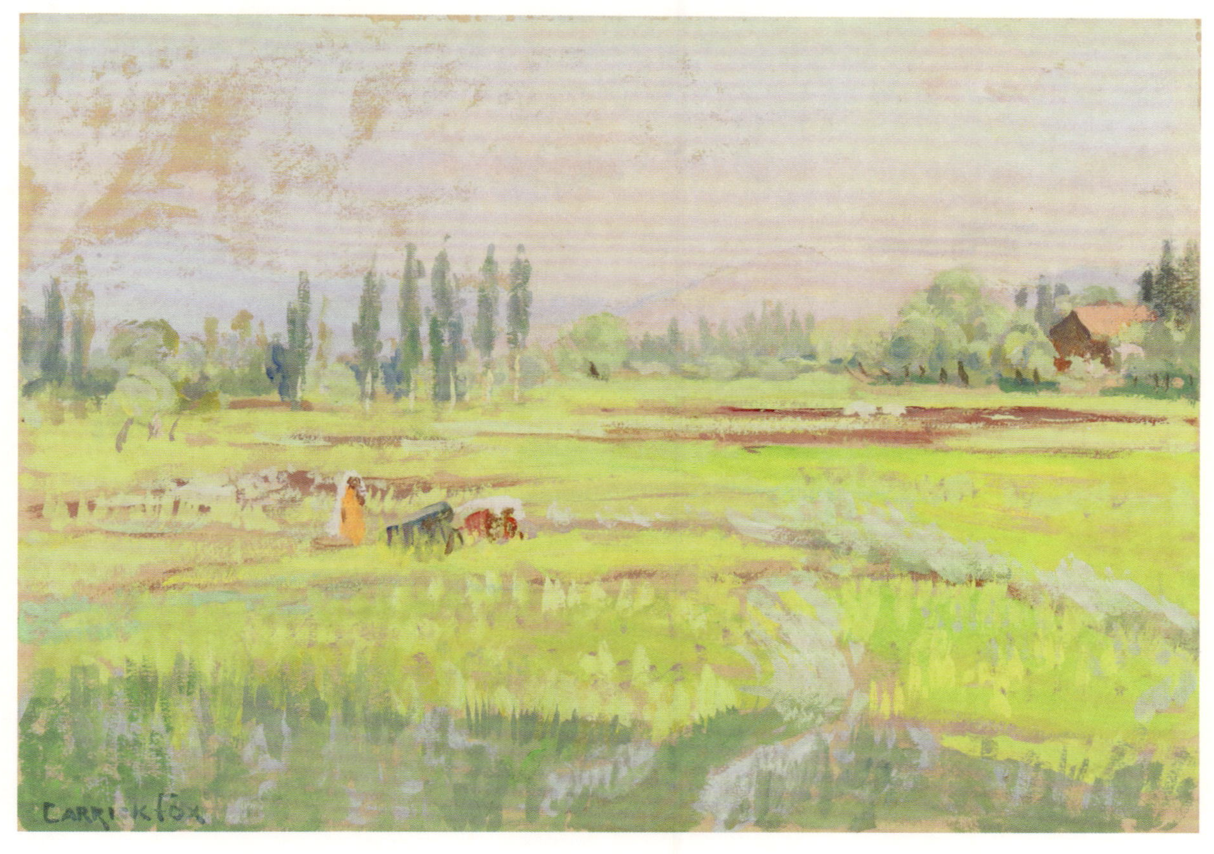
CARRICK FOX

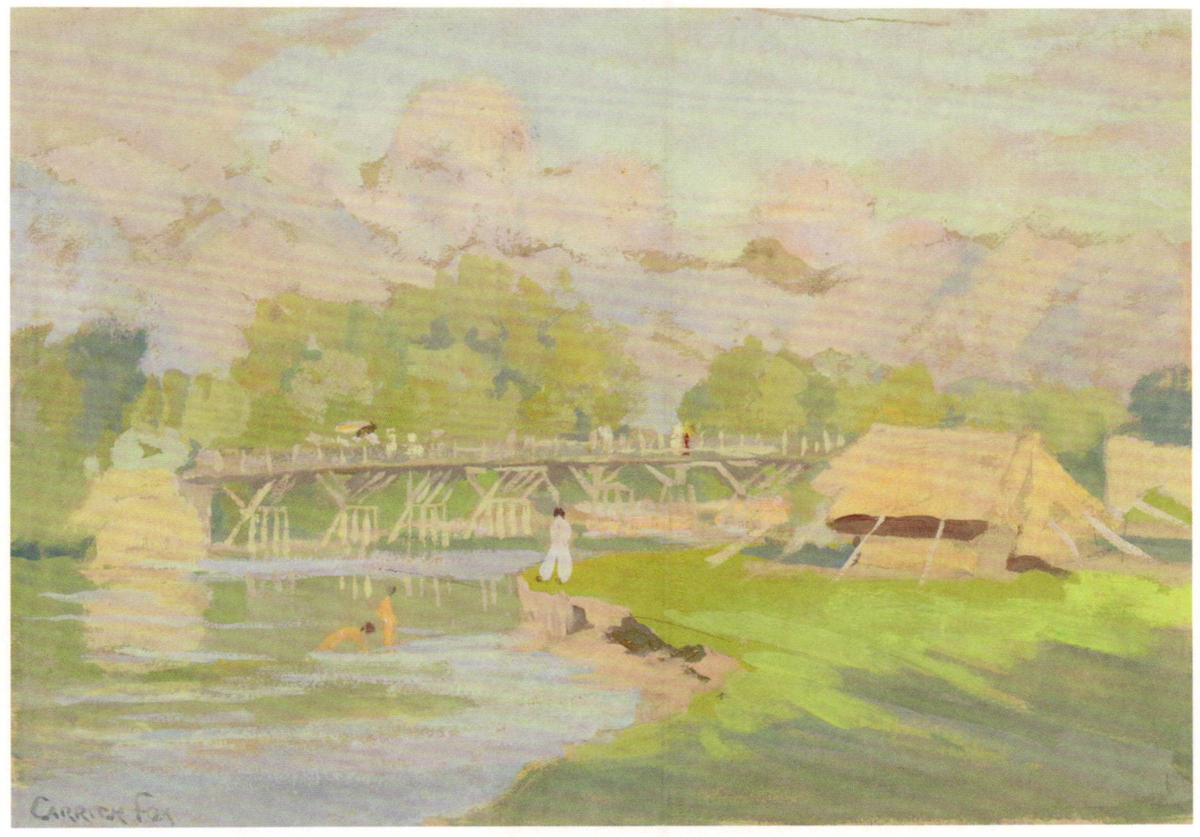
CARRICK FOX

At the time, Maureen was married to colonel Robert Milford Tweedy and, along with Carrick, they were friends of Hubert Evans, who was part of the Indian civil service and became a deputy commissioner.[201] Carrick's arresting, small painting *Deputy Commissioner's garden Agra, India* c 1935 (cat 76) conveys her avid appreciation of gardens. Painted in a post-impressionist manner, looking out from a veranda in shadow, the concentric circles of the pots are repeated in the circular garden beds, planted with vibrant red and purple blooms and bathed in light. Two figures in the distance amble through this contemplative space.

As a woman traveller, Carrick was resolute and her practicality was at times humorous. Tweedy, who as a schoolgirl in Paris had known Carrick, recalled meeting her 'eccentric aunt' at Delhi station. Tweedy was 'startled to see her descend from the train wearing an old-fashioned topee on her white hair and carrying a sweeper's basket: '"Aunt Ethel," we chorused, "what are you doing with a sweeper's basket?" "Carrying my chamber-pot of course. It goes with me everywhere".' Tweedy also remembered Carrick's resourceful nature:

> Well over sixty, and a widow, she made up in enterprise what she lacked in money. When this useful commodity ran out she used her skill as an artist and suggested to the railway company she did a series of posters for them, to which they agreed. On the proceeds she managed to get to Kashmir, the hard way certainly, but she got there. She travelled by the ordinary country buses somehow managing always to have a seat by the driver.[202]

Reflecting on her time in India, Carrick told a reporter she had 'travelled hundreds of miles by bullock wagon and pony to reach rare scenery.' Twice she took part in holy pilgrimages, one entailing a twenty-mile trek across rocky ground to a deep Himalayan cave, 'which housed a giant block of ice that changed form mysteriously'.[203] It is remarkable that Carrick, in her sixties, would have taken part in the annual pilgrimage known as Amarnath Yatra, a month-long trek to the Amarnath Temple in a cave in the Himalayas, where the ice known as Shiva linga (or Ice Lingam of Lord Shiva) changes shape.[204] Carrick recalled that there she met 'the spiritual head of the Tibetan Buddhists' who, at the time, was 'a man viewed only by a handful of Europeans'.[205] These memories suggest Carrick's commitment to seeking, through spirituality, a deeper understanding of the world and herself.

In June 1939, prior to the outbreak of World War II, Carrick spent time living on a houseboat in Kashmir, an experience she found idyllic and inspiring, 'a paradise for painters'.[206] In interviews upon her return to Melbourne, Carrick remarked that she was assisted by local Indian people in moving to different locations along the river, enabling her to combine work with pleasure and to capture 'India's beauty on canvas' over several months.[207] In the course of her visits in the 1930s, she painted on the Jhelum River in Srinagar. In a key example of these works, *Le bac, Kashmir* (The ferry, Kashmir) 1937 (cat 77, pp 118–19), she depicts groups variously embarking onto a boat and floating down the river. As always, close observation informs the painting, with a variety of buildings providing distinct reference points along the journey. The atmosphere is informed by the lapping water, brilliantly conveyed through brisk brushstrokes. The figures are also evocatively depicted, their colours and shapes adding to a sense of unity. It is a painting about contemplation and states of being, reflecting a sense of the spiritual dimension of her experiences in India.

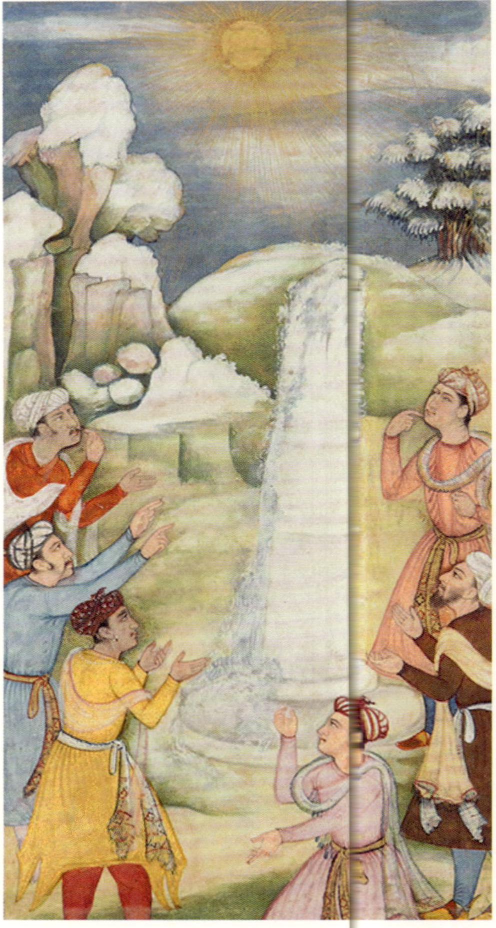

fig 29 *Mughal men admiring the miraculous ice lingam at Amarnath* c 1600, opaque watercolour and gold on paper, Aga Khan Museum

Opposite
cat 76 *Deputy Commissioner's garden Agra, India* c 1935, oil on canvas, Art Gallery of South Australia

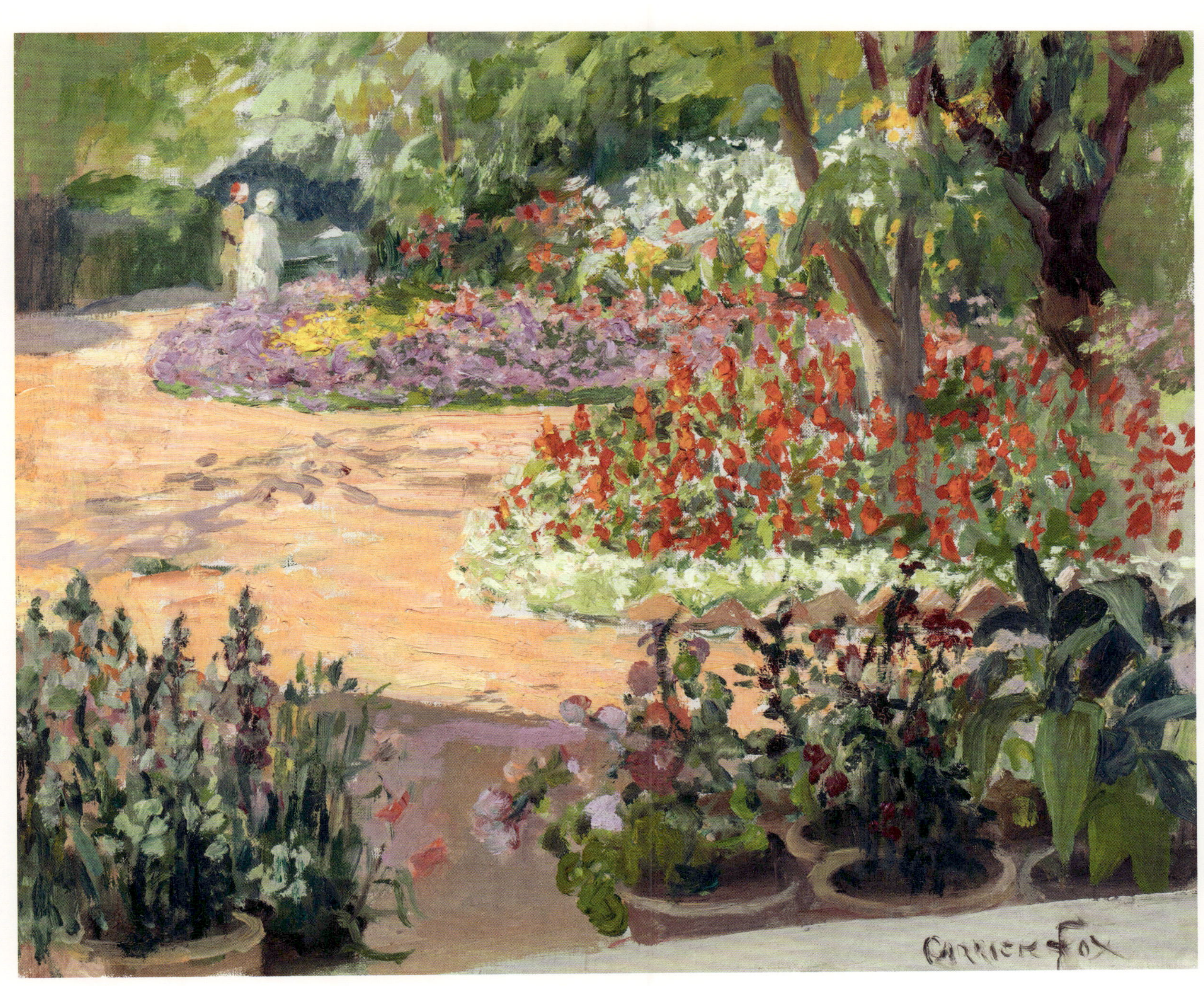
CARRICK FOX

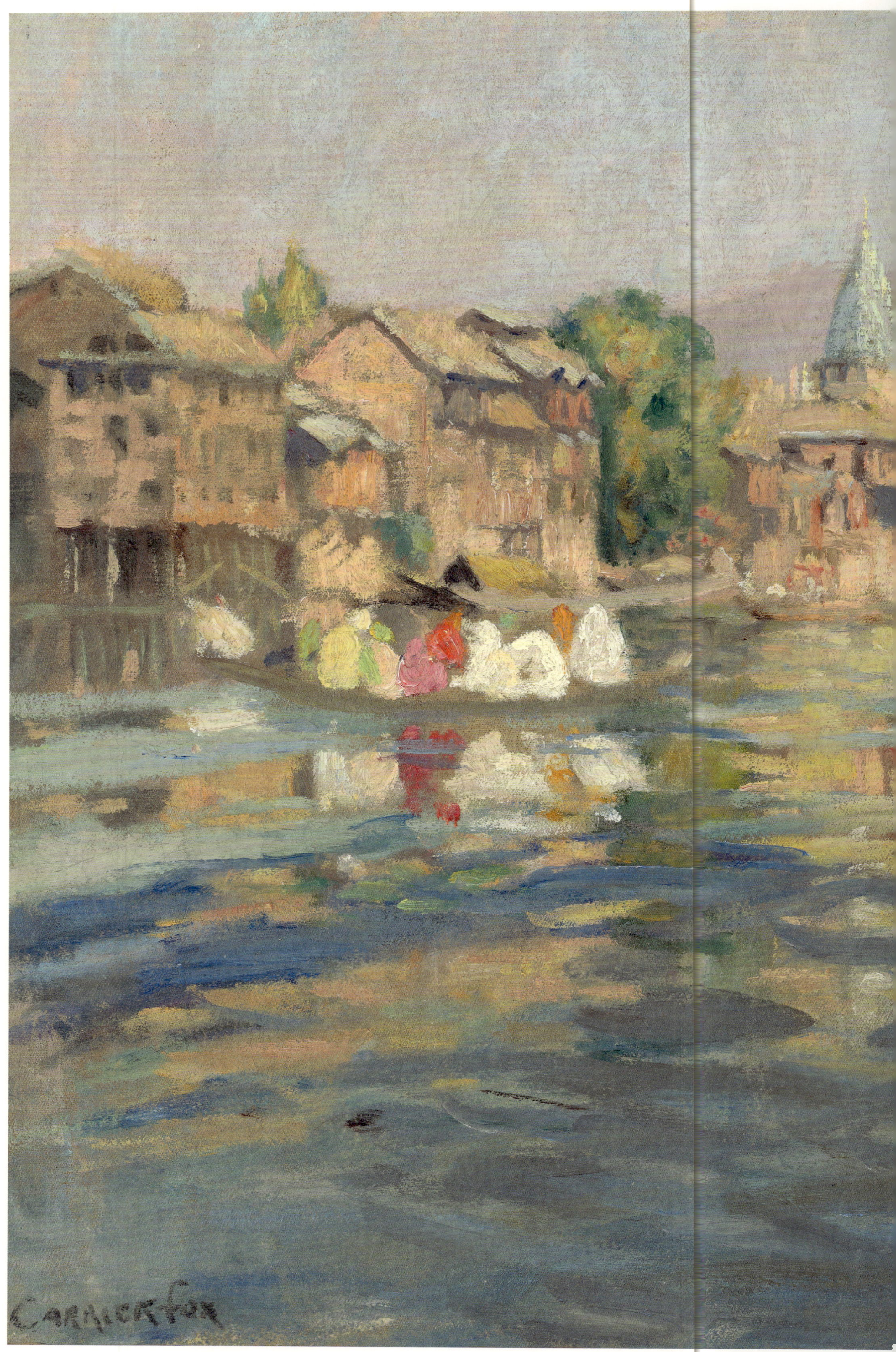

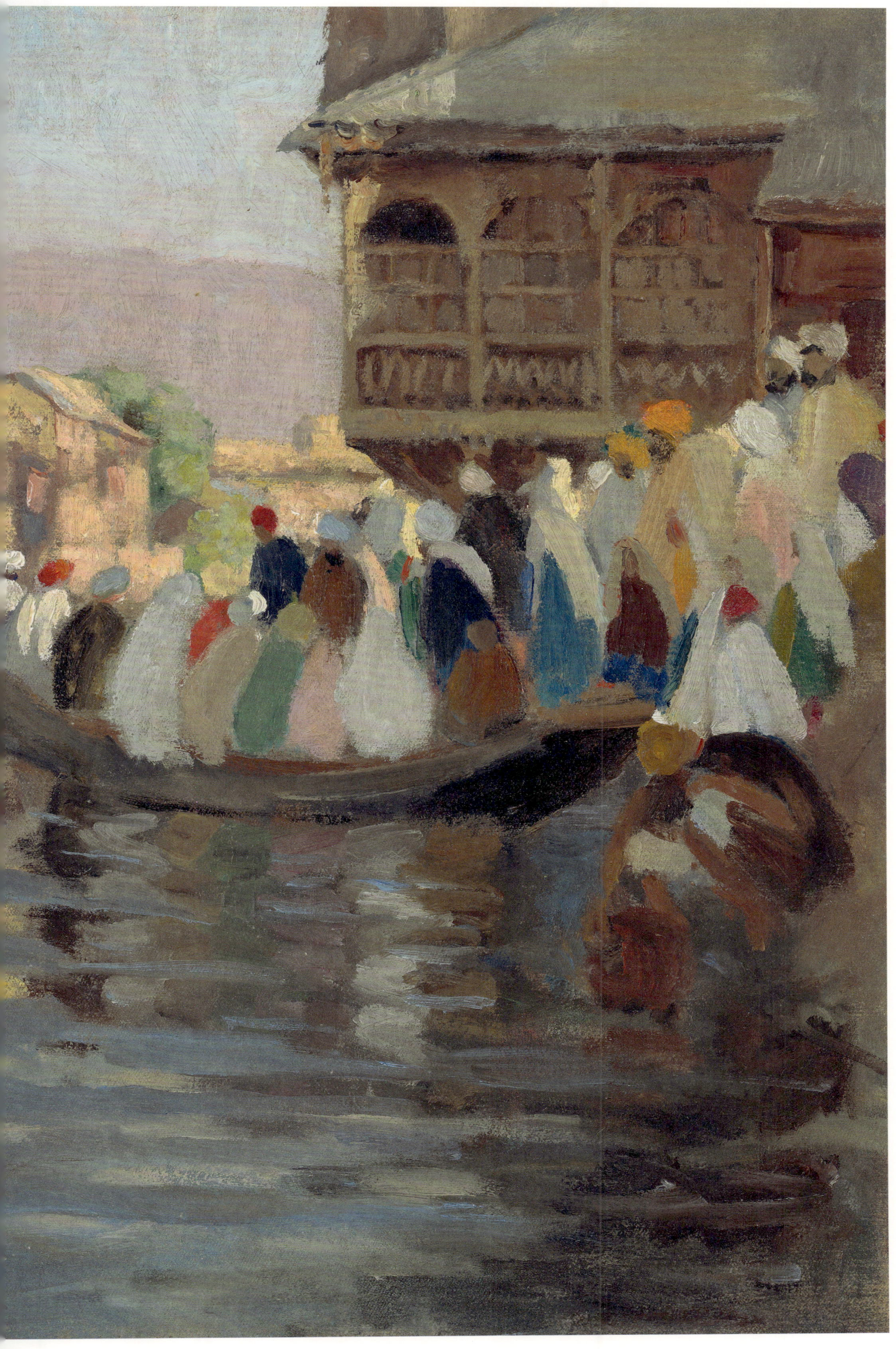

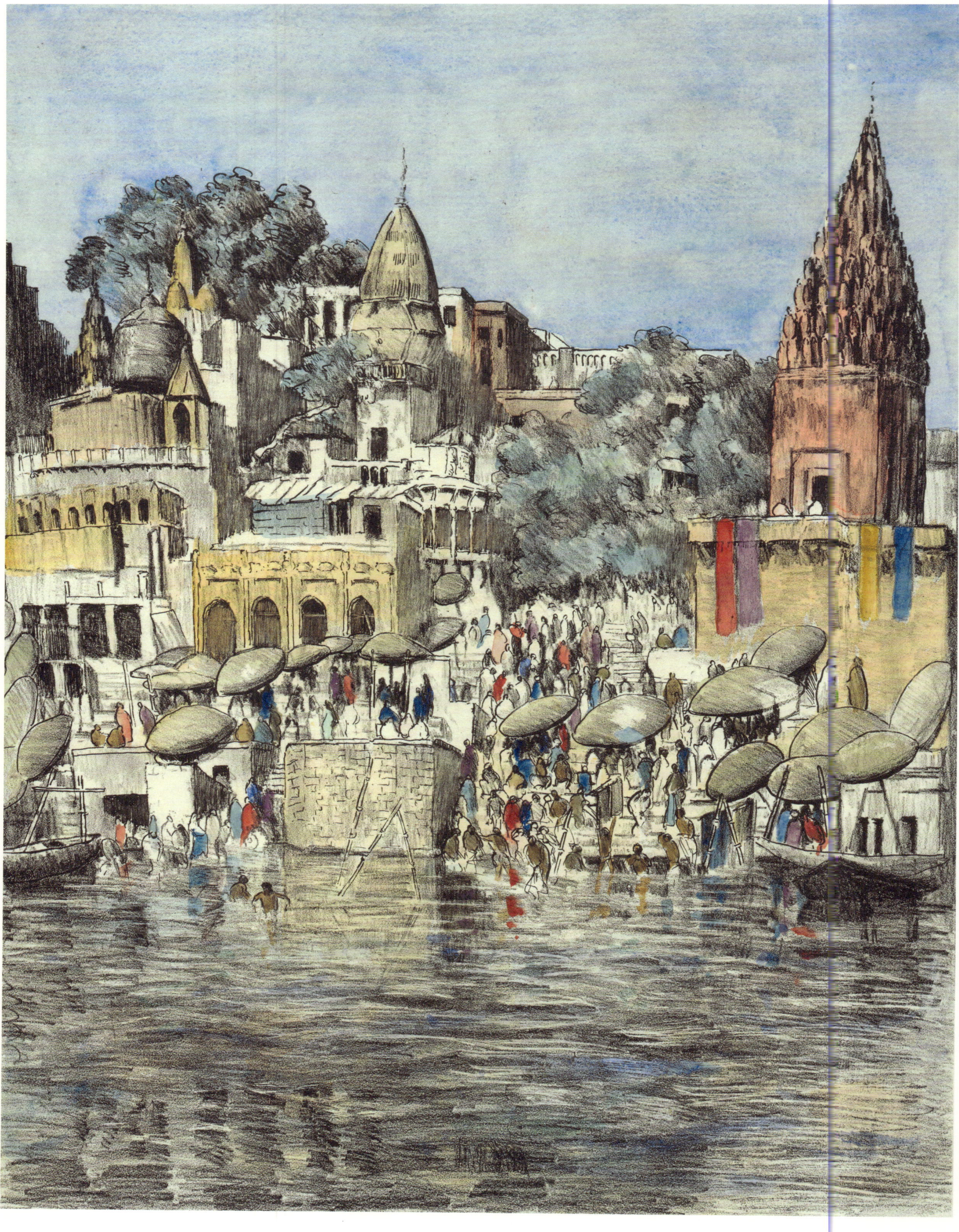

Previous
cat 77 *Le bac, Kashmir* (The ferry, Kashmir) 1937, also known as *Paysage d'Inde-le-bac* (Landscape at Inde-le-bac), oil on canvas, University Art Collection, Chau Chak Wing Museum, The University of Sydney

Opposite
cat 78 *Pilgrims bathing at Benares* c 1937, lithograph printed in black ink from one stone, hand-coloured in watercolour, National Gallery of Australia

Back in Europe the tide was turning, and Carrick's peace of mind would again be disrupted by war. In 1939 in France, where she was intending to return, there was disquiet—the Nazi approach was imminent. Meanwhile, in the artworld, a scenario was unfolding in Paris. Observing the rules of the blackout to avoid detection by the Germans, a convoy of lorries travelled without headlights through the dead of night, carrying precious cargo away from the Louvre, which was under threat of looting and destruction. Nearly all of the Louvre's significant sculptures were transported to a castle in the quiet countryside southeast of the Loire Valley, for the benefit of future generations. This was one of the reasons Carrick loved and supported France—there, culture mattered; of that, the French were in no doubt.

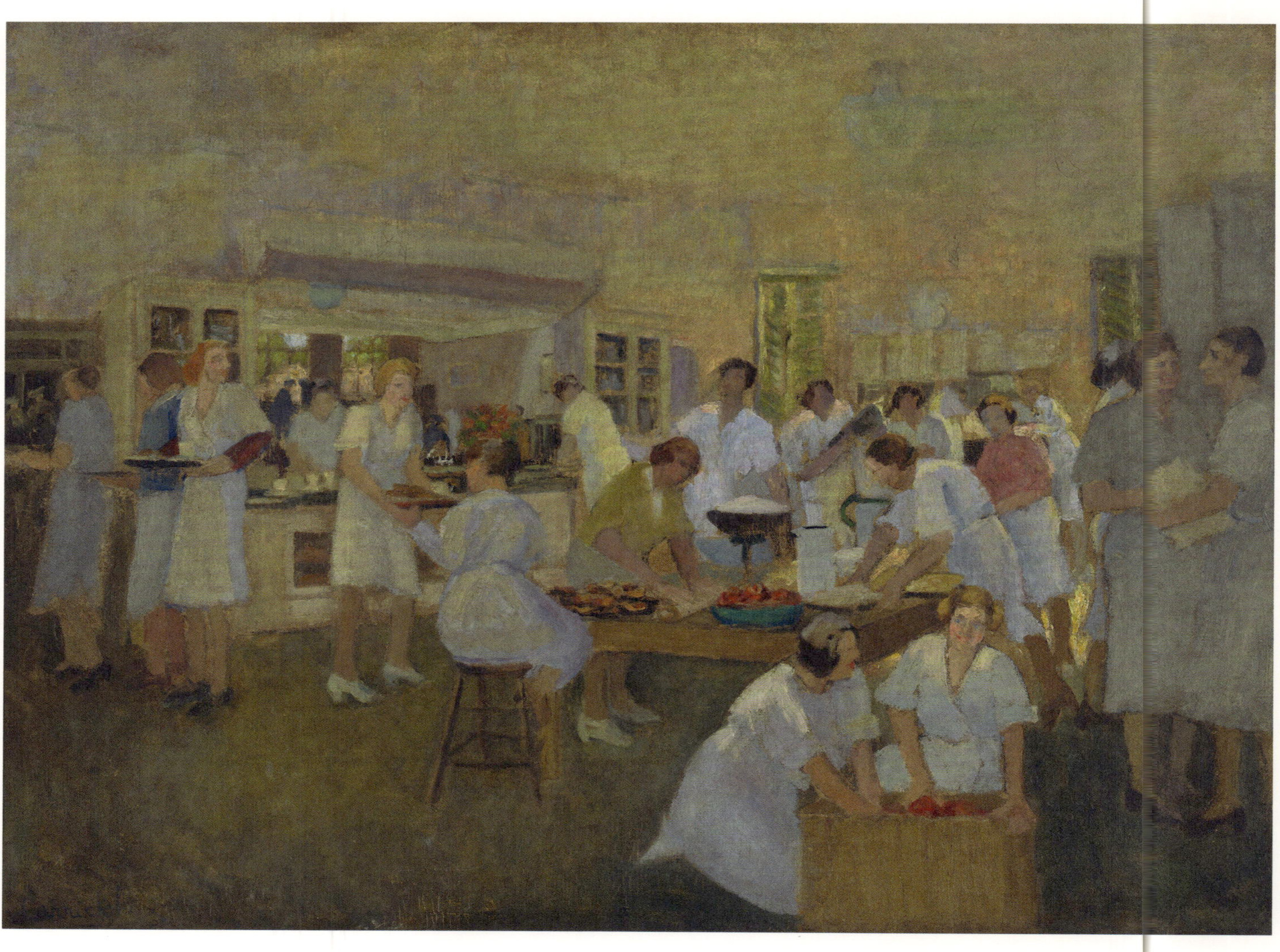

A continuing circle: 1939–1952

Never forget that life can only be nobly inspired and rightly lived if you take it bravely ... as a splendid adventure in which you are setting out into an unknown country, to meet many a joy, to find many a comrade, to win and lose many a battle.[208]

— **Annie Besant**

A report in *The Argus* on 23 October 1939 announced, 'One of the most interesting passengers to reach Melbourne from overseas yesterday was Mrs E Phillips Fox (Ethel Carrick).'[209] Carrick had intended to return to Paris after her travels in India. Instead, the outbreak of war in Europe meant that she chose to travel to Australia instead, arriving in Melbourne from Bombay (Mumbai). The rise of Nazism and the dramatic events of 10 May 1940, when the Germans attacked France, was of deep concern to Carrick. News had reached her with speed. On 19 June 1940 she wrote,

> Dear Fellow Artist,
>
> It is proposed to hold an exhibition of pictures as soon as possible, the proceeds to be given to the French Refugee Relief Fund, as a small thank[s] offering to tortured France, for all that French Art has given to us ... Will you help by giving AT LEAST one of your BEST pictures ... A number will be drawn by some responsible person, probably the French Consul. A general meeting will be held at the Victorian Artists' Society's room ... where the pictures may be sent.[210]

Around the same time that Carrick wrote her letter, thousands of refugees were fleeing Paris. Against the advice of the British, the government itself fled south on 10 June 1940—Marshal Philippe Pétain, facing the extent of the military assault on Paris, did not want a city of ruins. By 14 June it was declared an 'open city' and the German occupation began; it is still startling to see photographs of troops on tanks rolling through Paris. Given Emanuel Phillips Fox's Jewish background, it must have been spine-chilling for Carrick to learn of the extensive rounding up of Jewish people, including children, many of whom were sent to the concentration camps. Daily life for civilians in a

Opposite
cat 79 *The kitchen, Canberra Services Club* 1943, also known as *The canteen workers*, oil on canvas, collection of Rob and Jenny Ferguson

place that had encompassed difference and creativity was now under constant threat. Under Pétain, the French government retreated to Vichy. During this period, the French were quite literally on German time.

On the other side of the world, Carrick worked tirelessly. Her engagement echoed her efforts in World War I. On 16 July it was reported in *The Age* that the exhibition at the Athenaeum Gallery she had organised—with paintings donated by artists such as Arthur Streeton, Max Meldrum, AD Colquhoun, Amalie Colquhoun, Rupert Bunny, AME Bale and James Quinn—was a success.[211] Just after Christmas in 1940, Carrick wrote from Sydney to artist Sybil Craig in Melbourne: 'This is to wish you all a very Happy New Year. May it bring Peace before its close.'[212] Sadly, the war would drag on for years. Carrick was keen to support General de Gaulle's Free French Forces in London, set up in opposition to Pétain with the aim of defeating the German occupation of France.[213]

At the time, Carrick was living at The Manor, the theosophical residence in Mosman, and undertaking paintings of Sydney Harbour. She wrote, 'I miss the friendly meetings at no 5 but adore the beauty and quiet around me here.'[214] In September 1941, she wrote again to Craig: 'Tomorrow I go north for two months, where I hope to get some painting [done], if I haven't forgotten how to hold a brush.'[215] For the next three months she travelled across Queensland—Brisbane, the Glass House Mountains, Toowoomba and the Darling Downs, Coolangatta—then Tweed Heads in northern New South Wales. On 17 December Carrick stayed with Mrs Joubert (a theosophical connection) at her farm in Terranora. This picturesque location at the northern boundary of New South Wales was the subject of several paintings, all undertaken in 1941: *View from Joubert's farm*, *Towards the sea*, *Terranora and silver light* and *Terranora Lake*. The atmosphere of place is also captured in depictions of the Tweed Heads area (for instance, *From Kirra, North Coast* c 1941—cat 80), the delicately applied paint conveying lush, tropical vegetation with misty mountains in the distance. Carrick also painted the crystalline white sands at Coolangatta (cat 81) in such close-up as to make you feel like you could walk onto the beach alongside the wooden fenceposts and look out around the headland into the far distance.

Modest in scale, these painterly impressions were shown at the Athenaeum Gallery, alongside works by Fox, from late April until mid-May 1942. In the exhibition, Carrick's views of Queensland were in the company of her paintings undertaken in India, including of Nanga Parbat in the western Himalayas, one of the highest mountain ranges in the world. Considering Carrick's intrepid travel and spirit of independence, it must have been galling to read her experience referred to in *Queensland Country Life* as a 'housewife's paradise'.[216]

Carrick made three visits to Canberra in the early 1940s, with most of her works from the area undertaken in 1942 and 1943. In late October 1942, *The Canberra Times* reported that she had been staying in Canberra for the past few weeks as the guest of Patricia Tillyard of Red Hill. She was 'delighted with the spring beauty of Canberra and during her stay painted several pictures with plum trees as the main theme'.[217] Carrick stayed on two occasions with Tillyard, who had received an education in natural sciences at Newnham College, Cambridge and Trinity College, Dublin. She also served on the University of Canberra College Council (1942–45) prior to the establishment of the Australian National University.[218] Carrick and Tillyard, two outspoken women committed to helping others, had much in common.[219]

Opposite, top to bottom
cat 80 *From Kirra, North Coast* c 1941, oil on paper, HOTA Gallery Collection

cat 81 *Rainbow Bay, Coolangatta* c 1941, oil on canvas, collection of Jim Haynes OAM and Robyn McMillan

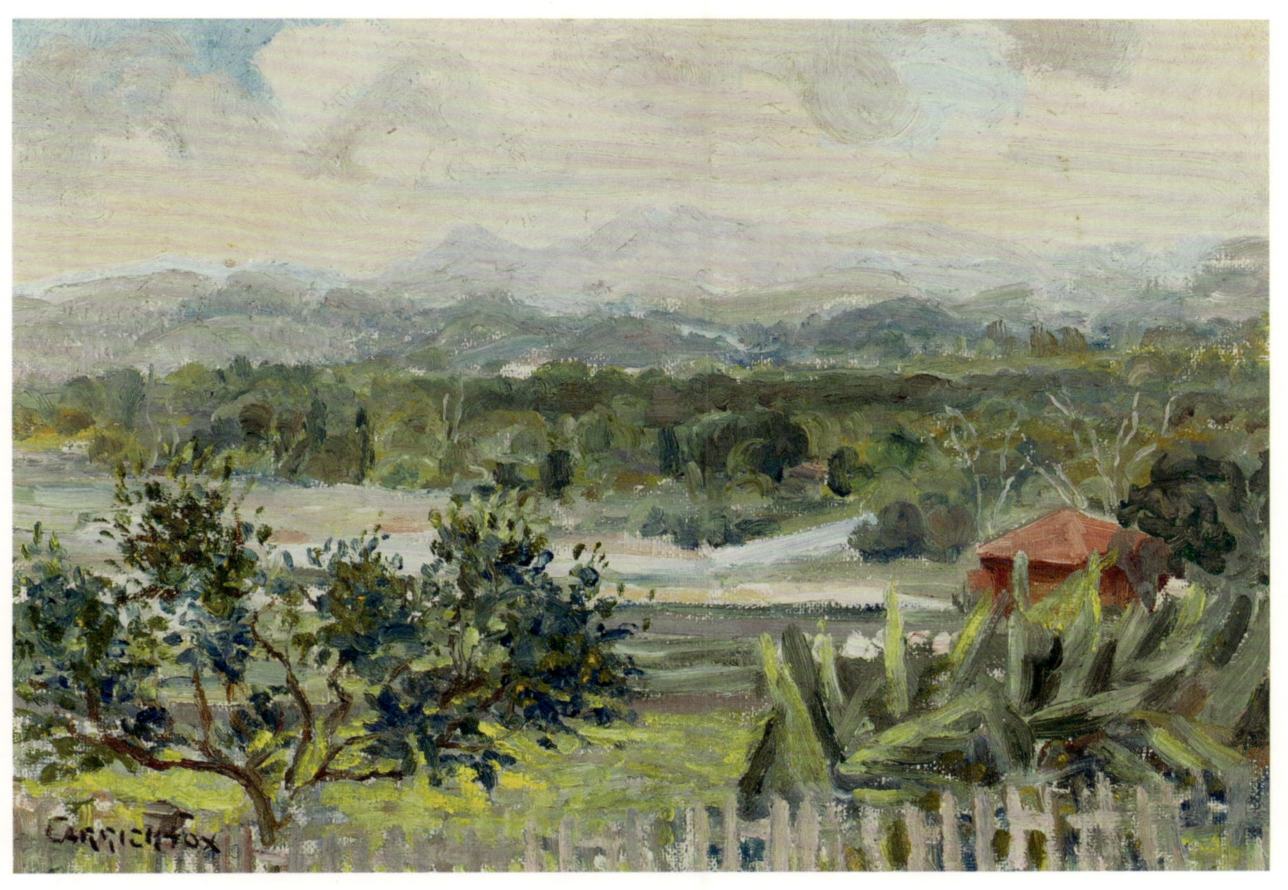
CARRICK FOX

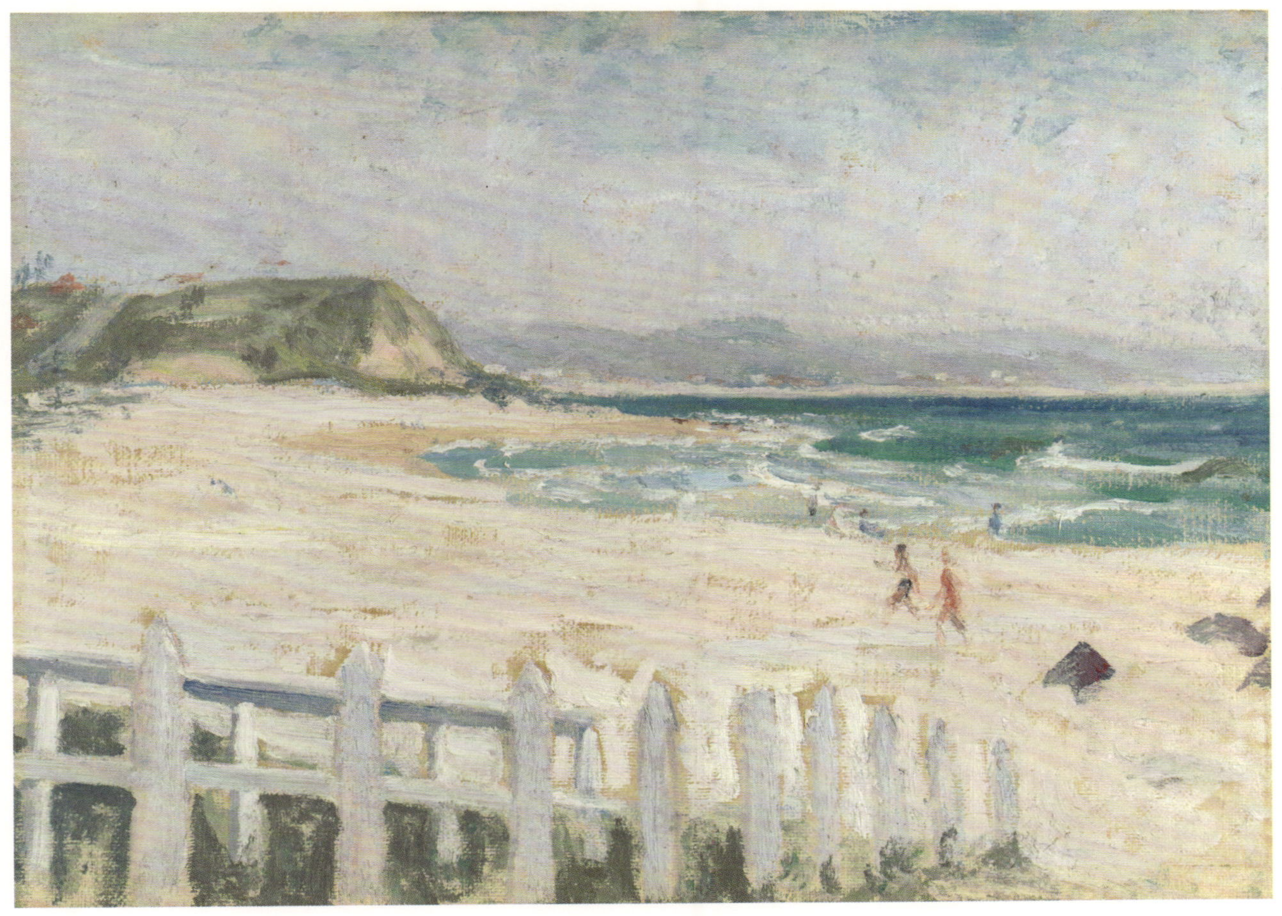

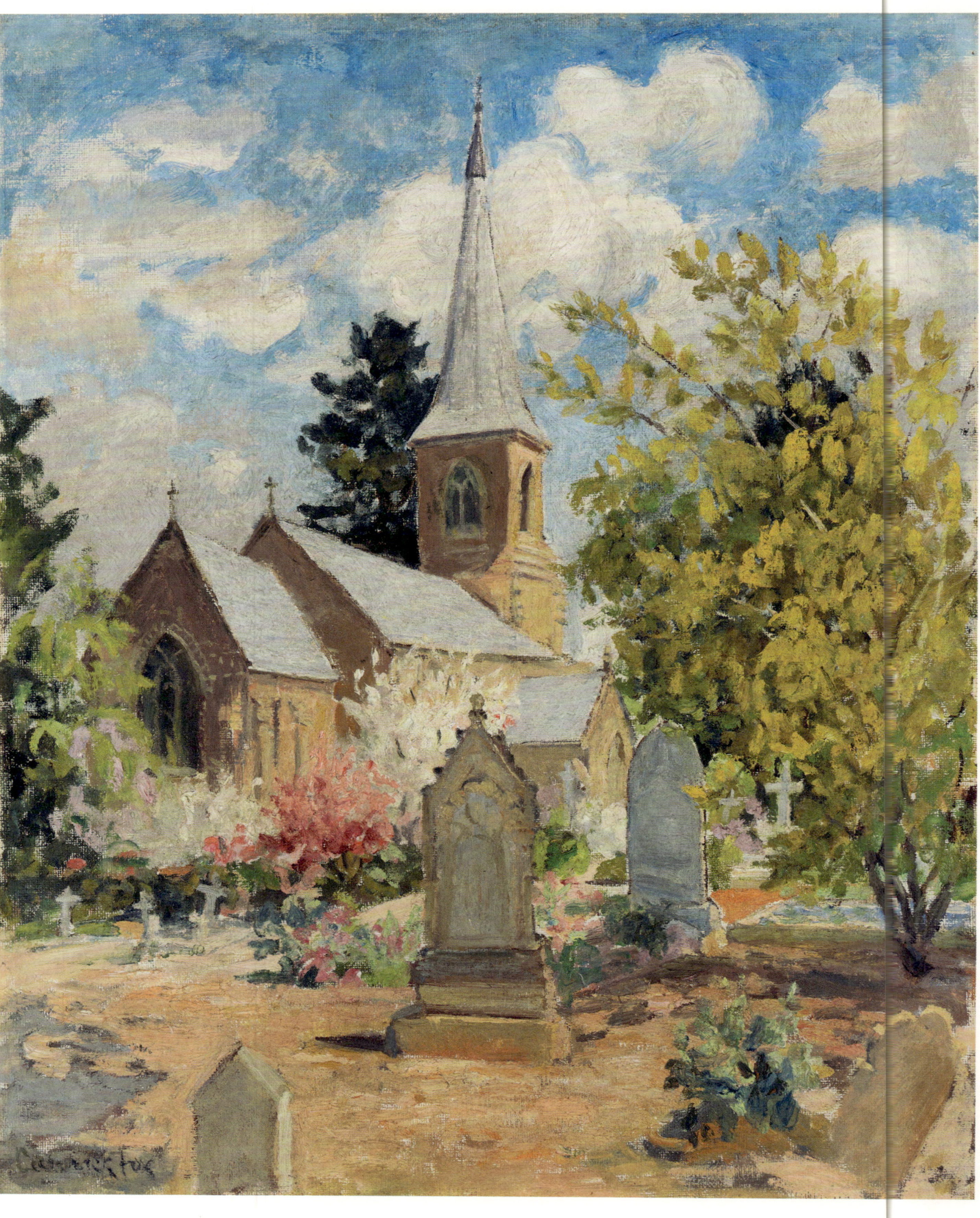

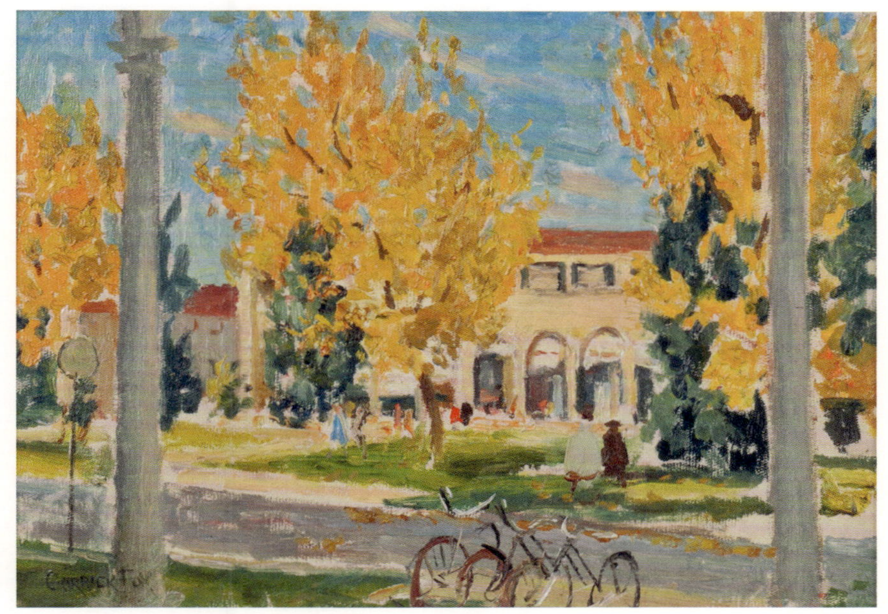

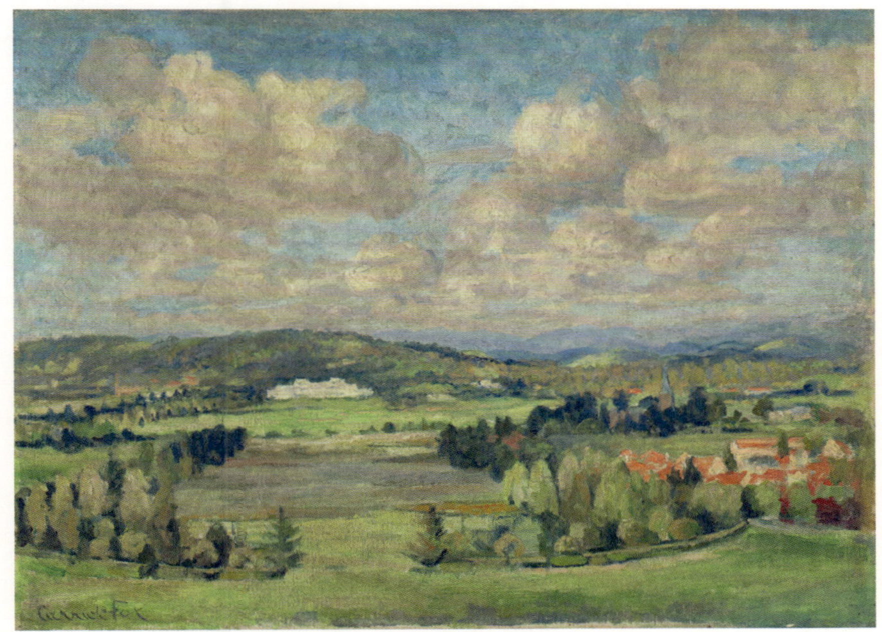

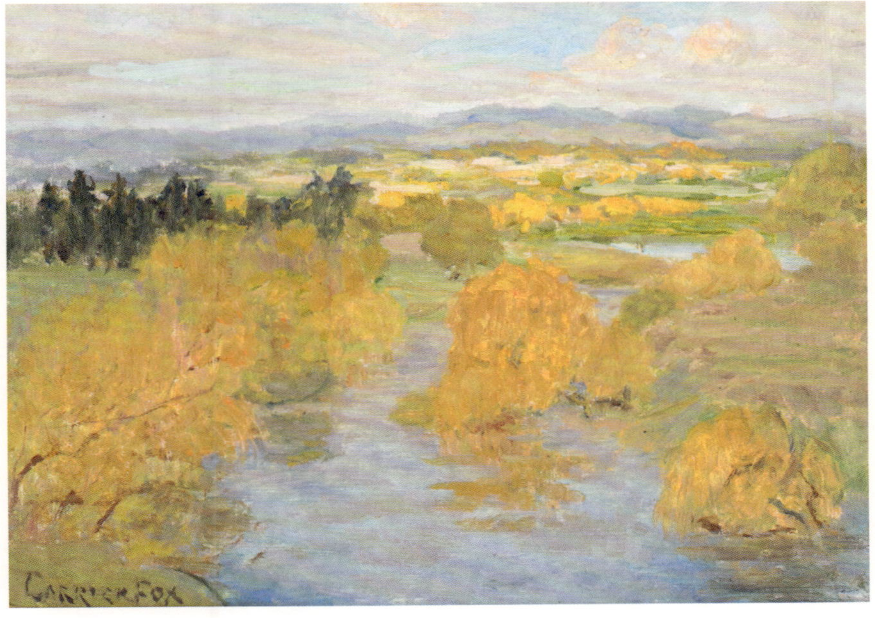

Opposite
cat 82 *St John's Church, Canberra* 1942, oil on canvas, Canberra Museum & Gallery

Top to bottom
cat 83 *Colonnades of Canberra's civic centre* 1943, oil on canvas on board, Canberra Museum & Gallery

cat 84 *Canberra* c 1944, oil on canvas, National Library of Australia

cat 85 *Molonglo* c 1943, oil on board, University Art Collection, Chau Chak Wing Museum, The University of Sydney

Carrick painted a number of Canberra's landmarks, a notable example being *St John's Church, Canberra* c 1942 (cat 82, p 126), undertaken during her initial visit, given the spring blossom. Robin Tillyard, Patricia's husband, was buried at St John's Church in Reid, which predates the establishment of Canberra as a city by more than 70 years. Consecrated in 1845, it was modelled on the classic English village church, relating back to Carrick's early interest in ecclesiastical architecture. In the painting, the spire is set against the scudding clouds of a blue-sky day; the lightness of the blossoms set alongside well-established headstones and newer crosses suggests cycles of life and death—of lives long gone as well as young soldiers gone too soon.[220]

Another landmark subject for Carrick was Parliament House. Her painting *Canberra* c 1944 (cat 84, p 127) emphasises the way the national parliament is located within the natural environment—big skies, low and rolling Brindabella mountains, paddocks and formal plantings. The shimmer of white architecture against the hills suggests a utopian construct in the garden city designed by Walter Burley Griffin and Marion Mahony (both theosophists for a time). The idea of Canberra as the capital of Australia meshed with theosophical thinking, where it was hoped that state tensions would be overcome in a meeting place for all, as expounded in the theosophical journal *Advance Australia*.[221]

On Carrick's second visit to Canberra in late April 1943, she painted *Colonnades of Canberra's civic centre* 1943 (cat 83, p 127) in front of the Sydney and Melbourne Buildings: 'The yellow poplars and bicycles in the foreground are typical of the city, while her dappled brushwork captures a cool breeze and the many colours of a sunny autumn day in the nation's capital.'[222] On 22 May 1943, Carrick wrote to Sybil Craig from Patricia Tillyard's home: '[I've] been very busy, trying to get my work done. Canberra's chief snag is its weather, very changeable, & extremely windy & cold & wet to top up with!'[223] It was noted at the time that 'before she leaves, Mrs Fox hopes to obtain a picture of canteen workers in the kitchen of the Services Club'.[224]

Some of Carrick's most interesting paintings of this period depict women undertaking voluntary work as part of the war effort, such as *The kitchen, Canberra Services Club* 1943 (cat 79, p 122), representing a shifting focus from plein air works to collectives working indoors. Tillyard's close friend Lady Gowrie, wife of the Governor General at the time, was instrumental in establishing the Canberra Services Club in Manuka.[225] The purpose of the club, which opened in 1941, was to provide a place where service personnel could relax, enjoy meals and social functions, and access reading facilities.[226] Carrick's painting shows a radiant light spilling in soft yellows and pinks onto the uniforms of the canteen workers, some of which stand out in crisp shades of white. The workers themselves are absorbed in an array of routine tasks: unpacking produce, preparing food and carrying trays. Two women conversing amicably to the side provide an anchor point, while the shutters opening onto leafy greenery convey airiness. There is a tender affection in this alluring work of women playing their part in the war effort, with Carrick herself contributing by bringing this much appreciated experience to light.

The Tillyard modernist residence in Red Hill, 'The Spinney', was designed by architect Heather Sutherland, who drew up the plans as part of her work for Malcolm Moir in 1936.[227] Given Carrick's interest in still life at this time, the remarkable garden there would have been an inspiration. Pattie Wardle (née Tillyard) wrote, 'In the virgin soil the roses

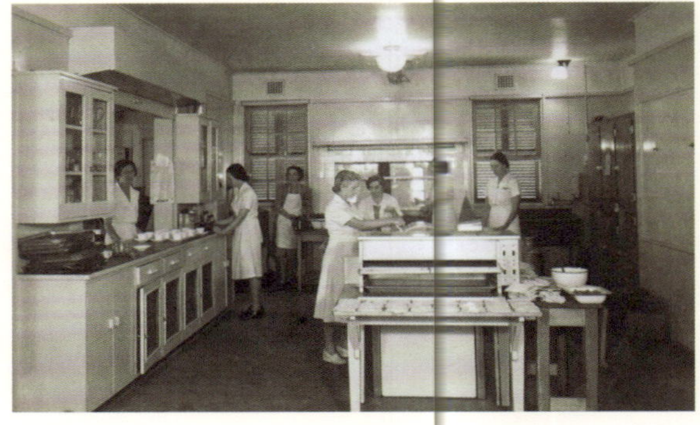

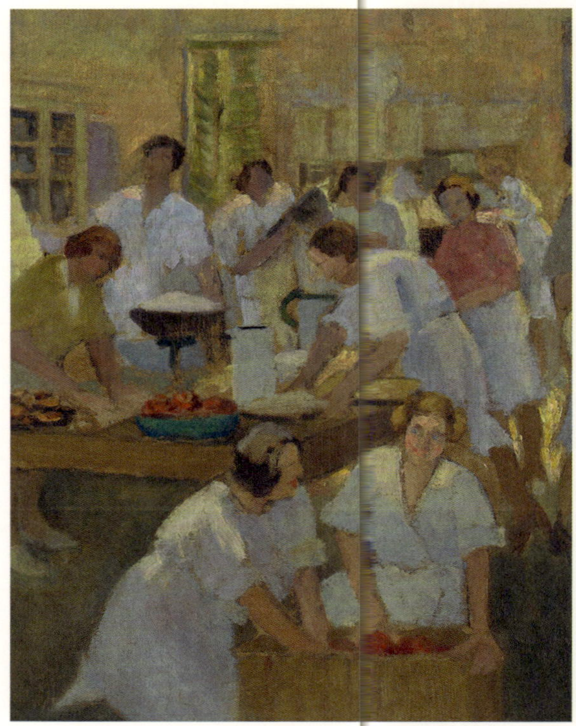

Top to bottom
fig 30 RC Strangman, *Seven women working in the Lady Gowrie Services Club kitchen, Manuka, Canberra*, c 1941, RC Strangman collection of photographic views of Canberra, 1930–60, National Library of Australia

The kitchen, Canberra Services Club 1943 (detail cat 79, p 122), also known as *The canteen workers*, oil on canvas, collection of Rob and Jenny Ferguson

Opposite
fig 31 Sybil Craig, *Women workers in the Paper Room (Fuse Section, Commonwealth explosives factory, Maribyrnong)* 1945, oil on canvas on board, Australian War Memorial

seemed to like, a Marion Manifold ran up the front wall of the house, and a row of hybrid tea roses—Ophelia ... Texas Centennial, President Hoover, Madame Dupont—was planted in the long bed between the driveway and the front lawn.'[228] Depending on the season, there were 'Shirley poppies' and 'all manner of flowering bulbs and a brick-paved area and plinth with a birdbath outside the living room's French doors and a bed planted with geraniums ... and there were lady Gowrie's fine flag irises given to Mother by that most loved Governor-General's wife ... during the war'.[229] It was from this garden that Carrick gathered fresh herbs and lavender for opportunity shops, raising funds for the war.

In 1944, Carrick returned to Canberra to set up an exhibition at the Masonic Temple. She was in communication with the Australian War Memorial and keen to show her work, aiming to do so during a parliamentary sitting time.[230] In the end, the situation was not ideal. Without a proper venue and in the absence of a hanging system, Carrick's 62 paintings were shown balanced on chairs! How bizarre, to consider her works 'taking a seat' for a mere couple of days in an exhibition opened by Baroness van Aerssen Beyeren, wife of the Minister of the Netherlands, and viewed by luminaries of the city.[231] It was noted at the opening that proceeds of the exhibition were donated to the Australian Red Cross and Services Welfare Association.

Carrick's commitment to the war effort was conveyed in a story in *The Age* in 1944, which commended the 'interesting series of voluntary women war workers, in which Mrs Fox has painted as a tribute to the splendid work being done by women who do not wear service uniforms'.[232] Coming in for special mention was Carrick's *Papier mâché, Red Cross Auxiliary in Sydney* c 1944 (cat 126, pp 222–23) in which she reveals one of the lesser-known activities of the war effort: using papier mâché as a substitute to replace equipment and utensils that were increasingly difficult to obtain.

Carrick, like many of her friends, continued to raise funds in the aftermath of the war, setting aside divisions in the artworld for the greater good. A case in point was the *French Comfort Fund exhibition* in 1946 at David Jones' Art Gallery in Sydney and Myer Art Gallery in Melbourne. With Carrick as Honorary Organiser, fellow members on the executive committee included her good friend Frankie Payne, also known as Mrs Clinton (Industrial Art Society); Erik Langker (President, Royal Art Society); Lloyd Rees (Society of Artists); Jerrold Nathan (President, Australian Art Society) and Peter Bellew (President, Contemporary Art Society). The democratic nature of this grouping is clear, with representatives of the traditional and contemporary coming together for a good cause.

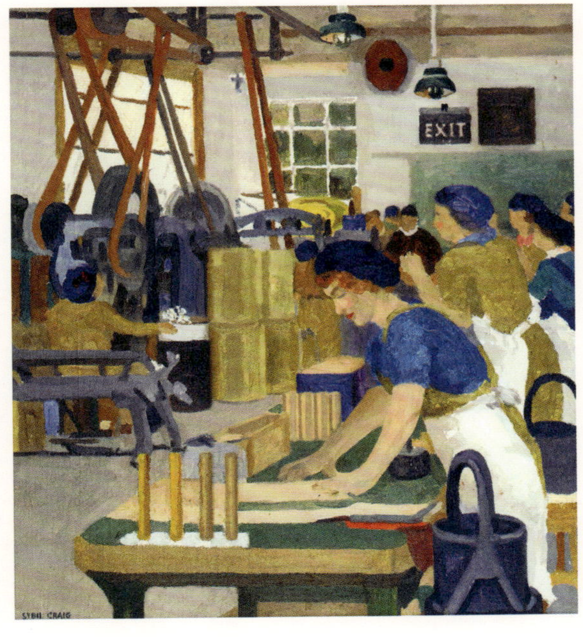

Alongside her efforts supporting the war, Carrick continued to paint, and in November 1944 she showed work alongside Sybil Craig and Jean Sutherland at Kozminsky Galleries in Melbourne. A review in *The Herald* remarked that the three exhibitors each contributed 'her own distinctive style',[233] while another in the *The Age* noted: 'Mrs Fox's contribution consists of landscapes from a number of countries ... France, Italy, Austria, North Africa and India have all been drawn on, and have yielded very pleasing subject matter. Mrs Fox is gifted with a full, yet subtle, color sense, and an eye for the picturesque.'[234] During this period, Carrick worked in studios on Pitt Street in Sydney and Bourke Street in Melbourne.

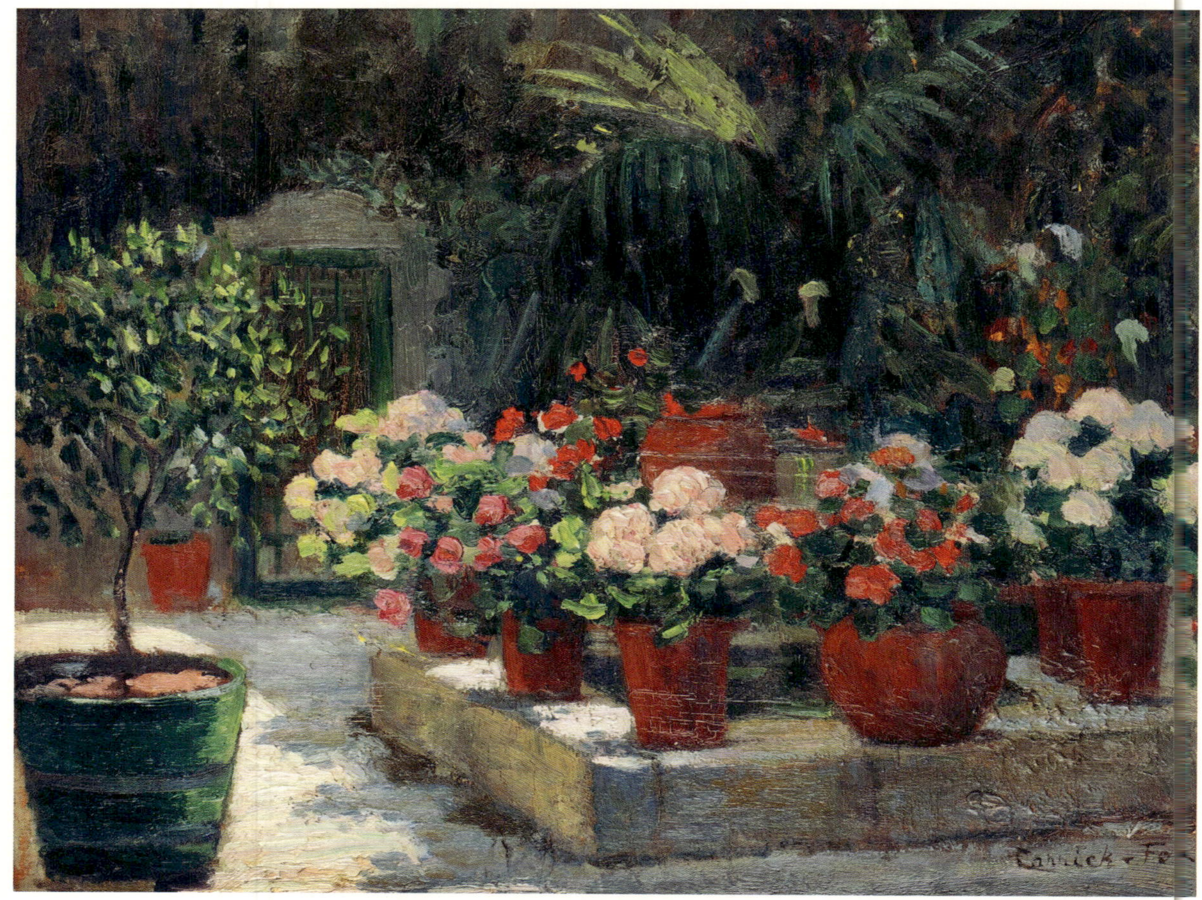

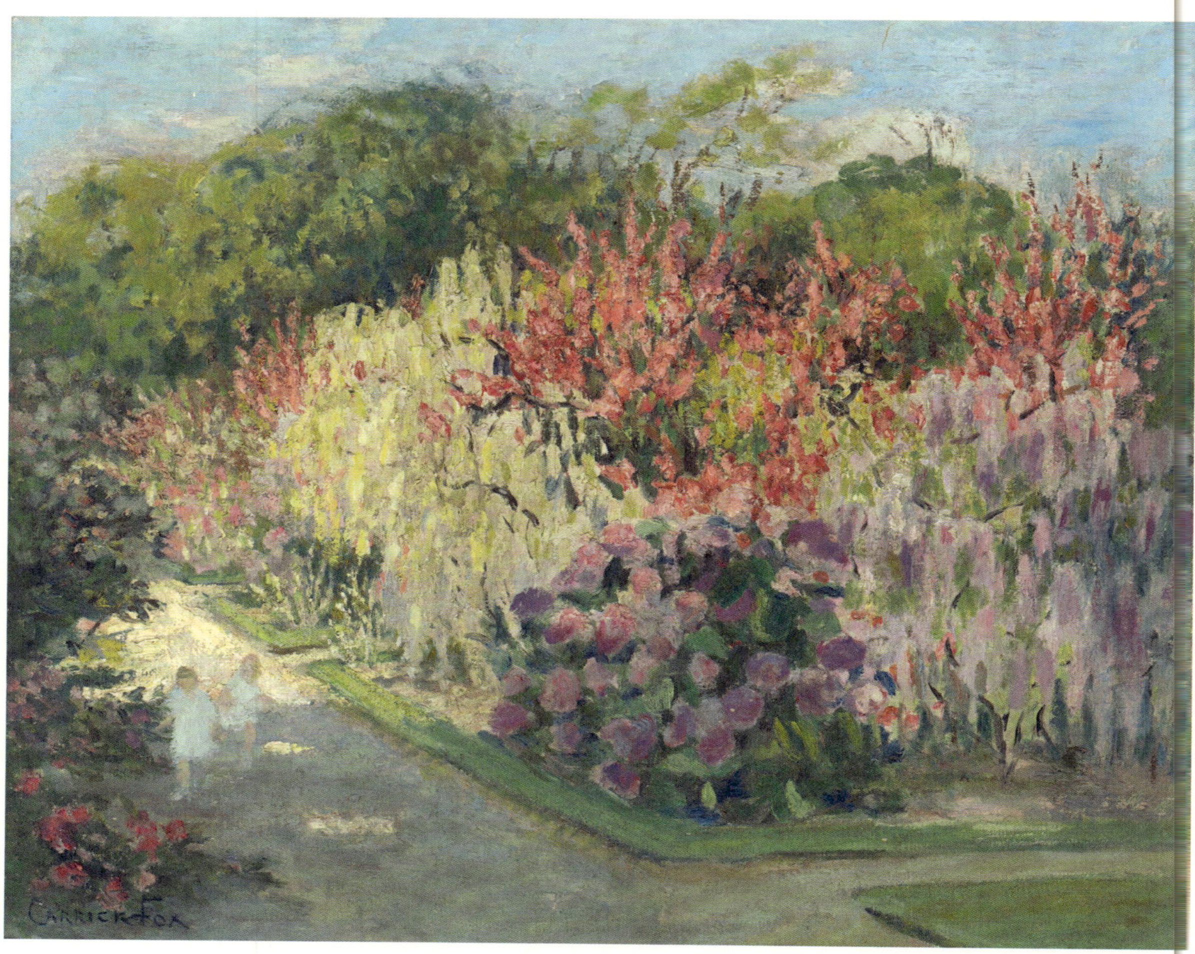

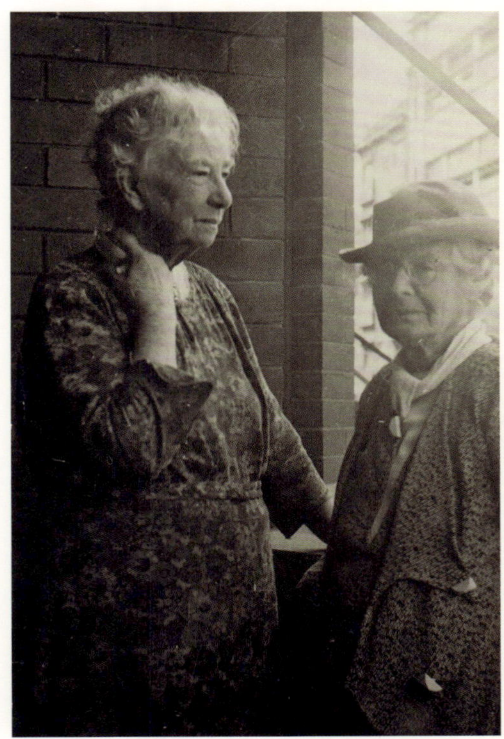

Opposite, top to bottom
cat 86 *Flower garden, Sydney* c 1944, oil on wood panel, Kerry Stokes Collection

cat 87 *In the botanic gardens* c 1945, oil on canvas, Benalla Art Gallery

Above
fig 32 Joshua Smith, *Dame Mary Gilmore and Mrs Phillips Fox*, c 1950–51, photograph, State Library of New South Wales

There was a palpable enjoyment of shared friendships during this time. In a letter from her studio at 70 Pitt Street in Sydney, Carrick wrote to Sybil Craig in Melbourne:

> I hope the days will soon be warm enough for you to work outside, in lovely half-moon bay. I've found another couple of gouaches done in France. I'll bring them over ... Tell me about other peoples' work too. I'm interested to know of all the people we know ... The weather is lovely now, the Harbour as blue as blue, + a pearly tone over all in the morning + a glorious glow in the late afternoon. Well, I'm sure the sunsets at St Kilda are very beautiful too. Have you seen a friendly spot that would do for me when I come over ...[235]

In another letter, dated 26 December 1945, sent after her return to Melbourne, Carrick again wrote to Craig, inviting her to tea: 'I am going to have a few friends & give a few Kashmir experiences'.[236]

Into the late 1940s, Carrick's circle of friends was ever-expanding and diverse. Some contacts came through theosophical communities, including Dorothy Bray, a resident of The Manor at the same time as Carrick and the typist for renowned author and social activist Dame Mary Gilmore (fig 32 and fig 56, p 235). Gilmore's insights into Carrick as an artist were largely informed by Bray, with whom she was connected on a more day-to-day basis. Gilmore wrote in a diary entry: 'Miss Bray came this morning and brought me a spray of rosemary from Mrs Phillips-Fox. She says Mrs Phillips-Fox paints with such self-absorption that she never even sees the people about her watching her as she paints. (She works a lot in the open.)'[237] In 1948, Archibald-winning painter Joshua Smith was concentrating on Gilmore's portrait. On 16 September, Gilmore wrote: 'Joshua Smith for a sitting, Mrs CB Maxwell and Mrs Phillips-Fox to see the painting. Mrs Phillips-Fox is greatly impressed.'[238]

It was Smith who took the photograph of Carrick and Gilmore at the respective ages of seventy-six and eighty-three—two indomitable women, defying the odds. The photograph shows them side by side, Carrick looking at the photographer through her round spectacles. She wears a dapper hat and a stylish jacket that looks handmade. In a diary entry dated 5 July 1948, Gilmore provides an amusing account that also captures a sense of camaraderie, even at life's end:

> Miss Bray with Mrs Phillips-Fox's account of Jane Price's death and the funeral. She just went out in sleep. Friends had a beautiful wreath made for the funeral. As they followed they noticed the number of men, and thought how well the men artists had turned up! At the crematorium they found they had followed the wrong funeral. Too late to go after Jane Price, they demanded the wreath back and took it home. Miss Bray and Mrs Phillips-Fox had no sense of shock over the matter, as they both thought how Jane Price, herself, would have laughed over the mishap.'[239]

In 1947, in the annual spring exhibition of the Victorian Artists Society's and the Melbourne Society of Women Painters and Sculptors exhibition, Carrick exhibited a 1907 work of the Luxembourg Gardens (cat 16, p 40). It was as though she was reflecting on her past, recognising that inspirational moment in her career, 40 years prior, as a young artist in Paris.

On 7 September 1944, Carrick heard the news that her apartment at 65 Boulevard Arago in Paris had been looted by the occupying Germans and that many of her husband's paintings had been taken. In 1949, at the time of her exhibition at John Martin's Art Gallery in Adelaide, a report noted the 78-year-old Carrick

> ... will revisit Paris to recover some of her drawings which she believes were among the few things left untouched by the Nazis when they looted her flat in the Latin Quarter. Only other remnants were her green-tiled stove and one silver salver.[240]

While she initially hoped to return to Europe in 1945, with the intention of setting up an artists' colony in the south of France,[241] Carrick remained in Australia until 1950. Along with a sense of trepidation at visiting her Parisian apartment knowing it had been looted, she was intent on seeing Emanuel Phillips Fox's retrospective come to fruition. As her communications with Hal Missingham reveal, she had long been advocating for this milestone exhibition.[242] The *E. Phillips Fox Interstate Exhibition* opened at the Art Gallery of New South Wales in late March 1949, travelling to the Queensland Art Gallery, National Gallery of Victoria and Art Gallery of South Australia. It was a dream come true in Carrick's quest to promote Fox's art and she was delighted that the Art Gallery of New South Wales acquired a treasured work by him, *The ferry* c 1910–11 (fig 40, p 161), in the same year.

In 1950, Carrick travelled on the Italian liner MS *Surriento* to Tangier, where she planned 'to stay with old friends, Dr and Mrs de Marquette, both of whom are doctors of philosophy, before returning to Paris'.[243] As she was suffering from acute rheumatism, it was touch and go whether she would make it onto the ship. Her visit to Dr Jacques de Marquette, was perhaps also inspired by the republication, in 1949, of his book *Introduction to comparative mysticism*.[244] Like Carrick, he was a theosophist and vegetarian, so they would have had much in common—and no doubt she enjoyed returning to North Africa after more than two decades.

Carrick's sense of adventure was unabated in old age. Now in her late seventies, she spent time in Paris and London. In a letter to Ola Cohn dated August 1951, she wrote that she went to Nice in February of that year. It is most likely during this visit that Carrick undertook what were among her last paintings of flower markets. This recurring, much-loved subject had evolved across decades; these late works revealing more modern attire, and an increased level of abstraction and freedom of expression. As always, the key touchstones of umbrellas create dynamic rhythms, while bunches of flowers add radiant colour. Yet, in contrast to the brilliant hues of *Flower market southern France* c 1951 (cat 88), *French flower market* c 1951 (cat 89, p 134) recollects her early interest in Manet's use of black, applied here in bold, solid strokes; this reflection on the past perhaps also pre-empts the sense of an ending. After Nice, at the age of seventy-nine, she was on the move again, wanting to make every minute count while she was still able to travel.

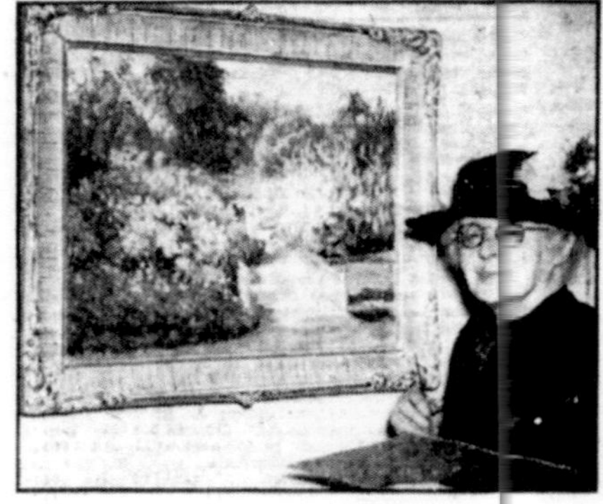

fig 33 *Ethel Carrick at the opening of her exhibition at John Martin's Art Gallery, Adelaide*, 1949, photograph in *The Advertiser*

Opposite
cat 88 *Flower market southern France* c 1951, oil on canvas on board, University Art Collection, Chau Chak Wing Museum, The University of Sydney

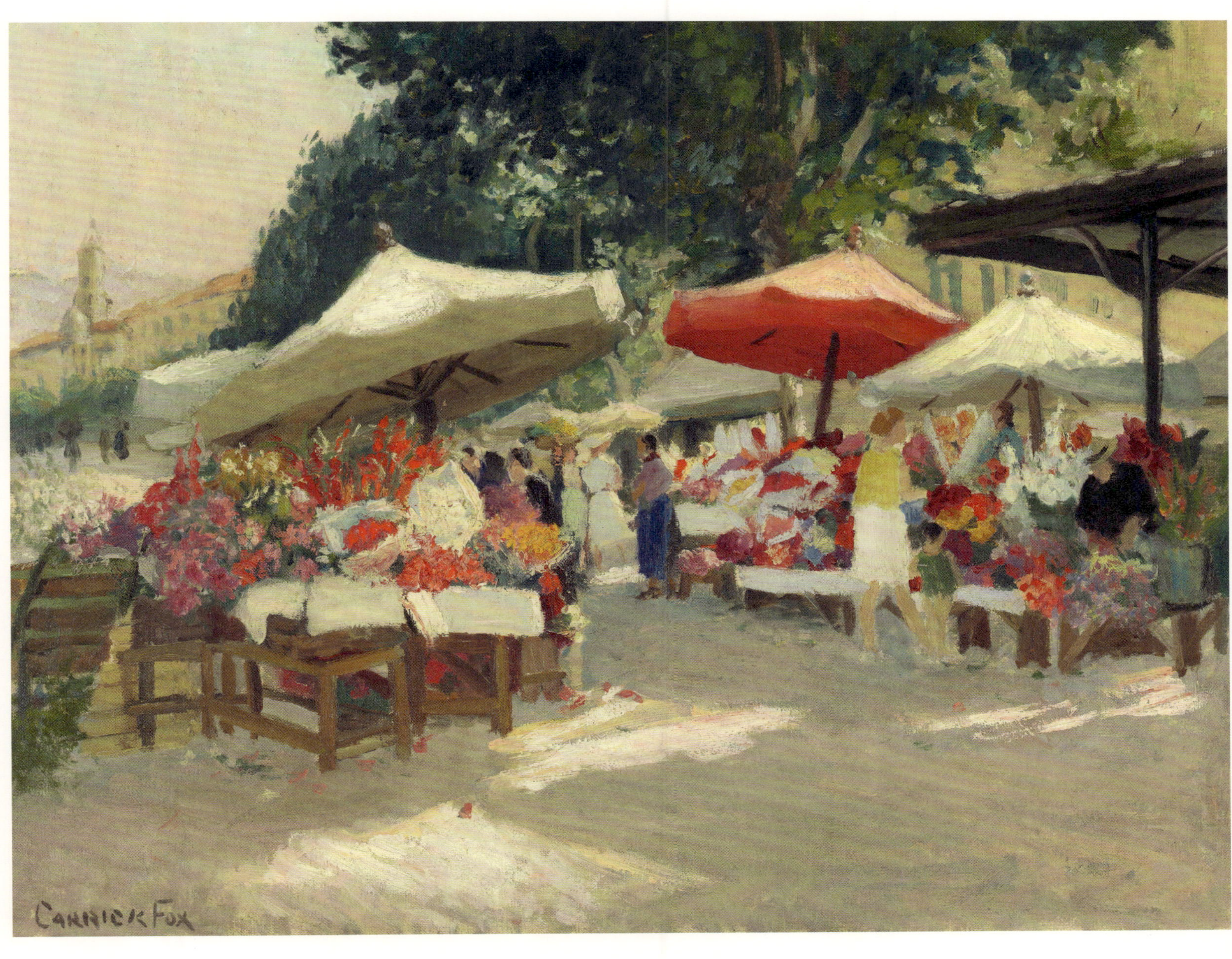

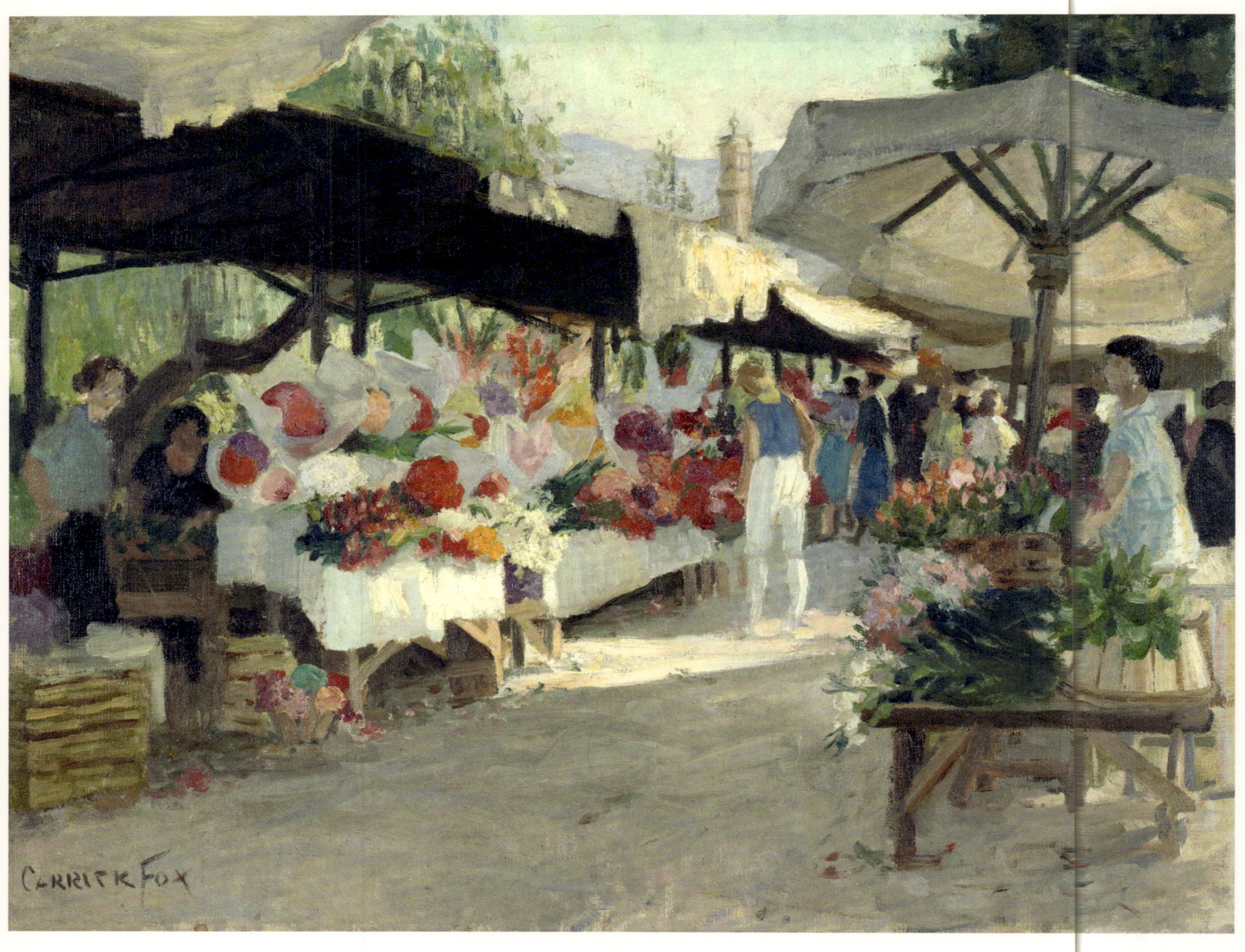
CARRICK FOX

Carrick shared her intrepid passion with Ola Cohn:

> Half way to Rome [I] decided to go there, of course you've been there! How I wish I'd gone earlier in my life—spent 3 weeks there. Then went by autocar to Assisi, one week, it was like living in another world, then only a short time in Perugia, a few days in Florence (where I'd stayed many years ago), San Gimignano & Siena—but one wants a year or two there—I do wish it were possible that all our young students who really want to know could visit & study at these wonderful places.[245]

Carrick also noted that she had bought 'a quantity of photographs' to show when she returned to Australia.

In January 1952, a letter she wrote to Irene (Renée) Fox suggested the need to slow down (a little): 'At present I'm in the south of France, resting as much as possible some miles above Nice right in the country, living the life of a cabbage ... I have a big room, with a fine view right across to the sea.'[246] She also noted that she had been busy working on some 50 lithographs (presumably hand-colouring), which she planned to bring back to Australia.

Carrick had let her Boulevard Arago apartment go in July 1951, but she was missing it.[247] 'I took a studio apartment with a tiny garden in the compound where I used to live ... but I want a place of my own.'[248] In a letter to Renée Fox, she wrote that she was planning a visit to Australia in 1952.

> I'm returning by the Dominion Monarch (Shaw Savill Line) which should leave London about the middle of May ... So glad Mannie's [Emanuel's] work is still being shown in the different capitals. I do hope a book will be published ... I've been exhibiting in the Royal Scottish Academy Society of Women Artists and the Royal Institute of Painters.[249]

Touchingly, the work shown at the Royal Scottish Academy in Edinburgh was *Australian gum blossom* c 1948 (cat 90, p 136).

With no intention of giving up the ghost, Carrick left Southampton for Melbourne aboard the SS *Dominion Monarch* on 1 May 1952. Upon her arrival in June she went to stay at the Lyceum Club, where she took ill. On the way to St George's Hospital in Kew she had a cerebral haemorrhage, dying a few days later.[250] She was eighty years of age. With no regard for her remarkable artistic contributions, the occupation on her death certificate was noted as 'home duties'. In a letter to Renée Fox, Ethel's sister Hilda reflected:

> Ethel's death was a very great shock for us all. She seemed, although much older, when I said good-bye just before she sailed, to be so full of vim & her arrangements for the future ... to have once more a flat in Paris.
>
> I had the day before the news arrived received a very bright and cheerful letter from her after she arrived—but she did mention that owing to the rough weather she had to be carried off on a stretcher.[251]

Opposite
cat 89 *French flower market* c 1951,
oil on canvas, Australian National University Art Collection

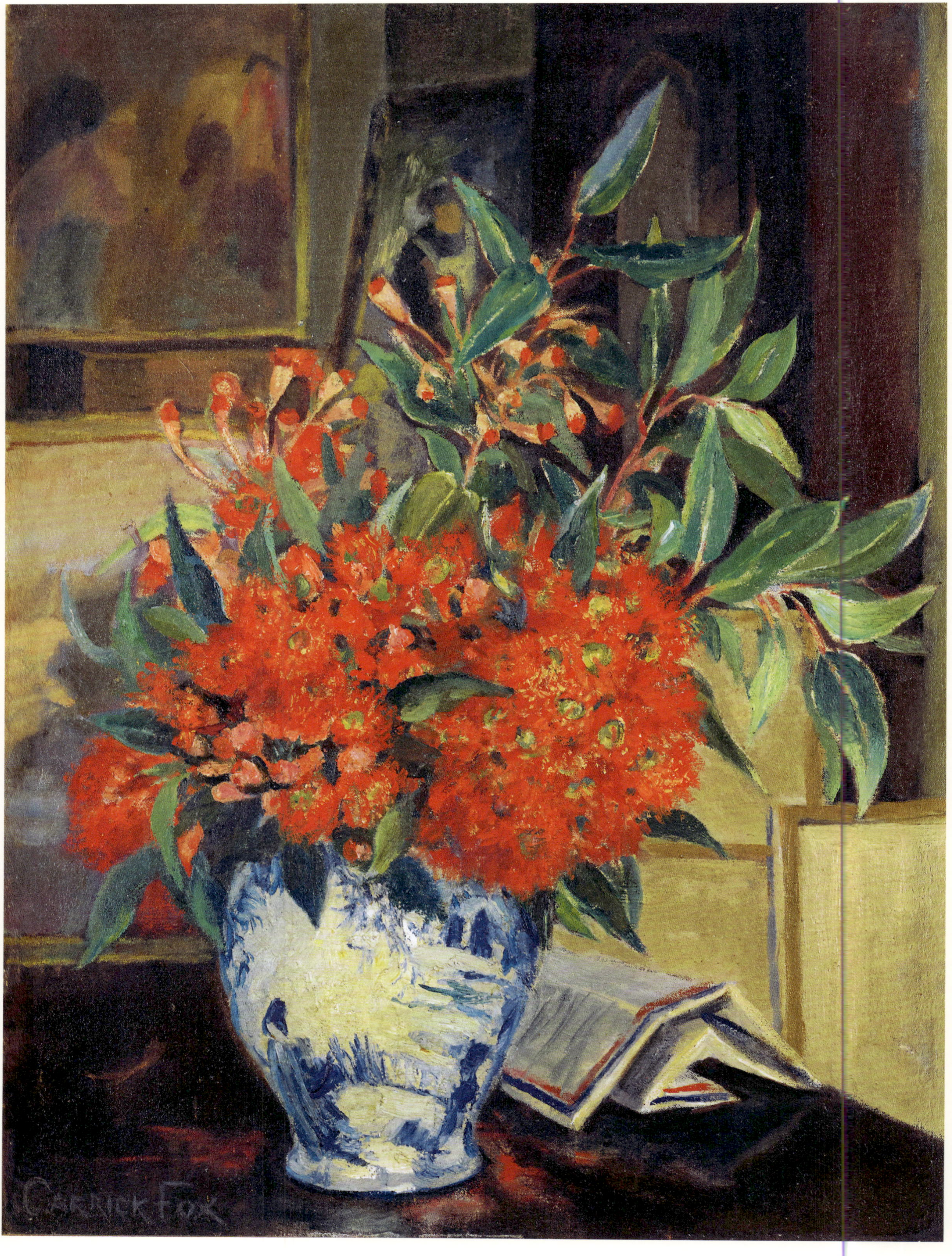
CARRICK FOX

Opposite
cat 90 *Australian gum blossom* c 1948, oil on canvas, The Wesfarmers Collection of Australian Art

An obituary for Carrick noted: 'In spite of advancing years she retained a vital and gracious personality which was reflected in her work. She retained also a keen interest in the work of the younger generation of Australian artists, holding very definite views on modern developments in art. She will be remembered by a wide circle of friends in Australia.'[252]

Taking an overview of Carrick's exhibitions, from the late 1930s up until her final years, it is striking to consider the range of her subject matter and locations. In an exhibition at Cooling Galleries, London (alongside works by Phillips Fox) and two large solo shows at Athenaeum Gallery, Melbourne in 1942 and 1944, she exhibited oils, gouaches and lithographs inspired by her ongoing travels from Srinagar to Canberra and much more between. Also featured were works such as *The quay at Dinard* 1911–12 (cat 102, p 159) and *Laveuses algériennes (Algerian women washing clothes in a stream)* c 1911 (cat 111, pp 176–77) which, like old friends, were still there keeping her company. Also, just as she returned to favoured subjects in her art, so she continued to return to favoured places, including the United Kingdom and France as well as Australia, where she felt a deep sense of connection. Certainly, by the time of her last visit to Melbourne she was considered by many to be an Australian, as she still is today. Yet, as she moved through the world, Carrick's life and art transcended fixed boundaries.

This is perhaps best encapsulated in *Le bac, Kashmir* (The ferry, Kashmir) 1937 (cat 77, pp 118–19). As we reflect upon this dream-like, floating world in the context of Carrick's broader output, we come to the important realisation that across many different contexts her works embrace diversity over disharmony—a central tenet of Jiddu Krishnamurti's teachings. In each location in which she worked, differences are clearly observed and articulated. At the same time, there is a feeling that, ultimately, we are all trying to find our way, united in a flow of luminosity and shadow, energies and presences, informing our inner lives and endless circles of connection.

Dr Deborah Hart is the National Gallery of Australia's Head Curator of Australian Art and curator of the *Ethel Carrick* retrospective. She is a widely published art historian and has written several acclaimed monographs. Commencing her career as an education officer at the Queensland Art Gallery (now Queensland Art Gallery | Gallery of Modern Art [QAGOMA]), Meeanjin/Brisbane, she has worked across a wide range of contexts, including in state and regional galleries and as guest curator on projects including the Asia Pacific Triennial (QAGOMA) and an exhibition exchange between Australia and Taiwan for the Museum of Contemporary Art Taipai and the University of Wollongong, Woolyungah/Wollongong. Since her appointment at the National Gallery as a senior curator in 2000, Hart has curated numerous exhibitions including *Joy Hester and friends* (2001); *Grace Cossington Smith: a retrospective exhibition* (2005); *Andy and Oz: parallel visions* (2007), also shown at The Andy Warhol Museum in Pittsburgh; *Fred Williams: infinite horizons* (2011); and *Hugh Ramsay* (2019–20). She also co-curated a number of significant shows including *Know My Name: Australian women artists 1900 to now* (2021–22), *Jeffrey Smart* (2021–22) and *Know My Name: making it modern* (2023). Dr Hart has also been responsible for recommending key acquisitions for the national collection, including significant works by women artists—Ethel Carrick among them.

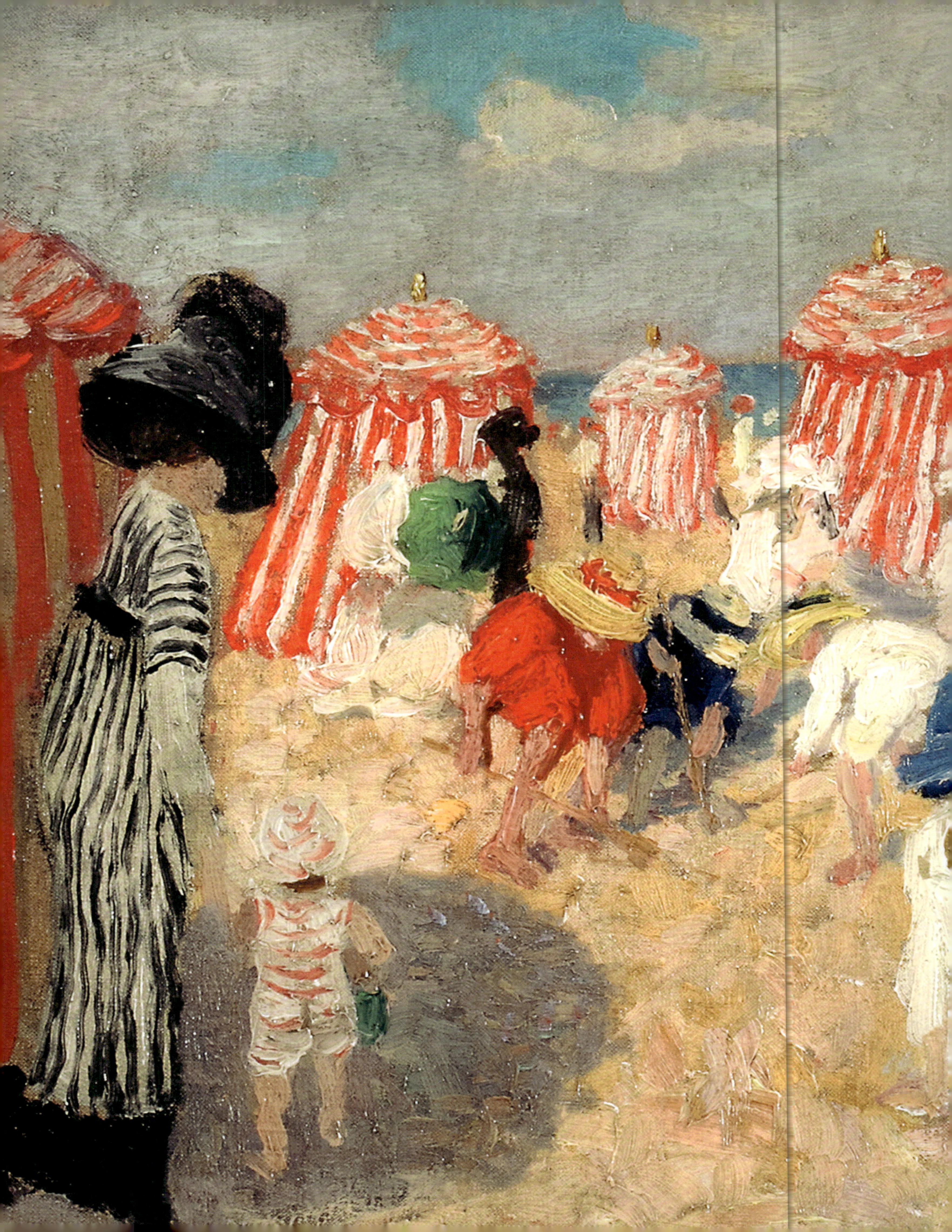

Seeking sunlight: Carrick and Fox's artistic marriage

Angela Goddard

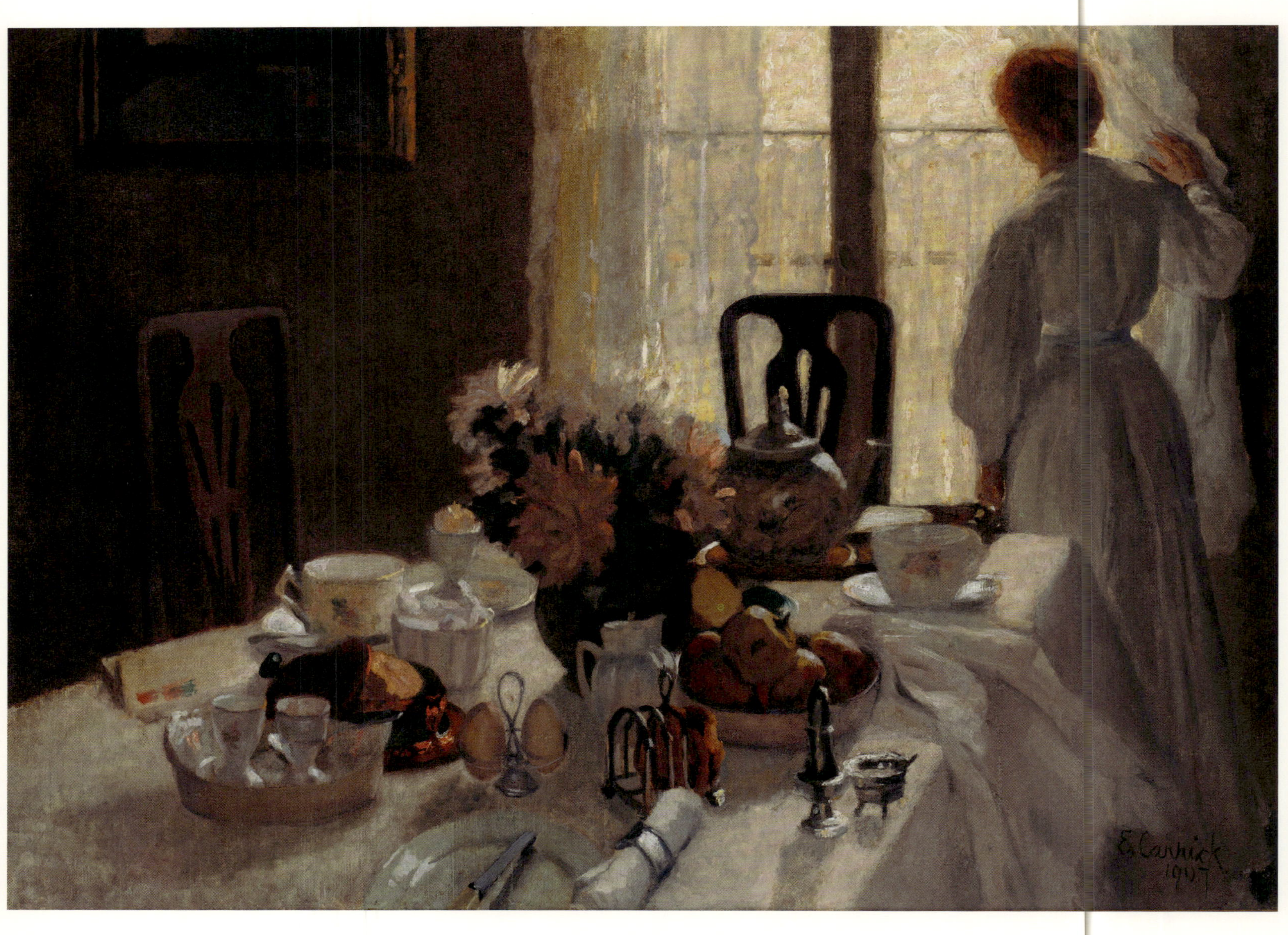

Ethel Carrick and Emanuel Phillips Fox were a dedicated, hardworking artist couple whose marriage offers a fascinating insight into the social mores of the early twentieth century. Together they were restless travellers, heading to well-known artistic holiday locations favoured by the middle classes. Though their age gap was only seven years, their ambitions, exhibition contexts and audiences diverged. Comparing their works at several key points of their marriage reveals fascinating similarities and differences; it is an enlightening lens through which to view Carrick's social and artistic milieu and her individual artistic contribution.

Carrick (born 1872) and Fox (born 1865) met on a sketching trip at St Ives, Cornwall, around 1901. Carrick had graduated from the Slade School of Fine Art, after studying under Henry Tonks and Fred Brown in the 1890s and early 1900s. Fox had been in England since 1901. Both hailed from large families. She came from a middle-class English Anglican family, one of nine children whose father, a draper, had died in 1899. Fox was born into the Jewish faith and had a supportive family, despite an absent father. She was financially comfortable and, like many women artists from the Slade, well supported by her family in her artistic ambitions. He relied on commissions and teaching for income, along with financial support from his brothers.

The couple wed on 9 May 1905 in the stylish Arts & Crafts and late-Victorian Gothic Anglican St Peter's Church in Ealing. The *British Australasian* reported a roll-call of prominent Australian artists who were invited, including Violet Teague, Tudor St George Tucker, Bernard Hall, Arthur Streeton, Bertram Mackennal, Dora Meeson and George Coates, George Lambert, John Longstaff, Tom Roberts and Rupert Bunny.[1] Their wide and international milieu also incorporated the St Ives–Newlyn circle, with Algernon Talmage from St Ives and his wife, Cornish artist Gertrude Rowe, in attendance; as well as English artists, such as George Clausen; French and American artists living in France; and Carrick's Slade classmates, including Hilda Fearon.

The wedding was timed to coincide with the Royal Academy of Arts annual summer exhibition, which included Fox's *The harvest field* 1905 and a portrait of his new wife *Ethel, daughter of the late AW Carrick, Esq* c 1904 (fig 7, p 32).[2] The happy couple then settled in at the leafy artist residence at La Cité Fleurie, at 65 Boulevard Arago, surrounded by the supportive creative community of Montparnasse, Paris.

Previous
Sur la plage (On the sands), Dinard 1911 (detail cat 97, p 149), oil on wood panel, private collection

Opposite
cat 91 *The breakfast table* 1907, oil on canvas on board, private collection

Fox had observed plenty of marriages among the art students at the National Gallery Art School in the 1880s and early 1890s, including those of Walter James Anderson and Theo Tuckett, Alexander Colquhoun and Beatrix Hoile, Arthur Boyd and Emma Minnie á Beckett, and John Llewellyn Jones and Lalla Corbett.[3] In Paris, the Foxes were also surrounded by artist couples. In many cases, the arrival of children diminished the careers of the wives—such as in the case of Edith Susan Gerard Anderson, a promising student of Fox's and the model for many of his major works of the period. Introduced by Fox to Theodore Penleigh Boyd, Anderson married Boyd in 1912. While she continued to paint, she didn't achieve substantial artistic recognition after her marriage, especially after their children Pat and Robin arrived. As Hilary Taylor points out, women artists of the period faced many challenges after completing their art education:

> **So great was the unspoken difference between the opportunities and expectations of women and men, even at the Slade, that it would seem that under no circumstances could these women have practised as artists in a way comparable to their male colleagues.[4]**

The Foxes did not have children, and we can only speculate as to whether this was by design or circumstance.

For the Foxes, the infrastructure of marriage offered both security and support—and, despite challenges, Carrick enjoyed Fox's positive encouragement. He boasted of her achievements to friends, writing in 1908: 'My wife has been very successful at the Autumn Salon—four pictures hung on the line and all sold—so if this sort of thing goes on I shall have to take a back seat!'[5] This was despite his more critical appraisal of the general standard of the work exhibited at the Salon d'Automne. A few years later, in 1911, Fox wrote to Hans Heysen: 'There is a lot of talk here about the post impressionists—I am sure you would not like them, nor could you feel any interest in the Autumn Salon, which claims to be the coming art—God help it, if it turns out to be so.'[6] However, Fox omitted Carrick from his disapproval. Later in the same letter, he notes that she 'is doing some very interesting and personal stuff. She is *sociétaire* (full member) of Autumn Salon and is very keen on modern outlook'.[7]

The Foxes each directed their work towards different audiences. By 1910, Fox was *sociétaire* of the Société Nationale des Beaux-Arts and regularly showed at the Royal Academy. Carrick's training at the Slade had produced several accomplished and highly admired structured interiors—such as *The breakfast table* 1907 (cat 91, p 140), which speaks back to her early training even though it was completed after her arrival in Paris. But Carrick quickly moved into a more modern arena. As a *sociétaire* (member) and then *juriste* (a member of the selection jury) of the Salon d'Automne—and a member of the progressive artist cooperative l'Union Internationale des Beaux-Arts et des Lettres from 1908—she sought out more modern exhibition contexts for her work, such as *Le Musée du Peuple*, a large exhibition of contemporary art organised by the fauvist Alexis Mérodack-Jeanneau in Angers in 1907, which also included works by Cézanne, Rousseau and Kandinsky. Outgoing and socially adept, Carrick would be active in several groups and societies of women artists in Paris and Australia throughout her life.

Carrick and Fox's marriage coincided with tremendous changes in social and political life for middle- and upper-class women in the first decade of the twentieth century. These 'new women' were able to move

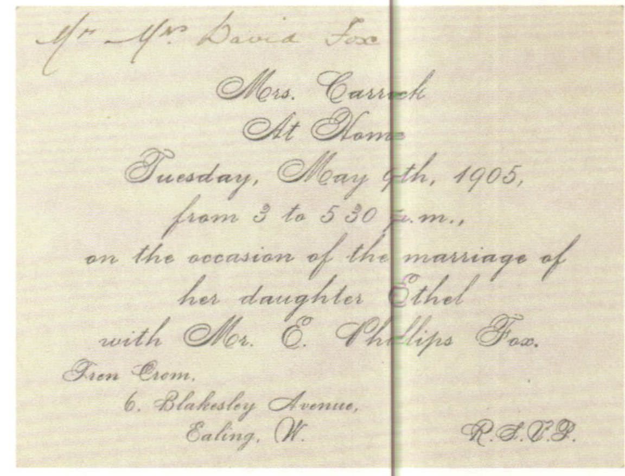

Mr & Mrs David Fox

Mrs. Carrick
At Home
Tuesday, May 9th, 1905,
from 3 to 5.30 p.m.,
on the occasion of the marriage of
her daughter Ethel
with Mr. E. Phillips Fox.

Tren Crom.
6. Blakesley Avenue,
Ealing, W.

R.S.V.P.

fig 34 *Invitation to the wedding of Ethel Carrick and Emanuel Phillips Fox, addressed to Emanuel's brother and his wife, Mr and Mrs David Fox*, 9 May 1905, Len Fox Papers, State Library of New South Wales

Opposite, top to bottom
fig 35 Emanuel Phillips Fox, *Art students* 1895, oil on canvas, Art Gallery of New South Wales

fig 36 Emanuel Phillips Fox, *A suffragette* 1911, oil on canvas, University of New South Wales

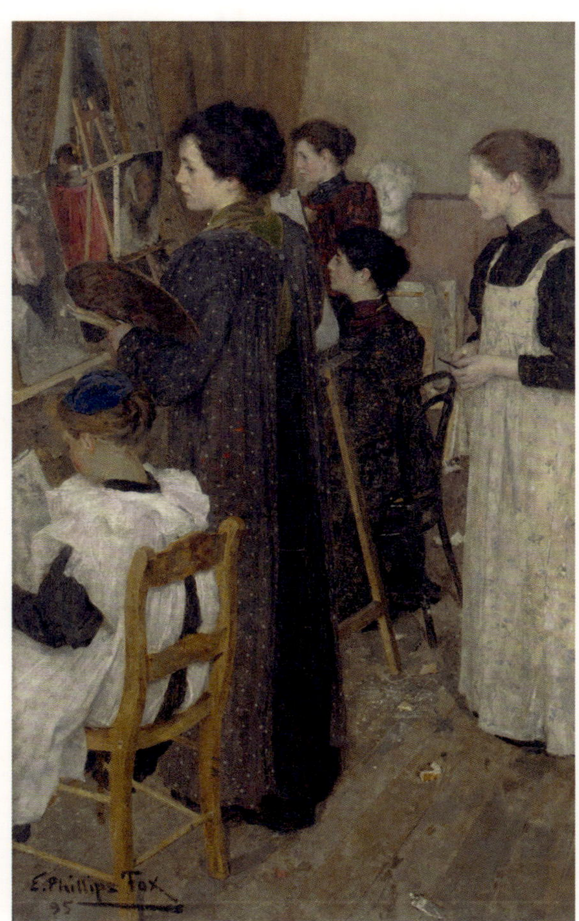

more freely, physically and socially, than ever before. They also politically agitated for voting rights, social reform, higher education and employment, as well as engaging in new forms of leisure and entertainment.

Women were the major focus of both artists' works, yet in vastly differing ways. After marriage, Fox no longer explored the classic impressionist subjects of rural labourers or peasants that featured in his earlier works. For the most part, he depicted women in domestic middle-class settings in leisurely and assured poses, rarely working, apart from delicately tending to a child or reading a book or letter. Carrick preferred to capture women in the streets, often depicting working women selling fruit, vegetables and flowers, or buying produce. She also presented nannies and nursemaids tending to children in parks, such as the Luxembourg Gardens, and at the beach. In addition to working women, Carrick captured well-to-do women relaxing in groups or promenading in fashionable dress. Key examples include her Luxembourg Gardens series, such as *In springtime, Luxembourg Gardens* 1907 (cat 16, p 40) and *In the Luxembourg Gardens, Paris* c 1908 (cat 22, p 47), and her beach scenes, such as *Seaside promenade, south of France* c 1910 (cat 37, p 68) and *Sur la plage (On the sands), Dinard* 1911 (cat 97, p 149). Her women are active, and often captured with a few strokes that don't particularise or identify them—they are types within a crowd.

Despite his work taking a more academic and Edwardian approach, Fox was progressive in his social values and attuned to conveying subtly complex social and intellectual ideas. Back in Australia, he set a major work *Art students* 1895 (fig 35), in the studio at the Melbourne School of Art in the Cromwell Buildings, Bourke Street, which he had co-founded with Tudor St George Tucker. Many of their students were women, and identified in this work are budding artists Cristina Asquith Baker in a spotted smock, Etta Phillips behind her, and Ina Gregory on the right in a cream smock. Unlike most of Fox's later works, here these women are working—absorbed in their tasks, their smocks are paint-flecked and the floor is strewn with debris. Its informality and matter-of-factness are striking, as is the heroic scale of the women occupied with their canvases. Perhaps due to its subject matter, the painting didn't sell in his lifetime—it was purchased by the Art Gallery of New South Wales in 1943.

Around 1909, Fox painted two large canvases of the same subject—a mother and child—both titled *Bathing hour*. He adjusted the shadows across the two versions; in the later work, *Bathing hour (L'heure du bain)* c 1909 (fig 37, p 148) the mother's coppery hair is set alight in the late-afternoon sun, her diaphanous empire-line dress sliced by a shadow dominating the foreground.[8] Fox's biographer, Ruth Zubans, notes that he often depicted an idealised woman: a mother at the secure and reassuring centre of the family yet always enclosed or contained, restrained in some way by her surroundings.[9] *Bathing hour* is unusual for the child's casual nakedness, and the fact that she is tended to by her mother rather than by a nanny. Virginia Spate has argued that by contrasting the girl's nakedness and the mother's flowing robes with the more restrictive formality of the women and children promenading in the background, the painting can be read as subtle commentary on social mores of the period.[10]

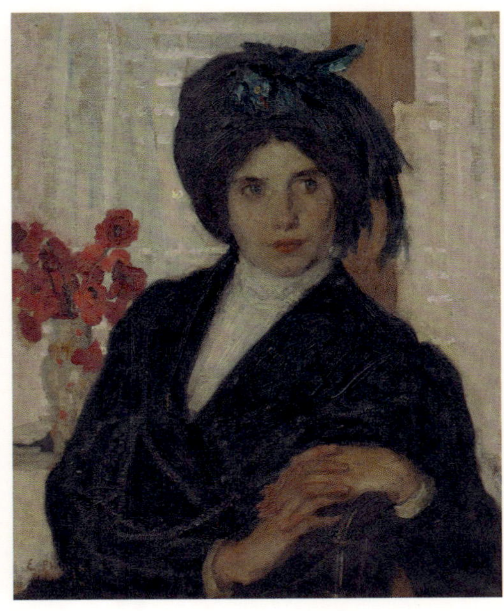

Several individuals in the Foxes' circle of family and friends were working towards women's suffrage. The most likely identity of the subject in Fox's *A suffragette* 1911 (fig 36)—painted in Paris in the same year as the inaugural International Women's Day—is Fox's cousin Marion Phillips.

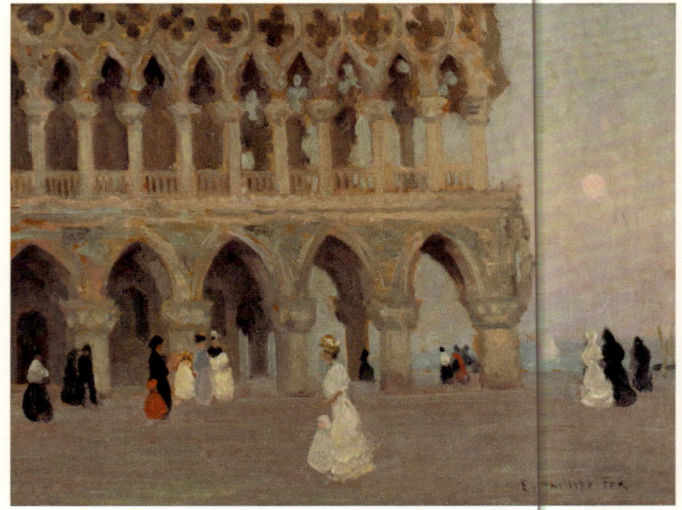

cat 92 Emanuel Phillips Fox, *Venice afterglow* c 1907, oil on board, University Art Collection, Chau Chak Wing Museum, The University of Sydney

Opposite
cat 93 *St Mark's Venice* 1907, oil on board, University Art Collection, Chau Chak Wing Museum, The University of Sydney

An outspoken feminist and member of several suffragette groups, she would later be the first Australian woman to enter the House of Commons of the United Kingdom.[11] Zubans describes the work as an unusual one for Fox, for its contemporary political currency. He showed the work in the 1913 Société Internationale,[12] at a time when aspects of the suffragist movement were increasingly militant, leading to arson attacks, property damage and prison hunger strikes.

As Mary Eagle points out, 'Fox's style underwent an upheaval after his marriage and move to Paris in 1905. For a few years he explored several styles and was more eclectic than he had been or was to be afterwards.'[13] These key representations of progressive women in Fox's oeuvre emerged after, and seemingly as a result of, his marriage.

It was when they were travelling that the couple's work aligned most, and when their influence on each other can be obviously discerned. Fox's long familiarity with plein air painting, through many summers spent at Charterisville, near Melbourne, in the 1890s, brings a relaxed quality to his French sketches, conveying the couple's restless and nomadic summer searches for pleasing subjects and sunlight. Indeed, Fox and Carrick's practices converge most closely in their manner of working outdoors. Fox used panels for painted sketches while travelling, later working up elements of these sketches into large canvases in his studio but rarely exhibiting the sketches. Carrick would paint quickly, often on small wooden panels, both at home in Paris and while travelling, occasionally completing studio paintings on canvas.

The couple's trip to Venice in 1907 shows their alignment. Fox's *Ship in sail, Venice* 1907 has clear and authoritative architectural structure, with light and colour drenching the scene. Swift brushstrokes model the sails of the ship and the mother and child walking along the lower right. Fewer Venice scenes by Carrick survive, but her panel *St Mark's Venice* 1907 (cat 93) shows a group of figures promenading along the canal front from the Piazza San Marco towards the church of San Giorgio Maggiore, with gestural strokes indicating movement and energy.

During the Belle Époque, thousands of holiday makers would gravitate to the seaside resorts in the summer. The Foxes generally sought out the northern coastal towns of Dinard and St Malo in Brittany, and Trouville and Deauville in Normandy. Casinos, horse races, hotels, restaurants and boutiques were sources of entertainment, and promenading on the beach and bathing in the sea presented many motifs for the Foxes to paint.

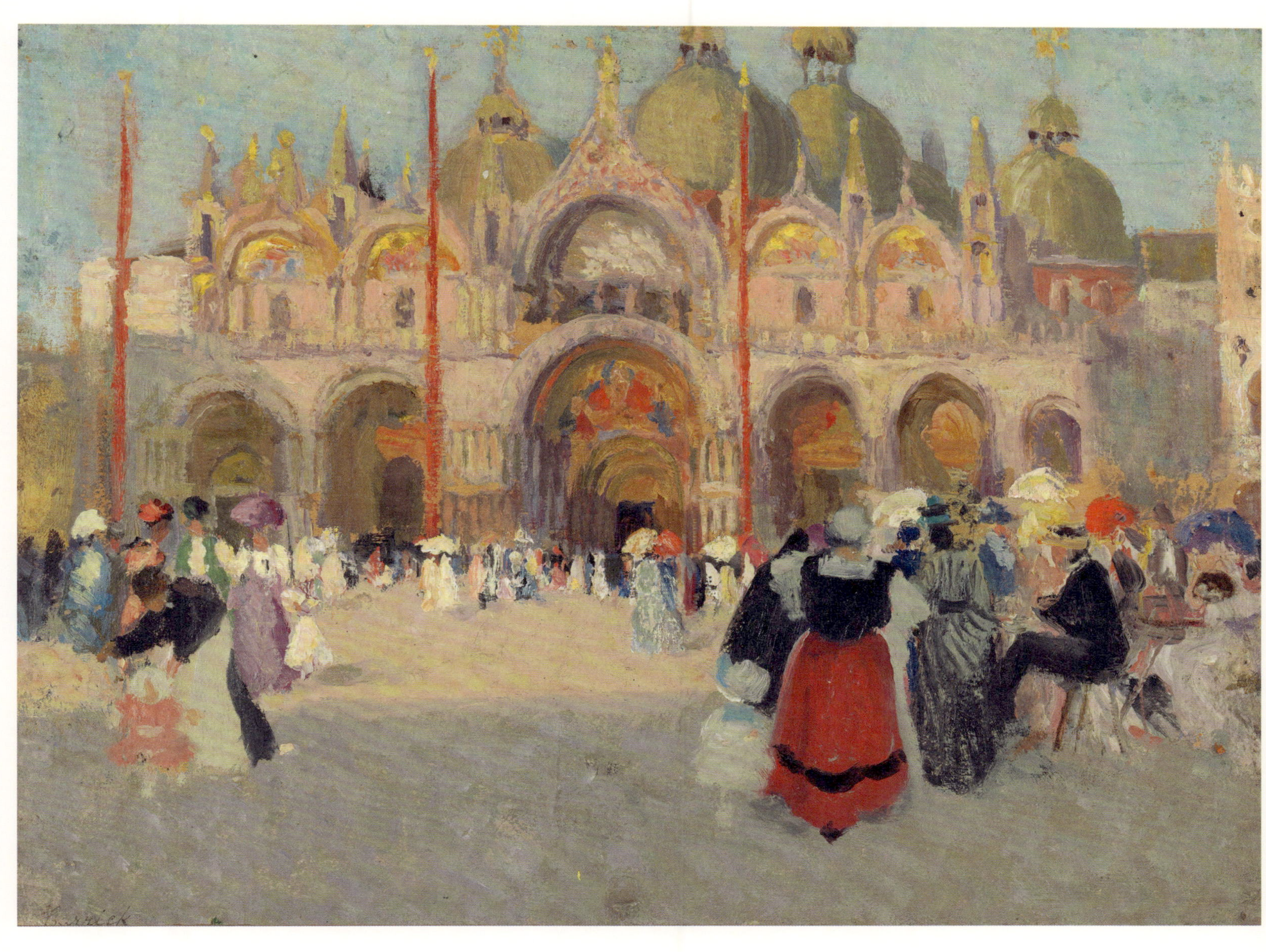

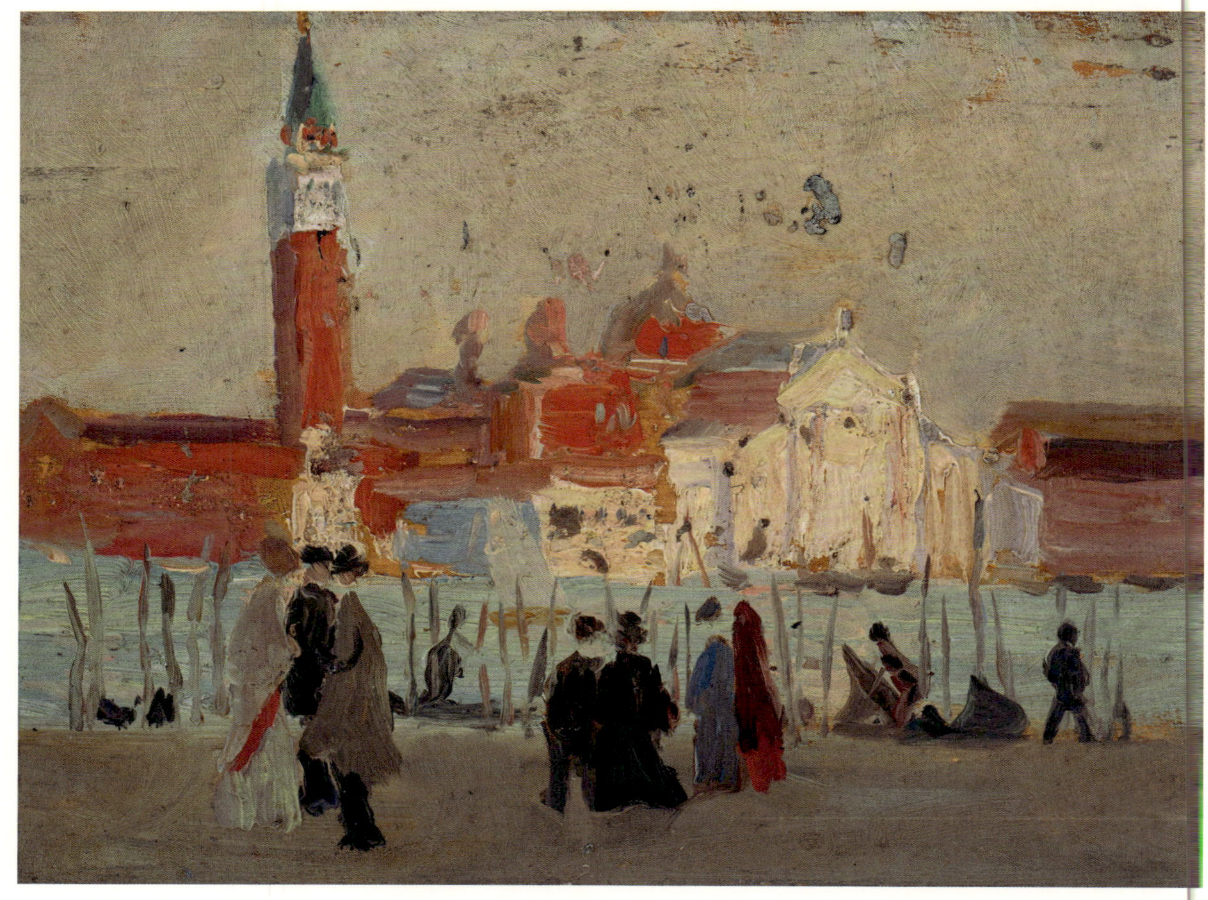

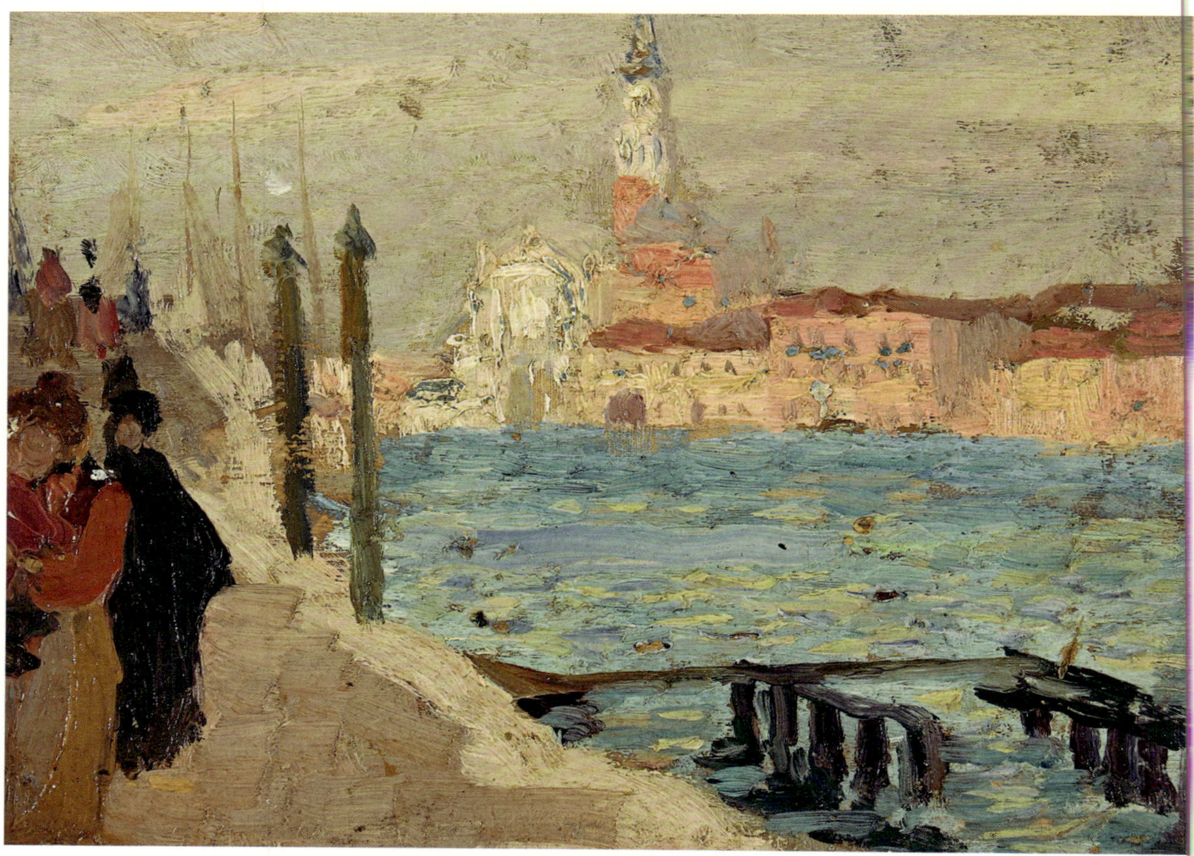

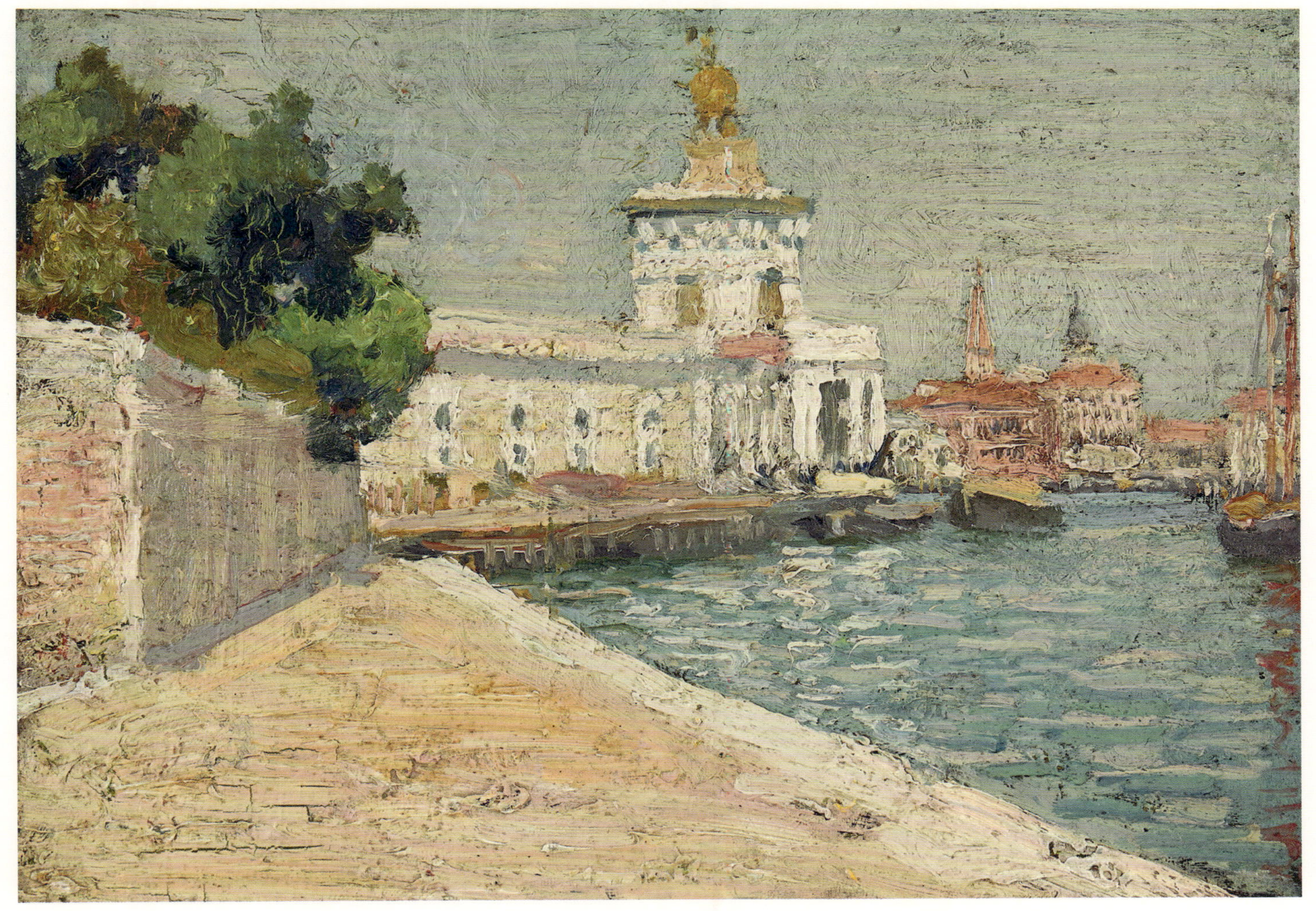

Opposite, top to bottom
cat 94 *Venice* c 1907, oil on wood panel, Castlemaine Art Museum

cat 95 *Venice scene* 1907, oil on panel, Shepparton Art Museum

Above
cat 96 *Building by river with boats* 1907, oil on panel, Shepparton Art Museum

Carrick and Fox's sketches at beachside resorts demonstrate many similarities in execution, but subtle differences in subject choices. Both use strong diagonals to structure their compositions and provide focus. Carrick's *La marée haute à Saint-Malo (High tide at St Malo)* c 1911–12 (cat 101, p 157) and *The quay at Dinard* c 1911–12 (cat 102, p 159), and Fox's *The ferry* c 1910–11 (fig 40, p 161), all offer an elevated viewpoint looking down on the scene. This was a favoured device of Carrick's when composing larger paintings, while Fox tended to pull in closer on smaller singular figures or groups in both his sketches (like *On a French beach* c 1909 and *On the sand* c 1910) and larger studio works. Carrick did not work in Fox's academic manner, and produced several beach sketches where the light is often dappled, unsettled and indistinct, restlessly leading the eye around the compositions.

Together, the Foxes also sought sunlit subjects beyond Europe. As Ursula Prunster has observed, 'the East, as locale and as idea, was a place of freedom for the Antipodean traveller–artist'.[14] The Foxes took a painting trip to North Africa in 1911, visiting Algiers and Bou Saada in Algeria, and Tangier in Morocco before returning home via Spain. In North Africa, Carrick would have had a very different experience to Fox. Like other women—including her Australian friend Hilda Rix Nicholas, who travelled to North Africa the following year—Carrick was restricted in her movements and access to public spaces. Art historian John Pigot has asserted that women painters perceived the region from 'a different point of view from that of their male colleagues', although their need to 'claim and construct the Orient as a European "other" was as fundamental to their project as it was to that of the men'.[15]

Fox did not fall into the usual trope of odalisques and harem scenes prevalent in the work of many male European artists of the time—his study *Moroccan girl* 1911, for instance, tends more towards whimsical portraiture than exotic fantasy. Both Carrick and Fox also produced many market crowd scenes, often painting side by side—we see the same square in Carrick's *Arabs bargaining* c 1911 (cat 108, p 170) and Fox's *A market in the desert* 1911 (fig 38, p 151) and *Street scene, Bou Saada* c 1911, although the latter is from a higher viewpoint, perhaps a hotel window. These were unusual subjects for both artists, in that they depict predominantly the world of men engaged in the commerce of the market. In Fox's work particularly, the crowds are indistinct rather than individualised, studies in volume and architectural features with energetic brushstrokes, blazing sunlight and rich colour—qualities more closely associated with his wife's work.

Carrick's extraordinary, semi-abstract *Laveuses algériennes (Algerian women washing clothes in a stream)* c 1911 (cat 111, pp 176–77) arrays glistening bodies around a stream at the bottom of a steep hillside. With light bouncing around the canvas the heat is palpable, and the women's exposed, muscular arms and legs are suggested by confident paint strokes. The scene feels intimate, with the women at ease and partially uncovered in Carrick's company. Most are firmly at work, apart from one figure on the left pausing to hitch up her skirt and rest in the heat. It's a scene that plays off exoticism, and this power differential is of course emphasised, but Carrick focuses on light and colour rather than titillation. This is Carrick at her best, capturing a fleeting scene of women at work in short strokes and blocky colour.

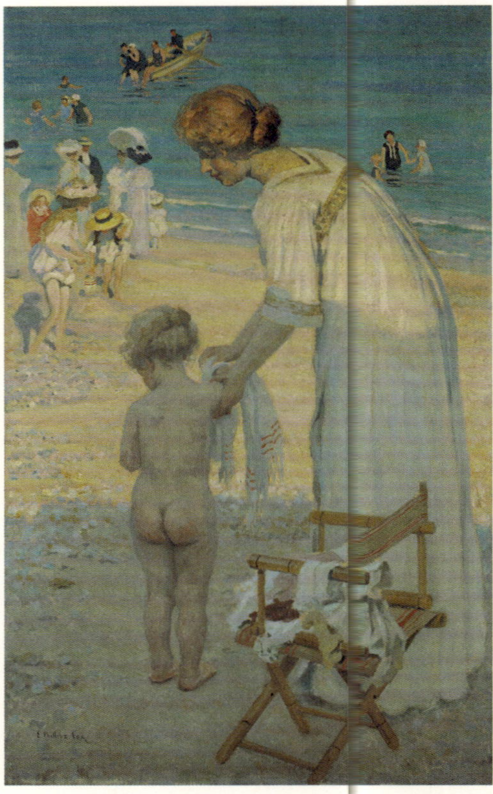

fig 37 Emanuel Phillips Fox, *Bathing hour (L'heure du bain)* c 1909, oil on canvas, Queensland Art Gallery | Gallery of Modern Art

Opposite
cat 97 *Sur la plage (On the sands), Dinard* 1911, oil on wood panel, private collection

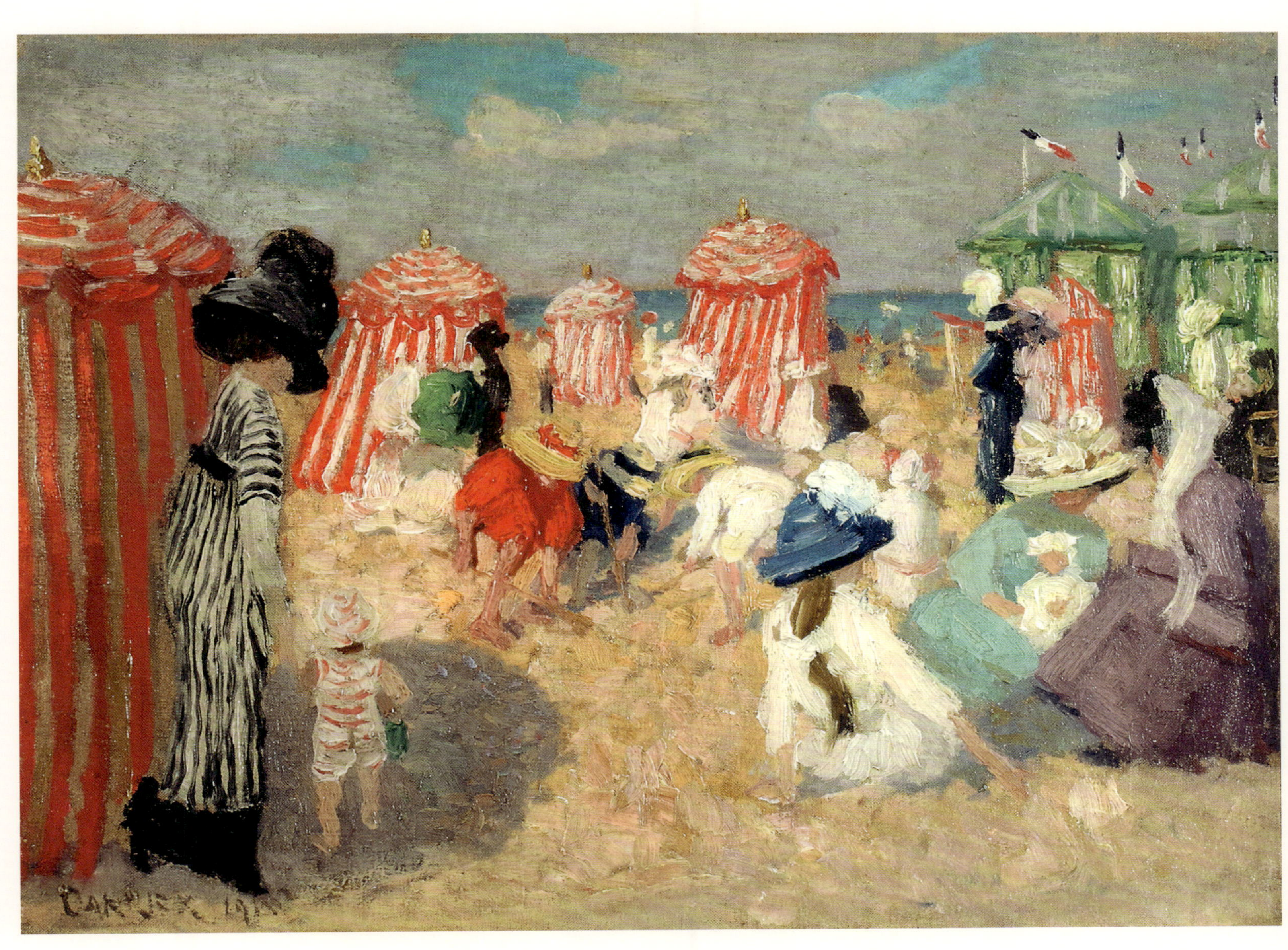

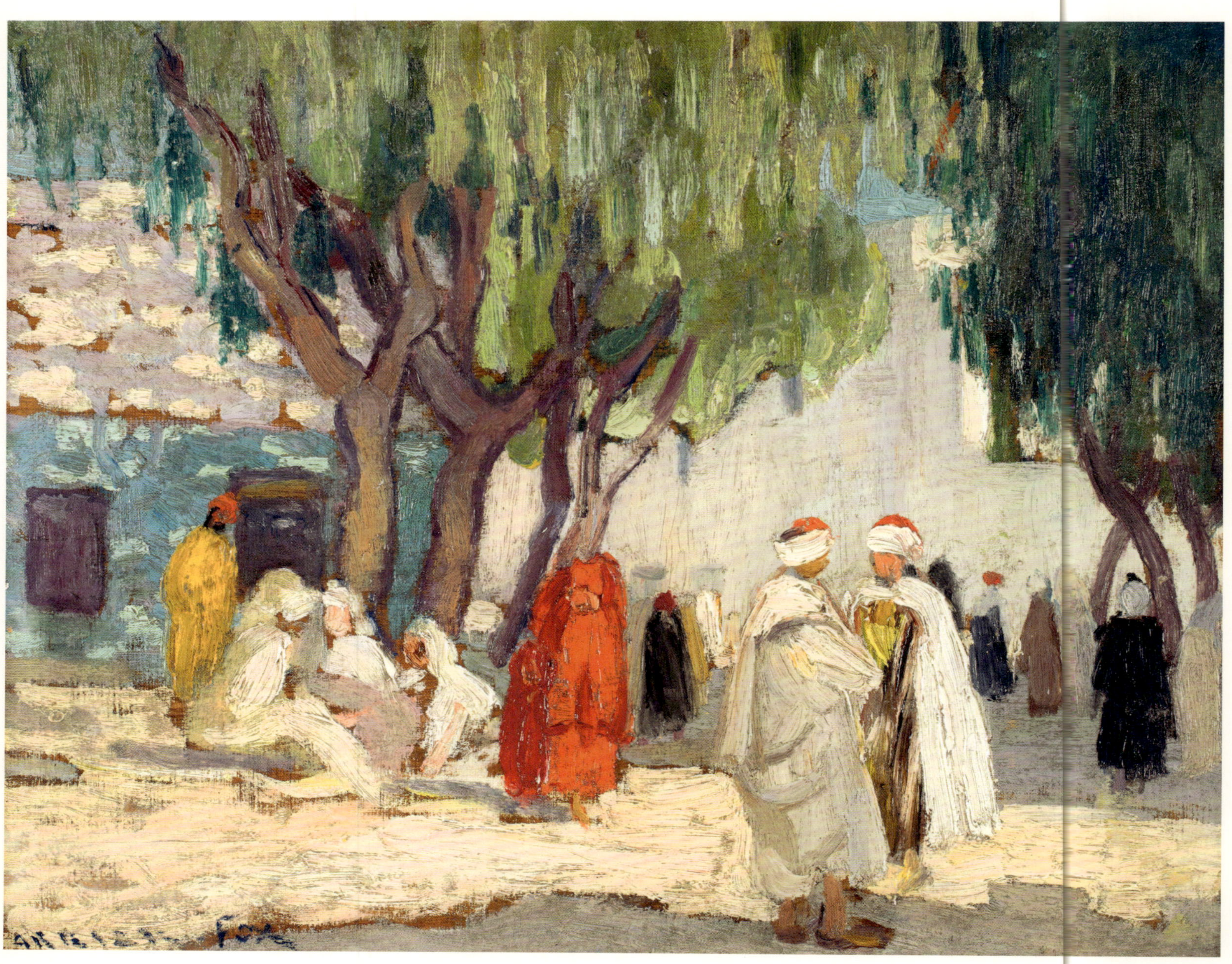

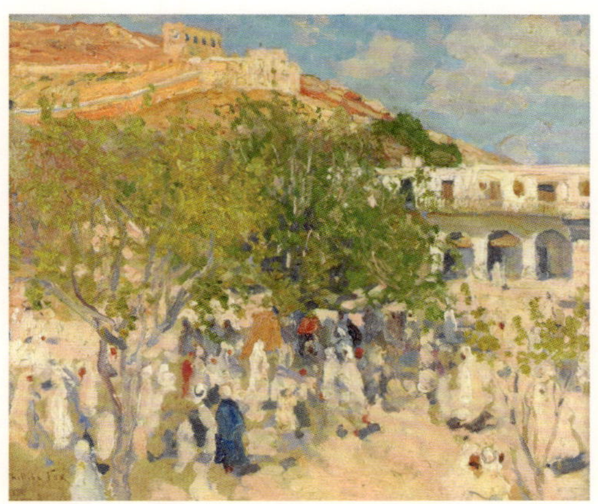

fig 38 Emanuel Phillips Fox, *A market in the desert* 1911, oil on canvas, New England Regional Art Gallery

Opposite
cat 98 *Morning in Kairouan* c 1919–20, oil on board, University Art Collection, Chau Chak Wing Museum, The University of Sydney

The Foxes took their North African works to Australia in 1913, holding several exhibitions, conducting painting trips and seeking commissions for Fox. In 1914, the outbreak of World War I not only delayed the couple's return to Europe, it also firmly changed the world they knew and depicted in their works. Then, in 1915, their idyllic cosmopolitan life together of art and travel completely disappeared with Fox's cancer diagnosis and subsequent death within days. Carrick's optimism, innovation and energetic approach to work and life took on a newfound precarity. She would later also spend World War II in Australia, supporting the war effort while the contents of her apartment in occupied Paris were auctioned by the Nazis in 1943, as she was the widow of a Jewish person. Becoming an Australian citizen in 1949, she continued her restless, nomadic life of art, travelling the world and capturing bustling modernity in her paintings.

After his death, Carrick became the steward and custodian of Fox's legacy. Tinges of her Edwardian period of security, delicate gentility and interiority remain captured in Fox's works, which Carrick resolutely promoted and sustained in the public eye. She worked tirelessly to place his work in collections, sometimes diminishing the significance of her own work in comparison.[16] By the time of Carrick's death in 1952, almost all of Fox's key works had been collected by major institutions, in large part due to her persistent lobbying of gallery directors. This would eventually lead to Ruth Zubans's 1995 catalogue and accompanying 1994 National Gallery of Victoria exhibition.

Such in-depth public recognition was slower for Carrick, and it is only in recent decades that her works have become more prominent in the public eye. Her French market scenes have been setting auction records since the late 1990s as most of her major works had been left in private hands, thus enabling them to circulate on the market and drive-up prices. Within the academic sphere, the work of several feminist art historians since the 1970s has been focused on uncovering overlooked women artists, leading to a more nuanced appreciation of the cosmopolitan Belle Époque period and shifting Carrick's characterisation as an English artist.[17] Moreover, it is only in recent years that her works have been regularly hung in permanent collection displays of Australian state and national institutions. This shift reflects an increased understanding that despite their brief marriage of only 10 years, Ethel Carrick and Emanuel Phillips Fox's shared dialogues and artistic union contributed to the vibrant worlds they brought to life for us.

Angela Goddard is a director, curator, writer and editor. In 2015, she was appointed Director of Griffith University Art Museum (GUAM), Meeanjin/Brisbane. She is also a board member of the Sheila Foundation, a foundation for women in visual art, and a former curator of Australian art at Queensland Art Gallery | Gallery of Modern Art, Meeanjin/Brisbane, where she curated *Art, love and life: Ethel Carrick and E. Phillips Fox*, in 2011. Recent exhibitions include *Duty of care*, Institute of Modern Art and GUAM (2024), co-curated with Stephanie Berlangieri and Robert Leonard; *r e a: NATIVE*, GUAM (2024); and *Taring Padi: Tanah Tumpah Darah*, GUAM (2024), co-curated with Alexander Supartono. Recent publications include *Richard Bell Reader: TATE Modern* (2023); *Richard Bell Reader: documenta fifteen* (2022), co-edited with Megan Tamati-Quennell; and *Gordon Bennett: Selected writings* (2020), co-edited with Tim Riley Walsh.

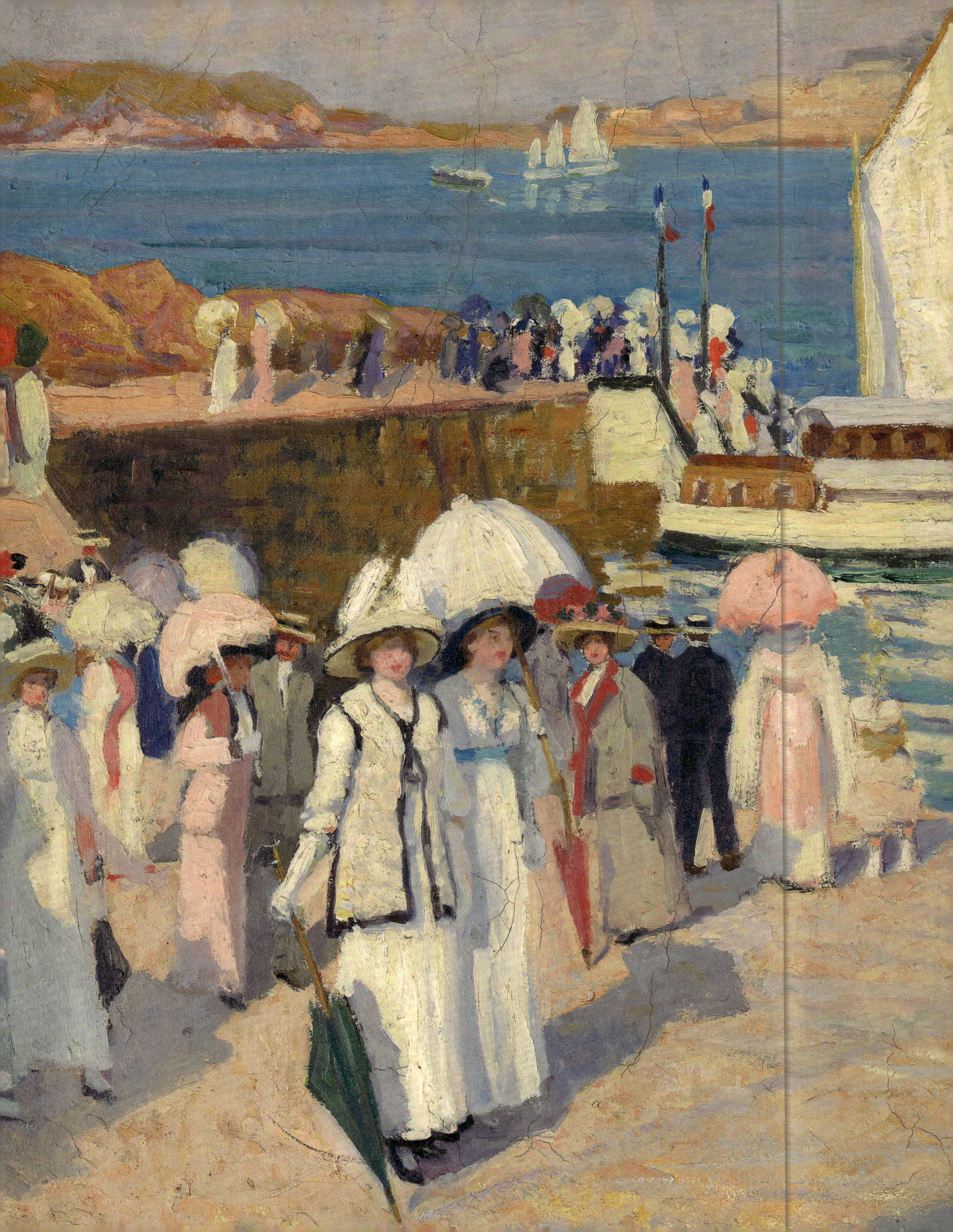

Sensations of summer: Carrick's French beach resort paintings

Denise Mimmocchi

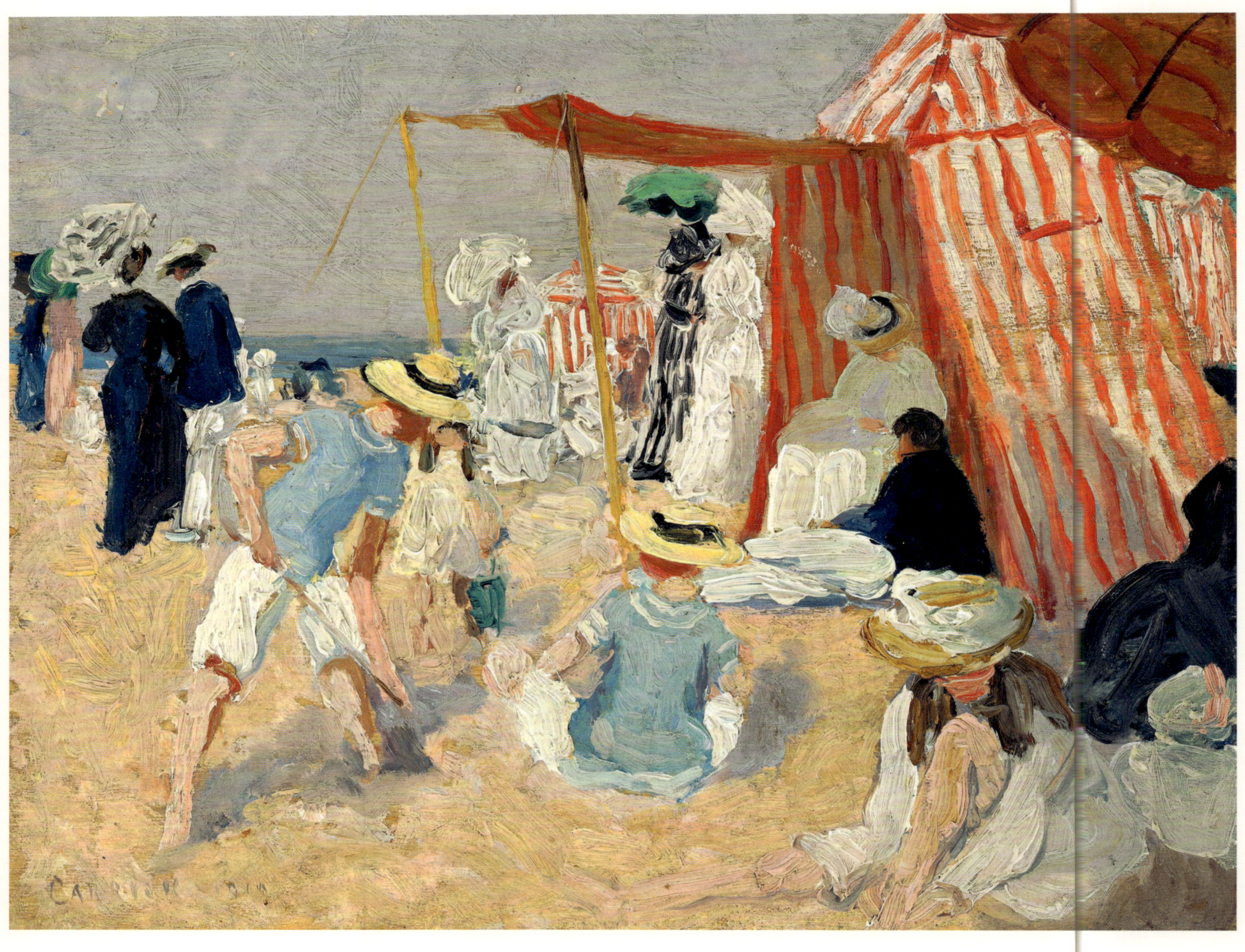

Between 1907 and 1913, Paris-based Ethel Carrick and her artist husband Emanuel Phillips Fox painted at various French coastal resort towns in Normandy and Brittany, and at Royan in the south. The French coastline, which had inspired artistic experimentation for earlier generations of modern painters, galvanised Carrick's elaborations on light, colour and movement. From these summer excursions, Carrick produced a series of arresting plein air sketches and accomplished studio paintings, transposing her aesthetic of urban modernity to take in the atmospheres and vacation culture of the seaside—and creating some of the defining works of her career.

The emergence of French Impressionism in the late decades of the nineteenth century coincided with the establishment of beachside resorts as popular destinations and new sites of middle-class leisure. By the early decades of the new century, paintings of fashionable beach-goers became entrenched in the modern cultural imaging of the French coastline. In the 1860s, Eugène Boudin had been a forerunner of such vacation subjects, and by the end of that century artistic innovators, including Claude Monet, had ushered in a new tradition of painting in which the sensations of summer light and water served as a backdrop to depictions of the relaxing tourist populous.

Carrick's beach resort paintings can be viewed as elaborations on and modernisations of this lineage of seaside art. She claimed the impressionists' emphasis on summer coastal atmospherics, and created paintings about the pleasures of place that are aligned to the Belle Époque ideal of languor, finery and elegance. However, as a painter 'very keen on the modern outlook', Carrick furthered the trope of vacation painting by enforcing her primary motif: the movement and milieu of the contemporary crowd.[1] In her resort works she created her own modern idylls, instilled with the poetics of summer, while envisaging the changing dynamics that mass tourism brought to the leisured spaces of the coastline.

Working at beach resorts opened a new realm of human activity for Carrick to paint. She was well-versed in painting the activities of the city, such as marketplace bustle or group gatherings in Parisian parks and gardens. Set against an ocean backdrop and with the influx of a different light, Carrick's resort paintings were infused with a renewed energy, one where time and the dynamics of the crowd appear slowed down but not completely relaxed.

Previous
The quay at Dinard c 1911–12 (detail cat 102, p 159), oil on canvas on plywood, National Gallery of Victoria

Opposite
cat 99 *Sur la plage* (On the beach) 1910, oil on wood panel, private collection

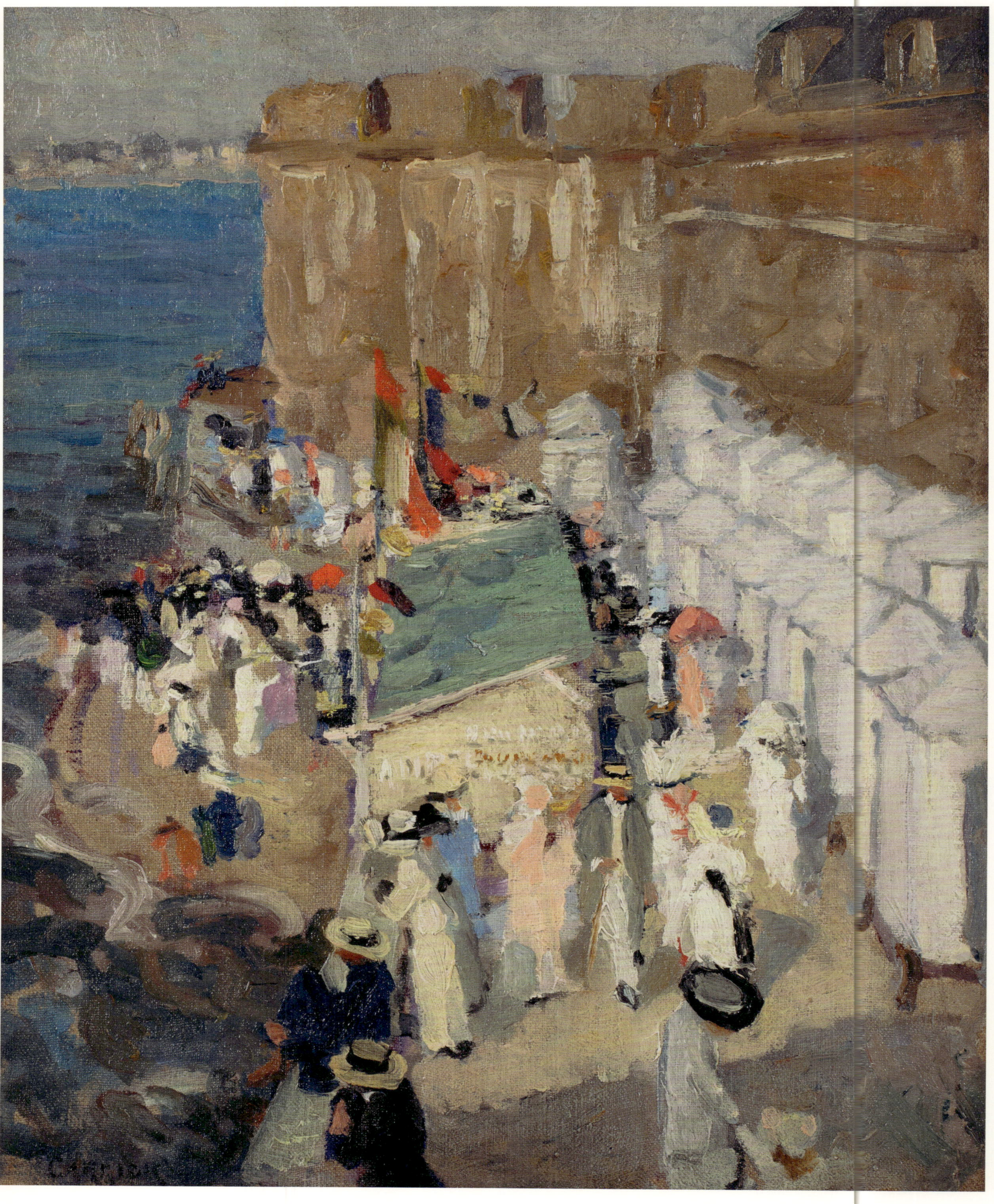

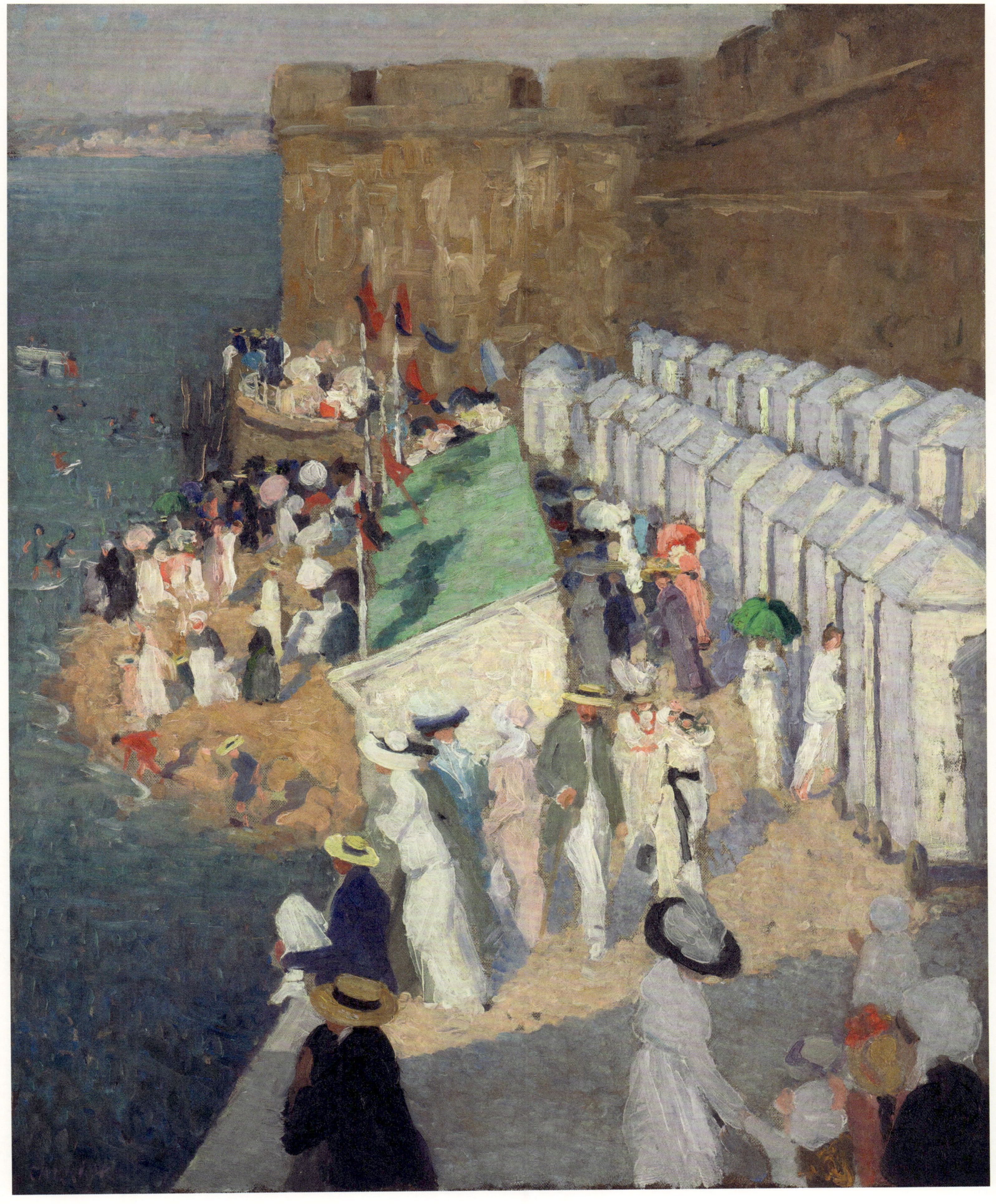

Carrick was an incessant traveller and there is, perhaps, something of the pace of her travels reflected in the tempo of her art, even as she imaged holiday scenes. In 1911, after a period spent moving between Spain, North Africa and the south of France, Carrick and Fox spent three weeks visiting St Malo and Dinard in Brittany, Trouville and Deauville in Normandy, and Royan on the French Atlantic coastline. The seaside trip was in part to aid Carrick as she recuperated from illness, but her output suggests that the artist fully applied herself to her work as the couple travelled. From this trip, Carrick created two major paintings, *La marée haute à Saint-Malo (High tide at St Malo)* c 1911–12 (cat 101, p 157) and *The quay at Dinard* c 1911–12 (cat 102). She completed both works in her studio and exhibited them in Paris in 1912.[2] These paintings, while connected in subject matter, differ in their emphasis, and suggest how Carrick negotiated between experimentation and the ideal as she evoked the French coast.

The fortified seaport town of St Malo on the English Channel coast remains known, as it was in Carrick's day, for the spectacle of its high tides—the once-described 'galloping' rush of water that rapidly claims the expanse of beach and instantly transforms the coastline. Carrick titled her painting *High tide at St Malo* to reference this phenomenon and included figures perched on the sea wall watching the event. But the tides are not the true subject of Carrick's work. Instead, it was the cluster of tourists that compelled her to paint what she considered to be her 'most successful picture of a moving crowd'.[3]

High tide at St Malo is an impressively composed work of human activity within a tightly compressed space. From a steep vantage point, Carrick pictures the crowd filing along the promenade, their movements receding into abstracted coloured patterns. For all the sun-filled delight of the work, there is a feeling of enclosure in the painting: the *taches* (touches) of figures are contained within the structured bands of fortress walls, the serried changing-huts and the blue ocean. Carrick ultimately holds to the forms of naturalism, but her attention to movement propels a quasi-abstracted space filled with light and colour.

Despite having all the hallmarks of plein-air spontaneity, *High tide at St Malo* was a studio creation, enlarged and adapted from a smaller composition that may have been painted on site, known as *Quay at St Malo* 1911 (cat 100, p 156). Comparing the two paintings reveals the way the artist transformed observed detail to abstracted effect, applying a series of small yet compositionally significant changes to enforce her key motif of movement.

In *High tide at St Malo*, Carrick adjusted the range of figures, adding, eliminating and enlarging people in her crowd to create a cleaner sweep of movement. The dotted spectacle of people instils the composition with an energised rhythm, with the unfolding shape of figures counterbalanced by the curve of sand and the rotund fortress. Among the high-keyed flourishes of summery fashion, Carrick includes black details of dress to act as grounding points in the composition and to lead the eye through the momentum of the crowd. She reduces details deemed unnecessary—on the fortress walls, the flags and rippling waters—and instead guides attention through the motion of figures.

Previous left
cat 100 *Quay at St Malo* 1911, oil on canvas, University Art Collection, Chau Chak Wing Museum, The University of Sydney

Previous right
cat 101 *La marée haute à Saint-Malo (High tide at St Malo)* c 1911–12, oil on canvas, Art Gallery of New South Wales

Opposite
cat 102 *The quay at Dinard* c 1911–12, oil on canvas on plywood, National Gallery of Victoria

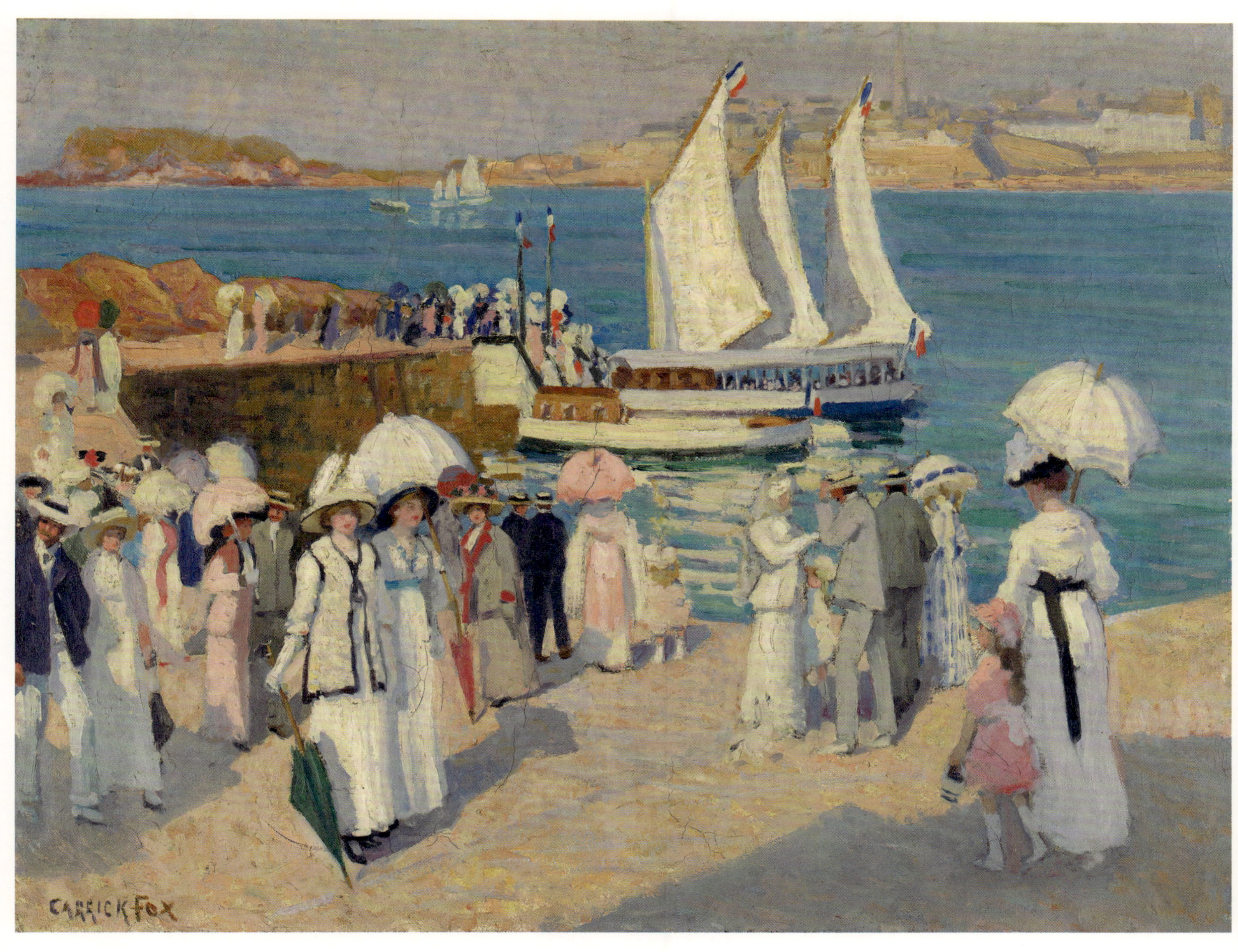
CARRICK FOX

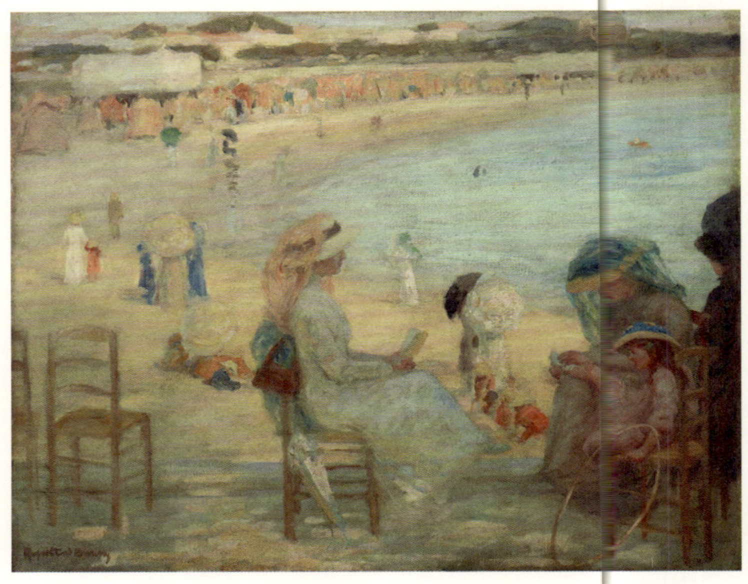

fig 39 Rupert Bunny, *On the beach (Royan)* c 1908, oil on canvas on hardboard
Art Gallery of New South Wales

While emphasising mass movement, Carrick does not forgo suggestions of individuals. Despite the abstracted flow of figures, a strong impression of the crowd's immaculate fashion remains—indeed, Carrick has a beautiful way of painting the features of hats in shorthand. While void of narrative, the picture is filled with human detail: characters of her crowd lean into their gait, ponder along the shores, and stroll at a summer's pace. We see playing children and their attendants, black-attired nannies, scattered throughout the scene.

Movement was Carrick's key motif, but *High tide at St Malo* is equally a composition of exuberant colour. The crowd is conveyed by patterns of impastoed pure pigments applied over an incredibly sparse ground layer, intensifying their impact. Figurative forms dissolve into this saturated, confettied colour, giving a sense of fleeting momentum. Central to Carrick's composition is a brilliant band of emerald green for the rooftop of the central beach hut. It was a pigment banned in 1900 due to the lethal toxicity of its arsenic component, but it remained sought after by artists—including Paul Gauguin, Vincent van Gogh and Paul Cézanne—for its distinct, non-naturalistic hue. Deliberately sourced by Carrick as the compositional centrepiece of her work, it adds a strikingly modern accent to her painting and marks her shift from the 'real' towards an abstracted and poeticised version of place.[4]

Carrick's resort paintings are scenes of bourgeois leisure, but they are not entirely calming. In her vignettes of tourist life, she paints people playing, pacing and parading along sands and beach promenades, giving an overwhelming sense of the action of holidays. In *Beach scene* c 1909 (cat 33, p 65), the striped patterns of dress combined with the red-and-white beach tents create a visual stir that is hastened, as with numerous other works, by Carrick's agitated brushwork. Her representation of children playing, such as within *Beach scene* and *Sur la plage* (On the beach) 1910 (cat 99, p 154), is energetic, the scenes anything but still—and the work of supervising women is noted.

Carrick's seaside scenes reveal the beachside holiday as a gendered arena. If Thea Proctor envisaged female zones of modern leisure as ones of languor and luxury, Carrick instead stresses their busyness. In another work, also titled *Sur la plage* (On the beach) c 1910 (cat 105, p 163), for instance, she depicts the toil of a nanny. These black-uniformed figures were as ubiquitous a presence in middle-class

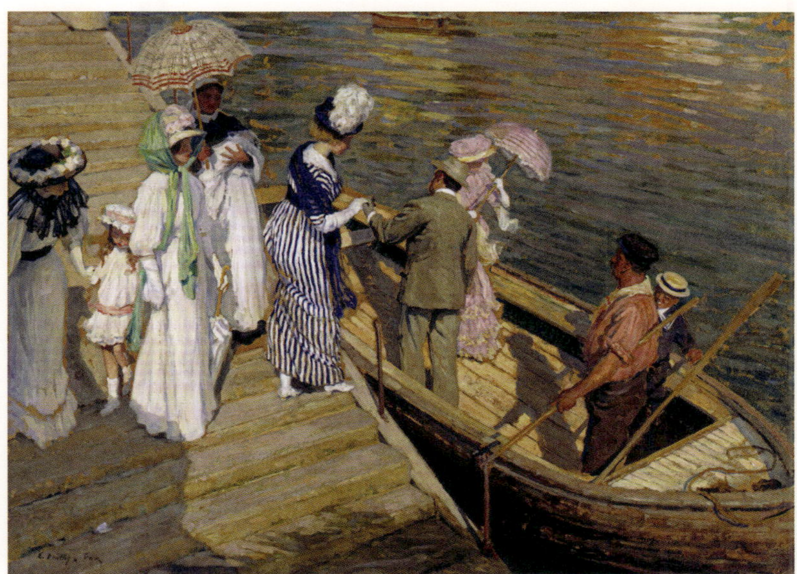

fig 40 Emanuel Phillips Fox, *The ferry* c 1910–11, oil on canvas, Art Gallery of New South Wales

vacations—and previously observable in Carrick's St Malo painting—as they were in scenes of daily life in Paris. The enjoyment of place, as Carrick's works remind us, is socially structured.

Overwhelmingly, Carrick's paintings image the seaside as crowded, marked by the vacationing influx. In *On the beach* c 1911 (cat 106, pp 164–65), the sands of Royan are filled with people and beach tents, leaving an impression of closeness. The tenor of Carrick's work is in marked contrast to that of her artist–friend and Australian expatriate Rupert Bunny, who had painted the Royan beach a few years earlier. In Bunny's *On the beach (Royan)* c 1908 (fig 39), the summer crowds are hazy, distant details, removed from the foreground female figure who is symbolically charged to embody the dreamy sensations of place.

Yet while Carrick's crowded vacation scenes are full and energised, they are not fraught. In her works, the 'Age of Anxiety' that James Gleeson once referred to had 'not yet dawned'.[5] Aligned with the sentiments of summer and the splendour of middle-class finesse, Carrick created her own poeticised repertoire of Belle Époque imagery. More than any other of Carrick's known resort works, *The quay at Dinard* (cat 102, p 159) services this ideal.

Dinard was a ferry ride across the emerald channel waters from St Malo and was the more opulent of the Brittany resort towns. For an artist who closely observed human activity as the basis for her works, the high-end parade of Dinard tourists proved an appealing subject for Carrick. She may have had in mind the elegant boating party of Fox's recently completed *The ferry* c 1910–11 (fig 40) as she considered the scene around Dinard's jetty landing for her painting. But *The quay at Dinard* is ultimately distinct in emphasis and execution from Fox's work. While the couple's seaside plein air sketches (like those from their North African trip that same year) are at times strikingly similar, *The quay at Dinard* is indicative of diverging studio practices. Carrick strayed from Fox's commitment to realism as she sought the modern sensations of colour, light and motion in her art.

The initial impression of *The quay at Dinard* is the immersive blue of the water, a colour that sets the tenor of this tribute to the luxuries of summer. Against this light-filled colour, Carrick adds the keynote of white dresses and sails, combining the sumptuous feel of refined fabrics and sun-drenched ambience. Her palette is one of bright, creamy, pastel hues, whites and pinks offset occasionally by black details of clothing.

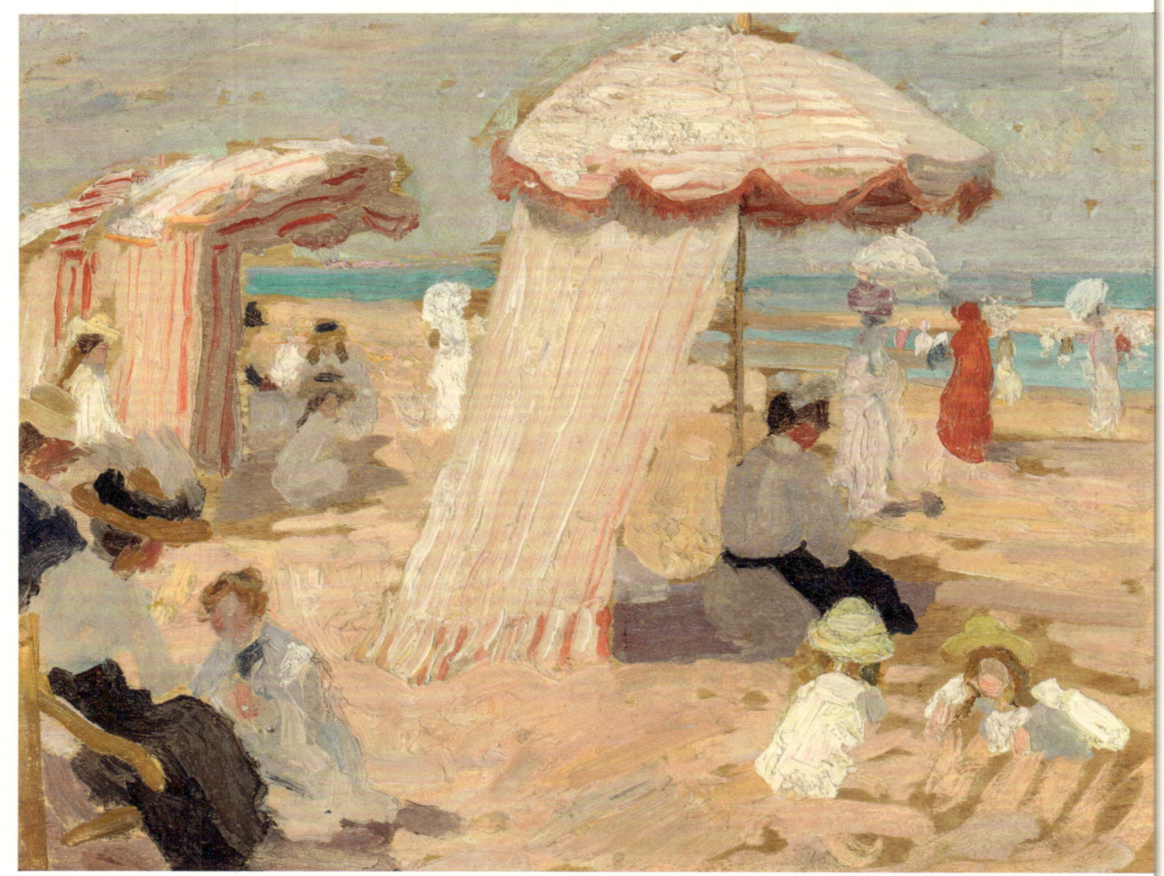

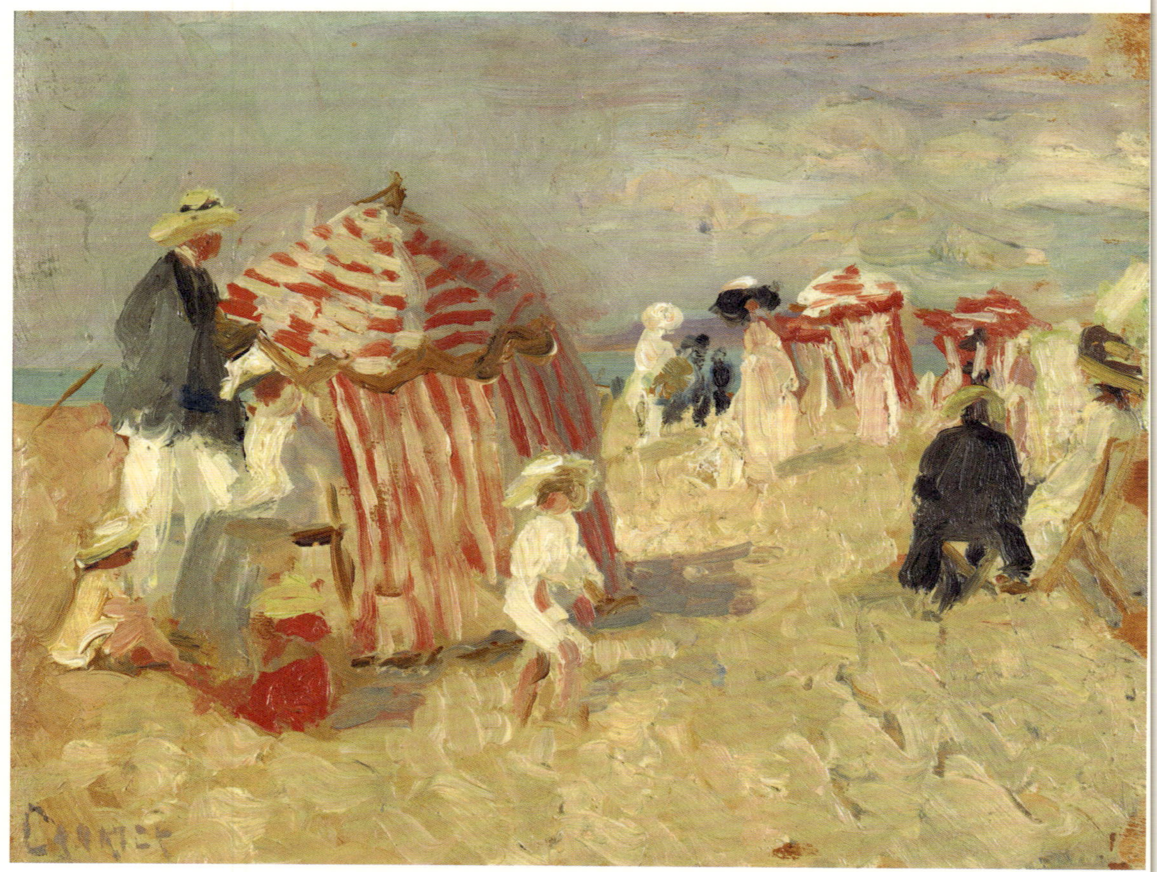

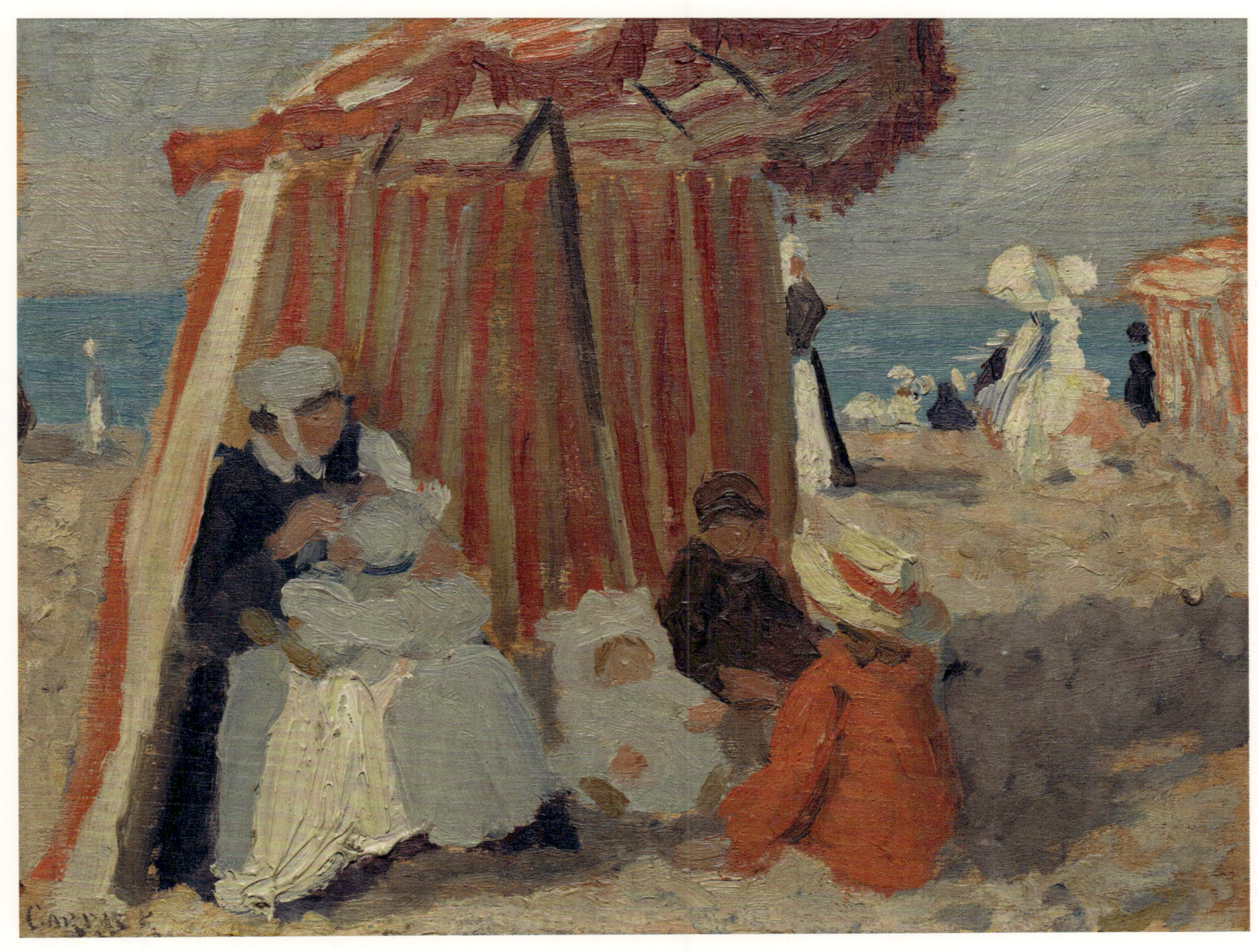

Opposite, top to bottom
cat 103 *Sur la plage* (On the beach) c 1910, oil on wood panel, Art Gallery of South Australia

cat 104 *On the sands* 1910, oil on wood panel, private collection

Above
cat 105 *Sur la plage* (On the beach) c 1910, oil on panel, Queensland Art Gallery | Gallery of Modern Art

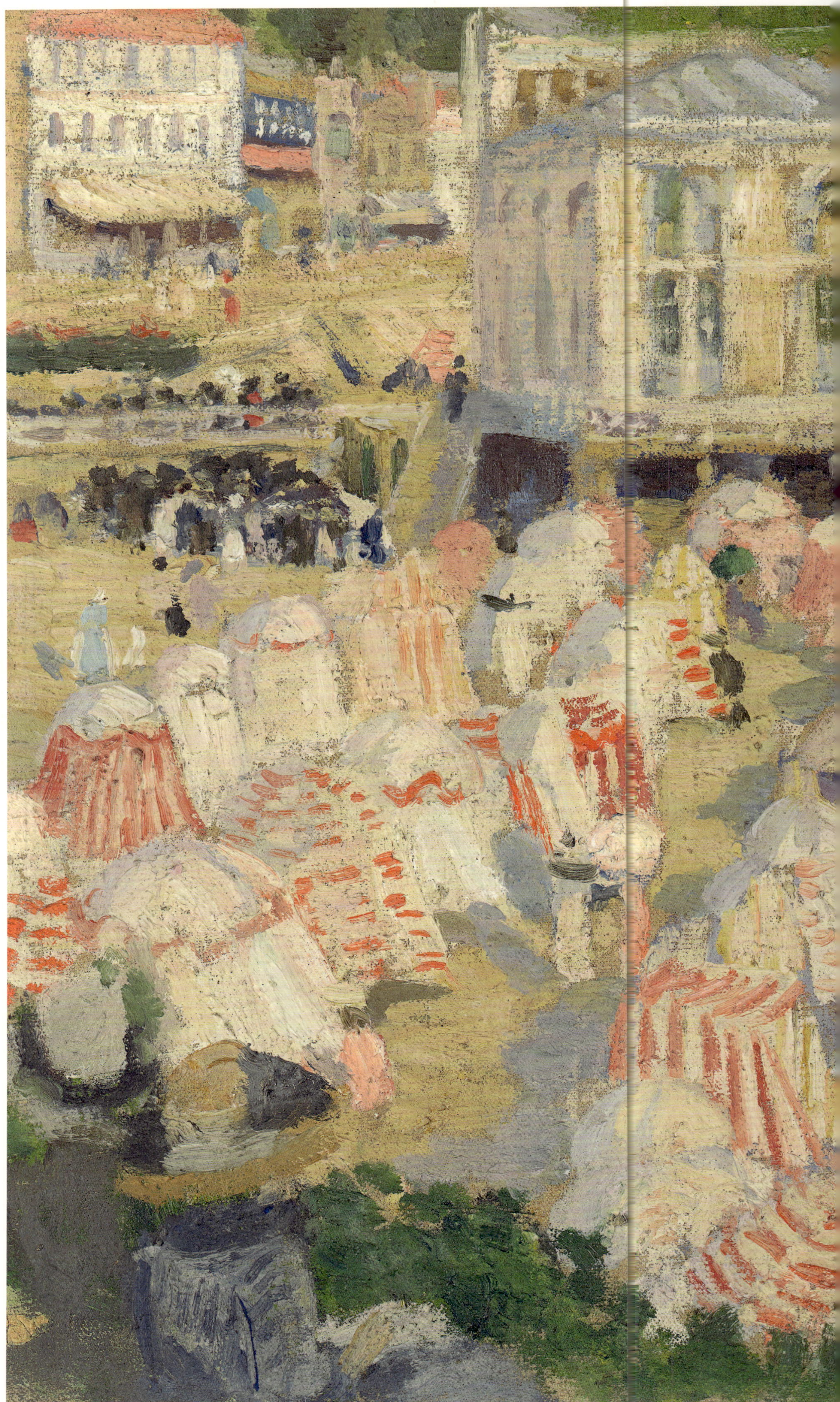

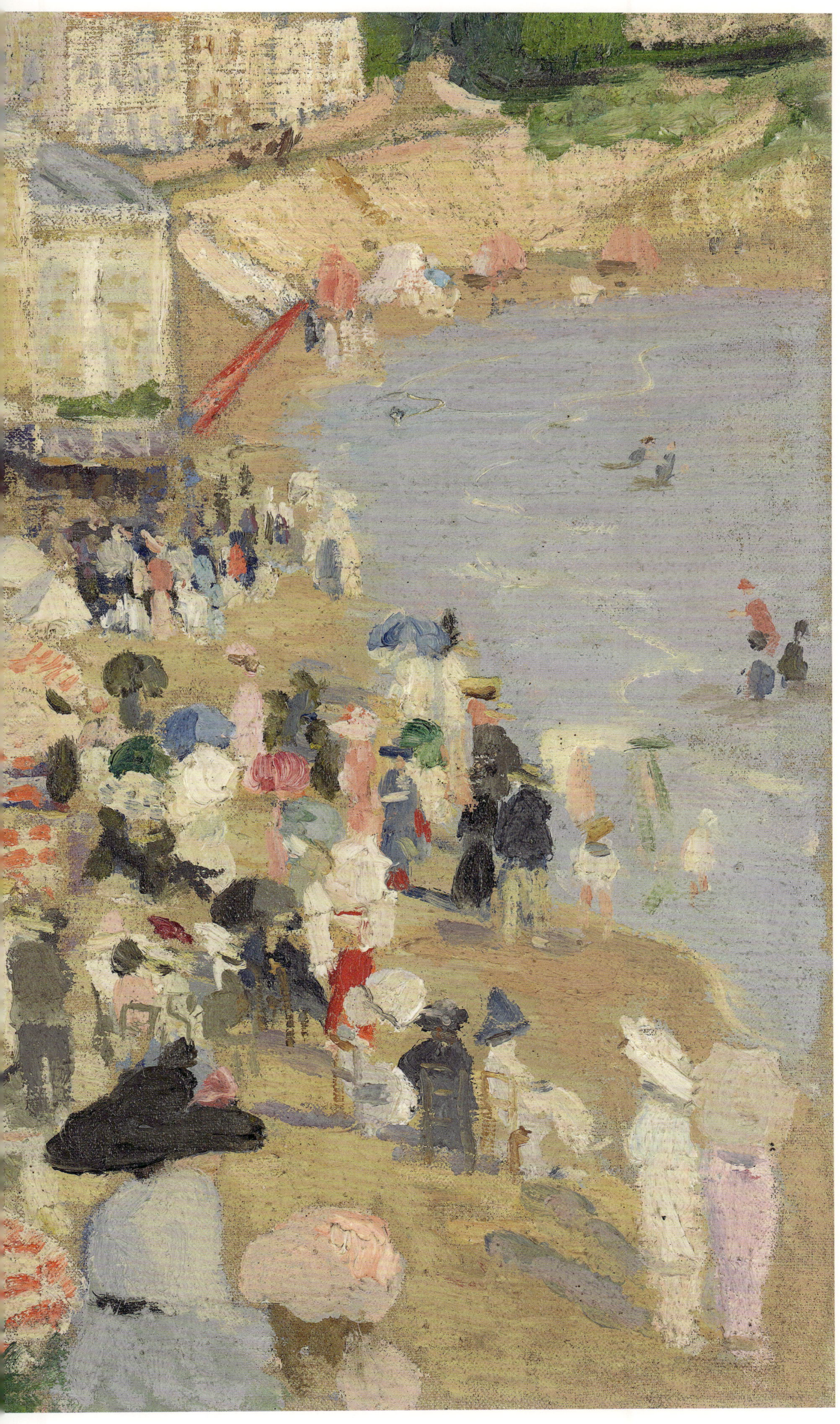

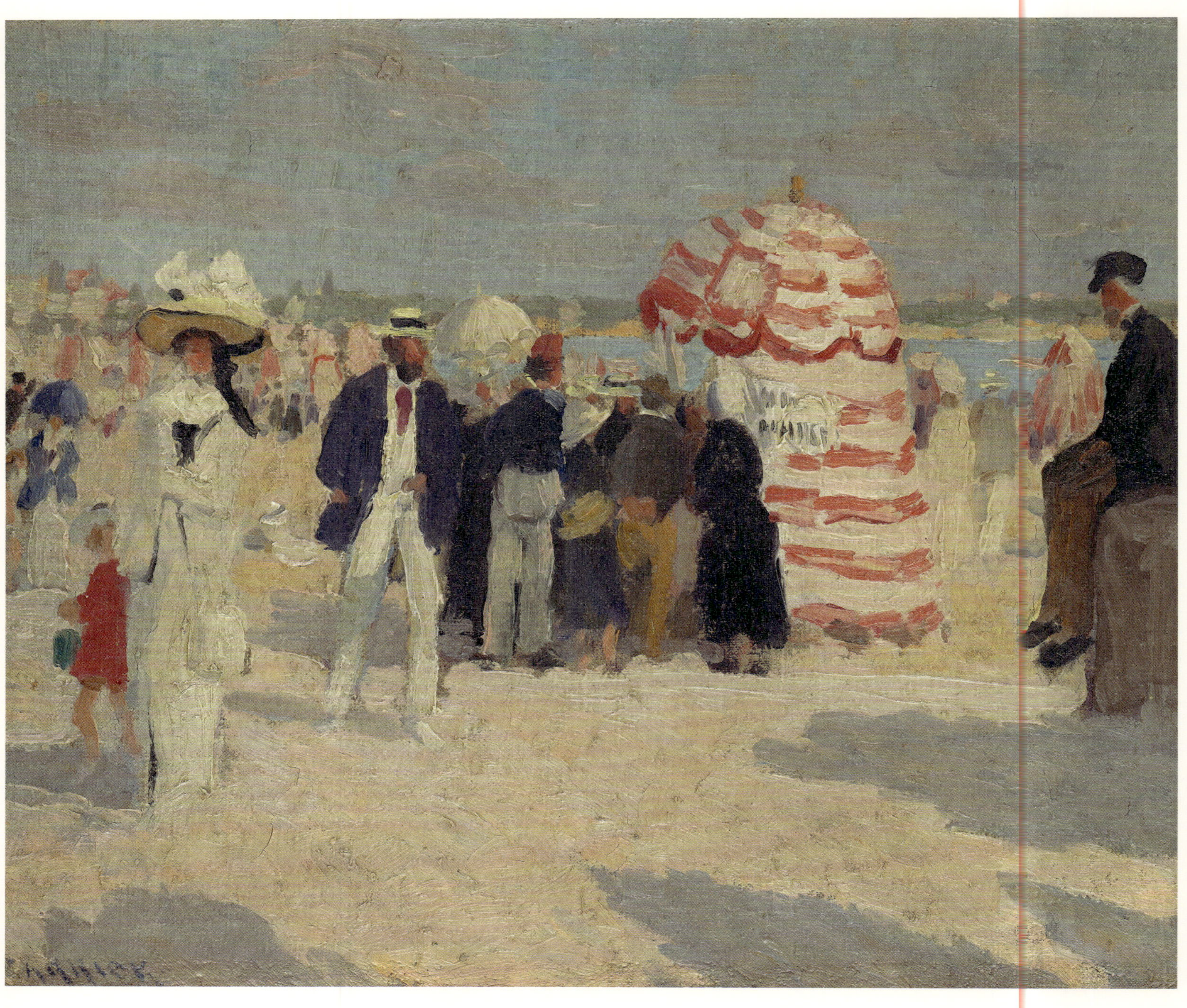

Previous
cat 106 ***On the beach*** **c 1911, oil on canvas, National Gallery of Victoria**

Opposite
cat 107 ***On the beach*** **c 1909, oil on canvas, Queensland Art Gallery | Gallery of Modern Art**

Unlike *High tide at St Malo, The quay at Dinard* is less about the fleeting than it is an evocation of time slowed down by the laid-back pace of summer. Carrick stills her crowd. Viewing them from a grounded level and without an abstracted sense of motion, she paints features of dress, smiling expressions and the cordial greetings of couples, details that add to the air of bourgeois leisure and elegance. There is a sense of performance to this manicured crowd, and the figures proceed like the extras of a film shoot. The mood is one of luxury, their movements are effortless. There is no sign of the working nanny in this opalescent spectacle of refinement.

High tide at St Malo and *The quay at Dinard* were among the paintings that Carrick brought with her when she and Fox visited Australia in 1913—and they featured in solo exhibitions in Sydney and Melbourne. Both paintings were enthusiastically received, and reviews noted the sense of light, warmth and motion that Carrick instilled in these paintings. Subjects of French holiday glamour, popular with audiences in Paris, would have also added to their appeal locally in Australia.

The exhilarating sense of modernity offered by Carrick's works, such as *High tide at St Malo*, was noted by the local press. With their 'vibrating light, colour and movement', her paintings showcased abstracted effect, 'eliminating the unessentials'.[6] It was a model of art that strayed from the stronghold of narrative and naturalism, pre-empting the developing modernisms that would flourish in Sydney during the war and interwar years.

In Sydney in 1913, Carrick would return to seaside subjects in a series of works at Manly and Balmoral. As in her earlier French paintings, Carrick was drawn to the movements of beachgoers. Among these works is *Christmas Day on Manly Beach* 1913 (cat 118, pp 194–95). After the experiences of French resort holidays, Carrick was perhaps struck by the casual approach to the beach-going public in Manly, painting the crowd amassed across the sands in casual dress and flocking to the water in the distance. Her beach scene remains a largely feminised zone. Removed from the parading bourgeoisie of Brittany, Carrick responded to the informality of these beachgoers with a marked sense of modernity, her composition emphasising the contours of the crowd, and the block colours and rhythmic arrangement she used to describe them.

Carrick's French beach idylls were painted during an era when the glamour and graciousness of bourgeois life cultivated the image of a Belle Époque. If Carrick's works played to this ideal, they did so with an emphasis on the rush of modern life. Hers were ultimately happy crowds, a humanity amassed but unburdened. Following the death of her husband, Carrick spent the majority of the war years in Australia. She returned to Paris in 1916 and resumed painting joyfully coloured works of flower stalls, corners of modern life seemingly removed from the trauma of conflict. But scenes painted at the Place de la Concorde reveal that the mood of Carrick's crowds had changed, the colours of life were now sombre. The world of idle summer delights had passed and the Age of Anxiety had arrived.

Denise Mimmocchi is Senior Curator, Australian Art at the Art Gallery of New South Wales, Gadigal Nura/Sydney. Recent exhibitions and publications include *Margel Hinder: modern in motion* (2021); *Tony Tuckson* (2018); *O'Keeffe, Cossington Smith, Preston: making Modernism* (2016), co-curator; *Sydney moderns: art for a new world* (2013), co-curated with Deborah Edwards; and *Australian Symbolism: the art of dreams* (2012).

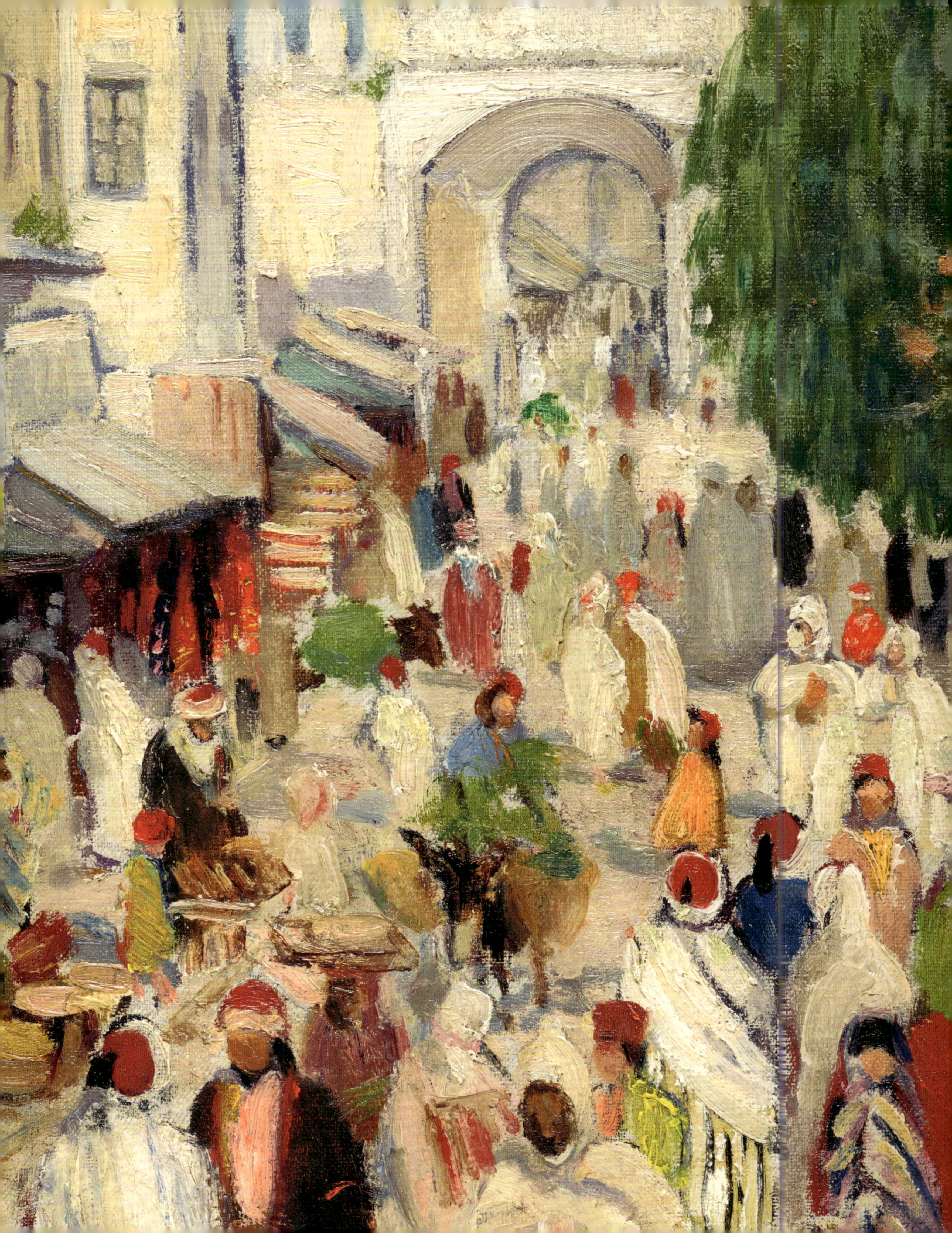

Light in the landscape: Carrick in North Africa

Emma Kindred

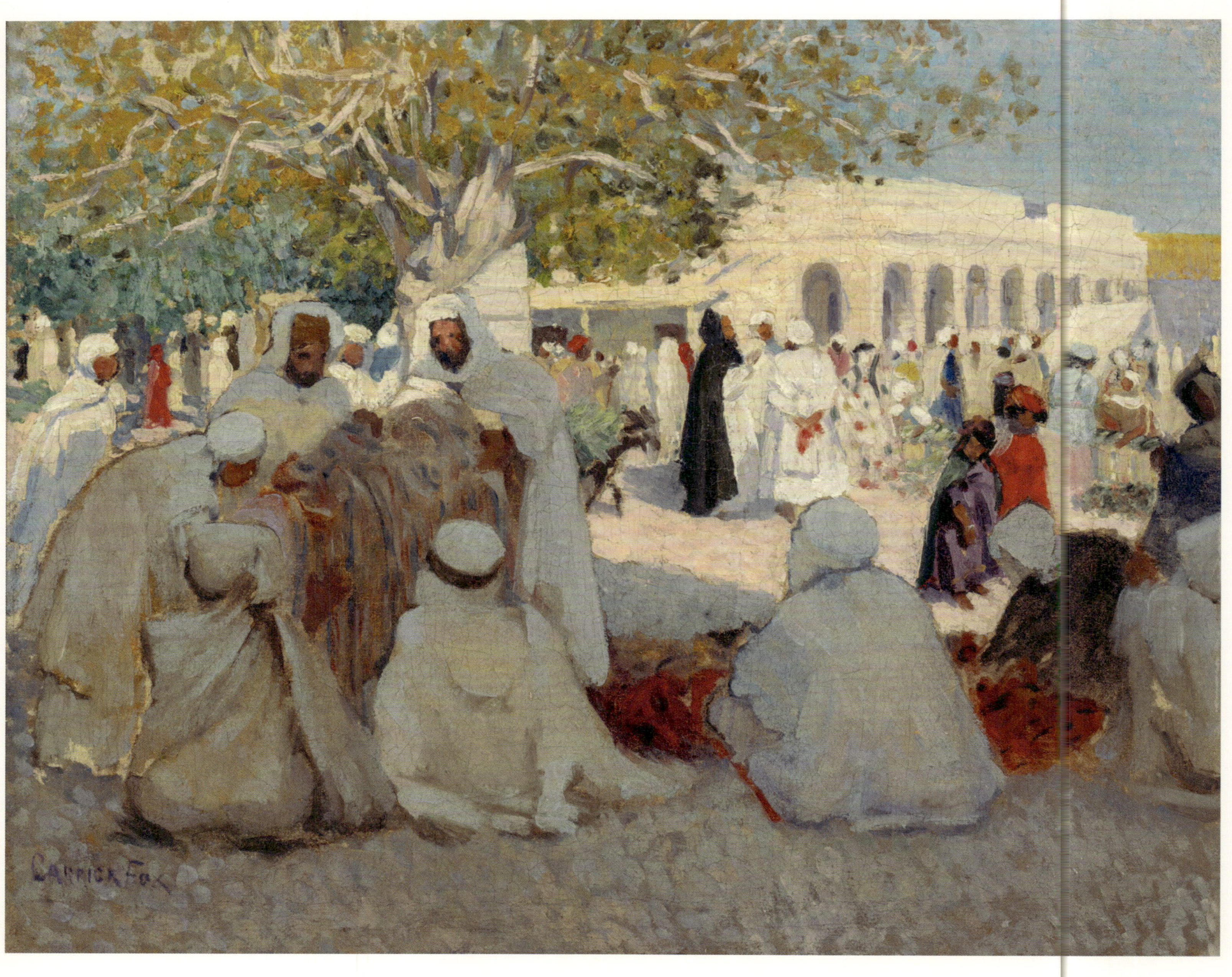
CARRICK FOX

When Ethel Carrick exhibited her North African paintings in Sydney in 1925, a reviewer praised her 'Algerian subjects ... distinguished by bold brush work and strong notes of color'.[1] Another applauded 'her skill in managing crowds in many street scenes about Tunis. These are real crowds, alive and purposeful'.[2] With a broad yet faithful rendering of space and architectural form, Carrick's work was inflected by a post-impressionist preoccupation with pattern and atmospheric texture. Over two separate journeys to North Africa, in 1911 with husband Emanuel Phillips Fox and again over the winter season of 1919 to 1920, Carrick sought out light in the landscape, capturing the brilliance and colour of the people and places she encountered.

While Carrick travelled extensively throughout her career, the 1911 journey signalled her first significant experience as a foreigner. Responding to an urban environment hitherto encountered only through the mediated gaze of Orientalist painters and photographers, Carrick drew on a painterly language honed in Parisian markets and French seaside resorts, engaging with the broader aesthetic possibilities of monumental architecture, and other elements of North African culture and peoples.

As a British-born Parisian resident, Carrick participated in Empire. Regions of French-held colonial North Africa, fashionable with painter–travellers in search of light and saleable subjects, had become a favoured destination for tourists seeking warmer climes. By the turn of the twentieth century, Tangier, Algiers and Tunis had sizeable European populations, functioning as centres of foreign commercial and diplomatic activity in North Africa before agitation for independence and decolonisation intensified after World War II. These coastal cities were reached by regular steamships departing Mediterranean ports. Travel literature promoted an interest in North Africa, known also as the Maghreb, generating expectations of a timeless land populated by picturesque 'types'. While American writer Edith Wharton lamented that 'Morocco still lacks a guide-book' in 1920, English-language guides published by Bradshaw, John Murray and Baedeker covered Carrick's destinations with various levels of detail.[3] These pocket-sized volumes 'mapped' what Derek Gregory describes as 'a double geography'.[4] Tourists wanted to experience sites with the comfort and security of familiar amenities, while also

Previous
A market in Kairouan c 1919–20 (detail cat 113, p 181), oil on canvas, Art Gallery of New South Wales

Opposite
cat 108 *Arabs bargaining* c 1911, also known as *Marché à Bou Saada* (Market at Bou Saada), oil on canvas, private collection

seeking reassurance that this modernity had not damaged or altered the exotic 'Orient' construct that such representation created and that they had come to see.

In the planning towards their 1911 trip, Fox was likely influenced by the travels of fellow Australian artists, as well as his teacher and celebrated French Orientalist painter Jean-Léon Gérôme. In 1883, Tom Roberts had gone on a sketching tour through Moorish Spain, returning to Australia with new approaches to capturing light and atmospheric effect.[5] In 1891, Charles Conder had sought refuge from illness in coastal Mustapha on the eastern outskirts of Algiers, and Arthur Streeton had spent two months painting in Cairo on his way from Australia to England in 1897.[6] Bessie Davidson made a painting excursion to Tangier in the company of Margaret Preston in 1906, and Hilda Rix Nicholas gained critical attention exhibiting the paintings and drawings completed during her journeys there in 1912 and 1914.[7] Anne Dangar spent six months in Morocco in 1939, with her work further afield in Fez, Marrakesh, Safi and Rabat made possible by changes granting increased access to foreign artists working in the French protectorate.

In the late nineteenth century, Australia's art-going public encountered Orientalist paintings acquired by the state galleries, including major works by English artist Sir Edward Poynter and French painter Nasreddine (Étienne) Dinet. Australian artist Robert Dowling's *A Sheikh and his son entering Cairo on their return from a pilgrimage to Mecca* 1874, painted following his journey to Egypt over the winter season of 1872 to 1873, was acquired by the National Gallery of Victoria in 1878. Dinet's *The snake charmer* 1889, purchased for the National Art Gallery of New South Wales in 1890, was popular with both critics and the gallery's visitors.[8] Painted in the Algerian town of Laghouat, the work was a favourite of Rix Nicholas, who was taken by how well her memory of North Africa matched 'the heat of that sun which throws back hot reflections from the gold earth'.[9]

Dinet had built a traditional Berber-style villa in Bou Saada, often welcoming visiting artists there when he was not spending the hot summer months in France. Though art business often took Dinet to the capital Algiers, Carrick and Fox likely encountered the artist during the six weeks they worked in Bou Saada.[10] Roger Benjamin has noted that Dinet's fluency in Arabic, along with his semi-permanent move to the oasis town and subsequent conversion to Islam, provided a very different Orientalist model than that of less-committed painter–travellers.[11] While no Australian artist engaged with the culture and society of North Africa to such an extent, *The snake charmer* (while more theatrically 'exotic' than any works by Carrick) was a reference point for those working directly from nature, like Fox and Carrick, who believed travel and the process of painting en plein air were vital. Though not associated directly with Impressionism, Dinet adopted an impressionist palette, and artists such as Roberts and Streeton emulated his approach when painting the dry, bleached Australian light. In 1890, French critic Georges Lafenestre noted that 'Algeria is a good school for colourists' and that Dinet was 'among the first to express the extraordinary and unexpected effects of the sun on the figures in the open air'.[12]

In 1906 Fox delivered a commissioned portrait of the Sultan of Morocco, Sultan Moulay Abdelaziz. Grace Joel wrote in *Art & Architecture* that Fox might be obliged to pay a visit to that part of the world to finish the work, but he likely relied on photographic sources.[13]

Opposite, top to bottom
cat 109 *Arab scene* 1920, oil on board, University Art Collection, Chau Chak Wing Museum, The University of Sydney

cat 110 *A street in Tunisia* 1920, oil on wood panel, private collection

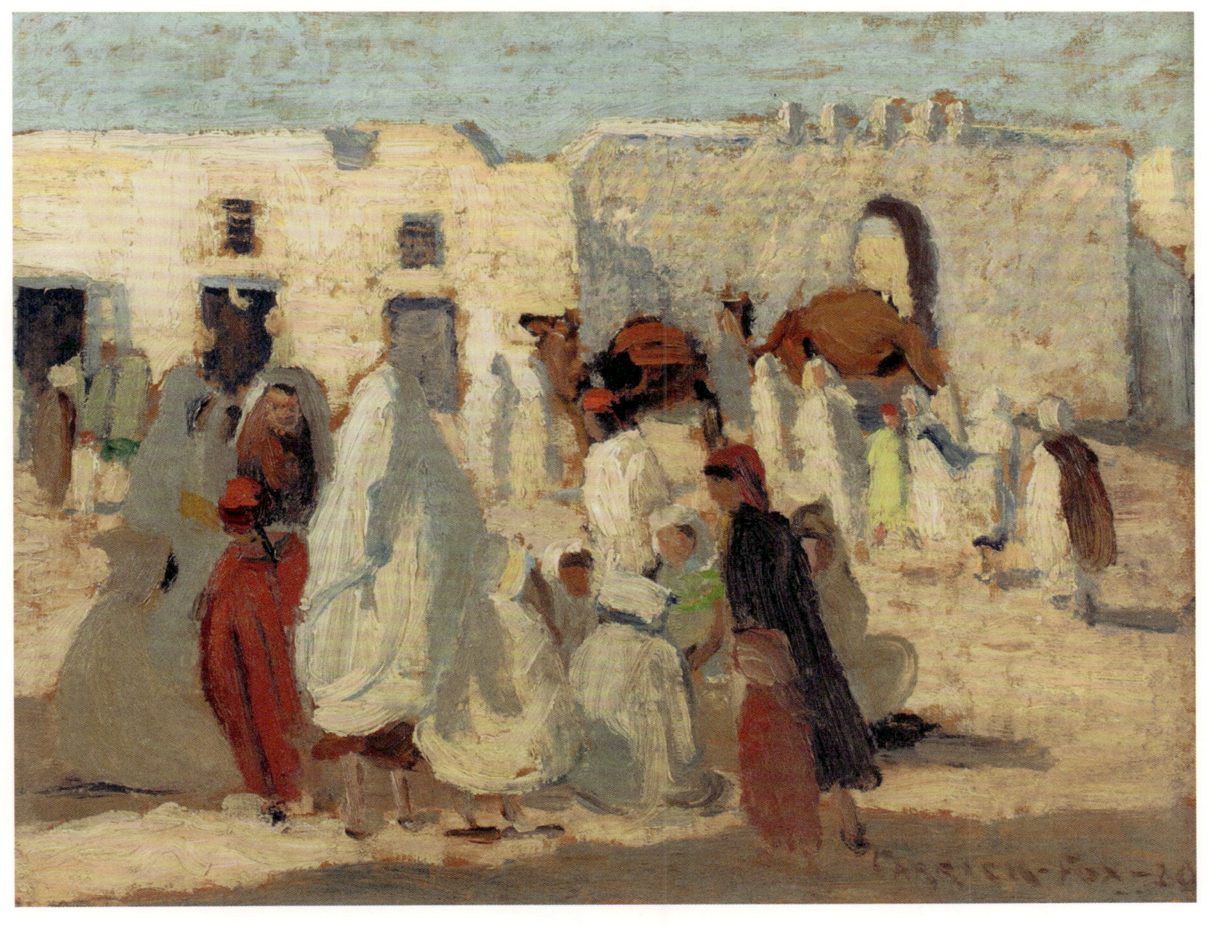
CARRICK-FOX-20

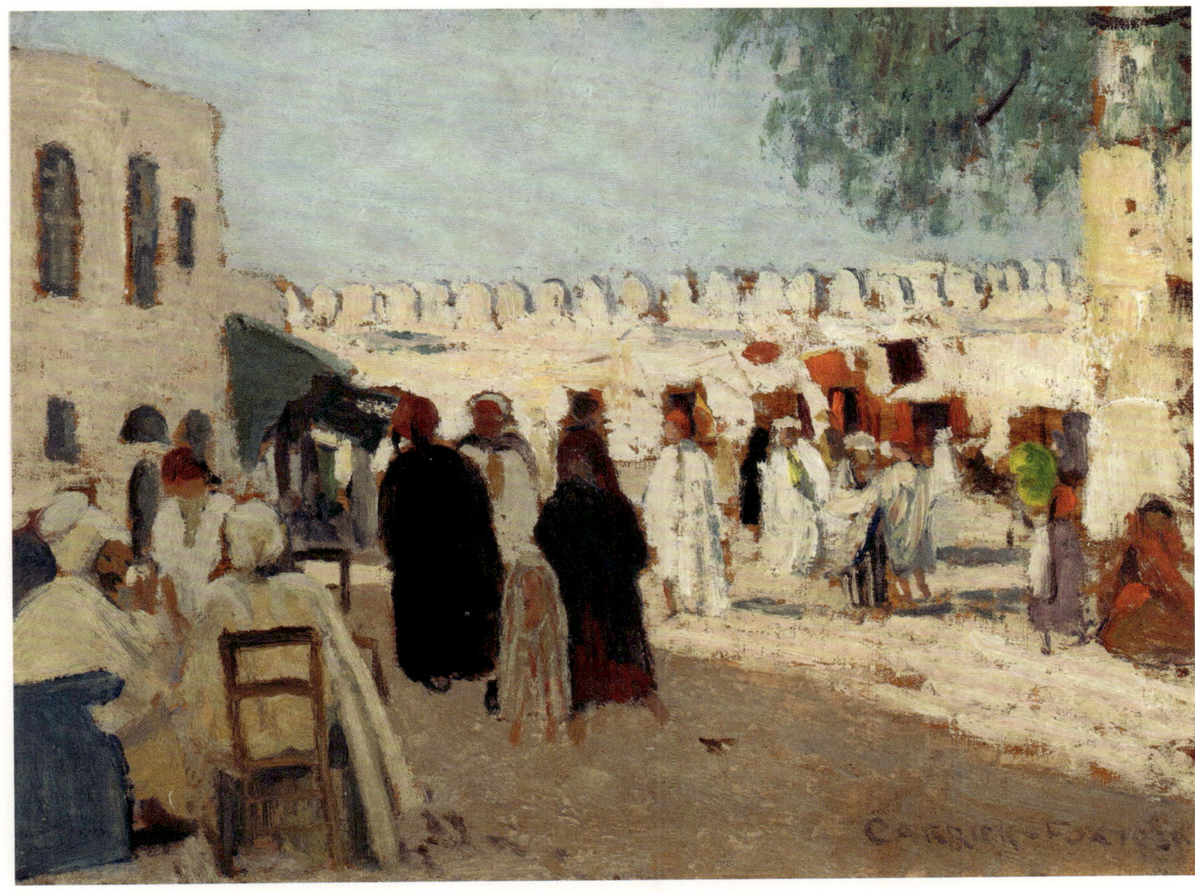

In May, *The Sydney Morning Herald* reported that 'Mr E. Phillip [Phillips] Fox has just completed a successful portrait (equestrian) of the Emperor of Morocco. This unfortunately he could not exhibit, as it had to be dispatched at once, to Morocco'.[14] While the completed commission has not been traced, an oil study bears the label of Sydney gallery Anthony Hordern & Sons, where it may have been exhibited. Fox's composition, with the Sultan mounted on a horse surrounded by the royal guard, repeated key motifs employed by other artists who had painted Morocco's sultans, including Eugène Delacroix's 1845 submission to the Paris Salon depicting Sultan Abd al-Rahman.[15] The rising forms of white architecture dominate, holding light that fills the scene from above. There is little evidence, however, to suggest that Carrick—or indeed Fox—travelled to Morocco in 1906, and it was not until their 1911 journey through North Africa that the artists would produce work of the region for exhibition in Paris and Australia.[16]

Headed for Algeria, Carrick and Fox departed Paris in mid-February 1911, sailing from Marseilles by steamship. They travelled south from the capital, 'motoring hard for eleven hours from Algiers to reach Bou-Saada', where they would paint for around six weeks.[17] *Baedeker*, the travel guide produced by German publisher Verlag Karl Baedeker, noted that the pre-Saharan town was a 'favourite resort of French painters of Orientalist subjects', and it became the location in which Carrick and Fox would establish themselves for the longest period.[18] With the opportunity to explore the sun-bleached oasis landscape and bustling markets, Fox wrote to his friend Hans Heysen that they were 'determined to get some settled sunlight—the last summer being no good at all in that respect'.[19]

When Carrick first exhibited her Algerian and Moroccan scenes in Melbourne and Sydney, gallery attendees were met with lively canvases. In broad areas of broken colour, she articulated the bright clarity of North African light across white stucco façades and shimmering crowds. A writer for Australian newspaper *The Argus* maintained that her works 'must be viewed at the proper focussing distance, say about five feet' so that the 'seeming[ly] hasty and heavy laden swift passages of paint will take form, gather, and make a delightful picture of the incident deftly caught and set down in a moment'.[20] Similarly, a review for Sydney's *The Newsletter* describing *Laveuses algériennes* c 1911 (cat 111, pp 176–77) noted that 'the space is too limited to see it properly' and unless visitors to the gallery were told to stand further away from the canvas, 'they simply can't see it'.[21] Carrick's flat application of pure colour 'put on in cubes and blocks' captures 'a tawny, bronze, brown sun-baked land, expressive indeed of the desert' against which the 'bright clothes' of the women 'glow'.[22] The technique creates a dynamism across the surface, with the reviewer describing the way the 'very slightly suggested' figures 'stoop and move their arms, and rest before you', while 'the swish of the water can almost be heard'.[23]

In his 1911 travel book *The Land of Veiled Women*, Scottish author John Foster Fraser exclaimed, 'the light is beautiful ... A few artists know of Bou-Saada, and come for the light'.[24] His description of a 'glare which eats up all detail' is realised in the vibrating surface of *Laveuses algériennes*.[25] The greens of date palms and cacti are repeated in grasses woven among the rocks, and in the garments worn by the women whose labour is at the centre of the scene. In reds, purples, blues and white, they find resolve against the brightness of the rocks. The *wadi* (stream) moves in curved strokes of blue that interrupt reflections settling on the surface of the water. Populated by Ouled Naïl women bathing and washing, the location was also used by photographers such as Swiss-born Jean Geiser, whose works were disseminated as postcards. Dinet and Alexis Auguste Delahogue exhibited paintings comparable to *Laveuses algériennes*, and French artist Marguerite Henriette Tedeschi's *The river bed, Bou Saada oasis, Algiers* 1910 (Falmouth Art Gallery) even depicts the same bend in the stream, with the curve of the rock wall visible to the left of the composition. Tedeschi's solitary figure, positioned at the water's edge, deviates from the works of Delahogue, Dinet and Carrick, which capture the action of a group of women. Carrick achieves a relaxed atmosphere within a paradoxically dynamic composition, with women bare-legged and bending towards the water while others rest on rocks or lay out colourful swathes of cloth to dry. Unlike the subjects of Dinet and Delahogue, there is no performance or titillation but rather a sense of real women genuinely at work.

Arabs bargaining c 1911 (cat 108, p 170) signals a shift in Carrick's approach to the crowd, with the composition focusing on an unfolding exchange. A review in Sydney's *The Newsletter* exclaimed that it 'has the very spirit of sale in it, and the colour of the East indeed, the tawny brown, tan, sunburnt, with a bright green, red, gold splash that makes it alive'.[26] In reaching shadows spanning the foreground, pomegranate merchants sit, their red fruit laid out on display. To the left, men wearing flowing white burnouses (hooded cloaks) hold up a length of woven cloth. Across the midground, bright sunlight washes over the bustling crowd. A donkey and its handler are painted in brief strokes, while a Berber woman stands near a row of arches wearing a *melhafa* (patterned robe) accented in colourful daubs of oil paint—similar to one that appears in *Laveuses algériennes*. Two figures dressed in red and purple are likely unmarried girls as they are not yet veiled. Sharing the same roughly 60 × 80 cm format as *Laveuses algériennes*, the work was completed for exhibition from a preparatory oil sketch. Together with a small group of other Algerian and Moroccan scenes, it hung in the Salon d'Automne in Paris and the Société des Peintres Orientalistes Français.

Carrick's oil sketch for *Arabs bargaining* was painted in Bou Saada's busy, French-built open market, which *Baedeker* notes was held on Mondays and Tuesdays. As at Biskra, the French military had built elegant arcades to promote local commerce on two sides of the Place du Colonel Pein. These peaceful transactions were overseen by the formidable fort of Cavaignac, clearly visible in Fox's *A market in the desert* 1911 (fig 38, p 151).[27] Painting on a canvas of similar dimensions to Carrick's sketch, Fox's *Street scene, Bou Saada* c 1911 was worked up from the same location.[28] This smaller canvas size appears throughout Carrick's and Fox's output from the 1911 trip, part of a group of pre-prepared supports brought by the artists. Writing to Heysen, Fox noted, 'We were in travelling order and I had fixed up a special box which turned out quite a success [and was also a] ... method of carrying our canvases.'[29] Commercially prepared tube paints also facilitated such intrepid painting excursions.[30] Fox described returning from the trip with 'a number of small sketches painted there—impressions of strong sunlight, full colour and atmosphere'.[31] The artists worked swiftly in brief, often thickly applied strokes, leaving parts of the canvas unpainted. In his letter to Heysen, Fox noted the sketches were 'painted at one go'.[32]

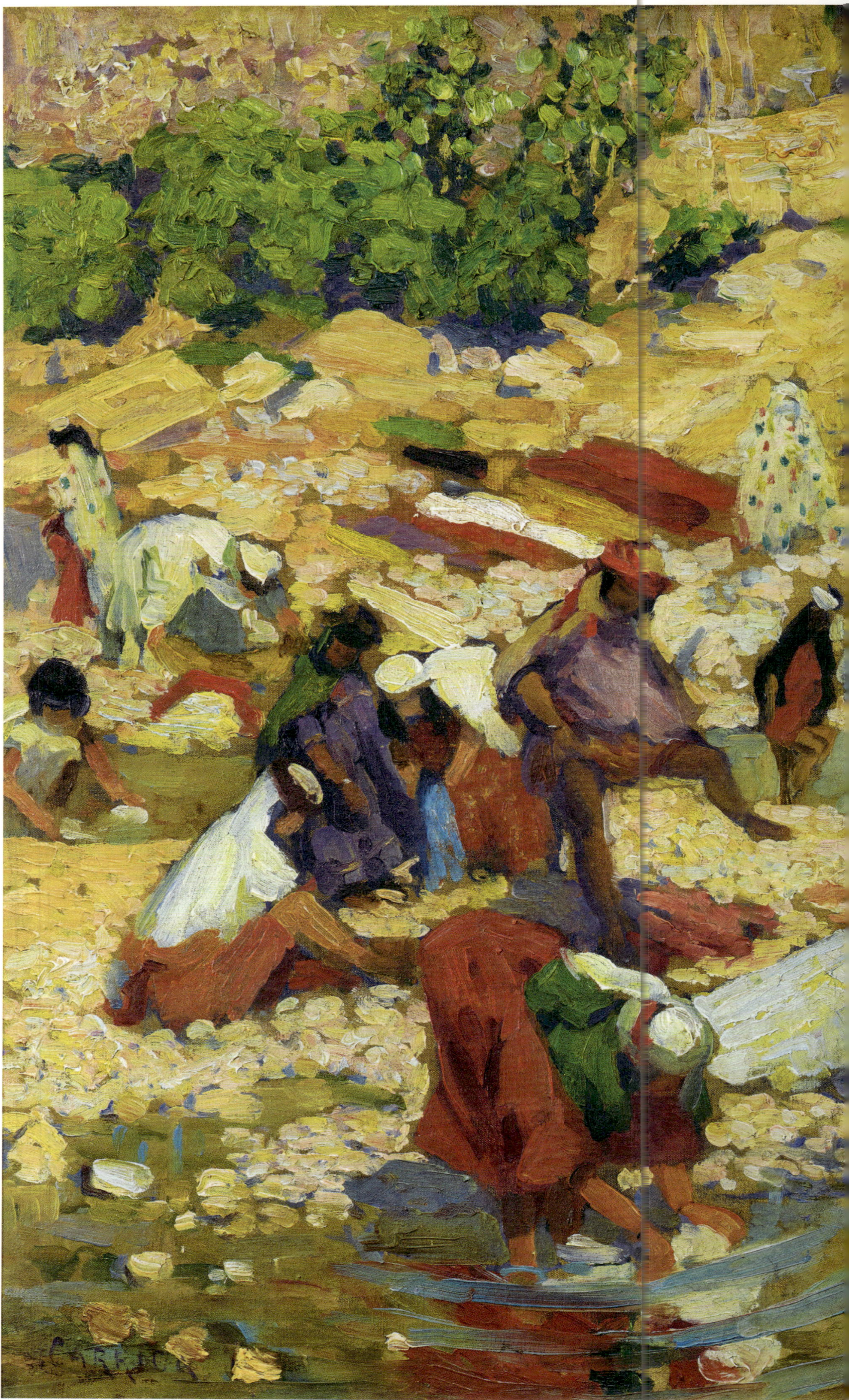

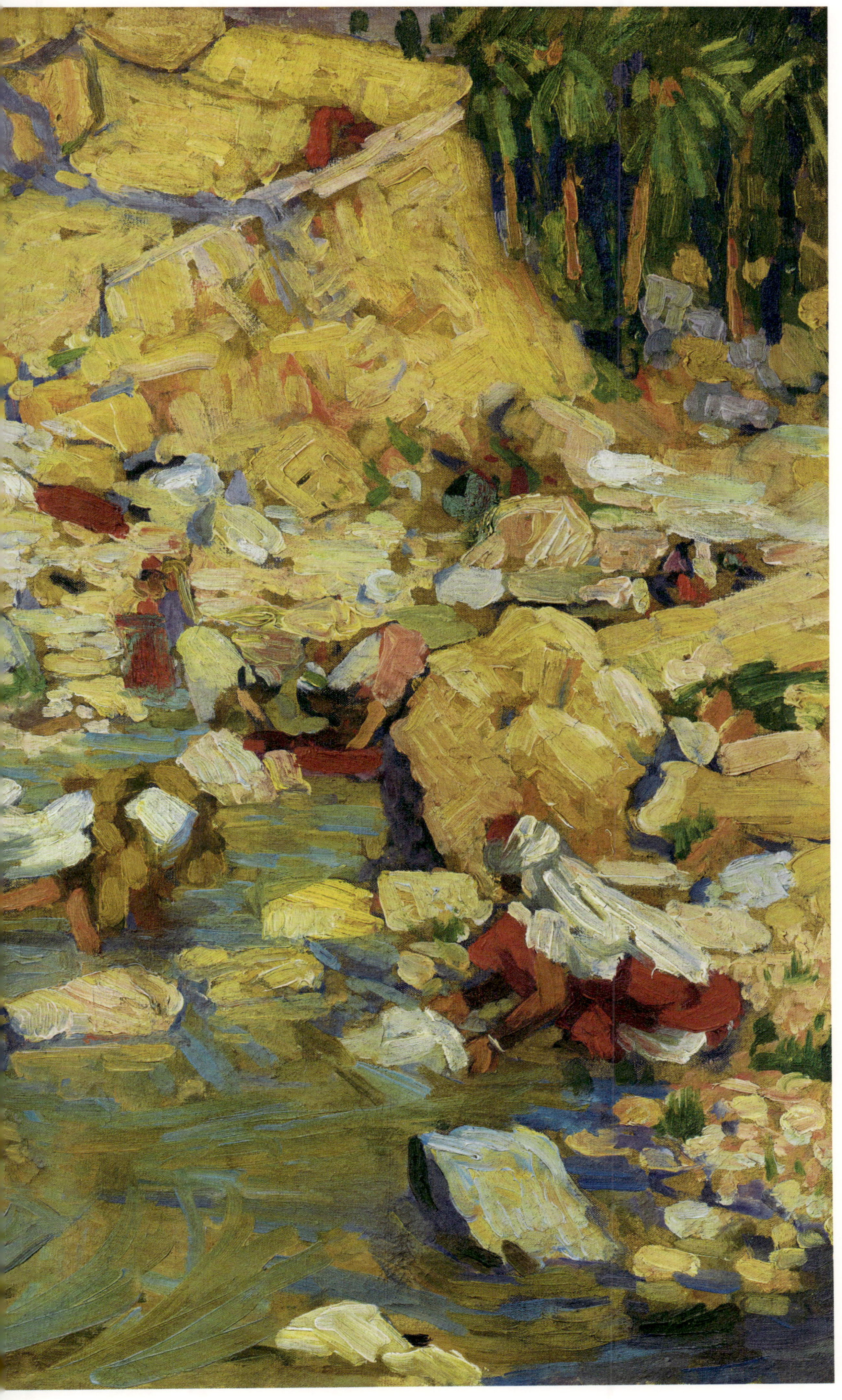

From Bou Saada, Carrick and Fox returned to Algiers before making their way to the Moroccan port city of Tangier, 'staying 3 or 4 days at each place ... and working everywhere'.[33] A reviewer for *The Argus* described Carrick's *The mosque at Tangier* c 1911 (cat 112) as 'one of the most delicate and graceful panels in the exhibition ... in a scheme of dainty yellow and blue, suggesting all charm of Eastern atmosphere, the cleverly placed figure adding everything to the sentiment of the composition'.[34] Blues and creamy yellows vibrate across the surface of the work, with vertical stretches of pale architecture that frame Rue Ben Abou leading to the marabout (a domed tomb for a Muslim saint) of Sidi Boukoudja in the upper medina. The white form of a women's billowing haik (an oblong cloth used as an outer garment) repeats this verticality. Carrick presents a sunlit vision of the marabout, its large dome picked out in white. The shrine is located below the walled casbah, the fortified zone with an outlook over the Straits of Gibraltar that contains Tangier's principal mosque with its high octagonal minaret, the Governor's Palace with its attached prison, and the graceful colonnade of the treasury.[35] That same marabout was painted and sketched by Henri Matisse the following year, in 1912.[36]

Popular with visiting artists since the 1830s, the treasury was painted by both Fox and Carrick. A reviewer for *The Newsletter* described Carrick's *Tangier Treasury* as 'cold, white, dazzling against the blue, broad as broad in touch, yet apparently every detail is there, so that I could describe it in detail'.[37] While her treasury painting has not been located, the review indicates that a similar palette to *The mosque at Tangier* was used, with the artist evoking the restrained architectural planes through cast shadows. Carrick's shimmering representation seems to break with the Orientalist tropes peddled by guidebooks such as *Bradshaws,* which described the town as having dirty, 'narrow, crooked' streets crowded with 'motley hordes'.[38]

Four years after the death of Fox, in the winter of 1919 to 1920, Carrick returned to North Africa, this time visiting Kairouan, the famous holy city of Tunisia. Following World War I, and now a widow travelling without the company of her husband, the experience of working in the markets and streets of the Maghreb was different. Of the crowds she encountered during her 1911 trip to Morocco and Algeria, Carrick had effused: 'I love the color, life, movement, and individuality of a crowd ... I've painted crowds in many countries. The best-behaved were the Arabs, who were dignified, polite, and superbly free from curiosity'.[39] In line with Carrick's observation, her friend Violet Teague noted in a 1913 review that the 'Arabs, too dignified to be curious, made way cautiously for the artists, and left them to paint in solitary peace—a lesson in good manners to a European crowd'.[40] While Carrick's crowds appear at a 'polite' distance, she described the second trip to Tunisia in less flattering terms. She found 'painting in the desert not all [how] the romantics picture it', commenting on crowds 'thick around you' and the 'heat and blinding sand'.[41]

A number of compositions painted during Carrick's time in Kairouan centre on the main street, which *Baedeker* notes was 'officially called Rue du Général-Saussier, enlivened by a picturesque crowd and numerous small shops'.[42] Punctuating the row of cloth-covered awnings that line the street in *A market in Kairouan* c 1919–20 (cat 113, p 181) is the arched Bab Djelladin (Gate of the Tanners) and the crenelated brick wall that surrounds the city.

Previous
cat 111 ***Laveuses algériennes (Algerian women washing clothes in a stream)*** **c 1911, oil on canvas, private collection**

Opposite
cat 112 ***The mosque at Tangier*** **c 1911, oil on canvas, collection of Philip Bacon AO**

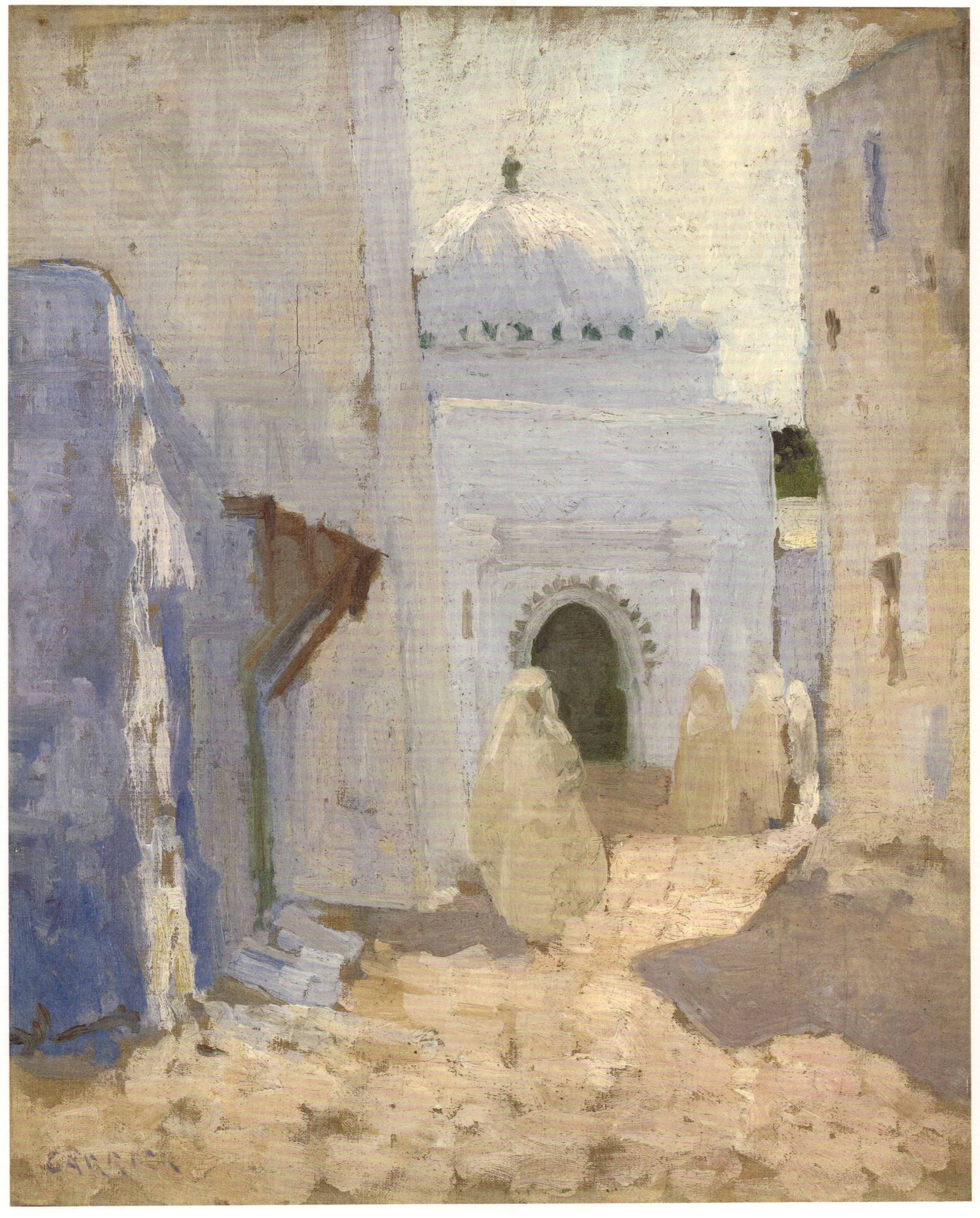

This bustling stretch of urban streetscape was a favoured view of artists, photographers and postcard publishers. While Carrick painted the Rue du Général-Saussier on a number of occasions, often from an elevated position, John Foster Fraser photographed the view from the angle of the street and Frances Nesbitt published her own watercolour version from the same aspect.[43] Of the street, Nesbitt noted, 'Though unusually wide and nearly straight it has a charm of line that makes the irregular grouping of minarets, mosques, and domes, set as they are amidst a tangle of booths, shops, and balconies, into a bewildering succession of ready-made pictures.'[44]

Drawn to the jewel-like colours and closeness of the market, Carrick expressed the dry heat of the sirocco wind in the assemblage of white architecture against a band of blue sky. With varying detail, figures are arranged across the foreground wearing the white or brown burnous and djellabas (loose-fitting robes) in blue, orange and red. White lengths of fabric are wound as turbans around the distinctive red fez. The brilliant greens of what is likely a peppercorn tree are repeated across both costume and the verdant tufts that lace rooftops.[45] Donkeys pass stalls piled high with fresh produce. With quickly applied notes of pure colour, Carrick finds rhythm in the movement of the crowd. There is little suggestion of the precinct suffering the perils of modernisation, an anxiety noted in *Baedeker* and by Nesbitt.[46] Like Rix Nicholas, Carrick's depictions of markets, mosques and urban streetscapes indicate a selective representation of such spaces, with any European presence excluded.

By employing a vertical composition in *North African street scene* c 1920 (cat 114, p 182) Carrick emphasised the visual dominance of the Djaama el Melek's minaret—off Rue Saussier near the goldsmith's souk—within Kairouan's urban landscape. Roger Benjamin has described such articulations of the archetypal street as a 'vertiginous optic', following a pattern set by contemporaneous photographers and painters who captured the hustle and bustle of narrow laneways through views that 'plunge up or down'.[47] The light that falls across the scene from the left also has the effect of elongating the central motif of the minaret, making it seem large and imposing. Mosques, particularly their minarets, often served as geographical markers to help navigate the winding and intersecting streets that threaded through the city. From the height of towering minarets, muezzins (criers who summon the Muslim faithful to the five daily prayers) perform the *adhan* (the call to prayer) heard in chorus across the city. These architectural structures announce the presence of the mosque within the urban streetscape, attracting the attention of the painter from a distance, long before the main building comes into view.

Carrick's painting describes the mosque's brick façade in square planes of creamy pink and yellow, with the edges of each face traced in fine lines of purple or left unpainted to reveal the warm midtone of the wood panel support. The calligraphic benediction set out in ornamental brickwork on the minaret—a broad treatment demanded by the architecture—has not been detailed. Painted in crumbly, dry oil paint, another of Carrick's Tunisian urban scapes, also titled *North African street scene* c 1919–20 (cat 115, p 183), shows a different mosque off Rue Saussier, the Djaama el Bey.[48] Its minaret rises above the streetscape as shimmer, holding the heat of the Algerian sun while shadows in pastel blues, pinks and mauve pool in the narrow street below. Across a foreground scrubbed in over the wood, figures are arranged in a pattern quickly and confidently expressed by loose strokes of brown, white and green.

Opposite
cat 113 ***A market in Kairouan*** **c 1919–20, oil on canvas, Art Gallery of New South Wales**

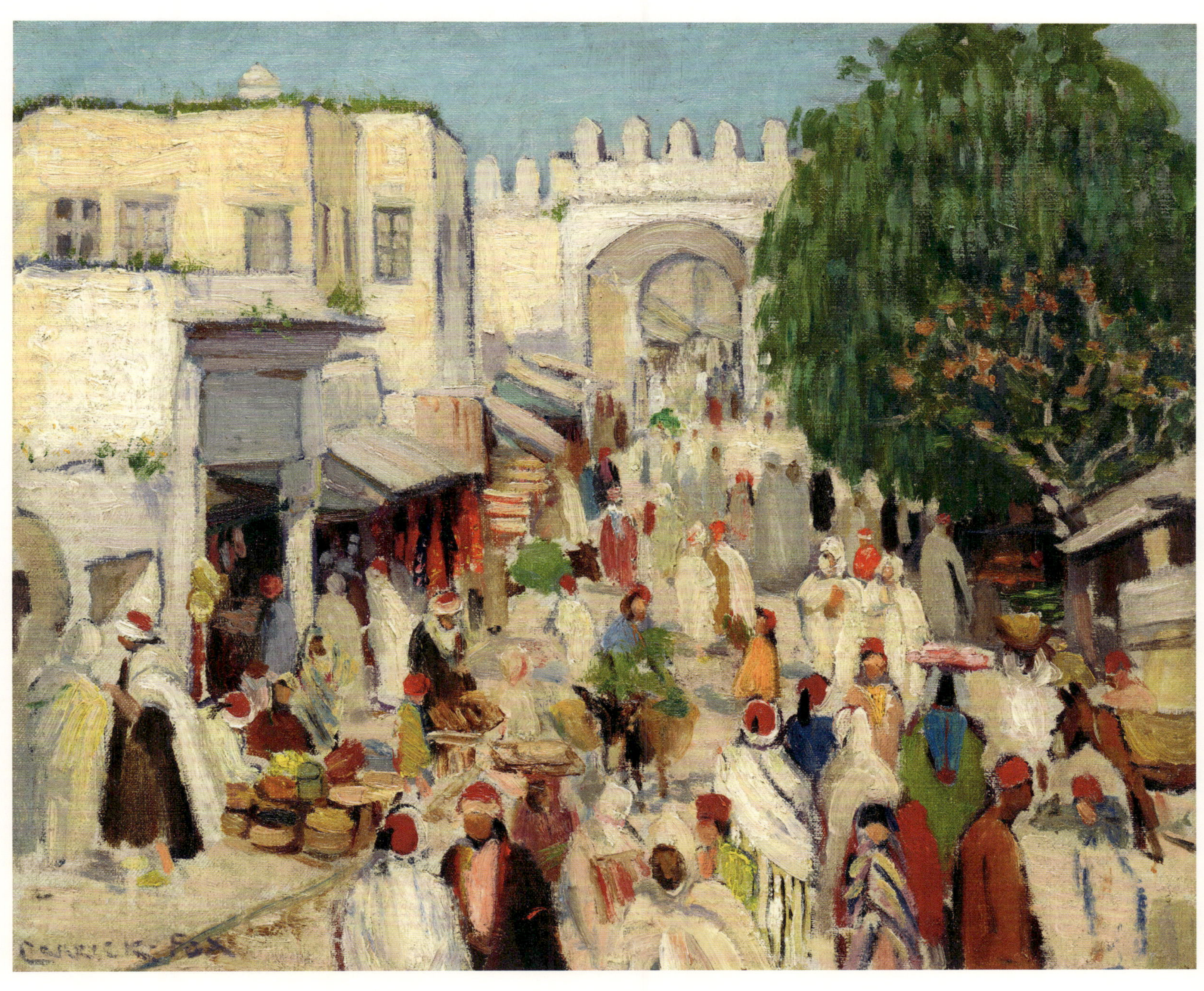

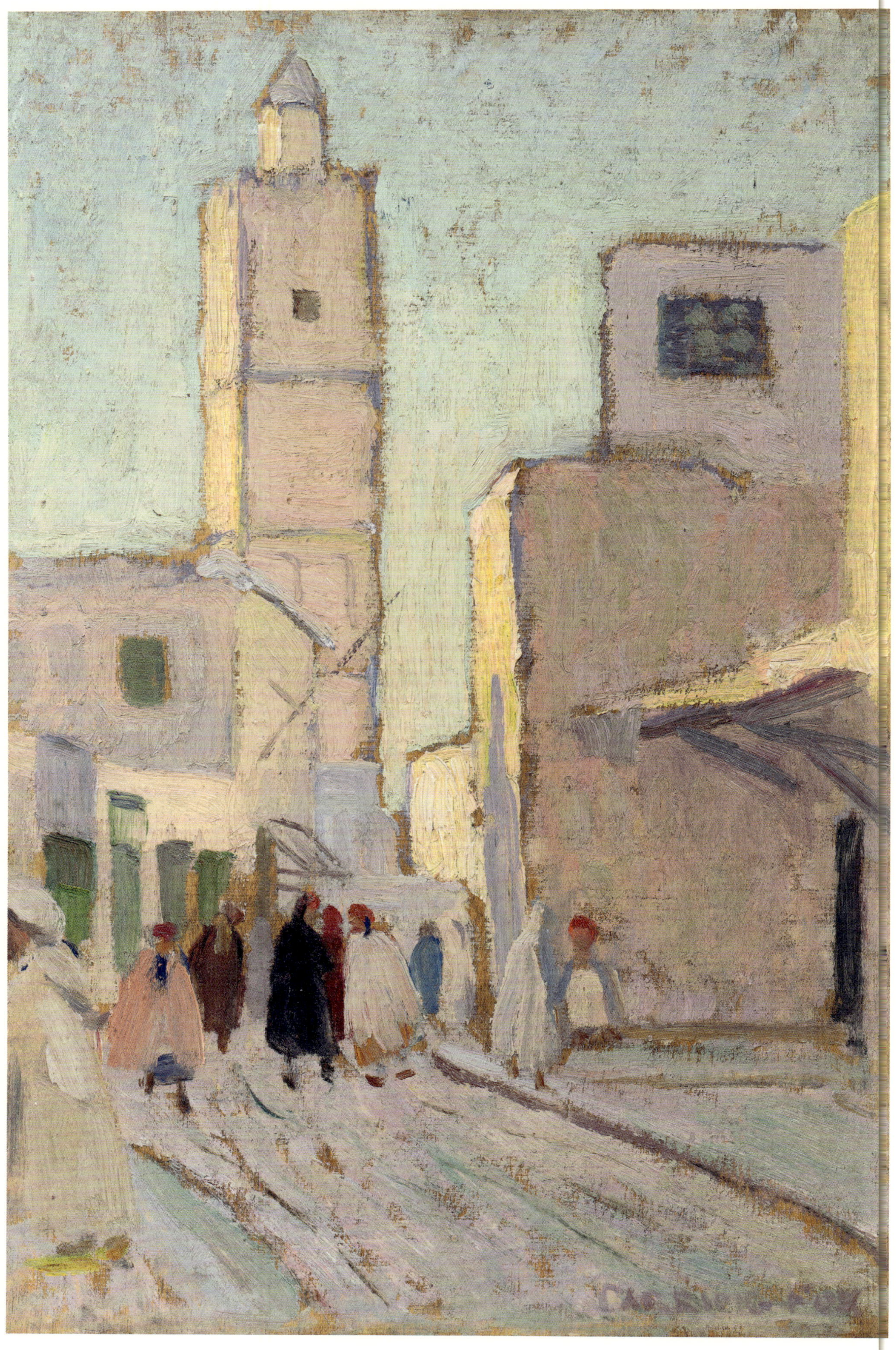

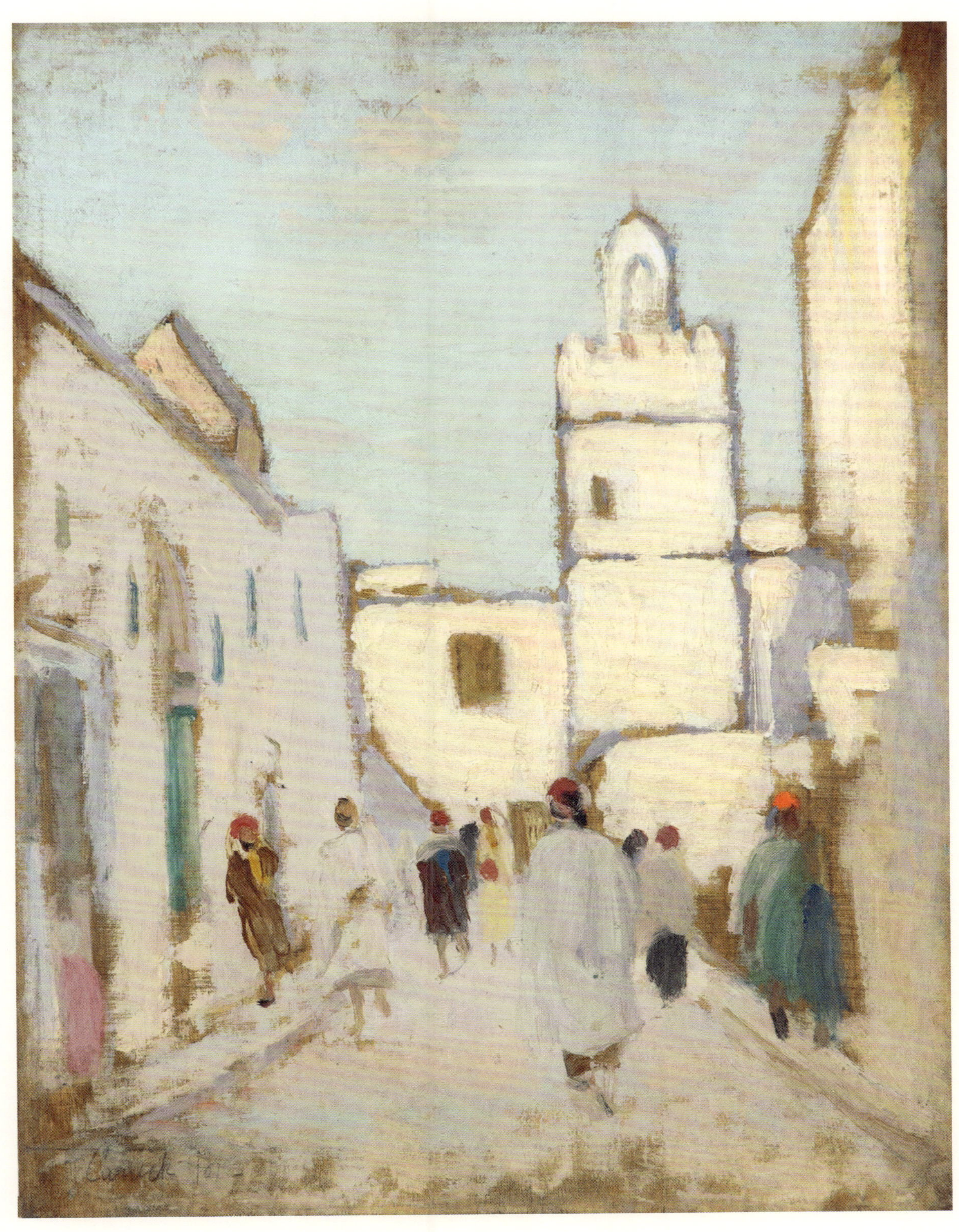

Opposite
cat 114 *North African street scene* c 1920, oil on panel, Art Gallery of Ballarat

Above
cat 115 *North African street scene* c 1919–20, oil on wood panel, Bendigo Art Gallery

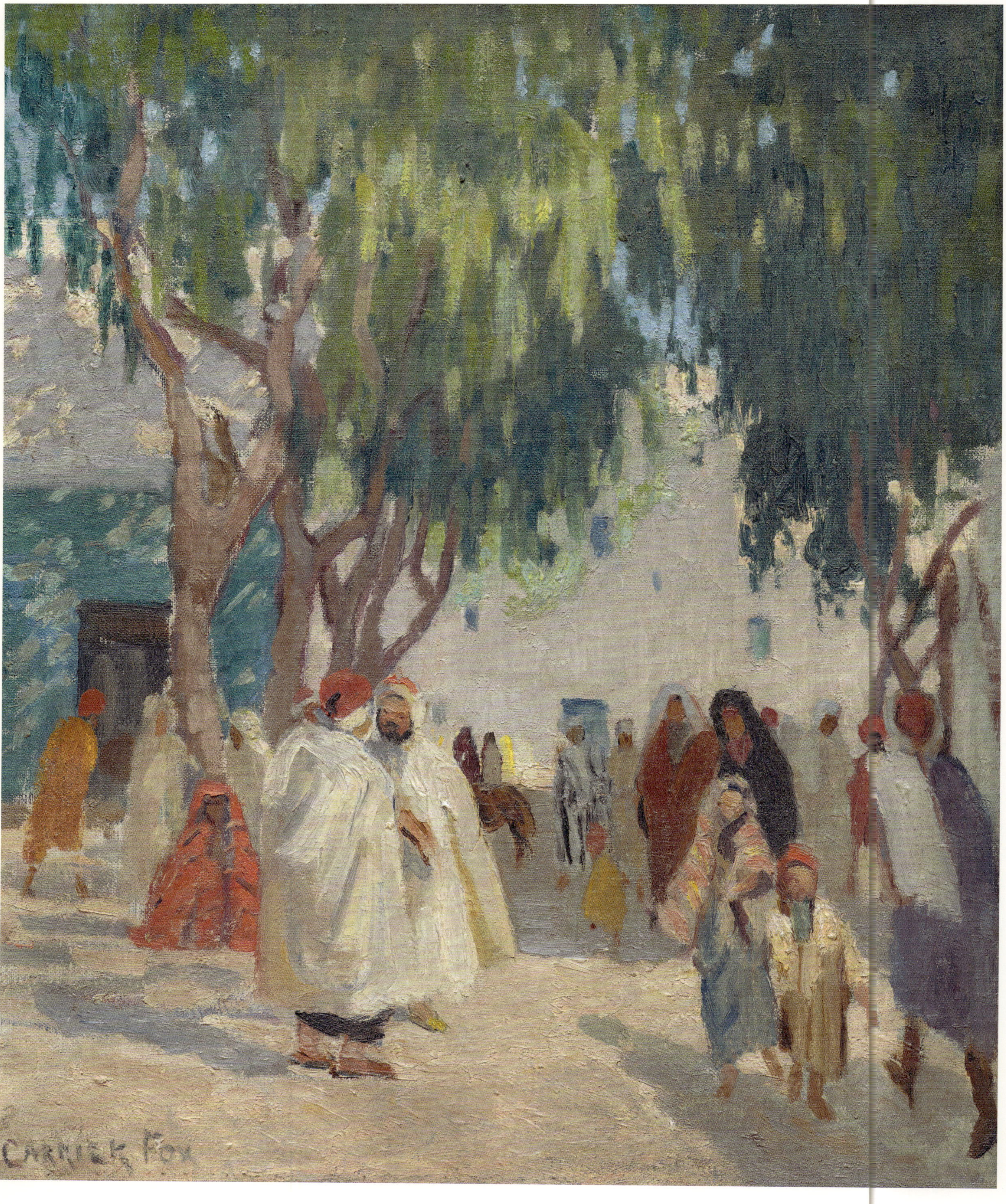
CARRICK FOX

Opposite
cat 116 *Street scene, Northern Africa*
c 1919–20, oil on canvas, private collection

For centuries, the mosques and market regions of North Africa served as potent signifiers of the 'Orient', understood by Western audiences as a distinctly Eastern expression of culture and religion, social interaction and commerce. They provided a backdrop rich in atmospheric effect for an artist drawn to the colour and energy of a crowd, 'alive and purposeful'.[49] Returning to Australia in 1925, Carrick remarked that 'the light in Australia reminds me of North Africa more than any other country I have been in'.[50] Carrick continued to travel throughout her life. Her experiences painting the sun-bleached landscapes, clustered architecture and vibrant crowds of the Maghreb helped her develop a visual language—bold and unflinching—that continued to find shape throughout her career. She brought a modern inflection to her paintings of North Africa, approaching a level of abstraction in her observations of people and place, as photographs of the time suggest. In March 1950, when Carrick was 78, *The Australian Women's Weekly* reported that she was returning to Morocco, 'bound for Tangier, where she plans to do some painting'.[51] While no works from this trip have been traced, the journey underscores Carrick's intrepid spirit and the sustained attraction North Africa held for the artist throughout her lifetime.[52]

Dr Emma Kindred is an art historian and curator. She is Curator at the National Portrait Gallery, Kamberri/Canberra; Honorary Research Fellow in the Discipline of Art History at University of Sydney, Gadigal Nura/Sydney; and Honorary Research Associate at the National Gallery of Australia, Kamberri/Canberra (where she was previously a curator). Her areas of specialisation are Australian art histories, artists as travellers, fashion in art and the use of decolonising methodologies in the museum and gallery context. Kindred's writing has been published in exhibition catalogues, books and academic journals, with recent essays including 'Some of the Cairo brightness: Arthur Streeton's Egyptian sojourn' in *Streeton* (Art Gallery of New South Wales, 2020) and 'An Australian incident: Tom Robert's Impressionism and the colonial project' in *Globalizing Impressionism* (Yale University Press, 2020).

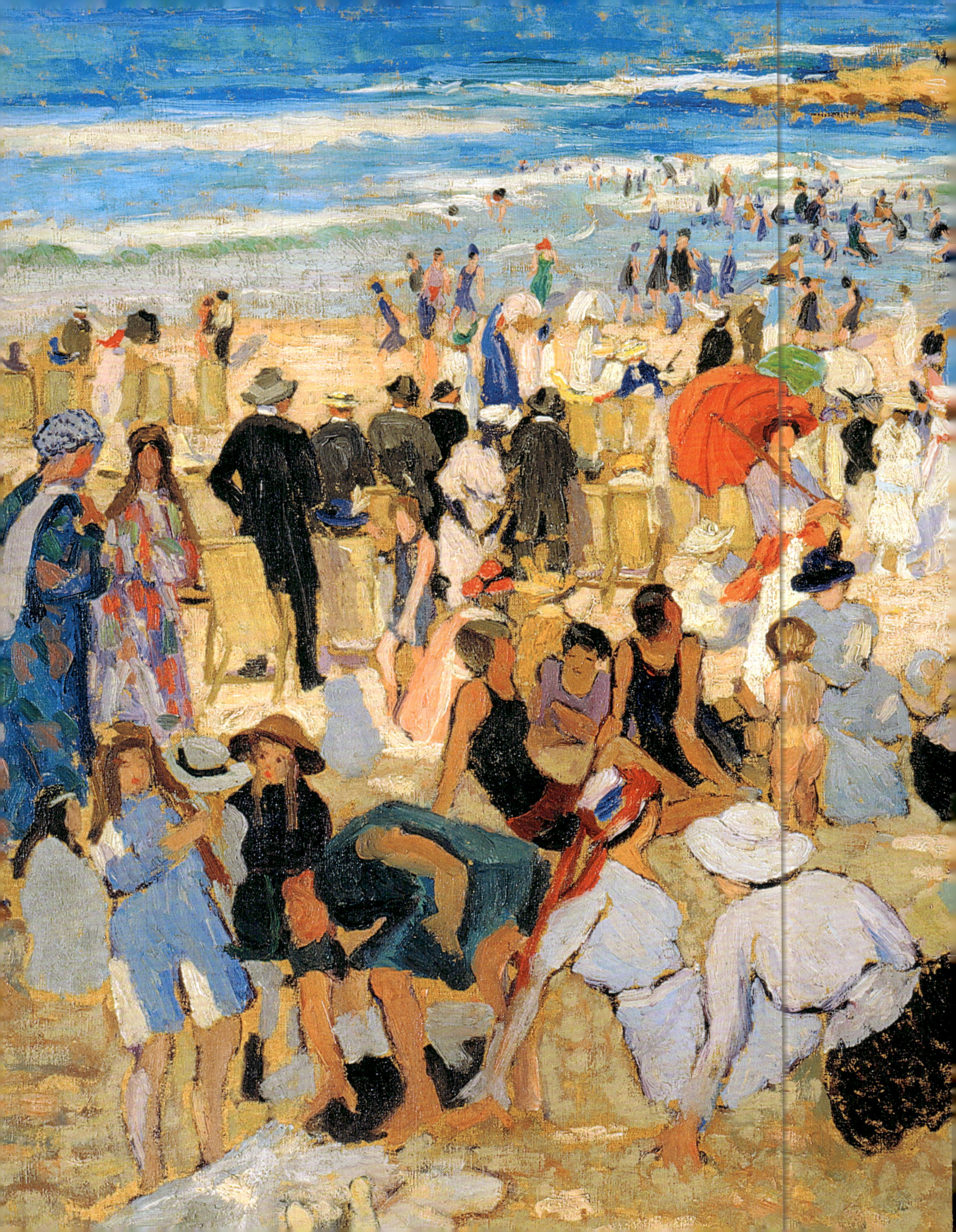

Aladdin's lamp for the artist: the Sydney summer of 1913

Rebecca Blake

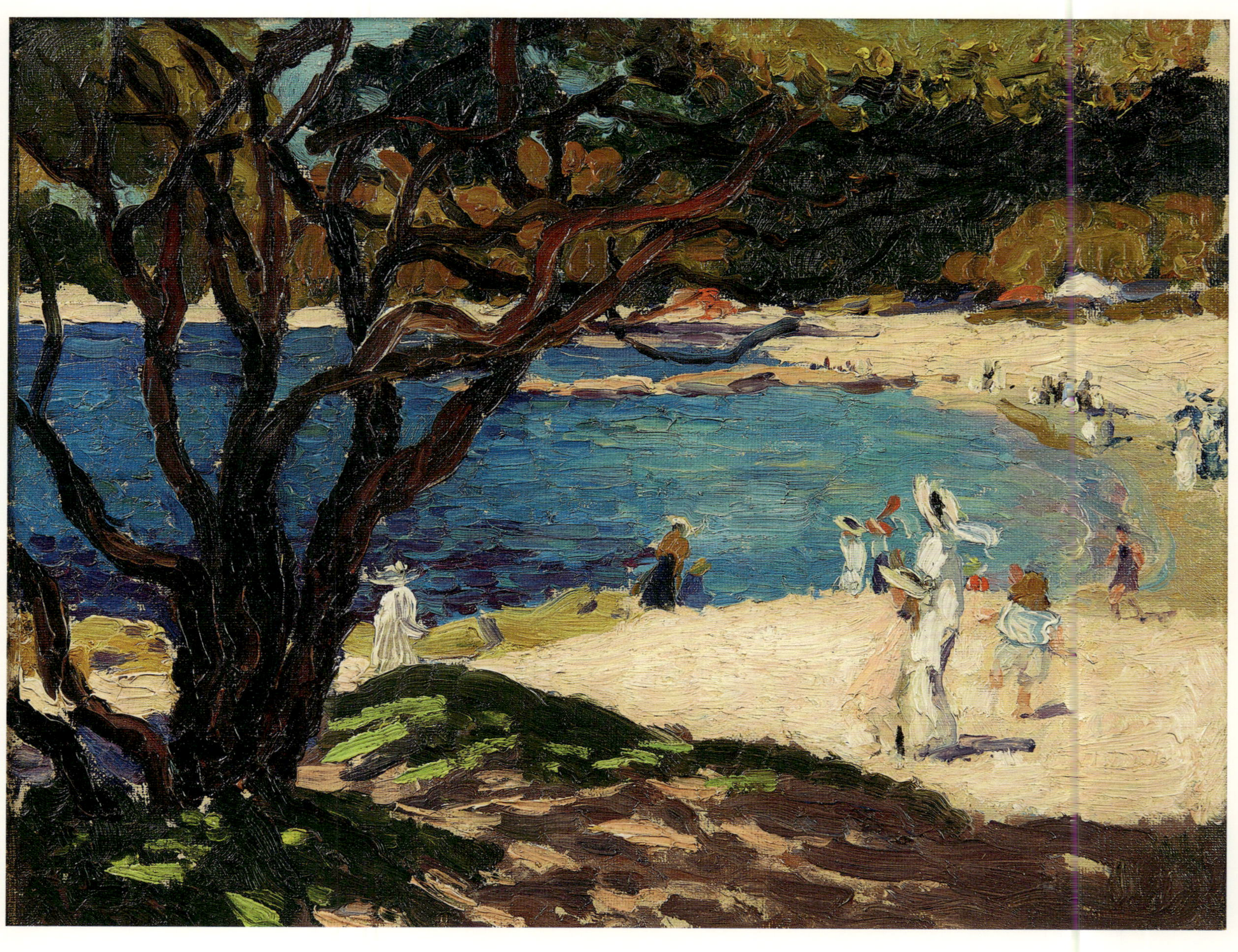

The summer of 1913 was a pivotal moment in the life and artistic career of Ethel Carrick. That season she moved to the beach suburbs of Cremorne and Manly, driven by a desire to paint—and experience the liberated lifestyle of—the Australian surfer girl. The vibrant beauty of Sydney's beaches provided her with endless inspiration, and the encounter fostered a connection with the North Shore that endured throughout her lifetime.

It was the peak of summer and Carrick was living in Manly, a stone's throw away from the water, accompanied by Australian artist Thea Proctor. Together, they spent endless hours swimming and exploring local beaches and rugged coastal cliffs. The artists dedicated themselves to their work, often heading out together before 6am to paint and explore the ever-changing environment. This time with Proctor dramatically influenced Carrick; her painting techniques became increasingly experimental and she forged her own artistic identity independent of her husband, Emanuel Phillips Fox. Carrick's beach scenes from this period are imbued with the freedom and exciting liberation associated with Australia's burgeoning beach culture.

On 2 August 1913, Carrick's immensely successful exhibition at Melbourne's Guild Hall gallery closed. Originally scheduled to conclude on 26 July, it was extended an additional week as many visitors were eager to see, and acquire, Carrick's work. As *The Daily Telegraph* revealed, 'she has quite eclipsed the record of any previous woman exhibitor and has out-distanced most of the men in regard to sales'.[1] Instead of resting on her laurels, Carrick quickly turned her attention to her next artistic endeavour: the beaches of Sydney. She travelled there alone (arriving on 14 August) while Fox stayed in Melbourne to finish his portrait of the Prime Minister, which was commissioned by the Art Advisory Committee for Federal Parliament House.[2] However, Fox was not far behind, leaving Melbourne on 23 September aboard the ocean liner RMS *Omrah* and arriving in Sydney two days later. The couple lived together at the Redcourt boarding house in Cremorne Point on the Lower North Shore. This two-storey federation-style guesthouse featured expansive vistas of the harbour and provided easy access to the city, located only 10 minutes by ferry from Circular Quay.

Previous
Christmas Day on Manly Beach 1913 (detail cat 118, pp 194–95), also known as *Manly Beach—summer is here*, oil on canvas, Manly Art Gallery & Museum Collection

Opposite
cat 117 *On Balmoral Beach, Sydney* 1913, oil on canvas on board, Mosman Art Gallery

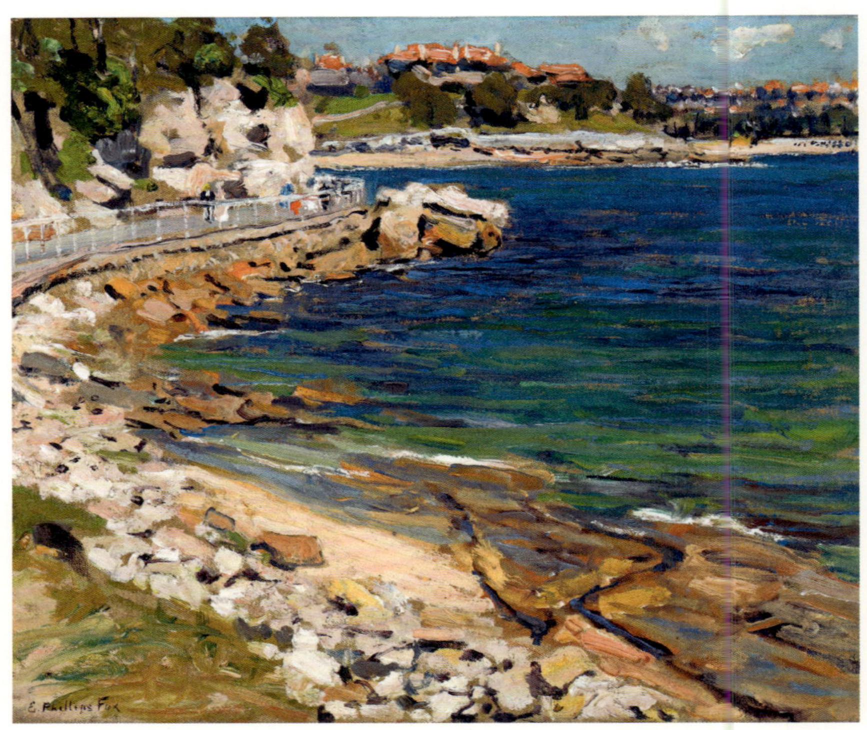

fig 41 Emanuel Phillips Fox, *Fairy Bower, Manly* c 1913, oil on canvas, private collection

Carrick's visit to Sydney was motivated by a deep desire to capture the city's vibrant beauty, describing it as an 'Aladdin's lamp for the artist'.[3] This was her second visit to the region and its iconic harbour beaches. During Carrick's first trip in 1908, she painted the bustling crowds along the Manly Beach promenade (cat 120, p 200), as well as families picnicking in Sydney's Royal Botanic Garden. Carrick was excited about the endless inspiration and told a reporter: 'Here I am going to paint, and paint, and paint all the beautiful things you have. I hope to do some [paintings] of your wonderful surf-bathing and the crowds going across the harbour. For your crowds are so pretty—so bright and dainty.'[4]

In September 1913, Carrick quickly set to the task at hand, creating works for her upcoming Sydney exhibition at Anthony Hordern & Sons gallery, scheduled for two months' time. She painted the beauty spots along the harbour, working en plein air with her palette and camp chair. During this period, she created the series of paintings *12 notes on Sydney Harbour*, as well as several seascapes—including *Dawes Point, Garden Island, Off Cremorne Point* and *On Balmoral Beach, Sydney* (all in 1913)—which were included in her Anthony Hordern & Sons exhibition. Her husband joined her on many of these painting excursions to Manly Beach, Balmoral Beach and Cremorne Point, working towards his own exhibition at the Royal Society's Art Rooms in mid-October.

Carrick's luminous harbour scenes capture the brilliant effects of Australia's intense sunshine, with an exemplary handling of light and shadow. In these works, the landscape dominates the composition, with crowds of sun-seekers captured from a distance. One of her major paintings from this period, *On Balmoral Beach, Sydney* 1913 (cat 117, p 188), is a vibrant impressionistic study of light and colour in jewel-like hues. The dabs of viridian green underneath the Moreton Bay fig reveal Carrick's exemplary skill in capturing the fleeting atmospheric effects of dappled sunlight. While the compositional style shares affinities with Fox's own harbour studies, such as *Fairy Bower, Manly* c 1913 (fig 41), Carrick's confident, loose brushstrokes demonstrate her unique impressionistic experimentation, bordering on abstraction.

On 4 November 1913, two days before the opening of her Anthony Hordern & Sons exhibition, Carrick injured her hand.[5] This was possibly a flare-up of her rheumatoid arthritis, a debilitating auto-immune disease that causes painful inflammation and stiffness of joints in the hands, knees and other areas of the body. Available medications at the time often provided little to no relief. They included cod-liver oil and iron as well as the drugs quinine and arsenic, both of which are now recognised as toxic.[6] Lifestyle modifications of hydrotherapy, a proper diet and resting in a warm and humid climate were typical recommended treatments. Carrick was plagued by crippling flare-ups of her condition throughout her lifetime. In May and June 1922, she underwent rheumatism treatment in the thermal waters and healing mud baths of Dax, in the south of France,[7] and in February 1950 she travelled to the warm climate of Tangier, a trip triggered by a severe attack of rheumatism in her right knee. Carrick wrote to Hal Missingham, telling him that it was 'horribly painful. The Dr said he'd get me on board. But it was touch & go'.[8] Living at the seaside was rejuvenating for Carrick; the warm climate and high humidity was necessary for her respite and healing.

While Carrick waited for her hand to improve, she informed the Australian media about her desire to paint the surf bathers at Manly Beach. *The Lone Hand* revealed Carrick's plan to 'spread her palette sumptuously to catch the Australian surfing girl as she frolics in the long white curl of the blue Pacific'.[9] A fortnight later *The Bulletin* reiterated this, writing that Carrick 'is now going to paint the surfing girl at Manly as she sees her, so the Paris Salon is likely to hang an Australian mermaid or two on its walls next year'.[10] Carrick's desire to paint for an extended period at Manly Beach was shared by her husband. On 5 November, Fox wrote from Redcourt in Cremorne to William Henry Gill: 'We shall be going to Manly to do some work soon ... I hope to get a few good seascapes—the colour is very fine at Manly.'[11] While both artists shared the same desire to paint this iconic region, Carrick's thematic focus differed from that of her husband. Her priority was not seascapes but the surfer girl and Sydney's burgeoning beach culture. The Australian surfer girl that Carrick describes was not the stereotypical bronzed goddess that dominates Australian culture today, but a woman with newfound freedom, liberated from the social strictures that dictated appropriate dress and leisure activities.

The first decade of the twentieth century featured dramatic changes to the rules regulating public conduct on Sydney's beaches. While ocean bathing at Manly Beach had long been popular, swimmers were required to wear a neck-to-knee outfit and daylight bathing was banned.[12] It was not until 1903 that Manly became one of the first Sydney suburbs to officially allow daylight bathing. While the stipulation to wear neck-to-knee swimming costumes remained, beachgoers frequently elected to breach the rules in favour of more practical forms of clothing. By 1908, one newspaper revealed that 'there are probably not half a dozen costumes in Sydney which would cover the body from neck to knee'.[13] As early as 1908, the Canadian swimming costume, which featured regularly in Carrick's 1913 Manly Beach paintings, was advertised in Sydney newspapers, and soon became a staple for men and women alike. The women's 'Canadian' consisted of a close-fitting tunic of dark material and a pair of trunks, which often left a wide margin above the knee. Regulations also governed how individuals behaved on the sand, with bathers expected to move directly between the water and the dressing sheds. Although sunbaking and loitering in swimwear was banned, bathers at Manly Beach frequently ignored these rules. There were regular reports that 'men and women loitered on the beach for hours' in their swimming costumes.[14] Over the following years, enforcement of regulations continued to wax and wane but one thing that remained consistent was the independent spirit of Sydney's beachgoers, who refused to have their seaside activities excessively regulated.

In the opening decade of the twentieth century there was extensive media coverage of Australian surf bathing and the newfound freedom of surfers at Manly Beach. The image of the liberated surfer girl was disseminated throughout England and Europe in artworks such as Percy FS Spence's illustration *Shooting the breakers at Manly Beach, Sydney, New South Wales* 1906. This image was reproduced in British newspaper *The Graphic* in 1906, as well as in tourist accounts of surfer girls at Manly, such as AR Rose-Soley's article 'The Australian girl: after many years', which was published in several British newspapers in 1910, including *The Queen*. Rose-Soley wrote:

> Sydney is tremendously proud of its surf bathers and we went across the bay to Manly on purpose to see them. There was no mistake about this being the genuine article—love of the water for the water's refreshing sake. None of the witching costumes that you see flirting with French waves, none of the floating ribbons and stockinged limbs that dawdle on an American beach, no hats to preserve the face from freckles ... she has been enjoying herself extremely, battling with the waters, 'shooting' the crested wave, and has acquired a fund of joyous energy wherewith to take her daily task.[15]

The summer of 1913 provided Carrick with the opportunity to experience her own liberating transformation in her identity as an artist. That November she gave an interview to a reporter from *The Sun*, revealing that she had developed an artistic autonomy separate to her husband: 'Now, although I still hold the same appreciation of his artistic powers, I think for myself as well, and hear other people's views on a subject before I decide.'[16] Carrick was a woman born before her time, often described by friends and family as possessing a rebellious spirit.[17] The newfound freedoms associated with Australia's burgeoning beach culture offered an exciting liberation, which Carrick was eager to experience and document.

By 22 November 1913, Carrick's hand had healed and she moved to Manly. Once again able to take up the brush and palette, she quickly got to work creating plein air studies of the bustling beach crowds. In December, Carrick was joined by her friend Thea Proctor. They both lived at 'Queensland House', a guesthouse at 10 Bower Street in Manly. The accommodation was only a short walk to the water, and Carrick and Proctor would often head out before 6am to paint and surf bathe.[18] Together they passed the days swimming and exploring local beaches, as well as dedicating themselves to their work—witnesses often saw the pair scrambling over the cliffs near Manly, endeavouring at all hours of the day to capture the ever-changing perspectives, highlights, tones and atmosphere.[19] While Carrick and Proctor were dedicated to their work, they also appeared together at a few important social events. On 12 December they attended the NSW Institute of Architects fifth biennial exhibition. One newspaper reported that 'Ethel Phillips Fox and Thea Proctor tore themselves away from Manly for the occasion. Handsome Thea, swathed in sapphire blue, looked so much like one of her own French fan fantasies'.[20]

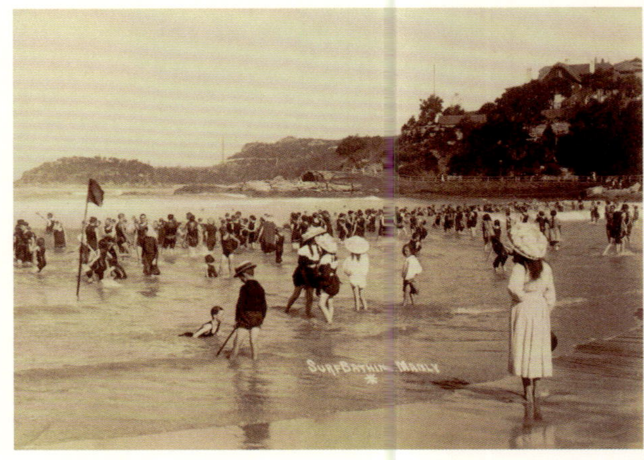

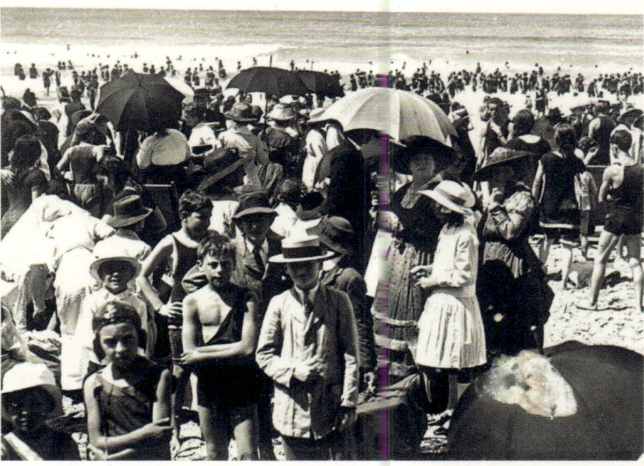

Top to bottom

fig 42 Unknown photographer, *Surf bathing, Manly*, c 1900–10, albumen photograph, State Library of New South Wales

fig 43 Frank Bell, *Crowd at Manly Beach*, 1900–20, albumen photograph, Northern Beaches Council

At Manly Beach, Carrick painted several plein air studies of crowds of sun and sand worshippers. In these works, she separates the canvas into three parallel ribbons of pale grey sky, luminous blue sea and golden sand. These horizontal planes are broken up by dense groups of beachgoers in pastel outfits who picnic and promenade along the water's edge. Carrick incorporates colour accents in the form of large umbrellas painted in vibrant, jewel-like tones. *Beach scene, Sydney* 1913 (cat 119, p 196) is a close-up study of two women relaxing on the sand underneath the shade of their umbrellas. In the background, swathes of men and women wearing Canadian swimsuits frolic in the surf and shoot the breakers amidst rolling waves.

In Carrick's studies, fully dressed beachgoers are depicted alongside bathers still wearing their swimming costumes. Although such behaviour was common, it defied the council's 'no loitering' rules and was considered rebellious. Even in November 1913, only a month before Carrick painted the bustling crowds at Manly, some municipalities proposed that sitting on the sand wearing a bathing costume should be classified as an offence. Luckily, this 'ridiculous' proposal was quickly vetoed.[21] Carrick's 1913 Manly Beach paintings capture the progressively relaxed attitudes of Australian beachgoers and the increasing social freedoms of the time.

Carrick's plein air studies were preparatory works for her major surf painting, *Christmas Day on Manly Beach* 1913 (also known as *Manly Beach—summer is here*, cat 118, pp 194–95), which captures people of all ages celebrating Christmas on the sand.[22] Painted from the vantage point of the southern end of Manly Beach, it overlooks swarming crowds of picnickers, sunbathers and swimmers frolicking in the water. Far off in the distance, the tiny figures of surfers battle the rolling waves of the Pacific Ocean. In the upper right corner is Manly Life Saving Club's mobile rescue tower. Installed only eight months earlier, it was a new and welcome addition for line and reel lifesaving rescues.

Hidden in plain sight amongst the busy Christmas day crowd are myriad representations of the Australian surfer girl that Carrick so desired to paint when she first planned her move to Manly. At the centre of the composition are two women with fashionably short hairstyles taking the liberty of sunbaking upon the sand in their Canadian swimsuits, joined by a toddler. Two more surfer girls can be seen on the far left of the composition, walking towards the water in their vibrant patterned kimonos, one with a towel draped over her shoulder. While they have not yet disrobed, their intention to swim is palpable. By 1912, the kimono was considered a fashionable staple in a woman's beach outfit.[23] Many bathers living close to the water found it convenient to walk to the beach donning a kimono or dressing jacket over their swimming costumes.[24] Carrick and Proctor may have worn similar kimonos on their short stroll from 'Queensland House' to the water's edge.

By 29 December 1913, Carrick had finished sketching the Manly surfers. Her husband travelled from Melbourne to join her on a painting expedition to the South Coast. The following year, Carrick exhibited her Manly Beach paintings for the first time at Athenaeum Gallery in Melbourne. *Christmas Day on Manly Beach* was the largest and most important work in the show and was accompanied by additional Sydney beach paintings *Crowds on the sands*, *Early morning surfers*, *Watching the bathers*, *On the sands*, *The road to the beach* and *Surfers 6am* (all undertaken around 1913).

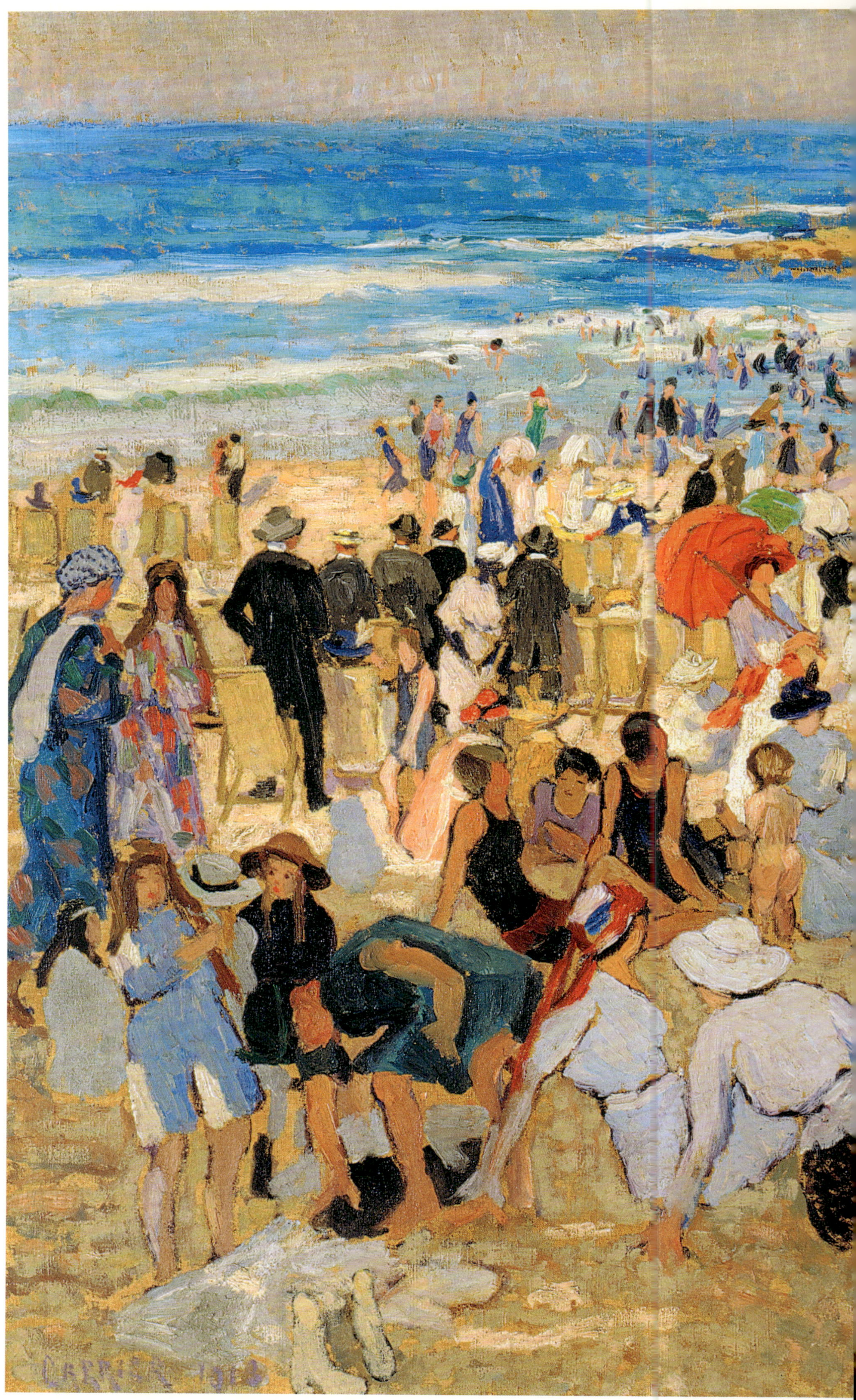

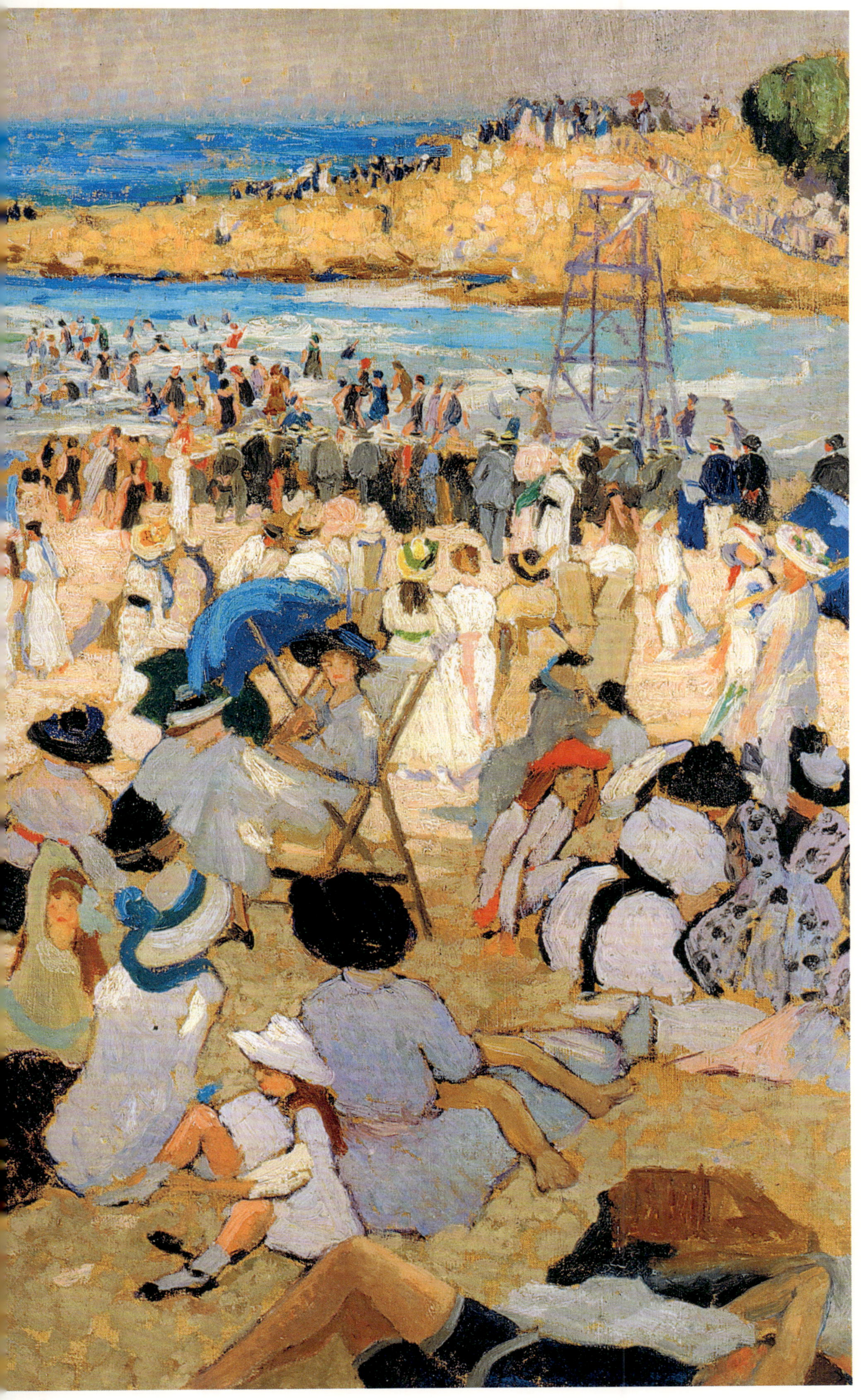

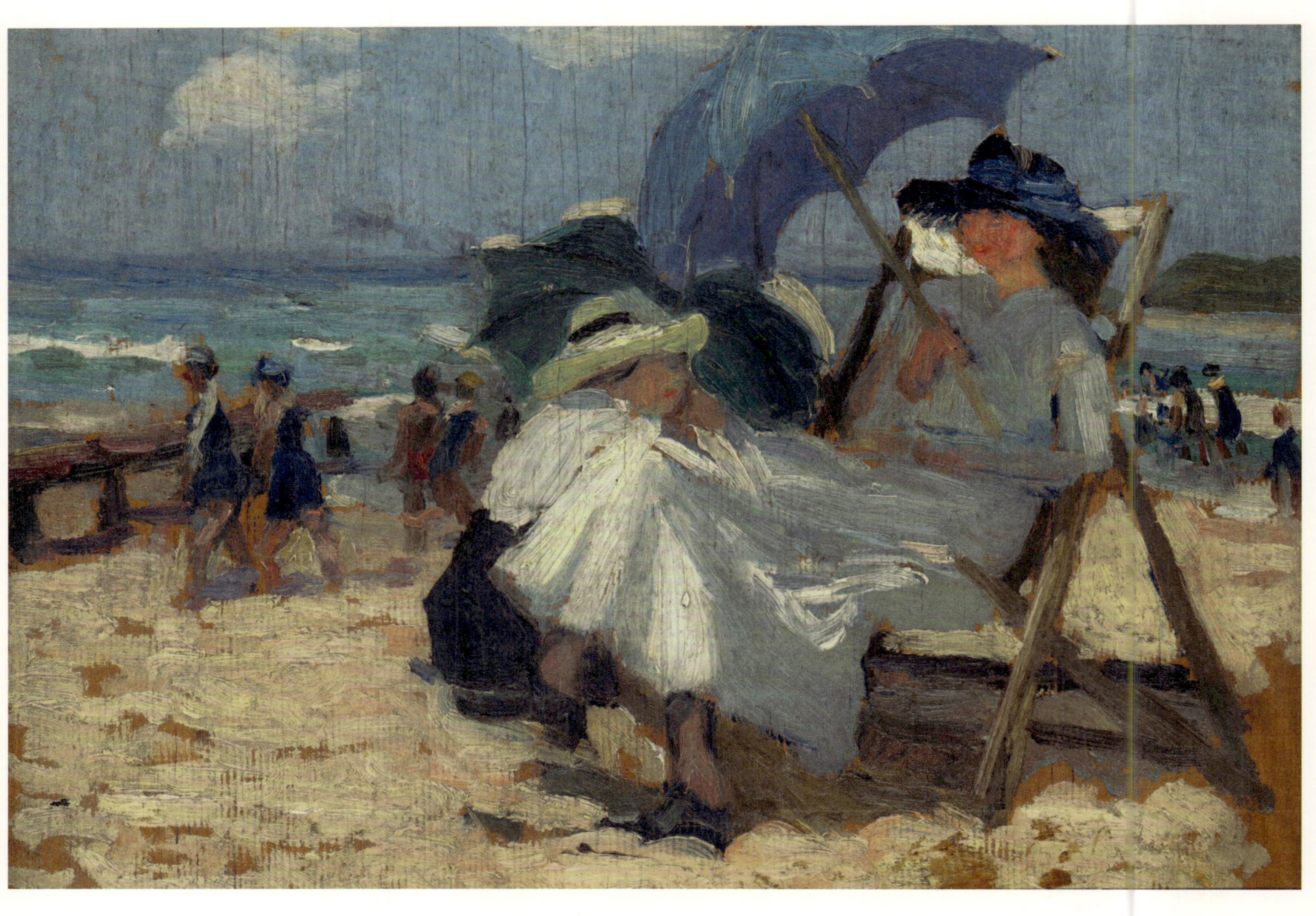

Previous
cat 118 *Christmas Day on Manly Beach* 1913, also known as *Manly Beach—summer is here*, oil on canvas, Manly Art Gallery & Museum Collection

Opposite
cat 119 *Beach scene, Sydney* 1913, oil on particle board, Benalla Art Gallery

When Carrick left Australia in 1916, she took her most important paintings back to Europe with her, including her Manly Beach paintings. That year, she exhibited *Christmas Day in Australia* c 1913, as well as *Early morning bathers at Manly* c 1913, at the Royal Institute of Oil Painters in London, where they were positively reviewed. Carrick's plan to exhibit her Manly Beach paintings in the Paris Salons was delayed due to their closure during World War I (1914–18). In 1919 the Salon d'Automne re-opened, and Carrick's desire to exhibit *Christmas Day on Manly Beach* may have been realised when she exhibited a work titled *Sur une plage australienne* (On an Australian beach), which could have been an alternative title.[25] What is known is that Carrick did exhibit *Christmas Day on Manly Beach* at the 1927 Exposition Internationale des Beaux-Arts de la Ville de Bordeaux under the title *La plage*, where it was awarded a diplôme d'honneur.[26] In 1933, Carrick brought *Christmas Day on Manly Beach* back to Australia with her. The following year, she wrote to the Director of Manly Art Gallery & Museum:

> **I have much pleasure in offering you on loan my picture of Manly beach painted some years ago. It has been exhibited in the Paris Salon & was awarded a diploma of honour at the last Bordeaux International exhibition.**[27]

Twenty-one years after Carrick first painted *Christmas Day on Manly Beach*, it returned from its European tour to its place of origin and was subsequently acquired by the Manly Art Gallery & Museum for their permanent collection. This quintessential painting demonstrates how vividly Carrick captured the beauty and spirit of Australia's burgeoning beach culture during the early twentieth century.

Rebecca Blake is Curatorial Assistant, Australian Art, at the National Gallery of Australia, Kamberri/Canberra. She is also a PhD candidate at the Centre for Art History and Art Theory at the Australian National University, Kamberri/Canberra. She has contributed articles and essays to numerous periodicals and publications including *Hugh Ramsay* (2019) and *Love & desire: pre-raphaelite masterpieces from the Tate* (2018).

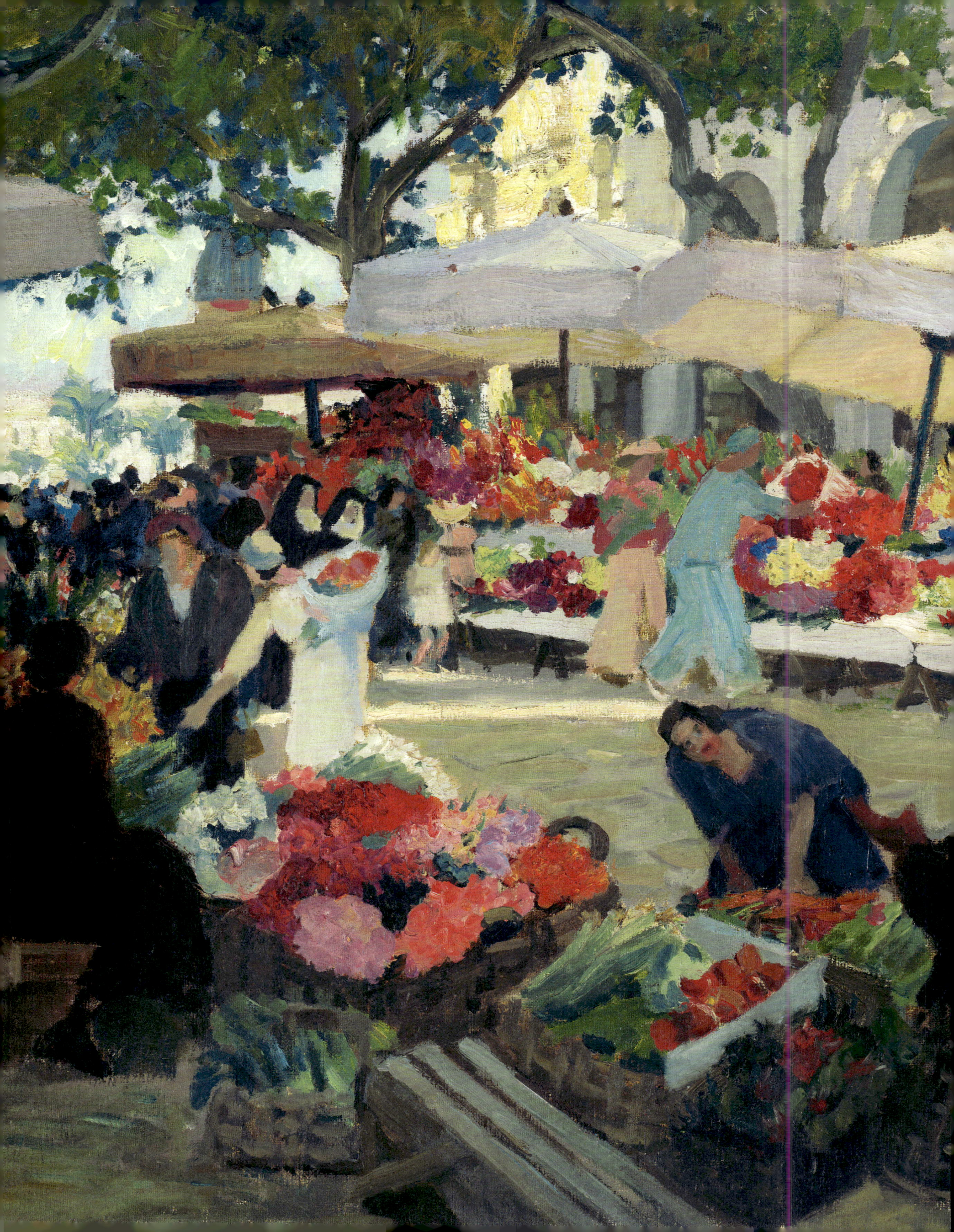

The Theosophical Society as a wellspring of inspiration

Jenny McFarlane

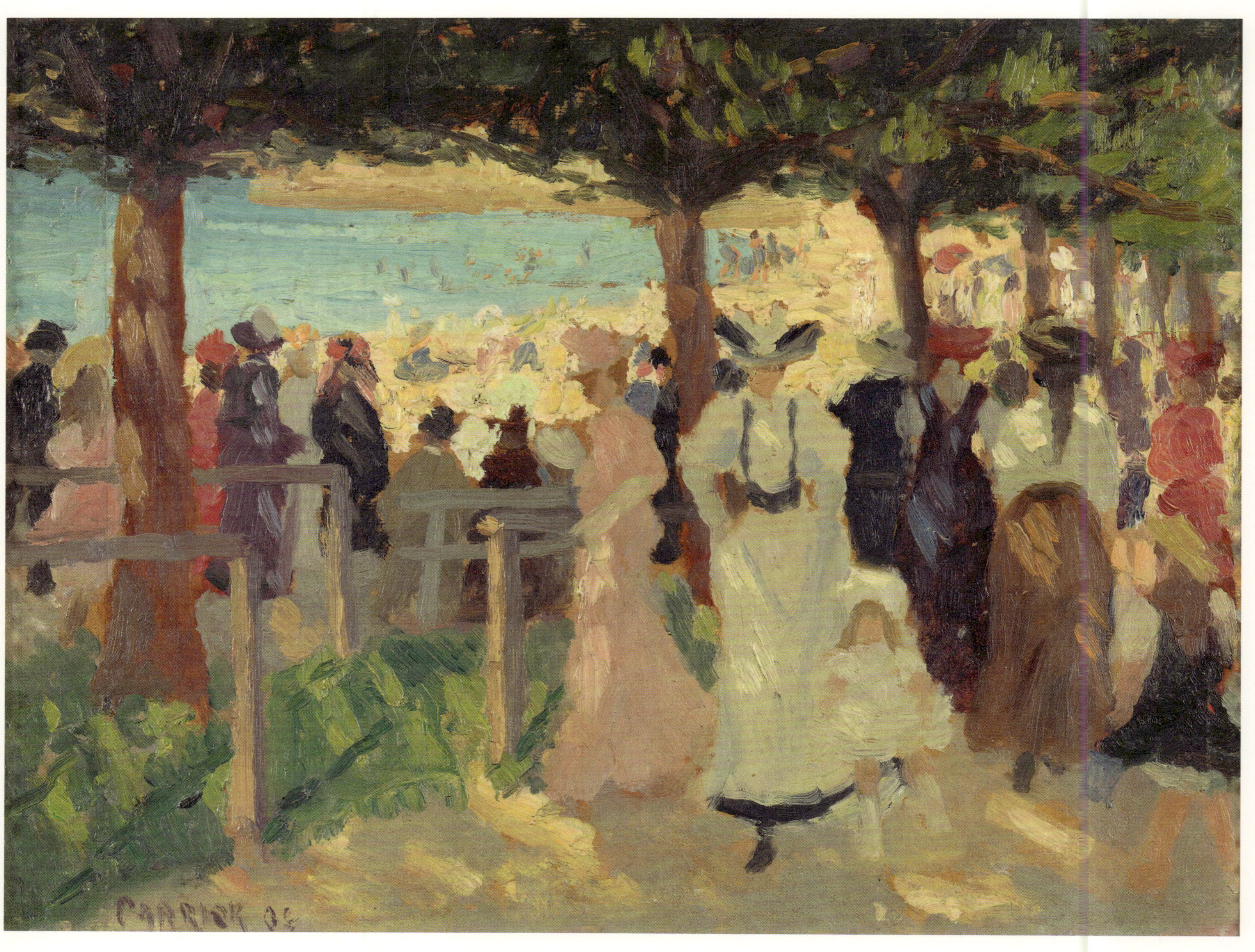

Mon verre n'est pas grand, mais je bois dans mon verre.
(My glass is not large, but it's the glass I drink from.)[1]

—Alfred de Musset, *La coupe et les lèvres*, 1833, quoted by Ethel Carrick, exhibition catalogue, 1913

When I read these words in 2002, it was as if Ethel Carrick spoke directly to me through the years. With this line from Alfred de Musset, she very clearly positioned her project as distinctive and intensely personal, not to be confused with the work of her husband or anyone else. She makes it clear, in the most literate and graceful way, that when she dips her cup into the bubbling wellspring of inspiration, that vessel is authentically her own. My research has led me to understand that a key source of her inspiration was the Theosophical Society.[2]

A crude summary of the three fundamental propositions of the Theosophical Society is truth in all religions, universal 'brotherhood' (extended to all of nature), and the powers latent in 'man'. In the early twentieth century, the Theosophical Society inspired many Australian and international artists who were exploring the nature of the real.[3] Carrick was a member from 1916 until her death,[4] but the Theosophical Society informed her paintings from as early as 1907 and contributed significantly to her professional success in Paris. During the period of Carrick's membership, however, the most significant psychic research was taking place in Sydney, giving her strong reasons to return to Australia after her husband's death and adopt the country as a home. Carrick's practice reflects these two centres.

In Paris, centre of the artworld in this period, Carrick rubbed shoulders with revolutionary artists such as Wassily Kandinsky, Alexander Scriabin, Nicholas Roerich, and Seraphin Soudbinine, for whom Theosophical writing and research opened new doors of creative inspiration. But Paris was not the centre for these avant-garde artists. Theosophical writing and research into the nature of the real were taking place in Adyar, Chennai (Madras) and Sydney, making these places the

Previous
In the Nice flower market c 1926 (detail cat 123, pp 210–11), oil on canvas, National Gallery of Australia

Opposite
cat 120 *La promenade* (The promenade) 1908, oil on wood panel, private collection

centres that mattered to this community. Carrick's familiarity with both Paris and Sydney would have brought her enormous personal cachet within this global community.

When restored to this context, Carrick's work embodies the complexities of the centre and periphery, showcasing the avant-garde stylistic innovations of Paris fully integrated with an alternative conception of the 'real', routinely explored in Sydney.

In Carrick's time, the Theosophical Society was not a small organisation. It was ubiquitous, and its ideas were widely debated in spheres as diverse as politics and the arts. Women artists in particular, such as Florence Fuller and Jane Price, were conceived as having a privileged status within its ranks. Jill Roe, whose work is the best source of information for anyone interested in the broader history of the Society in Australia, has shown that in 1911 Theosophical women were the 'best educated women of all religious groupings in this country.'[5]

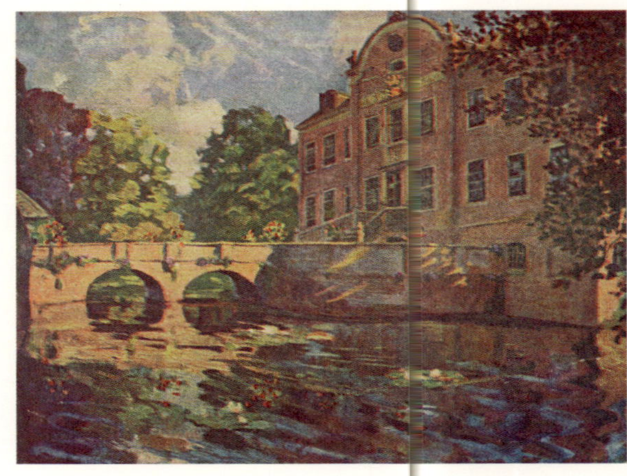

fig 44 Reproduction of Ethel Carrick's painting, *Castle Eerde, Ommen, Holland*, no date, in Len Fox Papers, State Library of New South Wales. Carrick joined the 3000-strong crowd at Castle Eerde, Ommen, Holland to hear Krishnamurti speak in 1927 and 1929.

The Theosophical Society was founded in New York in 1875 by Mme Blavatsky, William Quan Judge and the first president, Colonel Olcott. It was not the only organisation of its type, but it was the dominant organisation for artists in London, Paris, Amsterdam, Adelaide, Chicago, Melbourne and Sydney. Annie Besant succeeded Olcott as President in 1907; she had previously made her name as a militant advocate for women in the Bryant & May matchgirls' strike and as the author of a scandalous publication on contraception, amongst other things. Based in Adyar, Chennai (Madras), India, she travelled constantly, but her only daughter lived in Melbourne and her son-in-law, Ernest Besant Scott, would become the foundation chair of Australian History at The University of Melbourne. This gave the Theosophical artists and intelligentsia of Melbourne a particularly intimate relationship with the international organisation.

The charismatic character who led the Society with Besant was CW Leadbeater, and together in 1901 they published the influential *Thoughtforms*. However, the structured nature of the Theosophical Society that was comprised of discussion groups responding to local and touring lecture programs (which were often written up and shared through syndicated Theosophical journals) meant that these ideas had circulated well before this publication.

By 1914, Leadbeater was living at the Theosophical residence, The Manor, in the Sydney suburb of Mosman. In 1925, when Carrick arrived to hear the Society's promised new World Teacher (Jiddhu) Krishnamurti, The Manor was described by international travellers as the 'greatest of all occult forcing-houses', a place where participants could expect rapid spiritual 'advancement'.[6] Paris, by contrast, was a relative backwater for the Theosophical Society, apart from a few months in 1921 when Krishnamurti made that city his base.

When Ethel Carrick married Emanuel Phillips Fox in 1905, they established their marital home at 65 Boulevard Arago, Paris.[7] While Fox's network centred around the Americans in Paris, Carrick looked more to the Russians, French and Belgians she met in a Theosophical environment. Her neighbour at 65 Boulevard Arago, Seraphin Soudbinine, a favoured student of Rodin, was probably the first of Carrick's large network of Russian friends.[8]

At the time of Carrick's arrival in Paris he was engaged in a major art project alongside Jean Delville, a prominent lecturer on Theosophy and art since at least 1904, and composer Alexander Scriabin.

Each responded to Mme Blavatsky's vision of Prometheus in her book *The Secret Doctrine* (newly translated into French)—he was no longer presented as the 'thief of fire' but as the 'prophet light bearer'. Scriabin's symphony *Prométhée: Le poème du feu* (Prometheus: the poem of fire), which was innovatively designed to be performed with light projections corresponding to the notes being played, remains one of the most important works to have been inspired by the Theosophical Society. Delville's painting *Prométhée*, begun in 1904, was completed in 1907, and Soudbinine's *Vers la lumière* (Towards the light) in 1908. For critic Sébastien Clerbois, 'these works witnessed a subtle balance between two traditions: one symbolist, typical of the nineteenth century, the other belonging to the avant-garde of the twentieth century'.[9] It is hard to imagine that Carrick, the spiritually adventurous painter–pianist and future life-long member of the Theosophical Society, would have ignored these extraordinary projects.

From 1907 until her death, Carrick was a part of this extended Theosophical community, and the support of this network of artists would be immensely important for her professionally. In 1907, Carrick first exhibited with the artist's cooperative Union Internationale des Beaux-Arts, des Lettres, des Sciences et de l'Industrie, known familiarly after the title of their intermittent journal, *Les Tendances Nouvelles*. Her introduction almost certainly occurred through her neighbour Soudbinine. While Les Tendances Nouvelles was only one of the societies Carrick associated with (others included the Salon d'Automne, Les Quelques and the Royal Academy of Arts in London), it was important to her. She was elected a member in 1908 and would remain active within the group until its demise in 1914. The inspiration, owner and publisher of the journal Les Tendances Nouvelles was Alexis Mérodack-Jeanneau, a student of Gustave Moreau along with Matisse and Marquet. Under the nom de plume Gérôme Maësse he was also the journal's art critic.[10]

Mérodack-Jeanneau was immersed in the contemporary atmosphere of alternative spirituality within which the Theosophical Society was an important player.[11] The journal espoused theosophical ideas, including synaesthetic correspondences and a consistent interest in occult spirituality, with the artist conceived as a medium endowed with special faculties enabling them to see form as temporal and relative.[12] It celebrated Theosophical artists Jean Delville and Maurice Chabas,[13] as well as Marie Bermond, who was a founding member of the Society and also a central figure in the Paris Theosophical Society. Artists associated with Les Tendances Nouvelles at its founding exhibition in 1904 included Alexei Jawlensky, Wassily Kandinsky, Marie Bermond and Mérodack-Jeanneau (whose work had stylistic affinities with Fauvism).[14]

Les Tendances Nouvelles facilitated a departure from visible reality. Jonathan Fineberg locates the important influence of Les Tendances Nouvelles on Kandinsky as providing a framework within which he was able to negotiate a space between Symbolism and the avant-garde of the Fauves, a springboard for his later Theosophically-inspired abstraction.[15] According to Fineberg, Kandinsky came to understand 'Neo-Impressionism as a visual embodiment of the symbolist belief that colour and composition have laws of their own, independent of nature; thus he explored Neo-Impressionism as a vehicle for liberating colour.'[16]

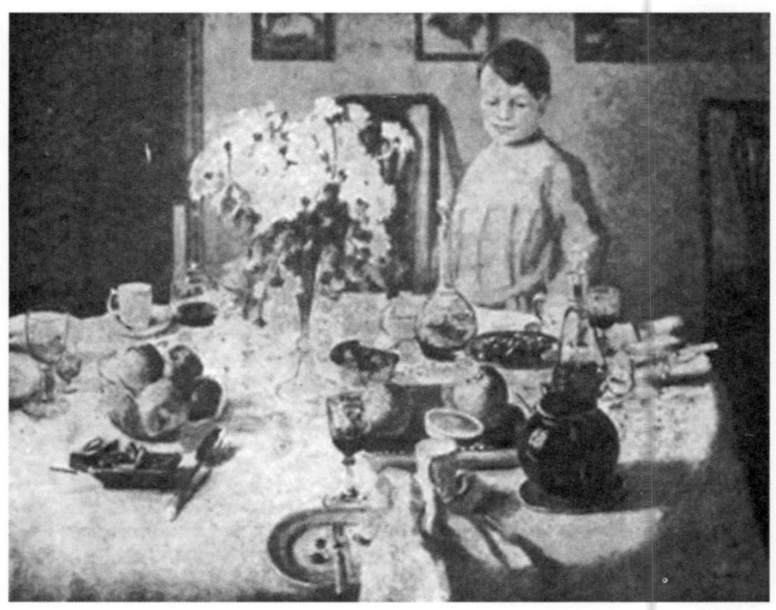

fig 45 Reproduction of Ethel Carrick's painting, *La table* (The table) c 1907 in *Les Tendances Nouvelles, vol 33*, 1907

Carrick showed her work in the second exhibition of Les Tendances Nouvelles in May to June 1907 in Angers. Known as *Le Musée du Peuple,* this exhibition featured 1 244 entries, including six works by Carrick[17] and 12 metres of wall space devoted to the black-edged, folkloric work of Wassily Kandinsky.[18] Carrick's work was well-reviewed by the press and *La table* (The table) c 1907 (fig 45) was reproduced in *Les Tendances Nouvelles*. This work strongly references her Slade training and is distinguished by sound competencies in many of the qualities that some Australian critics noticed in absentia, notably strong drawing. Interestingly, *La table* also exhibits the compositional concerns that would come to define Carrick's later work. There is an almost centripetal force concentrating energies at the centre of the work, a compositional inflorescence achieved through the arrangement of naturalistic detail. There can be no question of Carrick's academic competence. It is notable therefore that these naturalistic references would be consciously sacrificed in her later works for greater compositional energy and 'vibrational force'. This was a process perhaps already begun in the smaller canvases also referenced in the *Les Tendances Nouvelles* review—paintings of clear days in the Luxembourg Gardens, for instance, which demonstrate a moderated impressionist technique and a use of colour (rather than light) to define form.[19]

In Mérodack-Jeanneau's manifesto, *Le Synthétisme*, he describes the living energy of vibrating forces within the 'universal organism'.[20] Carrick's use of form and colour can be best understood against Mérodack-Jeanneau's call for the orchestration of coloured lines, zones of colour, vital rhythms, the definition of the relative movement of forms and the 'absolute movement of life'.[21] Indeed, Carrick's work should be seen in the context of this group of artists, who were reaching to represent a more profound reality, invisible to the human eye, where form and colour were conceived as metaphysical reflections of a unifying whole. Fineberg makes the crucial point that 'Les Tendances Nouvelles underscores the inadequacy of approaching modern art solely in terms of schools, "isms" or other closed concepts, pointing to the fluid exchange of ideas that animated intellectual life of the period'.[22] Carrick, Kandinsky and Mérodack-Jeanneau are united not by a stylistic connection but through a common concern to represent a more profound reality.

Carrick exhibited in the Salon d'Automne in 1906, 1907 and again in 1908, when Soudbinine was a *juriste*. In a letter to a friend, Fox would write, perhaps sourly, that 'my wife has been very successful at the Autumn Salon—four pictures hung on the line and all sold—so if this sort of thing goes on I shall have to take a back seat!'[23] The difference between Fox's conservative and Carrick's experimental communities is made explicit in *The Bulletin* 'Red Page' in May 1908:

> **There is an Autumn Salon, where all the conventions of painting are deliberately disregarded. The judges go on the theory that there are no rules in art; they will accept anything as long as it is a freak. Fox tells us that in this Salon the colour simply shrieks at you, and the drawing has a naivety of impression that looks like the work of a child of five.[24]**

By contrast, the review in *Les Tendances Nouvelles* paid special attention to Carrick's superior technique. [25] Following this exhibition, her work was noticed by Belgian curator Octave Maus, who was sympathetic to the ideals of Les Tendances Nouvelles.[26] Carrick was invited to participate in his 1909 Libre Esthétique exhibition in Brussels.

The Salon of La Libre Esthétique was a major international annual survey exhibition, widely acknowledged to have been insightfully connected with the international avant-garde. Forty artists were invited, including sculptors and printmakers. Pierre Bonnard's standing figure *L'eau de Cologne* 1909 was the iconic image of the exhibition. Other painters included Emile Claus, Paul Signac, HE Cross, Fernand Knopff, Odilon Redon, Auguste Renoir, Ferdinand Schirren, Maurice Denis, Théo van Rysselberghe and Édouard Vuillard.[27] The exhibition showcased symbolists, Les Nabis and the neo-impressionists associated with the transcendental scientist Charles Henry. It is likely that Carrick's association with Les Tendances Nouvelles led directly to her inclusion in this exhibition—she was introduced by Maus as 'Ethel Carrick, another newly arrived talent; tender, expansive and intellectual'.[28] She showed at least two works, *Marché aux fleurs à Venise* (Flower market in Venice) 1907 (cat 121, p 207) and *La promenade* (The promenade) 1908 (cat 120, p 200). The following years saw Carrick build on this early success, becoming a *sociétaire* of the Salon d'Automne in 1911 and a *juriste* in 1912.

Carrick's second trip to Australia in 1913 was a major turning point in her professional career. Upon her departure, her reputation in Paris was established, and she had strong, well-placed and active support within the Paris avant-garde. However, when she returned in 1916, a year after Fox's death, Paris was a war zone and would not really begin to recover until the 1920s. While she continued to find spiritual, intellectual and social support within the Theosophical community, and her practice continued to develop, she would never again enjoy the same level of organised professional support as she had in pre-war Paris. Her success in Paris did not travel with her to Australia; her achievements at the Salon d'Automne were presented as a sign of weakness rather than a strength, and she was often positioned as a poor shadow of her husband.

By July 1913, two months after her arrival in Melbourne, Carrick was driven to insist that the glass she filled from the inspirational wellspring was authentically her own. As she worked to reposition herself in a new Australian context, she found that her ambition to represent the unseen was largely misunderstood; only amongst Theosophical fellow travellers, did this ambition make absolute sense. Similarly, when

Kandinsky's revolutionary abstractions reached Australia the following year through the Theosophical press,[29] the Society's discussion groups were better positioned to understand the scale of Kandinsky's ambition than the established arts community. As a fellow exhibitor with Les Tendances Nouvelles (and similarly inspired by Theosophical precepts), Carrick's innovations, like Kandinsky's experimental abstractions, were largely misunderstood, overlooked and ignored.

After Fox's death in 1915, Carrick was encircled by a community of Theosophical women, including Ivy Brookes (the daughter of Alfred and 'Patti' Deakin, she was brought up in a family of spiritualists active in the Theosophical Society).[30] Soon after, in April 1916, Carrick travelled to England, crossing an ocean patrolled by warships. There, she saw her sister Jessie Platts' sons before they left for the Western Front; Jessie would soon relay spiritualist messages from her boys, who both became casualties of World War I.[31] Back in Paris on 5 December that same year, Carrick finally joined the Theosophical Society officially, sponsored by artist Marie Bermond and President Charles Blech.[32] Carrick may have attended the courses titled 'The astral world after death' and 'The mental world, thought forms and invisible aides', which ran that year in Paris. Like many of her generation, Carrick was sustained by the Theosophical Society through loss and war.

It is likely that Carrick would have been a fellow traveller with the Society for some time. How long she had known Marie Bermond before 1916 is difficult to tell. Certainly, Bermond was active in the Theosophical Society and had exhibited with Les Tendances Nouvelles as part of Soudbinine's artistic, Theosophical circle. Like Carrick, Bermond was an active feminist, traveller, social worker and spiritually inquisitive artist. It is hard to imagine that they would not have met before 1916. They would certainly have many conversations after this time at the new Studio Lodge, formed the following year. Carrick, Bermond and Maurice Chabas formed part of the intimate circle, publishing articles in the Theosophical press based on Lodge discussions—and these reflect instructively on Carrick's practice, past and present. The discussion group would also have attracted Soudbinine; sculptor Antoine Bourdelle; Jean Delville; Nicholas Roerich, *sociétaire* of the Salon d'Automne and collaborator on Stravinsky's *The Rite of Spring*; philosopher Réné Guenon; theorist of light and colour Charles Henry, for whom the major biographical source document remains the 1930 issue of the Theosophical publication *L'Étoile*; and perhaps American Theosophist, collector and curator Katherine Dreier. Then as now, the Society functioned more as a discussion group than an exclusive organisation. The Lodge would also have benefited from occasional visits from prominent Theosophists, especially in early 1921.

At the heart of the Studio Lodge's message for the artist was the idea of a universal 'brotherhood', a central unity, which was expressed in the physical world as form and colour.[33] The artist was conceived as a missionary whose task was to perceive this interconnectivity and, in representing it, raise other souls. Both Chabas and Bermond spoke of life as vibration; for Chabas 'the solid does not exist'.[34] Bermond was firm: 'There is no reality outside of ourselves.'[35] She saw life as movement, instability, continual change, a dynamic force in its subjective state. This is very visible in Bermond's own paintings, where life ripples across the figures in a manner reminiscent of her mentor, Bourdelle.

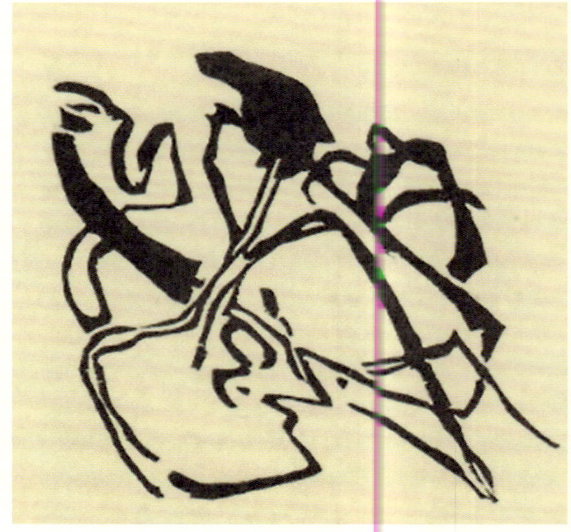

fig 46 Wassily Kandinsky, Vignette for 'Pyramid', woodcut, from *Über das Geistige in der Kunst* (Concerning the spiritual in art), 1911 , reproduced in *Herald of the Star* Nov 1914, p 627

Opposite
cat 121 *Marché aux fleurs à Venise* (Flower market in Venice) 1907, oil on board, private collection

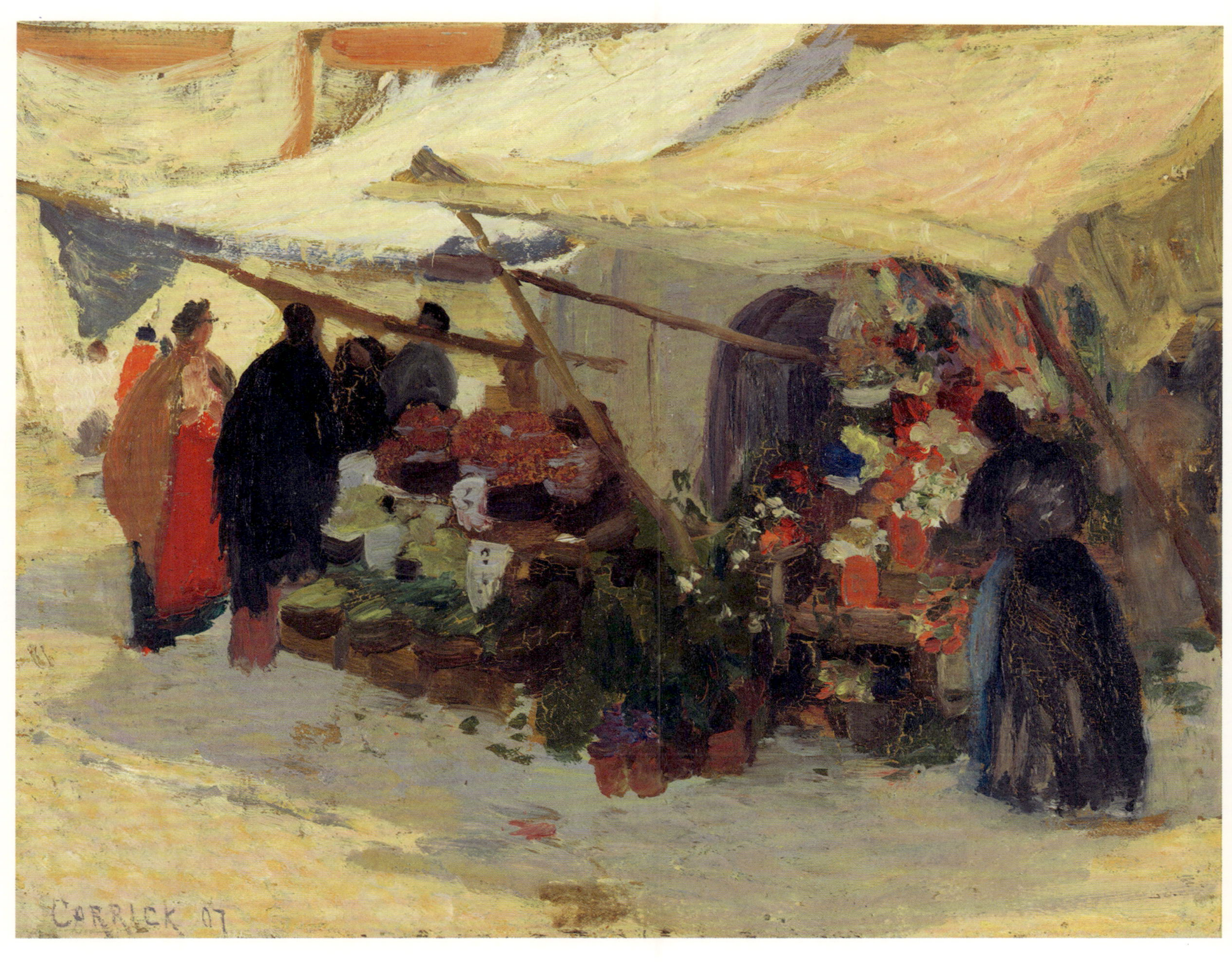
CORRICK 07

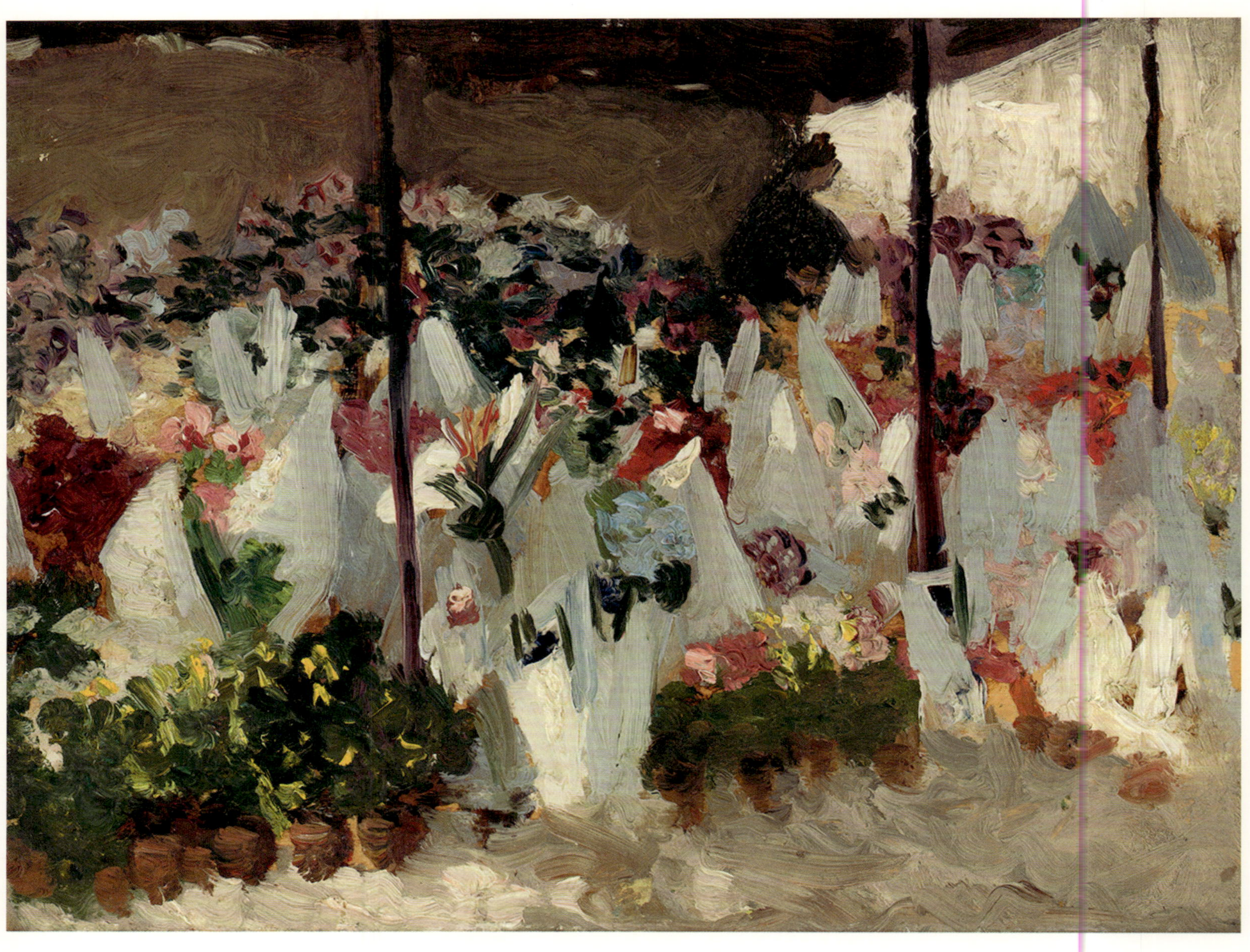

Carrick herself made this point during an interview in Adelaide in 1925. Answering an accusation that the work was unfinished, she argued for the representation of the invisible quality of the experience:

> **So called finish means arrested movement ... When you go out in the street and see a similar moving crowd try and remember how much (or little) detail you see while the people are moving.[36]**

In February 1925 Carrick left France aboard the SS *Oronsay*, once again bound for Australia. She arrived in Melbourne on 17 March 1925, shortly before Krishnamurti and Lady Emily Lutyens,[37] a friend of her sister Jessie. They were similarly en route for the National Theosophical Convention in Sydney, where they were the keynote speakers.[38] It was there that Krishnamurti and Leadbeater were reunited—surely one of the more emotional moments in the Theosophical Society's history. As anticipated, the politics of the event were tumultuous. Perhaps this is one reason that Carrick did not return to Adyar later that year with the Leadbeater contingent, when Krishnamurti publicly accepted the Theosophical Society's messianic role for the first time. On 21 December, Carrick was still at Stella Maris on Stanton Road, close to the Theosophical Garden School in Mosman and the newly constructed Star Amphitheatre in Balmoral.

Carrick's 1925 defence of her husband's work is useful in understanding what she herself valued. In her own introduction to his work, Carrick presented Fox as engaged in a similar quest to her own: 'Art to him was a sacred thing ... he painted as he felt, and gave to his canvas the inner truth, the soul of the subject.'[39] Yet contemporary Australian artist Lionel Lindsay felt Fox's work is best understood with an emphasis on physical engagement with the visible world:

> **The charm of life and the visible world more than sufficed his imagination, and his work is consistently personal, and at its rarest possesses a voluptuous quality which is, in truth, a reflection of the artist's mind.[40]**

One imagines with difficulty how such a statement would have been explained to Carrick's spiritually oriented Theosophical community, for whom a focus on the sensuous was evidence of a less spiritually evolved personality.

Carrick returned to Paris that summer via the south of France.[41] When she painted *In the Nice flower market* c 1926 (cat 123, pp 210–11), she had been an official member of the Theosophical Society for 10 years and, with much of the Society, was basking in the afterglow of Krishnamurti's assumption of the role of World Teacher. In light of Les Tendances Nouvelles and Lodge discussions, this work becomes a useful pivot to reflect on Carrick's practice.

Visible reality has been sacrificed to the representation of the 'absolute movement of life', the formal expression on canvas of the vital rhythms of the universe—a concept fully realised in this superb example of Carrick's mature work. As in her other crowd scenes, the flower market is merely a pretext for the representation of a different order of reality. Carrick creates harmony from the union of opposites; an oscillating, vibrating pattern of contrasting colour zones—hot colour and deep cool shade—holds our attention.

Opposite
cat 122 *Au marché* (At the market) c 1908, oil on Baltic pine panel, private collection

Following
cat 123 *In the Nice flower market* c 1926, oil on canvas, National Gallery of Australia

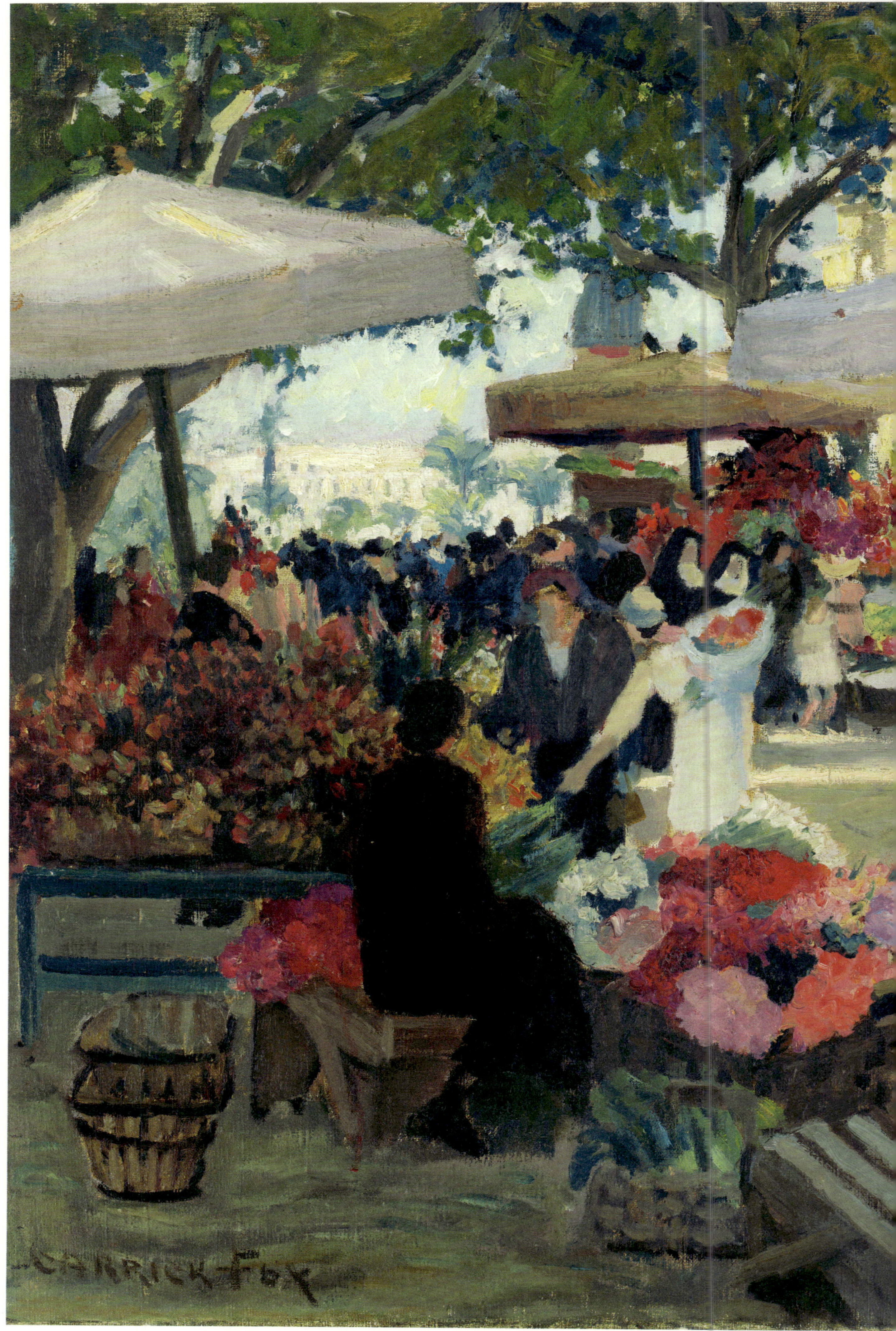

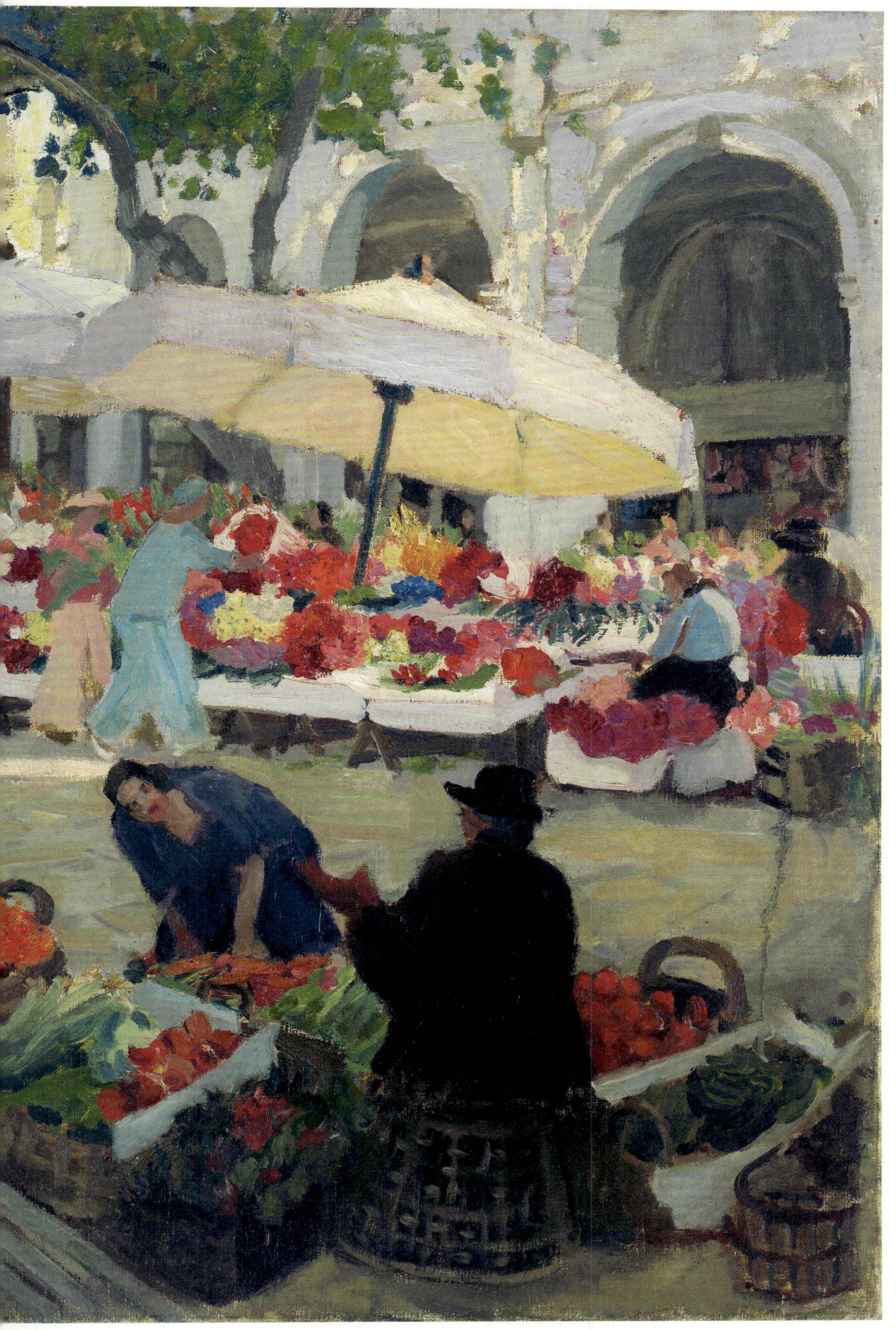

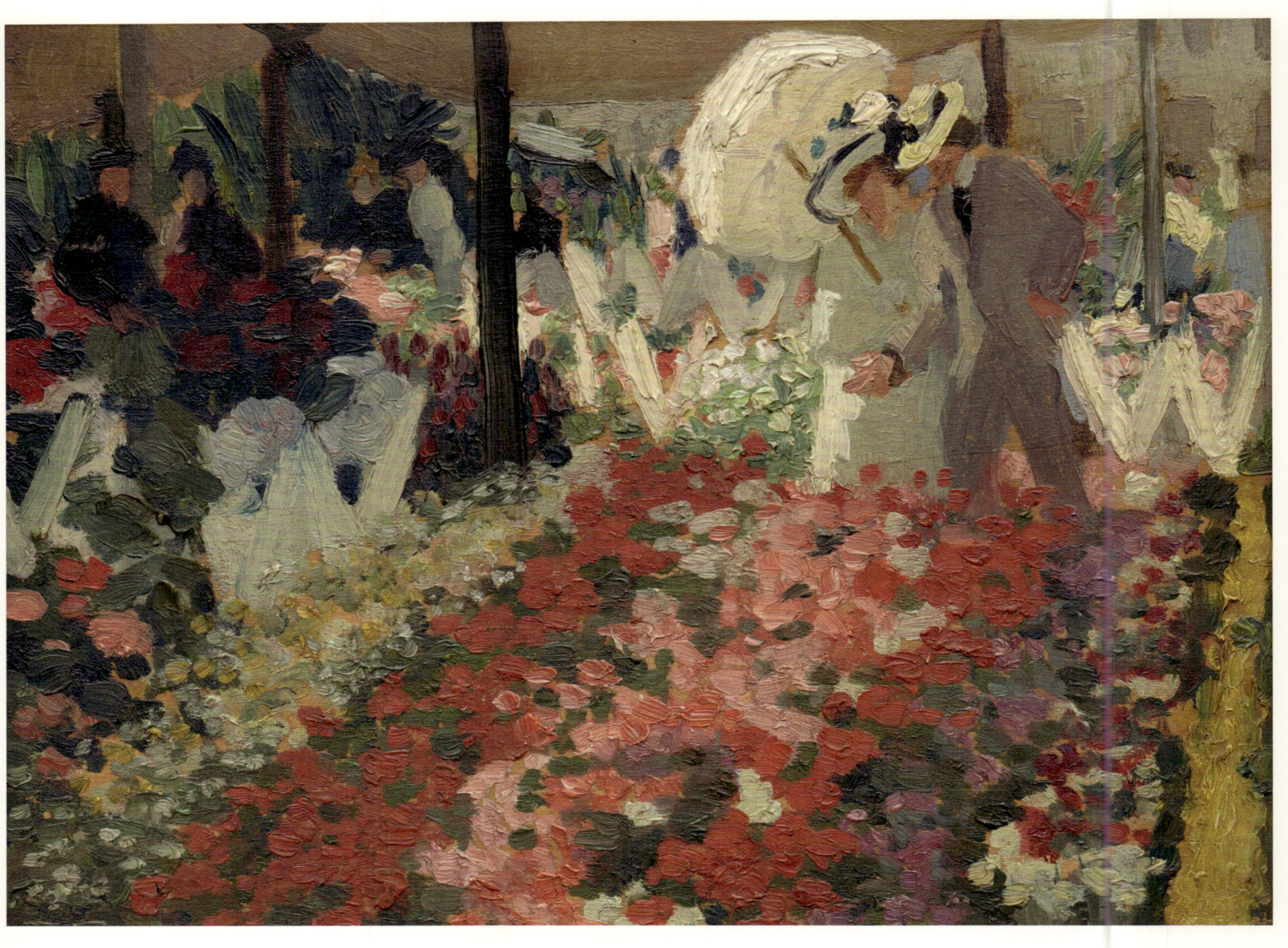

Opposite
cat 124 *Flower market (France)* c 1910, oil on wood panel, collection of McClelland

Coloured lines are boldly deployed as *repoussoirs*[42] and lines of force direct the eye. Her post-war work exhibits a new, volumetric quality; the umbrellas that close the composition at the top have fleshy, mushroom-like bodies and the white boxes and tablecloths cup the strong colours of the bouquets upwards with new mass. The arches, which are increasingly a feature of this period, lean forwards, as the dark colours at the front of the work push the eye into the centre of the composition. The whole fabric of the work is compressed, front to back, top to bottom, left to right. Lines of flight are closed by swatches of dazzling white, and the centre of the composition is full of wound-up bustle. The fortuitous combination of blooms and bright clothing is synthesised in happy, jostling brushstrokes barely distinguishable from each other. The flowers and frothy humanity are no longer subject to a hierarchy of being, but rather a Theosophical 'brotherhood' of being—microcosmic echoes of an interconnected whole.

The representation of life as vibration, carrying the deeper truth of a humanity networked with nature within a cosmic unity, is Carrick's special gift. Present from her earliest moments in Paris, this wellspring of inspiration found a point of connection with Soudbinine, artistic support in the ideas of Les Tendances Nouvelles and a spiritual home in the Studio Lodge of the Paris Theosophical Society.

By looking at Carrick's paintings through the lens of her sustained commitment to the Theosophical Society, we can recognise a commitment to the Society's vision of the cosmic unity and movement of life, discounting the visible to represent an unseen, more profound reality. Repositioned within her community of avant-garde artists, Carrick's personal and professional wellspring of inspiration was the same source that nourished many radical practices of the twentieth century, including her more famous colleague Kandinsky. Within this community, Carrick conceived of herself as a privileged individual with a clear responsibility to communicate her insights into a Theosophical truth. Among the avant-garde of the Salon d'Automne, Les Tendances Nouvelles, La Libre Esthétique and the Theosophical Society, Carrick's paintings communicated her vision of this invisible reality. To return to Carrick's chosen metaphor, the glass she dipped into this deep well was authentically her own. This important exhibition, as it brings us a better understanding of how Carrick viewed her own practice, is a fresh opportunity to drink this all in.

Dr Jenny McFarlane has curated diverse public collections in the Australian Capital Territory, including at the Canberra Museum and Gallery, the ACT Legislative Assembly and the Museum of Australian Democracy at Old Parliament House. She is currently the Canberra Health Services Curator of Arts in Health. McFarlane is the author of *Concerning the Spiritual: the influence of the Theosophical Society on Australian artists 1890–1934* (Australian Scholarly Publishing, 2012) and numerous articles and chapters in this field. Recent publications include 'Punk your graphics' in *eX de Medici: beautiful wickedness* (Queensland Art Gallery | Gallery of Modern Art, 2023) and 'Arts + health: new approaches to arts and robots in health care', a co-authored paper presented at HRI 2022: ACM/IEEE International Conference on Human–Robot Interaction at the University of Cambridge.

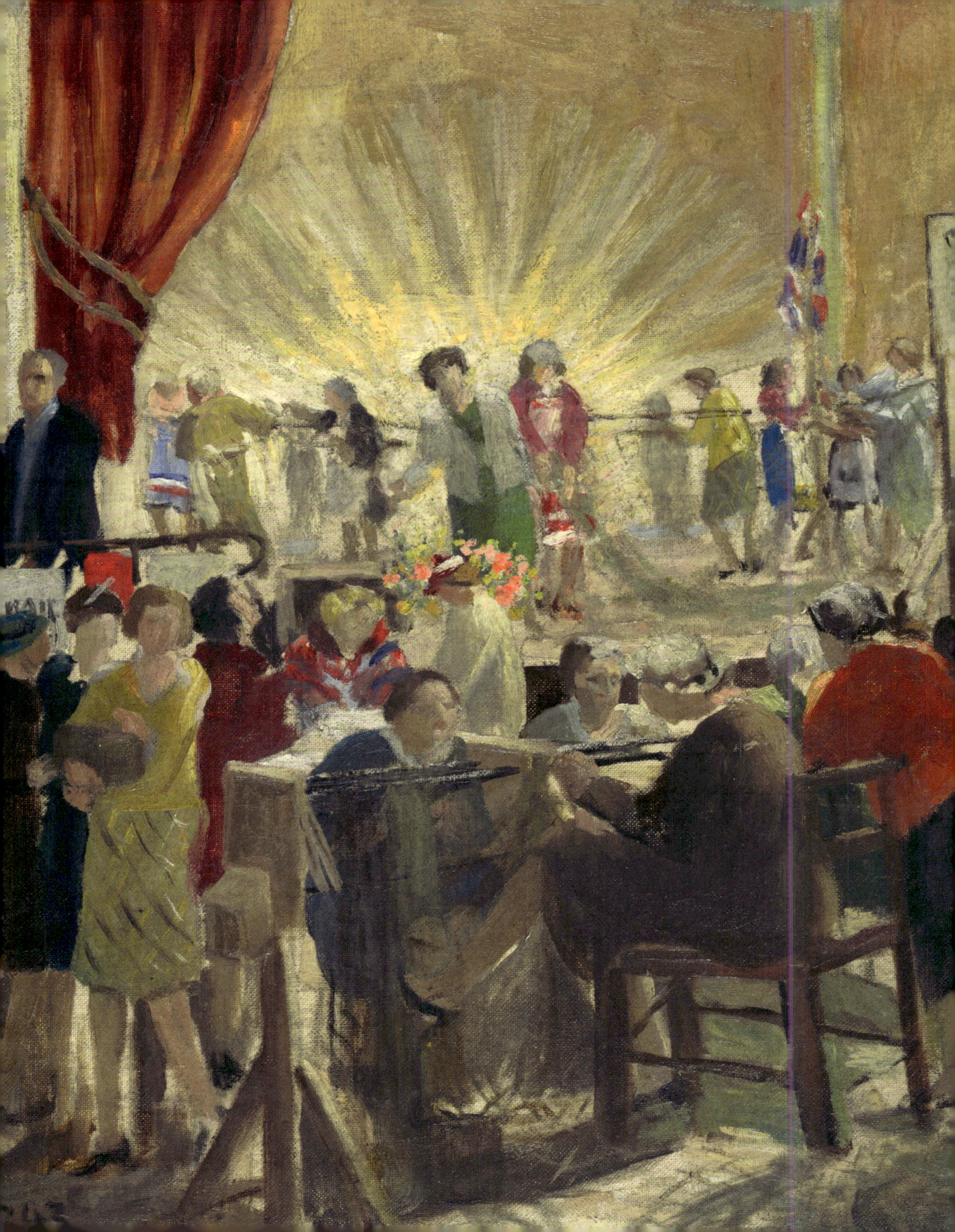

Sorrow and service: Carrick across the two world wars

Catherine Speck

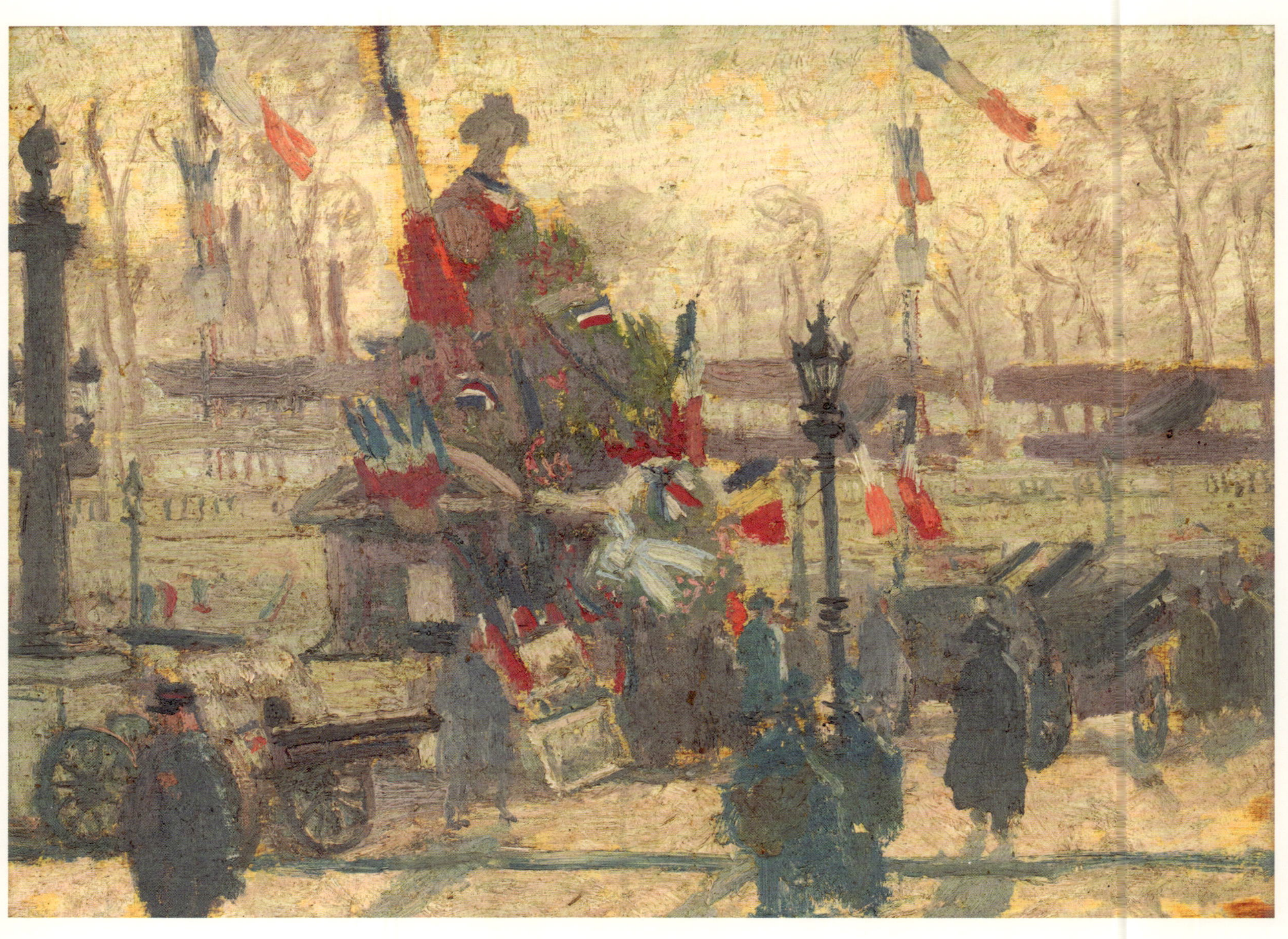

Ethel Carrick, a British-born artist who lived pre-war in cosmopolitan Paris, was very much a global citizen. In the apartment and studio complex she and her Australian spouse Emanuel Phillips Fox lived, at 65 Boulevard Arago in Montparnasse, there were artists from 30 nations.[1] The couple travelled to paint, and the subjects of their paintings were drawn from Paris and coastal resorts in France as well as across places in Europe and North Africa including Spain, Venice and Morocco. But during each world war, Ethel Carrick's movements were reduced to just two nations: Australia and France. These periods were spent avidly assisting—and, during World War II, documenting—war-relief efforts.

The Foxes were in Tahiti when World War I broke out. They headed to Melbourne, arriving in October 1914, and cancelled plans to return to Paris in December that year. Over the next few months they worked prominently to put their art to use in raising funds for the Red Cross, and in particular to acquire a lorry for the French Red Cross. Their sense of obligation to France was strong, as it was for many artists who once lived and worked there. American artist Cecilia Beaux, who credited her time in France for bringing light and colour into her painting, felt a similar impulse to help. Beaux donated money to an American volunteer ambulance corps in France and raised funds for the families of French artist–soldiers.[2] The Victorian Artists Society, of which Carrick and Fox were members, set about raising funds in all kinds of ways for the French Red Cross.[3]

Carrick also spent time in Sydney in 1915, where her infectious energy set in motion a plan for artists across the nation to come together as the Australian Artist Workers' War Fund—of which she became honorary secretary—to raise funds for the Red Cross. As Ruth Zubans has noted, Carrick was the perfect choice for that role—she was well-known in art circles and 'her social skills, her shrewd sense of how best to achieve results, and her forthrightness' set her apart.[4] In January 1915 she convened a meeting of Sydney artists in the Royal Art Society rooms, where they raised funds for a British Red Cross motor lorry.[5] She also convened a fundraising 'conversazione' in March 1915, the success of which was reported as largely due to her enthusiasm and energy.[6] She became part of a network of women artists engaged in the war effort, and even portrayed a group of volunteers in *Red Cross workers, Sydney Town Hall*, which she exhibited in 1916.[7]

Previous
National Defence League depot, St Michael's Hall, Sydney 1942 (detail fig 50, p 221), oil on canvas on cardboard, Australian War Memorial

Opposite
cat 125 *The statue of Strasbourg, Place de la Concorde, Paris* 1918, oil on wood panel, private collection

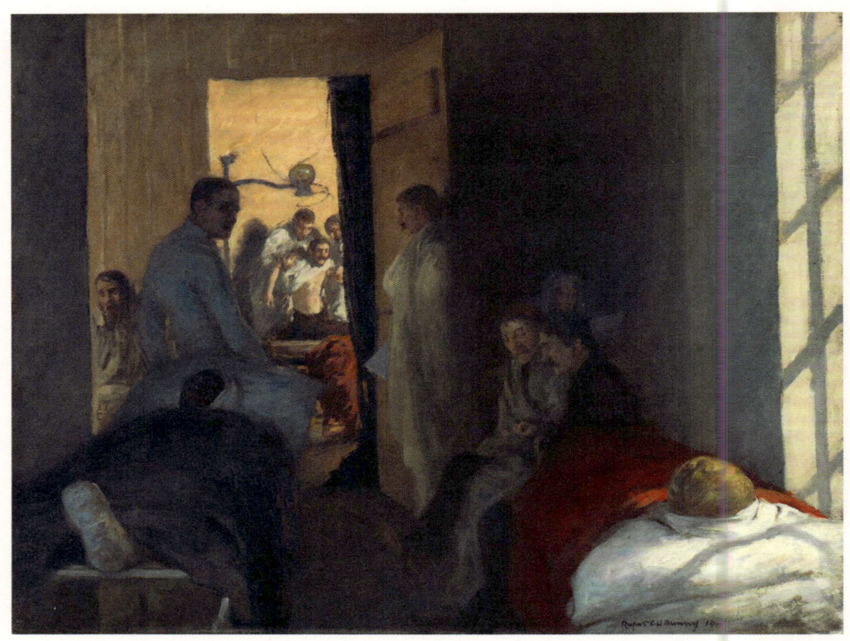

fig 47 Rupert Bunny, *Waiting to be X-rayed* 1915, oil on canvas, Australian War Memorial

However, Ethel Carrick's world changed on 8 October 1915 when her husband, Emanuel Phillips Fox, died suddenly in Melbourne following surgery for recently diagnosed cancer. Grief stricken, Carrick struggled coming to terms with Fox's death and her new circumstances; her circle of female friends—including Ivy Brookes in Melbourne and Bertha Merfield in Sydney—assisted her.[8] Once she had arranged a memorial exhibition for her late husband's work at the Athenaeum Gallery in Melbourne in February 1916 and an exhibition of her own work in Sydney in April 1916—with the proceeds donated to the French–Australian League of Help—she set off for London to visit family, then returned to Paris.[9] She arrived there in 1916.

It was a very different Paris to the one she had left; now it was cold and under siege. She lived through extreme food and fuel shortages and found it difficult to paint. In a letter to Ivy Brookes she wrote, 'We have passed through a very trying month of extreme cold—with coal very difficult to obtain. I never thought cold could be so cold! ... Potatoes are very scarce, I am going to plant as many as I can in our garden, also beans and peas.'[10] In happier times, this had been the lush and private garden setting for many of Fox's sun-filled paintings, especially his nudes, and some of her paintings too.[11]

Like Carrick, several of the artists in her circle who had remained in Paris took on war work. Rupert Bunny volunteered as an orderly at the American Hospital of Paris in Neuilly, where the experience of ferrying the injured affected him deeply. American expatriate artist Elizabeth Nourse, who Bunny and Carrick knew from Anglo-American artist circles, described what she called 'the blackest hour', when the fighting was just outside Paris and 'they brought into the hospital 7500 wounded'.[12] Little wonder one of the few paintings Bunny produced, *Waiting to be X-rayed* 1915 (fig 47), is so grim, depicting the wounded in a dim light. Bessie Davidson, who like Carrick had exhibited with Les Quelques, joined the Red Cross and took on nursing work at Auxiliary Hospital 108 on Rue Molitor in Auteuil, where she volunteered to work with typhoid patients.[13] Carrick herself visited Belgian refugee children housed in a nearby convent, possibly the same children American expatriate artist Elizabeth Nourse was assisting.[14]

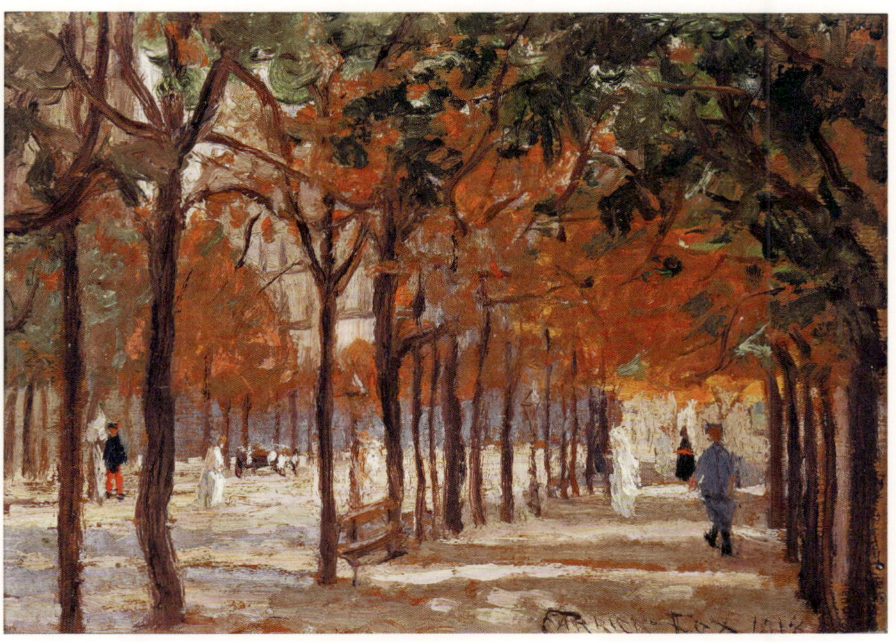

fig 48 *Luxembourg Gardens* 1918, oil on panel, private collection

Carrick felt unable to paint during this time, writing to Ivy Brookes: 'I have not painted yet, but hope to when brighter days come.'[15] She joined the cause of assisting Serbian prisoners and asked Ivy Brookes to do what she could from Melbourne to raise funds. She kept up her connections to Melbourne, and exhibited a large number of paintings in the exhibition her friend Violet Teague arranged for the French Week appeal in July 1916, and again for the 1918 French Red Cross exhibition *Salon des Poilus*.[16]

Once peace was declared, Carrick completed a small number of paintings depicting the Armistice, including *The statue of Strasbourg, Place de la Concorde, Paris* 1918 (cat 125, p 216), which shows one of its eight monuments, the Strasbourg statue, adorned with French flags celebrating the regaining of Alsace. Her melancholic *Luxembourg Gardens* 1918 (fig 48), so different from her pre-war versions, shows a sparsely frequented park in autumn, with patches of sunlight tentatively filtering through.[17] Just a few people and one lone solder are out walking, and the row of tree trunks suggests both the city and its people are exhausted. She exhibited these paintings in Sydney in 1925.[18]

Between the wars, Carrick maintained a presence in Australia, visiting and exhibiting. In 1933, at the time of her exhibition in Melbourne, a reporter from *The Age* described her as 'well-known to the Australian public'.[19] She was in Kashmir when World War II broke out in September of 1939, and by October was back in Australia.

As during World War I, Carrick was involved in numerous ways of raising funds for the war effort, including donating half the proceeds of a large exhibition of her and Fox's works at Athenaeum Gallery, Melbourne in April 1942 to the Red Cross.[20] One of the most ingenious schemes she devised, as a member of the artists' sub-committee for the Lord Mayor's Red Cross Appeal, was selling gum leaves preserved in gelatine and adorned with patriotic slogans in gold paint.[21] These were sold for a gold coin on Red Cross Flag Day in Melbourne in March 1940.[22] Artists from all societies came together and donated paintings for a fundraising exhibition to mark the occasion.[23]

By 1941, Carrick was busy promoting the Free French cause, as much of France was now occupied by Nazi Germany. When visiting Brisbane in September that year to raise funds for the cause of General de Gaulle, she spurred on support by referring to the efforts of the artistic community in Melbourne, which had recently contributed paintings for an art union exhibition that raised £300.[24]

Carrick also applied for the prestigious position of official war artist in October 1942 to record women's war-time activities, a natural choice given her long association with women's groups in Paris and Australia.[25] In her letter of application she was remarkably modest, listing just some of her many achievements, including being an *'Associé du Salon de la Nationale des Beaux-Arts*; and *sociétaire du Salon d'Automne*'.[26] Her choice of subject matter was very topical—Prime Minister John Curtin had just recently announced, in December 1941, the extensive employment of women in industries where men were not available to maintain production. Moreover, women's divisions in the armed services were forming in 1941 and 1942, and women were volunteering in all kinds of ways to support and join the war effort.

Timing was not on her side, however, and her application was unsuccessful. The machinery of government was moving slowly in these changing times and though by the end of 1941 Ivor Hele, Harold Herbert and Frank Norton had been appointed as war artists, it wasn't until mid-1942 that the Australian War Memorial Director, Lieutenant Colonel John Treloar, was seconded into running the Official War Art Scheme. This saw the appointment of four more male artists to the role of official war artists: William Dargie, Roy Hodgkinson, Murray Griffin and Lyndon Dadswell.

Despite Sydney Ure Smith—chairman of the War Art Council of Sydney, to which Carrick belonged—suggesting to Prime Minister Curtin in April 1942 and Treasurer Chifley in July 1942 that they use a much wider demographic of artists 'to record what they see ... and in this group should be women artists',[27] it wasn't until 1943 that Nora Heysen became the first woman to take up duties as an official war artist, followed by Stella Bowen in 1944.[28] Despite this, the Official War Art Scheme was clearly not keeping abreast of the widespread contribution of women on the home front. Sybil Craig, the third woman appointed to the role of official war artist, completed paintings of munitions workers and a small number of studies of women working in the Australian Comforts Fund—including *Voluntary worker (Mrs Desbrowe Annear)* 1945 (fig 49), which depicted its subject immersed in knitting. Late in the war, almost as an afterthought, Treloar arranged for Craig to portray four senior Red Cross women in a painting she completed in 1946, once a supply of pastels was secured.[29]

Carrick's earlier call to record women's war-time activities was going largely unheard, and with the Australian War Memorial also unresponsive, in 1942 she herself set about recording women's voluntary activities in Victoria, the Australian Capital Territory and New South Wales in a set of five paintings.

One of the five, *National Defence League depot, St Michael's Hall, Sydney* 1942 (fig 50), portrays a busy, convivial scene of women making much-needed camouflage nets. Some are immersed in knotting the twine, some are chatting. Others work on the stage of the church hall illuminated by the Anzac image of a rising sun, while red curtains frame the entire scene. Carrick was a theosophist, living then in their community at Mosman, and the rising sun image framing the women can also be

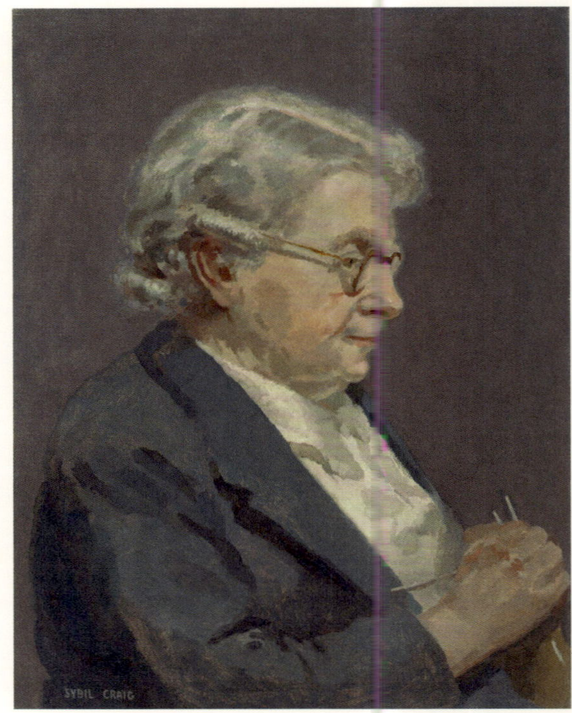

fig 49 Sybil Craig, *Voluntary worker (Mrs Desbrowe Annear)* 1945, oil on canvas on cardboard, Australian War Memorial

Opposite
fig 50 *National Defence League depot, St Michael's Hall, Sydney* 1942, oil on cotton, Australian War Memorial

read as a theosophical sign of energy, creativity and devotion. There is a warmth in the painting, generated by the rhythm of red from the curtains on the stage to patches in the women's clothing, and a deep sense of purpose in the women at work. The glow from the rising sun suffuses the entire scene and conveys a vibrating life force.[30] Carrick was masterful in depicting a crowd, as William Moore has observed, but it was the energy of the crowd as the visible expression of the absolute movement of life that fascinated her as a theosophist.[31]

St Michael's Hall was the city depot for the National Defence League on Hunter Street, and it adjoined St Michael's Flats, once a base for theosophical leader CW Leadbeater.[32] The subject of making camouflage nets was very topical at the time—nets were urgently needed and hundreds of women went each week to St Michael's Hall, and to numerous other centres, to donate their time.[33] The National Defence League alone had 119 centres and 10 000 members.[34] The craft of camouflage-net making was developed by camouflage expert WJ Dakin. Some nets were made up of 10 000 knots, but 'it was an unforgivable sin to do a granny knot or a slip knot. Double reef knots or weavers' knots are the ones permitted'.[35]

Along with camouflage-net making, Carrick selected various women's activities to record, including women of the Red Cross Auxiliary making papier mâché hospital equipment (cat 126, pp 222–23), volunteers cooking and serving meals in the Canberra Services Club (cat 79, p 122), and the Anzac Fellowship of Women assembling much-needed garments to send to England for distribution. She exhibited the five oil paintings as part of the exhibition *Pictures by the Late E Phillips Fox and E Carrick Fox* at Athenaeum Gallery, Melbourne in February 1944, then in Canberra in September that year as part of her larger solo exhibition.

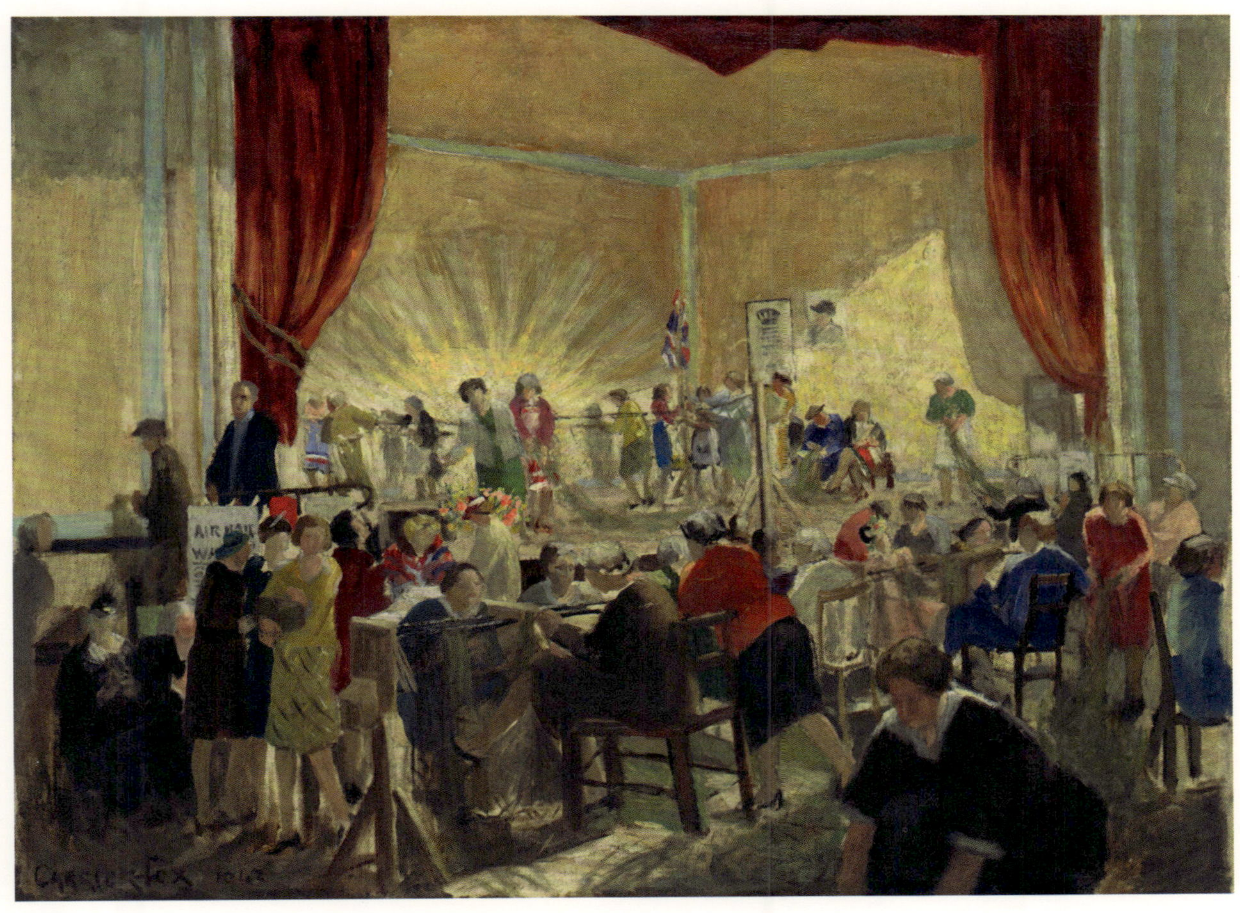

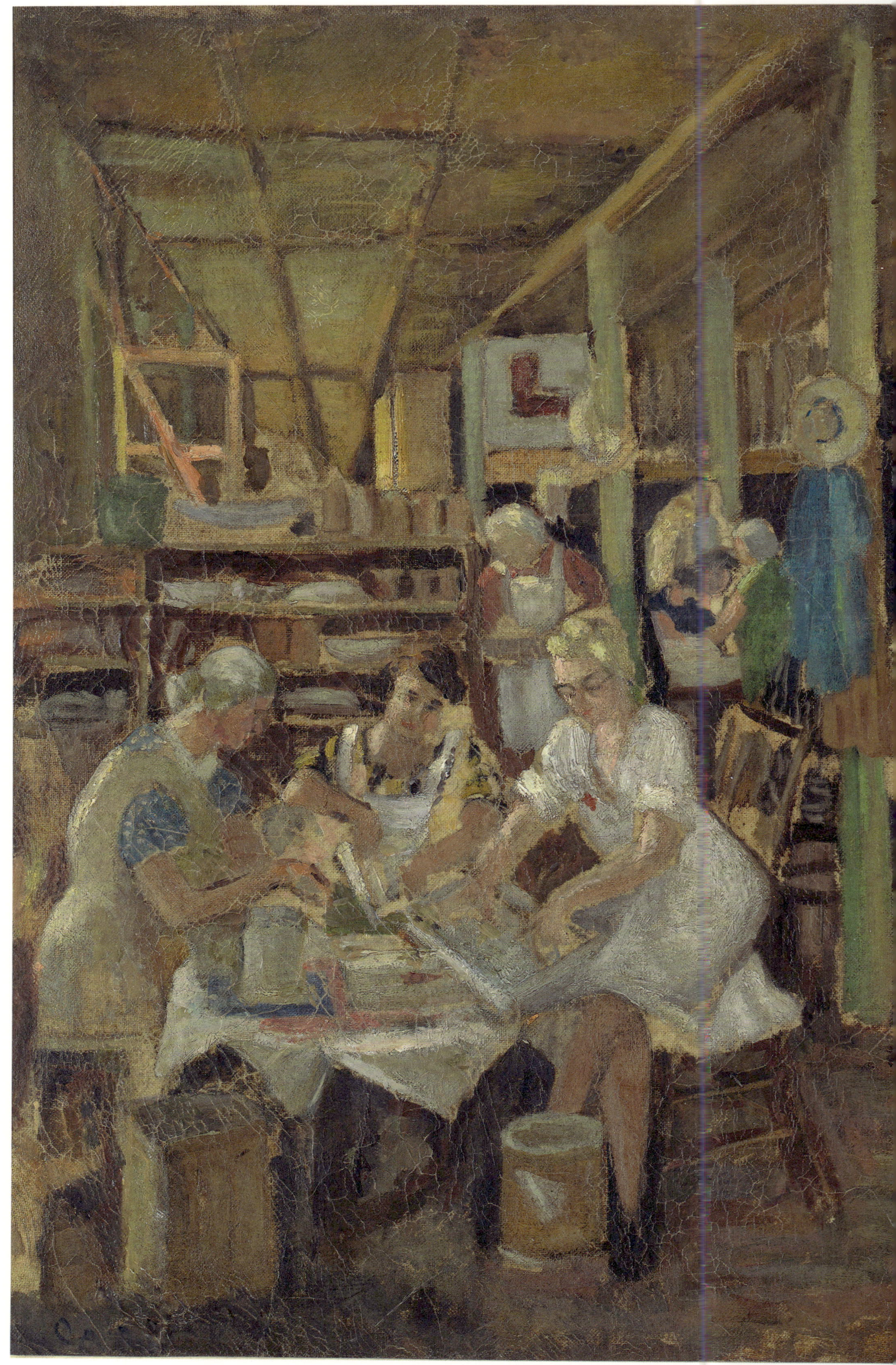

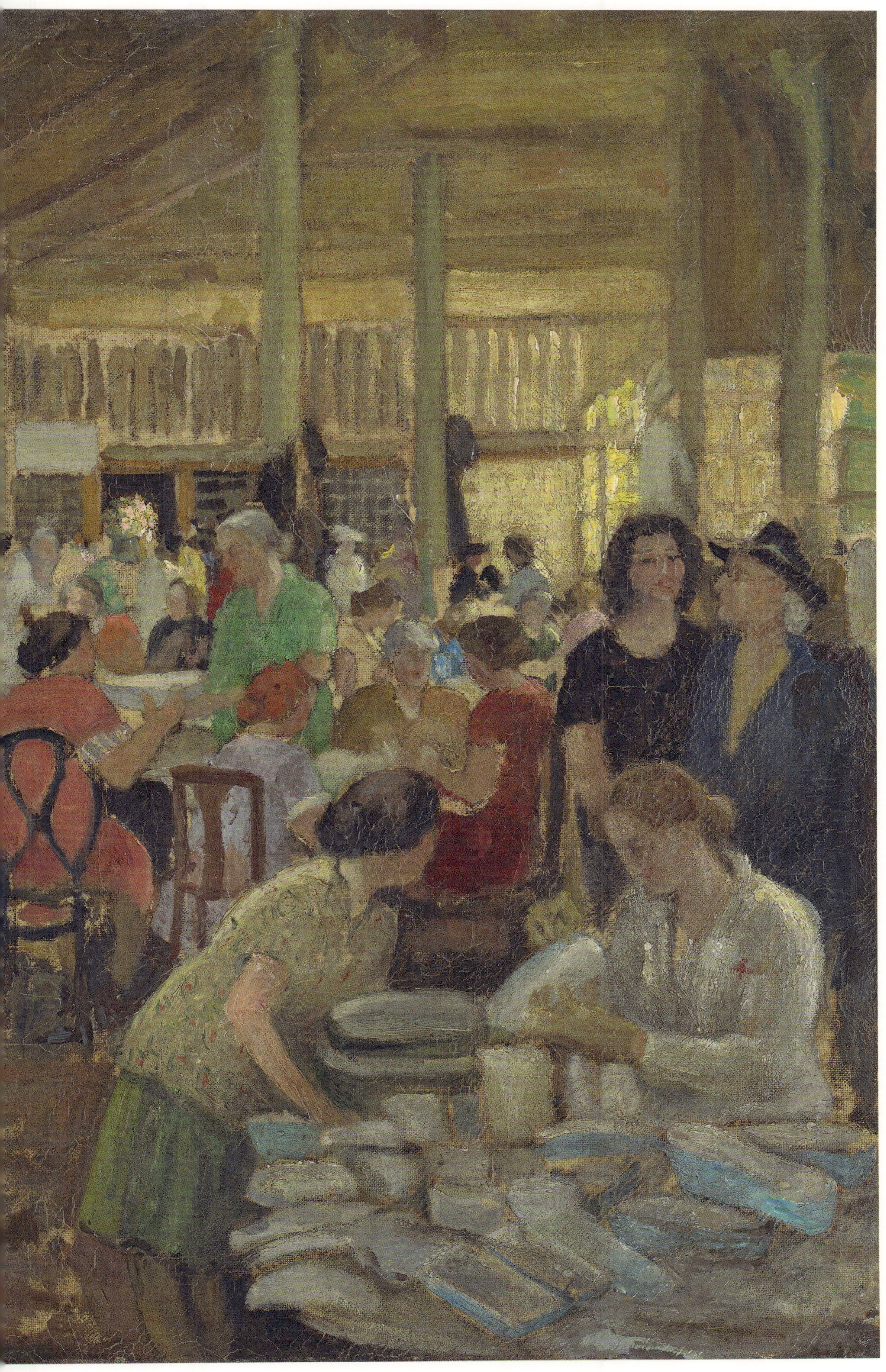

For the Canberra exhibition, she contacted Arthur Bazley, the acting director of the Australian War Memorial, explaining that she would be showing the work of 'five different groups of voluntary women war workers' and asking if she could store the work with him prior to the exhibition.[36] No doubt she did this as a way of ensuring that he would look over her paintings. This indeed transpired—there was damage to the lid of one of the three crates containing the paintings, so Bazley inspected the paintings themselves for damage and reported that there was none.[37]

At the time, Canberra was not the easiest of cities in which to find an exhibition venue. The only venue she could secure was the Masonic Temple but it did not have any means to display the paintings, so they were placed on chairs. Despite this, a reviewer said that 'her pictures are remarkable, for their sensitiveness and brilliance of colour, her five groups of ununiformed voluntary women war workers are major works, and especially interesting as records'.[38] True to form, Carrick arranged for the proceeds from the exhibition to go to the Red Cross and the Services Welfare Association. Carrick also showed three of the paintings in the large *Australia at war* exhibition shown post-war in each state gallery.

Carrick was not the only woman artist attuned to recording how women and the wider community were assisting the war effort. Dorrit Black's *The wool quilt makers* c 1941 (fig 52) shows a Red Cross group of women in Adelaide making quilts from scraps of fabric to send to families in England who had lost everything in the shelling of their cities. Grace Cossington Smith also completed several paintings of war-time activities, including *The flag in the room* 1941 (fig 51). In it, she depicts an empty armchair—this family is too busy to sit and read when patriotic duty calls, as signalled by the prominent British flag on display. Cossington Smith's sister Madge is visible through the open door in the next room, sewing items for the Red Cross.

Near the end of the war, Carrick became Honorary Organiser of the *French Comfort Fund exhibition* in Sydney so that she could focus on raising funds for artists in Paris, including expatriate Australians who had stayed on. Conditions there were harsh, food was rationed, and essentials such as milk were hard to come by. She developed an

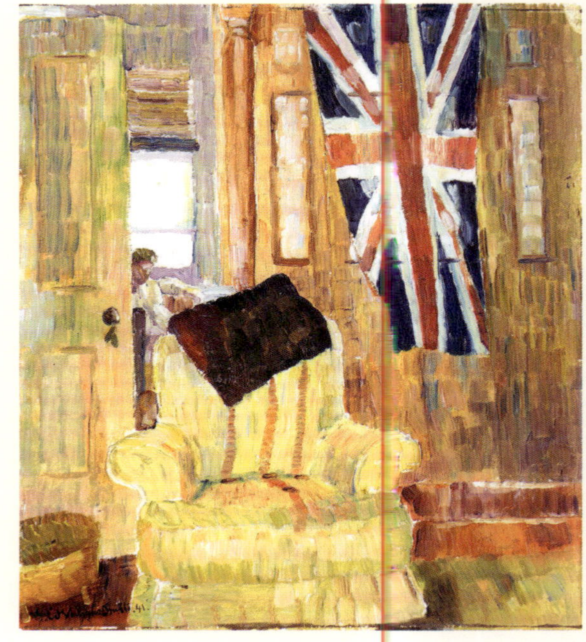

Previous
cat 126 *Papier mâché, Red Cross Auxiliary in Sydney* c 1944, oil on canvas, The Bastiaan Collection

Above
fig 51 Grace Cossington Smith, *The flag in the room* 1941, oil and pencil on cardboard, Australian War Memorial

Below
fig 52 Dorrit Black, *The wool quilt makers* c 1941, linocut printed in five colours from five blocks, National Gallery of Australia

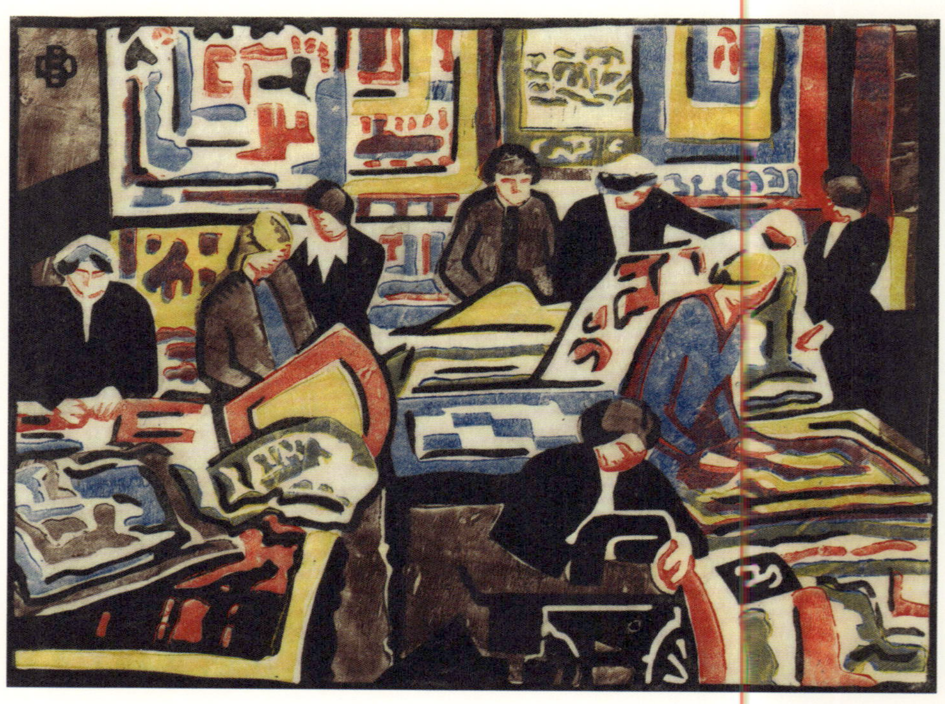

ambitious scheme for an art union, and asked the Art Gallery of New South Wales director, Hal Missingham, to circulate it to gallery directors around Australia.[39] Adelaide's *News* praised the scheme, writing that it 'is sure to receive enthusiastic support and artists and collectors will rush to make contributions when called upon for our debt to French art is immeasurable'.[40] The Sydney event, in which 100 artists donated their paintings, was held in David Jones' Art Gallery in February 1946; the Melbourne iteration was held the following month.

When Ethel Carrick's *National Defence League depot, St Michael's Hall, Sydney* was finally acquired by the Australian War Memorial in 1977, the organisation began the task of redressing the lack of work by women artists about home-front life during war time. The painting was one of the first acquired by curator Judith McKay, on the grounds that Carrick was a significant artist from a generation of women who had been overlooked. It was also noted that Carrick and her husband Fox were instrumental in raising money for the Red Cross during World War I, 'and it is regrettable that the War Memorial does not have one example of these public-spirited artists' war-time art'.[41] What was overlooked in these comments is that Carrick's patriotic work continued unabated through World War II.

Carrick's work across both world wars of the twentieth century encompasses only a small number of paintings because women artists were not appointed as official war artists in World War I, and in very limited numbers in World War II. Undeterred, she had the vision to complete a set of five paintings documenting the work of women on the home front, providing a much-valued eyewitness record. She was also bold enough to have them stored at the Australian War Memorial prior to being shown in 1944, where her work is now collected and recognised. But what has been little appreciated is the other side to her wartime work: her relentless and energetic fundraising for various war-related causes in Australia and France, writing letters variously from Mrs Ethel Carrick Fox and Mrs E Phillips Fox. Carrick successfully occupied the roles of charitable benefactor, respectable artworld figure and professional artist.

Catherine Speck is an art historian, writer, critic and curator. She is Professor Emerita of Art History and Curatorship at The University of Adelaide, Tarntanya/Adelaide, and a Fellow of the Academy of Humanities of Australia. She also convened and taught postgraduate programs in art history, and curatorial and museum studies with the Art Gallery of South Australia, Tarntanya/Adelaide, from 2002 to 2020. She is a member of the Fay Gale Centre for Research into Gender, the JM Coetzee Centre for Creative Practice, the Adelaide Critics Circle (Visual Arts) and a regular exhibition reviewer for *The Conversation*. Recent essays include 'The 1970s: Progressive, passionate and provocative' in *The Adelaide art scene 1939–2000* (2023), with Jude Adams; 'The total war and the role of women' in *The Great War and global media* (Los Angeles County Museum of Art, 2023); and 'On working as an Aboriginal museum director and curator of the Berndt Museum' in *Crosscurrents in Australian First Nations and non-Indigenous art* (2023), with Vanessa Russ.

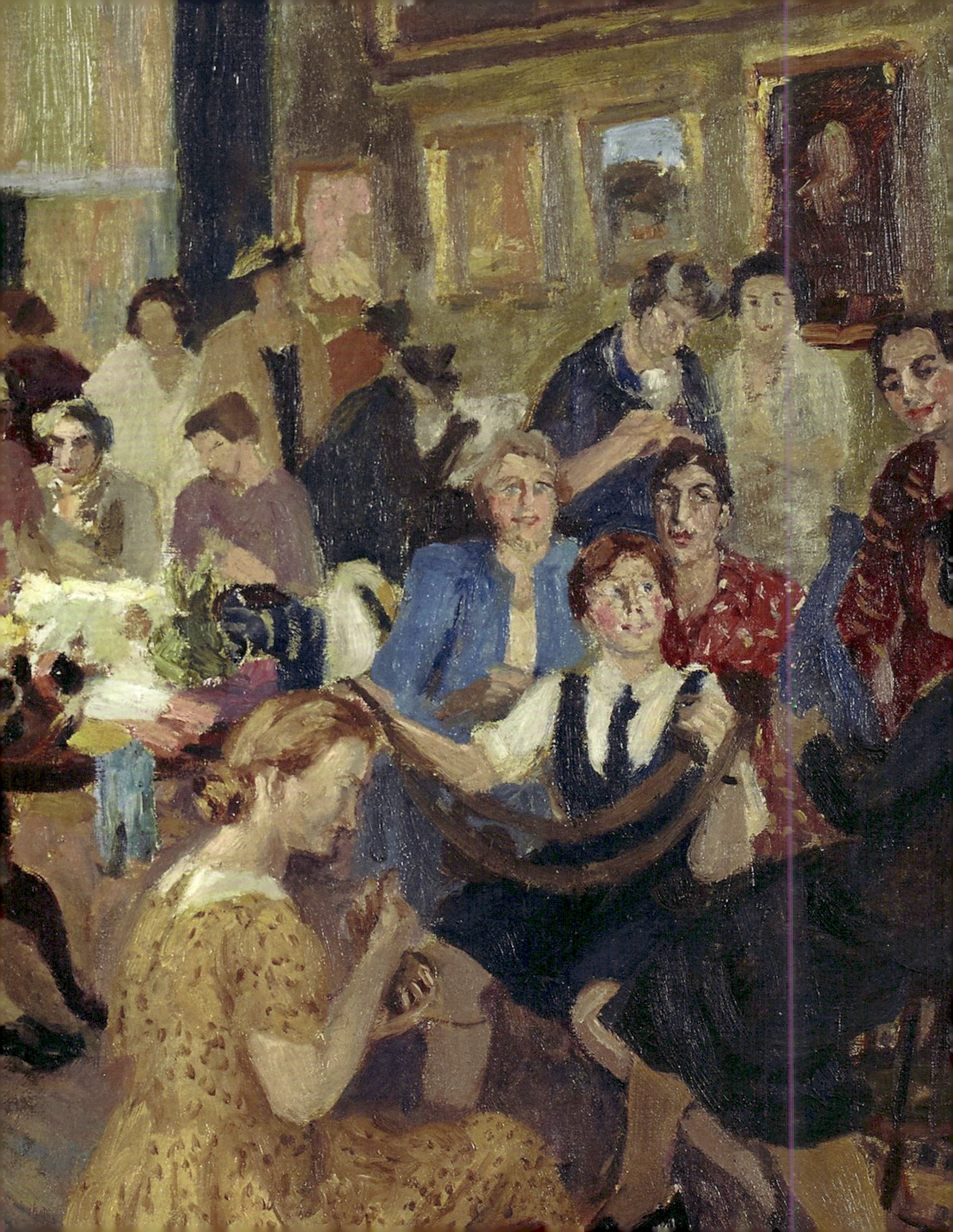

Friend, mentor, inspiration: Carrick's impact on Australian women

Juliette Peers

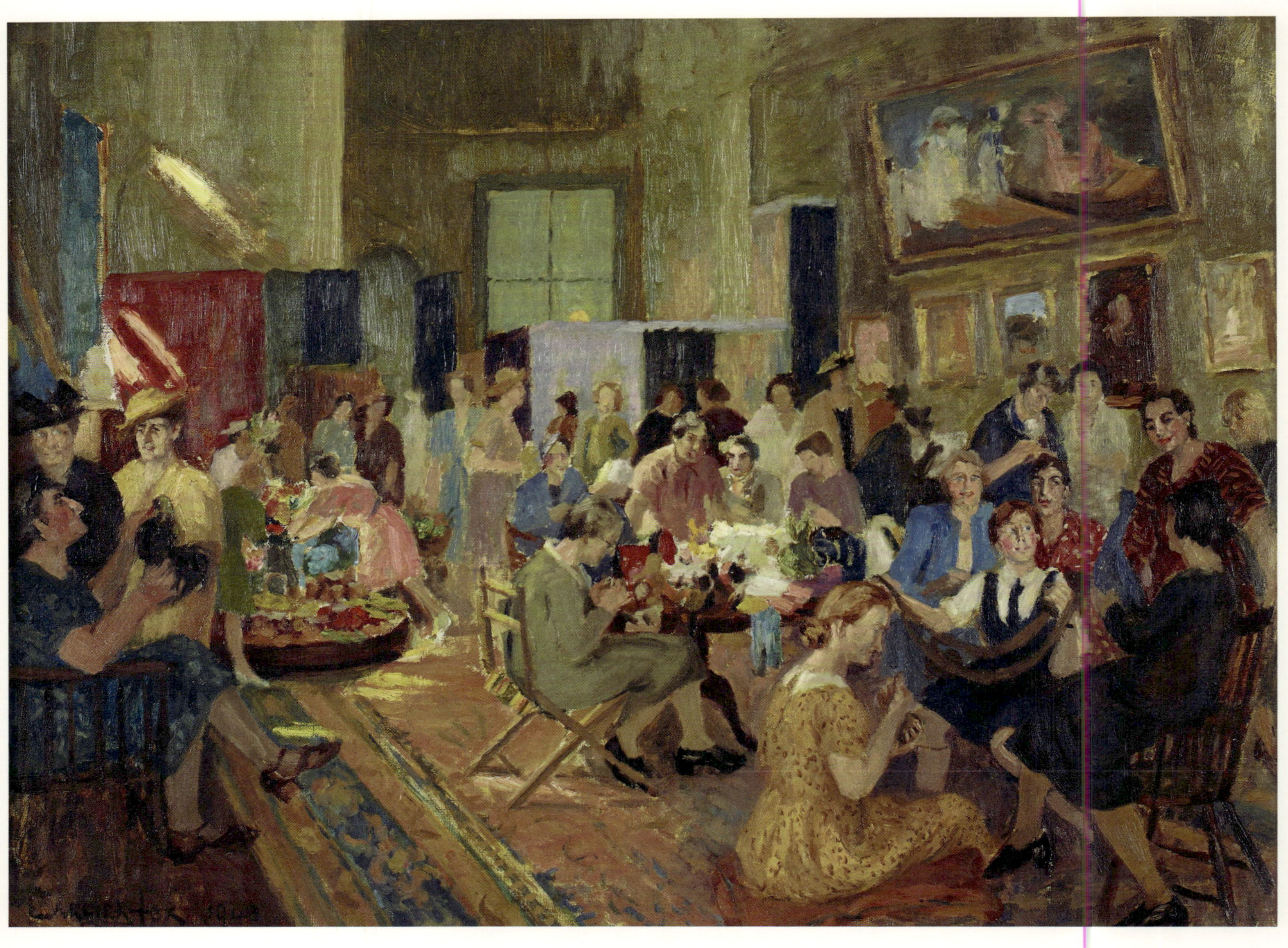

Longstanding bonds of friendship, values and professional interests shared with many Australian women artists thread through Ethel Carrick's life and art. Her relationship with Australia's oldest surviving organisation for women artists, the Melbourne Society of Women Painters and Sculptors (MSWPS), founded in 1902,[1] stretched from 1908 to 1951 and is of particular significance. One artwork, part of her major 1940s cycle of paintings depicting Australian women's contributions to the war effort, captures an afternoon meeting of the MSWPS' enterprising National Service Group. The MSWPS bound Carrick to Melbourne and offers a means of re-thinking received stories about Carrick as a disconsolate, lonely widow disenfranchised by her husband's family.[2] Moreover, through the MSWPS, Carrick befriended a younger generation of Australian artists, creating a transgenerational dialogue.

Carrick's impact on her contemporaries is best exemplified by the 1908 reception organised in her honour by the MSWPS. Not only was this gala evening the most formal and public gesture in their first decade of operation, moving them to the centre of Melbourne's artworld, but it was also a rare, unqualified affirmation of the public and social value of woman artists in federation-era Australia.[3]

> Mrs E. Phillips Fox was the guest of honor at an enjoyable at home given last night by the Woomballano Art Club [the previous name of the MSWPS, which changed by 1922], in the Victorian artists' rooms. Many representative artists were present and ... Mrs Fox on her arrival was presented with a bouquet of pink and white heather on behalf of the club ... Mrs Fox's show of pictures at Bernard's gallery has attracted considerable attention among local artists, and that she had many admirers at the Victorian artists galleries last night was amply proved.[4]

Connections to the Lyceum Club and her extended family of in-laws further underpinned Carrick's frequent presence in Melbourne. Accounts of her mixing socially with cousins and other relatives shift notions of her unpopularity within her Australian family. Dr Constance Ellis—a Phillips cousin, pioneering female obstetrician and foundation member of the Lyceum Club—provided accommodation for Carrick in Melbourne;[5] three Phillips cousins performed in the concert at the reception organised in Carrick's honour in 1908;[6] and a nephew, Moerlin Fox, attended her exhibition opening in 1949.[7]

During Ethel Carrick and Emanuel Phillips Fox's first visit to Australia together, the well-liked landscapist Montague Brown, who was Clarice Beckett's step-uncle, organised a reception for the couple.

Previous
Voluntary service 1943 (detail cat 127), oil on canvas, private collection

Opposite
cat 127 *Voluntary service* 1943, oil on canvas, private collection

This event was described by the *Melbourne Punch* as 'a large and brilliant gathering of the artistic community of Melbourne', including Walter Withers, John Ford Paterson and John Mather. Hans Heysen, a fellow student with Brown in Paris who would go on to develop a strong friendship with Fox, was also present.[8] Melbourne newspaper *The Age* reported that 'a very enjoyable evening was spent by a large number of guests' with Carrick, and that she had 'made many friends since she came to Victoria'.[9] Throughout their 1908 trip, and again in 1913, the Foxes were welcomed at elite social events in Sydney as well as Melbourne.[10]

Other organisations hosted functions to celebrate Carrick over the years, including the Melbourne Lyceum Club in 1925,[11] the Adelaide Lyceum Club in 1925,[12] the Sydney Society of Women Painters in 1925[13] and the International Club in Melbourne in 1933.[14] Carrick herself organised a party at the Lyceum Club in 1925 for her Melbourne friends, including some of her in-laws.[15] The Lyceum Club became a frequent home base for Carrick and was closely associated with her Melbourne family, who were among the founding members in 1911—two cousins by marriage served as president, and one as treasurer.[16]

Carrick remained particularly close to one cousin, the artist Rosetta (Etta) Phillips,[17] now remembered more as a model for her famous cousin in Fox's *Art students* 1895 (fig 35, p 143) and *Reverie* 1903 (Musée d'Orsay collection) than as an artist in her own right. Phillips studied at the National Gallery of Victoria and with Fox in the 1890s. Later, around 1900, she travelled to Europe to further her art studies, including studying with impressionist Isaac Israels.[18] Returning to Melbourne, Phillips joined the MSWPS in 1904, her cosmopolitan professionalism enhancing the group's early years. When her father died in 1909, Phillips left Australia permanently and settled in Paris. There, she was part of the Foxes' circle and her activities, including regular acceptance in the Salons, attracted attention in the *British Australasian* and the Australian press. Sydney's *Daily Telegraph* emphasised the solidity of Phillips' status: 'A cousin of Mr Phillips-Fox, and in times of peace an artist of no mean talent.'[19]

Phillips undertook both charitable and cultural activities alongside Carrick and was known in France as a jeweller and miniaturist, as well as a painter. Unlike many Australians in Paris, Phillips also moved amongst North American expatriates, exhibiting with American artists and nursing in an American field hospital during World War I,[20] offering Carrick a further node of international connection in her working life as an artist. For Phillips, Carrick rendered perhaps her greatest act of assistance. When Phillips, like many intellectuals, artists and Jewish refugees in Paris, was complacent about the potential of German occupation in the lead up to World War II, Carrick—who had no illusions, post-*Kristallnacht*,[21] about Nazi policies—insisted that Phillips leave Paris (against the latter's wishes), most likely saving her life.[22]

Beyond her cousins, Carrick's friendships encompassed a wide range of women. Violet Teague was naturally gifted and accomplished artist, moving seamlessly, like Carrick, between Australian and European aesthetics. Teague was an exceptional figure painter, yet also versatile as an avant-garde printmaker and a painter of impressionist landscapes. Carrick may have been more dynamic than the poetic, retiring Teague,[23] whose strong literary and historical interests often found tangible expression in her works of art, tableaux vivants and pageants. Although this exploration of pictorial narrative differed from Carrick's pragmatic, abstracting practice, both women shared a lofty, empowered vision of

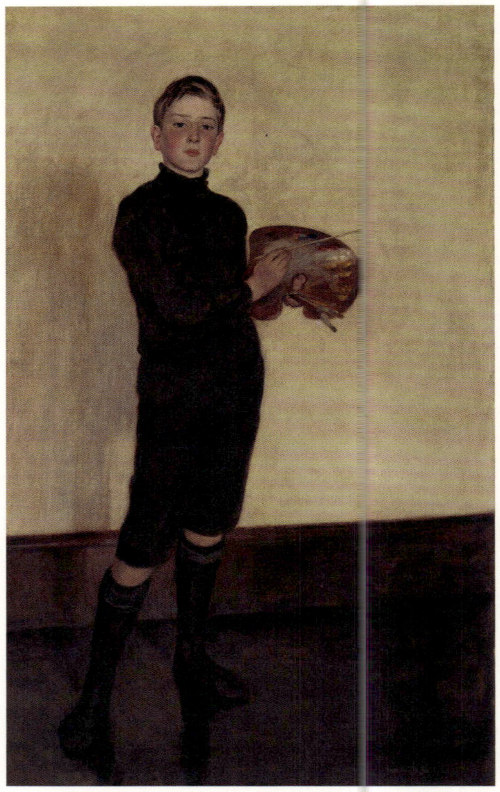

fig 53 Violet Teague, *The boy with the palette* 1911, oil on canvas, National Gallery of Australia

Opposite
fig 54 Ethel Stephens, *Honesty* c 1930, linocut, National Gallery of Australia

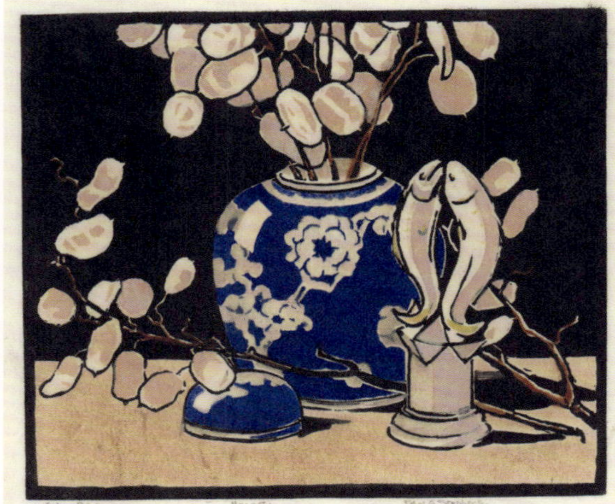

art's function, foregrounding the imbrication of the spiritually ethical within public life. Writing to Irene Fox in 1952, Carrick described Teague as her oldest Melbourne friend.[24] Teague was—like Bertha Merfield, Ina Gregory and Mary Meyer (a founder of the art circle within the Lyceum Club)[25]—a former student of Fox's. Indeed, Carrick became friends with all of these women, again complicating the construct of Carrick as an alien within Fox's circle of family and associates.

Another of her friends, the public-minded, feminist advocate Ethel Stephens, represented Carrick's more corporate working life. Stephens was a talented plein air artist who produced attractive, strongly designed modernist relief prints in the 1930s, after a third visit to France and England. From the 1890s onwards, Stephens worked to improve the status and visibility of women artists in Sydney. In 1892 she was elected to the committee of the Royal Art Society of New South Wales to represent its many female members.[26] She also helped found the Society of Women Painters in 1909 as well as advocating for craft and design in Sydney.[27] The pair met as early as 1908, when Stephens joined a contingent of Sydney women artists at the opening of Fox's solo exhibition, while Carrick had the honour of escorting the Government House party around the exhibition.[28] Stephens encountered Carrick again on the Foxes' return trip to Australia in 1913,[29] and they may have even connected earlier, in 1910, when Stephens was studying in France.[30] The two continued to correspond after Carrick's return to France, and Stephens published a letter from Carrick in the Sydney press in 1917.[31]

As with Carrick, Stephens' war-time activities were prodigious. Barely a fortnight after Australia entered the war on 4 August 1914, she had organised first-aid and nursing classes for Sydney women artists and was chairing meetings alongside the Governor General's wife, Lady Helen Munro Ferguson.[32] Stephens and Carrick worked for the same war-related charities, within art circles and amongst the general public,[33] with Carrick moving between Melbourne and Sydney before finally returning to Paris. When Stephens spent two years living in Paris, from 1920 to 1922, she took classes with Carrick.[34] In 1922, she actually moved into Carrick's apartment. The preference for high-key, strong, artificial colour in Stephens' later garden paintings could reflect an influence from Carrick, as well as from compositional motifs in the popular print media of the 1920s and 1930s. Stephens and Carrick, and Teague as well, framed their highly visible practices within a paradigm of public duty.

On the eve of World War II Carrick was travelling with plans to return to France, but when the war broke out in 1939 she instead returned to Melbourne. She was 'eager to try and repeat the effort made by her husband and herself during the last war',[35] joining the wartime charitable efforts of the MSWPS and other Melbourne artists. Being directly in contact with the MSWPS again launched a rich and expansive phase of her career. The painting *Voluntary service* 1943 (cat 127, p 228) depicts the MSWPS' National Service Group's massive fundraising efforts—the ongoing sales bazaar, gift shop, craft workshop and donation depot hosted by Polly Hurry (Mrs John Farmer) in her studio at 9 Collins Street.[36] Here, Carrick paid tribute to women she liked and knew. With buzzing activity and many women in brightly hued fashionable dress, the painting evokes the energy of the moment. Carrick also revived her old fundraising practice, as noted in *The Sun*: 'Mrs Fox organised the work of painting and decorating gum leaves for sale. Many of them had miniature scenes on them.'[37] In January 1940, Polly Hurry, Jean Sutherland, Sybil Craig and Lina Bryans sold painted gum leaves at Carrick's Collins Street stall;[38] in turn, Carrick assisted Bryans' 'lucky envelope' drive.[39]

Beyond fundraising, Carrick contributed to the MSWPS' creative and aesthetic impact on its contemporaries, especially in the late 1940s when a number of strong, high-profile women were exhibiting members. As reported in the daily Melbourne paper *The Argus*: 'Afternoon in the Luxembourg Gardens, a brilliantly coloured picture ... painted by Mrs Fox at an early stage of her career when she was in France 40 years ago. The figures in the picture are vital and graceful and an object lesson to most of our younger painters.'[40] The same could be said for Carrick's lively depictions of the same subject over the years.

Via the MSWPS, Carrick befriended a younger generation of artists, repeating the productive synergies and reciprocities seen in her earlier friendships and opening up hitherto overlooked transgenerational linkages in Melbourne art histories. An Australian pioneer of modernist sculpture in the early 1930s, and a pupil of Henry Moore, Ola Cohn's character rather than artwork linked her to Carrick.[41] Confident in her knowledge of materials and making, Cohn was publicly minded like Carrick, making significant bequests and taking charge of the fortunes of the MSWPS for 13 years. Both women followed alternative theologies; Carrick was a member of the Theosophical Society and while Cohn's spirituality was informal, Cohn still accepted uncanny, paranormal sensations. A letter written fewer than 12 months before Carrick's death suggests that they shared a keen consciousness of metaphysical values and traditions in art.[42]

Expressionist Lina Bryans was another significant MSWPS contact of Carrick's. Unconventional and with little concern for social proprietaries, Bryans was perhaps Melbourne's most singular and well-connected woman artist from the 1930s to the 1970s, bringing Carrick's network of associations into an identifiably contemporary milieu. Unlike many Melbourne women artists of the 1930s and 1940s, Bryans' reputation and profile remained high into the post-war era.[43] While not explicitly from the left side of politics, as were Mary Gilmore and Len Fox (Carrick's nephew), Bryans was a secular libertarian. Carrick's positioning as a free agent with links to radical factions in Australian cultural life—and whose practice was part of facilitating modernism in Australian art—is crystallised by her association with Bryans.

Other friends from the MSWPS whom Carrick supported and encouraged had less obvious synergies—although it is possible that Jean Sutherland's move back into practice and public life was informed by Carrick rebuilding her own career after the loss of Fox three decades earlier. Sutherland had initially undertaken lessons with her aunt, artist Jean Godlet Sutherland, and her second cousin, major impressionist Jane Sutherland.[44] She had then studied at the National Gallery School, where she won the travelling scholarship. She painted in a traditional style, inflected to advantage by the para-modernist, hard-edged classicism popular in Europe and England in the 1920s. Like many scholarship winners, from Winifred Honey to Douglas Green, Sutherland lost momentum after her early success, in her case possibly driven by poor sales and the fallout from a failed engagement to landscapist Ernest Buckmaster.[45]

Opposite
cat 128 *Luxembourg Gardens* c 1921, oil on canvas, University Art Collection, Chau Chak Wing Museum, The University of Sydney

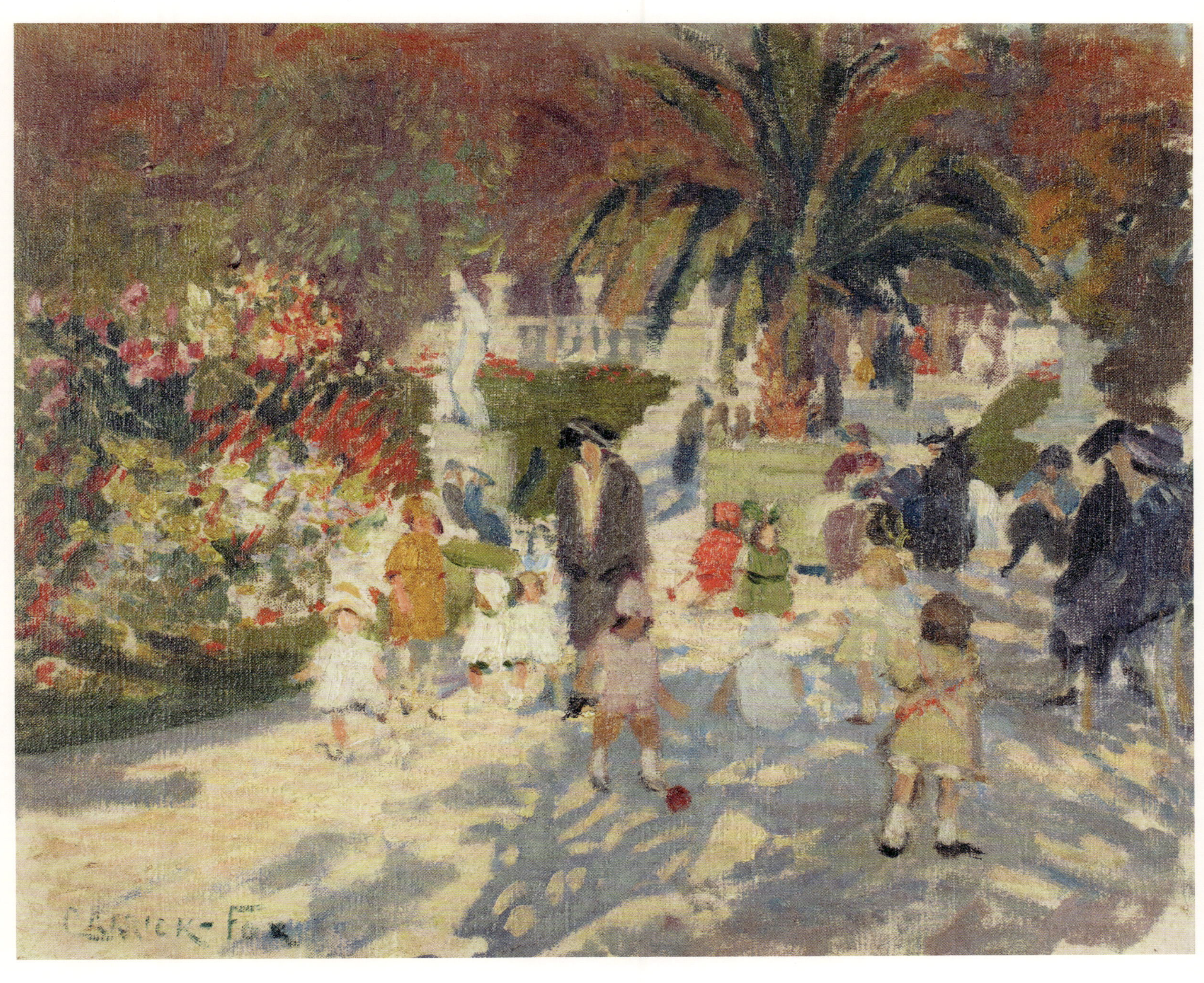

Living modestly on family income, Sutherland neither married nor needed to work; she inherited a house in Melbourne, where she provided Carrick with accommodation. In turn, Carrick encouraged Sutherland to be more involved with art and artmaking in Melbourne and so she joined the MSWPS where she met Sybil Craig, who became her closest artistic and personal colleague.

In her own words 'an advantaged child',[46] Craig, like Sutherland, had no impetus to sell works. A capable academic realist, in private Craig was drawn to spontaneous modernist experiments. Inspired by observing other artists and a short span of lessons in design at the Melbourne Technical College in 1935—more contemporary than the National Gallery School curriculum—she held these radical works back from exhibitions. Carrick's high colour, simplification of form, often shallow space and direct, rapid brushwork resonated with, and possibly guided, Craig's substantially self-taught interpretation of progressive art. Craig's papers also provide evidence that Carrick often visited the Craig family, who stored artworks for her and helped with her accommodation.[47] In 1944, Craig, Sutherland and Carrick held an exhibition at Kozminsky Galleries. This show with Carrick was one of the very few exhibitions, outside of artists' groups, in which either Craig or Sutherland presented work to the public.

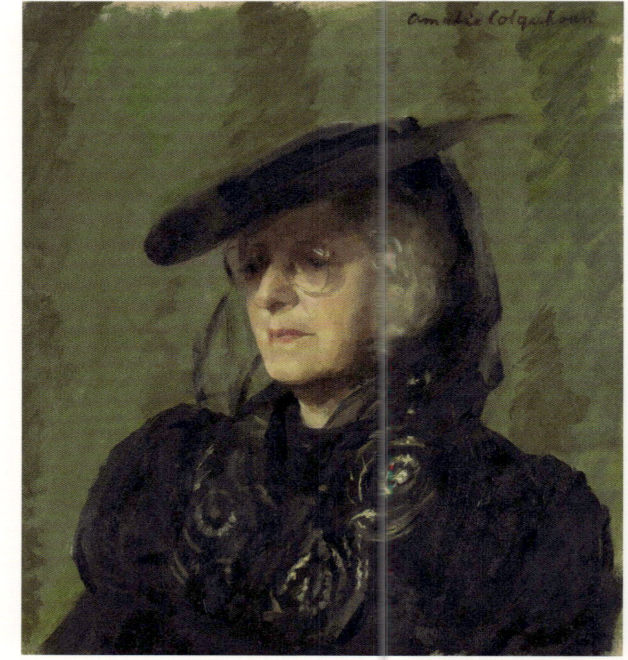

During this time, Carrick also renewed old friendships. Plein air artist Beatrice Colquhoun, who was on the MSWPS committee at the time of the 1908 reception, remained friends with Carrick for the next four decades.[48] In 1916, Carrick gave Alexander and Beatrice Colquhoun's studio as her contact address,[49] as she did with their son's studio in the 1940s,[50] and Beatrice was among the guests at Carrick's 1925 Lyceum Club party. Amalie Colquhoun, Beatrice's daughter-in-law, painted a striking portrait of an elderly but stylish Carrick in 1942 (fig 55)—now in the collection of the National Gallery of Victoria[51]—which conveys the slightly romantic, if not glamorous, persona that some contemporaries recalled in the 1980s. Alexander Colquhoun also suggested that Carrick had improved her husband's outlook, 'the bachelor artist melted in a large degree under the softening influence of a charming and socially minded wife'.[52] The Colquhoun family also dominated Carrick's 1940s fundraising efforts for French refugees: 'The name of Colquhoun often appeared, for, as well as "A.D." and his wife "Amalie," "A.D.'s" parents, "A" and "Beatrice," and his sister "Bess" were represented.'[53]

Living memories of Carrick survived from the 1940s into the 1980s and 1990s. Carrick was something of a Rorschach blot, amplifying and confirming the preoccupations of those who observed her. Her acuity, insight and interest in world affairs contrasted strongly with mainstream Australian expectations for women in the 1930s and 1940s, especially her scepticism of the British Empire and her understanding of the implications of Nazism. Len Fox admired Carrick's intellectuality and asked her to join the Communist Party of Australia—Carrick demurred, as she felt she was already committed to too many groups with theosophy, women painters and war work. However, she remained open to Marxism and Len Fox described her as 'a good fellow traveller'.[54] Carrick's left-leaning sympathies are also suggested by her friendship with writer and journalist Dame Mary Gilmore in Sydney in the 1940s.[55] A prominent figure in the Australian literary and political scene, Gilmore was the editor of the women's section of *The Australian Worker* (a newspaper produced in Sydney for the Australian Workers' Union between 1890 and 1950).

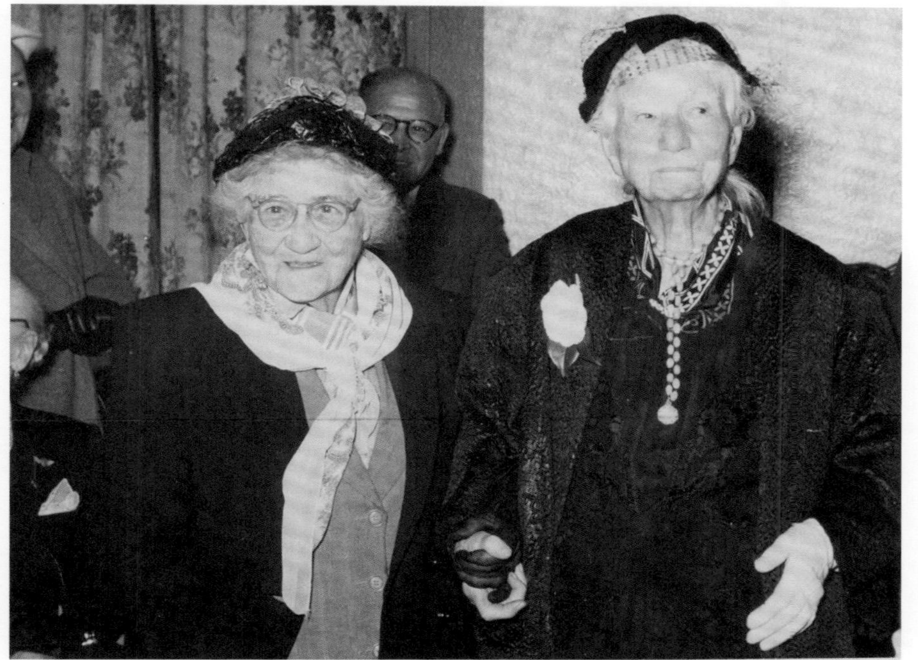

Opposite
fig 55 Amalie Colquhoun, *Mrs E Phillips Fox* c 1942, oil on canvas, National Gallery of Victoria

Above
fig 56 Unknown photographer, *Ethel Phillips Fox and Dame Mary Gilmore*, no date, photograph, State Library of New South Wales

For Annie Davison Oliver, Carrick represented an idealised degree of autonomy missing in her own life, as well as being public-minded and dedicated towards the causes that she espoused.

> She was a very small bright sort of person ... not exactly fussy, but very lively. She liked everything just so, always very brisk, always diving after things ... She was a very nice member [of the Society]. It was always Paris or Melbourne, Melbourne or Paris ... She had her apartment in Paris and whenever she needed a change, well off she'd go, and then she'd come back again.[56]

For Helen Ogilvie, Carrick personified modernism's struggles against a hostile conservative mainstream in Melbourne. Carrick, who was a fine and successful artist, was sidelined by the ignorant and conservative.

> She was rather a sad figure. She had had such a marvellous life overseas. She had lost her husband and was overlooked in Australia. I often saw brilliant oils in the window at Joels ... Riviera scenes, very bright. She had lived so long in France that her art was close to French styles.[57]

Assistance and encouragement also flowed in the other direction. Melbourne artist Bertha Merfield greatly supported Carrick in her profound grief after the death of Fox, talking her out of suicidal thoughts: 'I met them fearlessly and it seemed to stop the ideas.'[58] Sadly and tragically, in view of her life-changing assistance to Carrick, Merfield died in Melbourne falling out of a suburban train in 1921, overcome herself by unbearable circumstances. While discretely elided by some newspapers, her death was identified as suicide,[59] an open secret in the Melbourne artworld of the 1920s.[60] Like Etta Phillips, Merfield has little profile in curatorial memory, although she was an artist of significant achievement, trained in Paris and London, including at the Slade School of Fine Art.

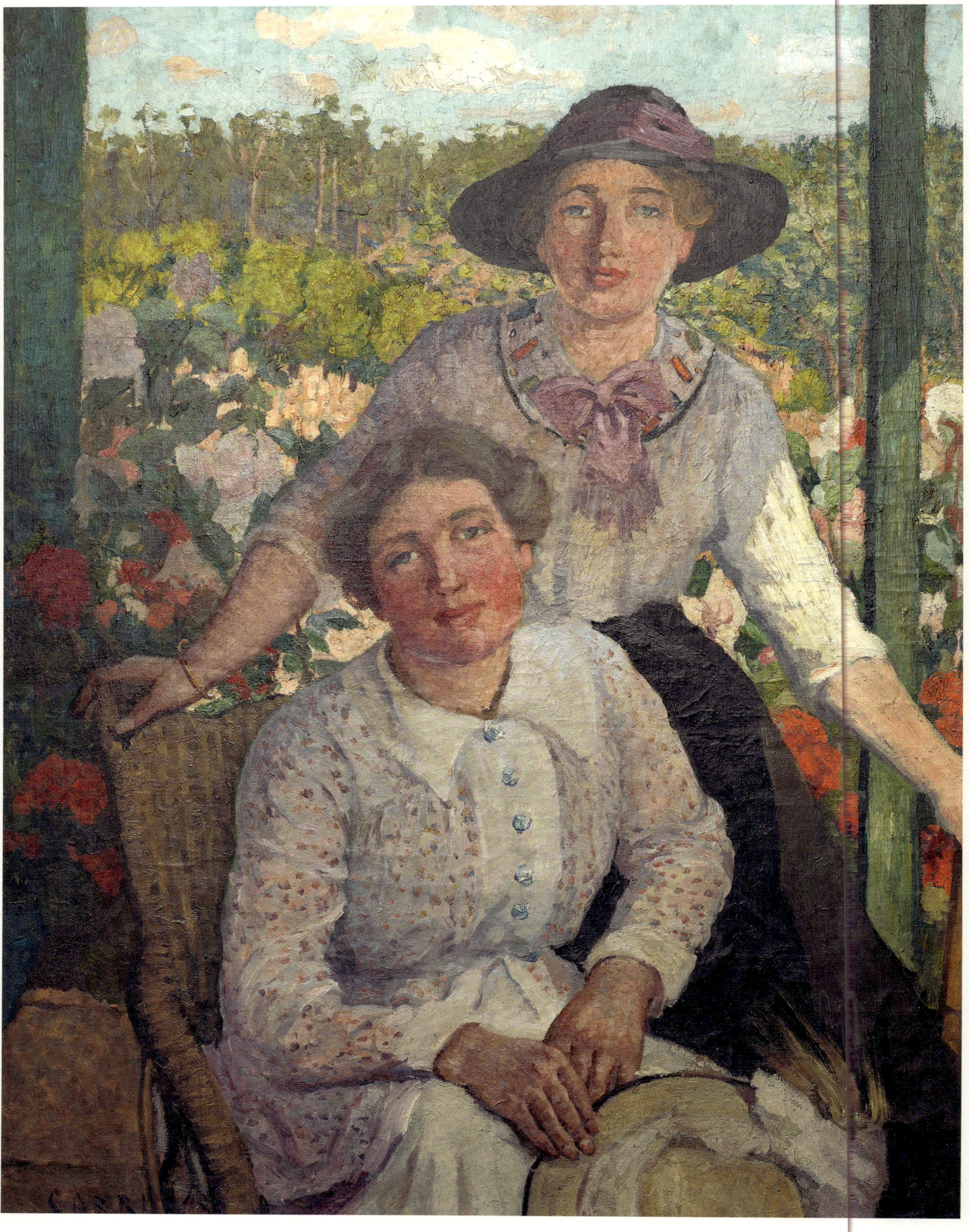

Opposite
cat 129 *On the verandah* no date, oil on canvas, private collection

In London she joined the Society of Mural Decorators and Painters, returning to Melbourne with a niche position as a muralist and early designer and receiving a number of prestigious commissions. The inaugural meeting of the Arts and Crafts Society was held in her Melbourne studio in 1908.[61] Over the years, many of Merfield's murals were destroyed as buildings were renovated or demolished, though her panel for the Nambrok estate homestead, an art nouveau bush scene, survives in the Gippsland Art Gallery.

These linkages offer more than sentimental anecdotes—they place Carrick within Edwardian and late Victorian transnational networks of professional, academic and creative women. Clubs and art organisations for women provided female travellers and students of some means with respectable, secure accommodation and workspaces when moving outside the family circle. Women, including women of colour, could travel between countries more freely than before, consolidating and leveraging professional opportunities. Feminist scholars have mapped this expansion of women's global mobility and career horizons,[62] and these unparalleled new opportunities significantly shaped and facilitated Carrick's later life and career. The Theosophical Society likewise facilitated productive bonds between creative and intellectual women of different cultures. Carrick's theosophical beliefs opened up a further vital and enriching network, distinct from her artist communities.

Popular and charismatic, Carrick moved among devoted colleagues and supporters in the Australian art community where she was a friend, mentor, influencer and networker. In turn, she enriched Australian cultural options during the first half of the twentieth century by holding exhibitions, placing her husband's works in public galleries, spearheading patriotic fundraising in both world wars, and guiding and supporting colleagues who lacked her secure, public self-positioning. Through many interviews and considerable press coverage, as well as appearances at public events, receptions, exhibition openings and meetings as she travelled across Australian states, Carrick constructed an expanded public profile for women artists. She was instrumental in amplifying and consolidating women's presence within and impact on Australian art from 1908 to 1951 to a degree that is only now receiving its due.

Juliette Peers is an art historian, curator and writer based in Wadawurrung/Central Victoria. Feminist art advocacy is central to her practice and includes writing, research and the growth and maintenance of archives and foundations. She is a life member of the Women's Art Register and has worked as a curator on projects with public galleries across Australia and in Europe, Britain and North America, including *Completing the picture: women artists and the Heidelberg era* (touring, 1992) and *Beating about the bush: a new lens on Australian Impressionism* (Art Gallery of Ballarat, Wadawurrung/Ballarat 2022). Peers taught design history at RMIT University, Naarm/Narrm/Melbourne from 1994 to 2019. She has curated several projects at the Art Gallery of Ballarat and is an associate curator at the Gippsland Art Gallery (Gunaikurnai Country/Gippsland).

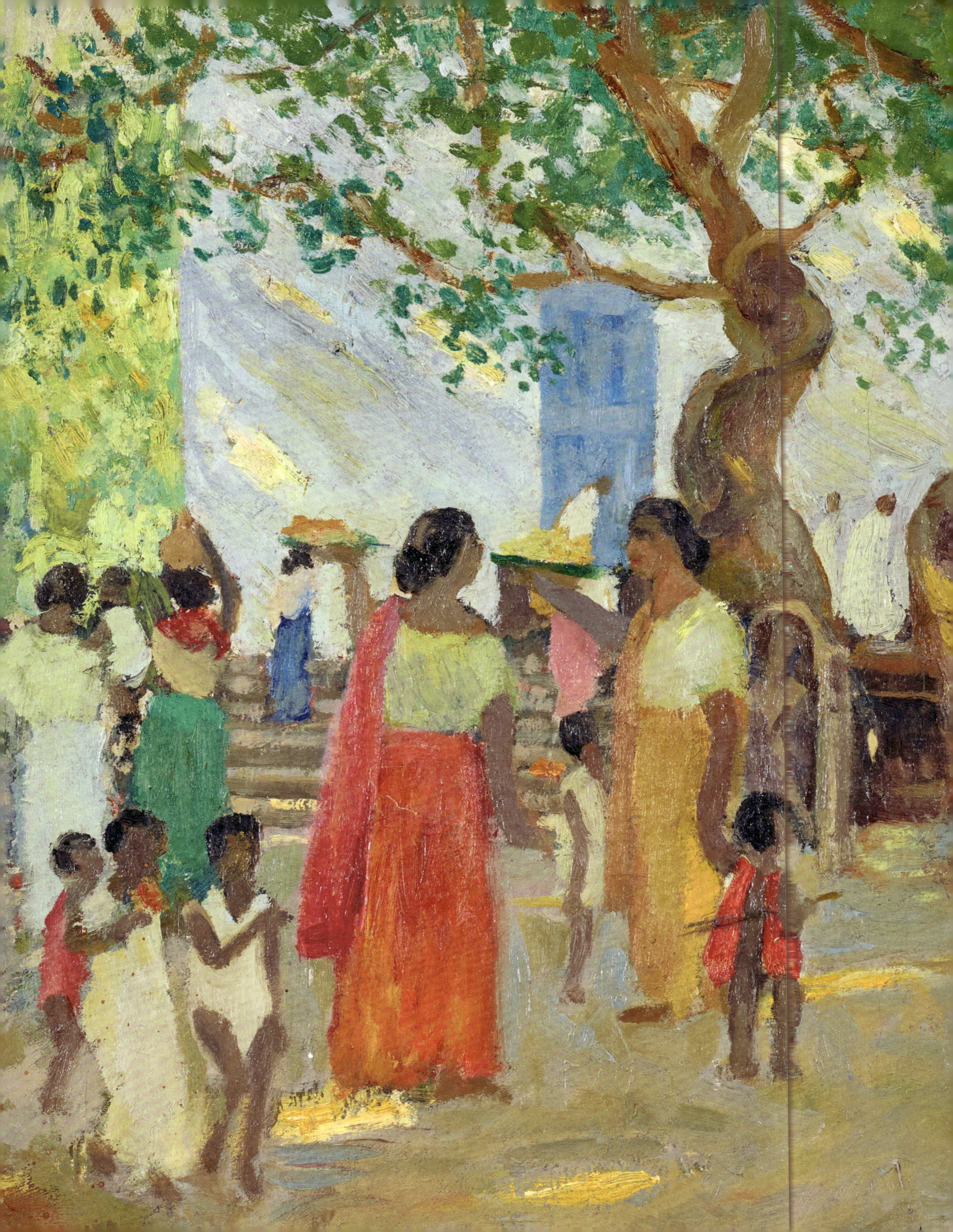

Chronology

Rebecca Blake

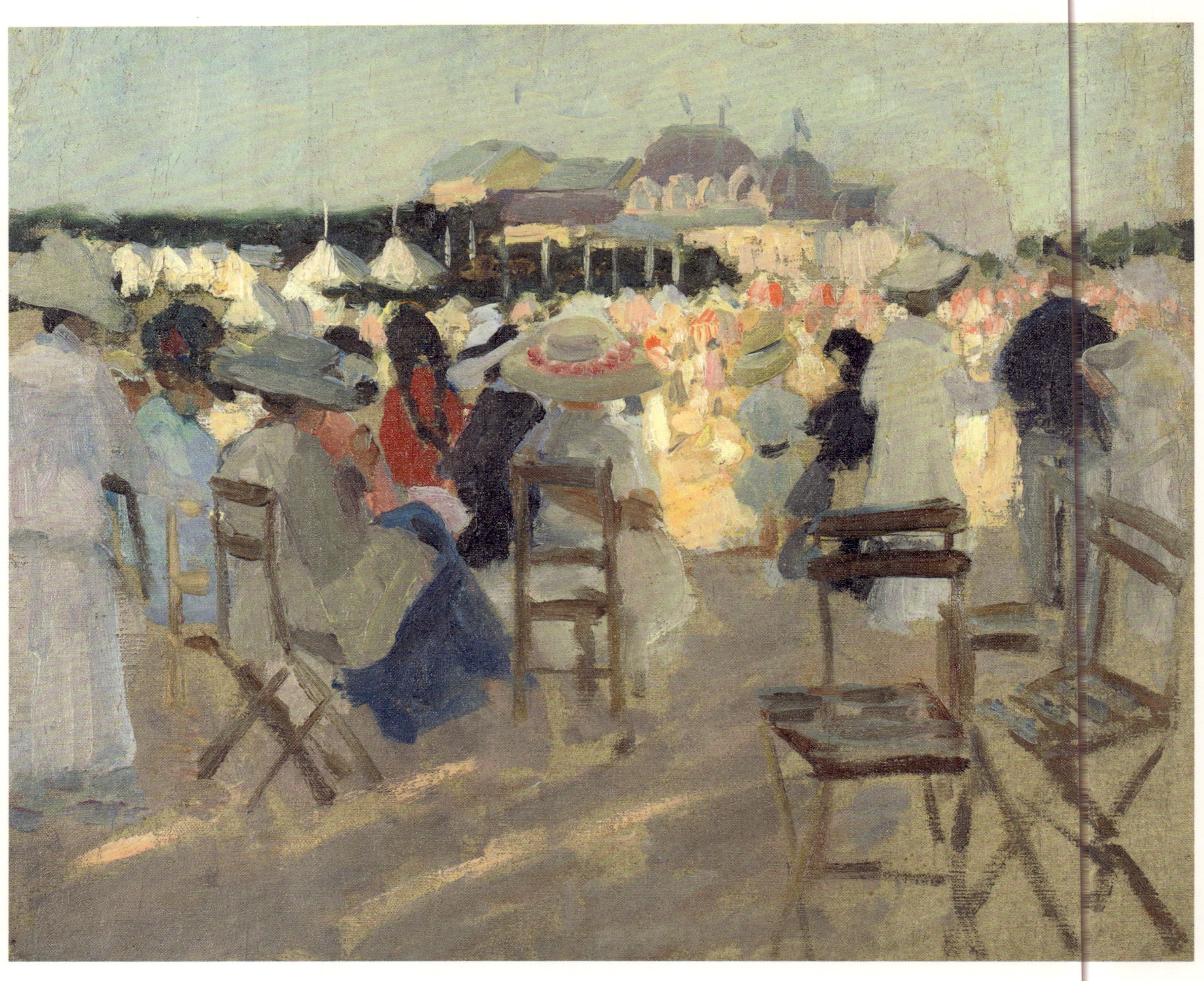

Previous
The market place c 1939 (detail cat 136, p 247), oil on canvas, private collection

Above
cat 130 *Band promenade* c 1910–12, oil on canvas on board, private collection

Note

This timeline centres around Ethel Carrick's artistic career and major life events. She had a rich social life, attending and hosting many gatherings and events with artists and other prominent figures of her time.

Key references for the chronologies in this publication include travel notes in social pages of Australian and British newspapers, particularly *The British Australasian*, and letters from Ethel Carrick and biographical notes held across numerous archives, chiefly the Len Fox Papers, State Library of New South Wales; the Papers of Sybil Craig and Papers of Ola Cohn, State Library of Victoria; Papers of Hans Heysen, Papers of Herbert and Ivy Brookes, and Diaries of Dame Mary Gilmore at the National Library of Australia.

1872

Ethel Carrick is born 7 February 1872 in Uxbridge, Middlesex, England. She is the second eldest daughter of nine children born to Albert William Carrick (1842–1899) and Emma Carrick, née Filmer (1846–1938).

1890s

Carrick lives at the family home Brookfield House, Uxbridge, Middlesex and studies with Francis Bate at Brook Green Studio, London.

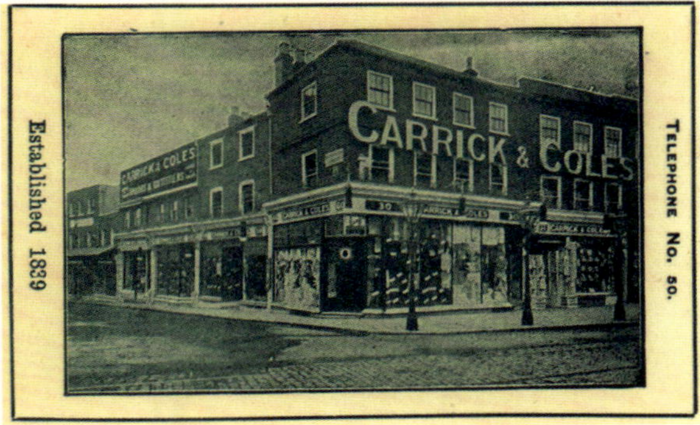

fig 57 *Carrick and Coles* c 1910, business card

1899

Carrick studies at the Slade School of Fine Art at University College, Gower Street, London from 1899 to 1904.

In the summer, Carrick attends St Ives Art Club with Slade peers Agnes Vyse, Hilda Fearon, Fanny Louise Coles and Gertrude Talmage.

1900

Carrick's family moves to 6 Blakesley Avenue, Ealing, and over the summer she stays with Slade friends at The Cabin, Westcotts Quay, St Ives.

1901

Carrick stays again at The Cabin, St Ives and meets her future husband, Emanuel Phillips Fox, on a sketching tour of Cornwall.

1902

Carrick travels to Caudebec-en-Caux, France, and paints *The market, Caudebec* c 1902. She likely sees Fox while in France.

1903

Carrick is awarded the Slade School Melville Nettleship Prize for Figure Composition. After graduation she attends the Newlyn School, Cornwall and models for Fox's *Reverie* 1903.

Carrick exhibits at the Society of Oil Painters, London and Society of Women Artists, London.

1904

Carrick summers in France and may visit Fox, who spends six months painting landscapes in a village near Chartres. They become engaged and spend Christmas together at Carrick's family home in Ealing, London.

1905

Carrick exhibits with the International Society of Sculptors, Painters and Gravers, London.

On 9 May, Emanuel Phillips Fox and Ethel Carrick marry at St Peter's Church in Ealing, London. They honeymoon in Cornwall before moving to 65 Boulevard Arago, Montparnasse, Paris.

1906

In London, Carrick exhibits at the Felix Art Club and The Royal Institute of Oil Painters. In Paris, she exhibits at the Salon d'Automne, and continues to exhibit there almost every year until 1938.

1907

In spring, Carrick and Fox visit Venice for some months, during which Carrick creates her Venice paintings.

In London, Carrick exhibits at the Royal Academy and The Royal Institute of Oil Painters. In Paris, she exhibits with the Société Nationale des Beaux-Arts for the first time, and continues to exhibit there almost every year until 1939. She exhibits at the international group exhibition *Le Musée du Peuple*, Angers, France.

1908

Carrick exhibits with women's group Les Quelques for the first time, and continues to exhibit there every year until 1911. By 1908, she is a member of the Union Internationale des Beaux-Arts, des Lettres, des Sciences et de l'Industrie.

Carrick and Fox travel from London aboard the RMS *Mooltan,* arriving in Australia in early February. In August, Carrick has her first solo Australian exhibition at Bernard's Gallery, Melbourne.

On 29 August, the couple leave Australia for France aboard the SS *Mongolia*, arriving in Paris by October.

1909

Carrick exhibits 10 paintings in *Seizième Exposition à Bruxelles*, La Libre Esthétique, Brussels. That summer they visit St Malo, Dinard, Trouville and Deauville.

1910

Carrick and Fox visit Dinard and St Malo. They also spend some of the summer in Royan.

1911

Carrick is made a *sociétaire* of the Salon d'Automne.

In the middle of February, she and Fox travel to Marseilles, Algeria, Bou Saada, Tangier, Cádiz, Seville, Cordova, Granada, Toledo and Madrid.

That summer they visit Dinard, St Malo, Trouville, Deauville and Royan. In September, Carrick works away from Paris without Fox, and in October they travel with a pupil to Montreuil.

1912

Carrick and Fox attend a reception hosted by the President of the French Republic at his official residence, the Élysée Palace in Paris.

In November, Carrick exhibits with the International Art Union, Roger Levesque Gallery, Paris and becomes vice-president of the group. In 1912 she is a judge at the Salon d'Automne.

Over the winter of 1912 to 1913 Carrick is unwell.

1913

Carrick exhibits her North African paintings at the Société des Peintres Orientalistes Français, Paris.

In April, the couple visit Sanary and Le Brusc before travelling to Australia aboard the SS *Orvieto,* arriving in Melbourne on 19 May. They stay at St Ives boarding house, South Yarra, and Carrick has a solo exhibition at Guild Hall, Melbourne.

In Sydney, she has a solo exhibition at Anthony Hordern & Sons. The couple move to Manly, and Carrick stays while Fox returns to Melbourne for Christmas. By 14 December, Carrick is living at a Manly guest house with Thea Proctor.

1914

Fox returns to Sydney and joins Carrick on a trip around New South Wales before travelling to Hobart via Melbourne.

In July, the couple travel together on a sketching tour of the South Pacific aboard the liner *Moana*. World War I begins and they return to Sydney late August, staying at Redcourt, Cremorne.

In November, Carrick attends the opening of the Society of Women Painters, Sydney, and paints the *Red Cross sewing depot* 1914 at the Town Hall, Sydney.

On 18 December, Carrick hosts a French tea charity event at the Women's Patriotic Club and she spends the Christmas vacation at Beecroft, Northern Sydney.

1915

Carrick and her friend Ethel Stephens are honorary secretaires of the Australian Artists Workers' War Fund. They organise a Sydney exhibition that opens 9 March and host a conversazione the following day to raise funds.

In early April, Carrick plans to leave Sydney to join Fox in Melbourne but she becomes unwell. Her doctor orders complete rest and she is admitted to Charlemont Private Hospital, Darlinghurst. By 24 May, Carrick has almost recovered and spends a few days out of town before returning to the Women's Patriotic Club in Sydney. She arrives in Melbourne by late July.

In September, Fox is seriously unwell. He has an operation at St Evin's Hospital, during which bowel cancer is discovered. On 8 October 1915, he dies in hospital. He is buried in Brighton Cemetery.

Carrick stays with Mr and Mrs Herbert and Ivy Brookes in Melbourne before travelling to Sydney to stay with Bertha Merfield and Mademoiselle Augustine Soubeiran.

1916

In February Carrick returns to Melbourne, staying at Fox's former studio, to organise the *Memorial Exhibition of Pictures by the late E. Phillips Fox* at Athenaeum Gallery, Melbourne, from 29 February to 18 March.

On 1 May she departs Australia aboard the liner *Omrah*, arriving at Plymouth in June. She exhibits her Manly Beach paintings at the Institute of Oil Painters, London and visits her brother Hartley Carrick, as well as her sister Jessie Platts. She then returns to her apartment in Paris.

On Christmas Day, Carrick and a few friends visit a Paris convent to present gifts to 150 Belgian refugee children.

1917

Carrick continues with the war effort, supporting Mr Hubert Daly, a pupil of Fox's, in sending parcels to soldiers. She writes to several friends in Australia, informing them of the dire state of Serbian soldiers and Belgian refugee children, requesting aid for starving Russian prisoners.

1918

Carrick sends away three cases of Fox's paintings when Paris becomes a target for German bombardment.

In autumn, Carrick and Madame Emma de Marquette (née Ward) found the Overseas French Homes League. They are joint honorary secretaries. Carrick writes to French sculptor Antoine Bourdelle to organise atelier visits, and Fox's cousin, Rosetta Phillips, volunteers for the group.

Carrick exhibits at the second l'Arc-en-Ciel exhibition, Galerie Goupil & Cie, Paris.

1919

Carrick and de Marquette host a successful Overseas French Homes League event at the Australian YMCA headquarters, Hotel Windsor, Paris, and organise visits to the atelier of French painter Lucien Simon.

Carrick visits St Jean de Luz, in the south of France, and winters in Tunisia.

1920

Ethel Stephens travels to Paris and takes up painting lessons with Carrick. The classes are held a couple of times a week and expand to include Vida Lahey, Alfreda Goninan and Jean Brennan.

Carrick travels to London to hold an exhibition of Fox's paintings at Walker Galleries, 118 New Bond Street, London, opening 10 May.

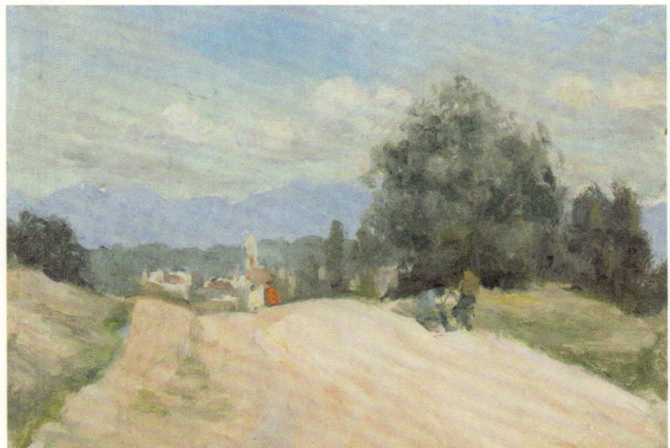

cat 131 ***Provençal landscape*** **no date, oil on artist board, University Art Collection, Chau Chak Wing Museum, The University of Sydney**

1921

In Paris, Carrick exhibits at the Salon des Indépendants and exhibits six North African paintings at the *Exposition de la Société Coloniale des Artistes Français.*

1922

Carrick is unwell over the winter, until the end of January. She exhibits one painting at the Salon of the Société Nationale des Beaux-Arts (*Au dessert* c 1922), which is reproduced in the official catalogue for the Salon.

Ethel Stephens moves into Carrick's apartment at 65 Boulevard Arago. In May, Carrick visits Dax, south of France, for rheumatism treatment.

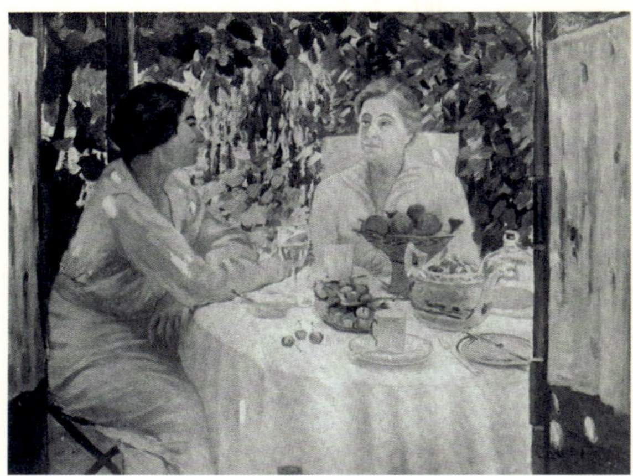

fig 58 Reproduction of Ethel Carrick's painting, *Au dessert* (At dessert) c 1922, also known as *Confidences*, in Société Nationale des Beaux-Arts exhibition catalogue, 1925

1923

In January, Carrick visits London with Bessie Gibson. In February, she holds a musical afternoon at her home in Paris; guests include Agnes Goodsir and playwright Oliver Madox Hueffer. She exhibits a portrait of Hueffer at the Salon d'Automne alongside a portrait of pianist Jean Batalla, which is hung on the line.

In March, Carrick hosts a welcome party for her friend and in-law, Dr Constance Ellis. In May, she visits London for the Royal Academy and to see Ivy Brookes, who later visits her in Paris.

In November, she shows in the *Group of Australian Artists* exhibition with Rupert Bunny, Bessie Davidson, Agnes Goodsir and Bessie Gibson at Panton Galleries, London.

1924

At the end of January, Carrick travels to Tyrol, returning to Paris at Easter. From May to June she visits Italy.

In late June, Carrick holds an 'at home' event to hear opera singer Miss Shelagh Nunn-Patrick. Guests include the artists Hilda Rix Nicholas and Roy de Maistre. On 6 July, Carrick and Hilda Rix Nicholas both attend a reception held by the Committee of the British Olympic Association at the Hotel Continental in Paris. Carrick has an interest in sport and runs a tennis club in Paris, which many of the Australian artistic circle belong to.

From September to December, she travels to London, staying with Miss EJ Jacobs and renting out her flat to General Golejewski and his family.

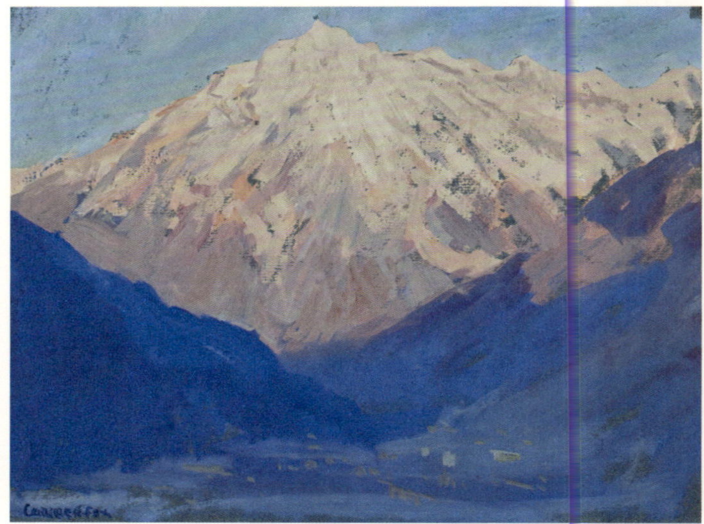

cat 132 *Mountain scene* c 1924, gouache on paper on board, Art Gallery of Ballarat

1925

Carrick attends the opening of Hilda Rix Nicholas's exhibition at Galeries Georges Petit, Paris, along with Rosetta Phillips, Shelagh Nunn-Patrick and Dorothy Richmond. Before leaving for Australia, she hosts a farewell party where French pianist Jean Batalla plays several pieces.

Carrick rents out her home and travels to Australia aboard the SS *Oronsay*, arriving in Melbourne 17 March. She stays with Dr Constance Ellis at New Grove, Wattletree Road, Malvern.

In April, she travels to Sydney for a Theosophical Society Convention. By May, she is back in Melbourne for her exhibition and stays with Ivy Brookes. In July, she travels to Adelaide for her exhibition and stays at the Queen Adelaide Club. Carrick returns to Melbourne and stays with Violet and Una Teague in Frankston, until 10 August.

By September she is in Sydney and stays at the Stella Maris flats, Stanton Road, Mosman. Ethel Stephens hosts an 'at home' event in Carrick's honour at The Society of Women Painters rooms, on 13 October.

In October, Carrick moves from Manly to Balmoral and stays until at least February 1926.

In November, she attends a party at Thea Proctor's studio. Other guests include Roy de Maistre, Hera Roberts, Jocelyn Garden and Adrian Feint. In December, she hosts a tea party at her studio at 10 Bligh Street.

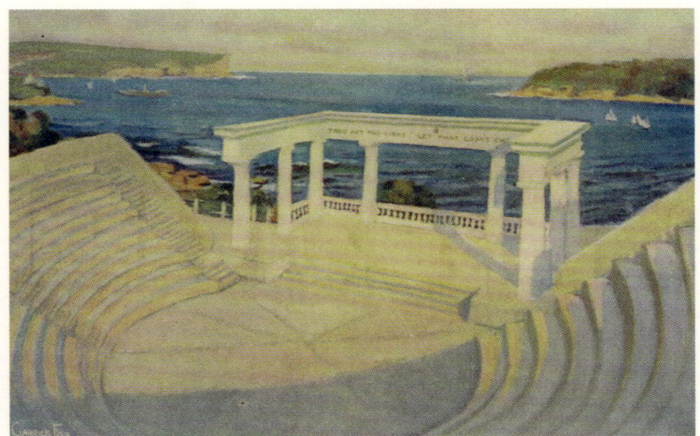

fig 59 Reproduction of Ethel Carrick's painting, ***Star Amphitheatre, Balmoral*** c 1925, Theosophical Society of Australia Research Library

1926

In January, Carrick advertises that she is taking on pupils for drawing and painting, and sells handmade batik shawls at the Roycroft Bookshop, Sydney.

Her paintings are exhibited in Europe while she is away, with works displayed in the foreign section of the Musée du Luxembourg, as well as the Women's International Art Club, London.

In April, she takes the overland train to Melbourne and joins the SS *Oronsay* bound for London. By October she has returned to Paris.

1927

By early 1927, Carrick is painting in Nice in the south of France and returns to Paris by 2 June.

In August, she attends the Theosophical Star Camp at Castle Eerde, Ommen, Holland. Three of her flower market paintings are exhibited at Galerie de la Palette Française, Boulevard Haussmann, Paris.

She also exhibits at the Exposition Internationale des Beaux-Arts de la Ville de Bordeaux, where she is awarded a *diplôme d'honneur* (diploma of honour).

1928

In March, Carrick holds a large party at her Boulevard Arago studio with her latest paintings on view. She attends a studio event where Russian dancer Sofia Fedorova performs, and an 'at home' event hosted by Agnes Goodsir.

In June, Carrick holds an exhibition of 22 paintings at Galerie de la Palette Française, Boulevard Haussmann, Paris. She sells her painting *Le marché aux fleurs à Nice* (the Nice flower market) c 1928, also known as *Coin d'une rue (Nice)* (Corner of a Nice street) to the French government (Musée des Beaux-Arts, Rouen).

1929

Carrick sends, by special invitation, two paintings to the Société des Amis des Arts de Bordeaux exhibition in Bordeaux, France. In February, she has a short visit to London.

Her work is included in a display of Australian artists in Europe at Australia House, London and she exhibits at the American Artists' Club, 107 Boulevard Raspail, Paris.

In summer, she is in Savoy, France, and returns to Paris 16 July. In August, she attends the Theosophical Star Camp in Holland and returns to Paris at the end of the month.

1930

Carrick exhibits *Le marché (Nice)* c 1927 with the Société des Amis des Arts de Bordeaux and briefly visits London in July.

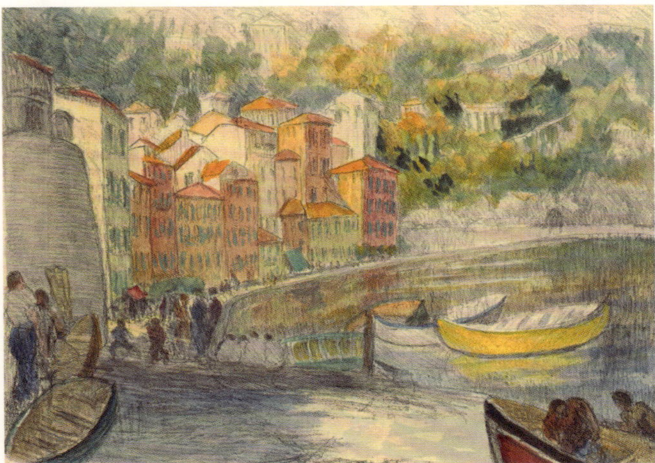

cat 133 ***A French harbour*** **c 1933, lithograph printed in black ink from one stone, hand-coloured in watercolour, Benalla Art Gallery**

1931

In Paris, Carrick exhibits two flower studies at a horticultural exhibition and a still-life, *Peonies* c 1930, at the *Exposition Coloniale Internationale*.

By December, Carrick is in London and stays until the end of March 1932.

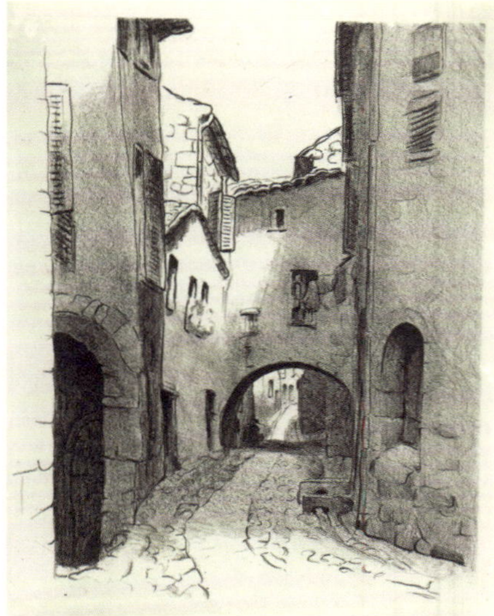

cat 134 *A street in St. Paul* c 1933, lithograph printed in black ink from one stone, Benalla Art Gallery

1933

Carrick travels from London to Australia aboard the liner *Ormonde* and arrives in Melbourne on 8 May. Her paintings are exhibited at the Salon Nationale des Beaux-Arts while she is away.

She has a solo exhibition at Everyman's Lending Library, Melbourne, opened by her friend Ivy Brookes. On 25 May, Brookes hosts an informal 'at home' at the International Club, Melbourne in honour of Carrick. In early August, Carrick leaves for Sydney.

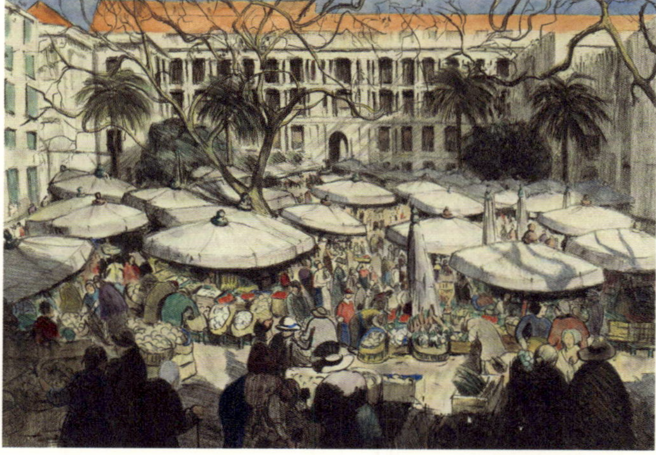

cat 135 *The fruit and vegetable market, Nice* 1933, lithograph printed in black ink from one stone, hand-coloured in watercolour, National Gallery of Australia

1934

Carrick is in Sydney until 7 February, at which time she leaves for Melbourne. On her last evening, she attends a gathering hosted by fellow theosophist Mrs Phyllis Campbell at Clifton Gardens.

She holds a joint exhibition with Fox's paintings at Athenaeum Gallery, Melbourne, before returning to Sydney to depart for Europe aboard the *Orama* on 24 April.

1935

In January, Carrick is in London staying at the private hotel at 8 Stanley Gardens, Belsize Park and meets with Bernard Hall before briefly returning to Paris.

She later returns to England to exhibit at the Royal Academy, London and visit her cousin Canon George at Devizes in Wiltshire, where she paints some portraits. She plans to travel to India that September.

1936

Carrick visits India (including current-day Pakistan), where she participates in several group exhibitions. On 27 and 28 May, she exhibits *Morning on the River Jhelum* c 1936 at the Srinagar Art Exhibition, Kashmir. On 27 July, she exhibits in a one-day group show at Nedou's Hotel, Gulmarg.

In December, Carrick is in Lahore, and attends an exhibition opening held by the Punjab Literary League. On the 19 December, she exhibits in a fine-art display at Foreman Christian College, Lahore.

On 25 December, Carrick has a large solo exhibition at the Club House of the Punjab Literary League, Lahore. The exhibition, organised by the Art Circle of the League, remains open until 1 January 1937.

1937

Carrick returns to Europe and exhibits her recent Indian painting *Le bac, Kashmir* (The ferry, Kashmir) 1937 at the Société Nationale des Beaux-Arts, Paris, and *A Parisian flower market* at the Royal Academy, London.

That summer she paints in Switzerland, returning to Paris by September.

1938

On 6 February, Carrick has surgery for appendicitis at the Hôpital Britannique Levallois-Perret, Paris.

Carrick holds *An Exhibition of Paintings by the Late E Phillips Fox and Ethel Carrick (Mrs E Phillips Fox)* at Cooling Galleries, London, 17–30 June, opened by Robert Gordon Menzies, Attorney-General of Australia.

1939

Carrick exhibits *Pont Neuf, Paris* at the Royal Academy, London. She is likely away travelling, as it is submitted on her behalf by James Bourlet & Sons Ltd, London.

By June, Carrick is in India. When World War II breaks out in September she is in Kashmir, and travels from Bombay to Melbourne aboard the SS *Strathmore*. In Melbourne, Carrick stays with Dr Constance Ellis.

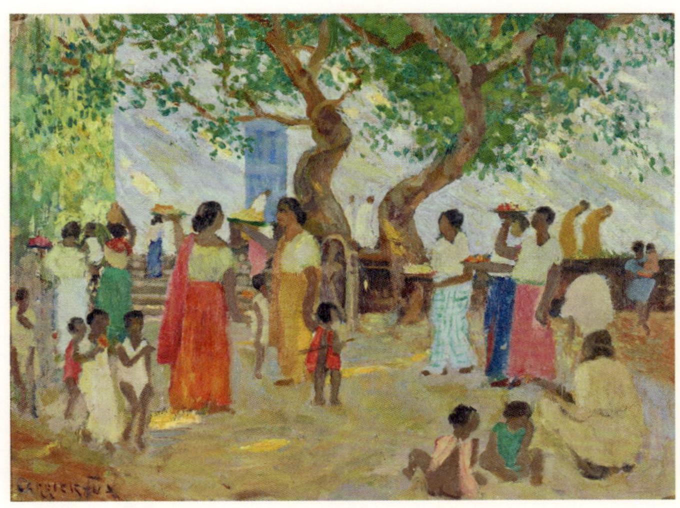

cat 136 ***The market place*** **c 1939, oil on canvas, private collection**

1940

In Melbourne, Carrick organises a charity exhibition at Athenaeum Gallery in her role as Honorary Organiser of the French Relief Fund, and assists the Women Painters National Service Group charity shop.

Carrick arrives in Sydney at the end of October and stays for several months living at The Manor, 1 Iluka Rd, Mosman.

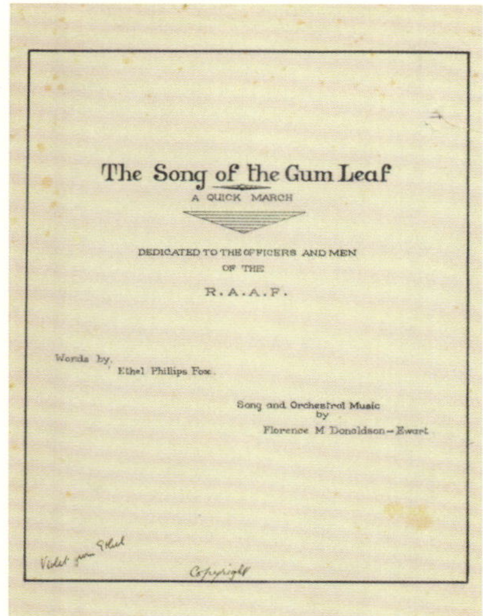

fig 60 **Ethel Phillips Fox (words) and Florence M Donaldson-Ewart (orchestral music),** ***The song of the gum leaf: a quick march*** **c 1940, sheet music**

1941

On New Year's Day, Carrick writes to Lionel Lindsay from The Manor to organise a meeting and congratulate him on his recent knighthood in the Federal New Year's Honours.

Carrick travels to Queensland and northern New South Wales for two months in September, visiting Darling Downs, Toowoomba, Coolangatta, Tweed Heads and Terranora.

1942

In mid-January, Carrick is in Melbourne and briefly visits Sydney before returning for her exhibition at the Athenaeum Gallery, Melbourne, from 27 April to 8 May. In October, Carrick exhibits with the Melbourne Society of Women Painters. That spring she travels to Canberra and stays with Mrs Patricia Tillyard, Red Hill.

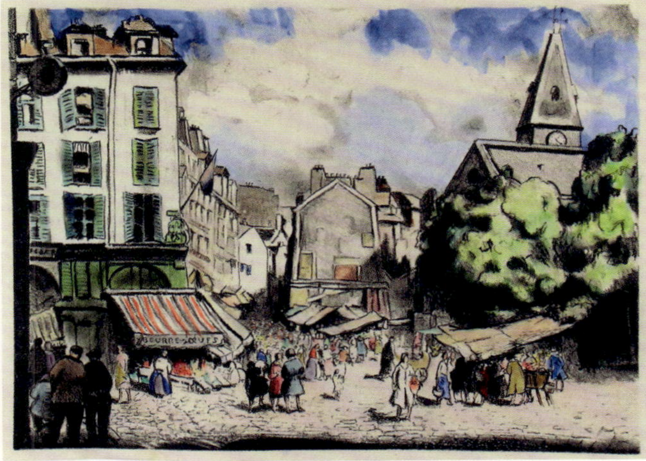

cat 137 ***La rue Mouffetard, Paris*** **c 1942, lithograph printed in black ink from one stone, hand-coloured in watercolour, Manly Art Gallery & Museum Collection**

1943

In early 1943, Carrick is in Sydney. By March, she is in Melbourne and shares Archibald Colquhoun's studio at 443 Bourke Street. In autumn she returns to Canberra, then visits Melbourne in early June before travelling to Sydney.

1944

Early in 1944, Carrick spends a week at Sybil Craig's beach house at Half Moon Bay, Port Phillip. She travels to Melbourne for her February exhibition at Athenaeum Gallery.

In August, Carrick travels to Canberra and stays at Hotel Canberra for her solo exhibition at the Masonic Temple, 7–10 September. She returns to Sydney before travelling to Melbourne for her group exhibition with Jean Sutherland and Sybil Craig at Kozminsky Galleries, 21 November – 11 December.

1946

Carrick and artist Frankie Payne are Honorary Organisers of the Artists Sub-Committee, French Comforts Fund, and coordinate an exhibition at David Jones' Art Gallery, Sydney to raise funds for struggling artists in Paris. They also coordinate a Melbourne exhibition at Myer Art Gallery in March.

1947

Carrick is in Melbourne and exhibits at the spring exhibition of the Victorian Artists Society, as well as the Melbourne Society of Women Painters at Athenaeum Gallery, Melbourne. Carrick spends most of the year in Melbourne.

1948

By April, Carrick is in Sydney and visits her friend Dame Mary Gilmore in Kings Cross. The pair meet as Carrick's theosophical friend Dorothy Bray, who also lived at The Manor, is Gilmore's typist. Carrick later attends one of Gilmore's portrait sittings with Joshua Smith.

In October, she stays at the Lyceum Club, Melbourne, and exhibits with the Melbourne Society of Women Painters at the Athenaeum Gallery.

1949

In May, Carrick visits Brisbane for the opening of the Emanuel Phillips Fox exhibition at Queensland Art Gallery, staying with Mrs Grifford Croll, sister of artist Frankie Payne.

She holds solo exhibitions at the Melbourne Book Club and John Martin's Art Gallery in Adelaide.

1950

On 22 February, Carrick travels to Tangier in Morocco aboard the MS *Surriento*. In June, she arrives in London and returns to Paris.

1951

Carrick moves into a different flat at 65 Boulevard Arago and travels to Nice, Grasse, Assisi, Perugia, Florence, San Gemigniano and Siena.

She exhibits with the Royal Scottish Academy, Society of Women Artists and The Royal Institute of Oil Painters.

1952

In May, Carrick travels from England to Australia and stays at the Lyceum Club, Melbourne. She plans to travel to Sydney, but this trip never eventuates. On 17 June 1952, Ethel Carrick passes away in Melbourne.

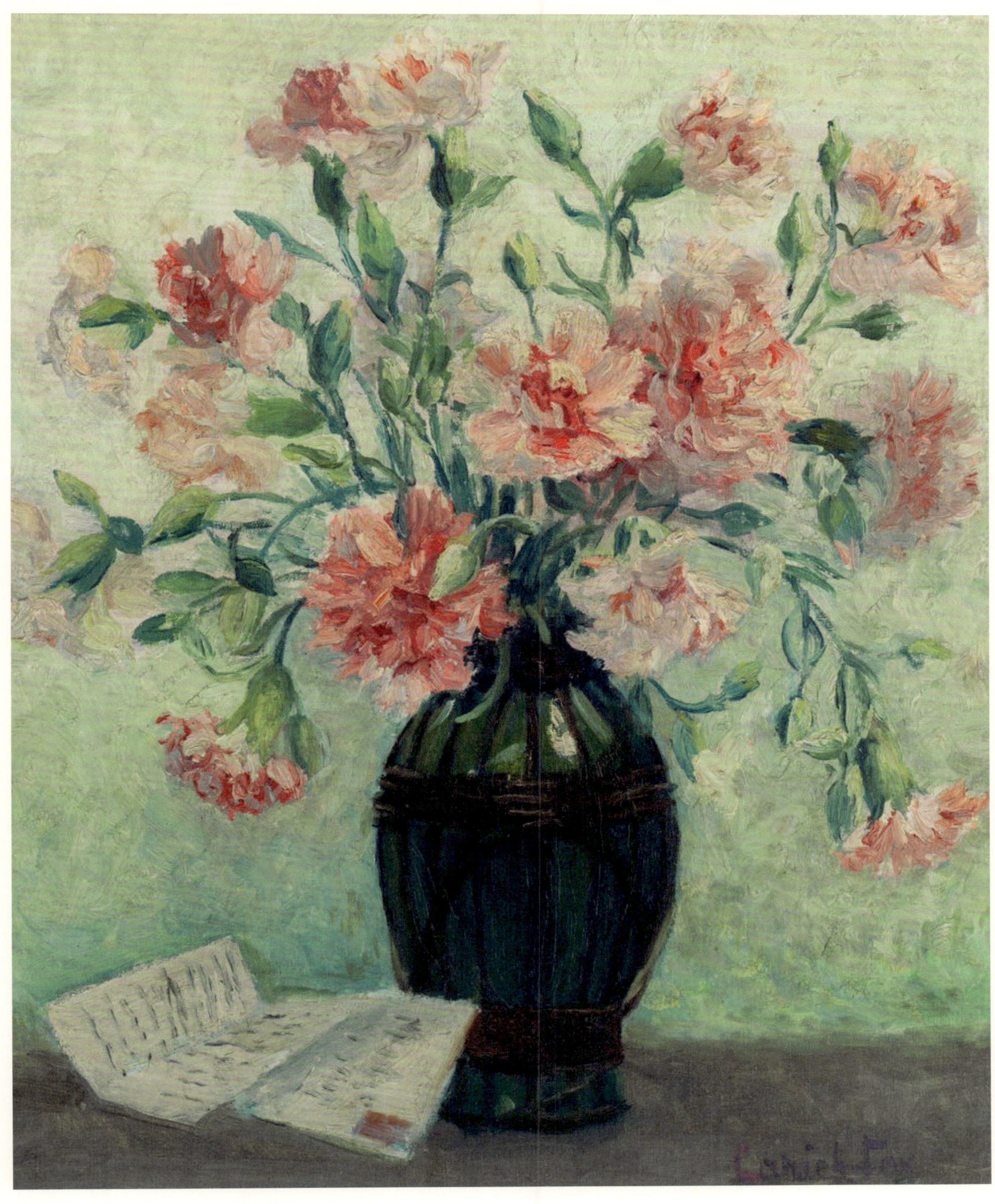

cat 138 *Carnations* c 1946, oil on canvas on board, National Gallery of Australia

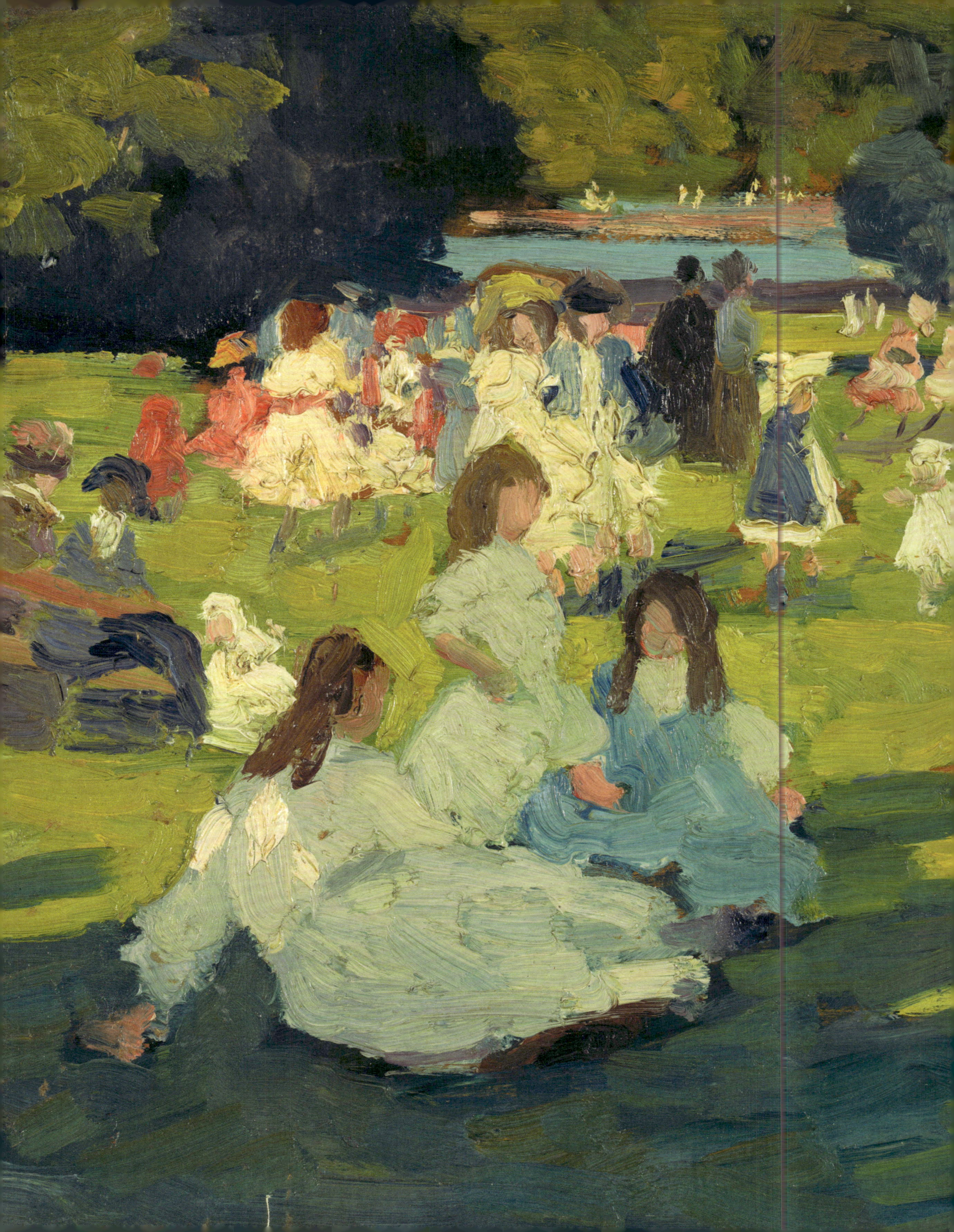

Notes

Exhibition history

Catalogue of exhibited works

Index

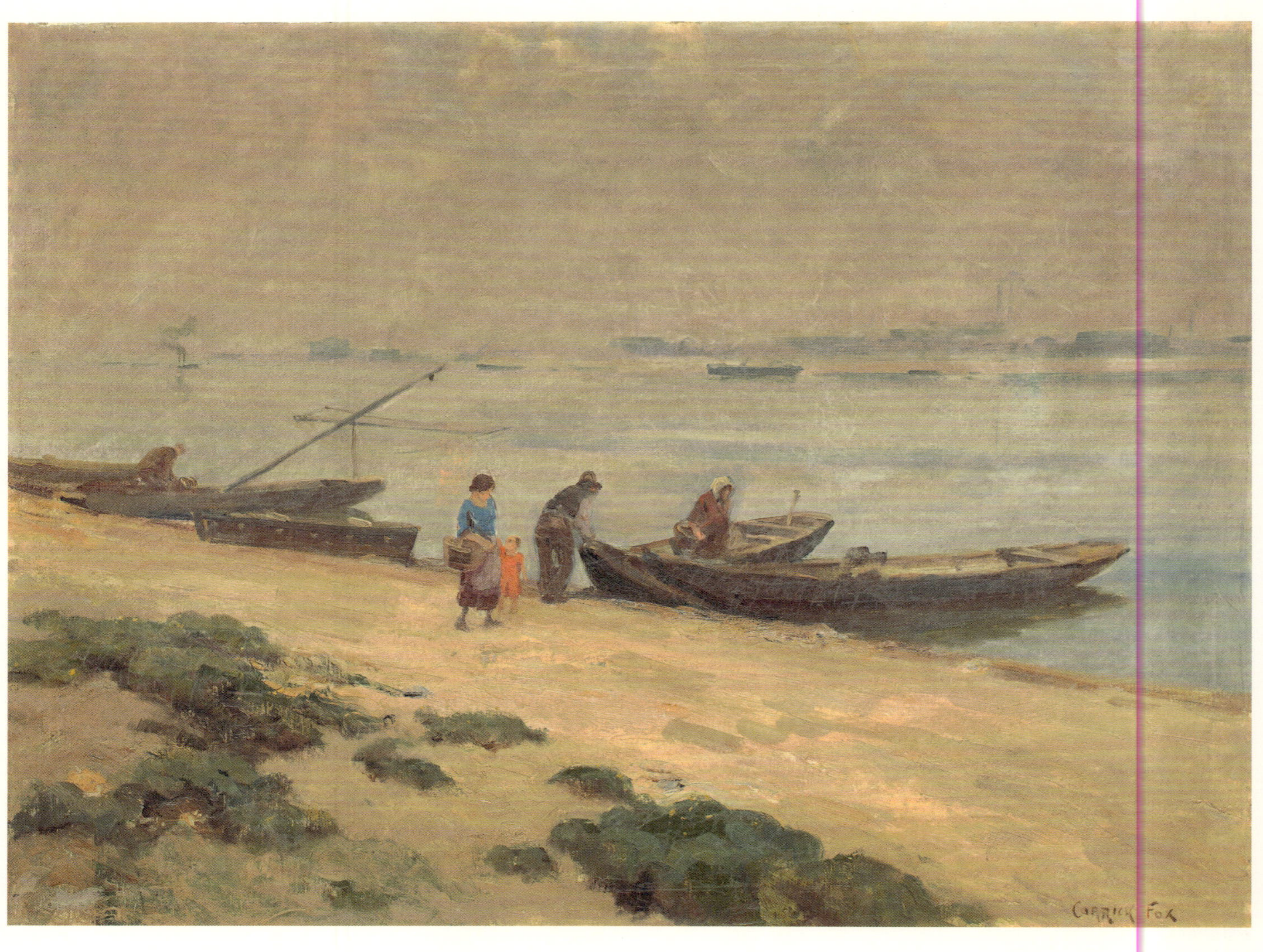

Previous
Esquisse en Australie (Sketch in Australia) 1908 (detail, cat 1 p 6), oil on wood, National Gallery of Australia

Above
cat 139 *Boats on a quayside* c 1912, oil on canvas, collection of Philip Bacon AO

Notes

First references to a source in each essay's notes are listed in full; repeated references within each essay are abbreviated.

Introduction

1 Ethel Carrick quoted in 'The Phillips-Fox Exhibitions', *The Bookfellow*, vol 2, no 10, 15 October 1913, pp 14–16, viewed 28 July 2024, http://nla.gov.au/nla.obj-842966617.

2 Thanks to Angela Goddard for this information, referred to in her essay in this publication.

3 I am grateful to the Gordon Darling Foundation for receipt of the Darling Travel Grant / International 2023, which allowed me to travel to the United Kingdom and France to undertake research. A lot of new information came from Carrick's letters; family accounts; the Slade School of Fine Art's archives and others pertaining to women artists; a visit to David Tovey in St Ives; the rich resource of Trove, including the *British Australasian*; and immigration records. I am greatly indebted to Rebecca Blake, who has worked closely with me on this project, for her excellent, painstaking research, which has enabled more accurate dating of events in Carrick's life and her art.

4 'Sketches of pictures in the society of oil painters', *The Queen*, Saturday 31 January 1903, p 29.

Ethel Carrick's life and art

Becoming an artist: 1872-1905

1 Edna Clarke Hall (née Waugh), unpublished memoir, Slade Archives, University College London, quoted in Alicia Foster, *Tate women artists*, Tate Publishing, London, 2004, p 82.

2 *Calendar session 1908–1909*, Taylor & Francis, London, 1908, p 196, quoted in Mengting Yu, *'A talented and decorative group': a re-examination of London's women artists, c.1900–1914*, PhD dissertation, Nanyang Technological University, Singapore, p 30.

3 Different published accounts of Carrick's life state that there were 10 children, but family and census records indicate nine children, with one child passing away at the age of five.

4 Philip Suter, *Suters Department Store History*, December 2013, viewed November 2023, http://www.philipsuter.co.uk/A_family_Business_Suters_Limited_1918_to_1928_2.htm.

5 Marcel Proust, *Within a budding grove*; vol 2 of *Remembrance of things past*, originally published in 1919, translated by CK Scott Moncrieff, Chatto & Windus, London, 1960, p 4.

6 Maureen Tweedy (née Mildford), unpublished family history, private collection, Norwich.

After Ethel Carrick's death her sister Hilda wrote, 'It still seems incredible that Ethel has gone from us. She possessed one of the most dominant personalities I have ever known—quite different from any other member of the family.' Hilda Carrick, letter to Irene (Renée) Fox, 29 November 1952, Len Fox Papers 1852–2001, State Library of New South Wales, Gadigal Nura/Sydney.

7 For example, the musical comedy *Two merry monarchs*, which opened at the Savoy Theatre, London, March 1910; and the publication Hartley Carrick, *The muse in Motley*, Bowes and Bowes, Cambridge, 1907. See 'Mr Hartley Carrick', *The Advertiser and Gazette*, 3 August 1928, p 3.

8 Tweedy, unpublished family history.

9 Mrs Clinton [Frankie Payne] quoted in a letter from the Union Trustee Company to the Director, National Art Gallery, Sydney, 28 May 1956, Ethel Carrick curatorial file, Art Gallery of New South Wales, Gadigal Nura/Sydney.

10 See Francis Bate's painting *The weeping ash* 1897, Reading Museum & Town Hall Collection, Reading, United Kingdom.

11 Slade Archives, UCLCA/4/1, University College London. Carrick was officially enrolled at the Slade in the years 1899–1900, 1900–1901, 1901–1902 and 1903–1904, and her name is absent in the University College London (UCL) calendar for 1902–1903. With thanks to Robert Winckworth, UCL Special Collections, London, for his assistance accessing this material.

12 Gwen John had also studied at the Slade but her final term, in 1898, ended prior to Carrick commencing.

13 Tessa Mackenzie (ed), *Art schools of London*, Chapman & Hall, London, 1895, pp 73–74.

14 University College London, *UCL Calendar for 1901–02*, Taylor and Francis, London, 1901–02, p 53, viewed June 2024, https://ucl.primo.exlibrisgroup.com/discovery/delivery/44UCL_INST:UCL_VU2/12356533620004761.

15 University College London, *UCL Calendar for 1904–05*, Taylor and Francis, London, 1904–05, p 14, viewed June 2024, https://ucl.primo.exlibrisgroup.com/discovery/delivery/44UCL_INST:UCL_VU2/12356533560004761.

16 With thanks to Dr Andrea Fredericksen, Curator, UCL Art Museum, London, for providing access to their collection of Slade School of Fine Art artworks.

17 During World War I, Tonks combined his medical and art skills to both help and depict wounded soldiers. See Emma Chambers, *Henry Tonks: art and surgery*, UCL Art Collections, London, 2002.

18 James McNeill Whistler *Symphony in white, no. 1: the white girl* 1861–62, National Gallery of Art, Washington, DC.

19 Carrick's visits are recorded in the local newspapers, *St. Ives Weekly Summary* and *Western Echo*. I am indebted to art historian David Tovey for sharing with me his considerable scholarship on the history of the artists who works in St Ives, including copies of the *St. Ives Weekly Summary*.

20 Angela Goddard, *Art, love and life: Ethel Carrick and E. Phillips Fox*, Queensland Art Gallery | Gallery of Modern Art, Brisbane, 2011, p 148.

21 David Tovey, *St Ives (1860–1930) The artists and the community: a social history*, Wilson Books, Gloucestershire, 2009, p 35.

22 Tovey, pp 289–91.

23 Tovey, p 249.

24 Tovey, p 251.

25 Tovey, p 251.

26 Tovey, p 92.

27 Arthur Burgess, letter to Muriel Coldwell, 8 September 1901, courtesy of the artist's grandson Stephen Bartley, quoted in Tovey, p 249. See Emily Carr's delicate depiction of Fearon in *And where is she at midnight* [?] *Why standing on the quay. Watching the boats with nut brown sails tossing on the sea* 1901–02, fig 5, p 24.

28 'Chit chat for women: a gifted woman', *The Advertiser*, 14 July 1925, p 10; Tovey, p 245.

29 The commission included the condition that 'the Trustees shall send to London, England, and commission a fit and competent artist to paint an Australian historical picture on the subject, either of Captain Cook's visit to Australia, or of Burke and Wills's expedition', J Lake, 'The new picture', *The Herald*, 4 December 1902, p 3.

30 Ruth Zubans, *E. Phillips Fox: his life and art*, Miegunyah Press, Melbourne, 1995, p 99.

31 Among them was Frances Hodgkins, born in New Zealand, who spent 1901 in Caudebec-en-Caux. Hodgkins wrote to her mother: 'Here I am settled down at last in Caudebec and very glad indeed to leave London and its many distractions ... I feel now as if I had really started to work in earnest, conditions are all favourable to work and I am living in an atmosphere of art, it is a very pleasant life we are leading and I wish time could stand still for a while. This is a charming spot full of quaint old streets & buildings and subjects in plenty for every day in the year.' Frances Hodgkins, letter to Rachel Hodgkins, 14 July 1901, *The Complete Frances Hodgkins Collection*, Auckland Art gallery Toi o Tāmaki, viewed June 2024, https://completefranceshodgkins.com/objects/29203/letter-from-frances-hodgkins-to-rachel-hodgkins.

32 On 19 August 1898, Pissarro had written to his son Lucien: 'Yesterday I found an excellent place from which I can paint the *Rue de l'Épicerie* and even the market, a really interesting one, which takes place every Friday.' Camille Pissarro, *Rue de l'Épicerie, Rouen* 1898, The Metropolitan Museum of Art, New York, viewed 14 May 2024, https://www.metmuseum.org/art/collection/search/437311.

33 Roger Butler, *Prints by Ethel Carrick*, unpublished manuscript, provided to the author on 23 November 2023. Butler notes that Carrick is not widely known as a printmaker but 'she experimented in printmaking in 1906 and was still thinking about it in 1951—the year before she died'. She produced very few etchings, concentrating mainly on lithographs later in her life.

34 This is referenced in Stephen Rainbird, *Expatriatism: a new platform for shaping Australian artistic practice in the late nineteenth and early twentieth centuries: a case study of six artists working in Paris and London*, PhD dissertation, University of Tasmania, nipaluna/Hobart, 2015, viewed 23 March 2024, https://figshare.utas.edu.au/articles/thesis/Expatriatism-a-new-platform-for-shaping-Australian-artistic-practice-in-the-late-nineteenth-and-early-twentieth-centuries-a-case-study-of-six-artists-working-in-Paris-and-London/23240576?file=40957499.

35 Emanuel Phillips Fox, letter to his sister-in-law Laura Fox, 10 Abbey Road, London, 29 December 1904, Margery Pitt Withers Papers, MS11231, State Library of Victoria, Naarm/Narrm/Melbourne.

36 Tom Roberts, letter to Walter Barnett, 39A Harrington Road, South Kensington, 7 January 1905, transcript in the private research papers of Dr Mary Eagle.

37 See Barbara H Weinberg, 'James McNeill Whistler (1834–1903)', in *Heilbrunn timeline of art history*, The Metropolitan Museum of Art, New York, 2000, viewed 29 February 2023, https://www.metmuseum.org/toah/hd/whis/hd_whis.htm.

38 Painting also reproduced in Zubans, p 114.

39 *The Age*, quoted in Zubans, p 114.

40 'Uxbridge', *Uxbridge & W. Drayton Gazette*, 20 May 1905, p 4.

41 *The British Australasian*, 11 May 1905, p 621.

42 'Mr Fox, the Australian Artist, intends to be married in the spring, and will reside permanently in Paris', *British Australasian*, 2 February 1905, p 152.

Discovering her vision: 1905–1915

43 Ethel Carrick quoted in 'Distinguished woman artist', *The Sun*, 9 November 1913, p 19.

44 Hilda Rix, letter to Rix Wight, no date, Hilda Rix Papers, National Library of Australia, Kamberri/Canberra, quoted in Brenda Niall, *The Boyds: a family biography*, Miegunyah Press, Melbourne, p 153.

45 The 1878 Paris Exposition was a world's fair and was the occasion for which the Eiffel Tower was built.

46 Coveted by developers, La Cité Fleurie was protected from 1973 thanks to the action of the painter Henri Cadiou (1906–1989), founder of the *Trompe l'oeil-réalité* movement who lived in workshop no 9. La Cité Fleurie, still serves as workshops and residences for artists. It is accessible during the 'Lézarts de la Bièvre' open days, every year on the second weekend of June, for artist studios in the 5th and 13th arrondissements. See Gilles-Antoine Langlois, *Walker's Guide 13th arrondissement, Paris, Parigramme*, 1996, viewed 14 May 2024, https://paris-promeneurs.com/la-cite-fleurie/.

47 'Through an artist's eyes: Mrs E. Phillips Fox returns', *The Herald*, 4 April 1925, p 12.

48 Ethel Phillips Fox, 'Studio life in Paris', *The V.A.S. Journal*, no 2, 1 May 1908, pp 1–2.

49 See Zubans, p 76.

50 *The Queen: The Ladies Newspaper and Court Chronicle*, 9 March 1907, p 428.

51 Phillips Fox, 'Studio life in Paris', p 1.

52 Tamar Garb, 'Revising the revisionists: the formation of the Union des Femmes Peintres et Sculpteurs', *Art Journal*, vol 48, no 1, spring 1989, p 63, viewed 14 May 2024, https://www.jstor.org/stable/776922.

53 Another nineteenth-century campaigner, Jean Alesson, analysed the numbers of women shown in the Salon, which was woefully low, noting in *Gazette des Femmes*: 'Rightly or wrongly, [the men] have judged for themselves the lion's share and treat women's work with excessive disdain.' Some, like Albert Wolff, agreed: 'Women are right to group themselves together because they are too often sacrificed in the Salons organised by men.' See 'Union des femmes peintres et sculpteurs', *Gazette des Femmes*, no 2, 25 January 1882, p 1, and A Wolff, 'Peinture et peintres', *Le Figaro*, 16 February 1883, p 1, both quoted in Garb, p 65.

54 Carrick noted in a review that she was the 'vice-president of the International Art Union in Paris'. Many of the names of these groups have similar titles and we know that she was definitely a part of the International Union of Artists. See 'Society doing things in Sydney', *The Australasian*, 15 November 1913, p 44.

55 A great admirer of Edgar Degas, Cassatt was a strong advocate for women in the face of the male bastions of power, including the Paris Salons, inspiring younger generations.

56 'Sunlight and motion', *The Herald*, 9 July 1913, p 7.

57 'Sunlight and motion', p 7.

58 Eleanor Norcross's exhibition was held at the Musée des Arts Decoratifs, Pavillon de Marsan, Louvre in March 1924. See Ann H Murray, 'Eleanor Norcross: artist, collector and social reformer', *Woman's Art Journal*, vol 2, no 2, 1981–82, p 5.

59 The Académie de la Grande Chaumière opened up significant opportunities for amateur and established artists alike. Among the Australians who studied there was Bessie Davidson, who made her home in Paris from 1910 and who showed in exhibitions with Carrick.

60 This is referenced in Stephen Rainbird, *Expatriatism: a new platform for shaping Australian artistic practice in the late nineteenth and early twentieth centuries: a case study of six artists working in Paris and London*, PhD dissertation, University of Tasmania, nipluna/Hobart, 2015, viewed 13 March 2024, https://figshare.utas.edu.au/articles/thesis/Expatriatism-a-new-platform-for-shaping-Australian-artistic-practice-in-the-late-nineteenth-and-early-twentieth-centuries-a-case-study-of-six-artists-working-in-Paris-and-London/23240576

61 Anna Todd, who divorced Carrick's brother Howard, was a determined woman whose interest in fashion involved a keen awareness of the French fashion houses of the day. 'With her flair for looking ahead Anna saw the day when the children of these hardworking citizens would demand more of life than their parents when the luxuries of one generation became the necessities of the next. Such a generation must be rising in Birmingham, better educated and with greater advantages and expectations than their parents.' Maureen Tweedy (née Mildford), unpublished family memoir, private collection, Norfolk.

62 Liliia Kornilieva, 'The signifying role of the dress in the novel "In search of lost time" ("A la recherche du temps perdu") by Marcel Proust', *Bibliotekarz Podlaski*, vol 54, no 1, 2022, p 184, viewed 14 May 2024, https://bibliotekarzpodlaski.pl/index.php/bp/article/view/674/801.

63 Maurice Denis' famous dictum in *Britannica*, viewed 14 May 2024, https://www.britannica.com/biography/Maurice-Denis.

64 Édouard Vuillard, *Jardins publics: la conversation, les nourrices, l'ombrelle rouge*, Musée d'Orsay, Paris, 1894, viewed June 2024, https://www.musee-orsay.fr/en/artworks/jardins-publics-la-conversation-les-nourrices-lombrelle-rouge-8015.

65 The nine panels became separated over time and *Under the trees* is now in the collection of the Cleveland Museum of Art, United States.

66 'Institute of oil painters', *The Westminster Gazette,* 16 October 1906, p 4.

67 Carrick later wrote in an unpublished biography on Emanuel Phillips Fox: 'In 1907, after despatching pictures to London (Royal Academy) & also to the Paris Salon [we] went down to Venice & worked there for a couple of months.' Emanuel Phillips Fox curatorial file, Art Gallery of New South Wales, Gadigal Nura/Sydney.

68 Quoted in Rebecca Andrews, 'Some early Australian artists in Venice', in *Venezia Australis: Australian Artists in Venice: 1900–2000*, Castlemaine Art Museum, Dja Da Wurrung Country/Castlemaine, 2005, p 12. Andrews notes that Hans Heysen arrived in Venice on 16 September 1902 for eight weeks of painting. Bessie Davidson (1879–1965) first visited in 1904 with Margaret Preston and returned many times. Streeton produced a very large number of Venetian subjects.

69 'Distinguished woman artist', *The Sun*, Sunday 9 November 1913, p 19.

70 *Table Talk*, 12 March 1908, p 25, quoted in Mary Eagle, *The oil paintings of E. Phillips Fox in the National Gallery of Australia*, National Gallery of Australia, Kamberri/Canberra, 1997, p 43. Eagle mentions that McCubbin had bought two paintings from the Foxes in Paris for the Abrahams brothers and Ethel Carrick listed a Fox painting, *Venetian colonade* [colonnade], in possession of Mrs Laurie Abrahams.

71 Frederick McCubbin, letter to Annie McCubbin, 7 August 1907, quoted in Andrew MacKenzie, *Frederick McCubbin 1855–1917: 'The proff' and his art*, Manna Gum, Lilydale, 1990, p 258.

72 Frederick McCubbin, letter to Annie McCubbin, 10 August 1907, quoted in MacKenzie, p 258.

73 The ship was destined for Melbourne but due to bad weather conditions they stopped in Adelaide instead.

74 Mary Eagle, interview with Mrs Louise Porker (née Fox, daughter of David and Irene Fox), 13 September 1988, private research papers of Dr Mary Eagle. Other letters in the Len Fox archive paint a more complex story. See Len Fox Papers 1852–2001, MLMSS 8085, State Library of New South Wales, Gadigal Nura/Sydney.

75 The Len Fox Papers reveal a highly complex family dynamic. See Len Fox Papers 1852–2001.

76 Letters in the Len Fox Papers indicate there was some antipathy from Irene Fox (who Carrick addressed as Renée) and others towards Ethel. However, as in many family situations, this is complex, not one-dimensional. For Irene and Ethel, Emanuel was the great bond between them and they communicated, largely about him, through to the end of Ethel's life. Irene also wrote to Hilda Carrick when Ethel died. Len Fox Papers 1852–2001.

77 'Distinguished woman artist', *The Sun*, 9 November 1913, p 19.

78 Carrick's close connections to the VAS, her generosity of spirit towards students, and her desire to foster opportunities was made evident in the article 'Studio life in Paris', *The V.A.S. Journal*, no 2, 1 May 1908, p 1.

79 '[W]hat makes this difference all the more remarkable is that Mrs Fox's talent is more of the masculine order than is her husband's.' Quoted in 'Melbourne doings', *The Daily Telegraph*, 20 May 1914, p 18.

80 'Parisian paintings—A blaze of colour—Mrs Fox's collection', *The Herald*, 4 August 1908, p 3.

81 'Exhibition of paintings by Mrs E. Phillips Fox', *The Age*, 4 August 1908, p 8.

82 Georges Seurat, *A Sunday on La Grande Jatte* 1884, Art Institute of Chicago, Chicago, viewed 14 May 2024, https://www.artic.edu/artworks/27992/a-sunday-on-la-grande-jatte-1884.

83 'Puck's girdle', *The Sydney Morning Herald*, 10 February 1909, p 5.

84 'La vie Artistique: Petit Salons, Les Quelques', *Le Matin*, 20 January 1909, p 4.

85 Octave Maus, preface essay in the exhibition catalogue for *Seizième Exposition a Bruxelles*, La Libre Esthetique, Brussels, 7 March 1909 – 12 April 1909. See transcription in *Database of Modern Exhibitions (DoME): European paintings and drawings 1905–1915*, last modified 27 July 2020, https://exhibitions.univie.ac.at/exhibition/210.

86 These works have since disappeared and so their dates and current locations remain unknown. The English translations of their titles are *Nurses and babies*, *A flower market in Venice*, *A market*, *The diabolo*, *The little rose* and *The promenade*.

87 The literal translation is not 'on the sands' but 'on the beach', but is within the same spirit, so we have kept the initial titling here. The alternative translation 'On the beach' has been used for other Carrick works with the French title *Sur la plage* and no English translation.

88 Letter from EPF to Hans Heysen, Hans Heysen Papers, NLA MS 5073/1/319A, cited in Zubans, p 182.

89 Mary Eagle goes further: '[Fox's work] was painted directly onto the wood panel ... There is no going back over the sketch a second time ... forms were modelled in solid areas of colour ... It shows Fox's earlier medley of many closely related colours ... but was painted in a manner closer to Carrick's "tonking" (after the Slade teacher Henry Tonks) whereby the paint was dabbed on and blotted to ensure a fast and even rate of drying.' See Eagle, 1997, pp 51, 52.

90 Michel Pastoureau, *The devil's cloth: a history of stripes and striped fabric*, translated by Jody Gladding, Columbia University Press, Columbia, 2001.

91 Emanuel Phillips Fox, letter to Hans Heysen, 13 September 1911, Papers of Hans Heysen, MS5073, National Library of Australia, Kamberri/Canberra.

92 See Roger Benjamin, *Orientalism: Delacroix to Klee*, Art Gallery of New South Wales, Sydney, 1997; Roger Benjamin, *Orientalist aesthetics: art, colonialism, and French North Africa, 1880–1930*, University of California Press, Berkeley, 2003.

93 It would appear that Rix Nicholas saw Carrick and Fox's North African works on a visit she made to their Boulevard Arago apartment.

94 Elena Taylor, 'Ethel Carrick 1872–1952', in Anna Gray, *The Edwardians: secrets and desires*, National Gallery of Australia, Canberra, 2004, p 151.

95 Jonathan Fineberg, 'Les Tendances Novelles, The Union Internationale des Beaux-Arts, Des Lettres, Des Sciences et de L'Industrie and Kandinsky', *Art History*, vol 2, no 2, June 1979, p 221.

96 Wassily Kandinsky, *On the spiritual in art*, 1911, translated in Kenneth C Lindsay and Peter Vergo (eds), *Kandinsky: complete writings on art, vol. 1 (1901–1921)*, GK Hall & Co., Boston, 1982, p 169.

97 *Les Tendances Nouvelles: Organe official de l'Union Internationale des Beaux-Arts, des lettres, des Sciences et de l'Industrie*, Quatrieme Année, no 39, 1908, p 834.

98 Ethel Carrick quoted in 'Distinguished woman artist', *The Sun*, 9 November 1913, p 19.

99 She later talks about de Maistre's very interesting colour 'inventions' in 'Women's views and news', *The Argus*, 20 March 1925, p 14.

100 Frances Hodgkins, letter to Rachel Hodgkins, 29 December 1911, Correspondence of Frances Hodgkins and family collected by Isabel Field, MS-Papers-0085-25, Alexander Turnbull Library, Wellington, New Zealand, viewed 14 May 2024, https://natlib.govt.nz/records/22715535.

101 'Mrs E. Phillips Fox's picture', *Punch*, 24 July 1913, p 41.

102 'Le Mois Artistique: Le Salon d'Automne', *L'Art et les Artistes*, vol 14, October 1911 – March 1912, p 87.

103 Stephen Rainbird writes with great insight and conviction about the radical nature of Carrick's art in *Expatriatism: A new platform for shaping Australian artistic practice in the late nineteenth and early twentieth centuries*, PhD dissertation, University of Tasmania, nipaluna/Hobart, 2015.

104 Although this work has been known as *Bull fight at Biarritz*, the location does not resemble Biarritz but looks more like the bullring in Lunel France. It is likely, as proposed by Rebecca Blake, to be *Impression of a bull fight*, Carrick's title for a painting of this subject exhibited in the Australian Art Association group exhibition in 1915.

105 Rainbird, p 213.

106 'The bullring remained a patriarchal space until the 1930s. *La Reverte* (Maria Salomé) was an exception, becoming in the early 1900s one of the public's most praised and adored bullfighters. In 1908, the government banned her because she was a woman. However, *La Reverte* shocked the world by taking off her wig and costume and revealing that she was actually a man, Agustin Rodriguez. Once the truth was revealed, the government allowed Rodriguez to continue as a torero.' Rainbird, p 215.

107 Carrick went on to say, 'a man who spoke French suggested, going next door to a boys' college and interviewing the principal. I did so, and he gave me a room for three days.' However, Carrick's paintings of courtyards suggest that she may have found other solutions that enabled her to connect with local women. See 'Distinguished woman artist', *The Sun*, 9 November 1913, p 19.

108 Zubans, p 183.

109 'A distinguished woman painter', *The Daily Telegraph*, 15 August 1913, p 15.

110 'The Australian painter, Mr E.P. Fox, who belongs unmistakably to the French school, scores one of the successes of the Salon; he exhibits six pictures, and those which are hung in the first room shine in comparison with the works that surround them. *Les Etudiantes* is a fine piece of work ...' 'Art in France', *The Burlington Magazine for Connoisseurs*, vol 19, no 98, May 1911, p 118.

111 'Australians in Europe', *British Australasian*, 4 July 1912, p 18.

112 Andrew Fisher (1862–1928) was an Australian politician and trade unionist who served as the fifth prime minister of Australia from 1908 to 1909, 1910 to 1913 and 1914 to 1915. He held office as the leader of the Australian Labor Party, and was particularly notable for leading Labor to its first federal election victory and first majority government.

113 'Mrs E. Phillips Fox's pictures', *Leader*, 12 July 1913, p 48.

114 'Mrs E. P. Fox's paintings', *The Argus*, 11 July 1913, p 5.

115 'Mrs E. P. Fox's paintings', p 5.

116 'Art note from Watt's city', *The Bulletin*, vol 34, no 1745, 24 July 1913, p 12.

117 'In other states', *The Daily Telegraph*, 6 August 1913, p 15.

118 'A distinguished woman painter', *The Daily Telegraph*, 15 August 1913, p 15.

119 Among them Carrick showed painterly sketches, which she described as 'notes'.

120 'Distinguished woman artist', *The Sun*, 9 November 1913 , p 19.

121 'Mrs Fox's paintings', *Evening News*, 7 November 1913, p 8.

122 'An interesting exhibition', *Australian Town and Country Journal*, 12 November 1913, p 57.

123 Vandorian [pseudonym], 'A woman's letter', *The Bulletin*, vol 34, no 1761, 13 November 1913, p 18. In the scrapbook she made during this time, she pasted newspaper cuttings of Carrick's shows.

124 See Rebecca Blake's essay in this publication.

125 'Pictures exhibited', *The Herald*, 4 May 1914, p 10.

126 For images of these works, see Zubans. *The ferry* is currently in the Art Gallery of New South Wales and *The arbour* in the National Gallery of Victoria.

127 'Social notes', *Leader*, 16 May 1914, p 51.

128 'Social notes', p 51.

129 Apart from exhibitions they would have seen, one of the former residents at the Boulevard Arago was George-Daniel de Monfreid, an artist and avid collector of Gauguin's art, and also executor of his will. Carrick and Fox would have been familiar with this legacy.

Fallow to flowering: 1915–1939

130 Charles Dickens, *A tale of two cities*, Houghton Mifflin Company, Boston, 1962, originally published in 1859, p 3.

131 'Modern art', *The Daily Telegraph*, 27 March 1915, p 8.

132 See 'Australian Artists' War Fund', *The Daily Telegraph*, 9 March 1915, p 8; 'Artists' War Fund soiree', *The Sydney Morning Herald*, 11 March 1915, p 8.

133 'Melbourne has been enlivened with various dedication days of recent years, both for charity and patriotism, but the arrangements for Australia Day, on July 30, promise to eclipse all former efforts. Commerce House, Flinders street, where Mr F.B. Jenkinson, hon. General organiser, has his headquarters, is a busy hive of industry. In one room are two well-known artists, Mr and Mrs Phillips Fox (Miss Ethel Carrick) sorting and preparing gum leaves. As an experiment Mrs Fox sold gum leaves as decorative favours in Sydney recently, at one of the street campaigns, and made a considerable sum. This has encouraged her to repeat the experiment. The women artists here are helping her with the scheme, and she is also anxious for others to assist, as she hopes to have 100 000 ready for Australia Day. The leaves are slightly stiffened, and gilded at stems and edges. On the surface, stamped in gold lettering, is the one significant word "Dardanelles," and the figures 1915 with patriotic ribbons.' From 'Getting grist for mill: Australia Day', *The Herald*, 20 July 1915, p 3.

134 'For Australia Day', *The Australasian*, 24 July 1915, p 4.

135 Alexander Colquhoun, 'E.P. Fox', undated notes, original in the possession of the family, photocopy in Violet Teague Papers, YMS14726, State Library of Victoria, Naarm/Narrm/Melbourne, quoted in Zubans, pp 170, 201.

136 Porker also noted: 'Poor Grannie Fox, a Rabbi's daughter, would have liked to have seen her son buried as a jew, but she let Ethel choose all arrangements, so my uncle was laid to rest in the Church of England section of the Brighton Cemetery.' Louise Porker, blue-bound folder, Len Fox Papers 1852–2001.

137 See Angela Goddard's essay in this publication.

138 Ethel Carrick, letter to Mrs Ivy Brookes, with SS *Levuka* written in the letterhead, 1915, Papers of Herbert and Ivy Brookes 1869–1970, MS1924/1/2584, National Library of Australia, Kamberri/Canberra. The letter has been edited here—it included mention of her being taken 'from that so-called "home"', referring to family tensions following Fox's death, when emotions were running high.

139 Bertha Merfield, letter to Ivy Brookes, 'Lulea', Elgin Street, Hawthorn, 3 January 1916, Papers of Herbert and Ivy Brookes 1869–1970, MS1924/1/2830, National Library of Australia, Kamberri/Canberra.

140 'The social circle', *Weekly Times*, 26 February 1916, p 9; 'Social notes', *The Australasian*, 26 February 1916, p 34.

141 Violet Teague, 'E.P. Fox and his work', *The Argus*, 26 February 1916, p 7.

142 Carrick helped organise Fox's memorial exhibition in 1916 and advocated fervently for the acquisition of his paintings by institutions for his retrospective exhibition (which occurred in 1949) and a substantial book with good illustrations, which happened after her passing. Len Fox wrote a small book on Fox, *Phillips Fox and his family*, Len Fox, Potts Point, 1985. Ruth Zubans wrote a scholarly, fully illustrated monograph: *E. Phillips Fox: his life and art*, Miegunyah Press, Melbourne, 1995.

143 This was a battle at Alba Kemal in Turkey as part of the Mesopotamia campaign that came about as a direct result of World War I, when the British Prime Minister was honouring a promise to Greece in relation to the Ottoman Empire.

144 Jessie Platts, *The witness*, fourth edition, Hutchinson & Co, London, 1920, p viii.

145 Platts, 1920, pp 15–16.

146 Ethel Carrick, letter to Ethel Stephens, published in *The Daily Telegraph*, 3 January 1917, p 4.

147 Jennifer McFarlane writes that 'in December that same year [1916], at 4 Square Rapp, in the shadow of the Eiffel Tower, Carrick finally joined the Theosophical Society officially. She was sponsored by Charles Blech and artist Marie Bermond.' See Jenny McFarlane, *A visionary space: Theosophy and an alternative Modernism in Australia 1890–1934*, PhD dissertation, Australian National University, Kamberri/Canberra, 2006, p 144.

148 Following his death, Carrick continued the practice of showing their works together in exhibitions. Ethel Carrick generally signed her paintings with her maiden name prior to Fox's death, after which she mostly joined his name with hers as Carrick Fox. Although there has been commentary over the years about a deliberate confusion between their works, she never signed her works Fox or Phillips Fox.

149 Ethel Carrick, letter to Ivy Brookes, Papers of Herbert and Ivy Brookes 1869–1970, MS1924/1/3642, National Library of Australia, Kamberri/Canberra.

150 Ethel Phillips Fox, letter to Ivy Brookes, 65 Boulevard Arago, 19 February 1917, p 4, Papers of Herbert and Ivy Brookes 1869–1970, MS1924/1/3141, National Library of Australia, Kamberri/Canberra.

151 'The League in Paris', *The Daily Telegraph*, 18 September 1918, p 5.

152 'Women's views and news', *The Argus*, 20 March 1925, p 14.

153 Carrick quoted in 'Women's views and news' p 14.

154 The de Marquettes were also theosophists. Madame Emma Jeanne de Marquette (née Ward) and her French son Jacques de Marquette were friends with Carrick, who visited Jacques de Marquette in Tangier in 1950. See Jacques de Marquette, *Confessions d'un Mystique Contemporain*, Panharmonie, Paris, 1965, p 12. See also 'Overseas French Homes', *The Sydney Morning Herald,* 13 June 1919, p 5, which reveals 'Madame de Marquette, the energetic French hon. sec, has a special link binding her to Australia, having spent five of her school years In Collins-street, Melbourne, where her father, Mr Henry Ward (a cousin of Sir Joseph Ward, of New Zealand), practised as a surgeon dentist.'

155 'Overseas French homes', p 5.

156 'Let's talk of interesting people ... distinguished artist', *The Australian Women's Weekly*, 10 February 1934, p 3.

157 See lettre autographe signée d'Ethel Phillips Fox à Antoine Bourdelle, 4 October 1918, Musée Bourdelle, Paris, B.1.24. C6.01, kindly provided by Claire Boisserolles, Chargée d'études documentaires, Responsable du centre de ressources documentaires, Musée Bourdelle, Paris. Carrick's aim was to 'give the boys to have the best impression possible of French people'. See Ethel Phillips Fox, letter to Ivy Brookes, 25 February 1919, Papers of Herbert and Ivy Brookes 1869–1970, MS1924/1/3497, National Library of Australia, Kamberri/Canberra.

158 Stephens was taking a refresher course at the Académie de la Grande Chaumière and Juliette Peers noted that Carrick was recommended by the teachers there. Juliette Peers, 'Fox, Ethel (Carrick)', in Delia Gaze (ed), *Dictionary of women artists*, Fitzroy Dearborn Publishers, London, 1997, p 546.

159 Alfreda Nellie Marcovitch, interviewed by Barbara Blackman, 27 March 1988, sound recording, National Library of Australia, Kamberri/Canberra, accessed June 2024, https://nla.gov.au/nla.obj-199142877/.

160 Alfreda Nellie Marcovitch, interviewed by Barbara Blackman.

161 Sotheby's, *Important paintings, Lot 34: Ethel Carrick Fox*, Sotheby's Australia, Sydney, 22 April 2008, pp 70–71, viewed June 2024, https://www.sothebys.com/en/auctions/ecatalogue/2008/important-paintings-au0719/lot.34.html.

162 Sotheby's, pp 70–71.

163 See 'A la galerie Goupil et Cie', *La Renaissance de l'art*, 1 March 1918, p 358; 'L'Arc-en-Ciel: Deuxieme Exposition', *Les Arts*, no 169, 1918, pp 20–24; and 'Un Exposition d'Art: A la Galerie Goupil et cie L'Arc-en-ciel', *Les Modes*, 1 January 1918, pp 5–7.

164 Phyllis [pseudonym], 'In the looking glass', *British Australasian*, 22 April 1920, p 11.

165 'La Bretagne aux Salons: Société Nationale des Beaux-Arts', *L'Ouest-Éclair,* 9 May 1921, p 1.

166 This painting could not be located but was praised many times in the press, including when it was shown in Australia.

167 'Mrs Fox with Miss Ethel Stephens, of Sydney, have had a flat and a studio in Rue D' Arago, Paris. Miss Stephens talks of returning to Australia at the end of the year.' See 'Social gossip', *The Herald*, 9 May 1922, p 9.

168 Ethel Phillips Fox to Violet Teague, 20 July 1920, Violet Teague archive, State Library of Victoria, Naarm/Narrm/Melbourne.

169 'Australians in Europe', *British Australasian,* 6 April 1922, p 16; 'Mainly about people', *The Daily News*, 15 May 1922, p 6.

170 'Artist and writer', *News*, 2 July 1925, p 1.

171 The closeness of Carrick's painting to the actual bridge is evident in photographs, even in contemporary photos of the bridge today.

172 At this time, the Order of the Star in the East was associated with the Theosophical Society, but the groups later separated. It is suggested that the amphitheatre was built specifically for Krishnamurti's address. The painting by Carrick could not be located at the time of writing. 'The amphitheatre was built in 1923 by the Theosophical organisation in Sydney. Dr Mary Rocke led the movement for its construction in order that Theosophists might welcome Krishnamurti' in 'Balmoral Amphitheatre', *The Sydney Morning Herald*, 15 January 1937, p 4.

173 While images remain of this painting by Carrick, it has not been traced. In 1924, the owner of Castle Erde, Baron Philip van Pallandt, gave the property to Jiddu Krishnamurti. In 1929 Carrick would have heard the famous speech when Krishnamurti renounced the Order of the Star in the East and withdrew from the Theosophical Society, still remaining close to Annie Besant.

174 'Chit chat for women: a gifted woman', *The Advertiser,* 14 July 1925, p 10.

175 'Wonderful pictures', *News*, 13 July 1925, p 9.

176 Carrick was unhappy about the lack of support from both public and private collectors and got offside with the press due to some of her comments. See Ethel Carrick, letter to Ivy Brookes, 29 July 1925, Queen Adelaide Club, Papers of Herbert and Ivy Brookes 1869–1970, MS1924/1/6054, National Library of Australia, Kamberri/Canberra. See also 'Adelaide for culture', *News*, 30 July 1925, p 1, where Carrick comments on the lack of culture in Adelaide. A retaliation is published on 5 August, stating, 'evidently Mrs E. Phillips Fox is a stranger in this beautiful city', from 'What our readers think', *News*, 5 August 1925, p 6.

177 Carrick originally wrote to Mr Mann in 1925 regarding Fox's *Art students* 1895, but the acquisition never eventuated. The offer was opened again when Carrick wrote to then Director, Mr John William Ashton, on 1 February 1943, offering Fox's paintings *Art students* 1895 and *A love story* 1903. *Art students* was acquired by what was then known as the National Gallery of New South Wales, in 1943, while his other (now famous) work *The ferry* c 1910–11 was bought in 1949. See Ethel Phillips Fox, letter to Mr Ashton, 1 February 1943, Emanuel Phillips Fox curatorial file, Art Gallery of New South Wales, Gadigal Nura/Sydney.

178 'Gossip from Sydney', *The Week*, 16 October 1925, p 26.

179 'Gossip from Sydney', p 26.

180 In October and December 1925, Carrick was staying in a block of flats, Stella Maris, on Stanton Road in Mosman. See Ethel Carrick, letter to Ivy Brookes, Stella Maris, Stanton Road, Mosman, 13.10.25, Papers of Herbert and Ivy Brookes 1869–1970, MS1924/1/6124, National Library of Australia, Kamberri/Canberra; and Ethel Carrick, letter to Mr Hans Heysen, Stella Maris, Stanton Road, Mosman, Sydney, 17 December 1925, Papers of Hans Heysen, MS 5073/1/1679, National Library of Australia, Kamberri/Canberra. That month Carrick was in Balmoral to paint the Star Amphitheatre, and at some point she moved to live in Balmoral; by April 1926 it is reported that Carrick 'has been staying at Balmoral for some time'. See 'Mrs Phillips Fox', *The Daily Mail*, 24 April 1926, p 11.

181 Ethel Carrick, letter to Ivy Brookes, Stella Maris, Stanton Road, Mosman, 13 October 1925, Papers of Herbert and Ivy Brookes 1869–1970, MS1924/1/6124, National Library of Australia, Kamberri/Canberra.

182 'Letters to Mariegold', *Sunday Times*, 7 February 1926, p 2.

183 *The Menton & Monte Carlo news*, 16 April 1927, p 13, viewed 23 August 2024, https://gallica.bnf.fr/ark:/12148/bpt6k45581733/f13.item.r=%22Mrs%20Phillips%20Fox%22.zoom.

184 See David Thomas, who has written excellent entries over many years, viewed 14 May 2024, https://www.deutscherandhackett.com/auction/lot/flower-market-nice-c1926.

185 It was exhibited as *La plage*. See reference to Carrick's original title in 'Social chatter', *Sunday Times*, 20 November 1927, p 15.

186 'For the home circle', *The Brisbane Courier*, 2 August 1928, p 19. When the painting *Le marché aux fleurs à Nice*, also known as *Coin de rue, Nice* was made part of the Rouen Collection, Carrick wrote asking for a colour image to show to her family in Australia, no doubt keen to prove to her sister-in-law Irene Fox, with whom she stayed in contact, that she was taken seriously in France.

187 Georges Bal, 'Paris art notes', *The New York Herald*, 9 June 1928, p 5.

188 'A garden in Paris', *The Register*, 14 July 1925, p 5.

189 Carrick also noted, 'We should also have a Renoir—but only a very good one. Some are very bad.' See 'More modern art needed', *The Herald*, 9 May 1933, p 10.

190 'Old masters and modern art "enriching dealers"', *The Herald*, 8 May 1933, p 1. Carrick continued: 'Railways stations, too, the first things to strike a traveller's eye, could take a hint from Switzerland, not only in Australia but in England and Europe generally. Some of the Swiss railway stations are masses of flowers.'

191 'The Parisian theatre,' *The Argus*, 23 November 1929, p 6.

192 'The palette,' *The Bulletin*, vol 54, no 2782, 7 June 1933, p 18.

193 See 'Art exhibition for mission', *The Herald*, 2 February 1934, p 19.

194 'Edwardian pictures—E. Phillips Fox show in the city', *The Herald*, 26 February 1934, p 8.

195 'She travelled widely in the East—we remember her visiting Adyar in 1935', quoted in 'Passed over', *Theosophy in Australia*, no 480, August 1952.

196 This display, which also included many objects and antiques, was connected with the golden jubilee programme of the Forman Christian College in Lahore. See 'College', *Civil & Military Gazette*, Lahore, 19 December 1936, p 8.

197 The Punjab Literary League brought together artists and other intellectuals for informal groups and salon gatherings where debates on art and aesthetics were undertaken. The group was founded by AC Woolner, the vice-chancellor of the University of Punjab. Jagtej Kaur Grewal reveals that the 'league played a significant role in enlivening the cultural scene in Lahore patronizing poets as well as visual and performing artists'. See Jagtej Kaur Grewal, 'Articulating a landscape for art: the works of Roop Krishna', *Proceedings of the Indian History Congress*, vol 75, 2014, pp 737, 741, viewed 2 April 2024, http://www.jstor.org/stable/44158455. The avant-garde Hungarian Indian artist Amrita Sher-Gil, who studied for six years in Paris, was in Lahore at the same time as Carrick. Sher-Gil returned to India in 1934, and in 1937 held a solo exhibition in Lahore at Faletti's Hotel. A reception in honor of Miss Amrita Sher-Gil was held at the Punjab Literary League club house on 30 November 1937. See P Foulda, 'Amrita Sher-Gil and Indian art', *Civil & Military Gazette*, 7 November 1935, p 15; and 'Reception to Miss A. Sher-Gil', *Civil & Military Gazette*, 28 November 1937, p 6.

198 Roop Krishna trained for three years at the Royal College of Art, South Kensington, London where he met his wife Mary Oldfield, who was born in West Ealing.

199 'Art exhibition in Lahore: work of Ethel Carrick', *Civil & Military Gazette*, 25 December 1936, p 9.

200 See Susannah De Vries, *Ethel Carrick Fox: travels and triumphs of a post-impressionist*, Pandanus Books, 1997, p 109.

201 Maureen Tweedy, who became a travel writer in the 1930s, married Hubert Evans in 1946 after she was widowed. Carrick's painting *Deputy Commissioner's garden Agra, India*, was passed down through his family before being gifted to the Art Gallery of South Australia.

202 Maureen Tweedy, *A label around my neck*, T Dalton, Lavenham, England, 1976, p 41. Carrick undertook a commission for poster designs from the Indian railways, as other women, such as Dorothy Newsome and Kathleen Nixon, had before her.

203 Harry Bennett, 'She still paints in oils at 77', *News*, 3 October 1949, p 4.

204 With thanks to Rebecca Blake for this information. See also Grace Knoche (theosophist), 'The mystic pilgrimage to Amarnath', *The Theosophical Path*, vol 20, January–June 1921, pp 566–76, viewed 14 May 2024, https://babel.hathitrust.org/cgi/pt?id=mdp.39015082585194&seq=602&q1=Amarnath. There were also several Australian articles on the pilgrimage, such as Miss CN Zujtshi MA, 'A journey to holy Amarnath', *Voice*, 1 February 1947, p 3.

205 Bennett, p 4.

206 See 'Visiting artist worker for Free French cause', *The Courier-Mail*, 18 September 1941, p 9.

207 'A housewife's paradise,' *Queensland Country Life*, 2 October 1941, p 6.

A continuing circle: 1939–1952

208 See Jone Johnson Lewis, 'Annie Besant, Heretic: the story of Annie Besant: Minister's wife to atheist to theosophist', *ThoughtCo*, viewed June 2024, https://www.thoughtco.com/annie-besant-heretic-3529122.

209 The report goes on to describe Carrick as 'widow of the first Australian artist to be elected a member of the Societe Nationale des Beaux-Arts (New Salon), and herself a distinguished painter.' 'The life of Melbourne: well-known painter returns', *The Argus*, 23 October 1939, p 7.

210 Ethel Carrick, letter, 'Delgetti' Park Street, South Yarra, 19 June 1940, Papers of Sybil Craig, box 40/6, MS13111, State Library of Victoria, Naarm/Narrm/Melbourne.

211 'Unique art union', *The Age*, 16 July 1940, p 10.

212 Ethel Phillips Fox, letter to Sybil Craig, 30 December 1940, Papers of Sybil Craig, box 40/6, MS13111, State Library of Victoria, Naarm/Narrm/Melbourne.

213 Also see additional quote: 'Mrs E. Phillips Fox, widow of the internationally famous Australian artist, and herself an artist of distinction under the title of Carrick Fox is a keen worker for the Free French cause. Mrs Fox, who is paying her first visit to Brisbane although she has been to Australia five times before, did a great deal of patriotic work in France during the last war. The Free French movement, she said, was receiving a great deal of support from the artistic community in Melbourne. She recently conducted an art union and exhibition of paintings by well-known artists, including a number by her late husband. By this means 300 was raised to assist the cause for General de Gaulle.' Cited from 'Visiting artist worker for Free French cause', *The Courier-Mail*, 18 September 1941, p 9.

214 Ethel Phillips Fox, letter to Sybil Craig, The Manor, Iluka Road, Mosman New South Wales, 30 December 1940, Papers of Sybil Craig, box 40/6, MS13111, State Library of Victoria, Naarm/Narrm/Melbourne.

215 Letter from Ethel Phillips Fox [Ethel Carrick] to Sybil Craig, September 1941, Papers of Sybil Craig, box 40/6, MS13111, State Library of Victoria, Naarm/Narrm/Melbourne.

216 'A housewife's paradise', *Queensland Country Life,* 2 October 1941, p 6.

217 'What people—are doing', *The Canberra Times*, 28 October 1942, p 4.

218 Patricia Tillyard was not awarded her degree at the time on account of her gender. Tillyard noted the need for a university in Canberra and advocated for the education of women. See 'Grand Dame of Canberra dies', *The Canberra Times*, 11 March 1971, p 8; 'Women who win profession equality', *The Canberra Times,* 16 January 1967, p 2.

219 Patricia Tillyard played a leading role in the developing city of Canberra from her arrival in 1928 with her husband Dr Robin Tillyard, a distinguished entomologist who had been appointed to establish one of the first CSIRO units in Canberra. She also did the illustrations for a number of his books, which included *Insects of Australia and New Zealand,* 1926. Sadly Robin Tillyard, who was both a scientist and an advocate of spiritualism, died in a car accident in 1937.

220 'As the federal capital grew around the little village church it was transformed from a country parish into one that reflected the power and influence of many of its parishioners, including Governor Generals and politicians.' Dr Malcom Allbrook, 'The tales of Canberra's oldest church', *ANU Reporter,* nd, viewed 4 April 2024, https://www.anu.edu.au/news/all-news/the-tales-of-canberras-oldest-church.

221 *Advance Australia* was a monthly magazine organised by the theosophist George Arundale, published from 1926 to 1929.

222 Canberra Museum + Gallery, *Colonnades of Canberra's civic centre* c 1943, viewed 14 May 2024, cmag.com.au/collection/items/colonnades-of-canberra-s-civic-centre/catalogue.

223 Ethel Carrick, letter to Sybil Craig, c/o Mrs Tillyard, Mugga Way, Red Hill, Canberra, Australian Capital Territory, 22 May 1943, Papers of Sybil Craig, box 40/6, MS13111, State Library of Victoria, Naarm/Narrm/Melbourne.

224 Given this correspondence, the painting can confidently be dated to the autumn months of 1943. 'What people—are doing', *The Canberra Times*, 28 April 1943, p 4.

225 The services club was also known as the Lady Gowrie Club for Servicemen and Women, or colloquially as The Hut.

226 It has been estimated that over one million meals were served there during the war years, staffed by volunteers, including 500 women. ACT Heritage Council, *Background information: Canberra Services Club*, October 2014, p 1, viewed 14 May 2024, https://www.environment.act.gov.au/__data/assets/pdf_file/0011/717176/Draft-Canberra-Services-Club-Background-Information-HCM-9.4.15.pdf.

227 Bronwyn J Hanna, *Absence and presence: a historiography of early women architects in New South Wales*, PhD dissertation, University of New South Wales, Gadigal Nura/Sydney, 1999.

228 Patience Wardle, 'The Spinney, 2 Mugga Way, Red Hill', *Australian Garden History*, vol 30, no 3, January 2019, p 22.

229 Wardle, p 22.

230 See Catherine Speck's essay in this publication. Carrick applied to be an official war artist and she also stored works at the memorial while trying to find a location for her show. A while after her visit to Canberra in 1943, Carrick wrote to Sybil Craig: 'My pictures are in Canberra—but I still have to find a place in which to show them so I'm going up shortly for a couple of days & hope to finalise matters—then when I know when Parliament will reassemble.'

231 'Art displays: facilities lacking in Canberra', *The Canberra Times*, 8 September 1944, p 2.

232 'Artist's tribute', *The Age*, 9 February 1944, p 3.

233 'Three combine in art show', *The Herald*, 20 November 1944, p 7.

234 'Art exhibition', *The Age*, 21 November 1944, p 5.

235 Ethel Phillips Fox, letter to Sybil Craig, 70 Pitt St, nd, Papers of Sybil Craig, box 40/6, MS13111, State Library of Victoria, Naarm/Narrm/Melbourne.

236 Ethel Carrick, letter to Sybil Craig, 443 Bourke St, 2 January 1946, Papers of Sybil Craig, box 40/6, MS13111, State Library of Victoria, Naarm/Narrm/Melbourne.

237 Dame Mary Gilmore, diary entry, 1948, p 405, Diaries of Dame Mary Gilmore, 1940–49, NLA MS 614, National Library of Australia, Kamberri/Canberra.

238 Dame Mary Gilmore, diary entry, 16 September 48, p 448, Diaries of Dame Mary Gilmore, 1940–49.

239 Dame Mary Gilmore, diary entry, 5 July 48, p 352, Diaries of Dame Mary Gilmore, 1940–49.

240 'Women's interests', *The Mail,* 1 October 1949, p 37.

241 'Women's news', *The Sydney Morning Herald*, 15 March 1945, p 6.

242 Ethel Carrick, letter to Hal Missingham, Director of the Art Gallery of New South Wales, 18 October 1948, Emanuel Phillips Fox curatorial file, Art Gallery of New South Wales, Gadigal Nura/Sydney.

243 'Artist drops in on Brisbane bound for France', *The Telegraph*, 25 February 1950, p 7.

244 *Introduction to comparative mysticism* was first published in 1944 and republished in 1949. As Rebecca Blake notes, Carrick was friends with Jacques de Marquette's mother, Madame Emma de Marquette, who she worked with on the Overseas French Homes project and who she also possibly went to Dax with, as they were there at the same time. See Jacques de Marquette's autobiography, *Confessions d'un Mystique Contemporain*, Panharmonie, Paris, 1965, p 82.

245 Ethel Carrick, letter to Ola Cohn, 65 Boulevard Arago, Paris XIII, 26 August 1951, Papers of Ola Cohn 1912—64, MS8506, State Library of Victoria, Naarm/Narrm/Melbourne.

246 Ethel Carrick, letter to Ola Cohn.

247 It would appear that she had recently sold her Boulevard Arago apartment.

248 Ethel Carrick, letter to Ola Cohn.

249 Ethel Carrick, letter to Irene [Renée] Fox, 25 October 1951, Len Fox Papers 1852–2001, MLMSS8085, State Library of New South Wales, Gadigal Nura/Sydney.

250 Janet Bomford, *Circles of friendship: the centenary history of the Lyceum Club*, Lyceum Club, Melbourne, 2012, p 115.

251 Hilda Carrick, letter to Irene [Renée] Fox, 8 July 1952, Len Fox Papers 1852–2001.

252 'Death of well-known artist', *Advertiser*, 20 June 1952, p 10.

Seeking sunlight: Carrick and Fox's artistic marriage

1 Wedding notice for E Phillips and Ethel Carrick Fox, *The British Australian*, 11 May 1905, p 621. *British Australian and New Zealand Mail*, May–June 1905, p 621.

2 The 137th exhibition of the Royal Academy of Arts, London, 1905, catalogue numbers 145 and 208.

3 Juliette Peers, 'Theodosia Anderson (1858–1933)', in *Into the light, recovering Australia's lost women artists 1870–1960: Into the Light Donor Circle Acquisitions,* Sheila Foundation Limited, Perth and Sydney, 2021, p 37, viewed 21 May 2024, https://sheila.org.au/wp-content/uploads/2023/03/Into-the-Light-Donor-Circle-Acquisitions-2021_WEB.pdf.

4 Hilary Taylor, '"If a young painter be not fierce and arrogant God ... help him": some women students at the Slade, c. 1895–9', *Art History,* vol 9, no 2, 1986, p 234.

5 Emanuel Phillips Fox, letter to HP Gill, 23 October 1908, Art Gallery of South Australia, Tarntanya/Adelaide.

6 Emanuel Phillips Fox, letter to Hans Heysen, 13 September 1911, Papers of Hans Heysen, MS5073, National Library of Australia, Kamberri/Canberra.

7 Fox, letter to Hans Heysen, 13 September 1911.

8 The first work—*The bathing hour* 1909, oil on canvas, 180 × 112 cm—is in the collection of the Castlemaine Art Museum, Dja Dja Wurrung Country/Castlemaine and the second—*Bathing hour (L'heure du bain)* c 1909, oil on canvas, 183.5 x 113.3 cm—is in the collection of the Queensland Art Gallery | Gallery of Modern Art, Meeanjin/Brisbane.

9 Ruth Zubans, *E. Phillips Fox: his life and art*, Miegunyah Press, Melbourne, 1995, p 159.

10 Virginia Spate, 'Nature and artifice: Emanuel Phillips Fox *Bathing hour*', in Lynne Seear and Julie Ewington (eds), *Brought to light: Australian art 1850–1965*, Queensland Art Gallery, Brisbane, 1998. Edited extract from Queensland Art Gallery | Gallery of Modern Art, nd, viewed 21 May 2024, https://blog.qagoma.qld.gov.au/emanuel-phillips-fox-the-culture-of-the-beach-bathing-hour.

11 Len Fox, *E Phillips Fox and his family*, Len Fox, Sydney, 1985, p 116.

12 Zubans, p 143; also see footnote 79, p 200.

13 Mary Eagle, *The oil paintings of E. Phillips Fox in the National Gallery of Australia*, National Gallery of Australia, Canberra, 1997, p 54.

14 Ursula Prunster, 'From Empire's end: Australians as Orientalists, 1880–1920', in Roger Benjamin (ed), *Orientalism: Delacroix to Klee*, Art Gallery of New South Wales, Sydney, 1997, p 52.

15 John Pigot, *Capturing the Orient: Hilda Rix Nicholas and Ethel Carrick in the East*, Waverley City Gallery, Melbourne, 1992, p 5.

16 'I want to lay stress on his work, which is so much the greater, my work is nothing in comparison with his.' Ethel Carrick quoted in Elizabeth Leigh, 'Life in pictures: Mrs Phillips Fox and her art', *Register*, 14 July 1925, p 4.

17 As Georgina Downey has pointed out, the Foxes and their circle 'found subjects in a cosmopolitan space that often transcended notions of national identity'. Georgina Downey, 'Cosmopolitans and expatriates', in *Art, love and life: Ethel Carrick and E Phillips Fox*, Queensland Art Gallery | Gallery of Modern Art, Brisbane, 2011, p 61.

Sensations of Summer: Carrick's French beach resort paintings

1 Emanuel Phillips Fox, letter to Hans Heysen, 13 September 1911, Papers of Hans Heysen, MS5073, National Library of Australia, Kamberri/Canberra.

2 *High tide at St Malo* was first exhibited at the Société Nationale des Beaux-Arts in April 1912, and *The quay at Dinard* at the Salon d'Automne in October 1912. Carrick first exhibited these paintings with the French titles *La marée haute à Saint-Malo* and *Sur le quai à Dinard*.

3 Ethel Carrick, letter to GVF Mann, Director, Art Gallery of New South Wales, 4 December 1913, Ethel Carrick curatorial files, Art Gallery of New South Wales, Gadigal Nura/Sydney.

4 See Simon Ives, 'High tide for the Belle Époque', *Look*, July 2010, pp 15–17.

5 James Gleeson, *Impressionist painters 1881–1930*, Lansdowne Press, Melbourne, 1971, p 114.

6 'Mrs E. P. Fox's paintings', *The Argus*, 11 July 1913, p 5; 'Pictures for the home, Mrs Phillips Fox's exhibition', *The Sydney Morning Herald*, 7 November 1913, p 7.

Light in the landscape: Carrick in North Africa

1 'Figure paintings: the Fox pictures', *Daily Telegraph*, 1 October 1925, p 7.

2 'Art exhibition. Some Phillips Fox pictures', *The Sydney Morning Herald*, 1 October 1925, p 10.

3 Edith Wharton, *In Morocco*, Charles Scribner's Sons, New York, 1920, p vii.

4 Derek Gregory, 'Scripting Egypt', in James Duncan and Derek Gregory (eds), *Writes of passage: reading travel writing*, Routledge, London and New York, 1999, p 119.

5 Roger Benjamin, Emilio Escoriza and Emma Kindred, 'Tom Roberts and Friends at the Alhambra', *Australian and New Zealand Journal of Art*, vol 15, no 1, 2015, pp 52–74.

6 See Emma Kindred, *Passages through the Orient: Arthur Streeton in Cairo*, PhD dissertation, The University of Sydney, Gadigal Nura/Sydney, 2012; Emma Kindred 'Souvenir and source: Arthur Streeton's Cairo through the lens', *emaj (electronic Melbourne art journal)*, vol 8, 14 April 2015; Emma Kindred, '"Some of the Cairo brightness": Arthur Streeton's Egyptian sojourn', in Wayne Tunnicliffe (ed), *Streeton*, Art Gallery of New South Wales, Sydney, 2020.

7 See J Hoorn, *Hilda Rix Nicholas and Elsie Rix's Moroccan idyll: art and Orientalism*, Miegunyah Press, Melbourne, 2013.

8 See *The Sydney Morning Herald,* 20 September 1890, p 65; *The Telegraph,* 8 January 1891, p 68.

9 WM, 'Artists' preferences—"The snake charmer" a favorite', *Daily Telegraph,* 1 July 1922, p 11.

10 Lionel Lindsay met the artist during his own visit in 1929. See Roger Benjamin, 'Lionel Lindsay's Maghreb', forthcoming in 2025.

11 Roger Benjamin, *Renoir and Algeria*, Yale University Press, New Haven and London, 2003, p 12.

12 Georges Lafenestre, 'Les Salons de 1890', *Revue des Deux Mondes*, vol 3, Paris, 1890, p 925, quoted in Roger Benjamin (ed), *Orientalism: Delacroix to Klee*, Art Gallery of New South Wales, Sydney, 1997, p 129.

13 Grace Joel, 'Australian artists in London: a reminiscence', *Art & Architecture*, vol 3, no 3, May–June 1906, p 99. 'It is highly unlikely Fox went to Morocco, which would normally mean travel to one of the royal capitals of Fez, Marrakesh or Meknes; c 1906 the country was in turmoil and few Europeans went to those places outside a military context. In 1907 the massacre of part of the small Euro population in Fez intensified the French military push to annexe Morocco.' Roger Benjamin, correspondence with the author, 2024.

14 'Australians in London', *The Sydney Morning Herald,* 9 May 1906, p 5.

15 Nadia Erzini and Stephen Vernoit, 'The palanquin thrones of the Alawite Sultans of Morocco', *Muqarnas Online*, vol 39, no 1, 2000, pp 289–316, viewed 2 March 2024, https://doi.org/10.1163/22118993-00391P12.

16 See John Pigot, *Capturing the Orient: Hilda Rix Nicholas & Ethel Carrick in the East*, Waverley City Gallery, Melbourne, 1993; Andrew Yip, 'Some settled sunlight: the Foxes in the Orient', in Angela Goddard (ed), *Art, love and life: Ethel Carrick and E Phillips Fox*, Queensland Art Gallery | Gallery of Modern Art, Brisbane, 2011.

17 Ethel Carrick quoted in 'Distinguished woman artist Mrs E. Phillips Fox. Painter of crowds', *Sun*, 9 November 1913, p 19.

18 Karl Baedeker, *The Mediterranean: seaports and sea routes, including Madeira, the Canary Islands, the Coast of Morocco, Algeria, and Tunisia*, Leipzig, 1911, p 270.

19 Emanuel Phillips Fox, letter to Hans Heysen, Papers of Hans Heysen, MS50723/1/319A, National Library of Australia, Kamberri/Canberra.

20 'Mrs E.P. Fox's paintings! Sand and sound impressionism', *The Argus,* 11 July 1913, p 5.

21 'Rare pictures. E. Phillips Fox', *The Newsletter*, 29 November 1913, p 5.

22 'Rare pictures. E. Phillips Fox', p 5.

23 'Rare pictures. E. Phillips Fox', p 5.

24 John Foster Fraser, *The land of veiled women: wanderings in Algeria, Tunisia & Morocco*, Cassell, London and New York, 1913, p 1.

25 Fraser, p 2.

26 'Rare pictures. E. Phillips Fox', p 5.

27 Baedeker, p 270.

28 Carrick's oil sketch for *Arab's bargaining* measures 38.2 × 46.2 cm. The canvas bears the stamp of Melbourne-based art-supplier W & G Dean.

29 Fox, letter to Hans Heysen.

30 Catherine Nunn, '"Less slick and not so clever": the materials and techniques of the Foxes', in Goddard (ed), 2011.

31 'Mr E. Phillips Fox', *The Argus*, 21 May 1913.

32 Fox, letter to Hans Heysen.

33 Fox, letter to Hans Heysen.

34 'Sane and sound impression', *The Argus*, 11 July 1913, p 5.

35 See Clifford Geertz, Hildred Geertz, Lawrence Rosen, *Meaning and order in Moroccan society: three essays in cultural analysis,* Cambridge University Press, Cambridge, 1979, p 235.

36 Jack Cowart, Pierre Schneider & John Elderfield, *Matisse in Morocco: the paintings and drawings, 1912–13,* National Gallery of Art, Washington, DC, & Harry N. Abrams, Inc., New York, p 64.

37 'Rare pictures. E. Phillips Fox', *The Newsletter*, 29 November 1913, p 5.

38 *Bradshaw's through routes to the capitals of the world and overland guide to India, Persia, and the Far East*, Henry Blacklock & Co., London, 1903, p 376–77.

39 'Distinguished woman artist Mrs E. Phillips Fox. Painter of crowds', *Sun*, 9 November 1913, p 19.

40 Violet Teague, 'Picture exhibition. E. Phillips Fox's art', *The Herald*, 21 June 1913, p 1.

41 'Life and pictures. Mrs Phillips Fox and her art', *Register*, 14 July 1925, p 4.

42 Baedeker, p 373. Named after General Saussier during the French colonial period, the street is known today as Avenue Habib Bourguiba.

43 Benjamin, *Orientalism*, p 149; Frances E Nesbitt, *Algeria and Tunis: painted and described*, A & C Black, London, 1906, p 211.

44 Nesbitt, p 211.

45 Peppercorn trees, genus *Scinus*, were likely planted by French authorities in the late nineteenth century to give shelter to Europeans unused to the harsh sunlight. Roger Benjamin, correspondence with the author, 2024.

46 Baedeker, p 373, cited in Nesbitt, p 212.

47 Roger Benjamin, *Orientalist aesthetics: art, colonialism and French North Africa 1880–1930*, University of California Press, Berkeley, 2003, p 40.

48 Henri Saladin, *Tunis et Kairouan*, H. Laurens, Paris, 1908, p 131.

49 'Art exhibition. Some Phillips Fox pictures', *The Sydney Morning Herald*, 1 October 1925, p 10.

50 Art exhibition. Some Phillips Fox pictures', p 10.

51 *The Australian Women's Weekly*, 4 March 1950, p 19.

52 I am grateful to Professor Roger Benjamin for his assistance identifying many of the sites in Carrick's paintings. This research was conducted with the support of the Australian Research Council grant 'Art and Cultural Exchange at the Strait of Gibraltar' [DP200103334], in which I am Partner Investigator.

Aladdin's lamp for the artist: the Sydney summer of 1913

1 'A distinguished woman painter', *The Daily Telegraph*, 15 August 1913, p 15.

2 RMS Omrah Passenger List, 26 September 1916.

3 'A distinguished woman painter', p 15.

4 'A distinguished woman painter', p 15.

5 'The world and his wife', *Sunday Times*, 23 November 1913, p 7.

6 'Will you tell me? Answers to questions asked by correspondents', *The World's News*, 21 December 1907, p 18.

7 'Mainly about people', *The Daily News*, 15 May 1922, p 6.

8 Ethel Carrick, letter to Hal Missingham, aboard the MS *Surriento*, 22 February 1950, Ethel Carrick curatorial file, Art Gallery of New South Wales, Gadigal Nura/Sydney.

9 'Mrs Phillips Fox', *The Lone Hand,* vol 13, no 79, 1 November 1913, p xxxvi.

10 'A woman's letter', *The Bulletin*, vol 34, no 1761, 13 November 1913, p 18.

11 Emanuel Phillips Fox, letter to William Henry Gill, Redcourt, Cremorne, Sydney, 5 November 1913, William Henry Papers, MS285/2, Mitchell Library, State Library of New South Wales, Gadigal Nura/Sydney.

12 Note that different beaches had different cut-off times for bathing. For example, in Waverley daylight swimming was banned between the hours of 8am and 8pm.

13 'Controlling ordinances gazetted: a neck-to-knee costume', *The Daily Telegraph*, 23 January 1908, p 9.

14 'The sun bath: strong measures contemplated', *The Daily Telegraph*, 15 December 1911, p 11.

15 Agnes Rebecca Rose-Soley, 'The Australian girl: after many years', *The Queen*, 24 September 1910, p 27.

16 'Distinguished woman artist', *The Sun*, 9 November 1913, p 19.

17 In an unpublished biography on Ethel Carrick Fox by her nephew-in-law, Len Fox wrote, 'I have learnt to look on Ethel as a leading artist, a gracious person, a rebel in many ways and a pioneer.' His older sister, Louise Porker, paralleled this, writing, 'I understand that she was the rebel of her family, and longed for more freedom.' Len Fox Papers, MLMSS 8085, Mitchell Library, State Library of New South Wales, Gadigal Nura/Sydney.

18 'Social gossip', *The Sun*, 14 December 1913, p 20.

19 'Social gossip', *Punch*, 18 December 1913, p 23.

20 'A woman's letter', *The Bulletin*, 18 December 1913, p 18.

21 'Harassing the bathers', *The Sun*, 21 November 1913, p 1.

22 The revised title is from new primary research revealing that the work Carrick donated to the Manly Art Gallery & Museum, and exhibited at the 1927 Exposition Internationale des Beaux-Arts de la Ville de Bordeaux, was originally titled *Christmas Day on Manly Beach*. See Ethel Phillips Fox, letter to Sir [Director of Manly Art Gallery], Lyceum Club, Melbourne, 7 February 1934, Ethel Carrick curatorial file, Manly Art Gallery & Museum, Gadigal Nura/Sydney; 'Social chatter', *Sunday Times*, 20 November 1927, p 15.

23 'Beauty on the beach', *The Prahran Telegraph*, 12 October 1912, p 7.

24 'Undressing on the beach', *The Daily Telegraph*, 3 January 1917, p 8.

25 Carrick had intended to exhibit her Manly paintings at the Salon d'Automne in Paris. See 'Men and women. Some personal paragraphs', *The Sun*, 25 November 1913, p 5.

26 'Social chatter', *Sunday Times*, 20 November 1927, p 15; see exhibition catalogue for Exposition Internationale des Beaux-Arts de la Ville de Bordeaux, 15 June – 15 August 1927.

27 Ethel Phillips Fox, letter to Sir [Director of Manly Art Gallery], Lyceum Club, Melbourne, 7 February 1934.

The Theosophical Society as a wellspring of inspiration

1 Alfred de Musset, *La coupe et les lèvres*, 1833, in Philippe Van Tieghem, *Musset oeuvres complètes*, Aux Éditions du Seuil, Paris, 1963, p 100. 'Mon verre n'est pas grand mais je bois dans mon verre' is quoted in Ethel Carrick, *Paintings by Mrs E Phillips Fox (Miss Ethel Carrick)*, exhibition catalogue, Guild Hall, Melbourne, 1913. Quote translated by the author.

The relevant section reads:

I do not usually pay much attention to the critics.
They are only insects and rarely sting.
They told me last year I imitated Byron:
You who know me recognise that this is not the case
I hate plagiarism like the plague;
My glass is not large, but I drink from my glass
While there is no honour today in being an honest man
I am certainly no grave robber.

In its original French:

Je ne fais pas grand cas, pour moi de la critique.
Toute mouche qu'elle est, c'est rare qu'elle picque.
On m'a dit l'an passé que j'imitais Byron:
Vous qui me connaissez, vous savez bien que non.
Je hais comme la mort l'état de plagiaire;
Mon verre n'est pas grand mais je bois dans mon verre.
C'est bien peu je le sais, que d'être homme de bien,
Mais toujours est-il vrai que je n'exhume rien.

2 Please note that in this essay capitalisation of Theosophy indicates a reference to the specific teachings and practices of the Theosophical Society rather than more general theosophical study.

3 Jennifer McFarlane, *Concerning the spiritual: the influence of the Theosophical Society on Australian artists: 1890–1934*, Australian Scholarly Publishing, North Melbourne, 2012 (based on author's own doctoral research, 2006, viewed June 2024, https://scholarly.info/book/concerning-the-spiritual-the-influence-of-the-theosophical-society-on-australian-artists-1890-1934/). While I am not a Theosophist, I find the Society's engagement with the arts an exciting area of research. See also Maurice Tuchman (ed), *The spiritual in art: abstract painting 1890–1985*, Los Angeles County Museum of Art, Abbeville Press Inc, Los Angeles, 1986; and Jennifer Higgie, *The other side: a journey into women, art and the spirit world*, Hachette Australia, Sydney, 2023

4 See the membership records of the Theosophical Society in Adyar, consulted by the author in April 2002.

Carrick's attendance at The Star Camp at Castle Eerde in Ommen, Holland in in 1927 and 1929 was recorded in 'Society', *The Sun*, 28 Aug 1927, p 4; and 'Australian artists in Paris', *The British Australian and New Zealander*, 11 July 1929, p 10. Carrick exhibited a painting of Castle Eerde in her solo exhibition at Galerie de la Palette Française, 5–19 June 1928, see 'Australians abroad,' *Sunday Times*, 5 August 1928, p 20. I would like to thank Rebecca Blake for kindly sharing this research into Carrick's attendances at Ommen.

Carrick also attended the Diamond Jubilee Convention in Adyar in 1935 as part of a contingent of eight people from the French section (*Bulletin Theosophique*, January 1935, p 45) and was again in India, Kashmir in 1939 (see 'Canberra paintings by Mrs Phillips Fox', *Canberra Times*, 7 September 1944, p 2). Theosophical Society membership records gave her address as The Manor on the 11 November 1940. This changed on 11 April 1947 when she transferred to Blavatsky Lodge in Melbourne, returning to The Manor on 24 September 1948. Carrick left money to various Theosophical organisations on her death.

5 Jill Roe, *Beyond belief: Theosophy in Australia 1879–1939*, New South Wales University Press, Sydney, 1986, p 185.
Note: this was re-published as Jill Roe, *Searching for the spirit – Theosophy in Australia, 1879–1939*, Marian Quartly (ed), Wakefield Press, Adelaide, 2020.

6 Mary Lutyens, *Krishnamurti: the years of awakening*, J. Murray, London, 1975, p 191.

7 Fox's own spiritual background included Mormon and Jewish inheritances. See Angela Goddard, *Art, love and life: Ethel Carrick & E Phillips Fox,* exhibition catalogue, Queensland Art Gallery | Gallery of Modern Art, Brisbane, 2011, p 146.

8 'Mrs E Phillips Fox returns', *Herald*, 4 April 1925, p 12.

9 Sébastien Clerbois, 'In search of the Forme-pensée: the influence of Theosophy on Belgian artists, between Symbolism and the avant-garde (1890–1910)', *Nineteenth-Century Art Worldwide: A Journal of Nineteenth-Century Visual Culture*, no 2, 2002, viewed 28 July 2024, 19thc-artworldwide.org/index.php/autumn02/259-in-search-of-the-forme-pensee-the-influence-of-theosophy-on-belgian-artists-between-symbolism-and-the-avant-garde-1890-1900.

10 Clerbois, p 68.

11 McFarlane, p 78.

12 Jonathan Fineberg, 'The history and character of Les Tendances Nouvelles', in *Les Tendances Nouvelles*: *Organe officiel illustre de l'Union internationale des beaux-arts, des lettres, des sciences et de l'industrie,* Da Capo Press, New York, 1980, p xxi.

13 Chabas's studio in 1900 was a meeting place for Maeterlink, Eduard Schuré, Leon Bloy, Camille Flammarion, Joséphin Péladan and René Guénon, whose writings would be important for Australian poet Harold Stewart. Péladan would later publish reviews as 'Sâr Merodack' in the Theosophical journal *Lotus Bleu* in 1895. The sculptor Antoine Bourdelle (1861–1929) was also a participant in the Rose + Croix salons and would, like many of his colleagues from this time, be significant in the Theosophical Society in the early years of the twentieth century.

14 For a full listing of this 53-member artist's cooperative salon see Jonathon Fineberg, *Kandinsky in Paris 1906–1907*, UMI Research Press, Ann Arbour, 1984, p 57, note 6.

15 Kandinsky's engagement with Theosophical concepts in Paris anticipates the more conventional 1908 dating of his mature abstract work. See Sixten Ringbom, 'Transcending the visible: The generation of abstract pioneers', in Tuchman, pp 131–53.

16 Fineberg, 1980, p xix.

17 Thanks to the National Gallery of Australia research team for this information.

18 Fineberg, 1984, p 71.

19 Claude Rozern, 'Quatre artistes', in *Les Tendances Nouvelles*, pp 673–74.

20 Finally published in 1914. See Fineberg, 1984, p 63.

21 The original French reads: 'la determination du mouvement relatif des formes et du mouvement absolu de la vie.' Alexis Mérodack-Jeanneau, 'Le Synthéthisme', *Les Tendances Nouvelles*, vol 62, 1914, p 1536. Quote translated by the author.

22 Fineberg, 1980, p xvii.

23 Emanuel Phillips Fox, letter to Harry Pelling Gill, 23 October 1908, quoted in Ruth Zubans, *E. Phillips Fox: his life and art*, Miegunyah Press, Melbourne, 1995, p 180.

24 Emanuel Phillips Fox, letter to Laura Fox, 28 December 1906, quoted in Zubans, p 179.

25 Gérard Mäesse, 'Review of the Salon d'Automne', *Les Tendances Nouvelles*, vol 39, 1908, p 834: 'Miss Ethel Carrick's work in this exhibition has attracted critical acclaim. Her paintings have been compared to bouquets of flowers; her work could not be more true or enchanting. The touching modesty of the artist conceals a true science in her way of seeing, in the juxtaposition of her brushstrokes, and in her grasp of the whole.' Quote translated by the author. In its original French: '*Mlle Ethel Carrick fait l'enthousiasme des amateurs. On a comparé ses tableaux a des bouquets de fleurs. Rien de plus juste et de plus aimable que cette expression. La modestie timide de l'artiste cache une science vraie de la manière de voir, de juxtaposer les touches et de comprendre.*'

26 Henri Breuil, 'Promenades à travers les Salons (Le Salon Unioniste)', *Les Tendances Nouvelles*, vol 49, 1910, p 1153.

27 MO Maus, *Trente années de lutte pour l'art: Les Vignt 1884–1893; La Libre Esthétique 1894–1914*, Librairie l'oiseau bleu, Brussels, 1926, p 395.

28 Maus, p 400. Quote translated by the author.

29 Huntly Carter, 'The spiritualisation of art', *Herald of the Star,* vol 3, no 2, 11 November 1914, pp 624–28. Theosophical journals circulated widely through the organisation; this review of Clive Bell and Kandinsky's books was illustrated with five abstractions by Kandinsky, including *Composition II* 1910.

30 Jessie Platts' good friend was the ardent Theosophist Lady Emily Lutyens, whose sister Constance Lutyens was the celebrated militant suffragette. Marion Phillips, Fox's cousin, was also an active feminist and wrote passionately on Annie Besant's 'great gift to humanity'. Other notable friendships included Violet Teague, Ivy Brookes, Bessie Rischbieth and Dame Mary Gilmore. Many of these women were themselves engaged with the Theosophical Society in one way or another.

31 Edgar Lovell Filmer Platts died in 1917 (1899–1917) and Captain John Carrick Platts died in 1920 (1897–1920). See Jessie Platts, *The witness,* Hutchinson & Co., United Kingdom, 1920. The copy of *The witness* in the Adyar Library is from CW Leadbeater's library.

32 Membership records of the Theosophical Society, consulted by the author in Adyar, April 2002. I would like to thank the Society for opening their archive to me.

33 Maurice Chabas, 'Du rôle sociale de l'art', *The Herald of the Star,* vol 3, no 7, 1914, p 397.

34 Chabas, p 398.

35 Marie Bermond, 'De l'art et de la vie, *Éditions de l'Étoile*, 1932, p 13.

36 Elizabeth Leigh, 'Life and pictures: Mrs Fox and her art', *The Register*, 14 July, 1925, p 4.

37 'Through an artist's eyes, Mrs E. Phillips Fox returns', *The Herald,* 4 April 1925, p 12. I would like to thank Mary Eagle, whose archive enabled me to construct the timeline underpinning this research.

38 The Theosophical Society Convention in Sydney opened on 9 April 1925.

39 Ethel Carrick, *Catalogue of paintings by the late E Phillips Fox and Ethel Carrick (Mrs E Phillips Fox),* exhibition catalogue, South Australia Society of Arts Gallery, Adelaide, 1925.

40 Lionel Lindsay, *Foreword to the catalogue of oil paintings by the late E Phillips Fox and Ethel Carrick (Mrs E Phillips Fox)*, exhibition catalogue, Anthony Hordern & Sons, Sydney, 1925.

41 Anonymous, 'Social gossip', *Sun*, 14 April 1926, p 13.

42 Elements in the foreground of a picture—usually also at the side—used to 'push back' the main scene and increase the sense of depth.

Sorrow and service: Carrick across the two world wars

1 'Through an artist's eyes: Mrs E Phillips Fox returns', *The Herald,* 4 April 1925, p 12.

2 Syvia Yount, *Cecilia Beaux: American figure painter*, University of California Press, Berkeley, 2007, p 182.

3 Anita Callaway, 'Violet Teague and the theatre of war', in *Violet Teague 1872–1951*, Beagle Press, Roseville, New South Wales, 1999, pp 73–81.

4 Ruth Zubans, 'A decade of travel in the life of Ethel Carrick Fox', *Art and Australia*, vol 36, no 1, 1998, p 90.

5 'Artists' War Fund: meeting at Royal Art Society', *The Sydney Morning Herald,* 29 January 1915, p 6; 'Patriotic funds: Artists' Fund', *The Sydney Morning Herald*, 6 March 1915, p 16.

6 'Artists' War Fund', *The Daily Telegraph*, 11 March 1915, p 8.

7 This painting, which has been lost, was exhibited in *Exhibition of oil paintings by Mrs E Phillips Fox*, Anthony Hordern & Sons, Sydney, April 1916.

8 Bertha Merfield was a former student of Fox's. See Zubans, 1998, p 90; Jenny McFarlane, *Concerning the spiritual: the influence of the Theosophical Society on Australian Artists 1890–1934*, Australian Scholarly Publishing, Melbourne, 2012, p 93.

9 The memorial exhibition was titled *Catalogue of pictures of the late E Phillips Fox* and Carrick's 1916 exhibition was titled *Exhibition of oil paintings by Mrs E Phillips Fox*, Anthony Hordern & Sons, Sydney, April 1916.

10 Ethel Phillips Fox, letter to Mrs Brookes, 19 February 1917, Papers of Herbert and Ivy Brookes 1869–1970, MSS1924/1/3/3141, National Library of Australia, Kamberri/Canberra. I am indebted to Rebecca Blake for these letters.

11 See Ruth Zubans, *E. Phillips Fox: his life and art,* Miegunyah Press, Melbourne, 1995, p 165.

12 Elizabeth Nourse quoted in Catherine Speck, *Beyond the battlefield: women artists of the two world wars*, Reaktion, London, 2014, p 44.

13 Penelope Little, *A studio in Montparnasse: Bessie Davidson: an Australian artist in Paris*, Craftsman House, Melbourne, 2001, pp 70–71.

14 Speck, pp 43–44.

15 Carrick, letter to Mrs Brookes, 19 February 1917.

16 See 'Exhibition histories: Ethel Carrick Fox', in Angela Goddard, *Art, love and life: Ethel Carrick and E Phillips Fox*, exhibition catalogue, Queensland Art Gallery | Gallery of Modern Art, Brisbane, 2011, p 162.

17 Ethel Carrick mentions some of these paintings in a letter to Mrs Brookes, 25 February 1919, Papers of Herbert and Ivy Brookes 1869–1970, National Library of Australia, Kamberri/Canberra.

18 William Moore refers to 'the armistice scenes in Paris' on show at Anthony Hordern & Sons, Sydney in 'Figure paintings: the Fox pictures', *The Daily Telegraph*, 1 October 1925, p 7.

19 'The art of Ethel Carrick', *The Age*, 24 May 1933, p 10. The exhibition was shown at Everyman's Lending Library, Collins Street, Melbourne.

20 'War portraits shown', *The Age*, 28 April 1942, p 4. Their joint exhibition was reported as 'one of the most important held in Melbourne for a long time'.

21 This idea was likely inspired by a similar scheme in World War I.

22 'Trees playing their part in our war effort', *The Herald*, 25 March 1940, p 7.

23 'Artists' Red Cross work', *The Herald*, 7 March 1940, p 26.

24 'Visiting artist worker for the Free French cause', *The Courier Mail*, 18 September 1941, p 9.

25 Ethel Carrick exhibited with the Society of Women Artists in London; exhibited with Les Quelques in Paris in 1908, 1909, 1910 and 1911; was the vice president of the Union of Women Painters and Sculptors in Paris; and was a member of the Melbourne Society of Women Painters and Sculptors.

26 Australian War Memorial Registry File 1942–45, AWM93 50/4/2/120, Australian War Memorial, Kamberri/Canberra. I am indebted to Lara Nicholls for sending me this file.

27 War art council memorandum, Australian Archives, A631/1, item 0130/2/1211, pp 4–5. See also Sydney Ure Smith, 'Art in war', *The Sydney Morning Herald*, 27 January 1943, p 5.

28 Both Nora Heysen's and Stella Bowen's appointments were approved in February 1943.

29 Lieutenant Colonel JL Treloar, letter to A Bazley, 14 October 1945, AWM93 205/2/34, Australian War Memorial, Kamberri/Canberra.

30 McFarlane, p 93.

31 William Moore, 'Figure paintings: The Fox pictures', *The Daily Telegraph*, 1 October 1925, p 7; cited in McFarlane, p 92.

32 St Michael's Hall and Flats at 69–71a Hunter St, Sydney was turned into a carparking complex in 1992.

33 'Experts will help you make camouflage nets', *The Sun*, 1 June 1941, p 25; 'Workers wanted to make camouflage nets, valuable war effort', *Yass Tribune*, 15 May 1941, p 1.

34 Patsy Adams-Smith, *Australian Women at War*, Nelson, Melbourne, 1984, p 346.

35 'The knotty problem of camouflage nets', *The Sydney Morning Herald*, 6 May 1941, p 9.

36 Ethel Phillips Fox, letter to Mr Bazley, 18 February 1944, Australian War Memorial Registry File 1942–45, AWM93 50/4/2/120, Australian War Memorial, Kamberri/Canberra.

37 AW Bazley, letter to Mrs Fox, 21 July 1944, AWM93 50/4/2/120, Australian War Memorial, Kamberri/Canberra.

38 'Canberra paintings by Mrs Phillips Fox', *The Canberra Times*, 7 September 1944, p 2; 'Art displays: facilities lacking in Canberra', *The Canberra Times*, 8 September 1944, p 2.

39 Ethel Phillips Fox, letters to Hal Missingham, 13 October 1945 and 6 December 1945, EP Fox file, Art Gallery of New South Wales, Gadigal Nura/Sydney; Ethel Phillips Fox, 'Relief to artist in France', EP Fox file, Art Gallery of New South Wales, Gadigal Nura/Sydney. I am indebted to Rebecca Blake for these letters.

40 'Aiding French artists', *News*, 20 October 1945, p 2.

41 See correspondence in relation to this acquisition in AWM 895/3/101, Australian War Memorial, Kamberri/Canberra. I'm indebted to Lara Nicholls for accessing these files.

Friend, mentor, inspiration: Carrick's impact on Australian women

1 Founded as the Students' Art Club, c 1902; then known as the Woomballano Art Club, 1905; then the Women's Art Club, 1913; then the Melbourne Society of Women Painters, 1930; and finally the Melbourne Society of Women Painters and Sculptors in 1954, and it continues under this title to the present day.

2 This point of view was disseminated widely in the 1990s through high profile sources, most notably Susannah de Vries Evans, *Ethel Carrick Fox: travels and triumphs of a post-impressionist*, Pandanus Books, Brisbane, 1997; and in academic literature such as Elin Howe, 'Ethel Carrick Fox: the cheat or the cheated?', in Mayanne Dever (ed), *Wallflowers and witches: women and culture in Australia, 1910–1945*, University of Queensland Press, Brisbane, 1994, pp 105–14.

Much could be said about the inaccuracies of these interpretations but here is a summary. Firstly, as all of Emanuel Phillips Fox's brothers married outside of their Jewish faith, the idea that religion alienated Carrick from her sisters-in-law or that the family resented her as an outsider to their faith and culture is not tenable.

Secondly, Len Fox and Mona Brand—whose memories of the Fox family were provided via interviews to writers researching Carrick in the 1990s—later verbally retracted and questioned the third-party interpretations of their memories, which somewhat distorted the public record around both Irene Fox and Ethel Carrick. Given that Fox's father was regarded as a ne'er do well and a parasite by Fox's mother's family, who supported his wife and children on the condition that he remained out of contact with them, there were pre-existing tensions in earlier generations of the Fox family.

3 Of course, the major *Australian exhibition of women's work*, 1907—a national and international display of women's art, applied art and other industries and activities at Melbourne's Royal Exhibition Building—was technically on a larger scale, but it could be defined as a separatist event. The reception to honour Carrick, by contrast, conformed to accepted mainstream protocols for celebrating high achieving male artists returning from overseas success.

4 'About people', *The Age*, 11 August 1908, p 7.

5 'Lyceum Club party', *The Australasian*, 9 May 1925, p 48.

6 'About people', p 7.

7 'The life: Melbourne', *The Argus*, 21 June 1949, p 9.

8 'Welcome to Lady Gibson-Carmichael', *Punch*, 13 August 1908, p 27.

9 'Social circle society letter', *The Leader*, 15 August 1905, p 45.

10 See 'Home & society', *Sunday Times*, 16 November 19[illegible]3, p 7. Guests included Miss Gurney and Augustine Sourbeiran, who supported Carrick after Fox's death and with whom she collaborated in wartime charity work. Fox was also honoured at this dinner.

11 An elaborate event, but one that Carrick was unable to attend due to ill health. See 'Art Circle Dinner', *The Sun News*, 21 August 1925, p 18.

12 'Over the teacups', *The Register*, 14 July 1925, p 4.

13 'Women painters', *The Sydney Morning Herald*, 14 October 1925, p 9.

14 'Women's realm', *The Australasian*, 20 May 1933, p 11.

15 'Lyceum Club party', p 48.

16 See Mark Duckworth and John C Gibbs, 'Morris Mondle Phillips (1870–1948)', *Australian dictionary of biography*, National Centre of Biography, Australian National University, Canberra, 1988, viewed June 2024, https://adb.anu.edu.au/biography/phillips-morris-mondle-8037. Also see AS Ellis, 'Constance (Connie) Ellis (1872–1942)', *Australian dictionary of biography*, National Centre of Biography, Australian National University, Canberra, 1981, viewed June 2024, https://adb.anu.edu.au/biography/ellis-constance-connie-6107; Janette Bomford, *Circles of friendship: the centenary history of the Lyceum Club Melbourne*, Australian Scholarly Publishing, 2012, pp 105–06, 108.

17 Juliette Peers, *More than just gumtrees: a personal, social and artistic history of the Melbourne Society of Women Painters and Sculptors*, Melbourne Society of Women Painters and Sculptors in association with Dawn Revival Press, Melbourne, 1993, p 265. Information on Rosetta Phillips collected from relatives, including Dr Archie Samuel Ellis, who consulted with Phillips' British relatives, informs this overview.

18 She published an essay on Israel in the *Trident*. See 'Some Melbourne Monthlies', *The Worker*, 2 July 1908, p 27.

19 'Y.W.C.A. in Paris', *The Daily Telegraph*, 20 October 19[illegible]5, p 6.

20 *New York Herald Tribune* [Paris edition], 25 March 1929, p 5. I am grateful to Rebecca Blake for locating this reference and sharing it. Phillips also had a solo exhibition at the American Arts Club later in the same year. See *British Australasian*, 9 May 1929, p 7 and 'Y.W.C.A. in Paris', *The Daily Telegraph*, 20 October 19[illegible]5, p 6.

21 *Kristallnacht* refers to the night of 9 November 1938, when German Nazis attacked Jewish people and their property. The name, literally translated as 'night of crystal', references the shattered glass left in the streets after these pogroms. The violence continued on 10 November, and in some places for several more days.

22 In conversation, Len Fox emphasised Carrick's awareness of the military and humanitarian danger of Nazism. British relatives of Etta Phillips recalled Carrick encouraging Phillips to leave Paris, saving her from deportation under Vichy France/Nazi rule and subsequent likely death. Carrick herself may have been in danger if she remained in France, but generally couples in mixed marriages were spared the full impact of the Final Solution until the very last months of the war. However, the seizure of Carrick's possessions at La Cité Fleurie on Boulevard Arago indicates that Carrick was certainly officially on the radar of Nazi antisemitism.

23 The latter's half-sister Una Teague also galvanised Violet Teague into a more public profile after the 1920s. Una Teague (and her mother Sybella, Violet Teague's stepmother), were known to Carrick and shared the same public, first-wave feminist energy. Una Teague was active in censorship and intelligence in Britain during World War I and also worked for Scotland Yard. After the war she became deeply involved with the welfare of refugees in eastern Europe and the Balkans and also showed interest in anthropology, especially of Australian First Nation cultures, and maintained links to Strehlow and the Hermannsburg Mission. See 'Una Sybella Teague', *South Australian Museum*, nd, viewed June 2024, https://www.samuseum.sa.gov.au/collection/archives/provenances/aa-322.

24 Ethel Carrick Fox, letter to Irene Fox, 2 January 1952, Len Fox Papers 1852–2001, Mitchell Library, State Library of New South Wales, Gadigal Nura/Sydney.

25 For details of the life and career of Mary Meyer see Juliette Peers, 'Place aux dames: women artists and historical memory', in Joan Kerr and Jo Holder (eds), *Past present: the National women's art anthology*, Craftsman House, North Ryde, 1999, pp 30–31; see also Bomford, pp 58–96.

26 'Miss Ethel A. Stephens', *Australian Town and Country Journal*, 17 September 1892, p 31.

27 See Juliette Peers' biography of Ethel Stephens in *Into the light: recovering Australia's lost women artists 1870–1960*, Sheila Foundation Limited, Perth and Sydney, 2021, viewed June 2024, https://sheila.org.au/wp-content/uploads/2023/03/Into-the-Light-Donor-Circle-Acquisitions-2021_WEB.pdf.

28 'Gossip for women', *The Telegraph,* 27 June 1908, p 4.

29 'Pictures for the home, Mrs Phillips Fox's exhibition, opened by Sir James Fairfax', *The Sydney Morning Herald,* 7 November 1913, p 7.

30 Stephens studied tempera painting overseas; see 'Miss Stephens' paintings', *The Sydney Morning Herald*, 5 May 1911, p 8. This was a medium that Carrick worked in as well, see 'Art circle dinner', *The Sun News,* 21 August 1925, p 18. Stephens would be a pupil of Carrick's in the early 1920s.

31 'For women', *The Daily Telegraph,* 3 January 1917, p 4.

32 See 'Red Cross Society: address by Lady Helen Munro Ferguson', *Kalgoorlie Miner*, 20 August 1914, p 8; 'Red Cross work: what women are doing', *The Sun*, 23 August 1914, p 3.

33 'In society and out', *The Sun*, 27 January 1915, p 3; 'In society and out', *The Sun*, 3 February 1915, p 4.

34 See Peers, 1993, p 25. In a letter from Ethel Carrick to Violet Teague, 8 June 1920, Carrick sent greetings to Teague's father. See also Alfreda Nellie Marcovitch, interviewed by Barbara Blackman, 27 March 1988, sound recording, 6004940, National Library of Australia, Kamberri/Canberra, viewed June 2024, https://catalogue.nla.gov.au/catalog/6004940.

35 'Travellers glad to land in Australia', *The Sun News*, 23 October 1939, p 39.

36 'Artist's tribute: woman war workers in paintings', *The Age*, 9 February 1944, p 3.

37 'Travellers glad to land in Australia', p 39.

38 'Splendid work for Comforts Fund', *The Age*, 25 January 1940, p 3.

39 'Art donations for Red Cross appeal', *The Herald*, 18 March 1940, p 10.

40 'Sculpture on show', *The Argus,* 25 October 1947, p 43.

41 Peers, 1993, pp 112–32, 206–07. For an overview of Ola Cohn's life see Barbara Lemon (ed), *A way with the fairies: the lost story of sculptor Ola Cohn,* RW Strugnell, Melbourne, 2014.

42 Ethel Carrick, letter to Ola Cohn, 6 August 1951, MS 8506 1024/3(b), State Library of Victoria, Naarm/Narrm/Melbourne. Their mutual dislike of extreme avant-garde art could suggest the belief sometimes adopted by those seeking spiritual and ethical values in visual art, that post-war abstraction, especially Abstract Expressionism, was mechanistic, capitalist vacuity. It is perhaps ironic retrospectively, considering the input that theosophy had into the development of non-representational art.

43 National Gallery of Victoria directors Sir Daryl Lindsay and Eric Westbrook and curators Brian Finemore and Jennifer Phipps were personal friends; Bryans organised public lectures for the 1961 loan exhibitions of JMW Turner and William Blake, marking the centenary of the National Gallery of Victoria, and the gallery offered a retrospective at their former Banyule campus in 1982.

44 Jane Sutherland (Jean Parker Sutherland's second cousin) ran art classes, later with the support of her cousin, artist Jean Godlet Sutherland. Since the 1890s, Jane Sutherland encouraged a number of women students to undertake fulltime study at the National Gallery of Victoria Art School, such as Elsie Barlow, Dora Serle and Jo Sweatman.

45 Roger Butler and Charles Nodrum, *Jean P. Sutherland (1902–1978)*, Deutscher Galleries, Melbourne, 1979.

46 Dianne Reilly, 'Sybil Mary Frances Craig (1901–1989)', *Australian dictionary of biography*, National Centre of Biography, Australian National University, Canberra, 2007, viewed June 2024, https://adb.anu.edu.au/biography/craig-sybil-mary-frances-12363.

47 See Ethel Carrick, letter to Mrs Craig, Black Rock, 20 March 1944, YMS 13111, box 40/6, State Library of Victoria, Melbourne. In the letter, Carrick thanks Craig 'for a very happy week spent with Sybil at your delightful cottage'. An undated sheet slipped into the Craig's visitors' book includes a quote from Ruskin by Carrick—see YMS 13111, box 36/4, State Library of Victoria, Naarm/Narrm/Melbourne.

48 See biography of Beatrice Colquhoun in Peers, 1993, pp 32, 208–10 and Peers, 2021, pp 24–33.

Another point of close connection between Carrick and the Colquhoun family was the Theosophical Society, of which two generations of the Colquhoun family were members, as was Beatrice Colquhoun's sister Marion Ferdinando. The Colquhouns were pivotal in organising an art circle for the Melbourne Theosophical Society in the 1910s and 1920s and the Society's Besant Hall in Collins Street hosted art exhibitions in the 1910s, a venture with which the Colquhouns appear to be closely associated.

49 Jenny McFarlane, *A visionary space: Theosophy and an alternative modernism in Australia 1890–1934*, PhD dissertation, Australian National University, Kamberri/Canberra, p 101.

50 See Ethel Carrick, letters to Sybil Craig, nd [c 1940s], State Library of Victoria, Naarm/Narrm/Melbourne. See also a letter from the Colquhoun's (Archibald and Amalie) Bourke Street Studio, 26 December 1945, YMS 13111 box 40/6, 4, State Library of Victoria, Naarm/Narrm/Melbourne.

51 Amalie Sara Colquhoun, *Mrs E Phillips Fox* 1945, oil on canvas 51.1 × 46.2 cm, National Gallery of Victoria, Naarm/Narrm/ Melbourne, viewed June 2024, https://www.artgallery.nsw.gov.au/prizes/archibald/1945/15356/.

52 Alexander Colquhoun 'Australian artists of the past: E. P. Fox', *The Age*, 22 October 1932, p 5.

53 'Melbourne chatter', *The Bulletin*, vol 61, no 3154, 24 July 1940, p 33.

54 Even though current activists tend to no longer regard theosophy as oppositional to imperialism but rather as a variant expression of imperialism.

55 Gilmore followed the Sydney artworld intently in the 1940s and welcomed many artists and other prominent people as visitors to her Sydney flat. See also Peter Edwell, *The Case that Stopped Australia,* Halstead Press, Ultimo, 2021, p 37.

56 Peers, 1993, p 25.

57 Peers, 1993, p 219.

58 Bertha Merfield, letter to Mrs Herbert Brookes, 3 January 1916, MS1924/1/2830, Papers of Herbert and Ivy Brookes, National Library of Australia, Kamberri/Canberra.

59 'Woman's suicide from train', *The Argus*, 30 September 1921, p 8.

60 Kathleen Mangan, in conversation with Juliette Peers, claimed that Merfield was distraught over a love affair with a married colleague, a prominent male artist of the day.

61 'Arts and Crafts Society', *The Age*, 21 March 1908, p 14.

62 Ros Pesman, *Duty free: Australian women abroad*, Oxford University Press, Melbourne, 1996, pp 1–17.

Exhibition history

This list includes all exhibitions known to feature Ethel Carrick's work during her lifetime and selected notable posthumous exhibitions, including two retrospectives. Often the group that have held the exhibition rather than an official exhibition name is listed.

Solo exhibitions

1908
Bernard's Gallery, Naarm/Narrm/Melbourne, 4–13 August

1913
Paintings by Mrs E Phillips Fox (Miss Ethel Carrick), Guild Hall, Naarm/Narrm/Melbourne, 11–26 July

Exhibition of pictures by Mrs E Phillips Fox (Ethel Carrick), Anthony Hordern & Sons (subsequently known as Anthony Hordern's Fine Art Gallery), Gadigal Nura/Sydney, 6–22 November

1916
Exhibition of oil paintings by Mrs E Phillips Fox, Anthony Hordern & Sons, Gadigal Nura/Sydney, April

1925
Exhibition of paintings by Ethel Carrick (Mrs E Phillips Fox), The New Gallery, 107 Elizabeth Street, Naarm/Narrm/Melbourne, 2–13 June

1928
Exposition Ethel Carrick, Galerie de la Palette Française, Paris, 5–19 June

1933
Ethel Carrick (Mrs E Phillips Fox) exhibition of pictures, Everyman's Lending Library, Naarm/Narrm/Melbourne, 24 May – 7 June

1936
Exhibition of paintings by Ethel Carrick (Mrs Phillips Fox), Punjab Literary League club house, Lahore, India [current-day Pakistan], 23 December 1936 – 1 January 1937

1949
Pictures by Ethel Carrick (Mrs E Phillips Fox), Melbourne Book Club Gallery, Naarm/Narrm/Melbourne, 20 June – 2 July

Exhibition of Pictures by Ethel Carrick (Mrs E Phillips Fox), John Martin's Art Gallery, Tarntanya/Adelaide, 4 – 18 October

1979
Ethel Carrick (Mrs E Phillips Fox): a retrospective exhibition, Geelong Art Gallery, 30 March – 4 May 1979; toured to SH Ervin Gallery, Sydney, 11 May – 3 June; University Art Museum, Meeanjin /Brisbane, 13 June – 5 July

Joint exhibitions with Emanuel Phillips Fox

1914
Paintings by E Phillips Fox and Mrs Fox (Ethel Carrick), Athenaeum Gallery, Naarm/Narrm/Melbourne, 5–16 May

1925
Pictures by the Late E Phillips Fox and Ethel Carrick (Mrs E Phillips Fox), South Australian Society of Arts Gallery, Tarntanya/Adelaide, 15 July – 3 August

Exhibitions of oil paintings by the late E Phillips Fox and Ethel Carrick (Mrs E Phillips Fox), Anthony Hordern's & Sons, Gadigal Nura/Sydney, 1–15 October

1934
Exhibition of paintings by the Late E Phillips Fox and Ethel Carrick (Mrs E Phillips Fox), Athenaeum Gallery, Naarm/Narrm/Melbourne, 27 February – 10 March

1938
An exhibition of paintings by the late E Phillips Fox and Ethel Carrick (Mrs E Phillips Fox), Cooling Galleries, 92 New Bond Street, London, 17–30 June

1942
Pictures by the Late E Phillips Fox and E Carrick Fox, Athenaeum Gallery, Naarm/Narrm/Melbourne, 28 April – 16 May

1944
Pictures by the Late E Phillips Fox and E Carrick Fox, Athenaeum Gallery, Naarm/Narrm/Melbourne, 8–19 February

Exhibition of Oil Paintings by Ethel Carrick (Mrs Phillips Fox), including works by E Phillips Fox, Masonic Temple, Kamberri/Canberra, 7–10 September

1945
Exhibition of Paintings by Ethel Carrick and E Phillips Fox, Macquarie Galleries, Gadigal Nura/Sydney, 14–26 March

1952
Collection of Pictures by the Late E Phillips Fox and E Carrick Fox, Leonard Joel, Naarm/Narrm/Melbourne, 26–27 September

1982
E Phillips Fox and Ethel Carrick: an exhibition of impressionist paintings, Castlemaine Art Gallery and Historical Museum, Dja Dja Wurrung Country/Castlemaine, 1 August – 5 September

1997
E Phillips Fox & Ethel Carrick, Deutscher Fine Art, Naarm/Narrm/Melbourne, 13 November – 6 December

2011
Art, love and life: Ethel Carrick and E Phillips Fox, Queensland Art Gallery | Gallery of Modern Art, Meeanjin/Brisbane, 16 April – 7 August

Group exhibitions

1902
Suffolk Street Galleries, London

1903
Society of Oil Painters, London, January
84 *The market, Caudebec*

Society of Women Painters, London
369 *Richmond Castle from the river*
403 *Rue de la Boucherie (Caudebec-en-Caux)*
599 *The dreamer*

1904
Felix Art Club, Alpine Club, London
Le marché (The market)

1905
International Society of Sculptors, Painters and Gravers, London
531 *Harmony in grey*

1906
The Royal Institute of Oil Painters, London, 15 October – 12 December
100 *An interior*
224 *Le marché* (The market)

Felix Art Club, Doré Gallery, Bond Street, London
two works titled *In the Luxembourg Gardens*

Salon d'Automne, Paris
296 *Portrait de Mlle M* (Portrait of Mademoiselle M)
297 *Étude* (Study)

Société Nationale des Beaux-Arts, Paris
232 *Le printemps* (Apple blossom)

1907
The Royal Institute of Oil Painters, London, 14 October – 12 December
286 *The breakfast table*

Salon d'Automne, Paris
272 *Jeune femme riante* (Young woman laughing)
273 *Marché aux fleurs à Venise* (Flower market in Venice)
274 *Marché aux fleurs* (Flower market)
275 *Marché aux faïences* (Pottery market)
275 *À Venise* (In Venice)
276 *Les enfants s'amusent* (Children playing)

Société Nationale des Beaux-Arts
245 *Le marché* (The market)

Le Musée du Peuple, Union Internationale des Beaux-Arts et des Lettres, Deuxième Congrès, Centre d'Art, Angers, France
788 *Le five o'clock* (Five o'clock tea)
789 *Le soir* (Evening)
790 *Marché aux fleurs* (Flower market)
791 *Au Jardin du Luxembourg* (In the Luxembourg Gardens)
792 *Au Jardin du Luxembourg* (In the Luxembourg Gardens)
793 *Au Jardin du Luxembourg* (In the Luxembourg Gardens)

Royal Academy of Arts, London
360 *Miss Amy Marks*

1908
Société Nationale des Beaux Arts, Paris
212 *Au Luxembourg* (In the Luxembourg Gardens)
213 *Au Luxembourg* (In the Luxembourg Gardens)

Les Quelques, Galerie des Artistes Modernes, Paris

Salon d'Automne, Paris
359 *La promenade* (The promenade)
360 *Au marché (esquisse)* (At the market (sketch))
361 *Esquisse en Australie* (Sketch in Australia)
362 *Esquisse en Australie* (Sketch in Australia)

The London Salon of the Allied Artists' Association, Royal Albert Hall, London, July – August
1594 *Forbidden fruit*
1595 *Jeune femme riante* (Young woman laughing)

1909
Seizième exposition a Bruxelles, La Libre Esthétique, Brussels, February
37 *Portrait de Mlle M* (Portrait of Miss M)
38 *Portrait de jeune femme* (Portrait of a young woman)
39 *La promenade* (The promenade)
40 *Nourrices et bébés* (Nurses and babies)
41 *Le diabolo* (The diabolo)
42 *La petite rose* (The small rose)
43 *Le marché* (The market)
44 *Marché aux fleurs à Venise* (Flower market in Venice)

Les Quelques, Galerie des Artistes Modernes, Paris, February
Jeune femme riant (Young woman laughing)
Pommiers en fleurs (Apple trees in bloom)
Au Luxembourg (In Luxembourg [Gardens])
Le diabolo (The diabolo)
and six other works

Salon d'Automne, Paris
257 *Nature morte* (Still life)
258 *Au Luxembourg: le diabolo* (In Luxembourg [Gardens]: the diabolo)
259 *Au Luxembourg: au mois de mars* (In Luxembourg [Gardens] in March)
260 *En Australie* (In Australia)

The London Salon of the Allied Artists' Association, Royal Albert Hall, London
221 *Au Luxembourg* (In Luxembourg [Gardens])
222 *Au Luxembourg* (In Luxembourg [Gardens])
223 *Au Luxembourg* (In Luxembourg [Gardens])

Victorian Artists Society winter exhibition, Naarm/Narrm/Melbourne
3 *Les chevaux de bois* (The carousel)
15 *Le diabolo* (The diabolo)
17 *The fruit market, Sydney*
29 *After lunch*
35 *La promenade, Manly* (The promenade, Manly)
38 *In the piazza, Venice*
126 *The farmyard*

1910
Société Nationale des Beaux-Arts, Paris
229 *Marché aux fleurs* (Flower market)

Les Quelques, Galerie des Artistes Modernes, Paris, February
several scenes of flower markets

Salon d'Automne, Paris
200 *Au Luxembourg* (In Luxembourg [Gardens])
201 *Effet blanc* (White effect)
202 *Sur la plage* (On the beach)

1911
Les Quelques, Galerie des Artistes Modernes, Paris, February

Salon d'Automne, Paris
250 *Laveuses Algériennes* (Algerian women washing)
251 *Un papillon* (A butterfly)
252 *Femme Arabe* (Arab woman)
253 *Vue à Cadix* (View in Cadiz)

Societé Nationale des Beaux-Arts, Paris
246 *Effet de contre-jour* (Backlight effect)
247 *Sur la plage* (On the beach)

1912
Société Nationale des Beaux-Arts, Paris
268 *La marée haute à Saint-Malo (High tide in St Malo)*
269 *Le Port d'Alger* (The Port of Algiers)

Salon d'Automne, Paris
295 *Jeune homme contre une fenêtre* (Young man in front of a window)
296 *Portrait de M. Penleigh Boyd* (Portrait of Mr Penleigh Boyd)
297 *Deux dames et un jeune poéte* (Two ladies and a young poet)
298 *Sur le quai à Dinard* (On the quay in Dinard)
299 *Marché à Bou Saada* (Market at Bou Saada)
300 *Marché Algérien* (Algerian market)

Exposition de la International Art Union, Roger Lévesque et Barbazanges, Paris, November

1913
21e Exposition de la Société des Peintres Orientalistes Français, Grand Palais des Champs-Élysées, Paris, 2–28 February
- **147** *Le Port d'Alger* (The Port of Algiers)
- **148** *La mosque de Tanger* (The mosque at Tangier)
- **149** *Une rue à Tanger* (A street in Tangier)
- **150** *Le marché de Bou Saada* (Market in Bou Saada)
- **151** *Le marché aux chameaux* (The camel market)

1915
Australian artists' War Fund exhibition, Royal Art Society Rooms, Gadigal Nura/Sydney, 9 March
- **2** *A French café*
- **8** *Apple blossom*
- **19** *Garden island*

Australian artists' War Fund exhibition, Athenaeum Gallery, Naarm/Narrm/Melbourne, opens 25 March

Australian Art Association 3rd Annual Exhibition, Athenaeum Gallery, Naarm/Narrm/Melbourne, 7–21 October
- **1** *A hot summer's day*
- **2** *Street in Tahiti before bombardment*
- **3** *On the quay*
- **4** *Waiting for the ferry boat*
- **5** *Arab women*
- **6** *Impression of a bull fight*
- **7** *Market scene in Tahiti*

1916
Art, antique and curio exhibition for the French Week appeal, Town Hall, Naarm/Narrm/Melbourne, 8–15 July
- **3** *On the sands*
- **4** *Sydney Harbour*
- **5** *A fair in the woods*
- **6** *A sunny cruise*
- **7** *A Sydney cove*
- **8** *Sanary*
- **9** *Yacht race (Sydney)*
- **10** *A Sydney beach*
- **11** *River Yarra*
- **12** *On the beach, Dinan* [Dinard]
- **13** *In Morocco*
- **14** *In Morocco*

The Royal Institute of Oil Painters, London, November
- *Early morning bathers at Manly*
- *Christmas Day in Australia*

1917
Royal Academy of Arts, London
- **291** *High tide at St Malo*

1918
Salon des Poilus, exhibition of pictures for sale in aid of the French Red Cross, Athenaeum Gallery, Naarm/Narrm/Melbourne, 6–20 July
- **25** *On the sands, Dinant* [Dinard]
- **26** *Charlie Chaplin in Tahiti*
- **27** *The white hat*
- **30** *Grass trees, Stanwell Park*
- **31** *The headland, Stanwell Park*
- **34** *A sunny cruise*
- **36** *Family life in Tahiti*
- **40** *Evening*
- **41** *Stanwell Park*
- **94** *Sanary*
- **95** *In Morocco*
- **96** *Chartres*
- **97** *The quarry*

Deuxieme Exposition de l'Arc-en-Ciel, Groupe Franco-Anglo-Américain, Galerie Goupil & Cie, Paris, 8 October – 3 November
- **58** *Portrait*
- **59** *En Australie* (In Australia)

1919
Salon d'Automne, Paris
- **315** *Mme de Marquette* (Madame de Marquette)
- **316** *Mary (peint pendant le bombardement de Paris 1918)* (Mary [painted during the bombardment of Paris 1918])
- **317** *Coin du marché à Tahiti* (Market corner in Tahiti)
- **318** *Sur une plage australienne* (On an Australian beach)

1920
Société Nationale des Beaux-Arts, Paris
- **299** *Les baigneuses* (Bathers)
- **300** *Jour de l'an en Australie* (New Year's Day in Australia)
- **301** *Journée chaude (Australie)* (Hot day [Australia])

Salon d'Automne, Paris
- **393** *L'attenten* (The wait)
- **394** *La sourire* (The smile)
- **395** *Coin de mon jardin* (Corner of my garden)

1921
Société Nationale des Beaux-Arts, Paris
- **244** *Une Bretonne* (Portrait of a Breton woman)
- **245** *Journée de Septembre (plein air)* (September day [outdoors])

Salon d'Automne, Paris
- **366** *L'Alsacienne* (The Alsatian woman)
- **367** *Mme Alfred Thiroux* (Madame Alfred Thiroux)
- **368** *La rue Saussier Kairouan* (Rue Saussier in Kairouan)

Société des Artistes Indépendants, Paris
- **550** *Soucis* (Worries)
- **551** *Fleurs d'automne* (Autumn flowers)
- **552** *Dans le Jardin du Luxembourg* (In the Luxembourg Gardens)
- **553** *Monotype*
- **554** *Monotype*

Exposition de la Société Coloniale des Artistes Français, Société des Artistes Français, Grand Palais des Champs-Élysées, Paris
- **106** *Marché aux oranges (Tunis)* (Orange market [Tunis])
- **107** *Tête d'une Bedouine* (Head of a Bedouin woman)
- **108** *Kadijaj*
- **109** *Rue à Kairouan* (Street in Kairouan)
- **110** *Dans un souk* (In a souk)
- **111** *Mosquée à Kairouan* (Mosque at Kairouan)

1922
Salon d'Automne, Paris
- **411** *Jeune femme à la rose* (Young woman with rose)

Société Nationale des Beaux-Arts, Paris
- **170** *Au dessert* (At dessert)

Society of Women Painters, London, February

1923
The Pastel Society, London, January

Société Nationale des Beaux-Arts, Paris
- **190** *Nature morte* (Still life)
- **191** *Portrait d'une soeur Belge* (Portrait of a Belgian sister)

Salon d'Automne, Paris
- **284** *Portrait de M Oliver Madox Hueffer* (Portrait of Mr Oliver Madox Hueffer)
- **285** *Portrait de M Jean Batalla* (Portrait of Monsieur Jean Batalla)

Group of Australian artists, Panton Galleries, 43 Leicester Square, London, November

1924
Exhibition of Paintings and Sculptures by Australian Artists in Europe, Faculty of Arts Gallery, London, 23 June – 12 July
- **48** *Market Place at Merano*
- **49** *Merano*
- **50** *On the promenade*
- **51** *The snow mountain*
- **52** *Sunrise*
- **53** *Late afternoon on the Tyrol*
- **54** *Evening, Merano*
- **55** *The Roman bridge*

Société Nationale des Beaux-Arts, Paris
179 *Marie dans son jardin* (Marie in her garden)
180 *Soleil d'été* (Summer sun)

Salon d'Automne, Paris
314 *Le marché à Verone* (The market in Verona)
314 *La Vieux Pont à Florence* (The Old Bridge in Florence)

1926
The Pastel Society, London, January

Salon d'Automne, Paris
544 *Pivoines* (Peonies)
545 *Place Saint-Médard, Paris*
546 *Rue à Kairouan* (Street in Kairouan)
547 *Esquisse* (Sketch)
548 *Esquisse* (Sketch)

1927
Société Nationale des Beaux-Arts, Paris
224 *Marché aux legumes (Nice)* (Vegetable market [Nice])
225 *Marché aux fleurs (Nice)* (Flower market [Nice])
226 *Marché aux poissons (Nice)* (Fish market [Nice])

Salon d'Automne, Paris
344 *Marché aux fleurs, Nice* (Flower market, Nice)
345 *Cagnes*

Exposition Internationale des Beaux-Arts de la Ville de Bordeaux, 15 June – 15 August
La plage (the beach) also known as *Christmas Day on Manly Beach*—awarded *diplôme d'honneur*

1928
Société Nationale des Beaux-Arts, Paris
339 *Le printemps dans le Tyrol* (Spring in Tyrol)
340 *Marché aux fleurs à Nice* (Flower market in Nice)

Salon d'Automne, Paris
323 *Monte-Carlo*
324 *Anémones* (Anemones)

1929
American Artists' Club, 107 Boulevard Raspail, Paris
Vegetable market in Nice

Société Nationale des Beaux-Arts, Paris
287 *Intérieur* (Interior)
288 *Place Saint-Médard, Paris*
289 *Souvenir*

Salon d'Automne, Paris
236 *Le pont Napoléon, Paris* (Napolean Bridge, Paris)
237 *Chanson d'un oiseau* (A bird's song)

Exposés dans les salons de la Société des Amis des Arts de Bordeaux, Terrasse du Jardin-Public, Bordeaux
156 *Printemps dans le Tyrol* (Spring in Tyrol)
157 *Marché aux fleurs Hollandais* (Dutch flower market)

1930
Salon d'Automne, Paris
416 *Le Pont Neuf*
417 *Le quai des Orfèvres*
418 *Printemps sur le quai des Grands-Augustins* (Spring on the Dock of Grands-Augustins)
419 *L'aprèsmidi sur le quai des Grands-Augustins* (Afternoon on the Dock of Grands-Augustins)

Société Nationale des Beaux-Arts, Paris
371 *Tulipes* (Tulips)

Exposés dans les salons de la Société des Amis des Arts de Bordeaux, Terrasse du Jardin-Public, Bordeaux
129 *Le marché (Nice)* (The market [Nice])

1931
Société Nationale des Beaux-Arts, Paris
379 *Les femmes, l'amour et les fleurs* (Women, love and flowers)

Salon d'Automne, Paris
314 *Fleurs du jardin* (Garden flowers)
315 *Fleurs sauvages* (Wild flowers)

Royal Horticultural Society, Paris, May
2 flower studies

l'Exposition Coloniale Internationale, Paris
Peonies

1932
Société Nationale des Beaux-Arts, Paris
346 *Pivoines* (Peonies)
347 *Marché aux fleurs, Nice* (Flower market, Nice)
348 *Marché aux fleurs, Nice* (Flower market, Nice)

Salon d'Automne, Paris
257 *Tulipes* (Tulips)
258 *Anémones* (Anemones)

The Australian art exhibition, Macleod Gallery, Sydney, March
70 *The Market Place, Verona*

1933
Société Nationale des Beaux-Arts, Paris
378 *l'ete* (Summer)
379 *Le petit dejeuner* (Breakfast)
380 *Tulipes* (Tulips)

1934
An Exhibition by Melbourne painters, Athenaeum Gallery, Naarm/Narrm/Melbourne, 27 January – 10 February
25 *The flower market*

Salon d'Automne, Paris
302 *Le jour de la lessive* (Laundry day)
302 *Dans la cuisine* (In the kitchen)
302 *Une apparition dans les vignes* (An apparition in the grapevines)
302 *Fleurs d'automne* (Autumn flowers)

Anglo-American painters, Association Florence Blumenthal,
79 *Rue Madame, Paris, November*

1935
Société Nationale des Beaux-Arts, Paris
293 *Le corsage rose* (The pink corsage)

Salon des Tuileries, Paris
343 *M. Louis Ridel*
344 *Une rue à Nice* (A street in Nice)
345 *Fleurs de printemps* (Spring flowers)

Royal Academy of Arts, London
13 *A bunch of flowers*

1936
Necou's Hotel, Gulmarg, India, 27 July

Srinagar Art Exhibition, Kashmir, India, 27–28 May
Morning on the River Jhelum

1937
Société Nationale des Beaux-Arts, Paris
260 *Le bac, Kashmir* (The ferry, Kashmir)

Royal Academy of Arts, London
50 *A Parisian flower market*

Salon d'Automne, Paris
270 *Femmes musulmanes dans un jardin* (Muslim women in a garden)
271 *Portrait*

Art section of the Exposition Internationale, September

1938
Salon d'Automne, Paris
287 *Le marché, Darjeeling* (Market, Darjeeling)
288 *Le printemps dans le Tyrol* (Spring in Tyrol)

1939
Royal Academy of Arts, London
443 *Pont Neuf, Paris*

Société Nationale des Beaux-Arts, Paris
202 *Marché aux fleurs* (Flower market)
203 *Marché aux fleurs* (Flower market)

1942
Melbourne Society of Women Painters, 33rd annual exhibition, Naarm/Narrm/Melbourne, 13–24 October
124 *"Le pont Napoléon", Paris* (The Napoleon Bridge, Paris)

1944
Paintings by Ethel Phillips Fox, Jean Sutherland and Sybil Craig, Kozminsky Galleries, Naarm/Narrm/Melbourne, 21 November – 1 December
1 *The English church, Gulmarg*
2 *Evening in Kashmir*
3 *Planting rice*
4 *The wooden bridge*
5 *Early morning in Kashmir*
6 *Gathering clouds*
7 *Rice fields*
8 *Ganderbal Village*
9 *An old church tower*
10 *The bazaar, Kairouan*
11 *A street in Dax*
12 *Pollensa*
13 *White umbrellas*
14 *Market in Tyrol*
15 *Fruit blossom*
16 *The canal, Annecy*
17 *By the lake, Annecy*
18 *A corner in Dax*
19 *Col des Montets*

Exhibition of paintings (from private collections), Melbourne Town Hall, Naarm/Narrm/Melbourne, 24–28 March
47 *Flower market in Nice, France*

1945
Noted Australian Artists Loan Exhibition, Myer Art Gallery, 1–27 August
72 *The beach at Dinard*

Australia At War, touring exhibition
39 *Melbourne Women Painters' National Service group*
40 *N.D.L. Depot St. Michael's Hall*
41 *The kitchen, The Lady Gowrie Services Club, Canberra*

1946
French Comfort Fund exhibition, David Jones' Art Gallery, Gadigal Nura/Sydney, 20–28 February
29 *Nasturtiums*
30 *Peach blossoms at Canberra*
31 *French fish market*
32 *Carnations*

French Comfort Fund, Myer Art Gallery, Naarm/Narrm/Melbourne, 19–29 March

1947
Victorian Artists Society autumn exhibition, 430 Albert Street, Naarm/Narrm/Melbourne, 28 April – 11 May
11 *In a French market*
25 *The incoming tide*
42 *Voluntary workers*

Victorian Artists Society spring exhibition, 430 Albert Street, Naarm/Narrm/Melbourne, 29 September – 12 October
23 *In the Luxembourg Gardens, Paris*

Melbourne Society of Women Painters, 38th annual exhibition, 13–25 October
16 *Afternoon in the Luxembourg Gardens*
17 *Gum blossoms*

1948
Melbourne Society of Women Painters, 39th annual exhibition, Athenaeum Gallery, 19–30 October
9 *The glory of a garden*
10 *Morning, from Clifton Gardens*

1949
Melbourne Society of Women Painters, 40th annual exhibition, Tye's Art Gallery, Naarm/Narrm/Melbourne, 18–28 October
27 *Corner of a market place – Darjeeling*

1950
Melbourne Society of Women Painters, 41st annual exhibition, Athenaeum Gallery, Naarm/Narrm/Melbourne

1951
Royal Scottish Academy, Edinburgh
122 *Australian gum blossom*

The Royal Institute of Oil Painters, London, 15 October – 7 November
90 *French flower market*

Society of Women Artists, London
737 *In Sydney Botanical Gardens*

1952
Melbourne Society of Women Painters, 43rd annual exhibition, Athenaeum Gallery, Naarm/Narrm/Melbourne, 7–18 October

Catalogue of exhibited works

All works are by Ethel Carrick unless otherwise indicated. Works by Carrick are ordered first by media then chronologically. Works by other artists are then listed chronologically.

Carrick used similar or identical titles within groups of works and often changed them across different exhibitions. She rarely dated her works. New research for this publication has helped to more accurately date works from letters, newspaper reports, immigration records, exhibition catalogues and reviews from the time. Where a date is truly unknown, this is indicated by 'nd' (no date).

If works have not been titled by the artist but instead were named afterwards, or gained a popular reference name, these titles are represented in brackets in the list below. For ease of reading, bracketed titles have not been used throughout the running text or captions of the book. Where there are known alternative titles, these have been listed as well.

Please note that there are works mentioned in the text that come from exhibition records. It is sometimes unclear which particular work they are referring to, or the locations of the works are unknown. Where the work and its location is known, and that location is in a public institution, we have recorded this within the text.

Carrick's artworks with French titles have been listed with French titles first, followed by the translation in English in brackets. Where the English translation was also part of the original title, both the French and English translation is kept in italics.

Dimensions are height before width.

Ethel Carrick

England 1872 – Australia 1952

Paintings
The market, Caudebec **c 1902**
oil on canvas
51.4 × 61.3 cm
private collection
courtesy Smith & Singer Fine Art
cat 4 p 16

Richmond, Yorkshire **c 1903**
oil on canvas
47.5 × 57.8 cm
Art Gallery of Western Australia, Boorloo/Perth
purchased 1978
1978/0P24
cat 6 pp 22–23

Pumpkin sellers **c 1903–04**
oil on wood panel
22 × 30.5 cm
private collection
courtesy Lauraine Diggins Fine Art
cat 11 p 29

(*Vegetable market*) c 1904
oil on panel
26.2 × 35.2 cm
private collection
cat 12 p 30

Paris park scene **1906**
oil on board
26.7 × 34.9 cm
National Gallery of Australia, Kamberri/Canberra
purchased 1969
69.82
cat 19 p 42

Luxembourg Gardens, Paris **c 1906**
oil on wood panel
26.2 × 35.2 cm
National Gallery of Australia, Kamberri/Canberra
purchased 1976
76.361
cat 17 p 41

The breakfast table **1907**
oil on canvas on board
72 × 101.5 cm
private collection
courtesy Smith & Singer Fine Art
cat 91 p 140

Flower market **1907**
oil on wood panel
26.4 × 35 cm
National Gallery of Victoria, Naarm/Narrm/Melbourne
presented through the Art Foundation of Victoria by the late Major BRF MacNay and Mrs D MacNay, Fellow, 1994
A9-1994
cat 14 p 34

In springtime, Luxembourg Gardens **1907**
oil on wood panel
26.3 × 34.5 cm
University Art Collection, Chau Chak Wing Museum, The University of Sydney, Gadigal Nura/Sydney
donated by the estate of Neville Holmes Grace, 2018
UA2018.45
cat 16 p 40

Sunday in the gardens **1907**
oil on canvas
45.7 × 60.8 cm
Queen Victoria Museum & Art Gallery, Launceston
purchased with funds from the QVMAG Arts Foundation, 1987
QVM 1987:FP:0006
cat 15 p 39

St Mark's Venice **1907**
oil on board
25.2 × 34.2 cm
University Art Collection, Chau Chak Wing Museum, The University of Sydney, Gadigal Nura/Sydney
donated by the estate of Neville Holmes Grace, 2018
UA2018.52
cat 93 p 145

Marché aux fleurs à Venise **(Flower market in Venice) 1907**
oil on board
24.5 × 32.5 cm
private collection
cat 121 p 207

(*Chioggia, Statue of the Madonna, Venice*) 1907
oil on wood panel
35 × 26 cm
private collection
cat 26 p 50

***(Venice scene)* 1907**
oil on panel
23.6 × 33.1 cm
Shepparton Art Museum, Yorta Yorta Country/Shepparton
donated by Arts Victoria, 1998
1998.57
cat 95 p 146

***(Building by river with boats)* 1907**
oil on panel
23.6 × 33.1 cm
Shepparton Art Museum, Yorta Yorta Country/Shepparton
donated by Arts Victoria, 1998
1998.57
cat 96 p 147

***(Venice)* c 1907**
oil on wood panel
15.4 × 20.8 cm
Castlemaine Art Museum, Dja Dja Wurrung Country/Castlemaine
gift of Major BRF MacNay, 1978
G860
cat 94 p 146

***(Royal Avenue, Versailles)* c 1907**
oil on wood panel
24.8 × 33.2 cm
Castlemaine Art Museum, Dja Dja Wurrung Country/Castlemaine
gift of Major BRF MacNay, 1982
G829
cat 27 pp 52–53

***The table vase* c 1907**
oil on canvas on composition board
92.2 × 72.5 cm
private collection
cat 5 p 21

***The Spanish courtyard* c 1907/1911**
oil on canvas
36.5 × 44.5 cm
private collection
cat 42 p 78

Esquisse en Australie
(Sketch in Australia) 1908
oil on wood
26.3 × 35.3 cm
National Gallery of Australia, Kamberri/Canberra
purchased 2023
2023.67
cat 1 p 6

***La promenade* (The promenade) 1908**
oil on wood panel
26.2 × 35.2 cm
private collection
cat 120 p 200

***The market* 1908**
oil on wood panel
27 × 35 cm
private collection
courtesy Philip Bacon Galleries
cat 23 p 48

***The quay, Milsons Point* 1908**
oil on artist board
26.4 × 34.9 cm
National Gallery of Australia, Kamberri/Canberra
purchased 1975
75.111
cat 29 p 57

***Figures on a jetty* c 1908**
oil on board
25.5 × 32.8 cm
private collection
cat 28 p 56

***Esquisse en Australie* (Sketch in Australia) c 1908**
oil on board
27.4 × 35.6 cm
private collection
courtesy Philip Bacon Galleries
cat 30 p 58

***Luxembourg Gardens, Paris* c 1908**
oil on board
36 × 44 cm (framed)
Collection of GR Teague
cat 21 p 45

***Au marché* (At the market) c 1908**
oil on Baltic pine panel
27 × 35 cm
private collection
courtesy Lauraine Diggins Fine Art
cat 122 p 208

***(Luxembourg Gardens)* c 1908**
oil on wood panel
26.5 × 35.4 cm
private collection
cat 18 p 41

***In the Luxembourg Gardens, Paris* c 1908**
oil on canvas
46.4 × 61.6 cm
National Gallery of Victoria, Naarm/Narrm/Melbourne
purchased 1949
2049-4
cat 22 p 47

***Bull fight at Biarritz* c 1908**
also known as *Impression of a bull fight*
oil on canvas
38.4 × 45.6 cm
National Gallery of Australia, Kamberri/Canberra
purchased 1974
74.247
cat 41 p 77

***French flower market* 1909**
oil on canvas
51 × 61 cm
private collection
cat 25 p 49

***Concert in the Luxembourg Gardens* 1909**
also known as *Open-air concert*
oil on panel
26 × 34 cm
private collection
cat 38 p 72

***Luxembourg Gardens, Paris* c 1909**
oil on wood panel
24.5 × 34.5 cm
private collection
cat 20 p 44

***Beach scene* c 1909**
oil on canvas on cardboard
38 × 55.4 cm
National Gallery of Australia, Kamberri/Canberra
purchased 1976
76.1061
cat 33 p 65

***On the beach* c 1909**
oil on canvas
36 × 42 cm
Queensland Art Gallery | Gallery of Modern Art, Meeanjin/Brisbane
gift of the Margaret Olley Art Trust through the QAGOMA Foundation, 2011
2011.086
cat 107 p 166

***On the sands* 1910**
oil on wood panel
26.5 × 35 cm
private collection
cat 104 p 162

***Sur la plage* (On the beach) 1910**
oil on wood panel
27 × 35 cm
private collection
cat 99 p 154

***Sur la plage* (On the beach) c 1910**
oil on panel
27 × 35.2 cm
Queensland Art Gallery | Gallery of Modern Art, Meeanjin/Brisbane
gift of the Margaret Olley Art Trust through the QAGOMA Foundation, 2012
2012.355
cat 105 p 163

***Rue Mouffetard, Paris* 1910**
oil on canvas
38.1 × 45.6 cm
Kerry Stokes Collection, Boorloo/Perth
cat 32 pp 62–63

***The promenade* c 1910**
oil on board
25 × 33.2 cm
private collection
cat 36 p 68

***Sur la plage* (On the beach) c 1910**
oil on wood panel
26.5 × 35 cm
Art Gallery of South Australia, Tarntanya/Adelaide
gift of Aldridge Family Endowment, Frank Choate, Susan Cocks, Dr Michael Drew, Emeritus Professor Anne Edwards AO, Dr Michael Hayes, Lipman Karas, Edward Mansfield, Jacqui McGill, Jane McGregor, David Urry, Peter and Pamela McKee, Dr Joe Verco AM, Dick Whitington QC, Peter Wilson and Zena Winser through the Art Gallery of South Australia Foundation Collectors Club, 2018
20189P107
cat 103 p 162

Seaside promenade, south of France **c 1910**
oil on panel
26 × 35 cm
Art Gallery of Western Australia, Boorloo/Perth
purchased with funds from the Sir Claude Hotchin Art Foundation, 1993
1993/0109
cat 37 p 68

French village scene with figures **c 1910**
oil on panel
41.6 × 50 cm
Art Gallery of Western Australia, Boorloo/Perth
donated by Dr Harold Schenberg, 1992
1992/0220
cat 31 p 61

Market scene **c 1910**
oil on board
15.7 × 22 cm
Shepparton Art Museum, Yorta Yorta Country/Shepparton
donated by Arts Victoria, 1998
1998.0055
cat 13 p 31

Flower market (France) **c 1910**
oil on wood panel
26.5 × 35 cm
collection of McClelland, Bunurong Country/Langwarrin
gift to the State of Victoria by Major Basil RF MacNay
cat 124 p 212

Flower market **c 1910–12**
oil on board
26 × 35 cm
private collection
courtesy Philip Bacon Galleries
cat 24 p 48

(*Band promenade*) c 1910–12
oil on canvas on board
36.2 × 45.1 cm
private collection
cat 130 p 240

Quay at St Malo **1911**
oil on canvas
44.6 × 36.5 cm
University Art Collection, Chau Chak Wing Museum, The University of Sydney, Gadigal Nura/Sydney
donated by the estate of Neville Holmes Grace, 2018
UA2018.50
cat 100 p 156

Sur la plage (On the sands), Dinard **1911**
oil on wood panel
27 × 35 cm
private collection
cat 97 p 149

On the beach **c 1911**
oil on canvas
37.8 × 45.6 cm
National Gallery of Victoria, Naarm/Narrm/Melbourne
Herbert and Ivy Brookes Bequest, 1973
A18-1973
cat 106 pp 164–65

Arabs bargaining **c 1911**
also known as *Marché à Bou Saada* (Market at Bou Saada)
oil on canvas
68 × 81 cm
private collection
cat 108 p 170

Laveuses algériennes (Algerian women washing clothes in a stream) **c 1911**
oil on canvas
64.5 × 81 cm
private collection
courtesy Rex Irwin Art Dealer
cat 111 pp 176–77

The mosque at Tangier **c 1911**
oil on canvas
46 × 35.5 cm
collection of Philip Bacon AO, Meeanjin/Brisbane
cat 112 p 179

La marée haute à Saint-Malo (High tide at St Malo) **c 1911–12**
oil on canvas
79 × 64 cm
Art Gallery of New South Wales, Gadigal Nura/Sydney
purchased with funds provided by the Gleeson O'Keefe Foundation 2009
475.2009
cat 101 p 157

The quay at Dinard **c 1911–12**
oil on canvas on plywood
70.9 × 91.1 cm
National Gallery of Victoria, Naarm/Narrm/Melbourne
Felton Bequest, 1942
1136-4
cat 102 p 159

Women in a courtyard **c 1911–12**
oil on canvas
37.5 × 45 cm
private collection
cat 43 p 79

Jeune homme contre une fenêtre **(Young man in front of a window) c 1912**
also known as *Afternoon in the studio*
oil on canvas
99 × 70 cm
private collection
cat 40 p 75

Boats on a quayside **c 1912**
oil on canvas
60 × 80 cm
collection of Philip Bacon AO, Meeanjin/Brisbane
cat 139 p 252

Watching the Australian fleet coming through Sydney Heads **1913**
oil on canvas
38 × 46 cm
collection of Rob and Jenny Ferguson
cat 45 p 84

Watching the fleet from the Domain **1913**
oil on canvas
38.6 × 46.3 cm
private collection
courtesy Smith & Singer Fine Art
cat 3 p 10

Beach scene, Sydney **1913**
oil on particle board
33.5 × 25 cm
Benalla Art Gallery, Yorta Yorta Country/Benalla
gift of Pamela Davies, 2005
cat 119 p 196

Christmas Day on Manly Beach **1913**
also known as *Manly Beach—summer is here*
oil on canvas
81 × 100 cm
Manly Art Gallery & Museum Collection, Cameragal Country/Manly
gift of the artist, 1934
A0053
cat 118 pp 194–95

On Balmoral Beach, Sydney **1913**
oil on canvas on board
26 × 34 cm
Mosman Art Gallery, Borogegal Country/Mosman, Sydney
The Balnaves Gift, 2011
cat 117 p 188

On Circular Quay **c 1913**
oil on canvas on Masonite board
44 × 37 cm
Art Gallery of New South Wales, Gadigal Nura/Sydney
purchased with funds provided by the Australian Masterpiece Fund including the following major donors: Antoinette Albert, Atelier, Boyarsky Family Trust, Stephen Buzacott and Kemsley Brennan, Krystyna Campbell-Pretty AM and the late Harold Campbell-Pretty, Anne and Andrew Cherry, Sue and Sam Chisholm AM, Professor Maria Craig, Rowena Danziger AM in memory of Ken Coles AM, Davies Family Foundation, Peter and Robyn Flick, Kiera Grant, Greatorex Fund, Lindy and Robert Henderson, Jonathan and Karen Human, Alexandra Joel and Philip Mason, Carole Lamerton and John Courtney, Robyn Martin-Weber, Lawrence and Sylvia Myers, Vicki Olsson, Guy and Marian Paynter, Elizabeth and Philip Ramsden, Joyce Rowe, Penelope Seidler AM, Denyse Spice, Max and Nola Tegel, Philippa Warner, The WeirAnderson Foundation, Ray Wilson OAM, Women's Art Group and Rob & Jane Woods, 2023
301.2023
cat 44 p 83

At sunset **1914**
oil on canvas on cardboard
25 × 31 cm
National Gallery of Australia, Kamberri/Canberra
purchased 1977
77.15
cat 47 p 86

Rose Bay, Sydney Harbour **c 1915**
oil on canvas
27 × 32.5 cm
collection of Jim Haynes OAM and Robyn McMillan
cat 46 p 86

The statue of Strasbourg, Place de la Concorde, Paris **1918**
oil on wood panel
26.6 × 33.7 cm
private collection
cat 125 p 216

(Armistice Day) 1918
oil on wood panel
26 x 34 cm
private collection
cat 51 p 93

(Champs-Élysées) c 1918
oil on panel
23.5 × 32.5 cm
private collection
cat 50 p 93

(Place de la Concorde) c 1918–19
oil on canvas on Masonite
88.3 × 137.3 cm
private collection
cat 49 p 92

The market 1919
oil on canvas
75.9 × 100 cm
Moran Family Collection
courtesy Smith & Singer Fine Art
cat 53 pp 96–97

La plage française (The French beach) 1919
oil on board
21 × 32.2 cm
University Art Collection, Chau Chak
Wing Museum, The University of Sydney,
Gadigal Nura/Sydney
donated by the estate of Neville Holmes
Grace, 2018
UA2018.37
cat 35 p 67

French beach scene c 1919
oil on wood panel
22 × 33.2 cm
Castlemaine Art Museum, Dja Dja Wurrung
Country/Castlemaine
gift of Major BRF MacNay 1982
G858
cat 34 p 66

French interior with young woman c 1919
oil on canvas
112 × 86 cm
collection of Rob and Jenny Ferguson
cat 52 p 95

(Town square) c 1919
oil on board
23.5 × 36 cm
private collection
courtesy Philip Bacon Galleries
cat 48 p 88

(Morning in Kairouan) c 1919–20
oil on board
26 × 33 cm
University Art Collection, Chau Chak
Wing Museum, The University of Sydney,
Gadigal Nura/Sydney
donated by the estate of Neville Holmes
Grace, 2018
UA2018.48
cat 98 p 150

A market in Kairouan c 1919–20
oil on canvas
38 × 46 cm
Art Gallery of New South Wales,
Gadigal Nura/Sydney
purchased with the support of the Art Gallery
Society of New South Wales through the
Elizabeth Fyffe Bequest, 2021
1.2022
cat 113 p 181

North African street scene c 1919–20
oil on wood panel
37.5 × 29.4 cm
Bendigo Art Gallery, Dja Dja Wurrung
Country/Bendigo
gift of Arts Victoria, 1998
1999.1
cat 115 p 183

(Street scene, Northern Africa) c 1919–20
oil on canvas
46 × 38 cm
private collection
cat 116 p 184

Arab scene 1920
oil on board
26 × 33 cm
University Art Collection, Chau Chak
Wing Museum, The University of Sydney,
Gadigal Nura/Sydney
donated by the estate of Neville Holmes
Grace, 2018
UA2018.38
cat 109 p 173

A street in Tunisia 1920
oil on wood panel
26.5 × 35 cm
private collection
courtesy Philip Bacon Galleries
cat 110 p 173

North African street scene c 1920
oil on panel
31.6 × 20.5 cm
Art Gallery of Ballarat, Wadawurrung/Ballarat
gift of Major BRF MacNay of Argyll, Scotland,
nephew of the artist, 1998
1998.115
cat 114 p 182

Dans mon jardin (In my garden) c 1920
also known as *A corner of my garden*
oil on canvas
80 × 53 cm
University Art Collection, Chau Chak
Wing Museum, The University of Sydney,
Gadigal Nura/Sydney
donated by the estate of Neville Holmes
Grace, 2018
UA2018.41
cat 39 p 74

On the verandah nd
oil on canvas
112 × 86 cm
private collection
cat 129 p 236

Luxembourg Gardens c 1921
oil on canvas
38 × 46 cm
University Art Collection, Chau Chak
Wing Museum, The University of Sydney,
Gadigal Nura/Sydney
donated by the estate of Neville Holmes
Grace, 2018
UA2018.46
cat 128 p 233

A street in Dax, France 1922
gouache on paper
20.5 × 27 cm
private collection
cat 59 p 101

Cottages at Dax 1922
gouache on paper
20.5 × 28.5 cm
private collection
cat 56 p 100

Mont Blanc c 1924
oil on wood
26.1 × 35 cm
collection of McClelland, Bunurong
Country/Langwarrin
3.1982
cat 57 p 101

The Church Tower, Merano c 1924
gouache on paper
22.6 × 29 cm
collection of McClelland, Bunurong
Country/Langwarrin
1986.29
cat 58 p 101

Mountain scene c 1924
gouache on paper on board
23.9 × 31 cm
Art Gallery of Ballarat, Wadawurrung/Ballarat
purchased 1949
1949.3
cat 132 p 244

Ponte Vecchio, Florence c 1924
oil on canvas
49 × 59.5 cm
National Gallery of Victoria, Naarm/
Narrm/Melbourne
gift of Andrée Fay Harkness through the
Australian Government's Cultural Gifts
Program, 2020
2020.571
cat 55 p 98

The market place, Verona c 1924
oil on cardboard
50.5 × 60.7 cm
Tasmanian Museum and Art Gallery,
nipaluna/Hobart
purchased 1975
AG2801
cat 54 p 98

The Verlaine Memorial, Paris c 1925
oil on canvas
51 × 62 cm
private collection
cat 60 p 103

In the Nice flower market **c 1926**
oil on canvas
59.2 × 80.9 cm
National Gallery of Australia, Kamberri/Canberra
purchased 1972
72.128
cat 123 pp 210–11

Flower market, Nice **c 1926**
oil on canvas
60 × 73 cm
Art Gallery of New South Wales, Gadigal Nura/Sydney
purchased 1955
9118
cat 61 p 105

Flower market southern France **c 1926**
oil on board
52.5 × 80.0 cm
University Art Collection, Chau Chak Wing Museum, The University of Sydney, Gadigal Nura/Sydney
donated by the estate of Neville Holmes Grace, 2018
UA2018.44
cat 65 p 107

Flower stall **c 1926**
oil on wood
26.8 × 35 cm
Bendigo Art Gallery, Dja Dja Wurrung Country/Bendigo
gift of Arts Victoria, 1998
1999.2
cat 62 p 106

The fruit market, Nice **c 1927**
oil on canvas
81.8 × 100 cm
Kerry Stokes Collection, Boorloo/Perth
cat 73 p 113

Flower vendors, Nice **c 1930**
oil on cardboard
26.5 × 36.5 cm
Kerry Stokes Collection, Boorloo/Perth
cat 64 p 106

Peonies **c 1930**
oil on canvas
81 × 65 cm
private collection
cat 71 p 111

Tulips **c 1930**
oil on canvas
64.5 × 53.5 cm
private collection
cat 68 p 110

(*Flower piece*) c 1930
oil on canvas
54.7 × 46 cm
National Gallery of Australia, Kamberri/Canberra
purchased 1972
72.473
cat 67 p 110

Nasturtiums **c 1933**
oil on canvas
45.2 × 38.3 cm
The University of Western Australia Art Collection, Boorloo/Perth
gift of Mr and Mrs Zygmunt Horawicz, 1989
1989.21
cat 69 p 110

(*Mixed flowers*) c 1933
oil on canvas on board
41.5 × 36.5 cm
Collection of Dr Garry Helprin
cat 70 p 111

The wooden bridge **1935**
gouache on paper
26.6 × 37 cm
Newcastle Art Gallery, Awabakal and Worimi Country/Newcastle
gift of Dr Roland Pope, 1945
1957065
cat 75 p 115

Early morning in Kashmir **1935**
gouache on paper
27 × 38.6 cm
Newcastle Art Gallery, Awabakal and Worimi Country/Newcastle
gift of Dr Roland Pope, 1945
1957064
cat 74 p 115

Deputy Commissioner's garden Agra, India **c 1935**
oil on canvas
37.5 × 45 cm
Art Gallery of South Australia, Tarntanya/Adelaide
gift of Helen Bowden 2018
9P108
cat 76 p 117

Flower market southern France **c 1935**
oil on board
23.5 × 43 cm
University Art Collection, Chau Chak Wing Museum, The University of Sydney, Gadigal Nura/Sydney
donated by the estate of Neville Holmes Grace, 2018
UA2018.42
cat 63 p 106

A bunch of flowers **c 1935**
oil on canvas on plywood
60.8 × 50 cm
Queensland Art Gallery | Gallery of Modern Art, Meeanjin/Brisbane
Purchased 1943
1:0321
cat 72 p 111

Le bac, Kashmir **(The ferry, Kashmir) 1937 also known as *Paysage d'Inde-le-bac* (Landscape at Inde-le-bac)**
oil on canvas
46 × 69 cm
University Art Collection, Chau Chak Wing Museum, The University of Sydney, Gadigal Nura/Sydney
donated by the estate of Neville Holmes Grace, 2018
UA2018.49
cat 77 p 118–19

Roses **c 1938**
oil on board
34 × 44.5 cm
University Art Collection, Chau Chak Wing Museum, The University of Sydney, Gadigal Nura/Sydney
donated by the estate of Neville Holmes Grace, 2018
UA2018.51
cat 66 p 110

The market place **c 1939**
oil on canvas
46.5 × 61 cm
private collection
courtesy Smith & Singer Fine Art
cat 136 p 247

Australian gum blossom **c 1948**
oil on canvas
60 × 44.5 cm
The Wesfarmers Collection of Australian Art, Boorloo/ Perth
cat 90 p 136

Rainbow Bay, Coolangatta **c 1941**
oil on canvas
24.5 × 34.5 cm
collection of Jim Haynes OAM and Robyn McMillan
cat 81 p 125

From Kirra, North Coast **c 1941**
oil on paper
24 × 35.5 cm
HOTA Gallery Collection, Kombumerri Country/Surfers Paradise
gifted by the citizens of the Gold Coast to future generations, 2004
cat 80 p 125

St John's Church, Canberra **1942**
oil on canvas
49 × 39 cm
Canberra Museum & Gallery, Kamberri/Canberra
2016.22
cat 82 p 126

Voluntary service **1943**
oil on canvas
57.5 × 78 cm
private collection
cat 127 p 228

Carnations **c 1946**
oil on canvas on board
46.5 x 36.5 cm
National Gallery of Australia, Kamberri/Canberra
bequest of Dr Lee MacCormick Edwards 2015
2015.838
cat 138 p 249

The kitchen, Canberra Services Club **1943 also known as *The canteen workers***
oil on canvas
59 × 81 cm
collection of Rob and Jenny Ferguson
cat 79 p 122

Colonnades of Canberra's civic centre 1943
oil on canvas on board
25.4 × 35.4 cm
Canberra Museum & Gallery, Kamberri/Canberra
2012.1
cat 83 p 127

Molonglo c 1943
oil on board
24.5 × 35 cm
University Art Collection, Chau Chak Wing Museum, The University of Sydney, Gadigal Nura/Sydney
donated by the estate of Neville Holmes Grace, 2018
UA2018.47
cat 85 p 127

Canberra c 1944
oil on canvas
46.5 × 61 cm
National Library of Australia, Kamberri/Canberra
3255390
cat 84 p 127

Flower garden, Sydney c 1944
oil on wood panel
26 × 34.5 cm
Kerry Stokes Collection, Boorloo/Perth
cat 86 p 130

Papier mâché, Red Cross Auxiliary in Sydney c 1944
oil on canvas
57 × 73 cm
The Bastiaan Collection
cat 126 pp 222–23

In the botanic gardens c 1945
oil on canvas
50.9 × 61
Benalla Art Gallery, Yorta Yorta Country/Benalla
Ledger Gift, 1980
cat 87 p 130

Provençal landscape nd
oil on artist board
26 × 35 cm
University Art Collection, Chau Chak Wing Museum, The University of Sydney, Gadigal Nura/Sydney
donated by the Honourable RP Meagher through the Australian Government's Cultural Gifts Program, 2011
UA2011.21
cat 131 p 243

Flower market southern France c 1951
oil on canvas on board
52.5 × 80 cm
University Art Collection, Chau Chak Wing Museum, The University of Sydney, Gadigal Nura/Sydney
donated by the estate of Neville Holmes Grace, 2018
UA2018.43
cat 88 p 133

French flower market c 1951
oil on canvas
49 × 63.5 cm
Australian National University Art Collection, Kamberri/Canberra
gift of Dame Elisabeth Murdoch, 1957
cat 89 p 134

Etchings
(*Houses*) 1906
etching in black ink on paper
29.3 × 22 cm
Art Gallery of Ballarat, Wadawurrung/Ballarat
gift of Major Basil RF MacNay of Argyll, Scotland, nephew of the artist, 1998
1998.113
cat 8 p 27

(*Saint-Germain-des-Prés, Paris*) 1907
etching printed in black ink from one copper plate
30.2 × 22.2 cm
National Gallery of Australia, Kamberri/Canberra
purchased 1980
80.914
cat 9 p 27

Lithographs
(*The High Street, Oxford*) nd
hand-coloured lithograph
32.5 × 49.7 cm
Art Gallery of Ballarat, Wadawurrung/Ballarat
gift of Major Basil RF MacNay of Argyll, Scotland, nephew of the artist, 1998
1998.114
cat 7 p 26

The fruit and vegetable market, Nice 1933
lithograph printed in black ink from one stone, hand-coloured in watercolour
47.6 × 56.1 cm
National Gallery of Australia, Kamberri/Canberra
purchased 1994
94.146
cat 135 p 246

A street in St. Paul c 1933
lithograph printed in black ink from one stone
48.6 × 38.1 cm
Benalla Art Gallery, Yorta Yorta Country/Benalla
Major B MacNay Bequest gift of Arts Victoria, 1998
1998.13
cat 134 p 246

(*A French harbour*) c 1933
lithograph printed in black ink from one stone, hand-coloured in watercolour
37.1 × 55.3 cm
Benalla Art Gallery, Yorta Yorta Country/Benalla
Major B MacNay Bequest gift of Arts Victoria, 1998
1998.15
cat 133 p 245

Pilgrims bathing at Benares c 1937
lithograph printed in black ink from one stone, hand-coloured in watercolour
45.8 × 35.1 cm
National Gallery of Australia, Kamberri/Canberra
purchased 1976
76.1227.21
cat 78 p 120

La rue Mouffetard, Paris c 1942
lithograph printed in black ink from one stone, hand-coloured in watercolour
40 × 50 cm
Manly Art Gallery & Museum Collection, Cameragal Country/Manly
purchased 1980
cat 137 p 247

Emanuel Phillips Fox
Australia 1865–1915

Paintings
Portrait of Ethel Carrick Fox 1907
oil on canvas on board
53.5 × 44.3 cm
Art Gallery of Western Australia, Boorloo/Perth
gift of Sue and Ian Bernadt, 1989
1989/0161
cat 10 p 28

Venice afterglow c 1907
oil on board
26 × 34 cm
University Art Collection, Chau Chak Wing Museum, The University of Sydney, Gadigal Nura/Sydney
donated by the estate of Neville Holmes Grace, 2018
UA2018.52
cat 92 p 144

May and Mina Moore Studios
Australia c 1904–1928

Photograph
Portrait of Ethel Carrick c 1913–16
toned gelatin silver photograph
19.6 × 14.7 cm (sheet)
33.2 × 23.1 cm (mount)
Art Gallery of South Australia, Tarntanya/Adelaide
gift of Mrs W H Schneider, 1976
918Ph32
cat 2 p 8

List of figures

These figures are listed in the order they appear throughout the catalogue.

Dimensions are height before width.

Fallow to flowering: 1915-1939

A continuing circle: 1939-1952

Seeking sunlight: Carrick and Fox's artistic marriage

Sensations of Summer: Carrick's French beach resort paintings

Aladdin's lamp for the artist: the Sydney summer of 1913

The Theosophical Society as a wellspring of inspiration

Sorrow and service: Carrick across the two world wars

Friend, mentor, inspiration: Carrick's impact on Australian women

Chronology

Index

Page numbers in italics indicate illustrations.
English names of works are alphabetised without considering their articles (The, A).
This is the same for French articles (La, Le, Les, and Une).
Chronology and Notes have not been included in the index.

Acknowledgements

Curator's acknowledgements

First and foremost, I wish to thank Nick Mitzevich, Director of the National Gallery of Australia for the opportunity to curate the *Ethel Carrick* retrospective and undertake in-depth research towards this publication. Coinciding with the Know My Name initiative to celebrate women artists, we recognised that it would be timely to undertake a retrospective on her art for the first time in nearly half a century, given her importance in Australian art and beyond. Our sincere thanks both to the Gallery's Council and Foundation boards for their wholehearted commitment to this project. My thanks also to Adam Lindsay, Deputy Director, for his guidance, and to the Assistant Directors and Heads of Department across the Gallery, as well as Helen Gee and Sophie Hunter in Executive for their support.

Most especially, we acknowledge the very generous contributions and commitment of Prue McLeod and The Lansdowne Foundation (Major Patron), Roslyn Packer AC (Exhibition Patron), Fiona Martin-Weber and Tom Hayward (Supporting Patrons), and Marilyn Darling and the Gordon Darling Foundation (Publication Partner). We are profoundly grateful for their belief in Ethel Carrick's legacy and its importance to retelling the stories of Australian art, locally and globally. To this end I also sincerely thank the Gordon Darling Foundation for the wonderful support of a Darling Travel Grant (International) that enabled my curatorial travel to the United Kingdom and France to undertake important original research.

This exhibition and publication build upon the foundational work of Margaret Rich, curator of the first Ethel Carrick retrospective in 1979, with contributions from Ruth Zubans, who wrote a major monograph on Emanuel Phillips Fox; the great in-depth scholarship on Fox and Carrick by Mary Eagle; and the dedicated work of Angela Goddard who curated a memorable exhibition for the Queensland Art Gallery on both Carrick and Fox. I am most grateful to them for generously sharing information with me and for their kind support. I also appreciate Roger Butler's insights into Carrick's printmaking. Butler and Eagle were former senior curators at the National Gallery and I thank them and others for their stewardship of works by Carrick into the collection. Susanna De Vries wrote the first monograph on Carrick, discovering among other works, *French flower market* 1909 (cat 25, p 49), shown in this retrospective exhibition.

It is with much appreciation that I acknowledge the authors who contributed insightful essays to this publication: Rebecca Blake, Angela Goddard, Emma Kindred, Denise Mimmochi, Jenny McFarlane, Catherine Speck and Juliette Peers. Their writing has contributed to our understanding of the complexities of Carrick's art and life story, which was so informed by a relentless passion for travel. We welcome their diverse viewpoints and spirit of ongoing enquiry and lively engagement. Together with those who have written about Carrick's artistic contribution over the years, they form a community which passes on the baton for future generations.

I am grateful for the expertise shared with me by Andrea Frederickson, Slade School of Fine Art, University College London (UCL), curator of collections (art); Robert Winkworth, special collections in the UCL library; David Tovey, author of numerous publications on artists' colonies of St Ives and Newlyn in Cornwall; and the team at AWARE (Archives of Women Artists Research and Exhibitions) in Paris. My sincere thanks to John Carrick and his partner Jean from Norwich, who kindly welcomed me into their home and shared information on Ethel Carrick's family history with me, and also to John Halfpenny and Kirsten Fox. My thanks also to Henri Loyrette, Catherine David, Angela Nevill, Nina Volz, Eleni Pantelaras, Alexandre Collex, Mary Linkins, Lucia Pesapane and Jennifer Higgie for meeting with me during my travels.

Major exhibitions are only possible with the great generosity of those willing to loan their works. We are most grateful to all directors and staff at public galleries and institutions who have contributed to research and loaned key works to the exhibition including: Michael Brand (Director), Wayne Tunnicliffe, Denise Mimmochi and Claire Eggleston, Art Gallery of New South Wales; Tony Ellwood (Director), Beckett Rozentals and Myles Russell-Cook, National Gallery of Victoria; Chris Saines (Director), Simon Elliott, Samantha Littley, Judy Gunning and Michael Hawker, Queensland Art Gallery | Gallery of Modern Art; Rhana Devenport (former Director), Tracey Lock and Elle Freak, Art Gallery of South Australia; Colin Walker (Director), Melissa Harpley and Emma Bitmead, Art Gallery of Western Australia; Ann Stephen (Senior Curator, Art), Michael Dagostino (Director), Katrina Liberiou, Maree Clutterbuck at the University of Sydney, Chau Chak Wing Museum; Tony Oates and team at the Australian National University Art Collection; Naomi Cass (Director), Jenny Long and Catherine Nunn at Castlemaine Art Gallery; Anna Wong (Director) and Virginia Rigney, Canberra Museum and Gallery; Louise Tegart (Director), Art Gallery of Ballarat; Eric Nash (Director), and Brenda Wellman, Benalla Art Gallery; Jessica Bridgfoot (Director) and Emma Busowsky, Bendigo Art Gallery; Susi Muddiman (Director) and team, HOTA (Home of the Arts), Gold Coast; Justine Ambrosio and team, Lawrence Wilson Art Gallery, University of Western Australia; Katherine Roberts, Manly Art Gallery & Museum; Lisa Byrne (Director) and team, McClelland; Lauretta Moreton (Director) and team, Newcastle Art Gallery; John Cheeseman (Director) and Kelly McDonald, Mosman Art Gallery; Shane Fitzgerald (Director) and team, Queen Victoria Museum and Art Gallery; Mary Mulcahy (Director) and Mary Knights, Tasmanian Museum and Gallery; Melinda Martin (CEO) and team, Shepparton Art Museum; and Dr Marie-Louise Ayres, Director General, National Library of Australia. Also to Jane Watters, Director, SH Ervin Gallery for her assistance.

Our heartfelt thanks to the many private collectors who have generously loaned treasured works from their collections: Philip Bacon AO, The Bastiaan Collection, Rob and Jenny Ferguson, Dr Garry Helprin, Moran Family Collection, GR Teague and the other private collectors in Australia and Britain who wish to remain anonymous. We are very grateful for loans from the Kerry Stokes Collection assisted by Erica Persak and Sarah Yukich; and The Wesfarmers Collection of Australian Art, supported by Helen Carroll. Thanks also to Alison Inglis from the Lyceum Club, which was an important base for Carrick.

I would also like to acknowledge the support of those who greatly assisted us with locating works for the exhibition and the publication: Philip Bacon AO and Lachlan Henderson, Philip Bacon Galleries; Geoffrey Smith, Smith & Singer Fine Art; Merryn Schriever, Bonhams Australia; Chris Deutscher, Damien Hackett, Fiona Hayward and Ella Perrottet, Deutscher and Hackett; John Albrecht (Chairman & Head of Important Collections), Leonard Joel along with Olivia Fuller and Georgina Lewis; Michael Blanche and Ruth Lovell, Lauraine Diggins Fine Art; Catherine Baxendale and Asta Cameron, Menzies Art Brands; and Lynda McLeod, Associate Director, Provenance Researcher & Head of Archives, Christie's, London. I am very grateful to David Cook, Andrew Crawford, Erica Drew, Mark Hughes, Rex Irwin, Annette Larkin, Justin Miller, Tom Silver and Cherie Silver, Ronan Sulich, Mary Teague and Elena Taylor. Theosophy was an important aspect of Carrick's life and we are grateful to Linda Oliveira, Pedro Oliveira, Richard Larkin and Jennifer Hissey of the Theosophical Society, for their assistance. We are also grateful to the State Library of New South Wales, the State Library of Victoria, and the State Gallery libraries for enabling in-depth research.

I am fortunate to work alongside an exceptional team of people at the National Gallery and appreciate the great contributions to this project of all involved, including some external colleagues. My sincere thanks to the dedicated, hardworking publications team including Penny Sanderson, publishing manager; Zoe Antony, managing editor; Sarah Gorey, editor; and Ashlea O'Neill, publication designer, for their care and attention to detail in bringing this catalogue to fruition, along with Ellie Misios, rights and permissions; and Sam Cooper, Eleni Kypridis and Brooke Shannon in imaging. I am deeply grateful for the hard work and ongoing support of the exhibition team: Dominique Nagy, exhibitions manager; Jane Marsden, loans registrar; Emma Doy, exhibition designer; and the team in conservation, including Jocelyn Evans (paintings) and Greg Howard for assistance with framing, Fiona Kemp and James Ward (works on paper). In our Foundation, Maryanne Voyazis and Tom Campbell have given great support to this project, as has Daryl West-Moore and the teams in Marketing and Communications, including Susie Barr, Kanesan Nathan, Keren Nicholson, Fiona Mcqueenie and Jess Barnes, as well as Marika Lucas-Edwards. My thanks also to the Research Library and Archive staff, Elizabeth Little, Jack Ennis, Simon Underschultz and Ellen Newton. It is most important to all of us at the Gallery to reach a wide and diverse audience and I am grateful to Georgia Close and our Learning and Access team, including Public Programs and the dedicated Voluntary Guides for their considerable ongoing support.

Very special thanks to Rebecca Blake, curatorial assistant, for her exceptional hard work and great contribution to both the Ethel Carrick retrospective exhibition and publication. Her detailed scholarly research into primary source material has directly informed a great deal of new research in this publication and is warmly acknowledged. I am profoundly appreciative for her dedicated work on all aspects of this project. My thanks also to my colleagues Rebecca Edwards (who curated a parallel exhibition on Anne Dangar), Tina Baum, Sarina Noordhuis-Fairfax and Alice Rezende for advice and assistance, as well as all those in the curatorial team in Australian Art for their kind, ongoing support. I am personally most grateful to Kirin Narayan for reading the manuscript and to Laurence and Graeme Hart, and Garrett Purtill for their unstinting encouragement.

While working on the publication, one of our wonderful private lenders sent me a quote by Carrick that he found particularly moving. It appeared in a catalogue for an exhibition of works by Carrick and Emanuel Phillips Fox at the South Australian Society of Arts Gallery in Adelaide in 1925. Carrick, who had returned from France to Australia wrote a foreword in praise of Fox's art, concluding: 'My own contributions to this Exhibition have been restricted by want of space, but some day, if you like, I will come again and show you more'. It is wonderful to have the opportunity to make this more fulsome showing of Ethel Carrick's own artistic contribution a reality.

Deborah Hart

— Exhibition Curator, Head Curator, Australian Art,
National Gallery of Australia

Supporters

Strategic Partners

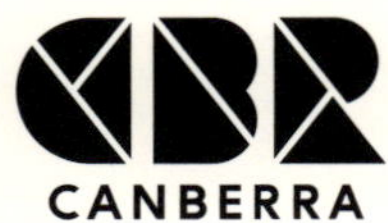

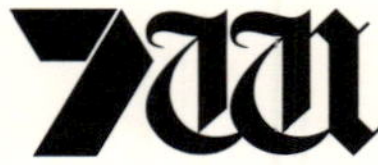

Major Partner

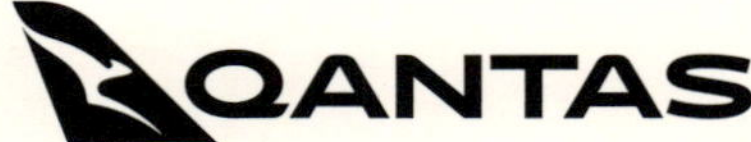

Major Patron

LANSDOWNE
FOUNDATION

Exhibition Patron

Roslyn Packer AC

Publication Partner

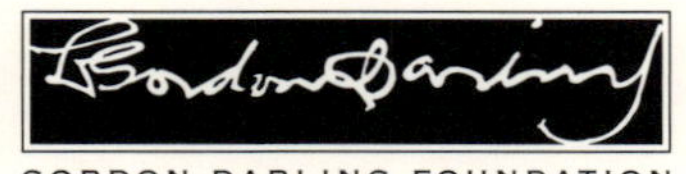

Supporting Patrons

Fiona Martin-Weber
and Tom Hayward

Promotional Partner

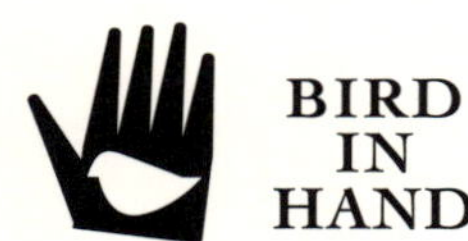

National Gallery acknowledgments

The Hon Anthony Albanese MP, Prime Minister of Australia

Governing Ministers
The Hon Tony Burke MP, Minister for the Arts
Susan Templeman MP, Special Envoy for the Arts

National Gallery Council
Ryan Stokes AO, Chair
The Hon Richard Alston AO
Esther Anatolitis
Ilana Atlas AO, Deputy Chair
Stephen Brady AO CVO
Helen Cook
Sam Edwards
Dr Nick Mitzevich, Director
Sally Scales
Prof Sally Smart

National Gallery Foundation
Stephen Brady AO CVO, Chair
Philip Bacon AO, Deputy Chair
Julian Beaumont OAM
Anthony Berg AM
Julian Burt
Terrence Campbell AO
Sue Cato AM
The Hon Ashley Dawson-Damer AM
James Erskine
Tim Fairfax AC
Andrew Gwinnett
Hiroko Gwinnett
John Hindmarsh AM
Wayne Kratzmann AM
The Hon Dr Andrew Lu AM
Dr Peter Lundy RFD, Secretary
Michael Maher
Dr Michael Martin
Dr Nick Mitzevich, Director
Roslyn Packer AC
Penelope Seidler AM
Ezekiel Solomon AM
Kerry Stokes AC
Ryan Stokes AO
Ray Wilson OAM

National Gallery Executive
Dr Nick Mitzevich, Director
Adam Lindsay, Deputy Director
Susie Barr, Assistant Director, Marketing, Communications and Visitor Experience
Sophie Gray, Project Director, Capital Works Taskforce
Alison Halpin, Chief Operating Officer
Felicity McGinnes, Chief Finance Officer
Helen Gee, Sophie Hunter, Elizabeth Smith, Lillee Keating and Wellin Pan, Directorate

Curator
Dr Deborah Hart, Head Curator, Australian Art

National Gallery Management Team
Samantha Braniff, Head of Partnerships, and staff
Jade Carson, Chief Information Officer, and staff
Georgia Close, Head of National Learning, and staff
Tracy Cooper-Lavery, Head of Art Across Australia, and staff
Terri Dwyer, Head of Human Resources, and staff
Mary Fisher, Head of Financial Accounting, and staff
Tayla French, A/ Head of Financial Planning and Analysis, and staff
Stefan Giammarco, Head of Visitor Experience, and staff
Deborah Hart, Head Curator, Australian Art, and staff
Greg Ible, Head of Estate Management, and staff
Magda Keaney, Head Curator, International Art, and staff
Elizabeth Little, Manager, Research Library and Archives, and staff
Marika Lucas-Edwards, Principal Content Strategist and Head of Digital, and staff
Elizabeth Malone, Head of Commercial Operations, and staff
Fiona McQueenie, Head of Communications, and staff
Dominique Nagy, Head of Exhibitions, and staff
Kanesan Nathan, Head of Marketing, and staff
Chris Reid, Head of Governance and Strategic Planning, and staff
Maryanne Voyazis, Head of Development and Executive Director, National Gallery Foundation, and staff
Debbie Ward, Head of Conservation and Registration
Daryl West-Moore, Head of Creative Studio, and staff

Photography credits
All reproductions are courtesy the National Gallery's digital team, excluding those who wish to remain anonymous, or are otherwise stated below.

photo Bo Wong: pp 22–23 (cat 6); photo © The Aga Khan Museum: p 116 (fig 29); © akg-images: p 36 (fig 8); image © Art Gallery of New South Wales: p 83 (cat 44), p 105 (cat 61), p 143 (fig 35), p 157 (cat 101), p 160 (fig 39), p 161 (fig 40), p 181 (cat 113); image courtesy BC Archives: p 24 (fig 5); image credit Birmingham Museums Trust: p 20 (fig 3); image courtesy Bonhams, Sydney: p 41 (cat 18), p 228 (cat 127); photo Oscar Capezio, The Australian National University: p 134 (cat 89); photo Angela Casey: p 39 (cat 15); photo Cultural Heritage Digitisation, London: p 50 (cat 26); image © Y. Deslandes /Réunion des Musées Métropolitains Rouen Normandie: p 109 (fig 24); image courtesy Deutscher and Hackett, Melbourne: p 154 (cat 99), p 190 (fig 41), p 219 (fig 48); photo Felicity Jenkins Photography: p 79 (cat 43); photo Robert Frith, Acorn Photo: p 110 (cat 69), p 136 (cat 90); image courtesy Getty Research Institute, Los Angeles: p 32 (fig 7); image © GrandPalaisRmn (musée d'Orsay) / Jean Schormans: p 46 (fig 12); photo Paul Green: p 87 (fig 22); photo Ian Hill: pp 52–53 (cat 27), p 66 (cat 34), p 146 (cat 94); photo David James: p 40 (cat 16), p 67 (cat 35), p 74 (cat 39), p 106 (cat 63), p 107 (cat 65), p 110 (cat 66), pp 118–19 (cat 77), p 127 (cat 85), p 133 (cat 88), p 144 (cat 92), p 145 (cat 93), p 150 (cat 98), p 156 (cat 100), p 173 (cat 109), p 233 (cat 128), p 243 (cat 131); Jessica Maurer Photography: pp 62–63 (cat 32), p 106 (cat 64), 113 (cat 73), p 130 (cat 86), p 247 (cat 137); image courtesy Kunstmuseum Bern: p 38 (fig 11); image courtesy Estate of Martha Stettler / Kunstmuseum Bern: p 38 (fig 10); image courtesy Lauraine Diggins Fine Art, Melbourne: p 208 (cat 122); image © Léon & Lévy / Roger-Viollet: p 60 (fig 15); image courtesy Menzies Art Brands, Sydney: p 72 (cat 38), p 100 (cat 56); digital image © 2007 MoMA, NY, image courtesy Scala Archives: p 206 (fig 46); image courtesy National Library of Australia, Canberra: p 80 (fig 20), p 112 (fig 26), p 127 (cat 84); image courtesy RC Strangman Collection, from the National Library of Australia, Canberra: p 128 (fig 30); image courtesy Northern Beaches Council Library Local Studies: p 192 (fig 43); image courtesy Philip Bacon Galleries, Fortitude Valley: p 48 (cat 23), p 58 (cat 30), p 88 (cat 48), p 173 (cat 110), p 179 (cat 112), p 252 (cat 139); Princeton University Art Museum / Art Resource, NY: p 37 (fig 9), p 69 (fig 17); photo Queensland Art Gallery | Gallery of Modern Art: p 111 (cat 72), p 148 (fig 37), p 163 (cat 105), p 166 (cat 107); image courtesy Shapiro Auctioneers and Gallery, Sydney: p 114 (fig 28); photo Shepparton Art Museum: p 31 (cat 13), p 146 (cat 95), p 147 (cat 96); image courtesy Smith & Singer Fine Art: p 10 (cat 3), p 16 (cat 4), p 21 (cat 5), pp 96–97 (cat 53), p 140 (cat 91), p 149 (cat 97), p 247 (cat 136); image courtesy State Library of New South Wales: p 54 (fig 13), p 131 (fig 32), p 142 (fig 34), p 192 (fig 42), p 202 (fig 44), p 235 (fig 56), p 247 (fig 60); image courtesy State Library of South Australia, Adelaide: p 132 (fig 33); image courtesy Philip Suter: p 18 (fig 1), p 241 (fig 57); photo TATE: p 64 (fig 16); photo Peter Waddington: p 125 (cat 80).

Copyright
We thank those who wish to remain anonymous, and the following:

© Estate of Amalie Colquhoun: p 234 (fig 55); © Estate of Grace Cossington-Smith: p 224 (fig 51); © Estate of Sybil Craig: p 129 (fig 31), p 220 (fig 49).

Published on the occasion of the exhibition
Ethel Carrick
7 December 2024 – 27 April 2025
National Gallery of Australia
Ngunnawal Country
Parkes Place East, Parkes
ACT 2600

A catalogue record for this work is available from the National Library of Australia.

Title: Ethel Carrick
Editor: Dr Deborah Hart
ISBN: 978-0-642-33510-4
First published: December 2024

Design: Ashlea O'Neill | Salt Camp Studio
Managing editor: Zoe Antony*
Publishing Manager: Penny Sanderson*
Text editor: Sarah Gory
Proofreader: Kay Campbell
French-language proofreader: Helen Curran
Indexer: Sherrey Quinn, Libraries Alive!
Imaging: Sam Cooper, Eleni Kypridis and Brooke Shannon*
Rights and permissions: Ellie Misios*
Pre-press: Adams Print
Printed by: Adams Print

* National Gallery of Australia

Cover art: cat 33 *Beach scene* c 1909, oil on canvas on cardboard, National Gallery of Australia